Deuteronomy in the Making

Beihefte zur Zeitschrift für die alttestamentliche Wissenschaft

Edited by
John Barton, Reinhard G. Kratz, Nathan MacDonald,
Sara Milstein and Markus Witte

Volume 533

Deuteronomy in the Making

Studies in the Production of *Debarim*

Edited by
Diana Edelman, Benedetta Rossi, Kåre Berge,
and Philippe Guillaume

DE GRUYTER

ISBN 978-3-11-126354-0
e-ISBN (PDF) 978-3-11-071331-2
e-ISBN (EPUB) 978-3-11-071341-1
ISSN 0934-2575

Library of Congress Control Number: 2021932004

Bibliographic information published by the Deutsche Nationalbibliothek
The Deutsche Nationalbibliothek lists this publication in the Deutsche Nationalbibliografie; detailed bibliographic data are available on the Internet at http://dnb.dnb.de.

This volume is text- and page-identical with the hardback published in 2021.
Typesetting: Meta Systems Publishing & Printservices GmbH, Wustermark
Printing and binding: CPI books GmbH, Leck

www.degruyter.com

This volume is dedicated to the memory of Philip R. Davies (1945–2018), our close colleague and project group member. We miss his flashes of insight, wit, and vitality and remember him fondly.

Foreward

This book is the result of a three-year grant (April, 2017–June, 2020) funded by the Faculty of Theology at the University of Oslo for a project entitled, "The Production, Purpose, and Ideology of Deuteronomy" ("Produksjonen, formålet og ideologien til femte Mosebok, Deuteronomium"). The members of the core working group have been myself, Diana Edelman, who served as the project leader, Kåre Berge, Philip Davies, Philippe Guillaume, and Benedetta Rossi. Philip's death was a huge loss to the group, but he attended early workshops and contributed enthusiastically to our brainstorming sessions. We are including the paper he presented at our first workshop, even though he died before he was able to revise and expand it for publication; Philip's ideas were stimulating even in preliminary form and have influenced our thought in many ways. We discussed the paper at length when he presented it, and observations and feedback we can remember we gave him at the time are included in the interactive editorial summary. The BZAW series editors have asked us to provide footnotes to his paper posthumously, which we have done to the extent we feel able and comfortable.

The project's publication plans include the present edited volume and a co-authored volume by members of the core working group. The present volume includes selected papers presented at our core group workshop in Oslo 28–29 May, 2017 and at the seminar group, "The Core of Deuteronomy," hosted by the European Association of Biblical Studies in Berlin, 7–11 August, 2017 and in Helsinki, 30 July–3 August, 2018. The seminar group was led by Philippe Guillaume and Kåre Berge initially, with my becoming a third leader once the research project was funded. Additional papers were solicited from certain scholars who attended the EABS seminars, from those who expressed interest in the project, and also by us on specific topics we thought were needed to round out the volume.

https://doi.org/10.1515/9783110713312-202

Contents

Part II: Case Studies on Textual Units or Themes within *Debarim*

Diana Edelman, University of Oslo, Oslo, Norway

Introduction

It is common for textbooks to describe the book of Deuteronomy as a law code (chs. 12–26) framed secondarily by narratives (chs. 1–11 and 27–34). This understanding has derived from the partial overlap in material in chs. 12–26 with what have been identified as legal formulations in Exodus and Leviticus, resulting in the commonly dubbed "Deuteronomic Code," (DC) "Covenant Code" (Exod 20:22–23:33) (CC), and "Holiness Code" (Lev 17–26) (HC), respectively. It also is based on the appearance of similar collections elsewhere in the ancient Near East. Scholars have tended to do comparative work between two or among all three biblical collections or between ancient Near Eastern collections and individual regulations in the three biblical collections.

Almost no work has focused specifically on the collection of materials in Deuteronomy 12–26, however, to try to understand if they contain an inner logic that might suggest an older purpose and setting as an independent composition prior to being framed to create the first version of the book of Deuteronomy. This was the original focus of the present volume. However, as the list of contributors expanded, along with the list of topics explored, it became logical to widen the focus to accommodate the collection more adequately. The astute reader will easily spot the papers whose main focus is on chs. 12–26 or some portion thereof and a possible identification of an *Ur*-composition and its possible function.

Contributors to the present volume have been asked to define what they consider to have been included in the hypothetical "core," and the answers are surprisingly varied. As Megan B. Turton helpfully notes in her essay, however, the very notion of a "core" is unclear in the larger scholarship on the book of Deuteronomy. Some in the field take it in a temporal sense to designate the earliest form of Deuteronomy, others to designate the casuistic portion of the legal collection (chs. 19–25). Yet others use it to designate whatever occupies a key central position within the book. Finally, there are those who would define the "core" by texts that are historically and theologically central to the message of the book. The varied answers within the present twelve essays reflect the ambiguity within the field at large.

The essays in Part One explore the production of the earliest form of the book in some cases (Philip R. Davies, Baruch Halpern, and myself) and the "core" in other cases (Bill T. Arnold, Graeme Auld, Kåre Berge, and Philippe Guillaume), in different ways. Davies starts with the prominence of the name Israel for the society envisioned in the book and then turns to the history of the

https://doi.org/10.1515/9783110713312-001

northern kingdom of Israel to understand the origin of the core and the book. He proposes the core resulted from a process of reasserting and redefining the identity of Israel, initially under King Jeroboam (I/II) who ruled in the eighth century BCE when new territories and population groups became part of the kingdom and needed to be acculturated. This existing core was expanded and reused for the same purpose after 722 BCE, when Israel ceased to exist and the kingdom and its historical core territory became the Assyrian province of Samerina. New population groups were introduced that needed to learn the customs and practices (collectively, *mišpaṭ*) associated with the local god of Israel.

As a challenge to the existence of an older, independent "core" that was secondarily framed, my article examines the genres used in the book and various formal structuring devices that have shaped the entire book. When this is done, chs. 12–26 or some lesser version of the verses currently contained within those limits do not stand out as likely to have existed in written form for some particular purpose. Themes and patterns cut across the "core" and the "frames." I put forward the very minority view, which I have been told is unlikely to be found persuasive, that the creator of the book was responsible for gathering together the collection of materials in chs. 12–26, no doubt drawing on older collections and compositions but also adding new material when it suited his purpose. I propose a date in the early Achaemenid period and leave open the possibility that its intended audience included members of the Samarian as well as Judean literati.

Berge presents a reading of the "core" as an exercise in resilience penned during Achaemenid imperial control. Such projects are by definition risky, but they call for disruptive change aimed at altering collective self-identity within a situation of contemporary imperial domination in a way obscured from those in power. He traces a number of reuses of royal ideology in the envisioned refiguration of Israelite society in the core, which advocates local autonomy and has as its point of reference the nuclear family. The annual pilgrimage to the moveable *māqôm* is modelled on the royal Achaemenid practice of traveling between royal palaces and providing feasts for dependent workers.

Halpern looks at the contents in his core form of Deuteronomy he dubs D622, defined as chs 5–28 but possibly chs 1–33, whether duplicated elsewhere or not. He finds the underlying purposes to be the addition of population to enact further a state-endorsed agrarian entrepreneurship and the creation of an "Israelite" identity based on public state-funded religious festivals and the concomitant elimination of phratry-based kinship identities reinforced by local lineage celebrations overseen by their *kōmer*-priests. While the latter already had been a policy in Judah after 701 BCE under Hezekiah and Manasseh, under

Josiah, whose court likely penned D622, target audiences included Samarians and Edomites as well as Judahites. He considers the chosen place for Yhwh's name to be an original element that was deliberately ambiguous in its phrasing, allowing for both a single place and any authorized place the king would designate. Altars remained in place in urban boroughs, now attended by Levites, who oversaw life-cycle events, lineage celebrations, commemorations, and other occasions for celebration among other duties.

Arnold, on the other hand, first focuses on the unparalleled material in the "Deuteronomic Code," seeking to see if it contains an identifiable ideological agenda that might point to the purpose of the legal material. It includes a chosen centralized sanctuary as an integral ideological element and sees the main ideology to be one god, place, one people.

In his two essays, Guillaume also looks at the contents as a whole but uses contradictions and inconsistencies to eliminate chs. 12:1–14:21; 16; 18:1–8, and 25:17–26:19 as secondary expansions within chs. 12–26. In the first essay in Part One, an original core is identified that centered on an annual family feast of unspecified length held at a mobile chosen place that changed annually but was always in a countryside setting to accommodate the numbers in attendance. The annual change of venue was to ensure that those who lived near the announced locale could profit from selling surplus food and animals to those who converted their non-tax tithe to silver. This would balance out the profits and losses over time for individual families that participated. In the second essay in Part Two, this core is associated with a *qᵉhal-yhwh* that consisted of entrepreneurial trading "brothers" within the larger "brotherhood of Israel" and their associated non-Israelite trading associates or "brothers," the Edomites and Egyptians.

Finally, Auld argues that the wording of many parts of the core of Deuteronomy, minus the secondary addition in 26:1–15, derives from the wording in a composition he has dubbed, *The Book of Two Houses*. This proposed written source contained a history of the Judahite monarchy and in his view, can be recovered from the material common to both Samuel-Kings and Chronicles. He argues the removal of non-synoptic material found in one or the other of these two compositions produces a coherent and complete earlier composition that both authors of the subsequent texts drew upon but supplemented in their own way. He believes the author of the core of Deuteronomy similarly drew on this source, using its vocabulary and certain phrases where appropriate to his own work.

Arnold provides a predominantly theological reading of the core and Davies one more associated with the history of religions and ethnicity. Guillaume provides a predominantly economic reading, while Halpern combines economic and identity-formation considerations with historical events during the late eight-seventh centuries BCE. Berge uses sociological theory and the history of Judah/Yehud to inform his reading. Auld's study is vocabulary-based more than focused on the underlying rationale of the text, while mine is a close literary reading that is genre-based. Arnold and Halpern postulate the core's composition in the late monarchic era but in different settings; under Hezekiah or sometime likely during the reign of Josiah. Davies and Guillaume propose a date after 722 BCE in the province of Samaria. Berge and myself propose a date in the early Persian period but do not specify if the location is Yehud alone or also Samaria; certainly, the orientation toward "all Israel" characteristic of the frames includes Samaria. Auld does not address the date of composition but implies a place of composition in Yehud, where *The Book of Two Houses* would have been written.

The understanding that chs. 12–26 comprise an original "law-code" necessarily requires their current function in the story-world as the stipulations to the covenant being contracted in the Plains of Moab to be a secondary adaptation. In such a case, in theory, any references within these chapters to events in the frame should be considered secondary to the original independent "core" material. Among the case studies included in Part Two of the present volume, this logic would require that Deuteronomy 18:15–22 be a secondary insertion (see the article of Megan B. Turton) and probably also that some or all of the laws connected with waging war in Deuteronomy 20:1–20 be removed from any hypothetical "core" legal collection (see the article of Martijn Beukenhorst).

Daniel Gräber, on the other hand, points out how the *gēr* is a category of liminal persons found "inside your gates" or "among you" in both the frames and the "core." The first appearance of the term in Deuteronomy 1:16 provides a legal definition that adapts the tradition in Exodus 18 about the institution of court proceedings to include cases between an Israelite and a *gēr*. As such, it prepares for and anticipates the regulatory references to the *gēr* in the core. This interesting situation could point to a later adjustment of the text, where a redactor either drew on the concept of *gēr* in the core to tie together the frames and themes more closely or one where he possibly added the *gēr* as a legal category into both the "core" and frame secondarily to adjust the book to the socio-legal needs of a later period.

In her first contribution on Levitical and Aaronide priestly rivalry, Benedetta Rossi focuses on two passages, Deuteronomy 10:6–9 in the "frame" and 18:1–8 in the "core," to uncover an inner priestly rivalry. She outlines rhetorical strategies in both passages that dialogue with P texts in order to challenge the exclusive authority of the Aaronide priests whereby the Levitical priests assert their status as a new priestly elite with exclusive control over the Torah, inheriting the authority of Moses. She considers both redactional additions that interrupt the existing contextual flow.

The possibility that the proposed older core document included additional materials that were omitted when it was adapted to serve as stipulations also must be acknowledged. Thus, in theory, the full original content of the hypothetical core document is no longer recoverable. We can only work with what we have and deduce from it a likely original function and life setting, hoping that if anything has been omitted, its absence has not skewed our perception of what that older written "core" was about.

It is possible to suggest what likely would be secondary expansions to any original core using various criteria, though not with absolute certainty, due to the lack of necessary confirming proof from mss. of earlier versions of the book or access to the archives in which the hypothetical original core document would have been kept. One example is found in the essay of Auld, where 26:1–15 is identified as secondary on the basis of the use of the positive command to prostrate oneself, which contrasts with the common command to prostrate oneself before other gods found elsewhere in the book, on the basis of unnecessary repetition of material already found in 14:22–23, and on the occurrence of the non-synoptic formula, "let his name dwell" vs. the synoptic "set his name there." Another is found in the first essay of Guillaume, where chs, 12, 16, 18 and 26 are identified as secondary because their portrayal of the *māqôm* as a temple-like institution where Levites collect priestly dues from sacrifices being offered contradicts the *māqôm* as a rotating, open-air facility without any Levites present, where Israelite families feast and rejoice annually before Yhwh as part of the dual tithing system presented in 14:22–29. Both scholars agree that part or all of ch. 26 is secondary, but they provide different rationales.

In addition to references to framing materials, if one maintains the common classification of the content of chs. 12–26 as a legal code or legal collection, then material that does not conform with the normal format of such collections known from elsewhere in the ancient Near East can be removed as secondary. All the paranetic material and the majority of the motive clauses should be removed, as well as second-person casuistic or conditional formulations and the majority of the second person apodictic or absolute formulations. The same applies to the so-called Covenant and Holiness Codes, which lack the paranetic material anyway (see the article of Edelman). This is the case whether one understands the collections to have served an academic rather than legislative function in either monarchic Judahite or post-monarchic Judean society. This is also the case whether one conceives of a legislative function in terms of statutory law or common law traditions.

If, on the other hand, one might want to rethink the classification of the core material and associate it instead with the stipulations of the vassal treaty or formal contract genre more generally, then the strong presence of the second person absolute formulations becomes normal and expected, as does the use of second-person "casuistic" or conditional formulations and even some motive clauses. However, the presence of third-person "casuistic"/paranetic material would need some form of explanation, since it was not standard practice in this context, and the paranetic material should be removed as secondary. Thus, what is present in chs. 12–26 does not conform to known practice for either the genre of the ancient Near Eastern legal collection nor to the international treaty/contract tradition. It already is a hybrid (see the article of Edelman).

Anyone examining the core as a self-contained literary unit must decide how to conceive of the original underlying document. Was it a legal collection that was expanded? Was it a set of stipulations that was expanded? Or, was it a document that already combined the traits of both genres and if so, why? This initial decision has important implications for what one decides to eliminate as secondary before deducing the purpose and life setting of the remaining, hypothetical "core."

There are currently a few main "schools" of thought concerning the compositional and redactional history of the book of Deuteronomy. Working chronologically, it is common for scholars to equate Deuteronomy with the scroll of the *torah* allegedly found in the temple in Jerusalem during repairs conducted during the reign of Josiah (reigned ca. 641–609 BCE; 2 Kgs 22:3–10). Those who do so either assume chs. 12–26 alone were found, as a "law code," or that something closer to the book was discovered, with an initial narrative framework already in place. These scholars usually go on to pose one or more exilic and post-exilic expansions or redactions, sometimes identifying two phases to the creation of the narrative frames: the inner frames first (chs. 5–11; 27) and the outer frames later on (chs. 1–4; 28–30). They consider the purpose of the frames to be to enhance the book's current hinge position as the closing to the five books of Moses (Gen-Deut) and as the opening to the Deuteronomistic History Collection (Deut-2 Kgs). They associate a final phase with the addition of chs. 31–34, whose purpose is to integrate the book more fully with Joshua to create a suitable ending to the narrative begun in Genesis with the divine promise of possession of the land of Canaan. Joshua narrates the conquest of most of the land by the tribes, creating a meta-narrative not limited to Genesis-Deuteronomy (the Pentateuch) but one that originally included the conquest (Hexateuch). Some argue Deuteronomy was inserted into this older meta-narrative, disrupting the original unity.

The essays of Davies and Guillaume offer a new argument for the possible northern origin of the Deuteronomy. Previous arguments had been based on a perceived coherence between Deuteronomy and northern prophetic tradition, especially Hosea. In addition, the references to the covenant ceremonies to be conducted at Mt. Gerizim and Mt. Ebal in Deuteronomy 11:29 and 27:2–12 had influenced some to propose a northern origin for the book. The minor emphasis on the ark, a prominent divine symbol in the cult of Judah, but a major emphasis on name theology instead also had been seen to point to a northern origin for the book.

While a post-722 BCE date had been proposed previously, opinions had differed over the place of composition. Some advocated a composition in Judah by Levitical refugees from the fallen kingdom of Israel, while others proposed its composition in the newly created province of Samaria. In the latter case, however, the underlying rationale for composition was a hope for the restoration of the monarchy following updated principles and practices after reflection over the demise of the kingdom. The new argument by Davies, adopted and expanded by Guillaume, avoids all the pitfalls of the previous arguments and provides a plausible socio-historical setting and rationale that will need to be addressed in future debates over the time and place of the composition of the book.

Another group of scholars rejects the historical reliability of the book-finding under Josiah and posits that the world-view expressed is best situated in a "post-monarchic" setting, given that the king plays such a minor role, becoming a pious student of *torah*-teaching. Some then posit the Neo-Babylonian period (ca. 586–539 BCE) and a minority the Achaemenid period (ca. 539–332 BCE) as the initial period for the composition of the earliest form of the book. Those who favor the Neo-Babylonian period also tend to accept one or more subsequent redactions, while those who favor an Achaemenid date acknowledge subsequent editing took place, but perhaps not as systematically as the traditional redactional layers that have been proposed. Some, however, probably would accept the idea that the "outer frame" (chs. 1–4; 28–30) was a subsequent addition aimed at integrating the book more fully into its current hinge position.

Some consider the call for the centralization of the cult to be a cornerstone of Deuteronomic ideology (e.g. Arnold, Auld), while others consider it to be either deliberately ambiguous (Halpern) or a secondary expansion (e.g. Guillaume; possibly so, e.g. Berge). Similarly, many scholars in the field remove the law of the king in Deuteronomy 17:14–20 as a later addition (e.g. Rossi in this volume), but not all. Some find room for it as original to the core (e.g. in this volume, Berge, Guillaume, Edelman).

The verses in Deuteronomy 2:4, 8 and 23:8 form the cornerstone of Guillaume's understanding of the creation of the original core and meaning of the phrase *qᵉhal-yhwh* in that document; yet other scholars would consider these verses to be secondary additions that deliberately allude to stories in Genesis concerning Esau/Edom, Jacob's brother. Particularly in the case of 23:8, which is part of a wider unit in 23:3–8 defining membership in the *qᵉhal-yhwh*, scholars have noted in reference to Egyptians entering the *qāhāl* in the third generation that there are deliberate allusions to similar stories in the Pentateuch involving the patriarchal sojourns in Egypt and even implicitly, the birth of Joseph's Egyptian sons, Ephraim and Manasseh, there (Gen). Similarly, the Moabites and Ammonites who are never to enter the assembly because they hired Balaam son of Beor to curse Israel provides a direct allusion to Numbers 21 or to a known written or oral Balaam tradition.

One's stance on whether all Levites were priests but not all priests Levites or whether all priests were Levites but not all Levites priests has important ramifications for viewing the role of priests vs. Levitical priests vs. Levites in the core and the frames. It will influence one's decision whether or not all three terms were deliberately being equated or if some were signaling discreet categories that allow the identification of editorial layers within the text (see the articles by Rossi and Auld).

A number of studies highlight the importance of being aware of the nuances of ancient Hebrew and not prematurely narrowing translations. Examples include אח and רע (Guillaume), הכהנים הלוים (Rossi), מצוה, חק, תורה, and עדות (Edelman), משפט (Davies and Edelman), עיר and שער (Berge and Halpern), כול (Halpern) and מקום (Halpern; Guillaume; Berge), חרם (Beukenhorst), גר (Halpern, Gräber), קהל יהוה (Halpern and Guillaume), מוסר, כהן, הזרוע והלחיים והקבה, חלק כחלק, and אשי יהוה (Rossi), and בחר (Turton). Translations into modern languages can, in fact, be quite misleading in their decisions to render with one meaning as opposed to another equally valid one. Given that biblical Hebrew is a dead language and that only a portion of the vocabulary that would have been used orally has been employed in writing the collection of biblical books, our ability to recover the full semantic range of a given term and idioms in which it would have been used is limited at best. All dictionary meanings ultimately are derived from contextual written use and from comparative usage in other ancient and modern Semitic languages.

The influence of different manuscript versions on understanding aspects of the growth of a text or its reception is raised as an issue by Auld, Beukenhorst, Guillaume, Graber, Halpern, Turton, and Rossi. The book of Deuteronomy exhibits relatively few variants in comparison with other books, especially Jeremiah. Even so, the differences among the MT, LXX, and Samaritan versions discussed in these essays bear directly on one's reconstruction of which reading is older and why and which is derivative and why. Textual criticism is an art, not a science; different conclusions can be drawn concerning the priority among a set of variant texts, depending on the principal(s) invoked in interpretation. Nevertheless, it is important to be aware when alternate readings exist in mss.

Some have little or no real impact on meaning, while others do. Should a scholar, however, create a hybrid text of a given book by systematically opting for one variant over another as they occur? Such as hypothetical text has no confirmed existence in the ancient world among a real community.

A more practical approach to variant textual traditions would be to read each manuscript as an embodiment of collective memory within a given community that used that manuscript as a written version of an authoritative, received tradition. While inevitably, some scribal errors will have crept in during manual recopying, the more significant variants can be seen to be updates and modifications of an older collective memory within the receiving community needing to use the past to address their current situation as well as the hoped-for future. In this case, one still cannot identify with certainty the "original" form of the memory, but one can read the Samaritan version, the MT version, and the LXX version, even with their minor differences among extant mss., as three versions of a common past that have been adapted over time to suit the needs of each community.

The issue of scribal compositional technique is briefly addressed in the contribution by Arnold. Within the field of Hebrew Bible/Old Testament, a number of studies have appeared in the last decade or so devoted to this important issue. Given the limited evidence for practices among the scribes responsible for the books now found in the collection comprising the Hebrew Bible/Old Testament, most turn to comparative evidence from Mesopotamia or Greece for analogy. The emphasis on scribal dependence on anterior texts, whether they are used in processes of compilation, expansion, adaptation, or integration, is an important reminder that formal scribal education in all ancient cultures would have involved a set of exemplary texts from different genres that likely were to be memorized. The components expected in a given genre, or the range of possible components, including mandatory and optional elements, would have been illustrated by the set texts but perhaps taught and learned separately. The likely existence of palace archives, temple archives, and personal scribal libraries would have meant that access to texts and documents beyond the set texts in the curriculum would have been possible in theory. Whether any or all of these collections survived the demise of both kingdoms in 722 and 586 BCE and remained accessible to those serving in the succeeding provincial administrations remains a point of debate. The tendency to overemphasize the derivative nature of scribal activity to the point that no credit is given for creativity or the ability of a scribe to compose a new composition or document that drew upon established patterns and genres needs to be resisted. My contribution raises this issue.

Finally, Benedetta Rossi's article on the reception and use of "legal" prescriptions in chs. 12–26 by the writer(s) of the book of Jeremiah reveals their containing literary strategies employed in subversive discourse, particularly irony. She notes that the authors presume the so-called frames of Deuteronomy and the emphasis in them on observance of Moses's *torah* and the conditions and requirements for securing return and restoration after exile. Thus, he or they were not working with a Ur-Deuteronomic "legal collection," if one ever existed, but with some form of the book that had the narrative frame (chs. 4 and 30 at least) in place. As she notes herself, her findings cannot prove nor disprove the possible existence of an earlier, independent "core" in some form or another. The irony leads to the subversive view that contravening *torah* opens the way to salvation and renewal.

The case studies presented in this volume are cumulative windows opening onto a vantage point that allows the reader to make a personal, informed decision about the nature of chs. 12–26. Six possible understandings of the rationale for and life setting of a "core" document comprising a large part of the content currently contained in chs. 12–26 are presented. Some results point in one direction and others in another. Certain readers undoubtedly will find these contradictory results frustrating, but they highlight the self-evident but sometimes overlooked fact that different presuppositions lead to different results. Readers of the volume are given the opportunity to think through what results would emerge in each case if a different set of presuppositions were applied and which solution they find most cogent and why. At the same time, the varied results can be used as an opportunity for a reader to examine his or her own presuppositions and why they are held. Is it because this is what was taught in undergraduate or advanced studies? Is it because it is the majority view? Is it the result of an independent, personal assessment of the material and issues? What data proves or corroborates this view over against other views?

It is time to move from the appetizer to the main courses! Bon appetit!

Palm Desert, 20 December, 2019

Part I: **Case Studies Relating to the Production of *Debarim***

Philip R. Davies †

From Where Did Deuteronomy Originate?

Instead of a *manifesto* for Josiah's reform, I propose that we view Deuteronomy as the product of a process of reasserting and redefining the identity of Israel within Samaria after 722 BCE. As such, Deuteronomy grew from an enterprise that was both Israelite-Samarian and post-monarchic, an enculturating project among recent immigrants into Samaria. Much in the same way that Israelites entered the land from elsewhere, the immigrants settled by the Assyrians (2 Kgs 17) find themselves in a land which they must come to regard as their own and as a divine gift.

I begin with an issue of method. Traditionally, literary-historical criticism aims to reconstruct the growth of the document by literary means. The procedure was fully developed in the nineteenth century as the only means of extracting historical data about Israelite history.[1] Since the introduction of archaeological data, including inscriptions, into the reconstruction of ancient Judahite and Israelite history and society, and in the light of recent research on empirical models[2] along with continuing differences of opinion on the dating of biblical literature, we should be more sceptical as to the extent to which we can retrieve the history of biblical texts through literary-critical analysis. My preferred approach, where it can be applied, is to begin with what we can know and infer from non-biblical sources of history, culture, and politics and consider where the possibilities for the creation of a particular text may lie. This approach primarily addresses the existence of such a text, particularly its ideology. The evolution of the text is the second topic, and, in my view, is discovered mainly through attention to major ideological disruptions rather than textual variations. How does this approach fit the book of Deuteronomy?

1 This approach became rooted in assuming and applying the Documentary Hypothesis.
2 E.g. Tigay, *Empirical Models*; Müller, Pakkala, and ter Haar Romeny, *Evidence*; Rezetko and Person, *Empirical Models*; Müller and Pakkala, *Insights*.

Note: This paper was presented by Philip at a workshop held in Oslo on 10–11 November, 2017. He was unable to revise it before his death on 31 May, 2018. The editors of BZAW asked that we supplement the few references he had originally included to make the article more helpful to colleagues. To the same end, since there was no formal conclusion in the original version, we have included an interactive editorial summary of the paper and its implications at the end of the article that includes the elements of our lively discussion of his ideas at the workshop that we can remember.

https://doi.org/10.1515/9783110713312-002

From the nineteenth to the twentieth century and still ongoing in the twenty-first century, Deuteronomy's origin has most commonly been assigned to the reign of Josiah, purely on the basis of the biblical narrative.[3] There is no non-biblical evidence of Josiah himself, let alone his policies, but scholarly proposals about a political, literary, and religious renaissance have been advanced on the basis of the account of his reign in 2 Kings 22–23.[4] The purpose of a law-code that defined an "Israel" and predicated its religion on a treaty between deity and the people, without the mediation of a king, whose role as lawgiver is removed, has been to a large degree explained by implausible speculation. The last two decades have seen a growing dissatisfaction with the Josianic hypothesis[5] and an inclination to consider a post-monarchic date,[6] but the search for an equally precise origin has yet to bear fruit.

One of the more useful suggestions of earlier Deuteronomic scholarship, originating with Adam Welch in 1924,[7] was that its content betrays an Israelite rather than Judahite origin. His proposal would mean a date of origin before the demise of the Judahite monarchy, which would still render Deuteronomy post-monarchic from the perspective of the kingdom of Israel. The possibility of a largely Israelite-Samarian content of the Pentateuch itself, it seems to me, has still not been fully absorbed into biblical scholarship. My preferred approach to Deuteronomy is first to ask why such a document – let us address the law-code without committing ourselves yet to the framework – might have come into existence in the first place. How it might have become associated with the reign of Josiah is probably one of the last questions to be raised.

Two major options present themselves: Deuteronomy may be understood either as a *manifesto* or as the literary *end-product* of an enterprise that was actually undertaken. The former option is more generally favored,[8] and certainly the Josianic explanation requires it, but explanations as to why and from where such a radical proposal should be written strike me as all completely implausible. Alongside the emasculation of the monarchy, the most problematic

---

3 De Wette, *Dissertatio critica*, 13–14 (footnote); de Wette, *Beiträge*, 168–179. See also Harvey and Halpern, "W. M. L. de Wette's '*Dissertatio*,'" 73–85.

4 So e.g. Römer, *So-Called Deuteronomistic History*, 49–55. See Arnold in this volume.

5 So e.g. Würthwein, "Die josianische Reform"; Na'aman, "Kingdom"; Davies, "Josiah."

6 So e.g. Pakkala, "Why Cult Reforms." Gustav Hölscher already had argued in 1923 that the book had originated in the postexilic period as a utopian program, so this minority view has had a long pedigree ("Komposition").

7 Welch, *Code*. He argued for a date in the early monarchy for most of the regulatory provisions and thought that the "code" had been deposited in a northern sanctuary, possibly Bethel, to dictate local practice in the adjoining region.

8 So e.g. Levinson, "Reconceptualization."

issue here seems to me the use of the term "Israel," assuming that this word has not be introduced at a later stage in the literary growth. I have argued that the adoption in Judah of "Israel" as a national identity does not predate the end of the Judahite monarchy itself, and I remain unconvinced by any alternative explanation.[9] The ethnic definition of "Israel" and its sharp separation from the "nations of Canaan," the latter *not* constituting neighboring populations but consisting of subjects of the monarch ruling the territory, seems a very strange kind of proposal under an independent or semi-independent monarch who would hardly have wished to exploit such ethnic opposition among his subjects. It may be that the distinction is rhetorical and seeks only to reinforce a ban on what were seen as "foreign" religious customs. But where the monarchy is ultimately in control of the cult, manifestos of this kind seem pointless.

Deuteronomy is more easily explicable as a literary work, with all the implications of temple and/or palace patronage in its production, if the work itself is not a manifesto seeking to change national self-definition but the "writing-up" of something that was already coming into existence. This "something" does not have to be conjectured, either: the story in 2 Kings 17:24–29 describes something that would fit this explanation of Deuteronomy quite well.

> The king of Assyria brought people from Babylon, Cuthah, Avva, Hamath, and Sepharvaim, and placed them in the cities of Samaria in place of the people of Israel; they took possession of Samaria, and settled in its cities. When they first settled there, they did not worship Yhwh; therefore, Yhwh sent lions among them, which killed some of them. So the king of Assyria was told, "The nations that you have carried away and placed in the cities of Samaria do not know the law of the god of the land; therefore he has sent lions among them; they are killing them, because they do not know the law of the god of the land." Then the king of Assyria commanded, "Send there one of the priests whom you carried away from there; let him go and live there, and teach them the law (משפט) of the god of the land." So one of the priests whom they had carried away from Samaria went and lived in Bethel; he taught them how they should worship (ירא) Yhwh. But every nation still made gods of its own and put them in the shrines of the high places that the people of Samaria had made ...

The story, which contains contradictions, is not, of course, to be taken as reporting a historical fact. But it may indirectly point to one, for it is explaining something that *is* a fact: the people of Samaria – or some, or many of them – continued to worship Yhwh, whether or not alongside other gods. This does not need arguing. The mention of Bethel is especially interesting: it is possibly intended to characterize Samarian Yahwism as a continuation of the idolatrous Yahwism with which the authors of Kings portray the royal cult of Israel. But no explicit

9 Davies, *Origins of Israel*, 105–71.

accusation of an idolatrous cult of Yhwh is, in fact, made. Another interesting feature of this account is the use of the word משפט, which, although more commonly plural in Deuteronomy, is used in the singular, too, and overall, more commonly than תורה. The translation "law" or "commandment" is too imprecise. It means "customs" or "way of doing things," the character that defines an ethnic group. It includes both social and cultic behavior.[10] The newly arrived populations are being taught how to behave like Israelites reasonably enough, since they are in the land of Israel where the god of Israel is at home and, it might be added, specifically at Bethel, where Jacob/Israel had established the cult of the "god of Israel" (Gen 28:10–22; 35:6–7).[11]

That an "Israel" persisted in Samaria is a fact; and the oracles of the early part of Jeremiah addressed to the "house of Israel" show that in the sixth century BCE, a more positive attitude than that of 2 Kings 17 was adopted.[12] But we are now dealing with a definition of "Israel" that is familiar from the Judahite-Samarian Mosaic canon: a people defined by ethnic descent but more importantly, by devotion to a particular god and the way of life he has prescribed. This is different from the known historical definition as a kingdom, which we find adopted in the books of Samuel and Kings and reflected in the use of the term ארץ ישׂראל, "land of Israel," in the Hebrew Bible (and echoed in the New Testament) to designate the territory of Samaria.

How "Israel" changes from being a political designation to an ethnic-religious term has been a matter of discussion for some time now, with various suggestions.[13] Obviously, after the disappearance of the kingdom itself and the cross-transportation of populations by the Assyrians, "Israel" could have no political or ethnic meaning. The ethnic could re-emerge, however, since ethnicity is a reflection of shared custom rather than the other way around. Should we conclude that a new understanding that "Israel" meant a particular set of social and religious customs and a particular cult arose after 722 BCE without any

10 For alternative proposals, see Edelman in this volume.

11 In his contribution to this volume, Halpern notes this mixed population in the North as well. although asserting a Josianic date of composition, he uses a similar logic to what Davies does here. Hoping to take over territory in Samerina as Assyrian power waned and put it under the same policy of agricultural entrepreneurship as had been implemented already by Manasseh and possibly Hezekiah in Judah, there was a recognition that a simplified sense of belonging to an expanded "Israel" based on public, state-funded religious events that broke the power of former phratries, including those of deportee communities in Samerina, was a key factor.

12 Davies, *Origins*, 116–26.

13 E.g. Knauf, "Bethel"; Na'aman, "Saul, Benjamin"; Na'aman, "Israelite-Judahite Struggle"; Fleming, *Legacy*; Finkelstein, "Corpus," 286–88.

social, political or ideological infrastructure, or was an ethnic understanding of "Israel" already in place during the monarchic period, which would provide a more realistic explanation for Israel's survival?

A recent study by Israel Finkelstein and Thomas Römer has suggested that, given the short timespan in which the city of Dan belonged to the kingdom of Israel, it can only have been Jeroboam II[14] who set up Dan, and thus Bethel also, as royal and national Yahwistic temples.[15] There was presumably a royal temple at the capital city of Samaria with its own cult, though whether it had the national or dynastic status that the cult of Jerusalem did in Judah can be doubted. Which deity was worshipped at these temples, or, perhaps more accurately, under what name was the deity worshipped? It was clearly a *national* god, the temples standing at the southern and northern borders of the kingdom. The association of Bethel with Jacob and the identification of Jacob as "Israel" suggests that the deity was the "god of Israel" (*'ĕlōhê yiśrā'ēl*) and that Israel was being defined ethnically by descent from a single ancestor. The political and the ethnic/cultural were being identified by means of this royal initiative.

This is the necessary conclusion, whether or not we date such a development to the early eighth century BCE, but such a date provides a plausible context. The mitigation of destabilizing competition among tribal components of the kingdom by encouraging a common ancestry could be attempted at any time, but the promotion of a sense of ethnic identity could consolidate the incorporation of neighboring areas into the kingdom of Israel under Jeroboam rather than conquest and mere submission to a Samarian monarch, while the Assyrian threat, though temporarily diminished, may have contributed to the phenomenon of "nationalism" as a response. Although Jeroboam's kingdom shrank after his reign, leading finally to the collapse of the kingdom in 722 BCE, the idea of an ethnic and religious "Israel" may have become sufficiently established to sustain an identity despite the loss of political identity and of population transportation. I have argued that it was precisely *this* ethnic definition of "Israel" into which Judah included itself in the absence of the Jerusalemite cult and under Benjaminite religious and political governance during Neo-Babylonian imperialism. I have suggested that the temple of Bethel might have served both provinces, offering a central (but not necessarily a single) home for the "god of Israel/Jacob."[16]

---

14 I am one of the few who prefers to think of him as Jeroboam I or the only Israelite king who bore that name.

15 Finkelstein and Römer, "Comments," 326–30.

16 Davies, "Origin," 4–5, 8–9; Davies, *Origins of Israel*, 159–71.

My hypothesis is that Deuteronomy is the product, not the starting point, of a process of reasserting and redefining the identity of Israel within Samaria. Bethel came to be located within Judah at some point after 722 BCE.[17] Once that happened, it could serve as a center for a cult now shared by giving physical expression to the incorporation of Judah into Jacob's family. It is this development that could explain how a new, anti-idolatrous, ethnically assertive and henotheistic (functionally monotheistic) cult of Yhwh, the god of Israel, came about in both Samaria and Yehud and how the Mosaic Torah literary project that more precisely defined this "Israel" became a joint exercise. Deuteronomy became part of this project at some point, if it was not part of its creation.

According to this hypothesis, Deuteronomy derives from an enterprise that was both Israelite-Samarian and post-monarchic in relation to the kingdom of Israel, which grew from developments under the Israelite monarchy. But at what point might we be dealing with a *document* that we could name "Deuteronomy"? The majority opinion is that the oldest form of this document was a collection of laws,[18] and at any point from 722 BCE onwards, the inscribing of those customs that defined Israel within Samaria might have taken place as part of the enculturation of newly transported populations as well as a reaffirmation of the essence of a post-monarchic national identity. I see no point in trying to reconstruct in detail the growth of this document; once in literary form, it most probably grew gradually thereafter, both by incorporating new "laws" and by acquiring a literary shape influenced by the well-established genres of royal law-code and vassal treaty. Its relationship to the *mišpāṭîm* of Exodus, the "Covenant Code," may be understood in several ways: Deuteronomy derived much of its content from an already existing legal code, which is the majority view;[19] Deuteronomy served as the basis for other biblical legal collections, as John Van Seters has argued;[20] or these are alternative literary out-

---

17 There are three logical options for when this former Ephraimite territory became reassigned to the tribal allotment of Benjamin and transferred from Israelite to Judahite or Judean control. The first is the reign of King Josiah, assuming he tested the weakening strength of Assyria by taking land on the northern border between Samerina and his kingdom. The second is in 586 BCE, when the Neo-Babylonians incorporated the kingdom of Judah into their provincial system; they could have adjusted the northern border with Samerina. Finally, the Achaemenid administration could have adjusted the northern boundary between the two provinces once it became the ruling imperial power. See e.g. Edelman, Davies, Nihan, and Römer, *Opening the Books of Moses*, 52–53.

18 So e.g. Kratz, *Composition*, 117–23.

19 So, e.g. Levinson, *Deuteronomy*; Otto, *Das Deuteronomium*, 236–364; Otto, *Deuteronomium 1–11*, 231–38.

20 Van Seters, "Cultic Laws."

comes of the same project, which I think is the preferable understanding. Indeed, André Lemaire has suggested that 2 Kings 17 may be understood as a reference to the Covenant Code.[21] I think the authors of Kings more likely alluded to Deuteronomy. Either way, the legal collections[22] are now embedded in a historical narrative about the origins of ethnic Israel. The latter narrative could have begun to be developed in written form under King Jeroboam and would form an essential part of any program of Israelite identity (re)formation through a common awareness and celebration of how the "nation" and its god were historically entailed. Deuteronomy's conversion of major agricultural festivals into commemorations of the founding event at Mt. Sinai/Horeb leads naturally to the idea that "laws" originated with that event and ultimately are attributable to Moses. But I note that in the account of Josiah's reform, the law book is not associated with Moses, an allusion that appears only in the summary notice of 2 Kings 23:25. My hypothesis says little about the literary history of Deuteronomy, but it offers some suggestions for the manner in which it achieved its extant form(s).

I end with an observation about the strong polemic against the "nations of Canaan" in Deuteronomy. It makes good sense in the context of a struggle to define non-Israelite behavior within Samaria as "foreign," as alien to the god who has given the people of Israel their land and to be stringently avoided and even hated. It is only "Israel" that can legitimately occupy the land. However, embedding this claim within a traditional Israelite story of origins creates a paradox: the Canaanites are indigenous and Israel is the immigrant, the exact opposite of the situation post-722 BCE. This might well be seen as an objection to the theory of Deuteronomy arising from an enculturating project among recent immigrants into Samaria. In response, I can only suggest that the Exodus tradition was already an intrinsic part of Israelite identity and so could not be effaced. But it could be turned to advantage. Long ago, as the founding story runs, the Israelites themselves had entered the land as immigrants (Deut 23:7). It is now the immigrants from elsewhere who find themselves in a land they must come to regard as their own. Being immigrants is no bar to being "Israelite." Rather, they can claim the land equally as theirs by divine gift. Cult, lifestyle, and asserted identity will not *override* ethnicity, but ethnicity will adapt itself to the contours of social and religious custom. Ethnicity is the code, except that through intermarriage, it necessarily imposes itself anyway.

---

21 Lemaire, "Reference."

22 I prefer not to use the term law.

Interactive Editorial Summary

In this seminal essay, Davies has proposed two potential settings for the creation and growth of a Deuteronomy originating in Samaria. He favors his new hypothesis that a form of the book in which the legal collection was placed in a historicizing framework was initially produced sometime after 722 BCE in the Assyrian province of Samerina. Its aim was to instruct the newly settled immigrants in the territory about the deity of the land and the customs associated with his worship as well as local social and judicial customs more generally. His preliminary idea was that these settlers would come to consider themselves Israelites and so be integrated into the existing cultural framework. This is a new theory that avoids the pitfalls of earlier proposals for a northern origin of the book surveyed by Cynthia Edenburg and Reinhard Müller.[23]

While Davies considers the strong polemic against the "nations of Canaan" in Deuteronomy to be a way to express immigrant behavior that falls outside Israelite custom that is to be abandoned if the newcomers are to become part of the post-monarchic, socially and ethnically reconfigured Israel, he did not directly address who the *gēr* would have represented in the text. His proposed historical setting for the book could equally allow as a primary aim the maintenance of already established socio-ethnic Israelite identity after the loss of the kingdom under the new provincial status as Samarians. Given the forced introduction of other ethnic groups within the territory, the references to the *gēr* who is to be included in the religious festivals of Yhwh Elohim, or as he prefers, Yhwh *'ĕlōhê yiśrā'ēl*, although this title is not used in Deuteronomy, might be to these new immigrants. They are not members of Israel, but they still need to honor the god of the land who provides them with agricultural bounty and increase in herds and flocks.[24] If any taxes were paid in the framework of such festivals, then they would have needed to attend for that reason alone.

Although Deuteronomy envisages the *gērîm* to live, like all Israelites, inside walled Israelite settlements, in reality, the wave of immigrants who arrived in 710–709 BCE under Sargon II would have been settled in communities of their own in destroyed or abandoned villages and towns or even some of them on farmsteads (2 Kgs 17:24, 27–31).[25] On the level of dispensing justice, then, it is

---

23 Edenburg and Müller, "Northern Origin?" He has not addressed how the form of the book made its way south in this essay, but based on his thoughts in *Origins*, his likely answer would have been that a copy was kept in the temple archives at Bethel while the sanctuary was still part of Samerina. See the end of this editorial summary.

24 For alternative proposals, see Graber in this volume.

25 For the origins of the new immigrants based on the names of their settlements in 2 Kgs 17:24, 27–31, see e.g. Na'aman, "Population Changes," 110–111; Younger, "Repopulation." For

likely that such settlements of *gērîm* would have been in full control of hearing and deciding internal disputes using their own elders and also having their elders negotiate binding decisions when a dispute involved a neighboring village or town, whether it contained ethnic Israelites or another ethnic immigrant group. It would only have been unresolvable cases that would have been referred to the judge at the *māqôm* (Deut 17:8–10), whose decision was final under penalty of death for Israelite or *gēr* alike. The judge would have functioned as a provincial appointee.

Davies secondarily entertains the possibility that an initial form of the book could have been produced already during the reign of King Jeroboam as part of an enterprise to create a sense of socio-ethnic identity after the addition of new ethnic groups to the kingdom through conquest and territorial expansion and possibly in the wake of Assyrian imperialism. This idea resulted from his reflection over the proposal by Finkelstein and Römer that under Jeroboam (II), national myths of origins were committed to writing and institutionalized at official royal shrines of the kingdom. The foundational myths included the Exodus story, attached to the Yhwh sanctuary in Samaria, and the Jacob narrative, attached to the sanctuaries of Penuel in Transjordan and Bethel in Cisjordan.[26]

On the one hand, as Davies notes, the idea of an ethnic and religious "Israel" may have become sufficiently established before 722 BCE to sustain an identity despite the loss of political identity and of population transportation. On the other hand, however, he did not take into consideration that an initial date for the *mišpātîm* framed in their current narrative of origins under Jeroboam suffers from the same weaknesses as a proposed date under Josiah. The creation of a law-code defining an "Israel" that predicated its religion on a treaty between deity and the people, without the mediation of a king serving as lawgiver, is hard to imagine in any monarchic period. If one wants to adopt an initial date of composition under Jeroboam, he or she will need to explain the initial shape and the subsequent post-monarchic adaptations that were made. Unfortunately, he did not have the opportunity to work through all the implications of such a possibility to refine or develop further his initial thoughts about this potential earlier form.

---

additional insight from two excavated cuneiform tablets, see Na'aman and Zadok, "Sargon II's Deportation." For changes in settlement patterns and material culture post-722 BCE, see Itach, "Kingdom of Israel," 67–73.

26 Finkelstein and Römer, "Comments," 326–30. Finkelstein has expanded the written compositions produced during the reign of Jeroboam II to include the majority of the hero stories reflected in the book of Judges and royal narratives about Saul, Jeroboam I, and Jehu ("Corpus," 268–80).

How the production of Deuteronomy relates to Davies's proposed Benjaminite History and collection of early forms of three prophetic books, Hosea, Amos, and Jeremiah, is unclear. He has argued that the Benjaminite document, written at Mizpah during the Neo-Babylonian period, provides a coherent history in which Benjamin plays the leading role. It began with Joshua's conquest of the territory around Benjamin, continued with a collection of tales of Israelite heroes, including the left-handed Benjaminite Ehud, went on to the judgeship of Samuel in Benjamin and ended with the anointing of the Benjaminite Saul as the first Israelite king. The inclusion of saviors from adjoining tribes, whether original or an expansion, anticipates the Israel ruled by Saul, while the Barak story might represent a further widening to include areas that became part of the kingdom of Israel in its subsequent history.[27] He also places the production of early forms of the three prophetic books at Mizpah, with source material for Hosea and Amos likely being taken from temple archives at Bethel.[28] His proposed initial composition of Deuteronomy relatively soon after the settlement of new immigrant groups in the province of Samerina would allow perhaps for a copy of this early form of the book to end up in the archives of the temple at Bethel before the site became reassigned to Judah and then accessed by Benjaminite scribes at Mizpah, the regional administrative center of Yehud during the Neo-Babylonian period.

Works Cited

Davies, Philip R. "Josiah and the Law Book." In *Good Kings and Bad Kings: The Kingdom of Judah in the Seventh Century BCE*, edited by Lester L Grabbe, 65–77. Library of Hebrew Bible/Old Testament Studies 393; European Seminar in Historical Methodology, 5. London: T & T Clark International, 2005.

Davies, Philip R. "The Origin of Biblical Israel." *Journal of Hebrew Scriptures* 5 (2005): article 17. https://journals.library.ualberta.ca/jhs/index.php/jhs/article/view/5746.

Davies, Philip R. *The Origins of Biblical Israel*. Library of Hebrew Bible/Old Testament Studies 485. New York: T & T Clark, 2007.

Edelman, Diana V, Philip R. Davies, Christophe Nihan, and Thomas Römer. *Opening the Books of Moses*. Sheffield: Equinox, 2012.

Edenburg, Cynthia and Reinhard Müller. "A Northern Provenance for Deuteronomy?" *Hebrew Bible and Ancient Israel* 4 (2015): 148–61.

Finkelstein, Israel. "A Corpus of North Israelite Texts in the Days of Jeroboam II?" *Hebrew Bible and Ancient Israel* 6, no. 3 (2017): 262–89.

27 Davies, *Origins*, 112–13.
28 Davies, *Origins*, 116–26, 161–71.

Finkelstein, Israel and Thomas Römer. "Comments on the Historical Background of the Jacob Narrative in Genesis." *Zeitschrift für die alttestamentliche Wissenschaft* 126 (2014): 317–38.

Fleming, Daniel E. *The Legacy of Israel in Judah's Bible: History, Politics, and the Reinscribing of Tradition.* New York: Cambridge University, 2012.

Hölscher, Gustav. "Komposition und Ursprung des Deuteronomiums." *Zeitschrift für die alttestamentliche Wissenschaft* 40 (1923): 161–255.

Harvey, Paul B., Jr. and Halpern, Baruch. "W. M. L. de Wette's *'Dissertatio Critica ...'*: Context and Translation." *Zeitschrift für altorientalische und biblische Rechtsgeschichte* 14 (2008): 47–85.

Itach, Gilad. "The Kingdom of Israel in the Eighth Century: From a Regional Power to Assyrian Provinces." In *Archaeology and History of Eighth-Century* Judah, edited by Zev I. Farber and Jacob L. Wright, 57–78. Ancient Near Eastern Monographs 23. Atlanta: Society of Biblical Literature, 2018.

Knauf, Axel. "Bethel: The Israelite Impact on Judean Language and Literature." In *Judah and the Judeans in the Persian Period*, edited by Oded Lipschits and Manfred Oeming, 291–349. Winona Lake, IN: Eisenbrauns, 2006.

Lemaire, André. "A Reference to the Covenant Code in 2 Kings 17:24–41?" In *Let us Go up to Zion: Essays in Honour of H. G. M. Williamson on the Occasion of his Sixty-Fifth Birthday*, edited by Ian Provan and Mark J. Boda, 395–406. Leiden: Brill 2012.

Levinson, Bernard M. *Deuteronomy and the Hermeneutics of Legal Innovation*. New York: Oxford University Press, 1997.

Levinson, Bernard M. "The Reconceptualization of Kingship in Deuteronomy and the Deuteronomistic History's Transformation of Torah." *Vetus Testamentum* 51 (2001): 511–34.

Müller, Reinhard and Juha Pakkala, eds. *Insights into Editing in the Hebrew Bible and the Ancient Near East: What Does Documented Evidence Tell Us about the Transmission of Authoritative Texts?* Contributions to Biblical Exegesis and Theology 84. Leuven: Peeters, 2017.

Müller, Reinhard Juha Pakkala, and Bas ter Haar Romeny. *Evidence of Editing: Growth and Change of Texts in the Hebrew Bible*. Society of Biblical Literate Resources for Biblical Study 75. Atlanta: Society of Biblical Literature, 2014.

Na'aman, Nadav. "The Israelite-Judahite Struggle for the Patrimony of Ancient Israel." *Biblica* 91 (2010): 1–23.

Na'aman, Nadav. "The Kingdom of Israel under Josiah." *Tel Aviv* 18 (1991): 3–71.

Na'aman, Nadav. "Population Changes in Palestine Following Assyrian Deportations." *Tel Aviv* 20 (1993): 104–24.

Na'aman, Nadav. "Saul, Benjamin and the Emergence of 'Biblical Israel.'" *Zeitschrift für die alttestamentliche Wissenschaft* 121 (2009): 211–224, 335–349.

Na'aman, Nadav and Ran Zadok. "Sargon II's Deportation to the Province of Samerina in the Light of Two Cuneiform Tablets from Tel Hadid." *Tel Aviv* 27 (2000): 159–88.

Otto, Eckart. *Das Deuteronomium. Politische Theologie und Rechtsreform in Juda und Assyrien*. Beihefte zur Zeitschrift für die alttestamentliche Wissenschaft 284. Berlin: de Gruyter, 1999.

Otto, Eckart. *Deuteronomium 1–11*. 2 vols. Herders Theologischer Kommentar zum Alten Testament. Freiburg im Breisgau: Herder, 2012.

Pakkala, Juha. "Why Cult Reforms in Judah Probably Did Not Happen." In *One God – One Cult – One Nation: Archaeological and Biblical Perspectives*, edited by Reinhard Kratz and Hermann Spieckermann, 201–35. Beihefte zur Zeitschrift für die alttestamentliche Wissenschaft 405. Berlin: Walter de Gruyter, 2010.

Person, Raymond F., Jr., and Robert Rezetko, eds. *Empirical Models Challenging Biblical Criticism*. Ancient Israel and Its Literature 25. Atlanta: Society of Biblical Literature, 2016.

Römer, Thomas C. *The So-Called Deuteronomistic History: A Sociological, Historical and Literary Introduction*. London: T & T Clark International, 2005.

Tigay, Jeffrey H, ed. *Empirical Models for Biblical Criticism*. Philadelphia: University of Pennsylvania Press, 1985.

Van Seters, John. "Cultic Laws in the Covenant Code and their Relationship to Deuteronomy and the Holiness Code." In *Studies in the Book of Exodus: Redaction-Reception-Interpretation*, edited by Marc Vervenne, 31945. Bibliotheca Ephemeridum Theologicarum Lovaniensium 126. Leuven University Press, 1996.

Welch Adam C. *The Code of Deuteronomy: A New Theory of its Origin*. London: J. Clarke, 1924.

Wette, Wilhelm M. L. de. *Beitrage zur Einleitung in das Alte Testament*. Halle: Schimmelpfennig, 1806–1807; English version: *A Critical and Historical Introduction to the* Canonical Scriptures of the Old Testament. Trans. Theodore Parker. Boston: Little and Brown 1843.

Wette, Wilhelm M. L. de. *Dissertatio critico-exegetica qua Deuteronomium a prioribus Pentateuchi libri diversum, alius cuiusdam recentioris auctoris opus esse monstratur*. Jena: Literis Etzdorfii, 1805.

Würthwein, Ernst. "Die josianische Reform und das Deuteronomium." *Zeitschrift für Theologie und Kirche* 73 (1976): 395–423.

Younger, K. Lawson, Jr. "The Repopulation of Samaria (2 Kings 17:24, 27–31) in Light of Recent Study." In *The Future of Biblical Archaeology: Reassessing Methodologies and Assumptions*, edited by James K. Hoffmeier and Alan Millard, 254–80. Grand Rapids, MI: Eerdmans, 2004.

Diana Edelman, University of Oslo, Oslo, Norway

Deuteronomy as the Instructions of Moses and Yhwh vs. a Framed Legal Code

1 Introduction

In this article I will focus on the literary templates belonging to various genres that potentially have been employed by the implied writer of Deuteronomy to create the book. My primary goal is to suggest whether the treaty, the legal treatise, instructions associated with wisdom, fictional autobiography, or testamentary literature is the dominating genre and the extent to which the others have been used as well by the writer to shape the literary product. My focus is not on the history of the compositional process of the book *per se*.

We have the final MT and LXX forms of Deuteronomy and only a few earlier versions of the book from mss. at Qumran, from which we need to work backward to try to understand the production of the book. Given the limited and insufficient evidence, all results are necessarily hypothetical. Nevertheless, any attempt to formulate an understanding of the likely intended purpose of the book needs to start with concrete mss. and the assumption that Deuteronomy was created as a piece of literature that was meant to convey a message to its intended audience. Structuring patterns, literary devices, and rhetoric would have been used to lead the audience through the narrative to a final resolution and what the implied writer would hope would be a clearly received message. Identifying where and how these appear and their implied effect on the audience is the first step toward comprehension and an unravelling of the writing process and the implied writer's purpose for writing. I am not denying the role of reader response in constructing meaning; I am asserting that some of the intentions of an implied writer can be deduced from careful attention to a narrative's construction and rhetoric.

Once this first step is completed, it is possible to take a further hypothetical step backwards to ask what sort of sources, oral or written, might have been available to the writer and if there is evidence that might indicate that one or more earlier sources have been incorporated whole or piecemeal by him to create this book. At the same time, one can ask if there is compelling evidence to identify any verses in the book as later additions because they interrupt the logical flow of the composition or contradict other material in the book. There might be later additions that do not fit these criteria, but they become almost impossible to identify if they blend in so well with the original style, flow, and ideology.

https://doi.org/10.1515/9783110713312-003

Past and current scholarship on Deuteronomy has tended to identify a legal "core," normally identified as chs. 12–26, as a self-sufficient unit that has been framed initially by 4:44–11:32 and 27–30 and then again subsequently with an outer frame consisting of 1:1–4:43 and 31–34. A central goal of the current volume is to provide case studies that shed light on the question of why Deuteronomy was written. As a result, an assessment of the current hypothesis concerning the creation of the book is a necessary step in my examination of the shaping of this piece of literature. I will address directly the question whether chs. 12–26 are likely to have constituted an independent composition at some point in time or whether they have been assembled for the first time in their current format by the implied writer of the book of Deuteronomy at the time he created the first edition of the book.

The purpose of chs. 12–26 or however one would define a hypothetical core can still be asked, whether one considers them to derive from an earlier, independent document or not. In the latter case, it might be possible to discern or propose an original purpose that became adapted when such a hypothetical document would have been used by the author of Deuteronomy, as ably demonstrated by the articles of Philippe Guillaume. Any possible prologue and epilogue would have been eliminated to allow for the collection of legal cases to serve as the stipulations within the treaty template. In addition, it would need to be argued that sermonic segments were introduced, as well as some narrative interludes (see Turton). There would be no way of determining what legal case material or unconditional commands might have been present in the underlying source but omitted by the author of Deuteronomy as inconsistent with his larger vision and purposes. This situation then poses a challenge in principle to any assumption that the earlier source contained only the current materials in those chapters. One would be assuming that the writer chose not to adapt the content by deletion, except for the introductory and concluding frames, but only by addition of the sermonic and narrative interludes. However, once one admits adaptations were made using both techniques, what would have prevented the deletion of original legal material or commands or the addition of new legal material or commands as part of the adaptation process?

Baruch Halpern's contribution, on the other hand, assumes that the original form of Deuteronomy, which he designates D622, already included some or most of the frame materials (chs. 5–28 or possibly–33) and that chs. 12–26, though built upon the Covenant Code as its source, could have been penned by scribes at Josiah's court. He offers a sustained case for situating its creation, along with D622, against historical events under Assyrian domination of the southern Levant in the late eight-seventh centuries BCE.

Bill Arnold's article provides an excellent comparison of the contents of chs. 12–26 with the "Covenant Code" (CC; Exod 20:22–23:33) and the "Holiness

Code" (HC; Lev 17–26). Summarizing the work of Benjamin Kilchör, there are 340 verses that comprise the material in chs. 12–26 after the frames in Deuteronomy 12:1 and 26:16–19 are eliminated. Of these, 110 are considered to be derived from or dependent on either the CC and/or the HC (32.3 %), and another 50 are related to texts in CC and/or HC, but the direction of dependence is impossible to determine (14.7 %). The remaining 180 verses contain material having no observable connection to other regulatory texts in the Tetrateuch (52.9 %).[1] Thus, even allowing room for disagreement over some arguments Kilchör has made to undergird the classification of certain materials in the first two categories, it is likely that at least half of the material in chs. 12–26 is unparalleled in the other so-called legal collections. In addition, it can be noted that only about half of the material in the CC has been taken up in Deuteronomy.[2] The unparalleled material provides a firm basis for discerning concerns within this these fifteen chapters, but the remaining legal material that interacts in some way with the CC and HC also needs to be included before a final assessment of Deuteronomic concerns and issues can be made. The differing emphases that are established in the different forms of an individual case law or command are vital for deciding if the differences found in the Deuteronomic versions reveal the same tendencies as are evident in the unique material or not. Scenarios of composition or redaction can then be postulated to account for the sameness or differences.

2 Preliminary Considerations

In trying to decide if an earlier independent "legal" source was used, or even if the writer was thinking in terms of such a source, the following considerations are relevant. First, references to the teaching (*tôrâ*) found in the "legal codes" in Exodus and Deuteronomy never claim Moses as its primary "author" or authority. It consistently is presented as Yhwh's teaching (Exod 13:9, 16:4, 28; 24;12, Deut 30:10; see also e.g. 2 Kgs 17:34, 37) or the teaching of Elohim (Exod 18:16, 20; see also e.g. Isa 1:10; Hos 4:6). Moses sets the divine regulations before the people as an intermediary (Deut 4:8, 44; see also e.g. Josh 1:7; 8:31, 32, 23:6).

1 Kilchör's proposed unique materials of the deuteronomic core are found in the following verses: **12**:6–12, 17–19, 26, 28; **13**:1, 2, 4–6, 8–13, 15–16, 18–19; **14**:1, 3, 20, 24, 28; **15**:3, 5–11, 13–14, 20–22; **16**:2, 5, 12, 14, 17, 20; **17**:3–4, 7–20; **18**:3, 6–8, 13–14, 17–22; **19**:8–9, 14, 17–20; **20**:1–20; **21**:1–6, 9–17, 19–20, 22; **22**:2, 5–8, 13–21, 23–27; **23**:2–3, 7, 9–10, 13–14, 16–19, 25–26; **24**:1–6, 11; **25**:3–4, 6–10, 17–19; **26**:4, 10–15.

2 For the list, see Fohrer, *Introduction*, 172.

Beyond these books, in line with this theology, Joshua 24:26 refers to the scroll of the book of Elohim, 2 Kings 10:31 refers to the *tôrat yhwh 'ĕlōhê yiśrā'ēl*, Nehemiah 8:18, 10:28, 29 to the *tôrat 'ĕlōhîm*, and Nehemiah 9:13 to the scroll of the teaching of Yhwh Elohim. 2 Chronicles 17:9 speaks of the scroll of the teaching of Yhwh carried by Levites who were commissioned to teach, and Psalm 78:10 refers to the *tôrat yhwh* and alludes to Deuteronomy's command via Moses to teach it to the children.

In addition, however, other books in the biblical collection designate this written teaching by the phrase, "the teaching of Moses" (1 Kgs 2:3; 2 Kgs 23:5) "the scroll of the teaching of Moses that Yhwh gave to Israel" (Neh 2:3), or to "the teaching, the scroll of Moses" (2 Chr 25:4). In the first case, in 2 Kings 23:5, the same scroll is referred to earlier in the narrative unit as the scroll of the teaching found in the temple of Yhwh, with no attribution of source (2 Kgs 22:8, 11; 23:24; see also 2 Chr 34:15, 19).

In most other instances, such references to the teaching of Moses are careful to qualify the description in such a way that makes it clear that Yhwh is the source of the teaching. 2 Kings 21:8 refers to the *tôrâ* that Moses my servant commanded them. Malachi 3:22 [4:4 Eng] refers to the *tôrâ* of my servant, Moses, which I commanded him at Horeb for all Israel. Daniel 9:11 and 13 refer to the oath and curse written in the law of Moses, the servant of Yhwh, which seems to refer to the book of Deuteronomy, and Ezra 3:2 and 2 Chronicles 30:16 refer to the *tôrâ* of Moses, the man of God and again in 7:6 to the law of Moses that Yhwh the God of Israel had given but then in 7:10 calls it the *tôrat yhwh*. Nehemiah 8:14 refers to it as the teaching that Yhwh had commanded by Moses and in 9:14, the *tôrâ* given through Moses in 9:14. Finally, 1 Chronicles 16:40 talks about things written in the *tôrat yhwh* that he commanded Israel and 2 Chronicles 33:8 to the *tôrâ*, statutes, and ordinances given through Moses, while 2 Chronicles 23:18; 31:3; and 35:26 refer to matters written in the teaching of Moses.

It is unclear if the expression, the teaching of Yhwh Sebaot, in Isaiah 5:24 or even the teaching of Yhwh in Isaiah 30:9 and 42:24 refers to an individual teaching, as the expression does in the books of Leviticus and Numbers, or presumes this *sepher* tradition. The same is the case for Jeremiah 6:19 and 8:8, 16:11, and 26:4, although the claim in Jeremiah 9:13, 26:4, and 44:10 that Yhwh set the teaching before the people might be intended to allude to the tradition of Moses as intermediary.

It is noteworthy that certain statements in subsequent books give the impression they are referring to the book of Deuteronomy explicitly. Joshua 8:34 refers to the reading of all the words of the *tôrâ*, blessings and curses, according to all that is written in the book of *tôrâ*. Also, Joshua 22:5 cites from Deuteronomy; "serve him with all your heart and all your soul." 1 Kings 2:3 refers to the keeping of Yhwh's statutes, his commandments, his ordinances, and his testimonies, as it is written in the teaching of Moses, so that you may prosper in all that you do and wherever you turn. This again alludes to language in Deuteronomy, not Exodus. So does 2 Kings 17:34, which alludes to the Song of Moses in Deut 33:4, 10, and the references to not wandering out of the land Yhwh gave the ancestors if they follow the law in 2 Kings 22:8 and 2 Chronicles 33:8. The regulation in Deuteronomy 24:16 about individual retribution is cited directly in 2 Kings 14:6 and 2 Chronicles 25:4 as being written in the scroll of the *tôrâ* of Moses in the first instance and in the *tôrâ*, the scroll of Moses, in the second. In 2 Kings 23:24, Josiah puts away the list of prohibited personnel in Deuteronomy 18, a list not found in Exodus but partially in Leviticus 19:31 and 20:6, 27. Isaiah 24:5 refers to the people violating the teaching, the statutes, thereby breaking the *bᵉrît ʿôlām*. Jeremiah 32:23 and 44:23 allude to the exile as the enactment of curses for not following the *tôrâ*. Malachi 2:8 talks of the corruption of the covenant of Levi, found in Deuteronomy 33, and Malachi 3:22 [4:4] refers to statutes and ordinances commanded at Horeb. Daniel 9:11 includes the confession, "So the curse and the oath written in the law of Moses, the servant of God, have been poured out upon us, because we have sinned against you." Nehemiah 10:29 states, "join with their kin, their nobles, and enter into a curse and an oath to walk in God's law, which was given by Moses the servant of God, and to observe and do all the commandments of Yhwh our Lord and his ordinances and his statutes." Finally, 2 Chronicles 19:10 also seems to allude to the referral of difficult cases to the temple staff in Deuteronomy. It appears that Deuteronomy and its regulatory section serves as the primary referential point in other books, not the so-called Covenant Code or Holiness Code.

3 The Basic Shape of the Book

According to Jeffrey H. Tigay, the book can be broken into an introductory heading, three discourses: 1:6–4:43, 4:44–28:69, and 29:1–30:20, and an epilogue of sorts about Moses's last days.[3] However, if we pay attention to where the narrator is introducing material other than in narrated asides,[4] the following sub-

3 Tigay, *Deuteronomy*, xii. Contrast the view of Norbert Lohfink, who speaks of four speeches and divides them as follows: Deut 1:1–4:43, 4:44–28:68, 28:69–35:52, and 33:1–29 (*Höre, Israel*, 15–16; "Bund als Vertrag," 218–21).

4 The narrated asides are found in 2:10–12, 2:15, 2:20–23, although this might be speech by Moses, and 10:6–9.

divisions in the text occur: 1:1–4:40, 4:41–26:19, and 27:1–34:12. The final section, however, contains much more third-person narration that does not serve to introduce asides, as it does in the first two sections. In the third section, third person statements by the narrator alternate with first person speech by Moses in most instances, but also with first-person speech by Moses together with the Levitical priests in 27:9–10 and by Yhwh in 31:16–21, 31:23, and 32:48.

The second subdivision, 4:41–26:19, has other recognizable structuring devices. A prominent one is the use of the repeated phrase, "Hear, O Israel," in 5:1, 6:4, and 9:1 that separates 4:41–11:32 from the *ḥuqqîm* and *mišpāṭîm* that appear in 12:1–26:15, forming a tripartite introduction within this section.[5] There is a mirror image of this phrase in the first subdivision in 4:1, which reads, "And now, O Israel, hear the *ḥuqqîm* and *mišpāṭîm* I am teaching you to do ..." Then, after their presentation, there is a brief report concerning declarations made in the wake of the presentation of the commands by Yhwh and Israel, which establish a formal agreement between them.

The material in 12:1–26:15 is set inside a frame that describes it as constituting *haḥuqqîm w^{e}hammišpāṭîm* in 11:32 and 26:16. Thus, these two verses delimit the extent of the section of regulations and legal cases while also defining their nature. This compound expression only occurs one more time within these chapters, in 21:1 in the section concerning the obligations of the king, which some have argued is a later addition. In addition, however, there are ten more occurrences of this compound expression in chs. 4–11 that anticipate and give a paranetic sense to the materials in 12:1–26:15. In five of these cases, the compound expression is summarized as or equated twice with *miṣwâ* (6:1, 7:11), once as *tôrâ* (4:8) and twice as *'ēdōt* (4:45; 6:20), while the variant phrase *ḥuqqîm* and *miṣwôt* appears three times, *miṣwôt*, *ḥuqqîm*, and *'ēdōt* once, and *ḥuqqîm* and *miṣwôt* occur alone once each.[6] The compound phrase returns again in 30:16, while *miṣwôt* and *ḥuqqîm* occurs in 28:15. Thus, the entire section in 12:1–26:15 is also seen to constitute a collective body of commands, which, in this case, are made by a divine superior to his subjects, Israel, and, secondarily, with lesser emphasis, as witnessing testimonies.

The materials in 12:1–26:15 are clearly distinguished from the "words" of the Decalogue in 4:13–14. The people heard the decalogue directly at Horeb; it contained commands laid upon them by Yhwh that subsequently were recorded

---

5 So e.g. McBride, "Polity," 238.

6 Deut 4:1, 5, 8, 45; 5:1, 31; 6:1, 20; 7:11; 11:1. Also, the variant combination *ḥuqqîm* and *miṣwôt* appears in 4:40 and 6:2, 10:13 and in 5:31; 6:1; 7:11: 11:1 *miṣwâ* is added as a third term; in 6:13 there is *miṣwôt, ḥuqqîm* and *'ēdōt* and in 6:60 *'ēdōt* is added as a third term. In 6:24 *ḥuqqîm* occurs alone and in 7:12 *mišpāṭîm* alone.

on the two tablets of stone. This material constituted the contents of a *b^erît*.[7] They are (re)presented orally in 5:6–21, and 5:22, 9:9–11, and 10:1–5 recall the history of their divine inscription twice on tablets. They are separate from the statutes and ordinances to be obeyed in the Promised Land in 12:1–26:15, which Yhwh commanded Moses to teach, and yet also deliberately included as still valid alongside the additional commands being presented.

Whether the point being made here is that the *ḥuqqîm* and *mišpāṭîm* in 12:1–26:15 are not divine words but an authorized interpretation of the Decalogue, as argued for example by Georg C. Macholz and Georg Braulik, is debatable.[8] They argue the indefinite form of the two nouns in 4:14 signals they are not reiterating another law in addition to the Decalogue and also that they are only valid in the land, while the Decalogue is binding always and everywhere. Their interpretation overlooks the possibility that the Decalogue can remain in effect always and everywhere while other independent commands can be made conditional in time or space alongside it. The ongoing validity of the Decalogue is upheld in the book both by its presentation in 5:6–21 and by the command to place the scroll of Moses beside ark that contains the tablets of the law, not inside it in place of the tablets, in 31:26. The latter is a divine artifact written by the finger of God (9:10), while the former is a man-made product meant to be used by and taught to humans as well as to serve as a witness or testimony, which includes the text of the two tablets.

What distinction is being maintained by using *ḥuqqîm* and *mišpāṭîm* to describe the material in 21:1–26:15, which otherwise is summarily classified as *miṣwâ*?[9] Christoph Levin has built heavily on Albrecht Alt's categorizations and has argued that *ḥuqqîm* represent cultic law and *mišpāṭîm* case law, while Calum M. Carmichael seems to be making a similar distinction when he proposes

---

7 Here consideration needs to be given to whether *b^erît* is used in the sense of the formal relationship that has been established between Yhwh and Israel or whether, instead, it might designate the written document containing commands from a superior to an inferior that could serve as the basis of a covenantal relationship but not represent the entire process that created such a relationship or a completed treaty. Specifically, in ancient Near Eastern practice, it appears these two things were separate entities in the Late Bronze period at least. So e.g. Beckman, "Hittite Treaties," 283.

8 Macholz, "Israel," 100; Braulik, *Theology*, 5–7. At the same time, it is clear that the Decalogue forms the basis of the Horeb covenant and that its validity is reaffirmed before the presentation and confirmation of the *ḥuqqîm* and *mišpāṭîm* forming the collective *miṣwâ* of a new covenant made on the plains of Moab in 28:69 [29:1], 9–14 [10–15].

9 Elsewhere in the Pentateuch, the alleged hendiadys *ḥuqqîm w^emišpāṭîm* appears once in Exod 15:25 in the singular and once in plural in Lev 26:46 alongside *hattôrôt* in a list of three elements. *Ḥuqqîm* appears alone in Lev 10:11 *b^eyad mošeh* and in Num 30:16, which God commanded Moses.

that *mišpāṭîm* apply to situations where secular jurisdiction can enforce a penalty for infraction, while *ḥuqqîm* refer to situations where secular jurisdiction is powerless to intervene, so that one must invoke prohibition, positive duty, and curse to gain compliance.[10] I would agree that *mišpāṭîm* represent collectively the casuistic law or conditional and relative legal formulations in these chapters expressed in both third and second person, since that formulation is thought to have derived from actual cases and their decisions. However, I find it more accurate to argue that *ḥuqqîm* refer to the other regulations formulated non-casuistically or unconditionally in second or third person, both positively and negatively, in these fifteen chapters.[11]

All extant "legal" collections from the ancient Near East are formulated casuistically, always in third person, with unconditional injunctions, prohibitions or regulations occurring rarely.[12] Conditional formulations in second person dominate the phrasing found in proverbs, instructional material associated with wisdom, a genre of Hittite regulations or sanctions, which also employed third person throughout, formal political agreements that include stipulations, private legal documents, and letters, while unconditional direct address formulated both positively and negatively is used in Hittite and Syrian treaty stipulations, wisdom instructions, disciplinary warnings, royal instructions and edicts, and tomb inscriptions.[13] If we turn to the meaning of the underlying root, *ḥ-q-q*, "to carve or inscribe," a more general categorization of *ḥōq*/*ḥuqqâ* would be a formal or official regulation or command that has been written down and has binding force.

Ḥuqqîm and *mišpāṭîm* are not used in 12:1–26:15 to describe individual legal regulations. *Mišpāṭ* in the singular is used more generally to refer to the just rendering of legal decisions, often translated "justice," and even in 17:8–11, whose wording refers to a hypothetical specific case, an actual case is not under review. The same applies to its use in 19:6, 21:22, 24:17, and 25:1. Nor does the term *tôrâ* appear in this section of commands except in 17:19–20, the "teaching" or instruction of the king. In these chapters there is a marked decrease in the appearance of *dābār*/*dᵉbārîm* in reference to Moses, except in his speech in

10 Levin, Über den 'Color Hieremianus,'" 118; Alt, "Die Ursprünge," 278–332; Carmichael, *Laws*, 41.

11 I am using the terminology developed by Rifat Soncino (*Motive Clauses*, 10–29), which offers a needed corrective to Alt's influential categories of casuistic and apodictic ("Die Ursprünge," 278–332).

12 For a list of where these formulations occur in the ancient Near Eastern codes, see Paul, *Studies*, 115, nn. 1 and 2 and Sonsino, *Motive Clauses*, 1980, 31, 34.

13 Sonsino, 36–38.

12:31 [13:1]. They contain almost no reference to the "promises to the fathers" and almost no direct divine speech. According to Casper J. Labuschagne, chs. 1–3 have ten references to divine speech, 4–11 eight references, 12–26 two references only, and 27–31 ten references.[14] These are a few trends that have been commented on before within chs. 12–26.

It is perhaps noteworthy that 12:1–26:15 is not co-extensive with the second speech of Moses, which occurs in 4:41–26:19, but a major component of it. This is particularly important to note because in 26:17–19, Moses ends this speech by informing the people that in the wake of hearing the *ḥuqqîm* and *mišpāṭîm*, "today" both Yhwh and they have made declarations that effectively put into effect the preceding contents that are subsequently described in 29:1 as the words of the *b^erît*. This exchange of declarations would seem to relate to the subsequent references to the oath, אלה, in 29:13 [14], 17 [18] and 19 [20]. It seems, then, that the author of Deuteronomy is envisioning a two-step process involving a set of formal commands or stipulations that are proclaimed before a declarative affirmation is made in order to enact a formal and binding pact.

The narrator reappears in 27:1, signaling the beginning of the final speech. Here, Yhwh's initial writing of the covenantal terms at Horeb in 4:13, 5:22, 9:10, and 10:2, 4, as recounted in the larger retrospective review with some anticipatory segments in chs. 1–11, is mirrored by the writing of the additional *tôrâ* by humans on the stones at Shechem in 27:3 and in the *tôrâ* scroll in 17:18 (anticipatorily), 29:21, 31:9, and 31:24. The command Moses gives in 31:19 to write the song found in ch. 32 as a witness against Israel that he performed his divine commission to deliver to them this instruction and his personal fulfillment of the command in 31:22 is a separate act of writing that is tangentially related to the writing of the book of teaching as another text meant to recall the covenant events on the plains of Moab.[15]

In the story world of the book, there is no set of sacrifices that serves as a third, concluding step to seal the covenant established "today." Instead, or in addition, after the people have entered the land, they are to make holocaust sacrifices and *š^elāmîm* sacrifices of well-being and enjoy a meal, "rejoicing before Yhwh," at Shechem. There, they will write "all the words of this *tôrâ*" on

14 Labuschagne, "Divine Speech," 375.

15 The act of human writing in papers of divorce (24:1, 3) is not directly relevant to this larger frame. The writing of "these words" on doorposts and gates in 6:9 and 11:20, however, is an imitative human act meant to recall divine regulations and actions. According to Ryan O'Dowd, Israel's writing has literal dimensions but is a mimetic symbol of their daily entrance into writing as a moral way of life (*Wisdom*, 83–84). In the latter two passages, *tôrâ* is appropriated, actualized, and applied as a continuing social exercise.

plastered stones (27:1–7). It is not fully clear if the exchange of declarations in 26:17–19 completed the covenant in Moab, making the events at Shechem a commemorative celebration of it, or whether in some way they are meant to conclude the agreement that was begun on the plains of Moab but not initiated formally until after the events to take place at Shechem. Ryan O'Dowd, for example, thinks that since a new speech begins in 27:1 and deals with events to take place at Shechem, the blessings and curses in ch. 28 are to be associated with a third covenant at Shechem, not with the covenant being made on the plains of Moab. At the same time, he sees this covenant to function as Kierkegaard's concept of "repetition"; "remembered events that become new."[16]

The two concluding poems are assigned different roles. The first in ch. 32 is described as a song that is to be memorized by Israel so it can serve as a witness against them when they break the set of commandments delivered by Moses to them on the plains of Moab. Its function within the book is harder to identify. Some have proposed it represents a genre dubbed "the covenant lawsuit" that they propose the overlord would have used to appeal to the gods who had served as witnesses to the treaty to point to the infraction before declaring war on the vassal as punishment for the infraction.[17] However, as Tigay points out, there is no mention of the covenant in the poem; instead, he thinks the poem portrays Israel as a recalcitrant child, not a rebellious vassal, and thus draws on family imagery and ideas of filial piety.[18] In addition, no infraction has yet occurred, even though it is anticipated that it will after Moses's death.

Autobiographies, fictional or actual, can include a dimension of self-defense or self-justification, so perhaps this can account for its presence (ch. 32). In anticipation of such rebellion, Moses is providing the song that is to be taught through the generations in Israel. When the people rebel and there are legitimate grounds for Yhwh to bring a covenantal law suit against them, this would in theory prevent the people from being able to shift blame onto Moses by claiming he did not instruct them properly. Thus, on some level, it serves as redundant proof that he has conveyed the *ḥuqqîm* and *mišpāṭîm* to Israel, alongside the written *tôrâ* scroll that contains the actual words. Since that is to be kept implicitly in the temple, beside the ark of the covenant, however, it is not directly accessible to the people, but the song is.[19]

---

16 O'Dowd, 87; quote from p. 88.

17 So e.g.; Huffman, "Covenant Lawsuit," 290–95; Harvey, "Le '*rîb*-pattern,'" 180–91; Wright, "Lawsuit," 41–58; Delcor, "Les attachés littéraires," 19–24.

18 Tigay, *Deuteronomy*, 29–30.

19 Ryan O'Dowd claims there is a deliberate contrast being set up concerning threats to distort Israel's knowledge in the second and third speech. The threats come from outside in chs. 12–26 but from inside in 29–32 (*Wisdom*, 92). This is an overgeneralization.

The poem in Deuteronomy 33, on the other hand, constitutes Moses's blessing, which serves as his last testament on the eve of his actual death. In some ways the entire book serves this function, but since it takes place in anticipation of his immanent death, it is more apt to describe the larger composition as Moses's collective farewell speech. The inclusion of the poem is logical within the context of a fictional autobiography set late in the life of the speaker. It is not a necessary component, but it is one that is appropriate in the context.

Finally, it is noteworthy that *hayyôm*, "today," is used thematically in all three sub-sections. The word appears in 1:39; 2:18, 2:25; 4:4; 4:8; 4:26; 4:39; 4:40 in the first subsection; 5:1, 5:3, 5:24; 6:6; 7:11; 8:1; 8:11; 8:19; 9:1; 9:3; 10:13; 11:2; 11:4; 11:8; 11:13; 11:26; 11:27; 11:28; 12:8; 13:19 [18]; 15:5; 19:9; 20:3; 26:16; 26:17; 26:18 in the second subsection; and 27:1; 27:4; 27:10; 28:1; 28:13; 28:14; 28:15; 29:9 [10]; 29:11 [12]; 29:14 [15]; 29:17 [18]; 30:2; 30:8; 30:11; 30:15; 30:16; 30:18; 30:19; 31:2; 31:27; 32:46 in the third subsection. Many uses appear in the stereotypical phrase, "the commandment (*miṣwâ*) that I am commanding you today." This is a unifying temporal feature that gives immediacy to the three speeches and has the rhetorical effect of urging the reader to take action in his or her situation alongside the audience in the story-world hearing Moses's speeches.[20]

4 The Law Code Template

German scholarship has tended to follow Martin Noth's understanding of the creation and expansion of the book of Deuteronomy. He argued that the original form of the book, *Urdeuteronomium*, consisted only of 4:44–30:20. Deuteronomy 1:1–4:43 was added as an introduction to the proposed Deuteronomistic History (Deut–2 Kgs) by including selected events from the period of the wilderness wanderings so that matters that would come up later in the narrative could be understood. Chapters 31–34, esp. 31:1–13 and parts of 34 (e.g. vv. 7–12, esp. v. 9), were also, in his view, Deuteronomistic anticipatory links to Joshua 1 and the larger, extended narrative.[21]

---

20 The possibility also should be considered that *hayyôm* has quasi-legal overtones in its use in many of these passages, where it might be intended to emphasize that the announcement of the stipulations and their formal acceptance by the people were to be put into force immediately, the same day. Paul Kalluveettil has pointed out that the idiom, *ntn* + *h*/*b*/*k* + *yôm* + *hazzeh*/*hahû* "indicates the coming-into-force of a juridical 'act'" (*Declaration*, 183). *Hayyôm hazzeh* occurs in 2:25, 11:4, and 26:16, but without the verb *ntn*, while a number of other uses emphasize choosing to follow the regulations today (pp. 183–85).

21 Noth, *Deuteronomistic History*, 13–16.

Noth offered a twofold explanation of the format for *Urdeuteronomium* as a speech by Moses whose main purpose was to convey the Deuteronomic law. First, the law already was formulated as first-person speech by Moses, and second, the writer had a preference for having characters in leadership roles use speeches in the wider History. He then stated there was a need for a summary of previous events from Horeb in the plains of Moab in the prologue to the laws, because their delivery was taking place at the end of the wilderness wandering period.[22] It seems, then, that Noth was arguing that the writer used an independent source comprising chs. 12–26 + 28 that already was framed in first person speech in the prologue and epilogue. He failed to comment on the fact, however, that while prologues and epilogues to "legal" collections typically are written in first person, all surviving examples of the contents of such collections from the ancient Near East are written in third person.[23]

In reading ancient Near Eastern examples of so-called "law codes" that have been preserved, it can be seen that two templates were used. The first had cases and verdicts alone, written in third person, while the second had a prologue and epilogue written in first person that framed the cases and verdicts in third person. Three examples of the first form that have survived are the so-called Sumerian Laws of Eshnunna (ca. 1770 BCE), with a superscription associating the laws with a King Dadusha (*COS* 2.130),[24] the Hittite laws, known from an Old Kingdom version (ca. 1650–1500 BCE) and a revised, expanded New Kingdom version (ca. 1500–1180 BCE) (*COS* 2.19),[25] and the Middle Assyrian laws (ca. 1076 BCE) (*COS* 2.132).[26] Examples of the second form that have survived are the laws of Ur-Namma of Ur (ca. 2100 BCE), which might have contained an epilogue but is known only from fragments,[27] the Laws of Lipit-Istar of Isin

22 Noth, *Deuteronomistic History*, 15–16.

23 The strict use of third person in legal collections has been noted before, by e.g. Gerstenberger, "Covenant," 43, n. 24; Paul, *Studies*, 122–23; Weinfeld, "Origin of Apodictic Law," 2, 63; Morrow, "Generic Discrepency," 138; Morrow, "*Fortschreibung*," 114.

24 See also Roth, *Law Collections*, 57–70. She notes that the introduction is similar to those found in Old Babylonian royal edicts and remissions.

25 See also Roth, 213–40.

26 See also Roth, 153–209. She also thinks the Middle Assyrian laws might have been compiled for the library of Tiglath-pileser I (ruled 1114–1076 BCE), of Ninurta-apil-ekur (ruled 1191–1179 BCE), or for the libraries of subsequent scribes (p. 154). The use of third person also occurs in Hittite "instructions" to various types of priests and temple officials, with interspersed second-person address, to commanders of border garrisons, with some second person address, and to the royal guard, all in third person (*COS* 1.83–85). Additional examples can be found conveniently in Miller, *Royal Hittite Instructions*. In Mesopotamian tradition, however, there is a preference for using first and second-person speech in such sets of instructions.

27 Finkelstein, "Laws," 66–82; Roth, *Law Collections*, 13–22.

(ca. 1930 BCE),[28] and the Code of Hammurabi of Babylon (ca. 1750 BCE) (*COS* 2.131).[29] The regulation sections of both templates are formulated as conditional propositions almost exclusively ("if ... then"), always in third person.

Noth was aware that one of the two templates for so-called law codes in the ancient Near East included a prologue and epilogue. He argued on the basis of the Code of Hammurabi that the inclusion of blessings and curses in Deuteronomy 28 was the result of an awareness of the practice of including both elements "at the end of the laws."[30] His delineation of the laws as running from ch. 12 to ch. 28, excluding ch. 27, rather than ending with ch. 26, as is more commonly suggested, apparently led him to move this aspect of the traditional epilogue into the law section proper. In his view, the text of the Code of Hammurabi had spread throughout the ancient Near East. Interestingly, however, he did not identify any influence of its prologue in Deuteronomy 12. Nor did he seem to consider the possibility that, when creating the current prologue in 4:44–49 and epilogue in chs. 29–30, the writer might have been influenced by this same template.[31]

The prologue of the law code template states that specific gods have named the king who is promulgating the collection to make justice prevail in the land, to abolish the wicked and the evil and to prevent the strong from oppressing the weak. The king then gives a list of his epithets and accomplishments, before returning to the divine command to provide just ways for the people and an assertion that he established truth and justice as the declaration of the land and enhanced the well-being of the people. Afterwards, the laws begin.

The contents of Deuteronomy 4:43–49 are not really comparable to what stands in the law code prologue. Instead, as Noth surmised, they set the scene for the events that follow, placing the speech on the eve of the conquest of Cisjordan.[32] Even so, he has not explained why his source used mostly second

---

28 Szlechter, "Le code de Lipit-Istar (I) and (II)"; Roth, *Law Collections*, 23–35.

29 See also Roth, 71.

30 Noth, *Laws*, 122–23. On p. 119, in n. 5, he explicitly states that the blessing and curses segment "certainly belongs to the original Deuteronomic law, and not to any added sections and yet contains a concluding chapter of blessings and curses." In support, he notes that the Holiness Code also ends with blessings and curses. Then, he argued that 28:1–69 originally followed directly after 26:16, 17*aba*, 18*a*.

31 In *Deuteronomistic History*, 31, n. 1, he suggested, "It is possible that Dtr.'s inclination to insert speeches is dependent on the extant form of the Deuteronomic law or at least influenced by it." Yet this comment still does not acknowledge the trend in law codes to state the principles in third person, not first or even second person.

32 Thus, the suggestion by Sigrid Loersch, for example, that Deut 5–11 would have constituted the expected prologue as an integral frame for the laws in chs. 12–26 since 28 is included as the epilogue, remains problematic (*Das Deuteronomium*, 36–37). She also cites the Code of

person singular and plural forms with occasional first-person language interspersed to express the legal principles conditionally. Of the 65 conditional statements in Deuteronomy 12:1–26:15 made with *kî* or *'im*, only 15 (19:11, 21:5, 21:18, 22:13, 22:20, 22:22, 22:25, 22:28, 24:1, 24:5, 24:7; 25:1, 25:2; 25:5, and 25:7), or 23 %, follow the ancient Near Eastern legal tradition that presents case examples and their verdicts in the third person. In most cases in Deuteronomy, second-person statements follow immediately to comment on the preceding case.

The epilogue of the law code template returns to the issuing king, who, after an introductory sentence in third person, claims in first person speech again to be the champion of justice who has written down his "just decisions" on a stela. The alleged blessings are for the brilliance of Enlil's countenance to be turned upon the one from above who does not do anything evil to it, damage his work or efface the inscription and put his own name on it (Lipit-Ishtar) or a long reign for any wise future ruler who does not reject his judgments, change his pronouncements or alter his statue (Hammurabi). Conversely, any king, *ēnu*-lord or *ensi*-ruler who does any of the listed things or induces an outsider to do so to avoid the curse is to be completely obliterated, with other calamities to befall him in a partially preserved final section that represents curses enacted by a series of deities, including Enlil, Ashnan, Sumukan, and Utu in the remaining legible lines (Lipit-Ishtar). Any future ruler who does any of these things is to be deprived of the shining glory of royalty, have his scepter smashed and his destiny cursed by Anu, father of the gods, and a range of other curses will befall him from Enlil, Ninlil, Ea, Shamash, Sin, Adad, Zababa, Ishtar, Nergal, Nintu, and Ninkarrak (Hammurabi).[33] Both extant epilogues include references to heaven and earth as well. Noth readily pointed out that these blessings and curses are laid on future kings in the Code of Hammurabi (and men of high stature as well in the case of Lipit-Ishtar), not the common people, and the shortness of the blessing contrasts with the longer list in ch. 28. He explained this anomaly by suggesting that the biblical writer attempted to add more balance between the blessings and curses.[34]

Hammurabi as her example. Its content does not correspond to that in the extant framed law codes, while the blessings and curses in Deut 28 are similar thematically to the extant law code epilogues but certainly not close in their wording or format. Loersch does not seem to acknowledge it was possible to have a law code without a prologue or epilogue, in which case the lack of a suitable prologue could have prompted both her and Noth to consider if ch. 28 might be serving a different function within the story world of the book and the development of the narrative. Does it belong to the second, fuller law book template as they were assuming, or perhaps a different template altogether?

33 Roth, *Law Collections*, 33–35, 133–40.

34 Noth, *Laws*, 122–23.

Braulik has accepted Noth's delineation of *Urdeuteronomium* but has a different understanding of the influence of the Code of Hammurabi on it.

> The exiles, however, probably experienced the just laws of the wise King Hammurapi as the highest achievement of any foreign culture. This is why the text of Deuteronomy contains parallels to the prologue and epilogue of the code of Hammurapi. These parallels are designed to show that Israel and its laws are superior even to this king and his impressive achievements. Most of the motifs and formulations in [chap. 4] verses 6–8 differ from the usual themes and expressions of Deuteronomy. Consequently, they occur seldom or not at all in the rest of the Old Testament.[35]

Thus, in his view, exiled Judahites gained direct knowledge of the Code while resident in Babylonia, not as a result of the wide diffusion of the text throughout the ancient Near East, as Noth had proposed.

Turning to other law collections in the Pentateuch, the Covenant Code (CC) in Exodus 20:22–23:19 contains a core section, 21:1[2]–22:16 [17], in third person, like other ancient Near Eastern law collections, which is framed by second-person segments in 20:22–20:26 and 22:17 [18]–23:19. Then, the Holiness Code (HC) in Leviticus 17–26 resembles Deuteronomy in having a majority of its sections in first person that deliver commands in second person (17:10–18:28, 18:30–19:5, 19:9–19, 19:23, 19:25, 19:25–37, 20:7–8, 20:19, and 20:22–26) but occasionally in third person (e.g. 20:1–6 and 20:9). However, it, too, has some interspersed segments in third person (17:1–9, 18:29,19:6–8, 19:20–22, 19:24, 20:10–18, 20:20–21, and 20:27) as in ancient Near Eastern casuistic collections and Deuteronomy. As already noted, the extant ancient Near Eastern legal collections contain primarily conditional formulations but have a few examples of unconditional formulations.[36] The latter are always formulated in third person like the caustic laws, however, never second person. In light of the presence of some third-person cases and verdicts in biblical collections, it can be concluded that the Judahite legal tradition did not differ from the international third person norm on purpose by using only second person to describe cases and their verdicts. As a result, the assessment that the original conception underlying Deuteronomy was that of a law book directed to an audience addressed in second person is highly unlikely.[37]

Logically, then, the collections of legal cases and expected actions in Deuteronomy 12:1–26:5 as well as Leviticus and Exodus to some extent would need

---

35 Braulik, *Theology*, 8–9.

36 Again, for a list of where these formulations occur in the ancient Near Eastern codes, see Paul, *Studies*, 115, nn. 1 and 2.

37 So e.g. Gárcia-Lôpez, *Le Deutéronome*, 14–16; Nielsen, *Deuteronomium*, 5–8.

to be seen as adaptations of the standard, third-person practice because they are functioning in a different capacity in their current locations in the books where they occur. None of the three so-called biblical law codes are legal treatises that belong to the same genre as what are commonly called ancient Near Eastern law codes. Even if content-wise, they reflect legal case decisions, when they employ first-person and second-person voice, they seem to follow the templates for instructions or for stipulations in formal agreements more than for legal codes. William S. Morrow has pointed out that within Akkadian scribal practice, second person unconditional formulations were used in treaties and loyalty oaths, prescriptive ritual texts, recipes, training texts, and royal decrees.[38]

In a seminal work, Berend Gemser made the important observation that no extant ancient Near Eastern law code includes motive clauses, which always are subordinate or dependent in structure and provide a justification or incentive for complying with a given regulation. In contrast, in Deuteronomy, 61 examples occur within 99 paragraphs in chs. 12:1–26:15.[39] Rifat Sonsino has modified Gemser's initial finding. He has noted that motive clauses are found in both conditional and unconditional legal formulations, alongside explicative notes and paranetic statements, and that though absent in most ancient Near Eastern "law codes," they are used in the Laws of Hammurapi and the Middle Assyrian Laws. He separates paranetic statements, whose purpose is to summon people to obedience and which can be formulated as independent clauses, from motive clauses, which Gemser failed to do, but includes dependently structured paranetic statements as examples of motive clauses. He provides a modified count of 111 motive clauses among the 225 prescriptions found in these chapters.[40] Their understandings corroborate the assessment of Gerhard von Rad that "Deuteronomy is not divine law in codified form but preaching about commandments."[41] The second person singular and plural address in Deuteronomy seems designed to persuade or convince the reader or hearer to act in a certain way, both as an individual (address in second person singular) and as a member of corporate Israel (address in second person plural).

---

38 Morrow, "Generic Discrepency," 140–47.

39 Gemser, "Importance," 97, 99.

40 Sonsino, *Motive Clauses*, 65–69, 93, 153–67.

41 Von Rad, *Studies*, 15.

5 The Vassal Treaty Template

The influence of the vassal treaty template on the shaping of Deuteronomy is commonly assumed or argued for. The plot of the book is about the making of a revised or new covenant (ברית) between Yhwh and Israel in the plains of Moab. Thus, logically, it would narrate events that would have conformed to such a formal process. When one examines the templates for oath-bound formal agreements known for the ancient Near East, however, it becomes apparent that there were regional differences and that traditions changed over time as well. Three regional traditions are available: the Hittite examples of the *išḫiul* from the Late Bronze Age (ca. 1550–1200 BCE), the Aramaic examples of the *adê* known from the Sefire treaties from the eighth century BCE, and the Assyrian examples of the older *rikšu* that evolved into the Neo-Assyrian *adê*.[42] It should be noted that in the Late Bronze tradition, common practice was to refer to a treaty using a pair of terms that translate "binding and oaths": *išḫiul* and *lengaiš* in Hittite and *rikiltu/rikistu/riksu* and *māmitu* in Akkadian, suggesting the document containing the stipulations was separate from the formal oaths sworn by the parties before the gods.[43] In Deuteronomy, the distinction is present, with the *ḥuqqîm* and *mišpāṭîm* collectively called the *miṣwâ* in 12:1–26:25 constituting the binding and references to the *ʾālâ* occurring separately in 29:13 [14], 18 [19], and 19 [20], constituting the oaths backed by curses.

Moshe Weinfeld considers the book of Deuteronomy to cohere more with the Hittite tradition than the Neo-Assyrian one. He points out that the provision for deposit of the tablets and the book of the Law in (sic!) the divine ark (10:1–5; 31:25–27) and the periodic recitation of the law before the public (31:9–13) and the king (17:18–20) are both found in Hittite vassal treaties but not in Neo-Assyrian ones. The historical prologue (Deut 1–11) also is absent from the *adê* tradition but present in the Hittite one. To this can be added the inclusion of blessings in the form of protection for loyal vassals as well as curses in the form of destruction for disloyalty, while the Assyrian tradition includes only curses.

---

42 For a discussion of the historical relationship among these forms, see e.g. Otto, *Das Deuteronomium*, 20–32; Morrow, "*Fortschreibung*," 114–16. A third point Morrow raises is that the Sefire treaties preserve the Hittite practice of having "discrete paragraphs of conditional stipulations [that] end with a repression formula" (115).

43 Beckman, "Hittite Treaties," 283. This observation had been made decades earlier by Viktor Korošec (*Hethitische Staatsverträge*, 26–28, 34–36). In the Iron Age, the Akkadian terms were replaced by the Neo/Assyrian phrase, (*ṭuppu*) *adê māmitu* or *adê tāmīti*, which retained both elements but adopted the Aramaic term for the element containing the sanctions, so e.g. Weinfeld, *Deuteronomy and Deuteronomic*, 67.

Weinfeld attributes to Assyrian influence the series of curses in Deuteronomy 28 that he says follows the order of the Assyrian pantheon, the laws of sedition in Deuteronomy 13, and the covenant-making with present and future generations (Deut 5:2–4) found in Esarhaddon's Succession Treaty (ESOD), lines 1–7 and 385–90.[44] However, the final element is found already in § A.i.19′–34′ of the Hittite treaty between Muršili and Duppi-Tešub (*COS* 2.17B), § A. ii.1–7 of the treaty between Tudhaliya and Šašgamuwa (*COS* 2.17C), and in § 17 of the Hittite treaty of Tudhaliya with Kurunta (*COS* 2.18). Thus, it is not unique to these two documents, which suggests it was a standard contingency that could be drawn upon in such situations rather than being an exception in the case of ESOD that was borrowed somehow by the author of Deuteronomy. In addition, the proposed parallels between ESOD §§ 10 and 12 and Deuteronomy 13:2–18 [1–17], on the one hand, and ESOD §§ 39–42 and 28:20–33, when examined, are superficial and point to both drawing on common ancient Near Eastern treaty and oath conventions. The latter does not reflect the order of the Assyrian pantheon.[45]

William S. Morrow argues for mixed influence from both the Aramaic and Neo-Assyrian oath-bound agreement traditions in the account of covenant-making in Deuteronomy. For him, the Aramaic tradition took over and passed on certain features from the Late Bronze Age covenant tradition known most fully from the preserved Hittite treaties. He notes on the one hand that in chs. 12–26, the overlord (Yhwh) is referenced in third person and the vassal (Israel) in second person, which reflects the most common compositional practice in the Neo-Assyrian *adê* in the seventh century BCE. Hittite practice was to reference the overlord in first person and the vassal in second person, which also was taken over into the Aramaic Sefire treaties and Esarhaddon's vassal treaty with Ba'al of Tyre. On the other hand, the inclusion of a short blessing formula as well as a short list of curses for keeping or breaking the oath was found in the Hittite tradition and taken over into the Aramaic Sefire treaties but was absent from the Neo–Assyrian *adê*, where longer lists of curses alone are invoked against the inferior part who would break the oath.[46] Thus, he is open to the possibility that Deuteronomy has been shaped by incorporating older, non-Assyrian elements from the Late Bronze oath-bound agreement that managed to become part of the Levantine Iron Age template. Ultimately in his view, "any putative older form [of the book] must reflect the composition of Deuteronomy as a treaty document," regardless of how one weighs the relationship of individual el-

44 Weinfeld, 66–67; Weinfeld, "*Bᵉrîth*." 267–69.
45 For a more detailed refutation of this position, see Edelman, "Saying Goodbye."
46 Morrow, "*Fortschreibung*," 115.

ements to known regional and temporal formal agreements that were sealed by oath.[47]

In the following discussion I will deal with standard elements found in each of the three regional templates but acknowledge that each document was adjusted to fit the situation so that the templates were not followed slavishly but were used as guidelines for the general ordering of the document. Since scribes in ancient Egypt used perishable papyrus as a writing surface during much of the existence of the ancient kingdom, no examples of its native treaty tradition have survived, so it cannot be included. This is unfortunate, since Egypt had controlled the southern Levant during the Late Bronze Age and its tradition logically might have been perpetuated by Canaanite scribes. It is possible, however, that an international treaty template had prevailed during this period, given the connected nature of the Late Bronze Age, examples of which have been preserved in Hittite archives.

If one looks at the Hittite template for a vassal treaty with its six standard elements, the following elements occur in Deuteronomy.[48]

1) The preamble, which in this case follows the Hittite tradition that begins, "These are the words of" + the name of the more powerful contracting king": 1:1–5, where Moses is the speaker on behalf of Yhwh and Israel is the other "receiving" partner. In contrast, Neo-Assyrian oath agreements open with the words, the *adê* of King PN + titles with PN or official titles.

2) The historical prologue that gives the background for the current imposition of the treaty: 1:6–11: 32.[49] As noted by Weinfeld, these prologues often refer to the past history of the relationship between the two parties and may dwell on the rebelliousness of the vassal's ancestors and its consequences. The same ideas are found in references to the promises to the fathers (Deut 4:37–38, 7:8, and 9:5) and to the rebellion during the wilderness wanderings (Deut 1:26–28, 1:43, and 4:3–5). There frequently is a reference in the prologue to the land given to the vassal by the suzerain and an urging of the vassal to take possession of it, found also in Deuteronomy 1:8 and 1:21, as well as to the boundaries of the assigned land.[50] S. Dean McBride, on the other hand, claims that the focus in this material on land signals it is not serving the function of a treaty prologue. He thinks the prologue should have told about Exodus events and

47 Morrow, 114.

48 E.g. Beckman, "Hittite Treaties," 284–86.

49 Dennis J. McCarthy limits the historical-paranetic prologue of the central treaty discourse to chs. 5–11. He considers 4:44–28:68 to be the basic draft of the book or the "core" that was expanded with the addition of later chapters (*Treaty*, 186).

50 Weinfeld, "*Beríth*," 267.

the making of the first covenant at Sinai/Horeb as the basis of the prior relationship, and neither appears.[51]

3) The stipulations: Deuteronomy 12:1–26:15, phrased primarily in first and second person.

4) Reference to one or more tablets and provision for deposit in the temple before the gods and periodic reading: Deuteronomy 10:1–5, 17:18–20, 31:9, 31:10–13, and 31:25–27. Provision for deposit of the tablets with the words of Yhwh Elohim in the divine ark that was to be kept in the temple occurs in 10:1–5. Provision for the deposit of "the scroll of this teaching" beside the Ark occurs in 31:25–27 as well as its conveyance to the priests and the elders in 31:9 and for the periodic recitation of the scroll before the public every seven years in 31:10–13. Meanwhile, the king is to study it daily (17:18–20).

5) A list of the gods that witness the agreement: 4:26, 30:19, 31:19–21, 31:25–28, and 32:46). In Deuteronomy, the sole deity that exists is the contracting superior party rather than a human king, which eliminates the possibility of divine witnesses. Nevertheless, Heaven and Earth are invoked as witnesses (4:26, 30:19, and 31:28), as they are in the Hittite treaty tradition (*COS* 2.17a, b; 2.18). In addition, the Song of Moses (32:1–43) serves as a witness against the Israelites (31:19–21; 32:46), as does the written scroll containing all the words (31:25–27 and 32:46?).

Finally, 6) curses and blessings: Deuteronomy 11:13–17, 11:26–28, and 27:14–28:45. The Hittite "blessings" consist of the protection of the gods who oversee the treaty and the curses, while the curses consist of destruction sent by those same deities on the king personally, his family, his city, and his land. They are generic, with no specific examples given. In contrast, here there are detailed examples of both blessings and curses, which go well beyond the Hittite custom in a vassal treaty.

It can be seen that all six elements occur in the narrative of Deuteronomy, although not in the exact order one would expect. The list of witnesses comes after the curses and blessings, although both of these elements are anticipated already in the historical prologue section, where they appear in the expected order: witnesses (4:26) and blessings and curses (11:13–17 and 11:26–28).

If the Neo-Assyrian *adê* template is followed instead, much less of the text is accounted for. I will work with the shorter list of seven elements proposed by Jacob Lauinger rather than the longer, eleven-element list derived by Simo Parpola and Kazuko Watanabe.[52] The point becomes clear even when using the

51 McBride, "Polity," 235.

52 Lauinger, "Neo-Assyrian Scribes," 286–87; Parpola and Watanabe, *Neo-Assyrian Treaties*, xxxv.

shorter list of expected elements: 1) preamble: Deuteronomy 1:1–5; 2) list of the gods: Heaven and Earth, the Song of Moses, and the larger scroll of *tôrâ* (4:26, 30:19, and 31:28); 3) stipulations: Deuteronomy 12:1–26:15; 4) curses only: Deuteronomy 11:16–17 and 11:28; 5) the words of the oath: missing, but a reference to the spoken words of both the people and the suzerain, Yhwh, is found in 26:17–19, as though a parity treaty were being established; 6) another series of curses: 27:14–26; 28:15–45, and 7) a final colophon: missing. The first list of witnesses is not in the expected sequence; it precedes rather than follows the stipulations. Under the missing oath, it can be noted the all but two references to a sworn oath in Deuteronomy have Yhwh as subject, not the people. The majority refer to Yhwh's having sworn to the fathers previously to give them land (1:8, 4:21, 6:10, 6:18, 6:23, 7:13, 8:1, 10:11, 11:9, 11:21, 19:8, 26:3, 26:15, 28:11, 30:20, 31:7, 31:20–21, 31:23, and 34:4) or to a covenant with the fathers (4:31, 7:8, 7:12 implicitly, 8:18, 9:5 implicitly, 13:17 implicitly, and 29:13 implicitly). Only in 28:9 and in the reference to Yhwh having spoken in 29:13 does it seem that Yhwh has sworn a current oath to the people. There are three mentions of a separate oath Yhwh swore at Horeb to destroy the people in 1:34–35 and 2:14. There are only two instances where the people swear, and in both cases, they are commanded always to swear an oath in whatever circumstance it might be required in the name of Yhwh only (6:13 and 10:20). In all extant examples of Neo-Assyrian *adês*, the suzerain never swears an oath to the lesser party. It is noteworthy, however, that in the Hittite treaty tradition, a mutual exchange of oaths took place in a ceremony in which the written contents of the treaty document was ratified (e.g. *COS* 2.17b).[53]

The remaining four elements in the longer list are: seal impressions after the preamble (#2 of 11); a historical introduction before the stipulations and after the oath that in their list comes after the list of divine witnesses and oath (#5 of 11), not after the stipulations; a violation clause (#7 of 11) before the first set of curses; and a vow (#9 of 11) between the two sets of curses. It also should be noted that Parpola and Watanabe position the oath immediately after the list of gods, before the historical introduction and stipulation, whereas Lauinger places it after the stipulations and first set of curses. If using the longer list, the seals would be absent, the historical introduction to the treaty stipulations found in two texts only would be ch. 11 perhaps, the violation clause would be Deuteronomy 27:10 for the ceremony to take place at Mt. Ebal and 28:15 for the ceremony on the plains of Moab, and the vow would be 26:18.

53 Altman, "Who Took," 178–84.

Finally, we will look at the Aramaic *adê* template represented on the first Sefire Stele, the longest and most complete of the three extant stelae.[54] It remains a point of dispute if this is a parity or a vassal treaty.[55] 1) A title, introducing the contracting parties: Deuteronomy 1:1–5; 2) a list of gods serving as witnesses to the agreement: Heaven and Earth, the Song of Moses, and the larger scroll of *tôrâ* (Deut 4:26, 30:19, and 31:28); 3) curses against the vassal if he violates the pact: Deuteronomy 11:16–17 and 11:28; 4) curses with accompanying rites: missing, 5) a restatement of the contracting parties that includes the sons and grandsons of both kings as well as the gods of both cities as contracting parties to the pact, plus an obligation to read out the treaty publicly: Deuteronomy 31:9–13 contains the provision for public reading and 6:1–3 might be loosely construed as a restatement of the contracting parties, but this element basically is missing; 6) the stipulations: Deuteronomy 12:1–26:15; 7) a statement the pact is to serve as a reminder or memorial for the future generations: Deuteronomy 29:13–27 [14–28]; 8) one "blessing" or non-curse, which resembles the Hittite tradition rather than the Neo-Assyrian one: Deuteronomy 11:13–15, 11:26–27, and 28:2–14; and 9) a few curses, which resembles the Hittite tradition more than the Neo-Assyrian one: Deuteronomy 11:16–17, 11:26, 11:28; 27:15–26, and 28:15–45.

As in the case of the Neo-Assyrian *adê*, only a few of the elements are lacking, but the sequence of their occurrence in Deuteronomy does not follow the Aramaic *adê* tradition closely, and there are many more blessings and curses in Deuteronomy than expected. Not all of the material in Deuteronomy is accounted for either, although the absence of a historical prologue in this tradition might be due either to an adoption of Neo-Assyrian practice on this point or to the nature of the Sefire pact as a parity treaty rather than a vassal treaty. Importantly, however, the inclusion of the gods of both cities as contracting parties alongside the human rulers in the second statement of the contracting parties provides a precedent for a deity as a contracting party in a formal treaty.

It appears that the author of Deuteronomy was familiar with a template for a vassal treaty that was much closer to that employed in the Late Bronze Age by the Hittite court than the subsequent ones used in the Iron Age by the Neo-Assyrian kings or by Aramean kings. How this template came to be part of Judahite scribal tradition needs a plausible explanation, as does the decision of the author of Deuteronomy to employ this older tradition and not use the Neo-Assyrian or even Neo-Babylonian templates that would have been more current in his own day, whether he wrote in the late monarchic, Neo-Babylonian, or

54 These are the subheadings proposed in Fitzmyer, *Aramaic Inscriptions*, 13–21.
55 Altman, "What Kind," 26–40.

early Persian period. Morrow's implicit suggestion that the Late Bronze tradition could have been maintained within the southern Levant during the Iron Age and used by the local polities there to establish treaties in the region prior to contact with the Assyrian imperial sphere is plausible;[56] the Aramaic tradition appears to have continued to employ it before absorbing some of the changes that were introduced in the Assyrian tradition.

It should be asked if the use of what resembles the older Hittite or Late Bronze treaty tradition but which might in fact have become the Judahite template in the Iron Age vs. the Assyrian or Neo-Babylonian tradition was due in part to the desire for a pattern where the superior party still could pledge and commit to action. In Hittite vassal treaties, the more powerful partner, the Hittite king, swore an oath to maintain the vassal in his position and to secure the possession of his heir, which was quite limited in terms of obligations in comparison to the vassal, who swore to uphold all the stipulations of the treaty.[57] The curses that would result from breaking the oath were only prescribed in writing for the vassal. Nevertheless, there are examples where the suzerain swore an oath to his vassal. Yhwh seems to bind himself to the obligation of maintaining Israel as his *'am s^egullâ* in 26:18 if the people obey his commands. Moses's teaching explains that this includes the divine blessings listed in 11:13–15, 11:26–27, and 28:2–14.

Or, is this due to the writer adapting the Assyrian-style treaty pattern that might have been taught in scribal education at the time of his writing? Perhaps coincidentally, some decisions taken to adapt the standard treaty pattern to describe the formal relationship between Yhwh and Israel ended up resembling the earlier pattern. As noted, the inclusion of explicit blessings and curses does not reflect the generalized Hittite practice nor Assyrian practice that had explicit curses only, without any blessings. Perhaps the writer wanted to include positive boons that would come from obeying Yhwh's *tôrâ* and not just negative consequences as part of his wider intention to motivate readers and hearers to agree and comply with the instructions being presented. This is a second possible option.

A third option is offered by Tigay, who prefers to see the writer of Deuteronomy to have used a covenant metaphor rather than a covenant template. He then suggests its background lies in a combination of two legal forms. The first is the ancient Near Eastern royal land grant, in which a king grants land or another gift to a servant and his descendants unconditionally and in perpetuity, and the second is the vassal treaty. He finds the vassal treaty inadequate be-

56 Morrow, "*Fortschreibung*," 214–15.
57 Altman, "Who Took," 178–84.

cause it only deals with Israel's obligation of loyalty to Yhwh but not Yhwh's concern for justice and human welfare as conveyed in the regulations for Israel's internal relations.[58] His observations would seem in some way to be getting at the same point raised above concerning the desire to include voluntary obligations committed to by the superior party at Sinai/Horeb for maintaining Israel as an *ʿam sᵉgullâ* in perpetuity, even if rebellion will lead to justified punishment.

Christian H. W. Brekelmans, on the other hand, finds the presence of the vassal treaty template in any form unlikely in Deuteronomy. He makes a few arguments in support. First, he notes that there is no suggestion that Yhwh is acting like a human suzerain who was extending his power to a place outside the center of his own existing realm and people; he is remaining at home among his people. Rather than representing a treaty, the texts that have been identified by him as echoing the treaty form are functioning instead to strengthen or maintain the existing relationship between Yhwh and his people by demanding loyalty. He also emphasizes that the first millennium *adê* form lacked both a historical prologue and blessings, which are present in Deuteronomy. In addition, both parties swear the oath, while only the vassal swore to the *adê*, and there is a mixture of law and covenant in Deuteronomy, while the normal stipulations of a vassal treaty were not laws.[59]

Brekelmans is splitting hairs to some degree by associating Deuteronomy possibly with a loyalty oath rather than a vassal treaty. The *adê* template was used in Assyria for both situations, as well as others, including "solemn promises by God to King," "a sworn agreement between gods," "a peace treaty between two great kings," and "an agreement against conspiratorial rebellion." The *adê* was a general term for "any solemn, binding agreement."[60]

Tigay feels a second governing metaphor is the one of father-child (5:7, 8:5; 14:1; 26:17, 29:12, 32:5–6, and 32:18–20), drawn from the vocabulary of marriage and adoption, since the covenant creates a family-like relationship.[61] However, he fails to point out that Hittite vassal treaties regularly employ this adoptive family fiction by having the stronger monarch be designated father and the weaker one son. Thus, it could be argued that the immediate source of this metaphor was the treaty form, where it also is employed, rather than an independent appeal to and metaphorical use of the concept of family. However, the father-son metaphor also is used in wisdom teachings, where a king or a sage

58 Tigay, *Deuteronomy*, xiv–xv.
59 Brekelmans, "Wisdom," 33–34.
60 Parpola, "Neo-Assyrian Treaties," 180–82; see also Lauinger, "Neo-Assyrian *adê*."
61 Tigay, *Deuteronomy*, xv.

is instructing his "son" in behavioral norms. It characterizes the teacher-pupil relationship in some ways, and there is a strong instructional dimension present in the book. Thus, there are multiple possible factors that could have influenced the decision to depict Israel as Yhwh's "children" in Deuteronomy.

A group of scholars has suggested that the origin of the unconditional formulations in second person in 12:1–26:15 is likely to be vassal treaty stipulations. They also are written in second person.[62] Thus, this could be used to bolster the suggestion that the primary template the author of Deuteronomy used to formulate the book was the vassal treaty. Moshe Weinfeld, however, has argued that since treaty stipulations are not legal ordinances, this origin for apodictic or unconditional formulations is not likely. Nevertheless, his alternate proposal to link the origins of apodictic formulations to the literary form of Hittite Instructions instead represents only a variation on a common ancient category of a binding agreement that included an oath.[63]

The Hittite Instructions are called *išḫiul*, a term referring to a formal pact or "binding" that corresponds to Akkadian *rikšu* and Hebrew *bᵉrît*. The same term is used in Hittite for a parity treaty or a vassal treaty. In this way, it very much corresponds to the Neo-Assyrian term *adê*, which can describe a vassal treaty, a loyalty oath, and other types of literature, as already explained. Weinfeld cites Zakutu's *adê* as a comparable Assyrian example, which was imposed on the royal family and court to support Assurbanipal,[64] and he might as well have cited Esarhaddon's loyalty oath *adê*, which was imposed on all citizens of Assyria to support Assurbanipal as his selected heir to the throne of Assyria as a more prominent example.

Weinfeld claims that in these various types of Hittite Instructions, the king "imposes the commandments and his subjects pledge the acceptance and the

---

62 E.g. Mendenhall, "Law and Covenant," 30. William S. Morrow rejects this source of influence for the unconditional formulations in the Covenant Code in favor of seeing them to stem from scribes working outside the palace, probably in some sort of cultic institution. He then concludes that early in the monarchy, a tradition developed to proclaim law and/or ethics in prescriptive genres, especially to cultic and military functionaries, as had been done in the Hittite sphere ("Generic Discrepancy," 148–50). By extension, his arguments would be applicable to the legal section of Deuteronomy.

63 So noted also by Morrow, "*Fortschreibung*," 116, which I discovered after reaching this conclusion from my own research into the issue. Here Morrow seems to have changed his opinion from his 1994 study, "Generic Discrepancy," where he rejected a derivation of the apodictic formulations from the treaty/loyalty oath tradition in favor of the Hittite Instructional material to cultic and military functionaries, not acknowledging both categories are described by the same terms in Hittite and Akkadian.

64 Weinfeld, "Origin of Apodictic Law," 69.

fulfillment of the commandments."[65] Yet, the three extant examples from the Hittite realm contain no reference to a formal pledge or oath. The first is directed to priests and temple officials (*COS* 1.83), whose opening twelve lines are too broken to reconstruct but whose colophon states "the first tablet of the rules of all the temple officials, of the kitchen attendants of the gods, of the farmers of the gods, and of the cowherds and shepherds of the gods, competed." Clearly then, there were additional tablets, so it is unclear if an oath would have been included in the final tablet. The second concerns instructions to commanders of border garrisons (*COS* 1.84) that opens, "Thus speaks his Maje[sty] ... thus let the border com[manders] be ..., after which follows a series of commands primary in third person but interspersed with second person address and command. The ending of the tablet is lost so it is unknown how many additional regulations were included or additional tablets and if there had been an oath included or not. The third text contains instructions to the royal guard (*COS* 1.85). The opening line is missing and only part of the second line remains. The rules are all in third person. The colophon reads, "First tablet of the Rules of the Guard, not finished." This also was a longer series of tablets, then, and might or might not have included direction concerning an oath. Thus, it becomes clear that Weinfeld's description of the inclusion of an oath as an integral part of this sub-category is derived solely from the Akkadian *adê* tradition, primarily from the single text of Zakutu's loyaly oath.

The absence of any oath in the preserved examples of the sub-category of the Hittite *išḫiul*, however, cannot be taken as definitive proof that such an oath might not have occurred in the final tablet of each series. An argument from silence here would be very unwise. As already noted, in the Late Bronze Age formal pacts were described by the phrase, "binding and oath." The native classification of these regulations under the ancient genre of *išḫiul*, which corresponded to the Akkadian *rikšu* and Neo-Assyrian *adê*, raises the question as to which element or combination of elements was central to the concept of these equivalent categories in different cultures. Was the inclusion of commands and regulations primary, or perhaps the formal signaling of acceptance through spoken words or the swearing of an oath afterwards to obey the rules, or both equally? The basic concept seemed to be a means of expressing the creation of a bond, contract, or formal relationship between two parties, who might have been equals or unequal, depending on the circumstances. Also, the specific situation requiring the bond would determine the rules or stipulations both par-

65 Weinfeld, 65. According to Ada Taggar Cohen, royal Hittite servants recited the words, "So be it!" when taking an oath of loyalty to the king ("Biblical Wisdom," 55), as evidenced in "The First Oath of the Soldiers" in *COS* 1, 165–67.

ties were agreeing to honor. It appears their content could take different forms but tended to be formulated in third person or second person, both primarily unconditionally but also sometimes conditionally, with the use of motive clauses. Whether the inclusion of the text of an oath or reference to an oath or verbal acceptance in the formal document would have been deemed necessary in all cases is unclear from the surviving evidence.

The term *b*ᵉ*rît* is used in Deuteronomy to describe five formal agreements: the event that took place at Horeb (Deut 4:13, 4:23, 4:31, 5:2, 8:18, 9:9, 9:11, 9:15 10:8, 29:24 [25], 31:9, and 31:25–26), future formal agreements with people in the land (7:2), all of Yhwh's covenants with Israel (7:9 and 7:12), the covenant with Levi (33:9), and the current event taking place on the plains of Moab (5:3, 8:18, 17:2, 28:69 [29:1], 29:8 [9], 29:11 [12], 29:13 [14], 29:20 [21], 31:16, and 31:20). Of these, it is likely that all would have involved the swearing of an oath or oral affirmation to obey the stipulated terms or agreed regulations in each case. Deuteronomy 26:17–19 are crucial verses that state that both Yhwh and Israel affirmed the terms set forth in chs. 12–26 on the plains of Moab via mutual declaration.[66] In the story-world in 29:11 [12] and 29:13 [14]), they are making a covenant and a "curse oath" on the plains of Moab. Here it is unclear if *b*ᵉ*rît* represents the written rules or terms and *'ālâ* the written curses that are part of an oath ceremony, being two discreet elements, or if they are synonyms, each being used metonymically to represent the regulations or stipulations together with the written curses to be activated if one breaks the rules. The former would make better sense, since a single term could otherwise have sufficed. [67]

The final three verses of Deuteronomy 26 become crucial, then, in determining if chs. 12–26 are being conceived of as binding instructional regulations or as the stipulated terms of a formal vassal treaty. They state that both parties, Yhwh and Israel, speak words that put into force the binding agreement created on the plains of Moab. The Akkadian loyalty oaths of Zakutu and Esarhaddon contain a series of pronounced curses against anyone who swears to uphold the pact but fails to do so. There are none against the superior party issuing the document, Zakutu or Esarhaddon. The use of the *hiphil* of the root אמר ("to declare") to describe the actions of both parties seems to be assuming a situation other than the formal invocation or intonation of one or more curses associated with the subsequent descriptive term *'ālâ*. Rather, it seems to express a

---

66 For the *hiphil* of *'mr* as a common juridical term signaling consent in the west Semitic world, see Vriezen, "Das Hiphil," 207–10.

67 For the meaning of *'ālâ*, see conveniently, Scharbert, "אלה," 261–67. Moshe Weinfeld assumes the first option, appealing specifically to the treaty-making tradition that refers to both elements (*Deuteronomy and Deuteronomic*, 2, 67).

form of mutual assent. Under the circumstances, it seems that 26:17–19 are not the formal closing to the segment of regulations and legal cases, the *ḥuqqîm* and *mišpāṭîm*, that began in 12:1 and end in 26:15 but a summary of what their function is in the story-world: they set the rules to be followed by Israel in its formal agreement being made with Yhwh on the plains of Moab. This means their function in the current narrative is as treaty or covenant stipulations.[68] This does not rule out their possible origin in an earlier source as a set of regulatory instructions, possibly with no accompanying loyalty oath, in a setting where a formal relationship is assumed to exist. A document similar to the various examples of royal Hittite instructions for groups of professionals would be possible.[69]

6 The Constitutional Genre

S. Dean McBride has argued that, rather than an example of the stipulations of the treaty genre, the "central document" in chs. 12–26 should be seen to constitute a unique genre, that of a constitution or "charter for a constitutional theocracy," with an outer frame that currently highlights this function for the core.[70] He notes that *tôrâ* should not be translated "teaching" or "instruction"; in his view, the latter two genres lack the normative, prescriptive force of the words presented that are more than admonitions or sage advice. The words announce sanctioned political policies incumbent upon both king and people, whose observance will influence the fate of the entire nation. Neither is *tôrâ* law alone, which is too narrow a translation. What is presented is not "the totality of particular categories of legislation and judicial practice appropriate to it."[71] In 4:45, *tôrâ* is epexegetically defined as treaty stipulations, *hā'ēdōt*, and the statutory rulings *haḥuqqîm wᵉhammišpātîm*. Like the first, the additional two uses of *'ēdōt* in the book in 6:17 and 20 seem to refer to the decalogue in 5:6–21. The second

68 Erhard Gerstenberger similarly has concluded that the fact that two thirds of the provisions in Deut 12–26 are formulated conditionally and only a third unconditionally is a direct result of their function. "The provisions are not so much case law but prescriptions stating what each partner it to do ..." in the treaty relationship ("Covenant," 43).

69 For a collection of these instructions, see Miller, *Royal Hittite Instructions*. Space precludes my inclusion of a discussion of the evidence that has been gathered by others to show that the establishment of a formal agreement between people and a god was not unique to Israel but was a known ancient practice.

70 McBride, "Polity," 235–36, 238.

71 McBride, 233.

phrase, understood as a *hendiadys*, is the standard way the writer describes constitutional matters that, "though fully sanctioned by divine authority, are promulgated only through the legislative agency of Moses."[72]

McBride argues that 1:6–4:40 do not read as a historical prologue to a treaty. Had the verses functioned that way, he would have expected them to have included a review of Moses's call and of Israel's deliverance from slavery. He calls them Mosaic memoirs. Instead, they narrate the sudden divine command to leave Horeb and conquer and settle in the land promised to the forefathers (1:6–8) and the civil administration set up by Moses and the tribes so that the commands could be carried out (1:9–18). Then, Moses ably demonstrates how national failure (1:19–46) and success (2:1–4:40) depend on implementation and maintenance of the decrees that will follow in the "core." He sees 4:44–49 as an editorial superscription and 5:1aα as a brief narrative introduction to a long foreward to the constitution that is presented in three parts, each beginning "Hear, O Israel," in 5:1aβ–6:3; 6:4–8:20 and 9:1–10:11 + 10:12–21:1 (238–39). Here he apparently is considering the mirror image of the phrase ("O Israel, hear") in 4:1 to be unconnected to these subsequent three. For him, the epilogue gives the same message as the Mosaic memoirs but now emphasizes, after his impending death, the responsibility of every Israelite (30:11–14; 31:9–13) as part of a democratized process of authoritative decision-making and its accompanying responsibilities.[73]

The point of a constitution, according to McBride, is to protect the rights of individuals, and 12:1–26:15 do that admirably. Suggesting a fivefold division, he sees the purpose of the first division, 12:1–28 to be "to identify the unique institutional locus of Israel's communal life" and of the second division, 12:29–17:13, to deal with national integrity defined by corporate institutions, rites, and judicial procedures. The third section, 17:14–18:22, delimits "the social authority that can be exercised legitimately even by divinely 'chosen' officers." The fourth, 19:1–25:19, illustrates responsible procedures and specific results in which "individual lives, livelihoods and personal liberties are at stake," while 26:1–15 prescribe "two liturgical acts which identify personal well-being and shared prosperity as reciprocal objectives of covenantal politics."[74] In traditional scholarship relating to Deuteronomy, this view of protecting individual rights would be understood to be illustrated by the focus on "brotherhood" and the rights of the underprivileged and resident aliens. However, the extant ancient Near Eastern law codes also contain specific cases with verdicts that illustrate

72 McBride, 233–34.
73 McBride, 236.
74 McBride, 240–43.

the protection of the rights of individual citizens as well as underprivileged classes. Thus, while the point is well-taken that *tôrâ* is not the equivalent of a comprehensive modern law code, 12:1–26:15 still present some selected cases and verdicts, as well as more general regulations for the behavior of individuals within society and corporate behavior meant to deal with threats to social cohesion, in second person. Except for the unprecedented paranetic material and the inclusion of regulations in second-person, some of the content of these chapters could be seen to be adapted from a so-called ancient law code in order to serve in their present instructional context. The observation by A. D. H. Mayes that "the influence of the covenant or treaty form is obvious," but this pattern offers "a basis and framework for a speech rather than for a covenant document"[75] could apply equally to an argument that 12:1–26:15 currently serve as covenant stipulations in a speech but are adapted from the law code form.

It is possible to argue that an intended function of Deuteronomy was to regulate community life and thus, it arguably would resemble what countries throughout the world today express via the genre, "constitution." However, it is difficult to distinguish a constitution from the known ancient Near Eastern law codes then, which frame the rights of individuals under monarchies and also present the king as the protector of the rights of the underprivileged and guardian of justice. Constitutions are not normally written as a series of speeches in the first person singular, as Deuteronomy is. Thus, to identify the genre of this work properly, we must relate it to the genres in use at the time it was created in the wider geographical context.

7 First-Person Narrative Templates

The function and impact of the first-person narrative in the book has received much less attention but is key for understanding the purpose of the book. First person narration was used in a wide range of ancient Near Eastern texts. It was common in royal inscriptions that related various deeds of a given monarch, including *adê* and treaty agreements between unequal partners, and in building inscriptions, in autobiographies, fictional or not, in court cases where testimony was recorded, in letters, in some contracts, in testaments, and in wisdom instructions.

When we turn to the book of Deuteronomy, more than one of these categories could apply. Fictional autobiography seems relevant, since Moses is re-

---

75 Mayes, "Deuteronomy 4," 41.

counting events he experienced with Israel from Mt. Horeb until arriving on the plains of Moab. At the same time, the narrative also functions as Moses's farewell speech at the end of his life,[76] similar to the farewell speech of Joshua (Josh 24), Samuel (1 Sam 12), David (1 Kgs 2:1–9), and the Testament of Jacob (Gen 49). It is the case that Deuteronomy 32, the so-called Words of Moses, serves this function more narrowly within the narrative plot, right before Moses's death, but the entire book also is set at the end of Moses's life. There is a witnessing aspect as well, where Moses is testifying to his unfair punishment in not being allowed to enter the Promised Land, where he blames the people for his actions that led to the divine pronouncement (3:23–26; 4:21–22; 32:49–51). This same aspect appears also in Samuel's farewell speech and Nehemiah's account of unjust accusations made against him and attempts on his life. Finally, the instructional aspect is present in Moses's constant admonitions about observing the divine *tôrâ* he is delivering and the consequences of following and not following it. The teaching is a source that produces wisdom and understanding in 4:6, even if, as Braulik notes, Israel is wise and discerning, not *tôrâ* directly.[77] The statement undeniably equates *tôrâ* and wisdom. Nothing is to be added to it or taken away from it in 12:32.[78]

7.1 Instructions

I would like to suggest that the instructional aspect was particularly important to the implied writer, but that other aspects of first-person compositions have

76 So e.g. Carmichael, *Laws*, 17, 23–25.

77 Braulik, *Theology*, 9.

78 Moshe Weinfeld links the farewell speech or testament genre with wisdom Instructions, especially Egyptian examples, intended for the future kings of Israel (*Deuteronomy 1–11*, 4). Subsequently, he expands his thoughts about Egyptian Instructions, focusing on those targeted specifically at the king, especially "Advice to the Prince,"(written in third person) and how the Hittite, Assyrian, and Egyptian kings were expected to comply with instructions written in books as a way to explain Josiah's eagerness to fulfil the words of the *tôrâ* discovered in the temple in 2 Kgs 22 as well as the command in Deut 17:19 for the king to read from his copy of the *tôrâ* his entire life so he will learn to fear Yhwh (56). He does not argue that the writer of Deuteronomy was deliberately fashioning Moses as a teacher of wisdom by drawing on elements of this genre, as I argue. In a subsequent section he points out how a number of verbal and conceptual ideas in Deuteronomy that are not found in the laws of P and H are found instead in wisdom literature. This insight leads him to suggest that scribes and "wise men" created Deuteronomy (62–65). The inclusion of ideas found in proverbial wisdom literature in the divine and Mosaic teaching sections would be consistent with a depiction of Moses as a wisdom teacher as well as a prophet and of Yhwh's words as wise teaching, not law *per se*.

also influenced the writing. Comparative examples of instructions and admonitions from Egypt and Sumer share the following characteristics. They are written by an authoritative, older person whose purpose is to relay instruction and wisdom to one or more younger individuals about human life, human nature, and codes of conduct that will be appropriate and result in a long, successful life, often but not always for those who held power and influence in the society. Much is written in second person, often imperative, but with first-person observations also interspersed.[79] Egyptian examples include the Instructions of Ani, which were written for the Egyptian middle class, not the upper class (*COS* 1.46), the Instructions of Ptahhotep, of Merikare, Amenemhet, Onchsheshonqy, and the Instruction of Amenemope (*COS* 1.47), which influenced proverbs. A Sumerian example is The Instructions of Shuruppak, which apply to secular life with little emphasis on religion or cult (*COS* 1.176), while a Babylonian example is the Akkadian Counsels of Wisdom, perhaps from the Kassite period (ca. 1595–1155 BCE).[80]

Turning back to Deuteronomy, some striking differences from the regular instructions occur that might lead some to dismiss this genre as present or influential at all, but the anomalies are contextual. The book contains both divine instructions being relayed to the people of Israel by Moses in his capacity as prophet and his own instructional teaching that builds upon what he as the speaker considers to be key elements of the divine teaching.[81] These latter are not primarily prophetic, even if one might consider the predicted exile to be *ex-eventu* prophecy. Rather, they are instructions to the nation for the future, when he will no longer lead them. The inclusion of this dual-level instruction accounts in part certainly for the failure of the teaching to sound like proverbial sayings in most instances, on the one hand, but also for the instructions in second person to the audience and its sermonic tone, with its warnings, admonitions, and promises of blessings for obedience to both the divine and his per-

79 This second-person link to similar prohibitive formulations in biblical legal collections has been highlighted by e.g. Gerstenberger, *Wesen*, 139.

80 Lambert, *Babylonian Wisdom*, 96–107. Motive clauses are present in this work. The command not to add to or take away from the teaching is not unique to the wisdom tradition; it also appears in the Hittite treaty tradition (*COS* 2.18, § 26).

81 Here the translation of the *piel* of *b-ʾ-r* in Deut 1:5 and 27:8 becomes relevant. The proposal to translate it according to the later Mishnaic sense of "expound" or "clarify," as found also in the noun *bîʾur*, "exposition or commentary," would fit my proposed context well, at least in 1:5. It works less well in 27:8, after the expounding has been completed, unless the point is that the divine words are to be written on the stones and then expounded in the way Moses has done in the book. However, it is not certain that this was the intended meaning of the two uses of the verb in Deuteronomy. See Edelman, "Metaphor."

sonal instruction and ill effects should both sets of teachings be ignored, on the other. As already noted, subsequent references to what likely is the book refer to it both as the scroll of the teaching of Moses but more often as the scroll of Elohim/Yhwh/Yhwh Elohim/Yhwh the God of Israel, which is consistent with this dual function within the text.

Another important link between instructional literature and Deuteronomy is the use of motive clauses in roughly 50 % of the regulations in chs. 12–26. Rifat Sonsino argues that the legislators who created the motive clauses in chs. 12–26 were directly influenced by the type of motivations that are integral to wisdom instructions and wanted to provide a pedagogically motivated rationale for the acceptance of the regulations by the audience.[82] They can be grouped into four subtypes by content: explanatory, ethical, religious, and historico-religious or religion, morality, wisdom, and law.[83] As noted earlier, motive clauses are present only in two legal collections, the Laws of Hammurapi and the Middle Assyrian Laws. They also are found in the Hittite Instructions (sanctions) for Temple Officials,[84] which, however, have been seen already to be a form of oath-bound pact rather than the type of Instructions being considered here. Nevertheless, motive clauses also occur in the Egyptian Instructions of Merikare (*COS* 1.35) and Instruction of Amenemope (*COS* 1.47) as well as the "Instructions of Šube-Awilum at Ugarit and the Words of Ahiqar.[85] This suggests the text of Deuteronomy as a whole, including the legal section, was meant to function instructionally and not primarily as a legal treatise.[86] Already in 1902, Samuel R. Driver pointed out that in the laws as well as the frame, the author's paranetic aim is clear as he develops the laws by referring to the moral purposes to

82 Sonsino, *Motive Clauses*, 120–27. He notes that motive clauses are used in a wide variety of ancient Near Eastern genres, including letters, popular proverbs, treaties, commemorative building instructions, royal inscriptions and edicts, contracts, and law suits (205–10).
83 For the first, see Gemser, "Importance," 103–110; for the second, see Carmichael, *Laws*, 35.
84 Noted explicitly by e.g. Gemser, "Importance," 111, n. 2. He dismisses this document and similar ones as not relevant for comparative purposes with biblical legal collections because of their very specific target audience. So also Weinfeld, "Origin," 64–65. However, he argues for the direct relevance of this document.
85 For the last two, see Sonsino, *Motive Clauses*, 169–70.
86 Erhard Gerstenberger has argued that biblical apodictic law formulations that constitute "rules for daily life" and "commandments for correct social behavior," found in Deut 22:1–12; 23:1; 23:16–26; 24:8–22; and 25:13–15, similarly had their origin in wisdom literature, not in the covenant treaty form. He compares them to Egyptian "instruction" literature, specifically Amenemope, Ani, and Merikare, and sees the early guardians to be fathers, tribal heads, wise men, and secondarily court officials but not priests or prophets. Thus, he links their origin to family ethos rather than covenant ideology ("Covenant," 47–51). In his view, the latter is a secondary development.

which they relate.[87] In addition, a comment by Duane L. Christensen highlights the integral nature of paranesis (e.g. in the form of motive clauses) within the legal collection: "The assumption that the original Deuteronomy is to be found only in chaps. 12–26 must be rejected. This section cannot be designated the real codex as opposed to the introduction (chaps. 6–11) since both of these sections share the same characteristic signs (*Numeruswechsel*, parenetic style, etc.)."[88]

Instructions often are classified as a form of wisdom literature.[89] Debate continues over whether we are justified in assuming the existence of a wisdom school or professionally grounded wisdom tradition in Judahite or Judean tradition. James L. Crenshaw, for example, argues for the existence of professional wisdom circles and a wisdom worldview.[90] R. N. Whybray proposes instead a common intellectual tradition focused on the life problems of individuals in relation to others in their communities on a daily basis. Its concern was "the present and future, including the fate of their children and descendants, and about the justice or injustice of their personal destinies."[91] Also challenging a professional wisdom tradition, Mark Sneed identifies wisdom as a mode of literature used to train young scribes that complemented other modes of literature in the curriculum of scribal education.[92] Regardless of how one views this debate,[93] it is apparent that there is a clear presence of wisdom-like elements in Deuteronomy.

While the nature and extent of such wisdom-like elements has been debated in previous scholarship, there is a general perception that it would be wrong

87 Driver, *Deuteronomy*, ii.

88 Christensen, *Deuteronomy*, lxix.

89 Weinfeld ("Origin," 64) rejects earlier proposals to derive the apodictic formulations from the exhortations of the wise by e.g. Gerstenberger (*Wesen*, 110–44) because these do not involve legal ordinances as such. Gerstenberger is connecting such prohibitive exhortations with the life setting of the clan and family (139–41). However, if the Egyptian examples I have cited are seen to belong to a wider category of wisdom literature, then a wisdom connection or origin would be possible, severed from Gerstenberger's proposed life setting and associated instead with a setting of scribal education for service at the court or in royal administration.

90 Crenshaw, *Old Testament Wisdom*, 28–29.

91 Whybray, *Intellectual Tradition*, 31, 33–43, 46, 54, quote from 69–70.

92 Sneed, "Is the 'Wisdom Tradition,'" 61–64, 71. His arguments are similar to those made subsequently by e.g. Yoram Cohen who, however, provides clear evidence for the use of Sumerian and Akkadian wisdom-type texts in the curriculum in scribal schools. Cohen also notes how three collections of these texts were subsequently quoted in Babylonian hermeneutical commentaries ("Why 'Wisdom,'" 42–56).

93 For more recent collections of essays on this debate, see e.g. Sneed, *Was There a Wisdom Tradition?* and Longman, *Fear of the Lord*.

to classify Deuteronomy as a wisdom book. Calum M. Carmichael, for example, states "D should not be categorized as wisdom literature, only as associated with it ... Moses' address to the children of Israel represents a conscious imitation of features found in a teacher-pupil setting."[94] Ryan O'Dowd concludes "... the strengths of the wisdom tradition are employed in Deuteronomy to accentuate the rhetorical and paranetic aims of the torah."[95] Even Weinfeld, who has presented the most sustained discussion of wisdom features in the book, seems to conclude in the end that Deuteronomy is closely related to wisdom literature, especially Proverbs, having been written by wisdom scribes, but is not wisdom literature *per se*.[96]

Barnabas Lindars notes the form of the book corresponds to a covenant renewal ceremony, but he also describes the paranetic material in the framework to constitute a series of sermons that use a didactic approach "in a manner reminiscent of the Wisdom tradition."[97] Jean Malfroy similarly comments on how "the allure of the book is essentially its oratory: '[the Deuteronomist] exhorts, pleads, stimulates, and multiplies promises and threats. Here, there are laws, but the Dt does not announce them calmly, sedately, in the fashion of a legislator; he recommends them with passion.'"[98] He then compares some of the strategies and phraseology in Deuteronomy to those used by a wisdom teacher both inside and outside Judah and Israel before concluding that the Deuteronomist deliberately assimilated the law of Yhwh to wisdom.[99] Calum M. Carmichael similarly finds "an affinity between the instructional setting of the Wisdom literature and the didactic intention of both the D laws and the rest of Deuteronomy."[100] He suggests the repetition found within chs. 12–26 is not the result of "a legislator's drafting different legal enactments at different times" but instead, the need of a teacher giving instruction to repeat a matter in different ways so hearers will absorb it.[101]

Lindars goes on to argue that the term *tôrâ*, which originally appeared only in the frame, with 17:18–19 an editorial expansion, is used to designate the entire corpus as a complete unit of "instruction" for people "to ponder and lay to heart," as though it were "the instruction of a father to his sons" (4:5–8).[102] For

---

94 Carmichael, *Laws*, 2.
95 O'Dowd, *Wisdom*, 47.
96 Weinfeld, "Deuteronomy," 256–57, 262.
97 Lindars, "Torah," 129.
98 Malfroy, "Sagesse," 58.
99 Malfroy, 59–65.
100 Carmichael, "Deuteronomic Laws," 198.
101 Carmichael, *Laws*, 37.
102 Carmichael, *Laws*, 130.

him, it is closest to the sense in which the word is used in Wisdom literature, as the instruction of wise men, vs. its use to designate a prophetic oracle or a priestly regulation. Even so, "the term retains its didactic overtones," and one could say "'the book of divine instruction' might represent the real meaning better than the usual translation, 'the book of the law'."[103]

Ada Taggar-Cohen recently has drawn attention to two sub-categories of Akkadian texts relating to wisdom. One, the "Instructions of Šūpê-Amēli," is a testamentary set of instructions from an elderly father to his son concerning pragmatic advice and directions about proper behavior, caring for family, and private property. The other, "Advice to a Prince," is written casuistically but includes instructions to the future king that emphasize his need to pay attention to a divine message and the desires and worship of the gods in order to avoid their punishment and their annulling of the treaties, which she sees to represent the framework of the civilized order. The Hittite text known as the Instructions of Hattušili I of Muršili similarly commands the prince to be careful about the business of the gods, their sacrificial loaves, libations, stews (?) and meal must always be available to them.[104] She concludes, "The very connection between obeying the command of a wise king and fulfilling the cultic demands of the divine world, stands at the core of royal success in controlling the land and making it strong."[105] She also notes that "the biblical texts combine the instructions of obedience to God with the obedience to father and mother, while the context of the text is instructions relating to mundane social issues as well as the service of the divine."[106] Here she cites Exodus 19–24 and notes they combine texts of instruction (unconditional formulations) with conditional laws in third person, but Deuteronomy 12–26 would have worked equally well, since it shares these characteristics.

Taggar-Cohen's emphasis on the inclusion of correct ritual behavior alongside rules of a successful life and well-being as an integral part of ancient Near Eastern wisdom is useful in putting the emphasis in Deuteronomy 12–26 on religious praxis into perspective. Since her examples where this emphasis applies are from the royal sphere, one should ask whether under the Judahite monarchy, a similar type of didactic royal instruction might have existed, which has been adapted and applied here to Moses as a substitute king and Israel as the "son" needing instruction.

---

103 Lindars, "Torah," 120–22, 130; quote from 131. In a similar vein, it can be noted that the verb למד appears in the Pentateuch only in Deuteronomy.

104 Taggar-Cohen, "Biblical Wisdom," 48–49, 52.

105 Taggar-Cohen, 58.

106 Taggar-Cohen, 51.

Stephen A. Geller has argued that Deuteronomy 4 has used "a wisdom form of argumentation" to argue against its own view that relying on experiential seeing on earth is the key to wisdom. Instead, hearing the Ten Commandments from heaven at Horeb becomes the primary source of wisdom, which is then made accessible to future generations through the unalterable scroll of the teaching of Moses that goes beyond normal advice or general guidelines for conduct instilled into pupils by a teacher. The novel ideology presented is that Israel's unalterable covenantal obedience ("just laws and judgements" in 4:8) that leads to life or death replaces conventional wisdom or becomes Israel's own form of wisdom.[107]

Certain scholars think that Deuteronomy 32, the so-called "Song of Moses," has been influenced by the royal court wisdom tradition. James R. Boston has argued the double invocation in the opening strophe is quite common in wisdom pericopes as well as in the introduction to a prophetic oracle, where it often is related to the teaching of justice and right conduct. A double invocation opens the formal teaching segment of the Egyptian Instruction of Amenemope (*COS* 1.47, III.10): "Give your ears, hear the sayings, give your heart to understand them," showing one use was in the context of the genre of Instructions. In his view, it likely was borrowed from a more original didactic setting. He argues that, in the song, a teacher who wants the wisdom of his own words to be listened to makes the appeal. There is no reference to divine authority, making it a form that could be called "the invocation of the teacher," which probably was associated with wisdom circles.[108] He also cites the appeal to fathers and elders in v. 7 as a possible allusion to the wise man, and he thinks that the assertion in v. 22 that Yhwh controls Sh'eol, which is found only in wisdom literature (Prov 15:11; Job 26:6, and Ps 139:7), represents a minority position reflecting wisdom influence. Finally, he cites a list of 17 words or expressions that in his view demonstrate significant linguistic affinities with wisdom literature before concluding that the cumulative evidence establishes a clear relationship between the "Song of Moses" and a wisdom tradition at home in the royal court.[109]

In assessing the arguments made above, Donn F. Morgan concludes the poem "reflect[s] a milieu in which wisdom and other traditions freely borrowed and utilized terminology and theological perspectives from each other."[110]

107 Geller, "Fiery Wisdom," 103–39, quote from 123. Much earlier, Gunnar Östborn had noted a change in Judaeo-Israelite wisdom from an "early" form shared internationally to a later one that absorbed *tôrâ*, creating a new ideal of Wisdom (*Tōrā*, 112–26).

108 Boston, "Wisdom Influence," 200.

109 Boston, 201–2.

110 Morgan, *Wisdom*, 54.

James L. Crenshaw considers vv. 12–14, which the author of Baruch 3:29–32a drew upon, to exhibit wisdom traits but does not otherwise discuss the "Song of Moses" or how extensive wisdom influence in it might have been.[111] Having rejected the existence of professional wisdom circles or sages or a wisdom movement, R. N. Whybray similarly finds words in the poem that can be considered exclusive to what he calls the intellectual tradition. However, he also considers it important to remember the caveat expressed by Georg Fohrer "that even when it can be shown that a speaker or writer has in fact made use of extraneous forms, this does not necessarily mean that his thought has been significantly influenced by them. His intention may have merely have been to refer to a well-known saying or mode of speech to communicate more effectively with his audience."[112] Crenshaw had expressed a similar caveat earlier: "Whenever a wisdom phrase or motif is found outside wisdom literature the scholar must determine whether or not the meaning has been changed."[113]

The following teachings have almost verbatim parallels in wisdom literature: the need for impartiality when rendering judgment in 1:17 (Prov 16:33),[114] the ban on moving a neighbor's landmark in 19:14 (Prov 22:28; 23:10–11; Job 24:2),[115] on having deceptive weights in 25:13–16 that also is in the Code of Hammurabi (Prov 11:1; 16:11, 20:23 but also in Lev 19:35–36; Ezek 45:10; Mic 6:10–11; Amos 8:5; Hos 12:8),[116] and on delaying the payment of vows in 23:22 (Eccl 5:3–5, 18:21–22; Prov 20:25).[117] Beyond these undisputed instances, however, additional passages in the book have been related to wisdom. For example, Jean Malfroy and Jeffrey H. Tigay find a parallel between Deuteronomy 8:5 and Proverbs 3:11–12,[118] while the use of the imagery of disciplining an unruly child in Deuteronomy 21:18 has been linked to Proverbs 13:24; 23:13–14, and 29:15 and

111 Crenshaw, *Old Testament Wisdom*, 187.

112 Whybray, *Intellectual Tradition*, 88–89, 154, quote from 73, summarizing Fohrer, "Remarks," 309–19.

113 Crenshaw, "Method," 133.

114 So e.g. Mayes, *Deuteronomy*, 125. Henri Cazelles pointed out that the ideas expressed here were part of an international wisdom tradition and similar to statements found in the Instruction of the Egyptian Vizier Ptahhotep (ca. 2375–2350 BCE) and the Edict of the Vizier ("Institutions,"110).

115 E.g. Nielsen, *Deuteronomium*, 193 and Tigay, *Deuteronomy*,183, though the latter gives general references to book of Proverbs, ancient Near Eastern law and Wisdom literature, and Plato's *Laws*.

116 So e.g. Tigay, *Deuteronomy*, 391, n. 39.

117 So e.g. Gerhard Von Rad, who connects it to Eccl 5:4–6 only but notes it is likely "a piece of advice from the sphere of proverbial wisdom" (*Deuteronomy*, 148), and Nielsen, *Deuteronomy*, 223.

118 Malfroy, "Sagesse," 59; Tigay, *Deuteronomy*, 93.

that of the glutton and drunkard in 21:20 has been seen to draw on stock imagery for insubordination that occurs in Proverbs 23:20–21 and 28:7.[119] The warning that an aggrieved husband will not accept a financial settlement from an adulterer in 22:22, implying it was a right, has been associated with Proverbs 6:32–35.[120] In 27:27, Tigay thinks the curse is based on the prohibition of moving landmarks in 19:4, while the combination of the blind, orphans, widows, and strangers as a grouping is found in Proverbs 23:10 and Egyptian wisdom literature and likely drew from this tradition.[121] He also suggests that the psychological incapacitation described in 28:29 that leaves the people unable to act wisely is a theme found elsewhere in Job 5:12–14, although there is clearly no direct quote at work here.[122] Gerhard Von Rad claimed 29:28 "sounds like a proverbial maxim which once dealt pithily with man's general relationship to what is secret and to what is manifest."[123] He also included the father/son relationship, the "binding" on the heart, teaching, and the "way" as examples of such maxims (cf. Prov 1:8; 6:21; 7:3). Gunnar Östborn has emphasized the use of "the way" as a paranetic theme in the historical retrospect in 10:12, 11:28 etc.[124]

Of the three categories of wisdom delineated by James L. Crenshaw, Deuteronomy deals with concerns addressed primarily by juridical and practical wisdom, which focuses on "human relationships in an ordered society and state."[125] His other two are nature wisdom and religious wisdom. Here, he has combined two of Roland E. Murphy's four categories without stating why or explaining how mastery of a craft or work-related skill logically coheres with juridical skill.[126]

Crenshaw rejects Weinfeld's proposal that the humanistic concern that typifies Deuteronomy derives from the wisdom tradition. In his view, the proposal is not based on the presence of ideological or stylistic elements that particularly and primarily typify wisdom literature.[127] Weinfeld's appeals to common terms like "see, hear, know, keep, law, and teach" as wisdom vocabulary do not meet his more stringent criterion.

119 E.g. Tigay, *Deuteronomy*, 197.
120 So e.g. Tigay, 207.
121 Tigay, 255.
122 Tigay, 264.
123 Von Rad, *Deuteronomy*, 180–81.
124 Östborn, *Tōrā*, 64.
125 Crenshaw, *Old Testament Wisdom*, 132.
126 Murphy's categories are judicial wisdom, nature wisdom, practical wisdom, and theologized wisdom ("Assumptions," 410).
127 Crenshaw, "Method," 131–33; Weinfeld, "Origin of Humanism."

Granting the former point and Crenshaw's important caveat "... that to call one wise is not to identify him as a sage,"[128] it is hard to escape the conclusion that Moses is being portrayed as a wise person. He acts as a teacher in his instructions to Israel and also shows his wisdom in his spelling out of the consequences for obedience to or rebellion against the extended divine teaching he is conveying as part of establishing a new covenant between Israel and Yhwh. It is correct that very little proverbial wisdom appears in Deuteronomy, and it is hard to demonstrate much formal influence of wisdom literature on the book using Crenshaw's criteria. On the other hand, however, if Stephen A. Geller is correct, then part of the ideological strategy being implemented by the author of Deuteronomy is to undermine the importance of any identifiable international wisdom tradition and replace it with *tôrâ*-based wisdom. To accomplish this goal, it is necessary to depict Moses as a sage-like figure whose "wisdom" is superior to that of other sages. In a similar way, Moses is depicted as an unparalleled prophet because of his unique role as transmitter of the divine *tôrâ* that serves as the stipulations of the second covenant and as its interpreter. I agree with Gerhard von Rad's conclusion: "the prophetic in Deuteronomy is merely a form of expression, and a means of making the book's claim to be Mosaic real."[129]

Another influencing factor on the style and format of the instructions or teaching is the decision to recount the covenantal events at Horeb, where Israel entered into a formal pact with Yhwh Elohim, as well as the new pact, described as a *b*ᵉ*rît* that involves an *'ālâ* (oath), being entered into on the plains of Moab (8:18; 29:2–15). The writer has deliberately employed the elements of a standard formal pact sealed by an oath. As a result, the divine teaching serves double duty as the stipulations section of the formal pact Israel must follow as Yhwh's "vassals" when they live in the promised land (12:1) and as divine instruction more generally in how to conduct oneself individually and corporately in order to live a long and successful life (e.g. 4:40, 5:30, 7:12–16, 11:9, 25:15, 26:28, 30:16, and 32:47) or to perish (4:26, 8:19–20, 11:17, 26:28, 28:63, 30:17–18, and 31:18). It is possible that the blessing sections in Deuteronomy derive from the Instructions template and not from the Hittite vassal treaty template, as has commonly been assumed, although it is equally possible that its presence is due to its belonging to both patterns.

---

128 Crenshaw, "Method," 133. Here he is building on the earlier comment by Roland E. Murphy that "wisdom language does not constitute wisdom" ("Assumptions," 104). At the same time, Whybray would agree with this aphorism but for a totally different reason: he rejects the existence of professional sages! I am more convinced by his arguments than Crenshaw's.
129 Von Rad, *Studies*, 69.

It is noteworthy that a copy of this scroll of teaching is to be deposited beside (*miṣṣad*), not in, the Ark (31:26), as a witness or testimony (עֵד) against Israel. For the writer of Deuteronomy, the Ark contained the tablets of the covenant written by the divine finger (4:13; 5:22, 9:10–11, 10:1–5). Their placement inside the Ark corresponded with the Hittite provision for treaties to be deposited in temples before the gods who oversaw the execution of the blessings and curses. Thus, the tablets with the Ten Commandments would seem to represent a copy of the formal treaty document, allowing the chest that held them to be called the ark of the *bᵉrît yhwh* (10:8).

The scroll of teaching represents something else, but what? It seems to serve as tangible, written proof that the Israelites had been instructed concerning appropriate behavior as members of the people of Israel and the consequences for obeying and not obeying. In this way, it somewhat resembles a contract that records the orally spoken words of the contracting parties, though we hear nothing from corporate Israel, except in 26:17–19, but rather from Moses as leader and prophet. Each side normally received a copy of a contract, which could be opened and read as necessary in case of a dispute.

In the storyline in Deuteronomy, the scroll reports the terms of a covenant established on the plains of Moab that contained additional terms that were revealed to Moses alone at Horeb but were to apply within the Promised Land. Like the tablets of stone, it functions as written attestation to a covenant between Yhwh and Israel, but to either a second covenant or to a renewed covenant with further stipulations. Unlike the tablets with the Ten Commandments that were to stay in the Holy of Holies where only the head priest could enter once a year, however, the scroll was to be taken out and read every seven years at Sukkot, reminding the people of what their ancestors and they must do as members of Israel (31:9–13). In this way, the scroll functions much like copies of a Hittite vassal treaty, with its provision in some instances that at regular intervals someone should read the text of the treaty deposited in the temple to the vassal king and his nobles or in public to remind them of their obligations. The stone tablets with the Ten Commandments, on the other hand, remained confined in the temple. To some degree, they are superceded by the scroll of teaching, which contains the Ten Commandments, leaving them in force, but which includes additional laws to be applied in the land as well.[130] In between readings from the witnessing scroll, individuals are to teach the Ten Commandments and other vital aspects of Moses's teaching to their children.

---

130 Barnabas Lindars thinks the intention of placing the book alongside the Ark containing the tablets is "to make the book a substitute for the Decalogue, or at least put it on the same level" ("Torah," 131).

Tigay comments on how the writer uses a rhetorical style well suited to oral presentation. Sentences contain assonance, key words, repeated themes, and stereotypical expressions, which typify oral presentation. The laws are free of technical details and so accessible to people of all backgrounds. The writer assumes that people must be persuaded to follow the laws, leading to the provision of explanations and underlying reasons to try to secure Israel's voluntary, informed compliance. Half the laws have accompanying explanations or motivational language showing their logic, justice, or consequences.[131]

F. Charles Fensham noted the closeness in style and contents between wisdom literature and law collections in the ancient Near East. While the first was used to teach people prescriptive norms and a policy for how to behave, the latter provided illustrations of infractions of those norms from actual legal cases, as well as their punishments. The policy found in wisdom literature is very similar to statements found in ancient law codes that included prologues and epilogues.[132]

7.2 Fictional Autobiography

The author of Deuteronomy also appears to have drawn on the template for a fictional autobiography. In a study of fifteen Akkadian examples, which also includes extant comparative literature from other ancient Near Eastern cultures, Tremper Longman, IIII establishes that the template for this genre had three elements. The first two were stable: a first-person introduction (self-identification) and a first-person narration of events experienced over time. The third and final element, however, had four options: blessings or curses, which seem to be derived from the template for royal inscriptions, the giving of donations to a temple or goddess, a didactic or advice-giving ending that readers were to apply to their own life, which links it to wisdom literature, and a *vaticinium ex eventu* prophetic ending.[133]

The first element seems to be lacking in Deuteronomy. The book opens with a third-person narrated statement (1:1–5), where Moses is named but not given any patronymic or more detailed genealogical introduction; it reads as though the audience knows this character already. "These are the words that Moses spoke to all Israel beyond the Jordan – in the wilderness, on the plain opposite

131 Tigay, *Deuteronomy*, xviii–xix.
132 Fensham, "Widow, Orphan," 129.
133 Longman, *Fictional Akkadian Autobiography*, 67, 86, 90, 101, 111, 164 for the three-part structure; 53–195 for discussion of examples of the four types of endings.

Suph, between Paran and Tophel, Laban, Hazeroth, and Di-zahab ..." The first-person narrative begins in 1:6 with "Yhwh our God spoke to us at Horeb, saying, 'You have stayed long enough at this mountain.'" However, an examination of Egyptian autobiographies shows that in that tradition, the introduction is in third person as here, not first person. Three well-known examples of non-royal autobiographical literature from Egypt, fictional or not, open with a third-person statement. "Sinuhe" begins: the Prince, Count, Governor of the domains of the sovereign in the lands of the Asiatics, true and beloved Friend of the King, the Attendant Sinuhe, says," before continuing, "I was an attendant who attended his lord ..." (*COS* 1.38). "The Shipwrecked Sailor" begins, "The worthy attendant said," and continues immediately with "Take heart, my lord! We have reached home." (*COS* 1.39). Finally, the "Report of Wenamon," whose status as a genuine or fictional report or autobiography continues to be debated, opens with a date and the name of the future speaker in third person. "Year 5, fourth month of summer, day 16, the day of departure of Wenamun, the Elder of the Portal of the Temple of Amun, Lord of thrones-of-the-To-Lands, to fetch timber for the great noble bark of Amun-Re, King of the Gods, which is upon the river and [is called] Amun-user-he." It then continues, "On the day of my arrival at Tanis ..." (*COS* 1.41), conveyed in first-person. Thus, the third-person opening of the book of Deuteronomy does not disqualify it from being framed as an autobiography; it suggests, however, that the author was aware that the opening could be in first or third person and opted for the latter.

The second and third elements of the Akkadian template are both present, however. The first-person account of Moses's experiences with Israel at Mt. Horeb and thereafter until reaching the plains of Moab spans the entire book, even if some narrated incidents appear to be flashbacks rather than in strictly chronological order. Of the four possible endings, it is clear that the writer has opted for the didactic one. As already noted, there are interwoven elements well before the conclusion that seem to relate to first-person Instructions, associated with what commonly is recognized to be wisdom literature. At the same time, blessing and curses appear thematically toward the end of the book.

8 Synthesis

The foregoing investigation into literary templates and their characteristics has yielded interesting facts that can allow the following observations to be drawn. First, it is highly unlikely that chs. 12–26 once constituted an independent legal collection that was taken up by the author of Deuteronomy and used wholesale to produce the larger book. Ancient Near Eastern law collections are all written in third person and consist almost entirely of conditional, "if ... then" formulations, with very occasional second person unconditional statements included. Also, only two of the extant law codes contain a few motive clauses. On this basis, any postulated underlying legal collection should be limited to the fifteen third-person conditional examples formulated with *kî* or *'im* in 19:11, 21:5, 21:18, 22:13, 22:20, 22:22, 22:25, 22:28, 24:1, 24:5, 24:7; 25:1, 25:2; 25:5, and 25:7, although one could perhaps be generous and add the additional thirteen odd unconditional third person formulations as well.[134] One would then need to decide if the remaining fifty second-person conditional formulations also should be assigned an ultimate origin in this same postulated collection or not. Why would some such exemplary cases be left in third person and others transferred into second person?

Eliminating the likelihood that a legal collection was the origin of 12:1–26:15, a more plausible possible explanation for those desiring to identify an independent source for this material would be that the contents of these chapters once constituted a collection of regulations for one or more occupational classes within the community of Israel or even for all its members. This would link it to the sub-category of the Hittite *išḫiul* that has been called somewhat unfortunately "instructions" in *Context of Scripture* (*COS*) by Hittitologists. A corroborative implication would be that the corresponding term in Hebrew, *b^{e}rît*, had a similar sub-category.

As argued earlier, the state of the preserved texts precludes our knowing if the words of a sworn oath longer than "So be it" had once stood at the end of the known examples of these written documents or not. However, since a formal treaty agreement was designated by the phrase "binding and oaths," it is possible that the *išḫiul* template was flexible enough to allow for the creation of a written document that contained commands alone, depending on its context of use, even if oaths would have been involved in its implementation. Were it not serving as a vassal or parity treaty but to present professional rules or terms of employment, then other elements like the historical prologue, provision for deposit, list of gods as witnesses, and blessings and curses would not need to be included.

This category of "instructions," better labeled "commands" or "sanctions," is to be distinguished from another genre called "Instructions" that belongs to wisdom-related literature because of its inclusion of a sworn oath as an integral element, if not in the text itself, then in the implementation of the document. In the Hittite tradition, such "commands" were formulated either completely in

134 17:6–7a, 17:12a, 17:13, 17:16–18:3, 19:4–6, 19:15, 19:16–18, 20:5–9, 23:1–3, 23:8, 23:10–11, 23:17, 24:16.

third person or in third person with second person formulations. Unconditional formulations predominate over conditional statements, and motive clauses are present.

A decision would need to be made about which verses in chs. 12–26 might need to be removed from this postulated set of oath-enforced regulations. In particular, should all references to entry into the land and events of the Exodus and Sinai/Horeb stay be removed as extraneous to this type of document? This hypothetical document would have no connection to the current story-world that is set on the eve of the occupation of the Promised Land after the Exodus, visit to Sinai/Horeb, and the wilderness wanderings. Thus, all such references currently found within the chapters would need to be removed as secondary insertions by the creator of the book. As noted by Martijn Beukenhorst in his article in this volume, the rules for conducting war would likely need to be removed, since their presence seems predicated on the setting in the story world. A logical beginning point for this hypothetical document might be 12:31 [32] or 13:1 since ch. 12 concerns events all explicitly to take place only after entering the land.

A second possible option for understanding chs. 12–26 as a hypothetical independent document would be to construe it to have constituted an example of the wisdom-related Instructions genre. This is a didactic genre that sets out to provide concrete examples of desired behavior and attitudes that will lead to a good life filled with blessing vs. a bad one beset by adversity. The unconditional formulations in second person address far outnumber the conditional casuistic formulations in either second or third person. In the Hebrew Bible, such instructions tend to take the form of proverbial sayings, but that might not have been the only format possible for such wisdom-related instructions, as seen from the wider ancient Near Eastern examples. The same decision about what to include or exclude from the collection, based on the influence of the setting created in the story world, would need to be made. There would appear to have been a fair amount of overlap between the conventions and general template used to create a set of royal instructions and wisdom-like instructions.

Having examined the possibilities for the author of Deuteronomy to have taken up a pre-existing document containing the majority of the material that he framed with a setting on the eve of the entry into the Promised Land, is it more plausible to assume such an independent document existed, or does it make more sense to argue that the author of the first version of the book would have assembled the materials in chs. 12–26 himself for the first time? Before one opts for the first alternative, a clear explanation of the original setting, function, and intended audience needs to be given, with some indication of what current material must be removed.

The second alternative, on the other hand, accounts immediately for what is present. In a setting on the eve of the occupation of the Promised Land, the regulations to be followed by Israel in the new phase of its existence are being formally announced in 12:1–26:16, followed by their binding acceptance via the people's declaration of acceptance in 26:17–19. They apply both individually and collectively. The inclusion of regulations that pertain to all spheres of society, civil, religious, military, and private, makes sense in the context and accounts for the approximately 50 % overlap in material with the "Covenant Code" and "Holiness Code" as well as the additional material found only in this set of regulations and the observations of a "constitutional-like" feel of the material. The overlap with the Covenant and Holiness "codes" and a few proverbs indicates the author drew on pre-existing oral and/or written material, and it is likely that some of the contents not duplicated elsewhere in Hebrew Bible texts also derived from similar sources. At the same time, it appears that pre-existing regulations and casuistic materials likely were adapted to reflect the particular ideological emphases the writer of the book wanted to convey (e.g. Deut 22:1 vs. Exod 23:4–5; Deut 23:20 [19] vs. Exod 22:24 [25]).

The close intertwining of source-critical presuppositions with exegetical principles in the field of Hebrew Bible studies has led to a preference for underplaying the creative contribution of biblical writers and even the denial of authorial status to those responsible for the biblical books in favor of a status as editors only. It is possible to propose that the majority of the material present in chs. 12–26 could have existed as an independent document belonging to the genre of instructions, royal or wisdom-like. But what is gained by postulating this earlier source over assigning the assembling of the materials in chs. 12–26 to the same person who created the preceding and succeeding narrative materials delivered primarily in a set of speeches made by Moses to Israel? All the regulatory material present is easily accounted for by the setting in the storyworld created by the initial creator of the book and the message he intended to convey to his audience through what he included in the set of regulations he assembled and presented using a predominance of unconditional statements, many motivational clauses, a few third-person conditional formulations that he usually followed with second-person motivational statements, and some second-person conditional formulations. Hypothetical earlier source documents and complex scenarios of the growth of the book over time involving multiple thematic redactions can certainly be constructed, as the articles by Philippe Guillaume in the present volume ably illustrate, even though the results are unprovable. It would be naïve to argue that the original form of the book is identical with the final form of the book, and a logical case can be made for alterations having been made in order to link the independent work into the meta-narrative sequence of the Enneateuch, with some smaller changes here and there as well. But the principle of Occam's razor is applicable here, given all the speculation involved, and that points to the person who created the book assembling 12:1–26:15 himself, using earlier written and oral sources in part but modifying them in some instances, as part of his overall plan.

Works Cited

Alt, Albrecht. "Die Ursprünge des israelitischen Rechts." In vol. 1 of *Kleine Schriften zur Geschichte des Volkes Israel*, 278–332. Munich: C. H. Beck, 1953.

Altman, Amnon. "What Kind of Treaty Tradition Do the Sefire Inscriptions Represent?" In *Treasures on Camels' Humps: Historical and Literary Studies from the Ancient Near East Presented to Israel Eph'al*, edited by Mordechai Cogan and Dan'el Kahn, 26–40. Jerusalem: The Hebrew University Magnes Press, 2008.

Altman, Amnon. "Who Took an Oath on a Vassal Treaty – Only the Vassal King or Also the Suzerain?" *Zeitschrift für altorientalische und biblische Rechtsgeschichte* 9 (2003): 178–84.

Beckman, Gary. "Hittite Treaties and the Development of the Cuneiform Treaty Tradition." In *Die deuteronomistischen Geschichtswerke. Redaktions- und religionsgeschichtliche Perspektiven zur "Deuteronomismus" Diskussion in Tora und Vorderen Propheten*, edited by Jan Christian Gertz, Doris Prechel, Konrad Schmid, and Markus Witte, 279–301. Beihefte zur Zeitschrift für die alttestamentliche Wissenschaft 365. Berlin: de Gruyter, 2006.

Boston, James R. 1968. "The Wisdom Influence upon the Song of Moses." *Journal of Biblical Literature* 87: 198–202.

Braulik, Georg. 1994. *The Theology of Deuteronomy: Collected Essays of Georg Braulik, O.S.B.* Translated by Ulrike Lindblad. BIBAL Collected Essays 2. Richland Hills, TX: BIBAL.

Brekelmans, Christian H. W. 1978. "Wisdom Influence on Deuteronomy." In *La Sagesse de l'Ancien Testament*, edited by M. Gilbert, 28–38. Bibliotheca Ephemeridum Theologicarum Lovaniensium 54. Louvain: Louvain University Press. Reprinted in *A Song of Power and the Power of Song*, edited by Duane L. Christensen, 123–34. Winona Lake, IN: Eisenbrauns, 1993. Citations are to the original version.

Carmichael, Calum M. "Deuteronomic Laws, Wisdom, and Historical Traditions." *Journal of Semitic Studies* 12 (1967): 198–206.

Carmichael, Calum M. *The Laws of Deuteronomy*. Ithaca: Cornell University Press, 1974.

Cazelles, Henri. "Institutions et terminologie en Deutéronome i 6–17." In *Volume du Congrès International pour l'étude de l'Ancien Testament, Genève 1965*, edited by P. A. H. de Boer, 97–112. Vetus Testamentum Supplements 15. Leiden: Brill, 1966.

Christensen, Duane L. 2001. *Deuteronomy 1:1–21:9, Revised*. Word Biblical Commentary 6A. Nashville: Thomas Nelson.

Cohen, Yoram. "Why 'Wisdom'? Copying, Studying, and Collecting Wisdom Literature in the Cuneiform World." In *Teaching Morality in Antiquity: Wisdom Texts, Oral Traditions, and Images*, edited by T. M. Oshida with Susanne Kohlhaas, 41–59. Orientalische Religionen in Der Antike 29. Tübingen: Mohr Siebeck, 2018.

COS = *Context of Scripture.* Edited by William W. Hallow. 3 vols. Leiden: Brill, 1997–2002.
Crenshaw, James L. "Method in Determining Wisdom Influence upon 'Historical' Literature." *Journal of Biblical Literature* 88 (1969): 129–42.
Crenshaw, James L. *Old Testament Wisdom: An Introduction.* Atlanta: John Knox, 1981.
Delcor, M. "Les attachés littéraires, l'origine et la signification de l'expression biblique 'prendre à témoin le ciel et la terre.'" *Vetus Testamentum* 16 (1966): 8–25.
Driver, Samuel R. 1902. *Deuteronomy.* 3rd ed. International Critical Commentary 5. Edinburgh: T. and T. Clark.
Edelman, Diana V. "The Metaphor of Torah as a Life-Giving Well in Deuteronomy." In *History, Memory, Hebrew Scriptures: A Festschrift for Ehud Ben Zvi*, edited by Ian D. Wilson and Diana V. Edelman, 317–33. Winona Lake, IN: Eisenbrauns, 2015.
Edelman, Diana V. "Saying Goodbye to the Theory of the Influence of Esarhaddon's Sucession *Adê* on Deuteronomy 13 and 28." In *Beside the Ark: Thinking about Deuteronomy outside the Box.* Edited by Diana V. Edelman, Benedetta Rossi, Kåre Berge, and Philippe Guillaume, forthcoming.
Fensham, F. Charles. "Widow, Orphan, and the Poor in the Ancient Near Eastern Legal and Wisdom Literature." *Journal of Near Eastern Studies* 21 (1962): 129–39. Reprinted in *A Song of Power and the Power of Song*, edited by Duane L. Christensen, 247–55. Winona Lake, IN: Eisenbrauns, 1993. Citations are to the original version.
Finkelstein, J. J. "The Laws of Ur-Nammu." *Journal of Cuneiform Studies* 22 (1968/1969): 66–82.
Fitzmyer, Joseph A. *The Aramaic Inscriptions of Sefîre.* Biblica et Orientalia 19. Rome: Pontifical Biblical Institute, 1967.
Fohrer, Georg. *Introduction to the Old Testament.* London: SPCK, 1978.
Fohrer, Georg. "Remarks on Modern Interpretation of the Prophets." *Journal of Biblical Literature* 80 (1961): 309–19.
García-López, Félix. *Le Deutéronome. Une loi prêchée.* Cahiers évangiles 63. Paris: Éditions du Cerf, 1988.
Geller, Stephen A. "Fiery Wisdom: Logos and Lexis in Deuteronomy 4." *Prooftexts* 14 (1994): 103–39.
Gemser, Berend. "The Importance of the Motive Clause in Old Testament Law." In *Adhuc Loquitur: Collected Essays of Dr. B. Gemser*, edited by A. van Selms and A. S. van der Woude, 95–115. Pretoria Oriental Studies 7. Leiden: Brill, 1968. Originally published in *Congress Volume Copenhagen 1953*, edited by G. W. Anderson, Aage Bentzen, P. A. H. de Boer, Millar Burrows, Henri Cazelles, and Martin Noth, 50–66. Vetus Testamentum Supplements 1. Leiden: Brill, 1953.
Gerstenberger, Erhard. "Covenant and Commandment." *Journal of Biblical Literature* 84 (1965): 38–51.
Gerstenberger, Erhard. *Wesen und Herkunft des "Apodiktischen Rechts."* Wissenschaftliche Monographien zum Alten und Neuen Testament 20. Neukirchen-Vluyn: Neukircherner Verlag, 1965.
Harvey, Julien. "Le '*rîb*-pattern', réquisitoire prophétique sur la rupture de l'alliance." *Biblica* 43 (1962): 172–96.
Huffmon, Herbert B. "The Covenant Lawsuit in the Prophets." *Journal of Biblical Literature* 78 (1959): 285–95.
Kalluveettil, Paul. *Declaration and Covenant: A Comprehensive Review of Covenant Formulae from the Old Testament and the Ancient Near East.* Analecta biblica 88. Rome: Biblical Institute Press, 1982.

Korošec, Viktor. *Hethitische Staatsverträge. Ein Beitrag zu ihrer juristischen Wertung.* Leipziger rechtswissenschaftliche Studien 60. Leipzig: T. Weicher, 1931.

Labuschagne, Casper J. "Divine Speech in Deuteronomy." In *Das Deuteronomium. Entstehung, Gestalt und Botschaft*, edited by Norbert Lohfink, 111–26. Bibliotheca EphemeridumTheologicarum Lovaniensium 68. Louvain: Louvain University Press, 1985. Reprinted in *A Song of Power and the Power of Song*, edited by Duane L. Christensen, 375–93. Winona Lake, IN: Eisenbrauns, 1993. Citations are to the reprinted version.

Lambert, Wilfred G. *Babylonian Wisdom Literature*. Oxford: Clarendon, 1960.

Lauinger, Jacob. "The Neo-Assyrian *adê*: Treaty, Oath or Something Else?" Vassal King or Also the Suzerain?" *Zeitschrift für altorientalische und biblische Rechtsgeschichte* 19 (2013): 99–115.

Lauinger, Jacob. "Neo-Assyrian Scribes, 'Esarhaddon's Succession Treaty,' and the Dynamics of Textual Mass Production." In *Texts and Contexts: The Circulation and Transmission of Cuneiform Texts in Social Space*, edited by Paul Delnero and Jacob Lauinger, 285–314. Studies in Ancient Near Eastern Records 9. Boston: de Gruyter, 2015.

Levin, Christoph. "Über den 'Color Hieremianus' des Deueronomiums." In *Das Deuteronomium und seine Querbeziehungen*, edited by Timoo Veijola, 107–26. Suomen Eksegeettisen Seuran julkaisuja 62. Helsinki: Finnish Exegetical Society, 1996.

Lindars, Barnabas. "Torah in Deuteronomy." In *Words and Meanings: Essays Presented to D. Winton Thomas*, edited by Peter R. Ackroyd and Barnabas Lindars, 117–36. Cambridge: Cambridge University Press, 1968.

Loersch, Sigrid. *Das Deuteronomium und seine Deutungen. Ein forschungs-geschichtlicher Überblick.* Stuttgarter Bibelstudien 22. Stuttgart: Verlag Katholisches Bibelwerk, 1967.

Lohfink, Norbert. *Höre, Israel! Auslegung von Texten aus dem Buch Deuteronomium.* Dusseldörf: Patmos, 1965.

Lohfink, Norbert. "Bund als Vertrag im Deuteronomium." *Zeitschrift für die alttestamentliche Wissenschaft* 107 (1995): 215–39.

Longman, Tremper, III. *The Fear of the Lord is Wisdom.* Grand Rapids, MI: Baker Academic, 2017.

Longman, Tremper, III. *Fictional Akkadian Autobiography: A Generic and Comparative Study.* Winona Lake, IN: Eisenbrauns, 1991.

Macholz, Georg Christian. "Israel und das Land: Vorarbeiten zu einem Vergleich zwischen Priesterschrift und deuteronomistischem Geschichtswerk." Unpublished habilitation, Heidelberg, 1969.

Malfroy, Jean. "Sagesse et loi dans le Deuteronome: études." *Vetus Testamentum* 15 (1965): 49–65.

Mayes, Andrew D. H. "Deuteronomy 4 and the Literary Criticism of Deuteronomy." *Journal of Biblical Literature* 100 (1981): 23–51. Reprinted in *A Song of Power and the Power of Song*, edited by Duane L. Christensen, 195–224. Winona Lake, IN: Eisenbrauns, 1993. Citations are to the original version.

McBride, S. Dean, Jr. "Polity of the Covenant People: The Book of Deuteronomy." *Interpretation* 41 (1987): 229–41. Reprinted in *A Song of Power and the Power of Song*. Edited by Duane L. Christensen, 62–77. Winona Lake, IN: Eisenbrauns, 1993. Citations are to the original version.

McCarthy, Dennis J. 1981. *Treaty and Covenant.* Analecta Biblica 21A. 2nd ed. Rome: Pontifical Biblical Institute, 1981.

Mendenhall, George E. "Law and Covenant in Israel and in the Ancient Near East". *Biblical Archaeologist* 17 (1954): 26–46.

Miller, Jared L. *Royal Hittite Instructions and Related Administrative Texts.* Edited by Mauro Giorgieri. Writings from the Ancient World 31. Atlanta: SBL Press, 2013.

Morgan, Donn F. *Wisdom in the Old Testament Traditions.* Oxford: Basil Blackwell, 1981.

Morrow, William S. "*Fortschreibung* in Mesopotamian Treaties and the Book of Deuteronomy." In *Recht und Ethik im Alten Testament. Beiträge des Symposiums "Das Alte Testament und die Kultur der Moderne" anlässlich des 100. Geburtstags Gerhard von Rads (1901–1971) Heidelberg, 18.–21. Oktober,* 2001, edited by Bernard M. Levinson and Eckart Otto, 111–23. Altes Testament und Moderne 13. Münster: Lit, 2004.

Morrow, William S. "A Generic Discrepancy in the Covenant Code." In *Theory and Method in Biblical and Cuneiform Law: Revision, Interpolation, and Development.*, edited by Bernard M. Levinson, 136–51. Journal for the Study of the Old Testament Supplement Series 181. Sheffield: JSOT Press, 1994.

Murphy, Roland E. "Assumptions and Problems in Old Testament Wisdom Research." *Catholic Biblical Quarterly* 29 (1967): 407–18.

Nielsen, Eduard. *Deuteronomium.* Handbuch zum Alten Testament 1.6. Tübingen: J. C. B. Mohr, 1995.

Noth, Martin. *The Deuteronomistic History.* Journal for the Study of the Old Testament Supplement Series 15. Sheffield: JSOT Press, 1981.

Noth, Martin. *The Laws in the Pentateuch and other Studies.* Translated by D. R. Ap-Thomas. London: SCM, 1966.

O'Dowd, Ryan. *The Wisdom of Torah: Epistemology in Deuteronomy and the Wisdom Literature.* Forschungen zur Religion und Literatur des Alten und Neuen Testaments 225. Göttingen: Vandenhoeck & Ruprecht, 2009.

Östborn, Gunnar. *Tōrā in the Old Testament: A Semantic Study.* Lund: Håkan Ohlsson, 1945.

Otto, Eckart. *Das Deuteronomium. Politische Theologie und Rechtsreform in Juda und Assyrien.* Beihefte zur Zeitschrift für die alttestamentliche Wissenschaft 284. Berlin: De Gruyter, 1999.

Parpola, Simo. "Neo-Assyrian Treaties from the Royal Archives of Nineveh." *Journal of Cuneiform Studies* 39 (1987): 161–89.

Parpola, Simo and Kazuko Watanabe. *Neo-Assyrian Treaties and Loyalty Oaths.* State Archives of Assyria 2. Helsinki: Helsinki University Press, 1988.

Paul, Shalom M. *Studies in the Book of the Covenant in the Light of Cuneiform and Biblical Law.* Vetus Testamentum Supplements 18. Leiden: Brill, 1970.

Rad, Gerhard von. *Deuteronomy: A Commentary.* Old Testament Library. Translated by Dorothea Barton. London: SCM, 1966.

Rad, Gerhard von. *Studies in Deuteronomy.* Translated by David Stalker. Studies in Biblical Theology 9. London: SCM, 1961.

Roth, Martha T. *Law Collections from Mesopotamia and Asia Minor.* SBL Writings from the Ancient World 6. Atlanta: Scholars Press, 1997.

Scharbert, Josef. "אלה." In vol. 1 of *Theological Dictionary of the Old Testament*, edited by G. Johannes Botterweck and Helmer Ringgren, 261–66. Translated by John T. Willis. Rev. ed. Grand Rapids, MI: Eerdmans, 1977.

Sneed, Mark. "Is the 'Wisdom Tradition' a Tradition?" *Catholic Biblical Quarterly* 73 (2011): 50–71.

Sneed, Mark, ed. *Was There a Wisdom Tradition? New Prospects in Israelite Wisdom Studies.* Ancient Israel and Its Literature 23. Atlanta: SBL Press.

Sonsino, Rifat. *Motive Clauses in Hebrew Law.* SBL Dissertation Series 45. Chico, CA: Scholars Press, 1980.

Szlechter, E. "Le code de Lipit-Istar (I)." *Revue d'assyriologie et d'archéologie orientale* 51 (1957): 57–82.
Szlechter, E. "Le code de Lipit-Istar (II)." *Revue d'assyriologie et d'archéologie orientale* 51 (1957): 177–96.
Taggar-Cohen, Ada. "Biblical Wisdom Literature and Hittite Didactic Texts in the Ancient Near Eastern Literary Context." *Journal of the Interdisciplinary Study of Monotheistic Religions* 14 (2019): 45–64.
Taggar-Cohen, Ada. "Biblical *covenant* and Hittite *išḫiul* reexamined." *Vetus Testamentum* 61 (2011): 461–88.
Tigay, Jeffery H. *Deuteronomy: The Traditional Hebrew Text with the New JPS Translation*. The JPS Torah Commentary. Philadelphia: Jewish Publication Society, 1996.
Vriezen, Theodor C. "Das Hiphil von *'amar* in Deut 26.17, 18." *Jaarbericht van het Vooraziatisch-Egyptisch Gezelschap (Genootschap) Ex oriente Lux* 17 (1963): 207–10.
Weinfeld, Moshe. 1977. "*Bᵉrîth*." In vol. 2 of *Theological Dictionary of the Old Testament*, edited by G. Johannes Botterweck and Helmer Ringgren, 253–79. Translated by John T. Willis. Grand Rapids, MI: Eerdmans, 1975.
Weinfeld, Moshe. *Deuteronomy 1–11: A New Translation with Introduction and Commentary*. Anchor Bible 5. New York: Doubleday, 1991.
Weinfeld, Moshe. *Deuteronomy and the Deuteronomic School*. Oxford: Clarendon, 1972.
Weinfeld, Moshe. "Deuteronomy: The Present State of Inquiry." *Journal of Biblical Literature* 86 (1967): 249–62.
Weinfeld, Moshe. "The Origin of Humanism in Deuteronomy." *Journal of Biblical Literature* 80 (1960): 241–47.
Weinfeld, Moshe. "The Origin of the Apodictic Law: An Overlooked Source." *Vetus Testamentum* 23 (1973): 63–75.
Whybray, R. N. *The Intellectual Tradition in the Old Testament*. Beihefte zur Zeitschrift für die alttestamentliche Wissenschaft 135. Berlin: Walter de Gruyer, 1974.
Wright, G. Ernst. "The Lawsuit of God: A Form-Critical Study of Deuteronomy 32." In *Israel's Prophetic Heritage: Essays in Honor of James Muilenberg*, edited by Bernard W. Anderson and Walter Harrelson, 26–67. New York: Harper & Brothers, 1962.

Kåre Berge, Faculty of Theology, University of Oslo

Cities in Deuteronomy: Imperial Ideology, Resilience, and the Imagination of Yahwistic Religion

1 Introduction

Cities play a remarkable role in Deuteronomy as the residential area of the population and the place where local judicial and civil activity takes place. This article investigates the role of cities in the civil system of the Israelite "state."[1] Two issues are of special concern: the local judicial system of the cities and their relation to *hammāqôm*. I will argue that Achaemenid royal ideology has been taken over and modified or altered to fit the new theology of the heavenly King of Israel in an act of resilience, the ability to resist imperial domination.

2 Cities and Gates: Deuteronomic Hallmarks

Urban life is documented in Deuteronomy as "cities" (ערים), occurring 57 times, and "gates" (שערים), appearing as שעריך "your gates" 27 times[2] or as lexemes appearing 58 and 34 times, respectively (Accordance search). "The place" (המקום) is not designated as a city any more than its location is specified. Therefore, it is not included in Table 1. Its relation with the Deuteronomic cities is discussed further below.

The discussion of cities in Deuteronomy by Don Benjamin convincingly describes Deuteronomic Israel as an urban culture. The notions of "the place" as the capital city of Jerusalem and of the opposition between retribalized cities and more feudal terms of the monarchy, are problematic.[3] The volume edited by Diana Edelman and Ehud Ben Zvi deals with several aspects of the biblical city, but scarcely with Deuteronomy.[4] Some studies of urbanism in Antiquity touch on biblical cities but hardly consider the specific place Deuteronomy

1 The term "state" is anachronistic but is hard to substitute, so I will use it in a general meaning also presented by, e.g., Bang and Scheidel, *Oxford Handbook of the State*, in their introduction (pp. 5–9 and 14–26): "premodern states, early states." See also Yoffee, *Myths*, 15–21.
2 Frese, "Land of Gates," 34, 44.
3 Benjamin, *Deuteronomy*, especially ch. 2.
4 Edelman and Ben Zvi, *Memory*.

https://doi.org/10.1515/9783110713312-004

Tab. 1: City and Gates in Deuteronomy.

1:22–3:12	Cities to be conquered and plundered
3:19	Safety for Ruben and Gad's wives and children in cities I am giving you
4:41–42	Transjordanian cities of refuge
5:14	Sabbath even for your *gēr* in your gates
6:9; 11:20	*Mezûzōt* at your gates
6:10	Fine cities you have not built
9:1	Cities fortified up to the heavens
12:12; 16:11.14	Rejoice at the *māqôm* with the Levite who is in your gates
12:12.15; 15:22	Eat meat in your gates
12:17–18	Eat tithes and firstlings at the *māqôm,* also with the Levite in your gates.
13:13–17	Destroy the entire idolatrous Israelite city
14:21	Give carrion to the *gēr* within your gates
14:27–29; 26:12	Store triennial tithes within your gates
15:7	Lend to your needy brother in one of your gates in your land
16:5	Do not eat Passover in your gates
16:18	Appoint judges and officers in all your gates
17:2–5	Stone the idolater in one of your gates
17:8	Refer a difficult case within your gates to the *māqôm*
18:6	A Levite may leave one of your gates
19:1–12	Set up cities of refuge in Cisjordan
20:10–20	Differential treatment of conquered cities
21:2–6	How elders of the city deal with bloodguilt in the countryside
21:19–21	Let the men of his city stoning the rebellious son at the gate
22:15–21	City elders must judge cases of premarital prostitution at the gate
22:23–24	Stone anyone guilty of premarital intercourse inside the city at the gate
23:17	Runaway slaves can settle down freely in one of your gates
24:14	Pay wages to your *gēr* who is in your land in your gates
25:7–8	The elders of his city should shame the reluctant brother-in-law at the gate
28:3, 16	Blessings and curses in city and field
28:52–57	Misery in your besieged gates
31:12	Assemble even your *gēr* in your gates to learn to fear Yhwh
34:3	Palm City

grants to cities.[5] Besides the literary perspective on urbanism in the volume edited by Lester L. Grabbe and Robert Haak,[6] Daniel A. Frese has done valuable work on the function of "the gates" in Deuteronomy.[7]

5 So e.g. Aufrecht, Mirau, and Gauley, *Urbanism*; Kemezis, *Urban Dreams.*

6 Grabbe and Haak, *Every City.*

7 Frese, "Civic Forum"; "Land of Gates."

The Hebrew word עיר may not necessarily designate a walled settlement. For instance, in 2 Samuel 2:3 it denotes the "cities of Hebron" (ערי חברון), which likely are smaller dependent villages and settled areas in the local region, but in Deuteronomy, the cities Israel is to conquer have high and inaccessible walls (Deut 1:28; 28:52). Once taken, these walls will shelter the wives and children of the Transjordanian tribes while their men go and help the other tribes conquer their own cities. In Canaan itself, Israel is not expected to destroy the cities it will take. Cities are a gift from Yhwh (Deut 3:19). In this sense, Deuteronomy is an exception to the supposed negative connotations of cities in the Bible.[8] To be sure, cities can be where some individuals or the entire population may be led astray (Deut 13:15–16; 17:2, 5).

Apart from Deuteronomy 3:5, where a difference between walled cities (ערי בצרות חומה) and unwalled settlements (ערי הפרזי) is marked, cities in Deuteronomy are often designated by the stock phrase "in your gates" (בשעריך), a synecdoche for an Israelite city in general. This idiosyncratic use of the term "gates" has one clear parallel outside Deuteronomy in Exodus 20:10 // Deuteronomy 5:14 and similar denotations in Jeremiah 14:2; 15:7.[9] 1 Kings 8:37 and Ruth 3:11, on the other hand, may denote the community of a town.[10] Although some authors propose a literal use of "the gates" to refer to actual city gates in Deuteronomy 23:17; 24:14; 26:12, this is hardly convincing.[11] Baruch Halpern (in this volume) distinguishes between plural and singular use of the word. He argues that the plural form "in your gates" refers to local neighborhoods of a city, like Akkadian *babu*, the place of a lineage operating as an extended family. In his view, the singular form, in contrast, refers exclusively to the place of judgment by the elders. However, Deuteronomy 16:18; 17:5, 8 contradict this.

The suggestion that in Deuteronomy 5:14; 12:12; 14:21, and 14:27 the word "gates" stands for "location" and "place," which would include settlements of any type, is doubtful; there is nothing that actively points in the direction of unwalled settlements.[12] That "there were probably more rural farmers than urbanites in ancient Israel"[13] does not imply that Deuteronomy does not differentiate between walled and unwalled settlements. What it shows is that Deuteronomy views all Israelites as city-dwellers. Rural hamlets, farmsteads, villages, and *hamulas*, central in modern Arabic ideas of local and community relations,

---

8 Roddy, "Landscape," 15–16; Anthonioz, "Cities," 30.
9 So Frese, "Civic Forum," 279; "Land of Gates," 34.
10 Frese, "Civic Forum," 295.
11 Frese, "Land of Gates," 40.
12 *HALOT* 4, 1,616.
13 Frese, "Civic Forum," 289.

do not appear in Deuteronomy.[14] And they need not appear, because the city includes the gardens, orchards, arable land, and grazing grounds around it, where the urbanites produce their sustenance.[15] Deuteronomy does not differentiate between city-dwellers and peasants. Agricultural versus non-agricultural activity is moot. The entire population is engaged in the production of food. Contrary to Leviticus 25:32, no difference is made between urban and rural property. As a whole, the city is simply viewed as the space where Israelites conduct their day-to-day life, including justice and custom, among *gērîm* and slaves.[16]

Nevertheless, Deuteronomy does not necessarily describe life as it was lived when the work was produced. Deuteronomy may rather reflect a utopian program, even if it is the culmination of a process and its codification rather than a mere proposal.[17] The Deuteronomic portrayal of cities lacks most architectural items associated with cities. There is a square (13:16), but the urban structures described by Frank S. Frick and in the volume edited by Natalie N. May and Ulrike Steinert are conspicuously absent.[18] The idea of a kingdom would normally include a capital with the acropolis, the palace, and at least one temple as the nucleus of the state, but there is nothing.[19] There is no stronghold, citadel, tower, acropolis, or temple; no palace and no monumental buildings, either in the cities or at the other locus of Israelite life, the "place" (*māqôm*).[20] The place toward which all Israelites converge to feast in front of Yhwh is never designated a city. There is a lone reference to "the house of Yhwh" in the book (בית יהוה, Deut 23:19 [18]), where one cannot use what is given to a prostitute or the purchase price of a dog as payment of a vow at this facility because both are abominations to Yhwh, but how it relates to the *māqôm* is unclear. Clearly, this is a cult place (Deut 26:2), but the communicative intention of the *māqôm's* anonymity should be accounted for. The commonly used expression to describe the gist of the *māqôm*, "cultic centralization," is too marked by 2 Kings 23.[21]

---

14 Frantzman, "Arab Settlement," 58.

15 Frick, *City*, 92; Faust, "Jerusalem's Hinterland."

16 It should be noted that Max Weber already had noticed the conspicuous aspect of the cities in Deut (*Ancient Judaism*, 65–69).

17 Davies, "Authority," 32.

18 Frick, *City*, 92–93; May and Steinert, *Fabric*. See especially the articles by Steinert on city streets (pp. 123–70) and Baker on urban morphology (pp. 171–88).

19 For these appurtenances of a kingdom, see Ahlström, *Royal Administration*, 4–6.

20 See also Thelle, *Approaches*, 95. It is correct that Deut "never mentions a house built for YHWH" (55), that is, in relation to *hammāqôm*, but where is the location of *bet yhwh* in 23:19 [18]?

21 Pekka Pitkänen uses the term "the central sanctuary" in opposition to local altars, seeing Shiloh and Jerusalem as candidates for the former (*Central Sanctuary*, 95–109). This model

The majority opinion holds that in 12:15 and 12:21, זבח refers to profane slaughtering.[22] Otto notes that the meaning of the verb זבח as "to conduct profane slaughter" in these two cases is unique. Elsewhere in Deuteronomy, it designates cultic, sacrificial slaughtering. He offers two arguments for the profane meaning in 12:15 and 21. First, the use of עלה in 12:12–14a is a contrastive reformulation of the altar law in Exodus 20:24. Second, *kol-hammāqôm* in Exodus 20:24 is replaced in Deuteronomy 12:15 by *b^ekol-s^e'āreykā* "in all your gates," which, according to Otto, designates walled cities and their surrounding villages.[23] In his interpretation, there is no space for local sanctuaries (*Heiligtümer*), not even for blessings, as in Exodus 20:24, because they are directly linked to profane slaughtering (Deut 12:16). One could add that the parallel wording found in 12:15b and 15:22b, which states that you, the clean as well as the unclean, can eat meat slaughtered within "your towns," as you would (meat from hunted) gazelle or deer, also indicates that the slaughter of animals from one's herds can be done at home without involving a priest or the turning over of sacrificial portions to Yhwh or his priest.

The distinction becomes reasonable if one construes the base meaning of the verb זבח as "to slaughter" rather than "to sacrifice," and lets the context determine the presence or absence of ritual elements.[24] In 12:15, 12:21, and 15:22b, there is no indication that local altars are in use. To be sure, there are Levites "in your gates" (Deut 16:11), but as noted above, "in your gates" is a synecdoche for an Israelite city in general, and any assumption the Levites are functioning in the cities as priests officiating at local sacrificial altars lacks tex-

---

presupposes a pre- and early-monarchic origin, which is rejected in this article. Eckart Otto denies any literary influence of the pre-exilic Deuteronomic centralization formula (12:13–19) on the original *Reformbericht* in 2 Kgs 23:4–14*, although he accepts such an influence on the exilic-postexilic Deuteronomistic redaction, for example, in Deut 12:2–3. He argues that 12:13–19 is influenced by "*der Jerusalemer Kultreinigung in 7. Jahrhundert*" (the purification of the cult of Jerusalem in the seventh century). Accordingly, in his view, the *maqom* clearly is the Jerusalem temple (*Deuteronomium*, 1,190). I will return to this issue later. He also anchors the Deuteronomic concept in the Neo-Assyrian royal festival meals (p. 1,191; so also Altmann, *Festive Meals*, 72–74). I pursue this line of thought in this article, but in relation to Achaemenid rather than Neo-Assyrian ideology.

22 So e.g. Otto, *Deuteronomium*, 1,183; Lundbom, *Deuteronomy*, 435, who talks about "simply 'slaughter', not '(slaughter to) sacrifice.'"

23 *Deuteronomium*, 1,184.

24 *HALOT* gives this as the first meaning and specifies that זָבַח זֶבַח is used when designating a cultic sacrifice. This replaces the older understanding in *BDB*, 257, which lists the first meaning as "slaughter for sacrifice" and the second as "slaughter for eating," with the claim that this is "connected also with sacrifice, as all eating of flesh among ancient Hebrews was sacrificial."

tual evidence. The legislation concerning priestly portions from sacrifices in 18:3 due to Levitical priests seems to confirm this same conclusion. It is only when a Levite goes up to *hammāqôm* and ministers there in the name of Yhwh his god like all his fellow Levites who "stand to serve" there before Yhwh that he is entitled to share allotted (temple) portions (18:6–8). The wording allows for a possible distinction in duties at *hammāqôm* between Levitical priests and Levites, but if so, it still indicates that those actively serving receive some sort of food portions, whether they are the ones enumerated in 18:3–4 for priests specifically or something less.[25]

3 Family, Tribe, or State: Who is in Charge?

The point of reference for the entire legal corpus is the nuclear family, not the tribe or the clan. The only explicit linkage of the city elders with the clan or tribe appears outside the core (Deut 31:28). In the core, nothing is said about the elders or the lineage/property. Tribes e.g. lineages occur as a point of reference for all Israel in 12:5, 12:14, 16:18, and 18:5. Their relation to elders is unclear. Whether or not elders in Mesopotamia were survivals of tribal practices,[26] the Deuteronomic elders are more akin to the elders in the organizational set-up of city-states than to those in a tribal organization. The latter looks superimposed and may be a re-tribalization of the idea of Israel.[27] This contradicts the claims of Johannes U. Ro that the Deuteronomic Code "attempts to materialize the benefits of the lay returnees" and that "the returned exiles" formed a self-governed (real as well as fictive) kinship community" within the territory of Yehud.[28]

Joseph Blenkinsopp has developed Max Weber's notion that the accumulation of power and wealth in cities would reduce the social significance of the lineage and its ethos in favor of the state bureaucracy. He has argued that the stipulations of the Deuteronomic code transfer allegiance from the kinship net-

---

25 As noted by William S. Morrow, "Deut 12:13–19 is a Dtn statement which articulates the principle that no legitimate sacrifice is to take place outside the *mqwm*" (*Scribing the Center*, 14). His investigation of subsequent uses of variations of the *māqôm* formula first introduced in ch. 12 in 14:1–17:13 confirms this initial statement (pp. 57–226). For an analysis of the roles of Levites and Levitical priests in Deut, see the first contribution by Benedetta Rossi in this volume.

26 Van der Mieroop, "Government," 124; *Ancient Mesopotamian City*.

27 Garfinkle, "Ancient Near Eastern City-States," 111–12.

28 Ro, *Poverty*, 61, 45, respectively.

work (clans, tribes) to a state-appointed local and central judiciary to reduce the authority of village elders.[29] This is repeated by Susan Ackerman. She argues that rural ancestor cults were dismantled and village culture discarded in order to weaken cohesion within clans. The aim would have been to strengthen state authority over taxation by disconnecting the individuals and the families from the patrimonial estates, the *nᵉḥālôt*.[30] The problem with these views is that the state and centralization are hard to find in Deuteronomy. The impotent and optional monarch of ch. 17 is hardly conducive to the notion of any kind of state.[31] The focus on the pilgrimage to the *māqôm* and the arbitration of difficult cases there (Deut 17:8) is balanced by the large space devoted to local autonomy. The notion of centralization is a vestige of de Wette's connection of *Ur-Deuteronomium* with Josiah's reform, to the point that the Deuteronomic *māqôm* was deemed to be none other than Jerusalem, complete with its king and temple.[32]

Given the on-going popularity of the notion of cultic centralization in Jerusalem,[33] it is crucial to underline that Deuteronomy envisions cities as having their local autonomy intact and viable. This stands in contrast to the lack of local power structures (i.e., the local dynasts, priesthood, the landed aristocracy, etc.) in Palestine at the end of the sixth century BCE or better, the lack of archaeological evidence of such power structures.[34] The problem is that the local structures evinced in Deuteronomy would leave few traces in the archaeological record, either architectural or epigraphic. As discussed above, Deuteronomy's cities are devoid of monumental buildings. As for the conspicuous economic activity taking place in its cities, it was either conducted orally, or Palestinian rains have long erased the ink.

Hence, we are faced with a fascinating dilemma. The economy Deuteronomy delineates in detail corresponds to a factual agricultural economy quite similar to what we know from Mesopotamia.[35] It is not peculiar to Deuteronomy:

> Babylonian villages, towns, and cities were characterized by councils of "citizens" who made determinations in certain legal cases. Whether or not something similar obtained

---

29 Blenkinsopp, "Deuteronomy," 4.

30 Ackerman, "Cult Centralization," 19–25. See also Schaper, *Priester und Leviten*, 109.

31 So e.g. Thelle, *Approaches*, 199.

32 So, e.g., the more recent position of Schaper, *Priester und Leviten*, 89 and *passim*. Anselm Hagedorn ("Placing [a] God," 193) is open to other solutions. Like my own work, he focuses on the functionality and its significance more than on identifying a specific place.

33 E.g. Tigay, "To Place."

34 Lipschits, "Demographic Changes"; "Achaemenid Imperial Policy," 29; Finkelstein, *Hasmonean Realities*, 53–57.

35 Postgate, *Early Mesopotamia*, 80–83, 276.

> in Assyria is not known. We might assume so, but such a body is not mentioned in any text. There is no popular assembly of any kind or any quasi-representative body that could make known the concerns of the people to their rulers. Perhaps the mayors played this role.[36]

Codex Hammurapi presents us with the picture of local administration of justice, in part by the elders of the village, in part by the mayor, and the possibility of taking a case to an upper court. At the same time, Deuteronomy might present a subversive picture, something completely different from the actual situation, some kind of utopia.

4 Deuteronomy, Imperial Ideology, and the Royal Garden

Deuteronomy's concentration on cities and their hinterlands reflects an imperial practice best known from the Achaemenid Empire. In principle, the Great King ruled the entire realm but in practice, the king "occupied the land in the immediate neighbourhood of the town, and the rest of the cultivated region which belonged to it."[37] The Persian kings Cyrus and Cambyses "endeavored to appropriate local traditions to their advantage over the long run and to present themselves as protectors of the sanctuaries. At the same time, this strategy required allowing the elites of the conquered countries to participate in the functioning of the new imperial order."[38]

Assuming the scribal elite behind Deuteronomy were able to participate in royal, imperial culture, one can expect Deuteronomy to focus on cities. Deuteronomy's depiction of the Promised Land as involving the takeover of towns, orchards, and cisterns resembles accounts and images of the kings' victorious endeavors told in texts and pictures.[39] Werner Berg has argued that Deuteronomy presents the land of Israel as God's garden.[40] His argument is based on the frames of Deuteronomy, but the abundant fertility appears also in the core (Deut 15:4–6). Mesopotamian royal gardens become a potent vehicle for royal propaganda from the ninth century BCE onwards.[41] Royal gardens somehow transmit

36 Bedford, "Neo-Assyrian Empire, 37.
37 Briant, *From Cyrus*, 419.
38 Briant, 79.
39 So e.g. Berge, "Agriculture."
40 Berg, "Israels Land."
41 So e.g. Stronach, "Garden."

their fertility to the entire land, and Persian kings located palaces amidst such gardens.[42]

In a similar way, Neo-Assyrian inscriptions display royal ideology with a focus on achievements of agricultural and horticultural abundance and constructed space such as cities, palaces, and temples.[43] In Deuteronomy, Yhwh is the great king, but instead of building cities, he delivers them ready-made to Israel with their fertile fields, gardens, and cisterns (Deut 6:10–12). As much as Assyrian and Persian royal ideology avers that the imperial deity is the ultimate owner of the land,[44] Deuteronomy presents Yhwh as the only patron of the land and its people (e.g. Deut 6:10–12, 7:21, 8:7–10; 11:12; 12:29–31).

The transformation of the conquered land to make it fit for the new political regime is also found in Anatolia. In Urartean inscriptions, the king "through his personal heroism, subdues the wilderness, establishing a built environment that is 'civilized' by virtue of its inclusion within the constituted political whole."[45] Mesopotamian sources present the royal garden as ideal space, a "dream world."[46] The king has a cosmic role in assuring fertility and the fruitfulness of the land.

Deuteronomy presents a more complex picture. The land is already fertile, but it is still somewhat uncivilized (Deut 9:4), while the wilderness is where Israel finds herself when Moses pronounces his Deuteronomic sermon. Moses's speech and subsequently the scroll that records it transform the undisciplined world of the Canaanites and make it fit for the Israelites. The concentration on cities is what is expected for a civilized regime. As a divine king, however, Yhwh needs not engage in building activity. The Canaanite cities become Israelite in one stroke of Moses's magic words. Just as Nebuchadnezzar II restored the *ziqqurrat* in Babylon,[47] Yhwh similarly sets up the *māqôm* as a privileged place of worship. Just as Urartean rulers claimed to have dismantled pre-existing polities and removed their inhabitants,[48] Deuteronomy's Israel shall dismantle Canaanite altars and slaughter the inhabitants of their cities (Deut 8:3). But the cities themselves are taken over.

42 Green, "*I Undertook*," 172.
43 Green, 127.
44 Bedford, "Neo-Assyrian Empire," 48; Wieshöfer, "Achaemenid Empire," 81.
45 Smith, *Political Landscape*, 162–65.
46 Green, "*I Undertook*," 62.
47 Borchhardt and Bleibtreu, "Aspektive," 487.
48 Smith, *Political Landscape*, 166.

5 The *Māqôm* and the Cities

Scholarly models of early states, as well as ancient Oriental royal ideology, testify to the idea that there needs to be some geographically unifying entity. Usually, this is a palace or a temple. The plurality of autonomous cities in Deuteronomy provides no such unifying entity. The *māqôm* is the place where Israel converges to become one.

Paradoxically, the *māqôm* is never identified with Jerusalem or with any other city in Deuteronomy.[49] The single location specified in the book for a cultic event is Mount Ebal/Gerizim (Deut 27:4–13), where plastered stones bearing "all the words/matters of this teaching" are to be set up/established. The only other architectural feature is a simple altar of undressed stones (Deut 27:5–6) that is to be used to offer holocaust offerings and to slaughter the peace offerings for a one-time celebration to take place there. Nowhere in these verses is this site designated "a" or "the" *māqôm*.[50]

In 17:8–9, however, the location of the court of appeals explicitly is at the *māqôm*, where the Levitical priests and the judge who will exist in those days will render a decision. The fact that Levitical priests are at the *māqôm* suggests that a permanent altar is located on site, if not also the building of Yhwh your god (23:19 [18]) The *māqôm* also is to serve as an annual site of pilgrimage three times a year, and usually, such sites have permanent cultic structures erected, even if they are not in use year-round. The text does not specify that the appeals court only convened during the times of pilgrimage; rather, the wording suggests that whenever the need for a verdict that could not be rendered at the

---

49 For a contrary position, see above, n. 21. Lohfink concludes his extensive literary analysis by stating that the combination of the centralization formula and *die Erwählungsaussage* cannot refer to any place other than Jerusalem, because throughout the Hebrew Bible, election of places is always exclusively connected with Zion/Jerusalem, never with other sanctuaries ("Zentralisationsformel," 318, 321). Whether this also applies to a possible *Vorform*, without the election phrase (e.g., Jer 7:12), is open to speculation. Lohfink's article also seems to imply a stand against Halpern's rather ambivalent interpretation of the centralization formula ("Centralization Formula," 35, 37). However, Halpern's observation that the older part of Deut 12, vv. 13–19, does not speak of a pilgrimage, is noteworthy; it could indicate a number of possible places of worship. For one assessment of Greenspahn's arguments for multiple places ("Deuteronomy") as insufficient to overturn the majority understanding that a single place is intended, see Arnold, "Deuteronomy." William Morrow favors the *māqôm* formulae in their various forms to intend a single, selected site, but not necessarily Jerusalem (*Scribing the Center*, 53–54). This discussion, although important, does not affect the main thrust of the present article.

50 The altar in 16:21 may be considered the altar before which a basket of first-fruits is to be presented 26:1–4, but it also could refer to local altars; so e.g., Bautch, "Altar,"; Lundbom, *Deuteronomy*, 527.

local level occurred, the case could be taken to the *māqôm*. This in turn points to a site that was to have Levitical priests functioning year-round, who could subsist on the priestly dues (12:11; 18:1, 3) from animals sacrificed in connection with voluntary vow and peace offerings (12:6, 11, 27) and firstlings from the flock and herd (15:19–23). A judge would also be present all the time. Hence, while assuming the *māqôm* was located in a city could be premature and might presuppose reading Deuteronomy in light of 2 Kings 23, modelling it as constructed space does not go beyond the evidence in the book or comparative anthropological studies of pilgrimage sites.[51]

Imagining the *māqôm* as a place for economic transactions such as taxation and tithes that would have been necessary to ensure its viability[52] is only problematic if one takes the wording concerning the consumption of the annual tithes during the pilgrimage feasts literally. Much discussion has taken place about whether the entire tithe was to be consumed by the family and other guests during the pilgrimage event[53] or whether implicitly, it was only a tithe of the tithe used for the feasting activities, with the remaining foodstuffs or silver being delivered to storage facilities at the *māqôm* either annually or two out of every three years, which is the common assumption. The reference to a tithe of the tithe in Numbers 18:26 makes explicit what might have been implicit in the tithing regulations in Deuteronomy for land-owners. The transactions involving silver in Deuteronomy 14:26 would be one activity in which the imperial treasury could have been involved.[54]

The frame supplements the economic and judicial presentation of the *māqôm* with a solemn reading of the Torah (Deut 31:9–12), a practice deriving from Moses's prophetic charisma (Deut 34:10). In both cases – core and frame – the *māqôm* is defined by its functionality very much like the cities in the legal core. Literary construction replaces actual constructed space.

6 Charisma and Homage

Max Weber's concept of charisma is closely related to the notion of social organization and institutions.[55] Charisma is defined as a sign of involvement with

51 So e.g. McCorriston, *Pilgrimage*, 56, 61–160.
52 So e.g. Dandamaev, "Neo-Babylonian Administration"; Altmann, "What Do the Levites," 231.
53 For a detailed argument in support of this view, see both contributions in this volume by Philippe Guillaume.
54 Briant, *From Cyrus*, 406–8.
55 Eisenstadt, "Introduction," ix.

the animating centers of society. The centers are constructed, cultural phenomena. Clifford Geertz has demonstrated that royal ideology combines both royal parades and travels that infuse places and areas with the royal aura or charisma to create order.[56]

Moses – the prophet who knew Yhwh face-to-face (Deut 34:10) – is endowed with a unique charisma. The order derived from Moses's charisma is evinced as a warning against false prophets and charismatics (Deut 13:1; 18:20–22) who may challenge the prophetic authority of Moses. These challenges are to be resolved through the thorough destruction of the idolatrous city (Deut 13:13–17). Moses's charisma is thus inscribed in the ritual, legal, and religious practice of each and every city.

Achaemenid texts equally present the king as possessing a divine charisma "in the most literal sense."[57] In a typically Weberian understanding, charisma is "a quality of an individual personality by virtue of which he is set apart from ordinary men and treated as endowed with supernatural, superhuman, or at least specifically exceptional qualities."[58]

Charisma elicits responses characterized by moral fervor "rooted in an attempt to come into contact with the very essence of being,"[59] i.e. an attempt to re-establish direct contact with the roots of cosmic and socio-political order. Royal charisma has the ability to transform the uncivilized and undisciplined natural world into a construction fit for human social life.[60] To do so, the king must travel from place to place, like the Persian "nomadic king" travelling with the entire administrative apparatus.[61] Strabo's mention of "a number of palace-cities, some with 'the treasure-house', the riches, and tombs of the Persians" (Strabo 15.3.3) portrays an empire that was more decentralized than kingdoms, obviously because it was too vast to be ruled centrally.

In Deuteronomy, the travels of the nomadic king are reversed. Instead of the king moving from place to place, the people go from their cities to the "king" – Yhwh Elohim – at his *māqôm* to offer homage. Yhwh does not tour the different cities to receive homage from his people. Thus, the families pay homage to Yhwh by banqueting in front of him (Deut 14:22–26). Deuteronomy's focus on cities is not about landscape. It is about staging power and charisma and thus creating order throughout the territory Israel inhabits.

---

56 Geertz, *Local Knowledge*, 124.
57 Lincoln, "Role of Religion," 226.
58 Eisenstadt, "Introduction," xviii.
59 Eisenstadt, xviii.
60 Smith, *Political Landscape*, 161.
61 Briant, *From Cyrus*, 186–91.

7 Redistributive Integration of the Cities

Theories of early states consider territorial centrality as essential to the state, while simultaneously including "redistributive integration, euergetism and liturgies, ... authority based on social contract, ... semiautonomous functioning of lower-order subsystems and ritual sanctification of corporate cognitive code" as other essential traits.[62] Central regulation of production and redistribution affects logistics as well as control of local customs. Deuteronomy's double tithing system (Deut 14:22–23 and 14:28–29) involves both the local city, where triennial tithes are stored and redistributed, and the *māqôm*, where some or all of the annual tithes are consumed during feasting activities, presenting some striking similarities with Strabo's report about Persian cultic meals:

> The Persians do not erect statues or altars, but offer sacrifice on a high place ... and when the Magus, who directs the sacrifice, has divided the meat the people go away with their shares, without setting apart a portion for the gods, for they say that the god requires only the soul of the victim and nothing else. (Strabo XV.3.13)

The entire consumption of sacrificial meats by the people is also found in several Persepolis tablets that end with the formula "and the kurtas [slaves] ate (the grain)," referring to rituals followed by a banquet.[63] The sacrifice and the accompanying banquet exalted the might and generosity of the king. The rejoicing and feasting before Yhwh at the *māqôm* during the pilgrimage events three times a year function like the royally sponsored Persian banquets. The difference is that in Deuteronomy, the sponsor is Israel's deity, Yhwh, not a human king.

8 Local Leadership and Local Customs

Deuteronomy refers to a number of groups endowed with official functions: the elders of the city, elders of Israel, a judge and judges (Deut 16:18; 17:9, 12), שטרים ("officers" Deut 16:18; 20:5–9), heads of the tribes (Deut 1:15), tribes and elders (Deut 29:9), elders of the tribes (Deut 31:28), a priest (Deut 17:12; 18:3; 19:17; 20:2; 26:3), and Levitical priests (Deut 17:[9],17:18; 18:1; 24:8; 27:9).

The elders of the city represent the *Gemeinwesen*, the tradition and local rules of conduct without undertaking judicial tasks.[64] They have executive and

62 Bang and Scheidel, in the prologue of *Oxford Handbook*, 25.
63 Briant *Cyrus to Alexander*, 246
64 Gertz, *Die Gerichtsorganisation*, 172, 222.

notarial functions, teaching and representing the ethos of the people. Contrary to the "elders of the cities," the "elders of Israel" (Deut 27:1, 31:9) or "your elders" (Deut 5:23; 28:10; 31:28) belong to the frame, where they appear as echoes of the core's elders of the city in a wider context of the overarching notion of "all Israel" of the Torah of Moses, much the same way as do the Levitical priests.[65]

Alexander Rofé has speculated that the appointment of judges and officials "in all your gates" (Deut 16:18) hints at local representatives of a royal or imperial administration.[66] In light of the situation in Mesopotamia, it is possible that the judges and officials appointed "in all your gates" reflect the competition between the governmental authority and the *puḫrum*, the local assembly,[67] as the respective domains of each authority were never clearly defined.[68] In this case, it is necessary to postulate the presence of some tension within Deuteronomy 12–26, with a challenge to local autonomy made by some ill-defined overarching authorities, in order to align the core's autonomous cities with the presentation of the tribal Israel of the frame.

The Levitical priests may also point to an intentional challenge to local autonomy. Contrary to the Levite who appears beside the *gēr*, the widow, and the orphan and plays no clearly defined role, the Levitical priests and the priests, sons of Levi (Deut 21:5) represent the supreme authority that the addressee is to obey in everything they teach (Deut 24:8). Their decisions take precedence over any local ruling. However, their ruling is to be sought only when local authorities cannot reach an agreed decision (Deut 17:8), so one could argue there is no intentional usurpation of authority but instead, an agreed hierarchy for judicial decisions.

It is impossible to decide if Deuteronomy's regulations related to the cities are local traditions and customs or mere literary creations illustrating the ideology of the authors. In some cases, one may argue for custom or tradition, for instance, when the Levites will get their portion to live from if they choose to go up and serve at the *māqôm* in 18:6–8. One may infer from 1 Samuel 1:13–14, 16 that there is custom behind this practice of priests receiving a portion of a sacrificed animal destined to supply meat for a feast.[69] On the other hand, the family laws in Deuteronomy 22:13–29 have close similarities with the Middle

---

65 Gertz, 225; Willis, *Elders*, 45; Wagner, "Beobachtungen," 407–11.

66 Rofé, "Organization," 96–98.

67 Seri, *Local Power*, 159–61.

68 Van de Mieroop, "Government," 144–45.

69 Thanks to Diana Edelman for making me aware of this possible connection. For priestly prebends, see the first article by Benedetta Rossi in this volume.

Assyrian law collections, and some other family laws even have exclusive parallels in the so-called Tablet A, § 12–16: Deuteronomy 21:17; 22:28–29; 25:11.[70] This might indicate that the family laws are not customary but partake in some trans-local, learned mutual relationship. On the other hand, it is very unlikely that the local administration of justice did not regulate family matters on the basis of custom and tradition.

9 Concluding Analysis: Resilience

Whereas Eckart Otto uncovers a subversive element of resistance in Deuteronomy's treatment of Esarhaddon's Vassal *adê* document,[71] I reject any dependence or use of the latter document in Deuteronomy 13 or 28 and find the concept of resilience more applicable to identifying the function of both the "core" and the wider book. By resilience, I mean the ability of Deuteronomy to resist imperial domination by envisioning another possibility of rule, a political imagination of renewal and transformation.[72]

The writers had to find ways not to provoke imperial authorities while, at the same time, calling for some disruptive change that would alter the collective self-perception and challenge social units to act, while limiting damage.[73] The concept of resilience comes into play when individual entities, regardless of whether these are individuals, groups, or states, must prove their ability to face the challenges generated by the turmoil of contemporary dynamics.[74] Resilience is not the acceptance of the status-quo. It is an act of resistance, a vector of response that investigates possibilities of change. It admits the vulnerability and risk of this project, which is clear throughout Deuteronomy but visible especially in chs. 13 and 18, which count with the possibility of opposition. Resilience depends on the ability or willingness of local authorities and of the population to adjust to the unifying ideas, religious ideology, and practice of the authorial elite in a way designated as "infrapolitics." In this sense, infrapolitics "describes the ways in which subordinate groups continue to wage a struggle against their subordination, but in a way obscured from the view of the domi-

70 Otto, *Deuteronomium*, 203–16.
71 Otto, "Deuteronomium als archimedischer Punkt"; *Deuteronomium*, see discussions of Deut 13 and 28.
72 Bourbeau and Ryan, "Resilience."
73 Naumann, Rampp, and Endress, "Introduction," loc. 155.
74 Naumann, Rampp, and Endress, loc. 320–21.

nant power."[75] Infrapolitics are thus a tactical choice born of prudent awareness of the balance of power.

Resilience as infrapolitics needs to be anchored and moored in the materiality of everyday life. The core is replete with presentations of everyday life (harvest, slaughter, borrowing, strays, and so on). The frames "reframe" life in the cities as fertility (Deut 28:3–20) without altering the figuration of Israel as dwellers in autonomous cities (Deut 28:52). Finding resilience in Deuteronomy requires identifying the presence of events perceived as disruptive. This is visible in the final part of the curses of Deuteronomy 28, but already in the warnings about the idolatrous city in ch. 13. Deuteronomy's program seeks to build social cohesion after a period of disaster. Deuteronomy's "laws" delineate in very practical ways what to do in order to rebuild Israel as a religious polity founded on Mosaic charisma without antagonizing any powers that be. I tend to interpret the failure to mention any imperial power, even if some figures in the text might serve its representatives, in terms of resilience: It is now time to rebuild an entity called Israel, now as a religious *polity* but completely founded on the Mosaic charisma and institution.

Works Cited

Ackerman Susan. "Cult Centralization. The Erosion of Kin-Based Communities, and the Implications for Women's Religious Practice." In *Social Theory and the Study of Israelite Religion: Essays in Retrospect and prospect*, edited by Saul M. Olyan, 19–40. Society of Biblical Literature Resources for Biblical Study 71. Atlanta: Society of Biblical Literature, 2012.

Ahlström Gösta W. *Royal Administration and National Religion in Ancient Palestine*. Studies in the History of the Ancient Near East 1. Leiden: Brill, 1982.

Altmann, Peter. "What Do the 'Levites in Your Gates' Have to Do with the 'Levitical Priests'? An Attempt at European-North American Dialogue on the Levites in the Deuteronomic Law Corpus." In *Levites and Priests in Biblical History and Tradition*, edited by Mark Leuchter and Jeremy M. Hutton, 135–54. Ancient Israel and Its Literature 9. Atlanta: Society of Biblical Literature, 2011.

Altmann, Peter. *Festive Meals in Ancient Israel*. Beihefte zur Zeitschrift für die alttestamentliche Wissenschaft 424. Berlin: de Gruyter, 2011.

Anthonioz, Stéphanie. "Cities of Glory, Cities of Pride: Concepts, Gender, and Images of Cities in Mesopotamia and in Ancient Israel". In *Memory of the City in Ancient Israel*, edited by Diana Edelman and Ehud Ben Zvi, 21–42. Winona Lake, IN: Eisenbrauns, 2014.

Arnold Bill T. "Deuteronomy and the Law of the Central Sanctuary *noch einmal*." *Vetus Testamentum* 64 (2014): 236–48.

75 Bourbeau and Ryan, "Resilience," loc. 4,358.

Aufrecht Walter E., Neil A. Mirau and Seven W. Gauley, eds. *Urbanism in Antiquity: From Mesopotamia to Crete*. Journal for the Study of the Old Testament Supplement Series 244. Sheffield: Sheffield Academic, 1997.

Bang Peter Fibiger and Walter Scheidel, eds. *The Oxford Handbook of the State in the Ancient Near East and Mediterranean*. Oxford: Oxford University Press, 2013.

Bautch, Richard J. "The Altar Not Destroyed in Deuteronomy 16.21." *Journal for the Study of the Old Testament* 20 (2016): 321–36.

BDB = Brown, Francis, S. R. Driver, and Charles A. Briggs. *A Hebrew And English Lexicon of the Old Testament*. Boston: Houghton Mifflin, 1906.

Bedford, Peter R. "The Neo-Assyrian Empire." In *The Dynamics of Ancient Empires: State Power from Assyria to Byzantium*, edited by Ian Morris and Walter Scheidel, 30–65. Oxford Studies in Early Empires. Oxford: Oxford University Press, 2009. Kindle edition.

Benjamin Don C. *Deuteronomy and City Life*. Lanham, MD: University Press of America, 1977.

Berg Werner. "Israels Land, der Garten Gottes. Der Garten als Bild des Heiles im Alten Testament." *Biblische Zeitschrift* 32 (1988): 35–51.

Berge, Kåre. "Agriculture, Space, and the Local as an Ideological Motif in Deuteronomy." In *Jeremia, Deuteronomismus und Priesterschrift. Beiträge zur Literatur und Theologiegeschichte des Alten Testaments. Festschrift für Hermann-Josef Stipp zum 65. Geburtstag*, edited by Andreas Michel and Nicole Katrin Rüttgers, 131–46. Arbeiten zu Text und Sprache im Alten Testament 105. St. Ottilien: EOS, 2019.

Blenkinsopp Joseph. "Deuteronomy and the Politics of Post-Mortem existence." *Vetus Testamentum* 145 (1995): 1–16.

Borchhardt, Jürgen and Erika Bleibtreu. "Aspektive und Perspektive im Neuassyrischen Flachbild." In *The Empirical Dimension of Ancient Near Eastern Studies*, edited by Gebhard J. Selz and Klaus Wagensonner, 477–542. Wiener offene Orientalistik 6. Vienna: LIT, 2011.

Bourbeau, Philippe and Caitlin Ryan. "Resilience, Resistance, Infrapolitics and Enmeshment." In *Resilience in Social, Cultural and Political Spheres*, edited by Benjamin Rampp, Martin Endreß, and Marie Naumann, loc. 4,161–735. Wiesbaden: Springer VS, 2019. Kindle edition.

Briant Pierre. *From Cyrus to Alexander: A History of the Persian Empire*. Translated by Peter T. Daniels. Winona Lake, IN: Eisenbrauns, 2002.

Dandamaev, M. A. "Neo-Babylonian and Achaemenid State Administration." In *Judah and the Judaeans in the Persian Period*, edited by Oded Lipschits and Manfred Oeming, 373–98. Winona Lake: Eisenbrauns, 2006.

Davies, Philip R. "The Authority of Deuteronomy." In *Deuteronomy–Kings as Emerging Authoritative Books: A Conversation*, edited by Diana V. Edelman, 27–47. Atlanta: Society of Biblical Literature, 2014.

Edelman Diana V. and Ehud Ben Zvi, eds. *Memory and the City in Ancient Israel*. Winona Lake: Eisenbrauns, 2014.

Eisenstadt, Shmuel N. "Introduction." In *Max Weber on Charisma and Institution Building: Selected Papers*, edited by Shmuel N. Eisenstadt, ix–lvi. Chicago: University of Chicago Press, 1968.

Faust Avi. "Jerusalem's Hinterland in the Eighth-Seventh Centuries BCE: Towns, Villages, Farmsteads, and Royal Estates." *Palestine Exploration Quarterly* 147 (2015): 283–98.

Finkelstein Israel. *Hasmonean Realities behind Ezra, Nehemiah, and Chronicles: Ancient Israel and Its Institutions*. Ancient Israel and Its Literature 34. Atlanta: Society of Biblical Literature, 2018.

Frantzman, Seth J. "The Arab Settlement of Late Ottoman and Mandatory Palestine: New Village Formation and Settlement Fixation, 1981–1848." PhD thesis, The Hebrew University, 2010.

Frese Daniel Allan. "The Civic Forum in Ancient Israel: Form, Function, and Symbolism of City Gates." PhD thesis, University of California, San Diego, 2012.

Frese, Daniel Allan. "A Land of Gates: Covenant Communities in the Book of Deuteronomy." *Vetus Testamentum* 65 (2015): 33–52. https://doi.org/10.1163/15685330-12301188.

Frick Frank S. *The City in Ancient Israel.* SBL Dissertation Series 36. Missoula: Scholars, 1977.

Garfinkle, Steven J. "Ancient Near Eastern City-States." In *The Oxford Handbook of the State in the Ancient Near East and Mediterranean,* edited by Peter Fibiger Bang and Walter Scheidel, 94–119. Oxford: Oxford University Press, 2013.

Geertz Clifford. *Local Knowledge: Further Essays in Interpretive Anthropology.* New York: Basic Books, 2000.

Gertz Jan Christian. *Die Gerichtsorganisation Israels im deuteronomischen Gesetz.* Forschungen zur Religion und literatur des Alten und Neuen Testaments 165. Göttingen: Vandenhoeck & Ruprecht, 1994.

Grabbe Lester L. and Robert D. Haak, eds. *'Every City Shall be Forsaken': Urbanism and Prophecy in Ancient Israel and the Near East.* Journal for the Study of the Old Testament Supplement Series 330. Sheffield: Sheffield Academic Press, 2001.

Green, Douglas J. *"I Undertook Great Works": The Ideology of Domestic Achievements in West Semitic Royal Inscriptions.* Forschungen zum Alten Testament 2.41. Tübingen: Mohr Siebeck, 2010.

Greenspahn, Frederick E. "Deuteronomy and Centralization." *Vetus Testamentum* 64 (2014): 227–35.

Hagedorn, Anselm D. "Placing (a) God: Central Theory in Deuteronomy 12 and at Delphi." In *Temple and Worship in Israel and the Ancient Near East: Proceedings of the Oxford Old Testament Seminar*, edited by John Day, 188–211. Library of Hebrew Bible/Old Testament Studies 422. London: T&T Clark International, 2005.

HALOT = Ludwig Koehler, Walter Baumgartner, and Johann J. Stamm. *The Hebrew and Aramaic Lexicon of the Old Testament.* Translated under the supervision of Mervyn E. J. Richardson. 4 vols. Leiden: Brill, 1994–1999. Accordance edition.

Halpern, Baruch. "The Centralization Formula in Deuteronomy." *Vetus Testamentum* 31 (1981): 20–38.

Kemezis, Adam M., ed. *Urban Dreams and Realities in Antiquity: Remains and Representations of the Ancient City.* Mnemosyne Supplements 375. Leiden: Brill, 2014.

Lincoln Bruce. "The Role of Religion in Achaemenian Imperialism." In *Religion and Power: Divine Kingship in the Ancient World and Beyond*, edited by Nicole Brisch, 221–42. Oriental Institute Seminars 4. Chicago: Oriental Institute, 2008.

Lipschits, Oded. "Achaemenid Imperial Policy, Settlement Processes in Palestine, and the Status of Jerusalem in the Middle of the Fifth Century B.C.E." In *Judah and the Judaeans in the Persian Period*, edited by Oded Lipschits and Manfred Oeming, 19–52. Winona Lake: Eisenbrauns, 2006.

Lipschits Oded. "Demographic Changes in Judah between the Seventh and the Fifth Centuries B.C.E." In *Judah and the Judaeans in the Persian* Period, edited by Oded Lipschits and Manfred Oeming. 323–76. Winona Lake: Eisenbrauns, 2003: 323–76.

Lohfink, Norbert. "Zur deuteronomistischen Zentralisationsformel." *Biblica* 65 (1984): 297–329.

Lundbom, Jack R. *Deuteronomy: A Commentary.* Grand Rapids, MI: Eerdmans, 2013.

May, Natalie N. and Ulrike Steinert, eds. *The Fabric of Cities: Aspects of Urbanism, Urban Topography and Society in Mesopotamia, Greece and Rome*. Culture and History of the Ancient Near East 68. Leiden: Brill, 2014.

McCorriston, Joy. *Pilgrimage and Household in the Ancient Near East*. Cambridge: Cambridge University Press, 2011.

Morris, Ian and Walter Scheidel, eds. *The Dynamics of Ancient Empires: State Power from Assyria to Byzantium*. Oxford: Oxford University Press, 2009.

Morrow, William S. *Scribing the Center. Organization and Redaction in Deuteronomy 14:1–17:13*. Society of Biblical Literature Monograph Series 49. Atlanta: Scholars, 1995.

Naumann Marie, Benjamin Rampp, and Martin Endreß. "Introduction: Resilience as a Perspective for the Analysis of Societal Processes." In *Resilience in Social, Cultural and Political Spheres*, edited by Benjamin Rampp, Martin Endreß, and Marie Naumann, loc. 167–90. Wiesbaden: Springer VS, 2019. Kindle edition.

Otto, Eckart. "Das Deuteronomium als archimedischer Punkt der Pentateukkritik. Auf dem Wege zu einer Neubegründung der de Wette'schen Hypothese." In *Deuteronomy and Deuteronomic Literature: FS CHW Brekelmans*, edited by Marc Vervenne and Johann Lust, 321–40. Leuven: Leuven University Press/Peeters, 1997.

Otto, Eckart. *Das Deuteronomium. Politische Theologie und Rechtsreform in Juda und Assyrien*. Beihefte zur Zeitschrift für die alttestamentliche Wissenschaft 284. Berlin: de Gruyter, 1999.

Otto, Eckart. *Deuteronomium*. 4 vols. Herders Theologischer Kommentar zum Alten Testament. Freiburg: Herder, 2012–2016.

Pitkänen, Pekka. *Central Sanctuary and Centralization of Worship in Ancient Israel*. Gorgias Dissertations Near Eastern Studies 5. Piscataway: Gorgias, 2004.

Postgate J. Nicholas. *Early Mesopotamia: Society and Economy at the Dawn of History*. London: Routledge, 1992.

Redford, Peter R. "The Neo-Assyrian Empire." In *The Dynamics of Ancient Empires*, edited by Ian Morris and Walter Scheidel, 30–65. Oxford: Oxford University Press, 2009.

Ro, Johannes Unsok. *Poverty, Law, and Divine Justice in Persian and Hellenistic Judah*. Ancient Israel and Its Literature 32. Atlanta: Society of Biblical Literature, 2018.

Roddy Nicolae. "Landscape of Shadows: The Image of City in the Hebrew Bible." In *Cities Through the Looking Glass: Essays on the History and Archaeology of Biblical Urbanism*, edited by Rami Arav, 11–22. Winona Lake, IN: Eisenbrauns, 2008.

Rofé, Alexander. "The Organization of the Judiciary in Deuteronomy." In *The World of the Aramaeans 1: Biblical Studies in the Honour of Paul-Eugene Dion*, edited by P. M. Michèle Daviau, John W. Wevers, and Michael Weigl, 96–112. Journal for the Study of the old Testament Supplement Series 324. Sheffield: Sheffield Academic, 2001.

Schaper, Joachim. *Priester und Leviten in achämenidischen Juda*. Forschungen zum Alten Testament 31. Tübingen: Mohr Siebeck, 2000.

Seri, Andrea. *Local Power in Old Babylonian Mesopotamia*. Studies in Egyptology and the Ancient Near East. London: Equinox, 2005.

Smith, Adam T. *The Political Landscape: Constellations of Authority in Early Complex Polities*. Berkeley: University of California Press, 2003.

Strabo. *The Geography of Strabo VII*. The Loeb Classical Library. London: Heinemann, 1930.

Stronach David. "The Garden as a Political Statement: Some Case Studies from the Near East in the First Millennium B.C." *Bulletin of the Asia Institute* 4 (1990): 171–80.

Thelle, Rannfrid I. *Approaches to the 'Chosen Place': Accessing a Biblical Concept*. Library of Hebrew Bible/Old Testament 564. London: T&T Clark, 2012.

Tigay Jeffrey H. "'To Place His Name There': Deuteronomy's Concept of God Placing His Name in the Temple." In *"Now It Happened in Those Days": Studies in Biblical, Assyrian and Other Ancient Near Eastern Historiography Presented to Mordechai Cogan on his 75th Birthday*, edited by Amitai Baruchi-Unna, Tova L. Forti, Shmuel Ahituv, Israel Eph'al, and Jeffrey H. Tigay, 1.17–26. Winona Lake, IN: Eisenbrauns, 2017.

Van de Mieroop, Marc. *The Ancient Mesopotamian City*. Oxford: Oxford University Press, 1997.

Van de Mieroop, Marc. "The Government of an Ancient Mesopotamian City: What We Know and Why We Know So Little." In *Priests and Officials in the Ancient Near East*, edited by Kazuko Watanabe, 139–62. Heidelberg: Universitätsverlag C. Winter, 1999.

Wagner, V. "Beobachtungen am Amt der Ältesten im alttestamentlichen Israel." *Zeitschrift für die Alttestamentliche Wissenschaft* 114 (2002): 391–411, 560–76.

Weber, Max. *Ancient Judaism*. Translated by H. H. Gerth and D. Martindale. London: Collier-Macmillan, 1952. Reprint 1967.

Wieshöfer, Josef. "The Achaemenid Empire." In *The Dynamics of Ancient Empires*, edited by Ian Morris and Walter Scheidel, 66–98. Oxford: Oxford University Press, 2009.

Willis, Timothy M. *The Elders of the City: A Study of the Elder-Laws in Deuteronomy*. Society of Biblical Literature Monograph Series 55. Atlanta: Society of Biblical Literature, 2001.

Wilson, Ian D. "Yahweh's Anointed: Cyrus, Deuteronomy's Law of the King, and Yehudite Identity." In *Political Memory in and after the Persian Empire*, edited by Jason M. Silverman and Caroline Waerzeggers, 325–61. Ancient Near Eastern Monographs 13. Atlanta: Society of Biblical Literature, 2015.

Yoffee, Norman. *Myths of the Archaic State: Evolution of the Earliest Cities, States, and Civilizations*. Cambridge: Cambridge University Press, 2005. 3rd printing 2007.

Baruch Halpern

What Does Deuteronomy Centralize?

What Does Deuteronomy Centralize? Citizenship. But how and where and why?

1 Deuteronomy's Entanglement

For two centuries, an unparalleled consensus of scholars has affirmed Wilhelm M. L. de Wette's view that Josiah's "'book' of the torah" was Deuteronomy. All challenges have failed. Evidence in Kings sufficiently identifies Deuteronomy as the big find of 622 BCE.[1]

The **book of the Torah** inspires **Josiah's reform**. Though de Wette refrained from pronouncing on the state of the copy in 622, the familiar phrase, "the ink was still wet," cues scholars to inspect Deuteronomy through the lens of his reform. Equally, we judge the reform by the book.

We tighten the logical spiral by choreographing the tango between the law-code and the report of Josiah's reform in Kings. This means matching Deuteronomy's institutional architecture, the arguably different book of the Torah, and separately, the reform, to a three-dimensional social geography.

Deuteronomy's explicit organizational hierarchy is not a purely Josianic invention. Aspects of the reform depart from the plan. From the specifics, many infer that Deuteronomy is the anterior text.[2] Several policies were pertinent long before Josiah published them. Institutions, intentional ambiguities, and the book's central concerns reflect an intention to loosen credit and dispose real property for countryside reclamation.

---

1 See Diana Edelman's study in this volume.

2 Tigay, *Deuteronomy*, xx–xxi. Further below, § 6.1.

Note: Heartfelt thanks to these colleagues, each of whose criticisms has transformed this offering: Diana Edelman and Philippe Guillaume, my inspirational editors, Amanda Walls, Sarah Cook, Randy Garr, Tyler Kelley, and a stellar panel led by David Schreiner at the Southeast Conference for the Study of Religion, Athens, 2020: Bill Arnold, Harold Bennett, Erin Darby, and James Wilson.

https://doi.org/10.1515/9783110713312-005

2 Restricting Sacrifice

2.1 The Flashpoint

The law-code starts with its main link to Josiah: centralized sacrifice. In the **reform report** (2 Kgs 23:1–25), Kings tells us how Josiah read it. Others' understandings can only be inferred.

Deuteronomy has a compositional history.[3] Behind **law-code** (Deut 12–26), core (4–28), framework (here, 1–3; 29–34) and book is a "book of the Torah," reportedly found and more surely published in 622 BCE. This amorphous entity, here D622, is the fulcrum in Eckart Otto's phrase, the "Archimedean point of Biblical Studies."[4] D622 may have almost no literary prehistory – reusing stored-up fragments – but we know it has an intellectual history.

2.2 The One, the Many, and the Few

Deuteronomy 12 limits sacrificial liberty by directing offerings to "the place where Yhwh chooses to assign his name." Scholars defend two interpretations:
1) Centralization, restricting sacrifices to a single location, or
2) Nucleation, restricting sacrifices to registered shrines.

Deuteronomy's model is the Covenant Code (CC; Exod 20:22–23:33): here, Yhwh declares, "in every place (*mqwm*) where I proclaim (*'zkyr*) my name, I will come to you and bless you" (or, in "each/any place"). Sacrifice, says our consensus, is licit wherever Israelites choose. But whether in CC or Deuteronomy, *Yhwh* sets or proclaims his name. Pre-modern readers saw no difference.

The Syriac, however, presents a variant: "... where *you* proclaim (*tzkyr*) my name." Here, Yhwh "come(s) to you" where *you*, not he, decides. This is the likely original.[5] People err mostly in their own interest, and laziness outproduces zeal: haplography dwarfs dittography in frequency and in length. The same principle dictates a preference for some mis-readings: reading *aleph* for *taw* in paleo-Hebrew here is like reading *waw* in 1 Samuel 14:5 **ywšy'* as a *resh*, vilifying Saul.[6]

3 Definitively, Vater, *Commentar ueber den Pentateuch*, 493–503.

4 Otto, *Deuteronomium 1,1–4,43*, 69–72.

5 See Hoonacker, *Sacerdoce lévitique*, 9–10, whose argument is supplemented here. Cf. also Johnstone, "Exodus 20.24B."

6 The *aleph-taw* interchange of *'zkyr/tzkyr* may underlie a number of pre-LXX variants in the Hebrew, presumably reflecting the letters' similarities in some paleo-scripts. Examples include Ira the Jairite and Ira the Jethrite in 2 Sam, Aruma and *tarmâ* in Judg 9, for which, see Halpern,

Confirmation bias among influential readers propagated the errors as emendations across communities preserving the text.

The change from "you proclaim" to "I proclaim" might post-date, or inform, Deuteronomy. Regardless, Deuteronomy takes CC's law as an expression of the same sentiment as the phrase for ownership, *nqr' šm PN ʿl N*, literally, "*PN*'s name is called over *something*." A place labeled with Yhwh's name is a place he calls his own.[7] If centralizing, Deuteronomy construes CC to prescribe a single location at any given time, perhaps with an icon like the ark. Only extra-textual theology distinguishes a place where Yhwh's name is proclaimed from a place he chooses for his name. Deuteronomy's Yhwh may be as profligate with his name as CC's.

Deuteronomy is read to support either centralization or nucleation:

12:5–6:

'l hmqwm	**A:** to the place **B:** *to whatever place*
'šr ybḥr Yhwh 'lhykm	that Yhwh ... chooses
mkl šbṭykm	**A:** from all your tribes **B:** *from any of your tribes*
lśwm 't šmw šm	to put his name there
lšknw	as its post[8]
tdršw	you will seek guidance
wb't šmh; whb'tm...	and come there; and you {may} bring...

12:14:

bmqwm	**A:** In the place **B:** *In whatever place*
'šr ybḥr Yhwh	where/that Yhwh chooses
b'ḥd šbṭyk	**A:** in one of your tribes **B:** *in any of your tribes*
šm tʿlh ʿltyk w...	there, you will send up your ... (offerings)

"Rise of Abimelek," plus Deut 33:2, *'šdt lmw* and the versional *'šrw 'lm*. 1 Sam 14:5 is almost a visual pun.

7 The phrase applies to Jerusalem (Jer), the temple (Jer and 1 Kgs), the ark (2 Sam), and the people (2 Chr); cf. e.g., 2 Sam 18:18; 1 Kgs 16:24; "city of David/Sihon." For the absence of a resumptive *ʿl* in Exod 20:24, cf. Deut's "the place where/that Yhwh chooses" with resumptive *b*^{e} 5 times and 19 times without the *b*^{e}.

8 With Sandra Richter (*Name Theology*, 53–63), 12:5 *šiknô* is nominal.

Theodor Oestreicher and Adam Welch raised the distributive (B) alternative for 12:14 in the 1920s.[9] Their philology remains unimpeached and has found regular advocates since. Deuteronomy 12:5 has been the sticking point. Even Welch felt that it demanded centralization. Here, Yhwh chooses a place "from all of your tribes." The phrase describes Jerusalem in Kings,[10] because it most nearly approximated Josiah's agenda of centralization.

But not on the basis of its wording. Norbert Lohfink observes formal ambiguity: "The place ... chosen from *kl* your tribes" could mean from multiple tribes. So, "the Levite" (18:4, 6, 7) is one of a class, Levi (18:1, 2), "chosen from all your tribes." The place can likewise represent a class of individual places chosen from various tribes.[11] Similarly, the repeated expression, "the Levite/*gēr* (both invariably singular) who is in your gates," refers not to a unique Levite, but to a distributed class.[12] Literally, 12:5 permits sacrifice in distributed locations.[13]

"From all your tribes" is a weak reed. Lohfink observes its application to selecting a dynasty, so it may refer to individuals. But picks from the same universe (tribes, Israel) also include *classes* of selectees.[14]

The case for centralization depends more on the context of 12:5. Deuteronomy 12:2–4 demands that Israel eradicate "all the places where the nations you supplant serve their gods" and "eradicate their name from that place" (after

9 In support of an untenable early dating: Oestreicher, *Grundgesetz*; "Dtn 12"; Welch, *Code*. For bibliography, see Paton, "Post-Exilic Date"; Greenspahn, "Centralization"; Arnold, "Deuteronomy 12"; Otto *Deuteronomium 12–23*, 1,166; for scholarly context, Otto *Deuteronomium 1–4*. The revisionist position is rooted in Martin Kegel's *Kultus-Reformation des Josia*, still notable for its sociological exegesis.

10 For the Solomonic schism and to blame Manasseh for Josiah's death: 1 Kgs 11:32; 14:21; 2 Kgs 21:7; Halpern, "Why Manasseh." The formulation's implication in Solomon's schism links it to a Josianic scaffolding in DtrH. It might, with the fief formula, be post-Josianic. On usage, cf. 1 Kgs 8:16, clarified in 2 Chr 6:5–6.

11 Objects in the expression, "to choose X from all Y," can be collective: Exod 18:25; Deut 18:5; Judg 20:34; 1 Sam 2:28; 2 Sam 10:9. Cf. Arnold, "Deuteronomy 12." "Choose for [himself]," always proprietary, occurs with the place only in 2 Chr 7:12; it occurs with Jerusalem in 1 Kgs 11:36, though not 11:32.

12 Oestreicher ("Dtn 12") compared this passage to the fugitive slave law of Deut 23:16–17. Comparison with 1 Sam 2:28 demands nuance as well.

13 Lohfink, "Zentralisationsformel,"301–303 and Greenspahn, "Centralization" against Welch, *Code*, 24–86. *Kl* as aggregate: Gen 6:19–20; Exod 18:21; as "any": Gen 2:19; Exod 33:6, *mkl h'm*; 1 Kgs 5:11; 8:38; Gen 20:13; Deut 16:21; 22:6; 12:2. As "each": Gen 2:16; 3:1; Deut 15:19. Classes can act as count nouns: Saul seeks David serially in "all the clans of Judah" (1 Sam 23:23).

14 As in Exod 18:25; Judg 20:34;1 Sam 24:3; 1 Kgs 5:27. For the argument, see Lohfink, "Zentralisationsformel," esp. 318–20, 324–28; Arnold, "Deuteronomy 12"; further, Otto, *Kontinuum* 112–22; Levinson, *Hermeneutics*, 6–52.

7:1–5, 25). In 12:5, once Israel clears the cultic clutter of aboriginal populations, Yhwh installs *his* name.[15]

Bill Arnold submits that the antithesis contrasts Yhwh's place with "places" *both* foreign *and* multiple.[16] Yet the focus is on distinguishing other gods' hallows from those appropriate to Yhwh. A contrast in the *number* of places is not explicit. The text does not demand centralization.

This same point holds for many of the arguments, or potential arguments, for centralization against nucleation. Other functions of Yhwh's place need not be at fixed locations: the appeals court or the priest receiving tithes. That Pesaḥ demands an overnight journey[17] may reflect nucleation. The material *never directly engages* centralization.

Perhaps more influential is an appeal to the argument that monotheism, as articulated in the Shema's "Yhwh is One," implies centralization. "One God, one shrine" makes for good sloganeering but deficient algebra. The text never connects the terms of the equation.

2.3 Judicial Centralization

Deuteronomy's highest court consists of "Levitical priests and the judge *'ăšer* (usually: "who") is in those days" (17:9).[18] In 19:17, disputants face Yhwh, priests, and "judges 'who' are in those days." The priests presumably supervise oaths, divination, and directions (*yrh*) for executing the ruling.[19]

For *'šr yhyh bymym hhm*,[20] Nachmanides invokes personnel rotation: "(the priest) who is on duty at the time."[21] Ibn Ezra provides for the pre-monarchic

---

15 Arnold, "Deuteronomy 12," with Lohfink, "Zentralisationsformel." For related texts, see Richter, *Name Theology*, esp. 41–63. Cf. the *zkr* of Amaleq (25:19 < Exod 17:14). The effaced name (in 12:4; 9:14; 25:6; 29:19) may connote a physical presence: the destruction (*'bd*; 12:2a and all of 12:3) involves demolishing monuments. For this tactic and Josiah, see Halpern, "Late Israelite Astronomies," 459–80.

16 See Levinson, *Hermeneutics* 28–34; Arnold, "Deuteronomy 12."

17 The command to "go to your tents" permits as much in Deut 33:18; Josh 22:4–8; Judg 7:8; 1 Sam 4:10; 13:2; 2 Sam 18:17; 19:9; 20:1, 22; and 1 Kgs 8:16.

18 Some mss. read and make explicit "priest *or* judge," preferred, e.g., by Malbim. On this passage and Deuteronomy's professionalized judiciary, see Otto, *Deuteronomium 12–34*, 1,477–80.

19 Oaths and testing demand Yhwh's presence (6:13; 10:20). Levites are the subject of the verb *yrh* in Deuteronomy. Those who investigate (with Sam, LXX, *dršw*) and report (*hgydw*) the verdict are the judges.

20 The singular, "'who' is in those days," may modify both functionaries in 17:9, as in 19:17, where Samaritan and Masoretic mss. also read "is" vs. MT and G "are." The phrase describes a priest at an altar at Yhwh's place in 26:3–4.

21 "Those days" suggests seasons or eras. The singular, "(that) day" is used for "when, then," as in Deut 4:15; 21:16, 23; 27:2; 31:17–18, 22.

era as well as the monarchy. He imagines circuit assizes, familiar from Samuel, the sons of "judges," and the Europe of his day. He renders, "(the priest) wherever he is" (not "who will be") at the time. Before Israel achieves serenity, Yhwh is still meandering.

Ibn Ezra would think Beersheba was one of Yhwh's places in 1 Samuel 8:2. Following Samuel-Kings, he believed Yhwh elected a permanent place later on. Might a party to Josiah's contract infer that the venue was moveable to a nearby town with a prestigious shrine and reputable judges? Social context might demand Ibn Ezra's reading, but the text does not.

2.4 Going the Distance

Those who infer centralization from accommodations for distant pilgrims contrast one center to a ubiquitous traditional cult.[22] Deuteronomy 12:20–25 ordains: "When (*ky*) Yhwh your god broadens your territory (*hrḥb gbwl*) as he promised you," eat flesh when (*ky*) you like.[23] "If (*ky*) the place where Yhwh ... set(s) (*śwm*) his name" is "too far," "*sacrifice* (*zbḥ*) ... and eat in your 'gates.'" The guidelines duplicate those blind to distance (12:15–16), and the continuation directs oblations to Yhwh's place. The best explanations account for the repetition, not the elaborate redundancy.

Other provisions for distance overcome it. Deuteronomy 14:22–27 introduces a workaround for tithes "if the journey is too much for you ... because the place ... is too far from you." You sell goods for silver and buy victuals at the place. You economize on time as well as weight.[24]

Nothing here discloses whether the law-code centralizes or nucleates. However, concern for distance also justifies "cities of refuge"; 19:1–7 allows for three sanctuary cities (six "if Yhwh widens your territory [*hrḥb gbwl*] as he swore to your fathers"): "Lest the distance be excessive." Distance to where?

Stefan Schorch, like most, thinks "the distance" is to an *exclusive* place.[25] In critical doctrine, asylum towns replace the many altars abolished by Jo-

---

22 Cf. Schorch, "Samaritan Version."

23 J's Decalogue is the source: *when* (*ky*) Yhwh supplants your predecessors, he *will* "broaden your territory (*hrḥb gbwl*)" to permit your confident absence (Exod 34:24; freely, "insulate"; cf. *'ereṣ raḥăbat yādayim*, "a sprawling country"). The formulation inspires Deut 5:21–22; Exod 20:17.

24 14:22–29. Deut's tariff, resuming discussion of offerings in 15:19 with firstlings, does not repeat the accommodation.

25 Schorch, "Samaritan Version." For cities of refuge, latterly, Gertz, "Deuteronomy and Covenant Code." Deut rereads CC Exod 21:13–14, "provide yourself a place to which he can flee," as licensing "*places*" outside Israel's original settlement, which may involve a comparative

siah.[26] That math can be starry-eyed. The institution guarantees fugitives a formal trial. It cools destabilizing local conflicts. However, few, if any, hinterland establishments reliably protected hunted strangers.[27] Three may be more than we think.

Deuteronomy's mantra, "the place that Yhwh chooses," also allows for mobility: in DtrH, the ark, even *en route*, marks the choice.[28] Towns are less elusive. The policy also deflects violent men from the capital. Yet DtrH places only one such town in Judah, albeit a well-defended one: the provision reduces distance and uncertainty.

In sum, 12:20–28 must invoke distance for a reason. For some, it implies a place abroad and even licenses a hewn altar. Rebuilding its temple after 407 BCE, the Elephantine community petitions Persian appointees in both Judah and Samaria for permission to *resume* holocausts.[29] Its delegations hoped for success, based on or despite Deuteronomy. The joint response omits mention of animal sacrifice in affirming service in the "house of the altar."[30] Persia, however, recognized Samaria's Gerizim compound and still later, the Leontopolis temple. Such institutions developed a liberal interpretation of 12:20–28.

All this evidence is inconclusive. But advocates of nucleation make no appeal to corollary provisions in the law-code. They occasionally invoke references to activity outside "the place that Yhwh chooses," but these are incidental to the cultic reorganization (§ 5 below). Altogether, the tea leaves favor centralization. The moral case for it becomes overwhelming only with Josiah's policy.

---

parsing of definiteness; and, "from my altar ..." as "[even] from my [single] altar, take him," separating the altar location from those places.

26 Wellhausen, *Composition*, 358 (Nachträge).

27 The imperative to save face for a sheltering god regularly elicits pressure to extradite, as in Hdt. 1.157–60; 6.28–29; 8.104–6. Tyler Kelley observes (in conversation, 3/2020) that the cities of refuge insulate the cult from such conflicts.

28 The Dtr accepts stone altars built for assemblies elsewhere (1 Sam 7:17; 6:26–28). The Dtr also purposefully omits ark travel after the Temple is built.

29 Porten and Yardeni, *Textbook of Aramaic Documents*, A4.7–8. The community equally observed the Pesaḥ.

30 Porten and Yardeni, A4.9–10. The term is not far removed from "house of *bāmôt*." Cf. 2 Chr 7:12 "house of sacrifice," a plainer expression.

2.5 Neither Here Nor There

> A wise man, therefore, proportions his belief to the evidence.
> – Hume

Two related questions arise: why does this controversy recur? Why is Deuteronomy so unforthcoming on centralization? Schorch fingers the unthinkable: if Deuteronomy is nucleating, he observes, it must be sloppily written or deliberately ambiguous. The legislator could have clarified Deuteronomy 12:5 by writing, "in any place Yhwh your god chooses," on the model of CC (Exod 20:23). But a single word would make centralization explicit, too. The code's most striking quality is its ambiguity.

Our unforthcoming author, too, uses CC to model his imprecise formula. The allusion is so transparent that a reader not privy to Josiah's plans might well assume that Deuteronomy, like its referent, allows multiple selected places, in parallel or in series; a traditionalist would intuit the former.

Of legislators, especially when innovating, we expect precision.[31] Ours never quantifies places. Nor does he suggest, like Jeremiah, that places are elected *seriatim*.[32] In passages covering institutions, his formulations waffle, especially those concerning the cult. In Deuteronomy as in 1 Kings 11:32, the writer resolves the question by applying election "from all" the tribes solely to Jerusalem. The Dtr's clarity about centralization confirms Schorch's alternative: Deuteronomy's ambiguity is intentional. The legislator has *chosen not to choose*.

The place is also unnamed.[33] But the silence is dictated by narrative logic, whether it is unique or not. Moses could not say what place Yhwh would choose, although here, too, he could have clarified with the phrase, "where it is in those days." Still, his reticence allows the Dtr and Jeremiah to claim places succeeded one another. It alternatively permits readers to infer nucleation.

The numerical ambiguity diverts attention from other relevant issues. Do CC's sumptuary regulations apply to state occasions at the place only?[34] More

---

31 On legal registers and deviations from formulae, see esp. Winand, "Words of Thieves"; Lohfink, *Hauptgebot*, 10. For Deut's reliance on older usage, see Otto, "False Weights," 131–32; "Ersetzen oder Ergänzen."

32 Against which, Schorch ("Samaritan Version," 25) understands Deut's precondition, "rest," to be satisfied with Joshua.

33 The fact has been used to date Deut's composition. For the early date, see Oestreicher and Welch (above); for the late, Gary Knoppers, "Northern Context."

34 Insightfully, van Hoonacker, *Sacerdoce lévitique*.

important is the neglected question about which offerings Deuteronomy clearly restricts: early audiences presumably appreciated the nuances (see below).

Likewise, the law-code demands the removal of *aboriginal* shrines, not Israelite foundations attributed to patriarchs or other heroes. Conversely, only 23:19, regulating votives, mentions "Yhwh's temple," again, not necessarily a central shrine but certainly a legitimate one, or branch of one. The code might banish peripheral chapels and hallows. Turning its polemic against Yahwist shrines would require the Dtr to expose these shrines as misappropriated locales. Divorced from Judges-Kings, Deuteronomy is unclear. What Deuteronomy does is provide destinations for specific imposts. It limits the sacrificial franchise.

2.6 What Deuteronomy Controls

> It is the nature of great events to obscure the great events that came before them.
> – Francis Parkman, *Montcalm and Wolfe*

It is just the opposite for texts.

Deuteronomy coyly clouds the number and permanence of places and the identity of condemned hallows. These subjects cohere with others where the regulation is more explicit.

After the "centralization" law (chs. 12–13) comes a cultic schedule, or tariff (14:22–16:17).[35] It regulates only three offerings. Two out of every three years, citizens deliver tithes to the place (14:22–29). Firstlings and the Pesaḥ are taken there annually (15:19–20; 16:5–6). Other visits require foodstuffs commensurate with one's budget (16:10, 17).[36]

Chapter 12 directs offerings to Yhwh's place. We infer that deviation activates the provisions of ch. 13: sacrifice conducted elsewhere is apostasy. Predecessors, after all, worshiped "on the high mountains and on the hills and under any maypole" (12:2–3). There is no mistaking the mandate: "you must altogether obliterate [them]."[37]

---

35 The law-code regulates exactions in sequence: ch. 12 where; 13 to whom; and 14 what. 14:22 begins the sacrificial tariff with tithes (15:1–18 explore related redistribution.) Firstlings follow in 15:19, and then other universal imposts through 16:17.

36 Glossing *lōʾ yērāʾû pānāy rêqām* (Exod 23:15; 34:20), still preserved in Deut 16:16 but instantly qualified by means.

37 *ʾbd tʾbdwn*. The infinitive signals thoroughness. On paragogic *nun*'s systematic modality, see Garr, "Paragogic *nun*." In Deut, it is capacitative or obligatory ("they *can* not see"; "which they *must* learn"). In 2nd-person address in main clauses, it is always obligatory ("you *must*"), as Jared Klein and I show in a study in preparation.

Three warnings follow. The first: "You must not do (*t'śwn*) the same to Yhwh. *Instead*, you resort to (*tdršw 'l*) the place ... come thither, bring [offerings] thither, and eat there in [Yhwh's] presence and rejoice in your every enterprise,[38] you and your households, because [Yhwh] has blessed you" (12:4–7).

The second warning is: "You must not do (*t'śwn*) just as we do here now, each whatever is appropriate in his view," before Israel has secured its homestead. Once it enjoys peace all about (12:8–10), "then, [Yhwh's] place, thither you bring anything I charge you, your [offering types], and you rejoice in [Yhwh's] presence, you and your sons, daughters, manservants, maidservants, and the Levite that is in your gates ..." (12:11–12).

Although 12:5 is the poster child for centralization, 12:6, 11, "thither you bring your [offering types]," usually taken as imperative or hortatory, could equally be permissive: while you may not bring offerings to former hallows, you *may* bring them to a, or the, place. And, are the offerings being regulated for calendared events or for individual or occasional ones, too?

The third caution straws the rhetorical chaff from the requisite wheat (12:13):

hiššāmēr lĕkā pen	Scruple to not (imperative)
ta'ăleʰ 'ôlôtêkā	incinerate your holocausts
bĕkōl māqôm 'ăšer tir'eʰ	in (just) any place that you see

Of the offerings list, only holocausts are unambiguously restricted to the place, by the use of the imperative. Deuteronomy 12:14 directs them, alone, to Yhwh's precinct: "Instead, in [Yhwh's] Place ... you incinerate your holocausts and there carry out anything that I charge you."

Here, Deuteronomy is explicit. The holocaust consecrates assemblies or foundations.[39] It invokes an *association's* patron divinity. That patron must be Yhwh of the place, or sacrifice is treason. Thus, traditionally, ostracism and finding new paymasters means "worshipping other gods" (1 Sam 26:19); in Deuteronomy, exile, too, means serving *state* gods "you have not known" or inherited. The holocaust is a litmus test of public worship.

---

38 *bkl mšlḥ ydk(m)*, restricted to Deut 12–28 (6 times), features a 2nd person plural only here. Certain passages (Deut 2:7; 14:29; 15:10; 16:15; 24:19; 28:12; 30:9) have *bkl m'śh ydk* in the same sense.

39 Exod 24:5; 32:6 (JE); Num 10:10; 29:39 (P); Josh 22:27; Deut 27:6 (inaugurating altar for *šlmym*, 27:7); Josh 8:31. In narrative, Judg 20:26; 21:4; 1 Sam 6:14–15; 7:9–10; 10:8; 13:9–12; 2 Sam 6:17–18.; 24:24–25; 1 Kgs 3:4, 15; 8:64; 9:25; 2 Kgs 10:25. For Qumran, see Schiffman, *Sectarian Law*, 191–210.

In these contexts, Deuteronomy resembles the notorious loyalty oaths Esarhaddon imposed around his Empire, as objects of reverence, in 672 BCE. Both the idea of *installing* Yhwh's name and the law-code's conception are reminiscent of these loyalty oaths as well.[40]

The holocaust is not the only regulated offering. "You cannot sacrifice the Pesaḥ in one of your gates" (16:5) has a counterpart in 12:17: "(Legally), you are not entitled[41] to partake in your gates of the tithe of your grain or wine or oil, or of the firstlings of your herd or flock, or of any of your [volunteered offerings]." The holocaust, the foundational civic offering, and Pesaḥ, the archetypal tribal totem, are confined to a state shrine.

Citizens at the precinct consume only a small share of a Pesaḥ, tithes, or firstlings. The positive command is, "Instead," you eat "in [Yhwh's] presence, in [Yhwh's] place." Likely, eating is permissive: legally, you cannot offer *this* food at home. You *must* pay carefully calculated tithes (14:22, plus 26:13–14). But you *may* dine once, in common, on firstlings, tithes or the Pesaḥ at Yhwh's place.

At the same time, Deuteronomy never bars citizens from eating meat at home. The practice has been mislabeled "secular slaughter," because the ritually impure may partake (12:15; cf. 23:10–17). But the term Deuteronomy employs for "secular slaughter" is "sacrifice" (*zbḥ*). One may celebrate away from the place (*mqwm*) as well: lineage celebrations, commemorations, rites of passage, and other occasions for feasting continued to find a place "in your gates." Deuteronomy imposes a cost on these affairs: they are not deductible. The place (*mqwm*) is not just for shared sacrifice. It is for taxes (12:5, 11, 17, 26). The tithe, which "I have removed from [my] house," is calculated from yield, without credits. So, the liturgy of the third-year tithe is a tax declaration: the citizen testifies "before Yhwh" – locally, to a Levite (14:28–29; 26:12–15): "I have eaten none of it *b'ny*, nor excluded any of it as impure, nor given any of it to the dead" (26:14). Provided the citizen bears the outlay, Rashi and Ibn Ezra saw that any of these activities was permissible.

---

40 For much of Esarhaddon's impact on Deuteronomy, see Otto, *Deuteronomium: Politische Theologie*. Taking Deuteronomy itself, however, as a loyalty oath is oversimplification, as demonstrated by Edelman in this volume and in "Saying Goodbye." Further below, n. 197.

41 "Cannot," here and in like contexts, is annulment. "You cannot ..." enthrone a foreign king (17:15); "disregard [others' property rights]" (22:3). Or, "he cannot ..." "promote the favorite wife's son ahead of the firstborn son of the scorned wife" (21:16); "divorce (a wife he defamed)" (22:29); or "take (his first wife) back" (24:4). So, Chr takes 1 Kgs 5:17, David "could not build a temple," as *legal* disqualification from the privilege. Similarly, Josh 9:19; Judg 11:35; 21:18; Jer 36:5. It is not used positively: even reluctant permission is expressed without the auxiliary (as in 17:15). Cf. CC *mšl*. "You cannot" corresponds in the singular to the plural vetitive with paragogic *nun*.

So, meals shared with the dead are not banned. In fact, the term, *zbḥym*, "sacrifices," in Deuteronomy's lists of what may be brought to the temple replaces the Exodus 20:24 term, "community sacrifices" (*šlmym*). Though Deuteronomy seems to ban abnormal sacrifice, it merely abjures official oversight of it.[42]

The point is, the strictures insinuated on what you may or must take to the place are more stringent than the literal prescriptions. The law-code seems to regulate all sacrifice, without doing so. This is very like its hesitation between centralization and nucleation. In both instances, ambiguity is its rhetorical strategy.

2.7 The Importance of Being Neither

This is ambiguity, not silence. Kings cites Deuteronomy as the book of the Torah that licensed centralization. What, then, does it mean when *Deuteronomy* does not resolve our ongoing differences over even its final intentions?

Ambiguity and vagueness are inclusive. They are implements for overcoming divisions among potential recruits, ploys for duplicity, or temporizations. Historically, they suggest a diverse public.

Not coincidentally, Deuteronomy presents itself and Kings presents Josiah's reform as requiring popular endorsement – in Israelite political theory, *imperium* comes from the folk.[43] 2 Kings 23 idealizes the enactment: as in Joshua 24,[44] the book of the Torah achieves legal force through citizens' formal assent.

Deuteronomy implements accepted norms: who muzzles threshing oxen? Where it proceeds from Samuel, CC, or J/JE, we see how it has applied them. Like CC (and J's Decalogue), it defines citizenship legally and ethically to unify stakeholders in *its* Israel. Deuteronomy, however, attenuates the role of extended kinship, which was under direct attack from Hezekiah's time.[45] Thus, the book discourages marks of parochial identities, such as demonstrative mourning. And, its rhetoric soars with the Shema: "Yhwh your god is a single Yhwh."[46] In its view, Yhwh's denominations are schismatic.[47]

---

42 The argument that Deut has secularized the word *zbḥ* (originally, and most persuasively, Levinson, *Hermeneutics*, 38) predicates that if activity does not pass state purity standards, it is not sacred.

43 This is the main thesis of Halpern, *Constitution*, esp. ch. 7.

44 Completing the agenda of Deut 29–31, usually but uncertainly assigned to Dtr.

45 For the social context, see Halpern, "Lineages."

46 So Levin, "'Color'," expounded by Aurelius, "Ursprung." For the interpretation, "Yhwh is One," see Lange and Eshel, "Shema' Yisrael." Johann Vater (*Commentar* 3.231) already had repudiated the analysis by Kennicott (*Editionis Veteris Testamenti Hebraici ad loc*). "Yhwh is One" is too nebulous to make for meaningful declaration.

47 Yhwh Shalom, of Teman, of Samaria, (of?) Hosts, Who Resides in Zion, El of Bethel, etc.

Deuteronomy's god is not localized. He is *only* the God of Israel: "Yhwh, your god," everywhere in Moses's speeches is the "venerable, portentous name" (28:58). He is "El//Yhwh, god of Israel" at Shechem (Gen 33:20; Josh 8:30), the same god in any manifestation.[48]

Unifying the body politic actuates Deuteronomy's concern with sedition (ch. 13) and apostasy (17:2–7) for gods of other *polities*. It demands declarations of identity with the body politic. The book recasts Hosea's attacks on profligate northern devotions to decry *state-endorsed* traditional worship.[49] Jeremiah and Ezekiel, in a move central to monotheisms, turn the critique on non-official devotions. Accordingly, Jeremiah's (44) partisans of the Queen of Heaven may chiefly be bereft of *civic* festivities, held by officials under Yhwh's aegis. Jeremiah, conversely, attacks the grass-roots devotions that they, legitimately in Deuteronomy's terms, have continued without state support.[50]

Uniquely, Deuteronomy presents itself as the elaboration of prime principles – its proprietary Decalogue.[51] This is also why Moses formulates the legal system (5:20–6:1). For authority, Moses quotes Yhwh directly (as 18:16–20). He nevertheless must win his audience by appeal to the passions and to reason. Like the books of pre-Socratics, Deuteronomy demonstrates ethereal wisdom by argument.

But, as in its debts to Assyria, Deuteronomy is the meeting-place of multiple intellectual vectors. Even derived from oracles, foundational law-codes require assent in Deuteronomy's world. The dossier of codes adopted by polities grows increasingly thick, from seventh-century Crete into the sixth century BCE. The likes of Solon and Lycurgus are invoked as lawgivers, and, their authority attaches, by common assent, to successors' enactments.[52] The constitution, or the

48 Roughly 300 "Yhwh, (Israel's) god." No other epithet is attached to "Yhwh."

49 See, e.g., Hos 4:13; Isa 1:29; Mic 1:5, and reused and new materials scaffolding DtrH. Hosea's view of state shrines, as Bethel, is more complex.

50 For the public/private divide and Deut, see again, van Hoonacker, *Sacerdoce lévitique*, 5–10; the same distinction occurs among tannaim in b. Sanhedrin 43b (11); cf. 6:5. Jer 44:15–19 is the soundest textual confirmation of Josiah's reform.

51 For Deut 5:6–21 as the source of Exod 20:2–18, see Auld, *Joshua, Moses and the Land*, 117–18. Deuteronomic shared diction: *gēr* and "gates"; *gēr* + pronominal suffix; *'ădāmâ 'ăšer* + *yhwh* + *ntn*; son + daughter + servant + maidservant + *gēr*; capacitative paragogic *nun* in a marked purpose clause, once otherwise in JEP and Former Prophets (Exod 11:7, E; 1 Kgs 8:43). Conversely, the interjection in Deut 5:5 might mirror what could be read as an aside between Exod 19:19 and 20:1 and thus postdate R-JEP.

52 See Aristotle, *Politics* 1,274a22b–26 for other lawgivers. For more recent discussions, see Smith, "Leges Regiae"; Gagarin, "Storytelling"; Chabod, "héros ordinaires." While CC's law binds the state, Deut's binds the state to enforce the laws, which it may not just interpret but also supplement with administrative rulings.

basic law, acquires an eponym and a tutor god to imbue it with lambent "wisdom and discernment" (Deut 4:6).

Through this mechanism, resonant with 1 Samuel, Deuteronomy slips in its most important innovations. The *instruction* remains Mosaic, even when changed.[53] For example, Samuel introduces kingship in the historiography. Moses does so in the law-code.[54] Israelites, like their neighbors, understood pseudepigraphy as metaphoric. In Judean jurisprudence, a Mosaic constitutional structure facilitates fulfilling Yhwh's demands. The theocratic system is timeless, unlike royal codes, treaties, and oaths. In the metaphor, it is the same, even when altered.

One conventionally put speeches in Moses's mouth. One could amend inherited rules, contrary codicil notwithstanding, in his voice. Yet the code revises the cult only tentatively. Deuteronomy never clearly confines Yhwh to a single place. It requires popular consent. At every turn, it permits, but does not impose, centralization. Deuteronomy, with all its self-justification and humanism,[55] is a campaign platform.

3 My World, by Moses

> It is in regarding social relations as physiological phenomena that I have conceived the project ...
> – Claude-Henri de Saint-Simon, *Lettres d'un habitant de Genève à ses contemporains*, 56–57

Since Deuteronomy and Kings claim the law-code requires subscription, we might ask, "Whose?" Deuteronomy answers in sociological categories, which we map onto historical ethnological commonplaces.

---

53 Lysias (Against Nicomachus 20.2) alleges, an engraver engaged by the polis took fees to add or delete provisions of what nevertheless remained Solon's laws. Like the authorial fictions, Deut 13:1 just articulates transactional metaphor.

54 Scholars since de Wette (*Beiträge*) derive Deut 17:14–20 from Samuel; so e.g. Bleek, *Introduction*, 236–37. Later, they recognized elaboration based on Kings; so e.g. Driver, *Deuteronomy*, lxii. Deut here works creatively from its sources in the same loose way it uses JE. Compare Zahn, "*Genre and Rewriting*."

55 Classically, Weinfeld, *Deuteronomy*, 282–97.

3.1 Deuteronomy Gives You Gates

Moses's first recollection in Deuteronomy concerns delegation. Departing Sinai, he installs officials and marshals[56] over nested units up to a thousand, by tribe (1:23). Unsurprisingly, he structures comparable courts (16:18–17:1): Magistrates and marshals you will appoint for yourself in all your gates, which Yhwh gives you, by tribe ...

The transition to sedentarism triggers a change in division from quantity to "gates." "Gates," like the population, are associated with more than justice. In "the gate," elders try cases; the citizenry execute judgment.[57] No like process transpires in "your gates." "Your gates" is not the plural of "the gate."[58]

Eckart Otto inaugurated the modern discussion of "your gates" with a comparison to Akkadian *bābu*, "gate," and *babtu*, an urban "ward" (here, "borough"). This represents both a residential quarter and the community organs providing limited local policing and governance, for which the synecdoche is the ward's name. Otto shows that it amounts to less than an entire city in Deuteronomy as well.[59]

The choice of the expression, "your gates," signals fresh orientation. It is distinct from "town" (*'yr*), the generic noun for "settlement": so, one moves toward the gate of a settlement, but not toward its "gates." The latter refers to quarters.

Physically, the "gates" are residential divisions. The (larger) town includes them as neighborhoods. Functionally, they have various aspects. So, elders, unmentioned inside the "gates," act at the level of town, tribe, or nation.[60] They participate in institutional spaces beyond the "gates." Towns, not "gates," offer refuge and treat derelict corpses. These "gates" are the smallest administrative unit that royal bureaucracy, or in Deuteronomy's narrative universe, the body politic, acknowledges: magistrates and marshals mediate the relationship.

Levinson, Otto, and Daniel Frese have recognized that "gates" are the parties constituting Deuteronomy's pact. Treating "gates" as autonomous corporations, they consequently apply the denomination to any settlement outside the capital.[61] Yet, as Otto points out, "gates" are wards, not towns.

---

56 *śry(m) wšṭrym*, 1:15. *šṭrym*, is found in E and Deut-Josh, not P.

57 21:19; 22:15; 22:24; 25:7. For the constitutional logic, see Halpern, *Constitution*, chs. 4 (111–23) and 7 (175–216).

58 For 17:2–7; 21:19, see below; peripherally relevant: 28:52, 55, 57.

59 Otto, "*ša'ar*, Gate," followed, except as noted, here.

60 Elders are identified with towns 36 times, 34 in DtrH. Only Deut ties them to tribes. On Deut 25:7, with elders resident in the "gates," see Otto, "*ša'ar*, Gate."

61 Levinson, *Hermeneutics*; Otto, "*ša'ar*, Gate"; Frese, "Land of Gates."

"Gates" is not a casual synecdoche for settlements: we see no interchange with *ʿîr*, "settlement." Otto's position, that towns can contain multiple gates, is also reinforced by 17:2–7. Earlier passages treat apostasy in cases of a charismatic, an extended family, and a town (13:2–18). For the individual and in the family, punishment is summary. Deuteronomy 17:2–7 covers cases inside "your gates," the otherwise unaddressed **borough**.

3.2 Gates and Houses

"Gates" are not "houses," culturally identified with mansions or extended family compounds (cf. Judg 18:14–15).[62] The third-year tithe goes from the house to "your gates," that is, from the private to the semi-public sphere (Deut 14:28–29; 26:12–13). The same outward progression is observed when the Shema enjoins display "on the jambs of your house and in your gates" (6:9; 11:19). Deuteronomy 17:2–5 treats apostasy "in one of your gates" as the omitted middle term between household and town in Deuteronomy 13. "Gates" are larger than an extended family.[63]

The group "you" bring to Yhwh's place includes children, slaves, and Levites (12:5, 18). Here and elsewhere, Deuteronomy calls it "your house(hold)" (14:26; 15:16, 20). To it, 16:11 and 16:14 attach tenants (*gēr*), orphans, and widows "among you" or "in your gates." The qualification, "who is in your gates," excludes the Levite and the marginal from individual households, extended families. They are instead common to an association of families, which Deuteronomy denominates "your gates."

These units are not accidents of residence. With Otto, it is as communities that they give legal status to residents. In Deuteronomy's system, if one does not belong "in your gates," one does not belong at all. The code rhythmically inculcates abstract communitarian norms, a cynic might say, because the state is offloading responsibilities onto locals.[64] Parallels to these boroughs, associations of extended families with dependent classes, have been referred to ethnographically as *expanded* families or **clan sectors** (the latter by Jack Goody): they congregate in their own quarters in towns or populate one or more villages and farms. Again, the expanded family mediates between the extended family

62 See Faust, "World of P."

63 "House denotes "compound" in 5:21; 6:9; 6:11; 11:6; 11:19; probably, 12:7; 14:26; 15:16, and 15:20; this may be what 24:5 exempts. A visiting ox (22:2) physically inside (*btwk*) "your house" implies a commodious property.

64 Otto, "*šaʿar*, Gate," 373–74 and Glanville, "Stranger," 612–13.

and the echelons of kinship we call the clan. In Deuteronomy, they mediate with the "town(ship)." The town(ship) is a section, a genealogical segment, of the landholding clan, though, by the logic of succession, its syndics share less blood than wine.

3.3 The Gates and the Clan Sector

In the clan sector, patriarchs preside over co-resident households, which include descendants; near relations, especially unwed females; and dependents. Some marriages demand a separate home, so the extended family may occupy a single manor house, a compound or, in some conditions, a cluster. Several "households" in concert comprise a district or quarter, the Arabic village *ḥamūla*, an endogamous family association where males are, distantly, "cousin" or "uncle."[65]

Judges 18 furnishes one scale on which a storyteller modeled the *ḥamūla*: "The men who were in the houses that were 'with' Micah's house" (18:22) are not compound-mates ("brothers") but occupants of adjacent structures.[66] Their posse unhesitatingly pursues six men and wordlessly declines confrontation with six hundred.

Other texts also gauge sizes. Samuel's banquet has thirty invitees (1 Sam 9:12–24), either because the storyteller imagines Ramah with three clan sectors or the Ramah district with thirty. Perhaps most relevant is the Pesaḥ. Not every male must offer a Pesaḥ, but surely every lineage must. A yearling sheep should feed about 150 adults (100–200 portions @ 225 g each). This oft-cited optimal number for friends to include in formal affairs[67] fits the clan sector.

In the land, succession to property and privilege was based on kinship bonds symbolized in cemeteries and multi-chamber tombs (including elite tombs at St. Etienne, for example). Through inheritance, clan sectors shared a

---

65 For the *ḥamūla* as "expanded family," see Cohen, *Arab Border-Villages*; Grossman, *Expansion*, 15–52, who documents comparable arrangements. The term "gate" persists as "ward" in some urban geographies, e.g., Beirut's Bab Idriss. On the "gates" generally, Otto, "*šaʿar*, Gate," 359–405; Frese, "Land of Gates." In 6:9, the sequence of house (compound) jambs and gates (residential districts) then yields movement in vv. 6–9 from the innermost outward.

66 Cf. Izbet Sartah II. For the rural manor house as an extended family dwelling, see Faust, "World of P." Micah's settlement is apparently unwalled – not a "town" but "these houses" (18:14). Micah's allies are not extended family ("brothers," "father's house"). The Danites and Jonathan the priest stand at "the entrance of the gate" – to Micah's compound.

67 For the classic formulation, see Dunbar, *How Many Friends?*

common shrine attached to graves. There, they memorialized those to whom they owed their moveable, immoveable, and personal properties.[68]

Functionally versatile, the clan sector organizes collaborative tasks and duties, political consensus, and exchange. Marshalling the services of dependents, especially slaves and affiliated metics (tenants, sg. *gēr*, and orphans), the group may develop specialties as a work crew. As a gang, it mobilizes as a militia squad.

The *ḥamūla* is a territorial-political-cultic-endogamic band: in politics, a bloc; in urban administration, a borough; in religion, a parish. Economically, it is a cooperative or a commune.[69] It corresponds to Moses's unit of ten.

3.4 Gates and the Lineages

But Deuteronomy isolates *ḥamūlas*, de-emphasizing extended kinship.[70] It embeds descent-groups in social realities. "Gates," though organized around and even physically congruent with lineages, include co-residents unaffiliated by descent. "Gates" are, accordingly, the locus of redistribution to the unfortunates Deuteronomy assigns them. The borough is the topical architectural articulation of a society.

In the borough, national obligations cannot be discharged. The citizen celebrates public festivals at the place (*mqwm*) with his household and various others.[71] The latter attach at the feasts to households, but the text connects them with the "gates."[72] The reminders to include the landless at festivals, explicitly Shavuot and Sukkot, reinforces the impression that they are fixtures. They are envisioned traveling with neighbors to the place. The communitarian ethic starts with tithes; these are notionally redistributed to the landless. Thus, the calendared occasions encourage integration in the borough's social fabric.

The tenant is a special concern.[73] In the wilderness, the tenant *in your camp* or *gates* attends the code's enactment (29:10; 31:12). They enjoy no entitlement

68 Halpern, "Lineages."

69 See Halpern, "Lineages"; Faust, "World of P," 173–218; for a valuable comparison, see Fales, "Composition and Structure," 45–60.

70 See above § 2.7.

71 See 16:11; 16:14; 14:28–29; 26:12–13. Levites in 12:12; 12:18; 14:27; 16:11; the tenant, orphan, and widow among you (*bqrbk*) join them in 14:29 and for Sukkot (16:14). At Pesaḥ, none is mentioned (16:5–7). The "tenant among you" shares first fruits (26:11 *bqrbk*).

72 See Lohfink, "Zentralisationsformel."

73 Sulzberger, *Labor*; Olyan, *Rites and Rank*, 74–81; Otto, *Gottesrecht*, 232–48; Friedman, *Exodus*, 200–3.

to local descent-group land (*naḥălâ*). So, to them one transfers defiling carcasses.[74] As tenants, escaped slaves (23:17) enjoy incontestable asylum.[75] But tenants attach to lineages from without, like Levites "in your gates." The household *hosts* the tenant "among you (*bqrbk*)" (16:11; 26:11, but not 12:12, 18). A citizen's "tenant (*grw*)" lacks the privileges of his "equal (brother)."[76]

Widows and orphans are also disadvantaged. Only "brother Hebrews" merit scheduled manumission: often this is equated with Israelites.[77] Yet the adjacent law cancels debt for "brothers," specifically colleagues (*rʿ*). Those with whom risk is thus shared are enfranchised citizens *in the borough*: insolvent kin "in one of your gates" (15:7) have claims on lineage solidarity, and the legal enforcement of debt is unusual, as in the *ḥamūla*. In the "gates," charity extends to the tenant.[78] Unsecured credit and debt relief remain within the core kinship network.

Overall, the marginal are not the responsibility of individual households, nor yet of towns, but collectively of households making up the cooperative of the borough. Residence, not kinship, is the organizing administrative principle.

Deuteronomy never directly attaches the concept, "gates," to kinship organization. It minimizes reference to kinship organization generally, so even the terms "clan" (*mišpāḥâ*) and "father's house" occur just once. It even desacralizes the lineage. "Gates," explicitly, are gifted to the sanctified tribes as part of Yhwh's land-grant.[79] Thus, tribes perform sacred duties, including enacting the covenant. The borough does not. "In your gates," the Pesaḥ, the national communal sacrifice, is void.[80] You *may* sacrifice in your gates (12:15, 21; 15:22) but forgo the holocaust, and purity rules need not apply. By such restrictions, Deuteronomy denies official standing to licit lineage celebrations, not least feeding the dead. Civic is not private religion. The appeal of "gates" as a nomenclature is its neutrality on both sacral and agnatic aspects of the clan sector.

---

74 Deut 14:21; the food given to a tenant or sold is thrown to the dogs in Exod 22:30. In Lev 17:15, it is universally edible, but consumers must clean up afterward.
75 Note also 24:14–15, "brother" and tenant hirelings. Glanville ("Stranger," 603–5) expertly exposes disputes concerning the *gēr*, showing that *gēr* denotes a legal status, not ancestry (cf. Deut 28:43).
76 1:16; 24:14. To tenants, compare Hammurapi's *muškēnum* and the classical metic; in 24:14; 28:43; 29:10 they are menial contractors. The Levite, orphan, or widow are never "yours."
77 For the discussion, see Rossi and Guillaume, "Law of Hebrew Slave."
78 Otto ("False Weights," 131–32) relates Deuteronomy's charity to the CC.
79 Deut 16:5; 16:18; 17:2; cf. 15:17. Boroughs are given by tribe in 16:18.
80 16:5–7; 12:17.

3.5 Town and Genealogy

Deuteronomy embeds the boroughs in an institutional hierarchy. Predictably, other texts use genealogical metaphor to describe hierarchy. Genealogy in our literature, therefore, exhibits two types. The administrative type is exemplified by P's rigidly segmentary lists. A less systematic, more dynamic view of identity underlies narratives in Judges and Samuel.

"Official" kinship structures – P's clans are tax districts in the Samaria ostraca – constitute a tiered stasis dissonant with the untidy dynamism of the organic kinship web. Only the administrative genealogy concerns Deuteronomy, and mainly for solemnities. JE, too, has only a sacred genealogy, stopping with the tribe. In defining institutions and structures topographically rather than socially, texts like Deuteronomy are early forays in political constitution. In its descent hierarchy, Deuteronomy layers household, tribe, and folk.[81] Its administrative hierarchy differs: borough, township, folk.

Ideal traditional divisions begin with the farmstead, a household, then the village, more than one household in a shared *ḥamūla*. This *ḥamūla* covers multiple farmsteads, one or two villages' worth, or wards. The town, usually walled, or the city, walled with a state garrison, contains multiple *ḥamūlas*. In Deuteronomy, the aggregate constitutes a **township**.

In descent-group geography, the *ḥamūla* is a residential chapter of a **phratry**. The **phratry** is the primary division of a township's assembly. Its chapters (four at Hebron, e.g.) exploit diverse opportunities. Crossing communities and zones, its members collaborate in ritual, administration, and, most importantly, common landholding.[82] The resultant collectives, built on preferential connection and exchange, are public partners in land transfers and socialize at township and regional occasions.

The relation between Deuteronomy's borough and the township is discernible. In boroughs, dispute resolution is local, among the households. The "ward" is also a seat of jurisdiction in Mesopotamia.[83] The *town's* elders are household patriarchs. "To the elders, to the gate" one comes for redress, especially in cases crossing lineages (22:14; 25:7).

Capital punishment involves "town" authority. So, should there be a traitor

> among you (*bqrbk*) in one of your gates that Yhwh your god gives you, who has gone and served other gods (elsewhere) ... which I have not commanded, and (if) you are informed,

---

81 In 29:17, the *mišpāḥâ* is "clan" or, probably, "clan sector" (Halpern, "Lineages").

82 As with the land sale by a clan's settled and nomadic divisions, whose chiefs are enumerated; see Boyer, *Textes juridiques*, 11.9–10, r 20–22.

83 Otto, "*ša'ar*, Gate," 367.

> and listen, and investigate adeptly, and, finally, the thing is proven true ..., then you will take that man or woman out to *your gates* and stone (him/her). (Deut 17:2–5)

Regardless where the infraction occurs, the guilty party *belongs* (*bqrb*) in the borough. When the body politic *hears*, and finds proof, they "take [the condemned] out" to the borough for execution. The display *addresses* the borough. But the *trial* is not in the borough: the town jurisdiction supervenes between the borough and the appeals court (17:8–13).

In another case, borough residents seek to execute one of their own. Deuteronomy 21:18–21 prescribes public shaming and death for the intractable son: his parents drag him out to "the elders of his town" *and* to "the gate of his place." The parents notify both township and borough, social distals and proximals.[84] But, in 17:2–7, fellow townsmen likewise must confront the borough in its manifestation as a clan-sector commune. Both capital cases reckon with the possibility that the borough is outside the town ("take [him] out to the borough"; "the gate of his place," not of the town): condemnees belong to boroughs but fall under the jurisdiction of townships. The town, traditionally, governs a territory.

In our imagination, monarchy supplants the city-state rather than eroding it. But "town" also means a township, including smaller settlements (e.g. 2 Sam 2:3; Isa 17:2). Such municipalities were epicenters of local jurisdiction. Bureaucratically, the township is a genealogical section (not sector) of an administrative clan: thus, the Samaria ostraca either aggregate remittances to clans or trace them to towns, segments of those clans.

The township was always a seat of political identity. Absalom hails travelers, "From which 'town' are you?" Replies signify "from one of the tribes of Israel" (2 Sam 15:2). The town's name indicated affiliation. Orphaned Beerothites fled to Gittaim, "and have been tenants there until now" (2 Sam 4:3). Nabal questions David's affiliation with a recognized township (1 Sam 25:10–11).

Outback ("wilderness") is assigned to towns as well, a commons beyond tillage, as to Gibeon or Beth Aven (2 Sam 2:24; Josh 18:12). Other such commons are in marginal zones but still within townships' purview.[85] So, Nabal was "a man in Maon," with an "enterprise in Carmel." His flocks graze the adjoining "wilderness of Maon," the township's free range.[86]

---

84 The interpretation of the ordinance in terms of Deut's institutional structure comes from Amanda LaMancha Walls, my wife. "Gate of his place," in its other occurrence (Ruth 4:10 MT), is the *ḥamūla* cooperative, not a physical gate.

85 Beersheba, Ziph, En Gedi, Tekoa: Gen 21:14; 2 Sam 23; 26:2; 2 Chr 20:20.

86 1 Sam 25:1, 21; cf. 23:25. Readers questionably take the tenant in Judg 19:16 for an Israelite whose business property (*m'śh*, as 1 Sam 25:1) is in Gibeah's tillage ("field").

Deuteronomy adapts this township's territoriality.[87] So, distance to the nearest town determines assessments for derelict corpses. Theoretically, townships, not family plots, cover the landscape. In contrast, P and Joshua clearly distribute land by tribe. Other texts sometimes ascribe "lands" to tribes: "the land of Naphtali" or "the broadener (*mrḥyb*) of Gad." They also belong to administrative clans (Hepher, Gilead), organic clans (Zuph), or non-Israelite towns (Laish, Tappuah). P and Joshua, on the other hand, present an administrative genealogy: legal succession programs geography.

3.6 What's in a Wapentake?

> Syng a song of Saxons
> In the Wapentake of Rye
> – *1066 and All That*

The relationship of townships with dependencies is also pertinent. 1 Samuel 25:2 describes "a man in Maon, whose doings were in Carmel." The district, Maon, encompasses the town or village of Carmel and, in 1 Samuel 23, Ziph and Ein Gedi. Maon is either a township or, positing a layer coordinating multiple townships, a **county seat.**

A county seat might be hypothesized from arrangements for outlying towns in the Arad letters. Likewise, in 701 BCE, Lachish and Tell Beit Mirsim represent different ends on the scale of positive royal presence. We believe that Lachish was the most important military post outside Jerusalem. Was it a township, or did it command a Shephelah catchment incorporating townships like Beit Mirsim?

These questions arise from the texts as well. The classic J and P administrative genealogies divide Judah into four primary tribal sections or administrative clans. Joshua 15 divides it into four topographical zones. And, in 701, rations distributed to Hezekiah's garrisons are stamped with the name of one of four towns (Hebron, Socoh, Ziph, and the much-unexplained *mmšt*), apparently representing the contents' regional provenance.[88] Their nomenclature for the regions differs: one difference recalls the Samaria ostraca, namely, the choice of municipal over genealogical designations. Such zones might produce their own

87 See Guillaume, *Land, Credit*, 17–53; Otto, *Kontinuum*, 80–81. In Ruth 4:10, it descends through the clan sector.

88 Manufacture in the Shephelah, overall comparative percentages of occurrence of each stamp, and the mixture of stamps at each site leave this as the prosaic explanation for the code. It has been widely mooted that the two- versus four-winged stamps may code the difference between oil and (concentrated) wine.

collection centers, reflected perhaps in the temple of Arad X, and more tantalizingly, in various eras, at Moza, Ramat Rahel, Arnona, and Gibeon. Such a role is perhaps also envisioned outside Deuteronomy for Levitical cities.[89]

Even if Samuel's Maon is a township, the system aggregating townships into counties has a precursor in regional designations, like "the land of Zuph," encompassing Ramah in 1 Samuel 9:13, or Cabul in 1 Kings 9:11–13. Joshua 15 subdivides Judah's four regions into a total of twelve counties. Its 110+ towns form groups of varying density. But at least in the northern reaches, we know that farmsteads and small villages far outnumber this list in the seventh century BCE. So the names listed are those of townships, classified for bureaucratic planning. Taking town names as those of townships also unblocks the riddle of town lists in Joshua 15–19: Joshua is not a Domesday Book.[90] It does, however, systematically divide Israel's territory.

Deuteronomy presupposes a background of township, and perhaps county or zone jurisdictions. Around this uncertain point revolves the question of cult consolidation: the law-code far more often contrasts "the place Yhwh chooses," directly and implicitly, with "your" profane "gates" than with alien hallows and never adduces higher organizational orders. What group assembled for ritual, identity affirmation and payments: township, county, region, or the capital alone? Philology holds no answer, for some reason.

4 Administering Citizenship

> Only he has a country who is a property owner or anyway the liberty and means to become one. He who does not have that has no country.
> – Wilhelm Weitling, *Garantien der Harmonie und Freiheit*

4.1 Borough Administration

Above the township perches the State. No intermediate clan or tribal structure appears. Tribes themselves are groupings only for national aggregation (as Deut 27:11–14; 33).

---

89 Diana Edelman, in correspondence, 2/2020, regarding P, Josh, Chr.

90 On the twelvefold division, with bibliography, Charles Christopher McKinny ("Administrative Division of Judah," 37) questions the efficacy of using survey results to date the lists, partly based on the mismatch addressed here. But administrative districting needn't change with new settlements or those that have grown over time, and if the Joshua lists reflect administrative, not organic social realities, the point is moot.

Borough officials (Deut 16:18–21) correspond to Moses's officers of tens. The king aside, these are the only officials nominated by the citizenry (also 1:12–15); like the king, they serve in concert with ritual specialists. Their social embedment is shielded by limits on physical shaming (25:2). Borough magistracy is a status, not a profession.[91]

These magistrates, household patriarchs, and borough marshals tried inter-*ḥamūla* cases as township elders (17:2–7). Stumped for a verdict, they are the "you" (sg.) who ascends to Yhwh's place. That law-court, or its surrogate, is the sole authority over conflicts between townships. So, beyond the township, jurisdiction is royal. As important, city hall is not necessarily Yhwh's place.

Yet the stress on "gates" has an unfamiliar aspect. Metaphor notoriously makes kinship terminology elastic. "Father's house" or even "house" denotes anything beyond a nuclear family. *'Elep*, a thousand, and *mišpāḥâ*, a large descent group, can be a clan or a clan section.[92] Texts refer to "tribes of (*šibṭê*) Benjamin" with their own *mišpāḥôt*.[93] The appropriation of "gates" as Deuteronomy's social, economic, and political isolates overhauls and recalibrates the administrative metaphor.[94] There is a Cleisthenic quality to the renaming.[95]

Introducing "gates" redefines population clusters formerly grasped as descent associations. The state, too, speaks kinship language, counting on its moral force to support marginal elements. But the legislator deemphasizes those bonds in his imagined landscape: as it did to prepare for 701 BCE, administration detaches itself from other extensive kinship sodalities. The borough is the zone into which it least intrudes.

---

91 Otto ("*ša'ar*, Gate," 399; *Deuteronomium 12–34* 1.1,477–80) infers professional jurists, as in E, where Moses appoints personnel (Exod 18:14–26; Num 11:16). In our interpretation, Levites and government specialists supplied expertise; hence, functional literacy increased status in commissioned echelons (Halpern, "Lineages," 79–82 § VIB).

92 Judg 6:15; 1 Sam 10:19; 23:23, military expression in Josh 22:14, 21, 30; Deut 33:17. On *mišpāḥôt*, cf. Judg 17:7–8; 18:2, 11.

93 Judg 20:12; 1 Sam 9:21; cf. 2 Sam 7:7. Benjaminite "tribes" apparently correspond to Judahite "thousands" in the more Benjamin-oriented source in 1 Samuel. P, in Num 4:18, speaks of the *šbṭ* of the *mišpāḥôt* of the Qehatite(s); P rarely uses this lexeme for "tribe" (Exod 28:21 = 39:14; Num 18:2), and may mean a faction.

94 See Otto, "*ša'ar*, Gate." The sense of commune is shared, as in 1 Kgs 8:37, perhaps Jer 14:2; 15:7. Houses never have gates, but, like gates, an entryway and doors. Towns never have doors.

95 Cleisthenes was a lawgiver remembered to have reformed the constitution of Athens by gerrymandering the city-state's descent associations into non-contiguous, mixed-descent voting divisions in 508 BCE, leading naive historians to dub him "the father of Athenian democracy."

4.2 Citizenship and Land

Each of Deuteronomy's townships has a seat, lending its name to the territory. But land registry operates primarily through the township (**3.5**). Townships collectively cover the entire countryside: it is almost inconceivable that a book as focused on landholding as Deuteronomy would leave portions of it unaccounted for.

A township census should thus capture landholders but not necessarily all members in Yhwh's assembly (*qāhāl*), or folk (*ʿām*). Citizenship, traditionally, requires induction into a lineage association, as betimes by post-pubescent circumcision. Inductees held equity in the common freehold, a *naḥălâ*, regarded as a "franchise" in Israel, itself called Yhwh's franchise. Privileged lineages allocated such portions to members. Thus, fathers "enfranchise" sons by endowing them with usufruct (21:16).[96] The franchise entails service and tax liability, giving one standing in sacral and deliberative assemblies (as in Judg 9:26–29).

Assemblies were mainly local.[97] The qualifications to participate in the assembly – field, residence, duties – were always local. Those without expectations of a *local* franchise are not *local* citizens. Citizenship in Deuteronomy starts with the borough.[98]

Displaced Israelites do not benefit from association privileges. This is not a novelty of demographic reconfiguration in the seventh century.[99] They have no voice in local assemblies, where the "folk" (*ʿām*) ratifies propositions put by "elders."[100] The local sacred assembly excludes tenants in Joshua 8:35 and others, including even local lineage members unable to sire franchisees, in Deuteronomy 23:2–9.[101] In the same way, Absalom and Hushai advise Absalom's

96 Deuteronomy innovates in making "land" the object of causative *hnḥl*, "apportion, endow" (cf. 1 Sam 2:8), followed in Jer, Ezek, 2 Isa and Zech, among others.

97 So, Gibeah in Judg 20; Jabesh in Judg 21; Shechem in Gen 33; 34; Judg 9; Hebron in Gen 23; Abel in 2 Sam 20; Libnah in 2 Kgs 8; also 1 Sam 9:12; 20:29, and cf. Deut 13.

98 As, again, Ruth 4:10.

99 Most of these structural components leave earlier reflexes on the ground as well as in texts: Stager, "Archaeology of Family"; Halpern, "Lineages"; Faust's observations ("World of P") on the extended-family compound versus the clan-sector quarter remind us that the architectural expression of homologous social entities varies by environment.

100 For the constitutional relation of elders and folk, see Halpern, *Constitution*, 187–216, ch. 7B. Elders are probably those with title to a franchise (*nḥlh*). So, ante-mortem property division might affect roles at different levels of proceedings.

101 The relationship of Deut 23 to citizenship was pointed out to me in conversation by Tyler Kelley, 6/2019.

war council but are excluded from its deliberations.[102] That citizenship or admission to the assembly was *ever* widespread in townships is unsure. In Deuteronomy, clients attach not to a family, but to the borough. Yet Deuteronomy formally welcomes tenants to a place at the communal table (and P at some even vaguer assembly) and dangles a prospect of enfranchisement.

5 The Sacred and the Gates

Although it woos tenant labor, Deuteronomy's enactment theoretically depends on the clan-sector householders who comprised assemblies in the various townships. These are unlikely to be well-disposed toward an unfamiliar social order. Indeed, Deuteronomy does not prescribe its administrative ladder but simply uses it.

The reform report (2 Kgs 23:4–25) thinks Moses wanted all hallows leveled but the Jerusalem temple. Deuteronomy bans holocausts, some consumption in the gates, and the Pesaḥ. What sacred activities remain in the gates? One key is the Levite.

5.1 Parish Shrines and the Gates of Dan

> It's cute! It's like a little clue.
> – *Sleepless in Seattle*

Yhwh is not entirely absent from the "gates." The measure erecting borough courts bars symbolic trees and betyls "adjoining the altar" that "you make for Yhwh your God" (16:18–17:1). This altar services oaths, divination, and expiation. Deuteronomy 17:1 forbids blemished sacrifice to Yhwh on it (cf. sacrifice in 12:15, 21). But 15:22 consigns blemished animals to the "gates" for eating. The altar is thus distinguished from the "gates."[103]

Too, every third year, the landed deposit tithes in the borough; the needy consume them.[104] The first recipients, Levites, are not themselves objects of

102 2 Sam 16:15–17:16, where the outcome is opaque to Hushai. For the same protocol in various texts, Halpern, *First Historians* 51–54.

103 See further Macdonald, "'Altar of Lord.'" In sequence, we have the court's erection (16:18–20), appurtenances (16:21–17:1), and procedure (17:2–7), before recourse to Yhwh's place (17:8–13).

104 14:28–29; 26:12–13. How does 12:17, "you have no right to eat in your gates the tithe ... and the firstlings ...," apply in the third year?

protective prescriptions or charity. They preside as citizens make declaration "before Yhwh," presumably at the altar (as 26:13). They oversee distribution.[105]

Before Deuteronomy, that altar may stand outside the quarter: 2 Kings 23:8 relates that Josiah demolished "the house of the high places of the gates that are at the entrance of the gate of Joshua, the (Jerusalem) township governor, which is to one's left in the city gate."[106] Taking "gates" with Deuteronomy, 23:8 tells us Josiah the Leveller targeted lineage – probably phratry – shrines in public spaces, limiting local kin-association advertisement.

There is an archaeological corollary. Five stelae stood in ancient Dan's interior gate plaza. John Emerton suggested the stelae were "high places of the gates."[107] Judges 18 reports, it is five scouts who discover Dan's icon, priesthood, and city. We should conclude, then, that Dan's spies represent the enclave's five founding lineages (*mišpāḥôt*, Judg 18:2, 11). Thus, P furnishes a spy per tribe, in a story probably shaped by ours.[108] Both P and Judges describe the scouts as distinguished men. The parallel is seemingly marred: P reports that Dan had one clan, named Hushim or Shuham.[109] Surprisingly, these and other major variants all represent anagrams of *ḥāmēš*, "five."

Multiple stelae also surround the gate at nearby Beth Saida.[110] These were the phratry stelae, clumped for use at a center (the *bamah* precinct) as descent groups convened: clans were not autarkic, and their gatherings facilitated commerce; there is no "house of (a single) *bāmâ*" because different associations use the facility. The phenomenon is widespread, each phratry needing its altar (§ 6, below). Classically understood, each stele represents a clan "baal" (here, totem divinity); the missing maypole stood in for Yhwh's *paredros* in the port, the

---

105 A hint of remoteness attends this tithe. For it, 26:15 asks Yhwh's blessing from his celestial den (<Ps 68:6; cf. Jer 25:30). In Deut, Yhwh acts from the heavens elsewhere only in 4:36 (<Exod 20:22); cf. 32:40; 33:26, 28. Appeal for remote aid may reflect distance between Yhwh and the local depository. He is more immanent when active.

106 OG preserves the phrase, "house of the high places of the gates"; G^B *ton oikon tōn pulōn* and MT *ʾt bmwt hšʿrym* have each suffered haplography from an original *byt bm(w)t hšʿrym*. Another OG plus places the shrine to one's left as one enters from outside. Though it looks (esp. the word, *ekkekentēmenōv*) like a gloss, it, too, may be original. Retroverted, *ʾyš bʾ bšʿr hʿyr mbḥwṣ*, the second word a victim of *homoioarkton*, the last either translational or suppressed with the loss of *bʾ*.

107 Emerton, "'High Places of the Gates,'" with "gates" taken as an architectural term.

108 By inference from Abraham Malamat's still-luminous article ("Danite Migration").

109 Num 26:42: "These are the sons of Dan by their clans: for Shuham (G, Samei), the clan of the Shuhamites. These are the clans of Dan according to their clans." Gen 46:23: "And the sons of Dan were/was Hushim (G Asom)."

110 On these precincts, see David Ilan, "Tale of Two Gates," suggesting a connection to Aramaean culture.

territory's progenitrix. Acolytes caparisoned them with seasonable raiment, including precious metals and gemstones, whence Deuteronomy's hope that donors not recover them.[111]

The altars, too, are those to which Deuteronomy denies stelae, when it relocates them from a civic precinct into the parish, physically or not. The reflex in Jeremiah 11:13 condemns Judah's gods, equal in number to its settlements, and altars for baals by its plazas. Here, the prophet may be ratcheting up Josiah's standards to include those inside the boroughs, to which Deuteronomy had already denied clan insignia.

5.2 Parish Levites

At the place (*mqwm*), the unaffiliated who join households are "in your gates" and "among you" (*bqrbk*), sharing group fortunes.[112] The local Levite, always "in your gates," is never "among you." Yet the legislator singles him out: when you are first directed to the place, he is the sole invitee from outside the household (12:12, 18). Especially for tithes and firstlings or for pledges, you take care *never* to leave the Levite behind (12:19; 14:27).

When at Yhwh's place, Levites "minister" (*šrt*) at will (18:6–7). They earn a cut from their borough's festivities at Yhwh's place (12:12, 18; 14:26–27). Why else does the provision precondition staff privileges for Levites eager (*'wh + npš*) to reach the place on attachment to an Israelite borough, *and thus service as a parish curate*?

Josiah alters this dispensation on the fly (2 Kgs 23:8–9). Levites get bonuses, like portioner canons in a collegiate church, in addition to fees from the clan-sector.[113] But Josiah refuses them license to sacrifice "on the altar of Yhwh in Jerusalem." The disparity is between the permanent transfer in Kings and the law-code's pilgrimage to the place (*bkl 'wt npšw*). Deuteronomy's feast was moveable.

Parish Levites carried enough weight to warrant a place at the public trough (10:9; 12:12; 14:27, 29; 18:1 [Gen 49:7], 8). The Levite occupies a niche, just as the

---

111 Deut 7:25–26; 29:16. On high-place trappings, see LaRocca-Pitts, *Wood and Stone*, 125–49.
112 16:11, 14. When physical, *qrb* is the "turf" from which guilt must be expelled, for Yhwh is "among (Israel)" (1:42; 6:15; 7:21; 31:17). Comparable is the "camp" (2:14–16; 4:3), where Yhwh patrols (23:15); cf. 29:10 (= tenants!). So it, versus the purely physical *twk*, implies conformity to local norms. The other passage where the underclass is "in your gates" is for the third-year tithe, eaten there (14:28; 26:12).
113 Deut 18:8, *lbd mmkryw 'l hā-'ābôt*. This may be one of the earliest deployments of *'ābôt* for lineages (Num 36:1; Josh 19:51; 1 Kgs 8:1; about 30 times in Ezra-Neh-Chr).

tenant, by scavenging carcasses or drawing water, fulfills roles degrading to the citizen.[114] Levites "who are in your gates" treat leprosy and notarize oaths and vows. They developed local ties (Judg 19). Although no more "your Levite" than "your widow" (cf. "your tenant"), they were probably apt to go native.

Levites conducted rites, including sacrifice, on behalf of the *ḥamūla*. The text insinuates that there was a Levite in every borough, whom one *at no time* leaves behind. The legislator implicitly casts the state as the party doing the insinuating.

On this model, the Levite's courtesy appointment at Yhwh's place was an opportunity for commensality in priestly quarters, with wages, reportage, and coordination, for socialization in the bureaucracy. The parish Levite supervising the ritual at Yhwh's place replaces an earlier ritual specialist who assisted at the township plaza for offerings by phratry "gates."

In the parish, according to 16:21, Levites supervise the altar precinct. They manage meal offerings and others seasonally. This side of the cult is more regular than animal sacrifice. And other categories of unrestricted sacrifice include expiatory offerings, public and private, the immanent benefit of which accrued mainly to the Levite. 2 Kings 23:9 betrays the same understanding: "the priests of the high places did not ascend to the altar of Yhwh *in Jerusalem*." The implicit, otherwise unnecessary contrast with other Yhwh altars points to the borough altar of 16:21. In Deuteronomy's "gates," Levites act as priests.

When Jeremiah caterwauls about altars at every plaza, he documents their use in boroughs' spaces to honor descent-group deities. Whether the spirits are offered meat or aromatics only, these altars conform to the letter of the law-code.

Surprisingly, Deuteronomy's demands affect animal sacrifice only at Passover, when firstlings, too, are delivered. To appreciate this, imagine that in a township's city, say Libnah,[115] a patriarch weds a son to a woman from another township. The feast involves two families' co-residents, neighbors, relations, business associates, dignitaries, and performers. Sacrifice must be made on the parish or township altar: Moses or no, *not* beseeching Yhwh's blessing would occasion unease.

Nor need the host welcome guests in a state of ritual impurity. The unblemished sacrifice is pure: the law-code is indifferent whether the impure partake. In a traditional world, distances traversed to attend life-cycle ceremonies are

114 For status conditioned on specialization, see Bond, *Trade and Taboo*.
115 At the moment, most plausibly Tel Burna, with bibliography in Shai et al., "Ten Years at Tel Burna," 83–84.

routinely celebrated in song, even commemorated.[116] Since non-Israelites defile the assembly (*qhl yhwh*), hosts isolate sacraments from taint. Guests, by etiquette as much as compulsion, join or avoid ritual elements. That this debased standards of purity seems improbable: "profane slaughter" changes little in ordinary life, except that the banquet can no longer be convened as a constitutional assembly, with a holocaust.

It was never Deuteronomy's intention to banish meat from the household or even the *ḥamūla* table. Its innovation was to outlaw exclusions from public sacrifice. State-dictated inclusiveness is a blow to the phratry and to the township, who now incorporate non-members in sacraments – and may not exclude them by offering a holocaust, demanding "purity" from all attendees.[117]

Overall, the Levites certify tithes "before Yhwh" at the borough shrine (26:13). They preside at lineage ceremonies like circumcisions[118] and festivals. The Levites in Deuteronomy minister to the borough: they are parish priests. Unlike their landowner patrons, borough priests are, ideally, agents in the matrix algebra of Yhwh's place.

5.3 Zeroing in on the Township

Removing clan insignia at altars, Deuteronomy superannuates phratries' rituals at the township seat. Does this mean that "the place where Yhwh chooses to put his name" was divorced from the town and altars that expressed social identity? As with the location of upper courts, application depends on the interpreter: the king, theatrically straitjacketed and chained, is free to choose.[119]

What expectations would poring over Deuteronomy's text raise in a traditional hills lineage head? The head knows Bethel was founded by Jacob/Israel or Abraham. Clan emblems are just as Israelite. Does this text ready readers for Josiah's atrocities at longstanding hallows?

---

116 As in Kgs, Pss and royal inscriptions. In July, 1972, Israeli co-workers at Khirbet Shema from Dabouriyyeh and Gush Halav invited four of us to a Druze and an Orthodox wedding, respectively. Both times, the singers adduced attendance all the way from America to emphasize the importance of the occasion. Per the style sheet: "Personal observation, (simultaneously) translated by Daoud and Yussef (last names long forgotten)."

117 Thus, holocausts attend the tribal blessing and cursing ceremony in Deut 27:6 but not the book's recitation before non-citizens in 31:10–13.

118 Association with Levi explains the choice of circumcision as a plot gimmick in two J tales (Gen 34; Exod 4:24–26).

119 On the king's restriction, see Markl, "Anti-King."

Some of the impact is open. Disallowing deductions for meals with the dead is an inroad on *ḥamūlas* and phratries. Those association meals helped especially the urban *ḥamūlas*, like Shechem's sons of Hamor, pack assemblies to apportion costs for festivals and public works.[120] Demographic dominance also allowed the city to attract phratry altars, whose custom was bound to suffer.

An obvious explanation for Deuteronomy's concern to cut out townships and phratries is that township assemblies were draining off resources. Expounding Deuteronomy,[121] Jeremiah 11:13 shares the concern: "the number of your *towns* are your gods." Deuteronomy's exactions circumvent the phratries and townships. Toppling the high places was Josiah's way of expressing support.

As W. Eugene Claburn recognized, tithes were originally civil imposts.[122] The centrality of tithes in the scheme is open: it is the first and the last assessment prescribed. Both statutes schedule local redistribution, and the first digresses into debt limitation. State agents at the place collected tithes and firstlings at Passover. Earlier, townships had drawn on these proceeds for local disbursement, sharing fitful levies with the crown. In Deuteronomy, the state has more predictable revenue. It seizes the township's income and leaves its liabilities.

Citizenship in Deuteronomy demands renewal at the king's agency. This implied inroads on township authority over land registry, which by implication, was a step on the way to restoration Yehud. But Deuteronomy acknowledges local sacrifices.

In the ordinary fabric of township life, sacrifice serviced professional healers and diviners, sealed agreements, expunged guilt, and fed associations. As conformist as Libnah might be, the township needed ritual. Formerly, royal appointment furnished the top staff, who also enjoyed custom and support. Township priests, like Jonathan the Mushite in Judges 18, could be fathers to prepossessing congregations. But royal subsidy was plugging a sinkhole of township institutions, where one phratry washed the others' hands and all sent their hands to the meat.

---

120 Judg 9; subliminally, even Gen 34. Still invaluable for its reflections on practical control at the assembly is Taylor, *Roman Voting Assemblies*.

121 John Skinner (*Prophecy and Religion*, 97–103) qualifies but validates the view as consensus. In a Jeremiah commentary, in progress, I add unacknowledged evidence that the oracle refers to Deut *ca.* 608 BCE.

122 Claburn, "Fiscal Reform," 13–16. E already consecrates tithes in the relation of Jacob to El of Bethel (Gen 28:22), suggesting that the idea was northern policy (versus Joseph in Egypt and 1 Sam 8), or reflects R-JE.

The new dispensation marks a third of the tithe for local redistribution. In the Levite-inspectors, Claburn saw tax collectors.[123] The legislator sends these community servants into the boroughs but awards them base pay from the chosen place (*mqwm*). The modest largesse propels their duty without undue friction. Josiah also (2 Kgs 23:5) cuts phratry priests from the crown budget.[124] Again, the obvious loser is the township.

Two cult installations probably reflect the imposition of similar strictures. The temple of Arad X was lavishly outfitted. In Stratum IX, someone lovingly retired the complex, interring an incense altar and steles with its adyton; in VIII, its large fieldstone altar, too, disappeared.[125] Similar claims are made about the steles, figurines, vessels, and fieldstone altar in the temple sealed under Moza's Stratum V.[126]

At Beersheba, a dressed-stone altar was dismantled, probably during the lifetime of Stratum III or with the construction of II. Its blocks were used in the base of a building abutting the gate in Stratum II.[127] Eighth-century Beersheba (IV–III) appears in two separate triads of sacrificial sites (Amos 5:5; 8:14), but P's later narrative omits it. Its altar may have had a long-distance draw, unsurprising given the location. To this heterogeneous pairing – Arad's regional temple and depot, Beersheba's altar – an addition has been mooted. In yet another category, and less certain, as Sabine Kleiman has shown, is a hypothetical decommissioned cult room in the Lachish III gate.[128]

These four installations were mothballed in the eighth century BCE, probably, as Ze'ev Herzog has underscored, under Hezekiah. The remains testify at

---

123 Cf. Claburn, "Fiscal Basis," 119; esp. Ahlström, *Royal Administration*, 47–56. Claburn blames Josiah's Reform on Levitical misappropriation (from 1 Sam?), but earlier evidence of their role, reach, or constitution is exiguous.

124 *kmrym*, 2 Kgs 23:5, at the *bāmôt, are best understood as lineage priests appointed for and from clans*. They need not be the astral priests in the continuation of the account. In any case, royal appointment in the towns suggests a parallel in Judah to practice in Israel, where Jeroboam makes priests for his *bāmôt*-precincts ("house(s) of *bāmôt*") of non-Levites in the towns of Samaria (below). So, in Hos 10:5 King Hosea's clan priests rejoice when Shalmaneser carries off Bethel's pan-Israelite icon. An etymological link to Akk. *kamāru*, "heap up," is not impossible, if offerings or altars are objects in mind.

125 Ze'ev Herzog, "Fortress Mound."

126 See Kisilevitz et al. "Moza"; Greenhut and de Groot, *Salvage at Tel Moza*.

127 Wall P12. Aharoni, "Horned Altar" and Yadin,"Beer-Sheba." Both thought the altar stood in Stratum II, which Aharoni linked to Hezekiah's reform and Yadin to Josiah's, by his "gate of Joshua." Definitively, see Herzog and Singer-Avitz, *Beer-Sheba III*, 1.172–76; 3.1,476–78 and references there. The wall in which the stones were found was repaired with the construction of Stratum II, as the town plan and the building's public character show.

128 Ganor and Kreimerman, "Gate Shrine at Lachish"; Kleiman, "Iron IIB Gate Shrine."

best to Hezekiah's urbanization.[129] But Arad presents, and Beersheba seems to, as evidence of state outreach to the country more than the township and phratry shrines Josiah addresses.

Closing state offices requires revisions. *In CC, Yhwh comes to you. In Deuteronomy, you schlepp to him.* Directing taxpayers to regional depots saves outlay. It also facilitated a change in collection. Historically, city-states collected revenues by settlement.[130] Ottoman authorities also recorded exaction by village, although collection was aggregated by district, like clans in the Samaria ostraca. In Deuteronomy, however, the self-organizing *ḥamūla* delivers direct to the state. Levites, debriefed in the place's Common Room, police delivery.

Deuteronomy generally walls official religion off from ethnic superstition. It removes "pilgrim" festivals from townships. It permits association fellowship meals (*šlmym*) at home but provides no subsidy; the budget for township feeding is capped at one third of its tithe. Like the phratries, the township, deprived of a legislative organ, can only exert social pressure for local governance. And even then, the state exacts concessions: channeling the subsidy to the borough, not the township; entitling all residents to participate in publicly-sponsored feasts; and dispensing with phratry insignia. Ritual associations were not to mark their separate identity: Israel was totalized. Practically, the old centers of organization, the townships, lost the most.

6 Deuteronomy's World

6.1 Deuteronomy before Reform

Deuteronomy's demands and Josiah's actions are differently nuanced, some part of which may be totted up to the purpose of the reform report in 2 Kings 23:4–25. Deuteronomy abhors infant sacrifice (12:29–31; 18:10), and Josiah pollutes a single *tophet* of indeterminate size. Deuteronomy keeps mum about tombs. Josiah wades in bones.[131]

---

129 Herzog, "Perspectives"; Moulis, "Hezekiah's Cultic Reforms." The sociohistorical bearings exclude Ahaz, for whose reforms, see Heth, "Stripping of the Bulls"; Halpern, "Lineages" (esp. 19–27, IIB-C), with background on Hezekiah's urbanization.

130 OB cases, conveniently, in Földi, "Property of City." As projection increased through networks, district authorities (city-states) interposed between the village and the center, in one or more layers.

131 See Halpern, "False Torah," with references, to which add the Esarhaddon oath curse, in Parpola and Watanabe, *Neo-Assyrian Treaties*, 2.46:445–46 (#6 § 47). Michael Jursa ("Söhne Kudurrus") showed the Assyrians desecrated the remains of Nabopolassar's grandfather;

Nothing in Deuteronomy targets Yhwh-friendly high places. It insists Israel destroy "places where [aborigines] served their gods." Its songs (chs. 32 and 33) mention *bāmôt*, "high places," as Israel's *assets*.[132] P, too, *values* Israel's high places.[133] It rephrases D622's edict against *aborigines'* high places.[134] Both distinguish others' hallows from our *bāmôt*.

But others' hallows, in the reform report and DtrH, *are those bāmôt*.[135] Even Solomon's chapels, untouched by Hezekiah, are labeled foreign; of three gods honored, only Ashtoret is autochthonous. Tacking alien gods onto accusations of alien atmosphere at the *bāmôt* is the reform report's innovation, or Dtr's.[136] Deuteronomy and P were more forbearing, rhetorically, like the treatment of icons in Arad IX.

Again, town *bāmôt* decommissioned, Deuteronomy (18:6–7) allows Levites to "minister" to their pilgrims at the place: "Scruple to not leave the Levite behind, all your time on your patch." The Levite cannot, however, mount Yhwh's altar (2 Kgs 23:9), doubtless because "to minister" does not stipulate "to sacrifice." Josiah weaseled through a loophole to transfer Levites permanently, some to Jerusalem. Again, the law soft-sells the event.

The direction of reception is evident. Josiah's report trumpets a vigorous enactment of Deuteronomy. Deuteronomy does not reflect the reform.[137] By the time of the report, that ink had dried.[138]

Natalie N. May ("Iconoclasm and Text Destruction," 15–16) linked it to the curse. Assyrian traces are extensive in Josianic Judah. Cf. nn. 41, 200.

132 For the history of scholarship, see Hardy and Thomas, "*Bɔmɔ*." Deut's *bmtym* differ: 32:13; 33:29 (> Isa 58:14). High places are, of course, Yahwistic elsewhere, as in Amos 7:9; Mic 1:5 (sg. *bmwt*, or short for their precinct? cf. Barrick, *BMH*, 98); 2 Kgs 18:22//Isa 36:7. Further, Barrick, *BMH*, 107–30.

133 And sanctuaries: Lev 26:30–31. Vater, *Commentar* 3.460.

134 Num 33:52, often excised for doing so, is P (Friedman, *Bible with Sources*, 304): it omits altars and maypoles, central to Deut, while adding cast icons and high places, absent from Deut's provisions.

135 I belabor the point in *First Historians*, 220–28.

136 Defended perhaps by exegesis of the enemy's *bāmôt* (33:29) and Israel's *bāmôt* (*drk* + *bmty*) being equated in destruction. The predictable implication is that Deut 12:1–4 and associated passages are Josianic, not inherited.

137 See n. 2 above.

138 DtrH also departs from Deut while elaborating on it. It supposes no place was chosen, except insofar as it housed the ark, which still travels for holocausts; perhaps each site was sanctioned by a Judge, as with Gideon and Samuel; or, that there was no place continually until Jerusalem. The place's election clause applies to Jerusalem starting with Solomon (1 Kgs 11:32; 14:21; 2 Kgs 21:7). See the summary by Paton, "Case for Post-Exilic Origin"; further, e.g. Hyatt, "Jeremiah," 158 on Deut 23:18 and 2 Kgs 23:7 *qĕdēšîm*; with resort to post-exilic insertions; Wazzana, "Law of King," 180–82 on Solomon's sin and Deut 17. Cf. Knoppers, "Rethink-

6.2 Deuteronomy's Intellectual Origins

Behind Deuteronomy loiters a century of experience with Assyria. By 738 BCE, having engulfed central Syria, Assyria redrew borders down to Tyre and Israel. In 734–732, it ripped through Damascus, across Galilee, and down to Gaza. In 724, Assyria occupied the rump Israelite kingdom, and in 722 probably the capital. Replacements for its population, deported in 720, arrived from abroad soon afterward.[139] Throughout the West, Assyria introduced its administrative systems.

Samaria's ethnic map after 720 BCE remains uncoded. Tiglath-Pileser had denuded Galilee and much of Gilead. However, Samaria's Assyrian governors stemmed from the highest echelons: one was the eponym for 690 BCE.

Governors were expected to maintain production and monitor trade. For such purposes, retaining olive and vine-tenders would be natural. Although reassignment was probably normal, it is unclear that Assyria deported more than the elite to distant locales: in 738 BCE, Menahem could levy fifty shekels each on 60,000 households; in 720, Sargon counts 30,000 individual deportees from the city, Samaria. How internal redistribution was conducted is opaque. Israelite craftsmen worked the olive industry at Ekron after Sennacherib.[140] These could, however, have defected as metics sometime after 734 or been reassigned after 701.[141]

The movement of Israelite craftsmen mirrors what Avraham Faust has seen as the migration of industrial processing from Israel to Judah to Philistia in the course of the ninth-seventh centuries BCE.[142] We may assume that guild specialists brought along processing equipment from a temporary location when Stra-

---

ing," esp. on Dtr's positive view of Solomon's wealth, and pp. 399–400 on Deut 31:9–13 vs. Josh 8:30–35 and 2 Kgs 23:1–3. Still, starting with key words like "gates" and "high places," Deut is never exactly Deuteronomistic. Jer and Ezek then exceed even Josiah's zeal for reform – limiting Yhwh to punishing individuals (Halpern, "Lineages," esp. 11–17, 57–91) like a human. Disparities between the DtrH and Deut are best explained by contextual difference, Deuteronomy's anteriority, or diegesis. They are a poor basis for stratifying Deut.

139 The evidence, from the "wedge-decorated" bowl (the wedges are more likely functional, for grating) to various tells, e.g. Rekhesh (Paz and Hasegawa, "Who Built"), Dotan, Hadid, Jemme, and es-Saidiyyeh, sustains the claim of replacement; the timing is inferred from Kings and Sargon. For a review of the evidence, see Aster, "Transmission," 34–40.

140 Sy Gitin ("Incense Altars") documents their diagnostic symbolic tradition.

141 Krzysztof Hipp, ("Fugitives," 59–63, 66–67) documents leniency toward skilled captives, and runaways' communities. For non-standard Israelite spelling on an ostracon, see Gitin and Aḥituv, "Two New Inscriptions," 225–26. There is no indication of their earlier presence at Ekron.

142 Faust, "Interests of Assyrian Empire."

tum IC was reconceived to accommodate them.[143] The policy was fraught: it would be odd were these biddable Israelites uncourted in Ekron's struggles with Hezekiah. They apparently prospered not far from native turf.

While they rewrote local Israelite land tenure, provincial authorities found themselves competing with Judah for agrarians' loyalty. One element of the response was to reappropriate Yhwh's old cult. In 2 Kings 17:24–29, Assyria dispatches an exiled priest to Bethel to mitigate maulings. That priest at Bethel is the counterpart to the priest who interred Josiah's "man of god" after such a mauling (1 Kgs 13:23–30). He looks every bit at home in a fairy-tale etiology, charming to Josiah's chancery. The most one can take from the account's inclusion is that Assyria underwrote a cult and priestly establishment, possibly from the 720s forward. Kings diagnoses the reason for this accommodation by projecting the logic of Josiah's Bethel policy onto Jeroboam's schismatic cult: "If this folk make a practice of going up to make sacrifices in the temple of Yhwh in Jerusalem, then this folk's mind will return to their master" (1 Kgs 12:26). Old hands left in place may have inducted new neighbors. Certainly, transplants had no natural bond to the province, especially as Assyrian power and budgets waned. Potential affinity for their high god's surviving state cult warranted counter-measures, with the desirable side-effect of deflecting Israelites from sending gifts and pledges to Yhwh on Zion.

Other hints of the competition come from Judah's side. As Israel tottered and fell (740–720 BCE), Judah positioned itself as a successor. For a century, it was prized as a coalition partner. Economically, it developed into an engine of intensified agriculture and long-distance trade. Culturally, it developed a burgeoning literary canon.

Even before 701, Israel's *land and population* figured in Hezekiah's ambitions (ca. 727–698 BCE). Isaiah's blueprint, before and after, frames Israel's reunification under the Temple's aegis: Judah, Israel's successor state and sometimes remnant, offers survivors Jerusalem's shelter.[144] The theme, shared with Micah, reflects an interest in capturing human resources. Prosperity follows Davidic ministration.

Early recruitment will mainly have targeted those experienced in ecologically appropriate production, as at Ekron. And, programmatic settlement was

---

143 The perils of moving might conversely explain plant equipment discarded and in secondary use (a press weight, e.g.) in IB, with earlier arrangements in IC less planned. See Gitin et al., *Field IV Lower*, 1–20. Note, though, that the dedicatory inscriptions are not standard Israelite but probably civic devotions for Šarrat-Ekron, *ptgyh*, or conceivably, Galilean.

144 With suggested dating in parentheses, Isa 29:13–24 (701 BCE); 10:20–23+11:10–16 (734–732/724–720 BCE, esp. 8:23; 10:28–32); 14:1–3 (729–689 BCE).

already underway in the Arad-Beersheba Valley.[145] It stands to reason that at least some Samarian defectors were stationed there.[146]

6.2.1 701 BCE and Other Contributions

In 701, Hezekiah herded Judah into forts and Sennacherib reassigned them as Assyrian assets. Most were probably deported: lineage ties in the period were abruptly abridged; family sizes shrank; Isaiah inferred that Yhwh's rejection of countryside cults had now reached Judah, especially in the towns.[147] The attack on Israel's extramural clan-cults resonated with Hosea and Amos, first to underpin emergency urbanization and afterward, to explain calamity.

Manasseh achieved eminence among Assyrian collaborators before the invasions of Egypt; by the 680s, therefore, he had engineered Judah's resurgence by dispatching gangs from Jerusalem. Judah's demography rebounded over the century, even before it regained the outer Shephelah. "Judah became a sort of Assyria in miniature through a policy of internal deportation. Systematic exploitation of agricultural and industrial resources was standard Assyrian strategy."[148]

Manasseh systematized specialized resource exploitation. Isaiah (2:4) and Micah (4:3) sloganeer about guns-into-tractors retooling. Manasseh codified or at least propagated these texts as guides to reconstruction. Claims that township sharps cheated people of their franchise especially justify land redistribution after 701 BCE.[149]

This situation proves crucial to Deuteronomy's intellectual origins. Judah's recovery depended on influx. To emerge from Samaria's shadow, farm labor was central to royal ambitions; Assyrian dominion accelerated economic differentiation and resource concentration. The labor pool most obviously accessible consisted of those omnipresent Samarian refugees on whom we are wont to

---

145 For an up-to-date regional picture (and a fresh eighth-century foundation), see Itkin, "Horvat Tov." The Negev forts were most likely wrecked *ca.* 701 BCE.

146 Thareani ("Forces of Decline," 212) discerns non-Judahites from pig bones at Aroer. Comparable pig-bone frequencies at Iron IIB Israelite settlements (Sapir-Hen et al., "Iron Age Pigs") support the possibility of Israelite defectors at the site.

147 Halpern, "Lineages," to which add e.g. Isa 7; 9:12; 10:11–12, 11:26; and 14:1–2.

148 We may assume that Assyria licensed Manasseh to site oil production facilities at Beth Shemesh, recapturing produce for Judah, as a reward after the invasion of Egypt in 672, at latest. The quote in the text is from Halpern, 397. Other aspects of this (1991) study need adjustment as well, I acknowledge gratefully to those who have engaged with it.

149 As in Hos 13:10 (judges); Mic 2–3.

blame, for a start, Jerusalem's expansion, the creation of JE, Deuteronomy, literary prophecy, *and* the fragments of northern dialect in biblical texts. I confess to intuitive skepticism about a cultural *Putsch* by shards of a shattered world, but the court had a voracious need for agriculturalists. Accordingly, Deuteronomy welcomes all Israelites to the assembly (*qhl yhwh*), delaying absorption only of those attached to neighboring territorial states (in Giorgio Buccellati's terminology).[150]

Of special interest here is a seventh-century proliferation of farming villages and farmsteads on Judah's northern by-ways, presumably incorporating deportees. Avraham Faust robustly links these estates and communes to Jerusalem's burgeoning appetite.[151] Massive oil production hubs at Ekron and Bet Shemesh also testify to intensification in the Judean hills, with facilities to convert the value into silver. Both of these projects presupposed Assyria's peace. Hezekiah and Manasseh, benefiting from Sennacherib's rural policy, transformed Judah into a city-state, wringing rent from its resources.[152]

State capitalism in a backward country is capitalism doubly backward. Success required integrating new trans-national networks. So, venturing outward into a Wallensteinian world system,[153] Jerusalem extended its internal reach. Rebuilt towns, like Beersheba and Lachish, reflect regimentation. In embracing modern agrarian policy, Judah contracted the pest of unremitting oversight reflected in Deuteronomy.[154]

Judah's ambition expresses itself in the publication of JE, conceivably for Hezekiah's uprising, but preserved and propagated under Manasseh for related purposes. Judah's cross-border appeal alternately rejected other cult manifestations of Yhwh and identified them with "Yhwh Sebaoth, resident on Mt. Zion" (Isa 8:18) or Shechem's "Yhwh, God of Israel." Yhwh had rejected Israel in favor of Judah, based on either its objects or its modes of worship. Sargon proved it by deporting Yhwh of Samaria.[155] Yet, competition remained from an autochthonous Samarian cult: as Gary N. Knoppers saw, Deuteronomy's primary contrast is between the two Yhwhs.[156] So Isaiah emphasizes that Yhwh intervenes

---

150 Deut 23:2–9; for the term, Buccellati, *Cities and Nations*.

151 Faust, "Impact"; further, *Judah*, 39–48, 160–62.

152 For a summation of centralization and the city-state, see Hansen, "Introduction," 19. Na'aman, ("Distribution," 172) introduces the apt comparison here.

153 Wallenstein, *Modern World-System*; Hopkins and Wallenstein, *World Systems Analysis*.

154 See Dion, "Deuteronomy 13."

155 Not Jeroboam's calves. Logic and Judg 18:30–31 and 2 Kgs 15:29 (but cf. 1 Kgs 15:20 with Dan on the same geographical horizon) suggest Tiglath-Pileser wound up with Dan's calf. Hos 10:5 implies Shalmaneser took Bethel's in the 724–722 BCE window.

156 Knoppers ("Northern Context") places the competition in a different setting.

not for Israel, but only for Judah: he inspires the myth of miraculous rescue from Assyria by passing off a payoff as God's deliverance (31:8), conveniently reinforcing Sennacherib's lies about Egyptian ineffectiveness in the battle of Eltekeh (1 Kgs 18–19). His contrast between the kingdoms' standing is not just self-congratulatory. Isaiah was promoting Yhwh in Zion.

The same contrast is a consistent motif in all the eighth-century prophets – Isaiah, Hosea, Amos, and Micah. The collection was published as a compendium.[157] It not only promises restoration through Zion; it traces Israel's fall to universal failings of politicians – irredeemable corruption compounded by ignorant arrogance; Isaiah presents Judah, in contrast, as prudent. The collection also treats cultic devotions in Israel and later in Judah's hinterland as nothing more than a cloak for worm-ridden rot. Yhwh, Hezekiah, and Assyria had bulldozed the pollution of generations. Isaiah and Manasseh sealed the rubble.

In materials from before 701 BCE, Israel's remnant includes both survivors of Assyrian deportation and Judah itself. This evolved in later rhetoric into a fuller identity of the two. But skirmishing with Yhwh of Samaria – or a successor manifestation perhaps – persisted. Prestige was the coin for attracting custom, and custom the currency of advancement. The realms of competition were those of healing, political prophecy, and the prestige of antiquity.

How rewarding oracles and petitions could be is inscribed in Classical history and framed on a thousand dedications. Elisha, the centerpiece in promoting Yhwh of Samaria under the Nimshides, was active in all three realms. The healing of the leper, Naaman, garners a highly-placed proselyte and stresses that Elisha is not in it for the money. The first cure by Yhwh of Zion in our literature comes when Isaiah outdoes Joshua at Gibeon by reversing time! Amid signs to Ahaz, sympathetic prophecy, and reminders of wonders at Gibeon and against Midian, Isaiah's "numen show" climaxes with death angels in Assyria's camp. These elements combine with sage political analyses and forecasts in the prophetic collection and, importantly, a concern for justice, all in service of Manasseh's program.

Manasseh's policies also left relevant territorial legacies. His intensified Negev settlement and fortification probably started with Israelites and Judahites; prosperity attracted new card-carriers.[158] When he recovered the Shephelah is unknown, but this came about by ca. 670 BCE, and more likely before.[159] Along the belt north of Jerusalem, too, the political border is unknown.

---

157 Freedman, "Headings," pursued in Halpern. "Sybil," 311–12, 334–35, n. 115.

158 See, however, Thareani-Sussely, "'Archaeology of Days of Manasseh'"; and, on the other hand, "Forces."

159 Ashkelon's rehabilitation comes before 690 BCE, when Sennacherib's inscriptions include it as a beneficiary of the campaign against Hezekiah. Leniency at Manasseh's accession or in

In 724–720, taking a maximal view of Israelite territory, Shalmaneser or Sargon gradually extended control to southern Benjamin, "flashing his hand at the (MT:) temple mount of Zion" while looking to Egypt. Isaiah 10 most naturally describes Assyrian dispositions at the border.[160]

Who was farming Benjamin? Possibly, Judahites and Benjaminites sheltered in Jerusalem in 701. Others may have been Assyrian transplants.[161] Refugees eventually abounded as hirelings. At some point, the Assyrian administration may even have put the territory at Jerusalem's disposal to support retooling. Its denizens, like Judah, were bound by Esarhaddon's pledge of allegiance. Isaiah (10:20) thought they could be induced to join the polity of Jerusalem. They are a primary object of social rhetoric for a century from 724 BCE.

Manasseh colors all over Deuteronomy. The book's society fits the seventh-century landscape, its reconfiguration for increased land use, and less architectural articulation of kinship in the towns. To this we may add the treatment of Levi: in Manasseh's regimen, Levites were apparently *assigned* by kings to localities (2 Kgs 23:8); depots like those at Moza, Arnona, and Ramat Rahel were designated for tithe delivery. And Assyrian influence is pervasive: Egyptophobia; the nomenclature for legal procedure (Deut 12:15; 17:4); the adoption of the "gates"-terminology, perhaps especially pertinent to millet-system colonies, or, in Judah, to incorporating Judahite, Israelite, southern and other transplants as farm communities. The specific curses of Deuteronomy 28, artifacts of an oath (*'ālâ*) of loyalty to the state, are shaped by the example of Esarhaddon in 672 BCE. The influence of Esarhaddon's curse on ancestors' remains permeates Josiah's propaganda.[162] It must have registered under Manasseh.

---

time through the offices of the pro-Assyrian Isaiah (the 701-campaign excepted) is possible; we should imagine occasional skirmishes over installations, especially in the central and southern Shephelah. For the Shephelah settlement, see Finkelstein and Na'aman, "Archaeology"; Faust, *Judah*.

160 In Isa 10:24–32, Assyria "strikes" Judah with a stick (v. 24) to restrain interference either in the march to Gaza in 734 BCE or the encounter at Raphia in 720 (the blow is sharper in 701; Mic 4:14). The passage is most often linked to 701, but see the more plausible approach in de Jong, "Window"; "From Legitimate King." At Nob, the march halts, though there is daylight left, to display an emblem (*yĕnōpēp yādô*) visible at Zion.

161 E. Axel Knauf and Philippe Guillaume rightly see the development of Benjamin as an eighth-century phenomenon, which they attribute to Israelites withdrawing southward; regardless of admixtures by residential zone, provincial authorities regulated settlement well into Asshurbanipal's reign (*History*, 110–11).

162 Above, n.131. Here again, Deuteronomy adapts a source, this time by transposition: in Esarhaddon's curse, the children grind parents' bone meal, whereas in Deut 28:53–55, parents eat children's flesh.

Starting with Hezekiah certainly, kings circumscribed clans' autonomy. They devalued association symbols – especially of clans and phratries. Contrary to the First Commandment, these stood between Yhwh and the folk.[163] Few clans survived 701 intact, when mass displacement outmoded existing administrative genealogies. How far Manasseh renewed the trappings of traditional religion inside Judah we cannot say. One would expect marks of royal presence on recovered and new lands. And, among whatever descent groups survived, Josiah withdrew earlier subventions for public activity.

Even if Deuteronomy has no pre-Josianic literary core, all the structural elements it describes and its deeper agenda of recruiting labor and promoting horticultural development reflect conditions obtaining through most of the seventh century. Even if first inscribed in Josiah's time, Deuteronomy codifies much established thought and practice.

6.3 The Josianic Element

The wording may be Josiah's. In fact, other than the CC and Esarhaddon's succession oaths, Deuteronomy's most influential sources may be bureaucratic jargon and royal rescripts. Peculiarities distinguish the guiding hand: distinctive deployment of paragogic *nun*; distinctive technical diction; an assortment of divine epithets marked by purposeful monotony; and the consistency of Moses's speaking voice, which Eleanore Reuter has shown is integral to the work.[164]

Multiple superficial indices point to Josiah's men. The provisions for ratification bookend with Josiah's covenant convention.[165] The text digresses in 12:29–31 (and 18:10) to ban child immolation, suppressed only by Josiah. Isaiah and Micah refer to the practice without censure as late as 701 BCE.[166]

---

163 The Hebrew of "You shall have no other gods before me" is *lōʾ yihyeʰ lĕkā ʾĕlōhîm ʾăḥērîm ʿal pānāy*: literally, "there will not be for you another god ahead of me." In D, compare the law prohibiting a father from awarding the prime inheritance to a second son *ʿl pny* the firstborn. Physically, a subject *ʿl pny* is interposed between a viewer's eye and the object of the compound.

164 Reuter (*Kultzentralisation*) demonstrates that Moses's voice is original to the composition. It follows that the reform report withholds Moses's name until 2 Kgs 23:25 as a revelation that, for those in the know, fulfills a suspended expectation, along the lines of the revelation of Jonathan's name in Judg 18, among other instances.

165 Deut 29:9–14; 30:11–20 (the immediate imposition); 31:9–13 > Josh 8:35// > 2 Kgs 23:1–3.

166 Isa 30:33; Mic 6:7. Cf. Hos 13:2, a criticism of "sacrificers of humans" for propagating herds. For earlier endorsements in E and Judges, see Walls, "Israel's Pagan Passover."

The Law of the King (Deut 17:14–20), which retrojects Isaiah's strictures on diplomatic relations with Egypt (Isa 31:1), insinuates a negative image of Solomon, the villain of both Josiah and the Dtr. Solomon's pharaonic alliance also intersects with Deuteronomy's antipathy to Egypt. Conceivably, Deuteronomy's ratification at Shechem (Deut 27; Josh 8; 24) evokes Israel's revolt. In scapegoating Solomon for the schism, DtrH concurs.[167] Connections to David are more positive: the ideal of Israel at the Euphrates leads *only* to Dtr's David;[168] likewise, the characterization of wilderness tenants (29:9–10) as woodchoppers recalls David's metic Hivite allies (Josh 9) against Saul.

Deuteronomy conditions centralization on rest (12:9–10). In DtrH, repose produces Solomon's temple. Its previous absence excuses Israel's *bāmôt* (1 Kgs 3:2–4). With the temple's completion, Kings refers to Jerusalem's choice as place.[169] Before, for Dtr, *places* are not illegitimate, just accoutrements and gods, or we would hear huffing about *bāmôt* as well as baals in Judges-Samuel.

Only the Rab-Shakeh (1 Kgs 18:22) defines Jerusalem's franchise as exclusive. Kings assumes it throughout:[170] *given* the temple, Solomon's *bāmôt* precipitated trouble, Israel's revolt, and more *bāmôt*. Only Josiah's reform erases Jeroboam's schismatic cult at Bethel *and throughout Israel*. Solomon is a historical-moral coupling between Josiah and Deuteronomy.

Josiah's part in our document is extensive. An abiding consensus acknowledges Deuteronomy's organization around "centralization."[171] To be fair, Deuteronomy's revisions to the CC entail minute accommodations, like securing septennial release by precluding discounted loans.[172] Overall, the book, with

167 See Wazzana, "Law of King," 180–82. The diagnostic feature here is wives (1 Kgs 11:1–3), not wealth (Knoppers, "Rethinking") or horse-trading (Isa 31:1), but all three contribute to the composite image.

168 Deut 1:7; 11:22–25; Josh 1:4, 7; these views derive from conventional, not contextual, interpretation of "the river" (2 Sam 8:3; Solomon in 1 Kgs 5:1,4; for the history, see Halpern, *David's Demons*, 243–59).

169 As though there had not previously been one in 2 Sam 7:7 > 1 Kgs 8:16. For Solomon as referent of the rest motif in Deut, see Paton, "Case for Post-Exilic Origin"; Levinson, *Hermeneutics*, 41–45.

170 Kgs connects the words "elect(ed) from all your tribes" to the temple, the schism, Manasseh, and Josiah. The invocation of the schism (1 Kgs 11, 4 times; 14:21) links it to Josianic scaffolding in Kgs, though like the fief formula, it may be a post-Josianic artifact. The others "Yhwh selected from all (Israel's) tribes" are a tribe (Deut 18:5) and priests (1 Sam 2:28). Cf. 2 Sam 10:9 for a parallel with multiple members in a chosen class.

171 Philologically exacting is Merendino, *Deuteronomische Gesetz*.

172 Deut 23:20–21 is a corollary of periodic debt release (15:1–3; 31:10). Cf. P's elaborate regulation of land value for the Jubilee and ban on interest (Lev 25:36–37 > Ezek 18:8–17; 22:12). Both traditions adapt Exod 22:24.

distinctive diction and divergent authorial and speaker's tones, evinces a uniform intellectual character as well.[173]

Deuteronomy has Hezekiah's and Manasseh's footprints all over it. But those we detect are the ones facing Josiah's way. Between Deuteronomy's draft, D622, and Josiah's reform report, a plausible narrative requires no significant interval.

6.4 *Josiah's Spoor*

It remains to consider Josiah's reform report with a view to Deuteronomy's application. Specific actions concern Jerusalem – as Yadin remarked when discovering Beersheba's altar in 2 Kings 23. Even the rescission of phratry priests' salary affects the Jerusalem district, as well as "towns of Judah" (23:5). It may include Solomon's befouled chapels (23:13–14). The only claims about Jerusalem's hinterlands, probably overlapping with these, are the collection of townships' priests and the pollution of *bāmôt*, where the priests made offerings, from Geba to Beersheba.

Read literally, 2 Kings 23:8 asserts that Josiah polluted two or more *bāmôt* in regions abutting the territories of Geba and Beersheba. Yet, it is not just difficult to find evidence of Josiah's cultic policy in seventh-century Judah, it is difficult to find any *public* cult. Second Kings 23:8 denominates an east Benjaminite town as Judah's northern border: reform in Jerusalem, after all, abuts Geba's district. Thus, in the genre, Solomon's *bāmôt* are singled out but count in the greater summary about profaning *bāmôt* from Geba to Beersheba. In light of this historiographic convention, which can be called the Tiglath-Pileser Principle after the king who raised it to an art form,[174] reform is less unbelievable than our impression of its comprehensiveness.

One site credibly connected with Josiah's reform often goes unmentioned. En Hazeva (Tamar) was a fort in the central Arabah. *Ca.* 650–580 BCE, authorities dug a pit inside an extramural building, depositing seven small altars (four miniature) and a plethora of paraphernalia, censers, incense stands, offering stands, some of which were anthropomorphic, one with a leonine mask, and vessel miniatures. Stelae lay on the building floor.[175]

---

173 For a review starting with Lohfink, *Hauptgebot*, see Otto, *Deuteronomium 1–4*, 146–85, to which add Reuter, *Kultzentralisation* on Deut as rediscovered autograph. Edelman's study in this volume demonstrates thoroughgoing adaptation to that context.

174 Halpern, *David's Secret Demons*, 116–18, 124–32.

175 See Cohen, "Fortresses"; Cohen and Israel, "Iron Age Fortresses"; Cohen and Israel, "Ein Hazeva"; "Excavations at 'Ein Hazeva," 83–85; Ben-Arieh, "Temple Furniture."

Ceramic and iconological parallels to Horvat Qitmit, an Edomite temple 45 km northwest, do not define ethnicity. Another extramural enclosure, in northern Moab, yielded similar items; the excavators suggested it serviced pastoral lineages.[176] Both sites may represent "house(s) [= precinct(s)] of high places" (*bêt bāmôt*), with altar service for several bands.[177] A Jordan Valley site, Tell Damiyah, features related contemporary icons.[178] Yifat Thareani makes a formidable case for Edomite ethnic affiliation.[179] At times, however, operative ethnic affinity transcends state jurisdictions. When states sweeten residence rules with preferential treatment, economic benefits flow from trade through a network exploiting licensed local affiliates. Thus, when clan names are shared among southern entities (Edom, Reuben, Judah, Levi) in Pentateuchal genealogies, odds are that those associations maintained a political presence across administrative boundaries.[180]

The En Hazeva shrine occupies a liminal location at the fort, in neutral space outside the king's town, on the models developed above.[181] The iconography has no martial overtone and owes nothing to the state. It reflects community among diverse regional elites. Sufficiently scrutinized, the materials reveal the reach of

---

176 For WT-13, see Dolan, "Site WT-13," adding use by travelers; for more on the comparison with En Hazeva, see Daviau, "Moab's Border"; "New Light." For an enlightening review of the ceramic analysis, see Jan Gunneweg and Marta Balla, "Provenience."

177 See Daviau, "Ḫirbet el-Mudēyine," 24–28; for WT-13's connection to descent groups, see Daviau, "Coroplastic," 6. The *bāmôt*-house might take the form of a building as at En Hazeva (or Lachish III, below). A further complex near a settlement has been recognized as a *bāmôt*-house at eighth-century Tel Nagila (Itzik Shai, *et al.* "Tel Nagila," 39). One structure was a hall with a betyl; the other was involved with food and possibly food service. The suggestion raises the question of the functional relationship between the *bāmôt*-house and the *marzēăḥ*-house. More often, the *bāmôt*-house is probably an enclosure, as in the cases of WT-13, al-Burnat, Dan, and, probably the "bull-site." How such installations service multiple clan associations may vary, and here, as with the temple, both the building and the precinct/compound are probably referents for Hebrew *byt (bmwt).*

178 Petit and Kafafi, "Beyond River Jordan."

179 Thareani, "Forces," esp. 212–14.

180 Earlier, compare the territorial Gad as Moabite in Mesha (attributed to Manfred Weippert, in seminar, by Ernst Axel Knauf, in correspondence) or Israelite (JEP, etc.). Cases of such shared clan names include in P's Edomite list (Gen 36:2–30) alone, Qorah, Kenaz, and Zerah. The systematic Edom is seventh century, and these entities in close proximity seem to be descent-groups on both sides. Surely, we would see a similar situation in Moab; P, of course, divides Edom, too, into two "ethne" (presumably, sedentary/enclosed nomad).

181 As a caveat, texts apply the term *bāmôt* to a variety of installations, depending on context. The lineage *bāmôt* seem mainly to be extramural. Some are more distant from a town (WT-13; al-Burnat) than others, reducing urban control of caucuses and rallies. Those by (En Hazeva, Beth Saida) or inside a gate (Beth Saida, Dan; perhaps Megiddo IVA, Lachish III, and similar enclosures "between the gates") reflect greater concentration around the fortification.

patriclans, and their dispositions, forms, and decoration probably distinguish among those clans.[182] Highland Judean traditions mark most of the table service and storage vessels in the fort. But the cooking pots, as often in the region, come from east of the Ghor, and the cult vessels from the Beersheba Valley: the culinary practice suggests distant solidarity, the cult regional solidarity.[183] Whatever else it represents – comparison to icon burial by Jacob spawns ruminations – the favissa at En Hazeva reflects and indicates that Kings' "*bāmôt* of gates" reflect an atavistic, non-state, self-organizing fellowship, i.e. the base observance of descent groups.[184]

The excavators tie the religious change at En Hazeva to Josiah.[185] The case does not involve a state altar, as at Beersheba, Arad, or Moza. Its closer affinity to the Lachish III inner gate room implies the latter was a repository for phratry gear, disarranged by Assyrian looters after the denizens were removed. Thus, miniature altars in Beersheba II residences remain: their styles vary by city quarter.[186] This, too, reflects different affiliations inside Deuteronomy's "gates." Civil practices and paraphernalia were not targets.

Similarly, Michèle Daviau has reported 28 limestone altars at Mudeyine: in the concentration, it is reasonable to see the rural population and especially small pastoral bands sheltering in the fortified city and bringing their lineage vessels and sacraments along, a phenomenon *not* witnessed, apparently, in Hezekiah's forts. But it is as likely that the Mudeyine town temple compound furnished a repository when these implements were not being unnecessarily transported.[187]

182 As Wolfgang Zwickel points out for "snake-house" model shrines and implies for others ("World of Cult Stands," 180, 186). In conversation (7/20), Blanche Harrup jested that the Qeiyafa model shrine's "binding" holes (Zwickel, fig. 14.30) relate to Samson's story.

183 Gunneweg and Balla, "Provenience"; Weinberger, "Provenance"; Thareani, "Forces," 213. The eastern cooking pot fabric I presume imparted a traditional flavor. At any entry to a new ancestral territory, it is conceivable that even strangers paid respect to the neighborhood gang's totems.

184 On reflexes of state versus non-state ("non-conformist") practice, see esp. Holladay, "Religion." Here, aspects of the objects may symbolize the clan. Yifat Thareani documents extramural remains from Beersheba to Mampshit as Bedouin markets ("Forces," 212), although fairs coincided mainly with other ceremonies. For the latter, see Franklin, "Entering the Arena," 97–99; reference in n. 50. Regardless, WT-13 and En Hazeva differ in attesting groups that had put down stakes, as members of the local economy.

185 Cohen and Israel, "Excavations," 83–85, with a questionable judgment that the objects were deliberately smashed, since they date both the building and the favissa to Stratum IV.

186 See the discussion with illustrations in Ziffer, "Altars and Art"; for the cube inscribed "priest" in South Arabian, see Bron, "South Arabian Inscription."

187 Still less likely is that the town enforced centralization. For the count, see Daviau, "Diversity in Cult," 440 and her general discussion of sites there.

The moveable kit at En Hazeva and WT-13 (the latter, a compound where kin-communities celebrated side-by-side, as at al-Burnat) evokes Hosea's bugbears.[188] Logically, we should imagine the gear set out at a nearby shade tree, preferably on a rise with an evening breeze; there, sacrifice on the CC-compliant temporary altars led to drinking and a meal in a pavilion, sometimes perhaps the *bāmôt*-precinct structure. The complex elucidates cities of refuge: *bāmôt* provided no haven, because *bamôt* were only occasional. Sometimes their phratry altars stood, perhaps fixed, at a center. Some may have been carried farther afield. But the Lachish gate chamber, a temporary storehouse for phratries' gear associated with the local "house of *bāmôt*," was not itself a place of animal sacrifice; neither was the structure at En Hazeva.[189]

Though the Mudeyine temple and Lachish gate, under state supervision, can hold a combination of implements, the *bāmôt*-compound is any area or structure, including an enclosure, where multiple kinship associations can celebrate. These invite lineage spirits and provide fare of their choice, each at its own station because each at its own cost. They do so, however, in a common location either together or severally, even on a nearby slope.

The temenos of the small altar for expanded family offerings must, however, be supplemented by temporary structures for animals. Their temenos can also serve the phratry, even the clan, repetitively or not. A *bāmâ* in the Reform report is where a phratry, clan, or township holds solemn assembly.[190]

The gear from these contexts does not scream "royal." Whether we consider it "foreign" depends more on our own categories than on historical ones. But the candidate sites for suppressed *bāmôt* – only En Hazeva in Josiah's case – and the three for altars, are all on Judah's edges. We remain uncertain to what degree Hezekiah left and Josiah persecuted "heterodoxy" in Judah's heartland. After his death, Jeremiah frowns even on Deuteronomy's parish altars (11:13). The alternatives are, however, indicated by the last movement of Josiah's reform.

7 Josiah's True North

Special orientation comes from the Reform report's crescendos: Solomon's high places and Bethel both were defiled with disinterred human remains. The elabo-

188 Esp. Hos 4:10, which Jer and Ezek cite.

189 Hemoglobin assays of the floors' makeup would adequately test this proposition.

190 The larger *bāmâ* at Bethel involves a constructed (*bnh*) feature, and that at Gibeon (1 Kings 3:4) should also be capacious, and extramural: these, like Jerusalem in Mic 1:5, host larger crowds.

rate forewarning about Bethel, with destruction and details about grave desecration,[191] stands in for a whirlwind cleansing of all Samaria by township. This campaign is portrayed not as a military but as a legal action, within the king's jurisdiction. Josiah invades Samaria, and Deuteronomy gives him legal cover.

When did this northern campaign occur? The grouping of specifics around Jerusalem suggests the report focuses on the king's proximity or autopsy, rather than sequence. By the time of Josiah's accession, Assyrian control in the west was waning. A few cuneiform tablets attest to the persistence of a provincial framework. But Manasseh, probably and Josiah's tutors, surely, were anticipating Assyria's decline by the 640s BCE. In the 630s, they transitioned from fantasy to planning.

Without adducing Chronicles, where reform begins in 632 BCE, it must have appeared by then that Samaria's government was hollow. Assyrian observances inspired tribal loyalty only in imperial representatives. The local territorial god was Yhwh, and Samerina underwrote its own, established form of Yhwh-worship – a point Kings minimizes. But Jerusalem had positioned itself as Yhwh's home residence since 720 BCE. Isaiah 18:7 calls it "the place of the name of Yhwh who resides in Zion"; Jerusalem had cultivated interest to the north, especially in Benjamin. As Assyria faded, Samaria was a natural temptation.

A half-century ago, scholars "usually" connected Josiah's northern revanche to Deuteronomy's provisions for Yhwh's "broadening" the land (12:20–27).[192] The connection applies to all of D622. The reform report says that Josiah "gathered all the elders of Judah and Jerusalem"; these lead to the temple "every citizen of Judah and the inhabitants of Jerusalem and the priests and the prophets and the whole folk" to enact the law-code (2 Kgs 23:1–3). Before he could impose it on Israel or Samaria, Josiah wanted backing from core stakeholders.

The DtrH sets the stage for Josiah early. First Kings 12:31 traces "house(s) of *bāmôt*" to Jeroboam, "in *Samaria*'s towns" (13:32), a phrase associated *only* with Jeroboam, the transplants, and Josiah. Samaria is elsewhere a city, not Israel. But Samaria, the Assyrian province, is where Josiah undid Jeroboam's arrangements. The Dtr claims Jeroboam recognized township phratries and provided them with sacred clubhouses. Priests at these state institutions, not recognized

---

191 The unnamed "man of God" denouncing Bethel (1 Kgs 13; 2 Kgs 23) is modeled on Amos, who also prophesied against the altar of Jeroboam (II); see Halpern, *First Historians*, 248–54. Note that Amos is refused the festival meal and told to celebrate in Judah, as in David's ostracism, to "serve another god." This is why the man of God can defy the divine injunction of 1 Kgs 13 against eating in Bethel: he believes it applied only to sanctified table fellowship.

192 So von Rad, *Deuteronomium* 67; subsequent citations in Levinson, *Hermeneutics*, 39, n. 33.

by Dtr as Levites, are phratry dignitaries both under Jeroboam and under Assyria (1 Kgs 12:31; 13:33; 2 Kgs 17:32).

Second Kings 17 picks up the thread: *bāmôt* marred every hamlet with regalia on hills and under trees (17:9–10). For mimicking those whom Yhwh "exiled" to make way for them (17:8, 11), Israel was in turn replaced by communities of diverse origin. These had guidance for placating Yhwh from a provincially-licensed priesthood at Bethel (17:24–29). The new communities made devotions to Yhwh and installed their respective ethnic gods (not state emblems) in towns' *bāmôt*-houses (17:29–33).

Second Kings 17:9, 29 establish that Assyria's settlers reuse Israel's civic *bāmôt*-houses. That they retain their own gods there alongside Yhwh "to this day" (17:34) occasions Josiah's destruction of the installations (23:19–20). Reform hagiography, unable to claim Josiah ground Bethel's calf to dust (Exod 32:20; Deut 9:21), has him instead do so to the altar and perhaps the *temenos* at Jeroboam's *bāmâ* (23:15). To reach Jeroboam's non-Levitic and idolatrous priests, he disinters them and burns their bone on the ravaged altar. And, he takes the performance to *bāmôt*-houses throughout Samaria.

Practically, Josiah's action repudiates Samarina's land registry: the discredited icons were the guarantors of descent lines. Deuteronomy smiles on appropriating fields, houses and towns (as Deut 6:10–11; 19:1; Josh 24:13), necessary for land reform already in Manasseh's Judah.

In the myth, Josiah undoes not just the sin by which Solomon divided Israel but those by which Jeroboam precipitated Israel's downfall. Kings goes even farther, advancing the myth of a revived Davidic Israel in Isaiah and Micah. Assyria's transplants should have assimilated and forsworn tribal gods. Their superstition, it claims, persists "to this day." Josiah's campaigns imposed the right myth on Samaria's towns. Cultivating Israelite identity in Samaria went from being a longstanding aspiration to a present assimilative strategy.[193] Not coincidentally, the main and perhaps only oracle Jeremiah places in Josiah's day starts by calling on Israel to rejoin Yhwh in Zion (Jer 3:6–4:2).

The transplants cling to old, foreign gods "to this day" in 2 Kings 17:34 because the *reconquista* remained a work in progress: the ongoing reform, as Cromwell's New Model Army would have seen it, probably continued in the north to 609 BCE. That is when Necho spiked the dream of a resurrected Israel, inducing theological nightmares.

Pacifying Samaria involved making new Israelites. Josiah promoted a cartoonish vision of public observances stripped of all local identity. Local Yhwh

193 For an alternative understanding of these events and the origin of Deuteronomy, see Davies in this volume.

manifestations had posed no problem for Hosea: the danger arises when they emblematize competing polities. But an alien influx obscures perceptions of polity and clan gods. The optics demand that Josiah suppress cultic display.

But the primary agenda of Deuteronomy and Josiah is *unity*.[194] Strictures on Israel apply to Judah. Here, Josiah outdoes Hezekiah: Hezekiah, we infer, had revised Judah's landscape, including some fleeting *bāmôt* and major shrines. Later, as at En Hazeva IV, new phratry shrines may have emerged. But Josiah broadened reform to include Israel.

Here is part of the explanation for ambiguity in Deuteronomy. The law-code has at least two arenas of application. Samaria is an ethnically-tessellated area, under foreign control, where Josiah's candidate for common allegiance is the established territorial god. The Benjaminite plateau alone was a prize that probably was not yet in Jerusalem's paws.[195] The other arena is a Judah long since disciplined to state entrepreneurship. A third may lie to Judah's southeast, where pastoralist populations enjoyed less confined networks, adaptable enough to have turned Edomite soon after, a fourth conceivably along the coast north of Ashdod.

The populations enjoy common standing: one law governs all residents. What difference the law makes to practice and how it is administered vary from case to case. The gear at En Hazeva registers respectful interment, like Arad's decommissioning. And the miniature altars in the Beersheba quarters might even suggest ongoing feasting at *bāmôt* in the absence of a civic cult center. Deuteronomy acknowledges the reality, even the legality, of earlier local practice. The Dtr memorializes state clerics in hinterland shrines (2 Kgs 23:5; 1 Kgs 12:31). The logic was familiar: kings, region-wide, patronized multiple cult establishments. Though renounced, the past retired gracefully. Differently put, the Deuteronomy that acknowledges offerings to the dead excluded some symbolic activities from civic regulation. The reform is not unattested: it is what we see in the ground.

The law-code best suits Josiah's plans for Samaria and his ambitions beyond. The loyalty oath was familiar to elites and levees, broadly. In practice, part of the appeal was to provincial administrators. This would explain why, by the author's choice, Deuteronomy 13 and 28 ring with Assyrian *intellectual* models from the cultural universe of Esarhaddon's oath.[196] The lawgiver's reap-

194 As Harold Bennett reminded me, in conversation, 2/20.

195 See recently Gadot *et al*, "What Kind" for the more probable scenario that Benjamin remained part of Samerina.

196 For the texts, see Lauinger, "Treaty, Oath, or Something Else?"; Ponchia, "*adê* Protocol and Administration"; Watanabe, "Innovations"; "Adoration of Oath Documents." Diana Edelman makes it plain that scholars' etiologies for elements shared by Deut and Esarhaddon's

propriations obscure uncited sources on casual consideration: the borrowing is of the genre, of ideas and their organization, a source for reappropriation, not reuse. Likewise, the curse targeting ancestors' bones, introduced by Esarhaddon, is absent from Deuteronomy 28 but enacted, somewhat transformed, in the Reform report.

Officials would relate to these segments in Deuteronomy as a benign variant on the same form. Like Esarhaddon's oath, Deuteronomy is administered at home *and* abroad. The adoption of the sacralized oath, bizarrely, preserves legal forms; in Esarhaddon's case, the instrument itself was divinized. Likewise, the "gates" terminology, applied as in Mesopotamian practice to both communities and built environments, adapts existing organization. Instruments of control leap out at us as limits on sacrifice, assembly, and local authorities. The concern with "other gods" and icons forecloses on fealty to other powers. The attack on the *bāmôt*, rhetorically linked to "other gods," blunts ethnic divisions of which colonial awareness probably ran high.[197] Applied to Samaria, Deuteronomy demands that all signs of a different identity be torn down, shattered, and burnt (cf. Gen 34!), though Josiah was far gentler at En Hazeva.

Even more telling are Deuteronomy's inducements. Here, ambiguous ecclesiastical arrangements play a role. The context dictates interpretation: Deuteronomy gives "Levites" staff privileges to squire clan-sectors to the place. Josiah, centralizing, *reassigns* "priests" there, not "Levites," deferring to D622. Second Kings 23:8 avoids reporting that relocation was forcible for the same reason, though collecting opinion-makers encourages conformity. In practice, too, Deuteronomy's slogans and formulae were adapted in different environments. The same may hold for licensing places inside and outside Israel's territory.

Ambiguity, the midwife of compromise, assured latitude to the crown and thus to Judah's elders. That Josiah sought consent for such magnanimity toward Samarians confirms that the ambiguity is directed to Judahite landowners. Thucydides would represent his submission eloquently, especially since Deuterono-

---

oath are overwrought, to defend, I suspect, against her position that the curses addressing like objects and the apostasy provisions derive (on both sides) from common contractual traditions of the time. She is surely right that the lawgiver's intent was to create his own arrangement, and to do so, drew on exemplars of the genre in which he was interested at the time. He drew, in fact, from various genres, legal ones and others ("Saying Goodbye"). His creativity can be seen in the division of 17:2–7 from Deut 13. But the choice of specific curse subjects from those traditions, in a cluster congruent with a cluster in the oath text, makes a relationship, direct or not, probable. Esarhaddon's loyalty oath was an iconic, public implement preserved and likely imposed under Assurbanipal among Assyrian citizens throughout the region. Awareness of it in Jerusalem, especially given elite collaborationists in Samaria, would be unsurprising.

197 For a useful comparison, see Prieto, *Forma Fenicia*.

my fuses justifications to social commentary to rules, in a way anticipating Ionian natural philosophy. Especially for recruiting allies in the north, Josiah sought backing in Judah.

Some inducements therefore naturally apply to Judah, as well as the north. Most of Deuteronomy 23:16–24:22 addresses issues concerning the deprived. Tenants deserve justice and dignity, though credit only against labor. Citizen privileges have material benefits. Limits on bond-service appeal to marginal lineages.[198] Septennial loan forgiveness is related. It is in the year of the release that Moses's torah is publicly recited. The coincidence is as substantial as it is symbolic (31:10–13), making the release a headline provision.

The rhetoric caparisoning the social program has a long history, of course, because it has a practical side. Deuteronomy is cushioning agrarian failure.[199] Its aim, a land rush, probably repeats an earlier experiment in Judah.

The policy promoting agricultural expansion and intensification was an inducement to seek citizenship: this would explain why the qualification "your brother" is added to the term, "Hebrew," when the slave release is adapted from CC. The rabbinic understanding of "Hebrew" as displaced person seems particularly apt for Samarians. And thus, struggling lineages are promised relief from debt-service. Small wonder that the slave in Deuteronomy seems not to be Israelite.[200] Such inducements now mainly faced northward, extending the reclamation Isaiah and Micah both foresaw. Further, Josiah targets the repositories of land claims, ancestral tombs, and the *bāmôt*-houses of the collectives in whom title to land was vested. He presumably repudiates provincial land-tenure and re-imposes Israel's traditional registry (preserved in P).[201]

We lack specifics on the campaign's progress. Still, Deuteronomy *morally equates Israel's deportation with its predecessors' extinction.* The Dtr adds historical comparison. In expecting adherence to the reformed Yhwh, Kings *includes Samaria's population in Israel.* It dangles a promise of god-given fields and even prefabricated houses (Deut 6:10; 19:2; Josh 24:13!) for extirpating signs of identity, especially alternative tribal loyalties as Sepharvaimites and so on, the only stable alternatives to Judah's Israel.

Deuteronomy 29:10 refers to tenants, in the camp, as woodchoppers and water-drawers, the same tenants who attend its recitation. The expression delib-

---

198 Deut 15:12–18 < Exod 21:2–10, but adding the qualification "brother" to the source. Hence, traditionally, "Hebrew" denotes displacement.

199 For the logic and operation of release, see Guillaume, *Land, Credit and Crisis*, 210–22.

200 Rossi and Guillaume, "Law of Hebrew Slave."

201 The same historical context generates the (administrative) geography in Joshua and perhaps P's clan genealogies.

erately invites comparison to the Gibeonites, whom Joshua incorporated as concessionaires at sacred assemblies (Josh 9:21–27). Tacitly, b. Yebamot 47b makes the connection to the Samarians: Moses's tenants "were holding onto their former ways," a phrase echoing Kings.[202] The nod to "Hivite" Gibeon, and thus Benjamin, invites revised appreciation of Jacob's land purchase and burial of gods (E, Gen 33; 35) and of Joseph's burial at Hivite Shechem, versus the warfare there depicted in J (Gen 34) and Judges 9. Long-integrated aboriginals furnish a model for recent arrivals, and for the body politic absorbing them. Those who remain insular do not fare as well as those incorporated in Jerusalem's reconditioned administrative genealogy.

Related to conflict as well is denying recognition to neighboring polities by sheltering runaway slaves, "Hebrew" or not (23:16–17). Even if this includes other regimes, it most immediately addressed defection in Samaria itself.

Deference to Samarian and to Israelite sensibilities is delicate and complex. So, reformists vilify the bogeyman Solomon, mainly by insinuation (including comparing Josiah's Passover to Joshua's); even symbolic concessions, however, were uncomfortable for Jerusalemite priesthoods.[203] Similarly, Deuteronomy takes expansion into account directly, but also in its specific provisions for acquired citizenship and its intellectual relationship to P.[204] Pondering these and similar aspects confirms the fruitfulness of an institutional approach and of the hypothesis. Here, one further complex of rhetoric and regulation stands in for the rest.

Scholars perennially ask why Josiah would saddle himself with the law of the King. The present approach furnishes context. The statute insinuates derision of Solomon. It also singles out traffic with Egypt, gesturing toward Solomon again. But this element has a practical side: Egypt was the sponsor of Josiah's competitors in Samaria and neighboring zones.[205]

Deuteronomy's most appealing feature is that it ***fixes** taxes*: their predictability serves economic development. The document also peddles a moderate, small government. The rhetoric is not entirely empty: royal self-indulgence

---

202 *ʾwḥzyn mʿśyhm hrʾšnym*; 2 Kgs 17:34, 40 *ʿśym + kmšpṭ(ym) hrʾšwn(ym).*

203 Did the Dtr insert fulfilment of the Judges's rest-motif at 2 Sam 7:1 to pre-empt the claim for Solomon? Josiah also outdoes David in 2 Kgs 23:21–25.

204 Two minuses in 12:20–28 illuminate the coexistence of sacrificial institutions after reform. Nothing is said of bringing Levites along. And, against both 12:5 and 12:14, the place that Yhwh chooses is not "from all/any" or "in one/any of your tribes." The following correspondences are tantalizing: "from one": 2 Sam 7:7; Deut 12:14; and "from all of your tribes": 1 Kgs 8:18, 44, 48; Deut 12:5. For P, provisions for land tenure and Levitical cities are crucial diagnostics.

205 A commitment to effacing Hezekiah's disastrous dalliance with Egypt registers in both Isaiah and Kings.

made lousy optics. But Deuteronomy's restrictions are not absolute, except the king's subjection to the torah. The rhetoric exploits vagueness, not ambiguity. Yet Deuteronomy is anything but vague about making its ethic of modesty a campaign plank.

Simultaneously, the reform report stresses violence against Samarian *bāmôt*-houses (2 Kgs 23:13–20), in contrast to Arad, En Hazeva, and Josiah's relatively mild "polluting" of Judah's *bāmôt* (23:8). Bethel and its seminary incarnated Yhwh's endorsement of Israel (with Gen 28). Undoing the Machiavellian arithmetic of Jeroboam's *native* heresy called for theatrics: it was chiefly symbolic, even as a statement of even-handedness. Josiah's action announced that he was not just the enemy of clan *bāmôt* or of transplanted divinities. He was stripping the religion of civic identity to its basics. Reform was modest and above all, economical.

Johann Severin Vater briefly commented on Deuteronomy's incessant drumming on the land.[206] Under Josiah, land demands investment, as in the aftermath of 701 BCE. It is at the heart of the enterprise of reform, identity-redefinition, and the ethic of citizens' individual dignity as part of a single, unmediated collective. And reform is the price of citizenship. Residential cooperatives abjure otiose historical identities in all civic domains. The new dispensation frowns on distinctions in ornament. *Even the king, Citizen Josiah, regards his subjects as equals* (Deut 17:20).

The promise is of the rule of impartial law, based on an unchanging, public, written text. The system attracts entrepreneurs, the engine of the reform's success. Like any campaign promise, this one is disingenuous. But it is the worthiest heir of reform: from the idea of text as authority arises that of constitutional government.

Conclusion

An institutional history from Ahaz to Josiah might look, in all, as follows:

From 734–622 BCE, Jerusalem invested in developing its southern and eastern fringes. To the north and west, it appealed for the custom and trust of elements identifying as Israelite. After the cataclysm of 701, the crown accelerated earlier efforts to repopulate the Negev, exploit the Arabah, and recover western tracts. Above all, land redistribution was lucrative and essential to recruiting new subjects. Ambition, and perhaps the accounting of the Assyrian resident at Ramat

---

206 Vater, *Commentar*, 3.412.

Rahel,[207] dictated administrative reorganization. This led to the mixing of historical and contemporary models, including Assyrian, to adapt traditional power arrangements. In Judah's central planning, the township system of Joshua 15 played a role. The crown continued appointing Levites (*khnym*) and phratry bigwigs (*kmrym*) as officiants at township *bāmôt*-complexes. These appointees reported incoming tithes and firstlings.

Some of D622's provisions may have been abstracted from administrative directives and records from this period. However, though the lawgiver calls on the Covenant Code for authority, he so thoroughly revises the relevant sectors, as in the case of Yhwh's place and its various district offices (including the type, "house of Yhwh" or bearing the soubriquet, "Yhwh, Inc.") as to abolish it. That strategy of echoing CC while twisting its meaning, a commonplace in constitutional argument, suggests that no more useful basis for argument presented itself or that we must conduct our search for sources without the crutch of their hypothetical diction and coherence. If D622 had a forerunner other than CC, it is lost. Even though CC permeates Deuteronomy 12–25, we can no more reconstitute it from Deuteronomy than we can the Gilgamesh cycle from the Akkadian epic.[208] There is little hope of our identifying otherwise unknown sources.

By the 630s, mandarins in Jerusalem were debating policy regarding the province of Samerina. Their tactics encompassed both promoting a national identity and forceful annexation as Assyria shifted resources and personnel to the eastern front. The crown hoped to co-opt erstwhile Assyrian officialdom and to absorb transplants by persuading township leaders to suppress tribal identities. In the south, meanwhile, they aimed to consolidate and enlarge Manasseh's success, particularly by enticing pastoralists and traders into the fold.

D622 was a result of their deliberations. It fell heir to heritages from Judah, Israel, Assyria, and elsewhere. It is still pertinent today that Moses adjured Israel, on the brink of the Conquest in Cisjordan, to shed old ways and other loyalties expressed by collective sacraments: like Jacob burying icons at Shechem, we all come with ancestral baggage.

In this system, ethnicity is not for display: the state limits public religion, and with it treasury funding, to one national god. So D622, as a program for integrating Samaria or Edomites and fugitive Egyptians, was intended to mix together peoples and make them one, all with the same god. Assyrian bureau-

---

207 The explicit suggestion by Berlejung, "Assyrians in West," 23, cited by Edelman, "Saying Goodbye," ms. fn. 20), is the best explanation offered for Ramat Rahel's early layers (VB and VA).

208 A point brought forcefully home in the opening chapter of Tyler Kelley's Ph.D. dissertation on P, in progress at the University of Georgia.

crats would recognize the sentiment, just as they would relate to segments related to vassal treaties, loyalty oaths, and civic organization in the document. Edom, Egypt's proxy in competing for southern trade against Judah, also had had its Assyrian residents. Defectors from Edom and Egypt were welcomed; those from allied polities (Moab and Ammon) were refused.[209] And although D622 does not impede incorporating Samarians into the assembly, neither does it resolve their status as citizen or tenant, a contentious issue. Here, perhaps rules of war (Deut 20:10–20) have some relevance, though their application is again not transparent.

D622 was free with symbolic capital, but husbanded latitude like a miser. The king, informed by Moses's directions and on prophetic advice, embodied the decision of the assembly. This allowed him, at his convenience, to designate regional locations for national ceremonies. Equally, he could compel subjects' attendance in the capital. Josiah requires appearance there at Pesaḥ in 622 BCE. No doubt, he maintained the custom in other years for Samarians. Collocation permitted senior officials to monitor the delegates, who may have been few; this was an especially useful tool in Joseph, the principal target once Josiah had reached Bethel.

Still, D622's stew amends Manasseh's administration to strip "non-Israelites" and Israelites alike of their distinctive ancestral insignia. The township in Judah had probably been stripped of legal autonomy since the time of Hezekiah. D622 formalized the status, more as a provision for new acquisitions than for surviving old ones. Thus P, facing these issues, instead invents a national funerary reserve at Machpelah to supplant clan ancestral hallows. Deuteronomy, too, devalues local citizenship, redefining responsibility by borough rather than by kinship association, for example, and assigning the tenant, including sharecroppers, to the commune. Inside Judah, the actual citizenry was intimately entangled in royal governance. On the fringes, however, and prospectively in Samaria, monitoring was a *desideratum*.

We know too little about Josiah's activities north of Benjamin to judge the relation of their progress to D622. In my view, we also know too little confidently to isolate layers within it, though these seem to exist. There are, however, some surmises to make about its publication.

On its recitation, D622 was probably distributed to Judah's officials and proclaimed in existing towns by Levites. Though scholars attribute different portions, isolated from the text, to various eras and circumstances, none has made a compelling argument for a redactional history, like that of Judges, that is exo-

209 Deut 23:4–9. For a careful survey, see Olyan, "Sie sollen nicht."

skeletal. Minimally, D622 encompassed Deuteronomy 5–28 and quite conceivably, all of chaps. 1–33: there is no change of language, except in poetic segments.

If D622 included chs. 29–31, it was written at the same time as, or just before, the reform report (2 Kgs 23:1–25): the connections run especially deep between them. Oddly, the account of Josiah's find, which occupies most of his regnal account, and of the reform sits uncomfortably with what succeeds (his violent death, for one) and precedes. The connections to Deuteronomy 29–31 suggest Josiah's actions and the account of them were scripted in accord with the book. Others will prefer to attribute the linkage to the Dtr, who wrote not long afterward; in the Josianic account, however, his hand is not so obvious as in free composition.

After Josiah's death (2 Kgs 23:25), however, the Dtr already was taking D622 to demand delivery of all oblations to Zion. Whatever his contributions to Deuteronomy 1–3; 29–34, and Joshua (e.g., ch. 23), he doubles down on the reform. He cites baal-worship, after 1 Samuel 7, only under Omrides and Manasseh, Judah having contracted the habit after Israel's demise, as in Jeremiah 2–4. Consistent with his perspective, the Host, too, had first infected Israel's preexilic practice and then entered Judah with Manasseh (2 Kgs 17:16; 21:3, 5). But his indictment of *bāmôt* only implies that they are aboriginal, reflecting an intellectual strand and perhaps a history celebrating Hezekiah or Manasseh. Jeremiah, and arguably Ezekiel, are even more radical. They apply D622's censure of public ceremonies to private life.

Possibly, the book of Joshua was assembled for the publication of D622. Their long-recognized coherence embraces the law-code's enactment at Shechem (8:30–35; 24), the chronological plot line, and several institutions.[210] Some features in Joshua reflect the Josianic agenda: not just the township system but the foregrounding of allotments for Judah and Joseph (Josh 14–17). Other elements, like the Levitical city system, appear to clash institutionally with Deuteronomy.[211] They invite a more complex perspective on that book's assembly.

---

210 The list includes cities of refuge, the Ebal altar, the public copy of the book, the allocation of clan land, and the presence of marshals and tenants in the community. Josh's town lists reflect common districting.

211 In P, Josh 21, and 1 Chr 6, the system contingently covers all regions. It coopts clan centers (Hebron for earlier Caleb, Qadesh) that Deut cuts out, four per tribe like the division of Judah. Replacing guaranteed rations in Deut 18:6–8, the Levitical city system disposes Levites at depots, without transfer to Jerusalem, and isolates Levites from descent groups. Josh 22 is less disturbing in terms of arrangements, and certainly less direct if meant programmatically. P wrestles with the same issues as Deut, and, had another century passed before an exile, only

A compelling, rather than possible, explanation of the literary continuum from Genesis to Kings has yet to emerge.[212] Like redaction-criticism in Deuteronomy, editorial theories rarely unpack a politics of transmission limited by the parameters of an evolving social matrix. But plausible inferences about editing must be embedded in an independent reconstruction of that matrix and the operation of its institutions. Whether Joshua and the frame of Deuteronomy predate the DtrH or not depends, thus, on the duration and extent of Josiah's forays and broadcasts into Samaria and just as much on relations to the other peripheries.

In the search for the context and goals of Deuteronomy, or Josiah, our discussion profits when we integrate social conditions, labor, ancestral gods, and the reductionist intellectual totalization and other limitations of the governors. The object of historical study, after all, is not technics in philology or archaeology, but a living landscape. In this, institutions' gravitational field warps our most historically specific relics, language, and other symbols, to sublimate metaphor, imprecision, and evasion into a usually aspirational and failed politics and governance.[213]

Works Cited

Aharoni, Yohanan. "The Horned Altar of Beer-sheba." *Biblical Archaeologist* 37 (1974): 2–6.

Ahlström, Gösta Werner. *Royal Administration and National Religion in Ancient Palestine.* Studies in the History of the Ancient Near East 1. Leiden: Brill, 1982.

Arnold, Bill. "Deuteronomy 12 and the Law of the Central Sanctuary *noch einmal.*" *Vetus Testamentum* 64 (2014): 236–48.

Aster, Sean Zelig. "Transmission of Neo-Assyrian Claims of Empire to Judah in the Late Eighth Century B.C.E." *Hebrew Union College Annual* 78 (2007): 1–44.

Auld, A. Graeme. *Joshua, Moses and the Land: Tetrateuch-Pentateuch-Hexateuch in a Generation since 1938.* Edinburgh: T. & T. Clark, 1980.

Aurelius, Erik. "Der Ursprung des Ersten Gebots." *Zeitschrift für Theologie und Kirche* 100 (2003): 1–21.

Ben-Arieh, S. "Temple Furniture from the Favissa at 'En Hazeva." *Atiqot* 68 (2011): 107–75.

Barrick, W. Boyd. *BMH as Body Language: A Lexical and Iconographical Study of the Word BMH When Not a Reference to Cultic Phenomena in Biblical and Post-Biblical Hebrew.* Library of Hebrew Bible/Old Testament Studies 477. New York: T&T Clark, 2008.

---

one of the two would likely have reached us. It is the passing of the elite concentrated on Jerusalem's acropolis that exposes internal divisions at court.

212 See Otto, "Deuteronomium 4" for an approach from fundamentals.

213 As Seth Richardson has repeatedly urged ("Before Things Worked," "Presumptive State," "Mesopotamian Citizen," and "Mesopotamian Political History").

Berlejung, Angelika. "The Assyrians in the West: Assyrianization, Colonialism, Indifference, or Development Policy?" In *Congress Volume Helsinki 2010*, edited by Martti Nissinen, 21–60. Supplements to Vetus Testamentum 148. Leiden: Brill, 2012.

Bleek, Friedrich. *An Introduction to the Old Testament, Volume 1*, edited by Johannes Bleek and Adolf Kamphausen. Translated by G. H. Venables. London: Bell, 1882.

Bond, Sarah E. *Trade and Taboo: Disreputable Professions in the Roman Mediterranean*. Ann Arbor: University of Michigan Press, 2016.

Boyer, Georges. *Textes juridiques*. Archives Royales de Mari 8. Paris: Imprimerie Nationale, 1958.

Bron, François. "A South Arabian Inscription: Part 1: The Inscription." In *Beer-Sheba III: The Early Iron IIA Enclosed Settlement and the Late Iron IIA-Iron IIB Cities*, edited by Ze'ev Herzog and Lily Singer-Avitz, 1,045–46. Tel Aviv University Nadler Institute of Archaeology Monographs 33. Winona Lake, IN: Eisenbrauns, 2016.

Buccellati, Giorgio. *Cities and Nations of Ancient Syria*. Studi Semitici 26. Rome: Instituto di Studi del Vicino Oriente, Università di Roma, 1967.

Chabod, Antoine. "Des héros ordinaires: Les législateurs légendaires grecs en contexte archaïque." *Cahiers des études anciennes* 57 (2020): 17–31.

Claburn, W. Eugene. "The Fiscal Basis of Josiah's Reforms." *Journal of Biblical Literature* 92, no. 1 (1973): 11–22.

Cohen, Abner. *Arab Border-Villages in Israel*. Manchester: Manchester University Press, 1965.

Cohen, Rudolph. "The Fortresses at 'En Ḥaṣeva." *Biblical Archaeologist* 57, no. 4 (1994): 203–214.

Cohen, Rudolph, and Yigal Israel. "Ein Hazeva – 1990–1994." *Hadashot Archaeologiyyot* 103 (1995): 110–16.

Cohen, Rudolph, and Yigal Israel. "The Excavations at 'Ein Ḥaẓeva / Israelite and Roman Tamar." *Qadmoniot* 29, no. 2 (1996): 78–92.

Cohen, Rudolph, and Yigal Israel. "The Iron Age Fortresses at 'En Ḥaṣeva." *Biblical Archaeologist* 58, no. 4 (1995): 223–235.

Daviau, P. Michèle. "The Coroplastics of Transjordan: Forming Techniques and Iconographic Traditions." In *Figuring Out the Figurines of the Ancient Near East*, edited by Stephanie M. Langin-Hooper, 1–12. Occasional Papers in Coroplastic Studies 1. United States: Association for Coroplastic Studies, 2014.

Daviau, P. Michèle. "Diversity in the Cultic Setting: Temples and Shrines in Central Jordan and the Negev." In *Temple Building and Temple Cult: Architecture and Cultic Paraphernalia of Temples in the Levant (2.–1. Mill. B.C.E.): Proceedings of a Conference on the Occasion of the 50th Anniversary of the Institute of Biblical Archaeology at the University of Tübingen (28–30 May 2010)*, edited by Jens Kamlah, 435–58. Abhandlungen des Deutschen Palästina-Vereins 41. Wiesbaden: Harrassowitz, 2012.

Daviau, P. Michèle. "Ḫirbet el-Mudēyine in its Landscape: Iron Age Towns, Forts, and Shrines." *Zeitschrift des Deutschen Palästina-Vereins* 122, no. 1 (2006): 14–30.

Daviau, P. Michèle. "Moab's Northern Border, Khirbat al-Mudayna on the Wadi ath Thamad." *Biblical Archaeologist* 60 (1997): 222–28, 251.

Daviau, P. Michèle. "New Light on Iron Age Religious Iconography: The Evidence from Moab." *Studies in the History and Archaeology of Jordan* 7 (2001): 317–26.

Dion, Paul-Eugène. "Deuteronomy 13: The Suppression of Alien Religious Propaganda in Israel during the Late Monarchical Era." In *Law and Ideology in Monarchic Israel*, edited by Baruch Halpern and Deborah Whitney Hobson, 147–216. Journal for the Study of the Old Testament Supplement Series 124. Sheffield: Sheffield Academic, 1991.

Dolan, Annlee Elizabeth. "Wadi ath-Thamad Site WT-13: A Hermeneutical Approach to Moabite Religion." PhD diss., University of Toronto, 2007.

Driver, Samuel Rolles. *A Critical and Exegetical Commentary on Deuteronomy*. 2nd ed. International Critical Commentary. Edinburgh: T. & T. Clark, 1896.

Dunbar, Robin. *How Many Friends Does One Person Need? Dunbar's Number and Other Evolutionary Quirks*. London: Faber and Faber, 2010.

Edelman, Diana Vikander. "Saying Goodbye to the Theory of the Influence of Esarhaddon's Succession *Adê* on Deuteronomy 13 and 28." In *Beside the Ark: Rethinking Deuteronomy outside the Box*, edited by Diana Edelman, Benedetta Rossi, Kåre Berge, and Philippe Guillaume, forthcoming.

Emerton, John A. "'The High Places of the Gates' in 2 Kings xxiii 8." *Vetus Testamentum* 44, no. 4 (1994): 455–67.

Fales, F. Mario. "The Composition and Structure of the Neo-Assyrian Empire: Ethnicity, Language and Identities." In *Conceptualizing Past, Present and Future*, edited by Robert Rollinger, 443–94. Proceedings of the Ninth Symposium of the Melammu Project Held in Helsinki/Tartu, May 18–24, 2015. Munster: Ugarit, 2018.

Faust, Avraham. "The Impact of Jerusalem's Expansion in the Late Iron Age on the Forms of Rural Settlements in Its Vicinity." *Cathedra* 84 (1997): 53–62.

Faust, Avraham. "The Interests of the Assyrian Empire in the West: Olive Oil Production as a Test-Case." *Journal of the Economic and Social History of the Orient* 54 (2011): 62–86.

Faust, Avraham. *Judah in the Neo-Babylonian Period: The Archaeology of Destruction*. Atlanta: Society of Biblical Literature, 2012.

Faust, Avraham. "The World of P: The Material World of Priestly Writings." *Vetus Testamentum* 69 (2019): 173–218.

Finkelstein, Israel, and Nadav Na'aman. "The Judahite Shephelah in the Late 8th and Early 7th Centuries BCE." *Tel Aviv* 31 (2004): 60–79.

Földi, Zsombor J. "The Property of the City, the Property of the King? A New Fragment of YOS 12, 321." *Hungarian Assyriological Review* 1 (2020) (preprint).

Franklin, Norma. "Entering the Arena: The Megiddo Stables Reconsidered." In *Rethinking Israel: Studies in the History and Archaeology of Ancient Israel in Honor of Israel Finkelstein*, edited by Oded Lipschits, Yuval Gadot, and Matthew J. Adams, 87–102. Winona Lake, IN: Eisenbrauns, 2017.

Frese, Daniel A. "A Land of Gates: Covenant Communities in the Book of Deuteronomy." *Vetus Testamentum* 65 (2015): 33–52.

Freedman, David Noel. "Headings in the Books of the Eighth-Century Prophets." *Andrews University Seminary Studies* 25 (1987): 9–26.

Friedman, Richard Elliott. *The Bible with Sources Revealed*. New York: HarperOne, 2003.

Friedman, Richard Elliott. *The Exodus*. New York: HarperOne, 2017.

Gadot, Yuval, Sivan Mizrahi, Liora Freud, and David Gellman. "What Kind of Village Is This? Buildings and Agroeconomic Activities Northwest of Jerusalem during the Iron Age IIB–C Period." In *The Last Century in the History of Judah: The Seventh Century BCE in Archaeological, Historical, and Biblical Perspectives*, edited by Filip Čapek and Oded Lipschits, 89–118. Ancient Israel and Its Literature 37. Atlanta: Society of Biblical Literature, 2019.

Gagarin, Michael. "Storytelling about the Lawgiver in the Athenian Orators." *Cahiers des études anciennes* 57 (2020): 33–44.

Ganor, Saar, and Igor Kreimerman. “An Eighth-Century B. C. E. Gate Shrine at Tel Lachish, Israel.” *Bulletin of the American Schools of Oriental Research* 381 (2017): 211–36.

Garr, W. Randall. “The Paragogic *nun* in Rhetorical Perspective.” In *Biblical Hebrew in Its Northwest Semitic Setting: Typological and Historical Perspectives*, edited by Steven E. Fassberg and Avi Hurvitz, 65–74. Publications of the Institute for Advanced Studies 1. Jerusalem: Magnes, 2006.

Gertz, Jan Christian. “Deuteronomy and the Covenant Code and their Cultural and Historical Contexts. Hermeneutics of Law and Inner-biblical Exegesis.” *Zeitschrift für Altorientalische und Biblische Rechtsgeschichte* 25 (2019): 187–94.

Gitin, Seymour. “Incense Altars from Ekron, Israel and Judah: Context and Typology.” *Eretz Israel* 20 (1989): 52*–67*.

Gitin, Seymour, and Shmuel Aḥituv. “Two New Cultic Inscriptions from Seventh-Century B. C. E. Ekron.” In *Marbeh Ḥokmah: Studies in the Bible and the Ancient Near East in Loving Memory of Victor Avigdor Hurowitz*, edited by L. Greenstein, Mayer I. Gruber, Peter Machinist, and Shalom M. Paul, 221–27. Winona Lake, IN: Eisenbrauns, 2015.

Gitin, Seymour, Trude Dothan, and Yosef Garfinkel. *Tel-Miqne-Ekron Excavations 1985–1988, 1990, 1992–1995: Field IV Lower – The Elite Zone, Part 2: The Iron Age IIC Late Philistine City*. Winona Lake, IN: Eisenbrauns, 2017.

Glanville, M. “The *Gēr* (Stranger) in Deuteronomy: Family for the Displaced.” *Journal of Biblical Literature* 137 (2018): 599–623.

Greenhut, Zvi, and Alon De Groot. *Salvage Excavations at Tel Moza: The Bronze and Iron Age Settlements and Later Occupation*. Israel Antiquities Authority Reports 39. Jerusalem: Israel Antiquities Authority, 2009.

Greenspahn, Fred. “Deuteronomy and Centralization.” *Vetus Testamentum* 64 (2014): 227–35.

Grossman, David. *Expansion and Desertion: The Arab Village and its Offshoots in Ottoman Palestine*. Jerusalem: Yad Ben-Zvi, 1994.

Guillaume, Philippe. *Land, Credit and Crisis: Agrarian Finance in the Hebrew Bible*. BibleWorld. Sheffield: Equinox, 2012.

Gunneweg, Jan, and Marta Balla. “The Provenience of 7th–6th Century BCE Cult Vessels from the Iron Age II Fortress at ‘En Hazeva using Instrumental Neutron Activation Analysis (INAA).” *Bulletin of the Anglo-Israel Society* 34 (2016): 57–72.

Halpern, Baruch. *The Constitution of the Monarchy in Israel*. Harvard Semitic Monographs 25. Chico, CA: Scholars, 1981.

Halpern, Baruch. *David’s Secret Demons: Messiah, Murderer, Traitor, King*. Grand Rapids, MI: Eerdmans, 2004.

Halpern, Baruch. “The False Torah of Jeremiah 8 in the Context of Seventh Century BCE Pseudepigraphy: The First Documented Rejection of Tradition.” In *“Up to the Gates of Ekron”: Essays on the Archaeology and History of the Eastern Mediterranean in Honor of Seymour Gitin*, edited by Sidney White Crawford, Amnon Ben-Tor, J. P. Dessel, William G. Dever, Amihai Mazar, and Joseph Aviram, 337–43. Jerusalem: Albright Institute of Archaeological Research and Israel Exploration Society, 2007.

Halpern, Baruch. *The First Historians*. San Francisco: Harper & Row, 1988.

Halpern, Baruch. “Jerusalem and the Lineages in the 7th Century BCE: Kinship and the Rise of Individual Moral Liability.” In *From Gods to God: The Dynamics of Iron Age Cosmologies*, edited by M. J. Adams, 329–424. Forschungen zum Alten Testament 63. Tübingen: Mohr Siebeck, 2009. Reprinted from *Law and Ideology in Ancient Israel*, edited by Baruch Halpern and Deborah Whitney Hobson. Journal for the Study of the Old Testament Supplements 124. Sheffield, Sheffield Academic Press, 1991.

Halpern, Baruch. “The Rise of Abimelek ben-Jerubbaal.” *Hebrew Annual Review* 2 (1978): 79–100.

Halpern, Baruch. “Sybil, or the Two Nations? Archaism, Kinship, Alienation and the Elite Redefinition of Traditional Culture in Judah in the 8th–7th Centuries B.C.E.” In *The Study of the Ancient Near East in the 21st Century: The William Foxwell Albright Centennial Conference*, edited by Jerrold S. Cooper and Glenn M. Schwartz, 291–338. Winona Lake, IN: Eisenbrauns, 1996.

Halpern, Baruch. “Why Manasseh is Blamed for the Babylonian Exile: The evolution of a biblical tradition.” *Vetus Testamentum* 48 (1998): 473–514.

Hansen, M. H. “Introduction: The Concept of City-State and City State Culture.” In *A Comparative Study of Thirty City-State Cultures: An Investigation*, edited by M. H. Hansen, 11–34. Copenhagen: Kongelige Danske Videnskabernes Selskab, 2000.

Hardy, Humphrey H., and Benjamin D. Thomas. “Another Look at Biblical Hebrew *Bɔmɔ* ‘High Place.’” *Vetus Testamentum* 62, no. 2 (2012): 175–88.

Herzog, Ze’ev. “The Fortress Mound at Arad: An Interim Report.” *Tel Aviv* 29 (2002): 3–109.

Herzog, Ze’ev. “Perspectives on Southern Israel’s Cult Centralization: Arad and Beer-sheba.” In *One God, One Cult, One Nation: Archaeological and Biblical Perspectives*, edited by Reinhard G. Kratz and Hermann Spieckermann, 169–99. Berlin: de Gruyter, 2010.

Herzog, Ze’ev, and Lily Singer-Avitz. *Beer-Sheba III: The Early Iron IIA Enclosed Settlement and the Late Iron IIA-Iron IIB Cities.* 3 vols. Tel Aviv University Nadler Institute of Archaeology Monographs 33. Winona Lake, IN: Eisenbrauns, 2016.

Heth, Raleigh. “The Stripping of the Bulls: A Reevaluation of Ahaz’s Role in Deuteronomistic Historiography.” Paper delivered at the Annual Meeting of the Midwest Region of the SBL. Notre Dame, IN, 11 Feb 2017.

Hipp, Krzysztof. “Fugitives in the State Archives of Assyria.” In *Change in Neo-Assyrian Imperial Administration: Evolution and Revolution*, edited by Natalie N. May and S. Svärd. *State Archives of Assyria Bulletin* 21 (2015): 47–77.

Holladay, John S. “Religion in Israel and Judah under the Monarchy: An Explicitly Archaeological Approach.” In *Ancient Israelite Religion: Essays in Honor of Frank Moore Cross*, edited by Patrick D. Miller, Paul D. Hanson, and S. Dean McBride, 249–99. Philadelphia: Fortress, 1987.

Hoonacker, Albin van. *Le lieu du culte dans la législation rituelle des Hébreux.* Ghent: Engeleke, 1894.

Hoonacker, Albin van. *La sacerdoce lévitique dans la loi et dans l’histoire des Hébreux.* London: Williams and Norgate, 1899.

Hopkins, Terence K., Immanuel M. Wallenstein, and associates. *World Systems Analysis: Theory and Methodology: Explorations in the World Economy.* Beverly Hills, CA: Sage, 1982.

Hyatt, J. Philip. “Jeremiah and Deuteronomy.” *Journal of Near Eastern Studies* 1 (1942): 156–73.

Ilan, David. “Iron Age II et-Tell/Bethsaida and Dan: A Tale of Two Gates.” In *A Festschrift in Honor of Rami Arav: “And They Came to Bethsaida …,”* edited by Fred Strickert and Richard Freund, 112–32. Cambridge: Cambridge Scholars, 2019.

Itkin, Eli. “Horvat Tov: A Late Iron Age Fortress in the Northeastern Negev.” *Tel Aviv* 47 (2020): 65–88.

Johnstone, William. “Exodus 20.24B: Linchpin of Biblical Criticism or Just Another Link between the Decalogue and the Book of the Covenant.” In *Reflection and Refraction: Studies in Biblical Historiography in Honour of A. Graeme Auld*, edited by Timothy H.

Lim, W. B. Aucker, Auld, and Robert Rezetko, 207–22. Vetus Testamentum Supplements 113. Leiden: Brill, 2007.

Jong, M. J. de. "A Window on the Isaiah Tradition in the Assyrian Period: Isaiah 10:24–27." In *"Isaiah in Context": Studies in Honour of Arie van der Kooij on the Occasion of his Sixty-Fifth Birthday*, edited by M. N. van der Meer et al., 83–107. Leiden: Brill, 2010.

Jursa, Michael. "Die Söhne Kudurrus und die Herkunft der neubabylonischen Dynastie." *Revue d'assyriologie* 101 (2007): 125–36.

Kegel, Martin. *Die Kultus-Reformation des Josia. Die Aussagen der modernen Kritik über II Kön. 23–24 kritisch beleuchtet.* Leipzig: A. Deichert, 1919.

Kennicott, Benjamin. *Editionis Veteris Testamenti Hebraici cum variis lectionibus brevis defensio, contra Ephemeridum Goettingensium criminationes.* London: Rivington, 1782.

Kisilevitz, Shua, Anna Eirikh-Rose, Hamudi Khalaily, and Zvi Greenhut. "Moza, Tel Moza: Preliminary Report." *Hadashot Arkheologiyyot: Excavations and Surveys in Israel* 126 (2014). Accessed August 30, 2020. https://www.jstor.org/stable/26604667.

Kleiman, Sabine. "The Iron IIB Gate Shrine at Lachish: An Alternative Interpretation." *Tel-Aviv* 47 (2020): 55–64.

Knauf, Ernst Axel, and Philippe Guillaume. *A History of Biblical Israel: The fate of the tribes and kingdoms from Merenptah to Bar Kochba.* Worlds of the Ancient Near East and Mediterranean. Sheffield: Equinox, 2016.

Knoppers, Gary N. "The Northern Context of the Law-Code in Deuteronomy." *Hebrew Bible and Ancient Israel* 4 (2015): 162–83.

Knoppers, Gary N. "Rethinking the Relationship between Deuteronomy and the Deuteronomistic History: The Case of Kings." *Catholic Biblical Quarterly* 63 (2001): 393–415.

Lange, Armin and Esther Eshel. "Shema' Yisrael. 'The Lord is One': How Its Meaning Changed." *Bible Review* 39, no. 3 (2013): 58–63, 69.

LaRocca-Pitts, Elizabeth C. *Of Wood and Stone: The Significance of Israelite Cultic Items in the Bible and its Early Interpreters.* Winona Lake, IN: Eisenbrauns, 2001.

Lauinger, Jacob. "The Neo-Assyrian *adê*: Treaty, Oath, or Something Else?" *Zeitschrift für Biblische Rechtsgeschichte* 19 (2013): 99–116.

Levin, Christoph. "Über den 'Color Hieremianus' des Deuteronomiums." In *Das Deuteronomium und seine Querbeziehungen*, edited by Timo Veijola, 107–26. Schriften der Finnischen Exegetischen Gesellschaft 62. Helsinki: Finnische Exegetische Gesellschaft in Helsinki, 1996.

Levinson, Bernard M. *Deuteronomy and the Hermeneutics of Legal Innovation.* New York: Oxford University Press, 1997.

Lohfink, Norbert. *Das Hauptgebot. Eine Untersuchung literarischer Einleitungsfragen zu Dtn 5–11.* Analecta Biblica 20. Rome: Pontifical Biblical Institute, 1963.

Lohfink, Norbert. "Zur deuteronomischen Zentralisationsformel." *Biblica* 65 (1984): 297–329.

Macdonald, Richard. "The 'Altar of the Lord Your God' in Deuteronomy 16.21: Central Altar or Local Altars?" *Journal for the Study of the Old Testament* 37, no. 4 (2013): doi 10.1177/0309089213475398, accessed 16 June 2020.

Malamat, Abraham. "The Danite Migration and the Pan-Israelite Exodus-Conquest: A Biblical Narrative Pattern." *Biblica* 51 (1970): 1–16.

Markl, Dominik. "Deuteronomy's 'Anti King': Historicized Etiology or Political Project?" In *Changing Faces of Kingship in Syria-Palestine 1500–500 BCE*, edited by Agustinus Gianto and Peter Dubovský, 165–86. Alter Orient und Altes Testament 459. Munster: Ugarit, 2018.

May, Natalie N. "Iconoclasm and Text Destruction in the Ancient Near East." In *Iconoclasm and Text Destruction in the Ancient Near East and Beyond*, edited by Natalie N. May, 1–32. Oriental Institute Studies 8. Chicago: Oriental Institute, 2012.

McKinny, Charles Christopher. "A Historical Geography of the Administrative Division of Judah: The Town Lists of Judah and Benjamin in Joshua 15:21–62 and 18:21–28." MA thesis, Bar-Ilan University, 2016.

Merendino, Rosario Pius. *Das Deuteronomische Gesetz: eine literarkritische, gattungs- und überlierungsgeschichtliche Untersuchung zu Dt 12–26*. Bonner Biblische Beiträge 31. Bonn: Peter Hanstein, 1969.

Moulis, David Rafael. "Hezekiah's Cultic Reforms according to the Archaeological Evidence." In *The Last Century in the History of Judah: The Seventh Century BCE in Archaeological, Historical, and Biblical Perspectives*, edited by Filip Čapek and Oded Lipschits, 167–80. Ancient Israel and Its Literature 37. Atlanta: Society of Biblical Literature, 2019.

Na'aman, Nadav. "The Distribution of Messages in the Kingdom of Judah in Light of the Lachish Ostraca." *Vetus Testamentum* 53 (2003): 169–80.

Oestreicher, Theodor. *Das Deuteronomische Grundgesetz*. Beiträge zur Förderung Christlicher Theologie 27. Gütersloh: C. Bertelsmann, 1923.

Oestreicher, Theodor. "Dtn $12_{13\,f.}$ im Licht von Dtn 23_{16f}." *Zeitschrift für die alttestamentliche Wissenschaft* 43 (1925): 246–49.

Olyan, Saul M. *Rites and Rank: Hierarchy in Biblical Representations of Cult*. Princeton: Princeton University, 2000.

Olyan, Saul M. "'Sie sollen nicht in die Gemeinde des Herrn kommen'. Aspekte gesellschaftlicher Inklusion und Exklusion in Dt 23,4–9 und seine frühen Auslegungen." In *Social Inequality in the World of the Text: The Significance of Ritual and Social Distinctions in the Hebrew Bible*, 173–85. Göttingen: Vandenhoeck & Ruprecht, 2011.

Otto, Eckart. *Das Deuteronomium. Politische Theologie und Rechtsreform in Juda und Assyrien*. Beihefte zur Zeitschrift für die alttestamentliche Wissenschaft 284. Berlin and New York: de Gruyter, 1999.

Otto, Eckart. *Deuteronomium 1–11. I. 1,1–4,43*. Herders Theologischer Kommentar zum Alten Testament. Freiburg: Herder, 2012.

Otto, Eckart. "Deuteronomium 4. Die Pentateuchredaktion im Deuteronomiumsrahmen." In *Das Deuteronomium und seine Querbeziehungen*, edited by Timo Veijola, 198–222. Schriften der Finnischen Exegetischen Gesellschaft 62. Helsinki: Finnische Exegetische Gesellschaft in Helsinki, 1996.

Otto, Eckart. *Deuteronomium 12–34. I. 12,1–23,15*. Herders Theologischer Kommentar zum Alten Testament. Freiburg: Herder, 2016.

Otto, Eckart. "Ersetzen oder Ergänzen von Gesetzen in der Rechtshermeneutik des Pentateuch." In *Die Tora. Studien zum Pentateuch. Gesammelte Studien*, 248–56. Beiträge zur Zeitschrift für altorientalische und biblische Rechtsgeschichte 9. Wiesbaden: Harrassowitz, 2009.

Otto, Eckart. "False Weights in the Scales of Biblical Justice: Different Views of Women from a Patriarchal Hierarchy to Religious Equality in the Book of Deuteronomy." In *Gender and Law in the Hebrew Bible and the Ancient Near East*, edited by Victor H. Matthews, Bernard M. Levinson, and Tikva Frymer-Kensky, 128–46. Journal for the Study of the Old Testament Supplement Series 262; Sheffield: Sheffield Academic, 1998.

Otto, Eckart. *Gottesrecht und Menschenrecht: Rechts- und literaturhistorische Studien zum Deuteronomium*. Beiträge zur Zeitschrift für altorientalische und biblische Rechtsgeschichte 2. Wiesbaden: Harrassowitz, 2002.

Otto, Eckart. *Kontinuum und Proprium: Studien zur Sozial- und Rechtsgeschichte des Alten Orients und des Alten Testaments*. Orientalia Biblica et Christiana 8. Wiesbaden: Harrassowitz, 1996.

Otto, Eckart. "*ša'ar*, gate." In *Theological Dictionary of the Old Testament*. Vol. 15, *šāḵar-taršîš*, edited by G. Johannes Botterweck, Helmer Ringgren, and Heinz-Josef Fabry, 359–405. Translated by David M. Green. Grand Rapids, MI: Eerdmans, 2015.

Parpola, Simo and Kazuko Watanabe. *Neo-Assyrian Treaties and Loyalty Oaths*. State Archives of Assyria 2. Helsinki: Helsinki University, 1988.

Paton, Lewis Bayles. "The Case for the Post-Exilic Origin of Deuteronomy." *Journal of Biblical Literature* 47 (1928): 322–57.

Paz, Itzik, and Shuichi Hasegawa. "Who Built Tel Rekesh?" *Biblical Archaeology Review* 45, no. 3 (2020): 34–40.

Petit, Lucas, and Zeidan Kafafi. "Beyond the River Jordan: A Late Iron Age Sanctuary at Tell Damiyah." *Near Eastern Archaeology* 79, no. 1 (2016): 18–26.

Ponchia, Simonetta. "The Neo-Assyrian *adê* Protocol and the Administration of the Empire." In *From Source to History: Studies on Ancient Near Eastern Worlds and Beyond Dedicated to Giovanni Battista Lanfranchi on the Occasion of his 65th Birthday on June 23, 2014*, edited by Salvatore Gaspo, Alessandro Greco, Daniele Morandi Bonacossi, Simonetta Ponchia, and Robert Rollinger, 501–26. Alter Orient und Altes Testament 412. Munster: Ugarit, 2014.

Porten, Bezalel, and Ada Yardeni. *Textbook of Aramaic Documents from Egypt*. 4 volumes. Jerusalem: Hebrew University, Dept. of Jewish History, 1986.

Prieto, Francisco Machuca. *Una forma fenicia de ser romano. Identidad e integración de las comunidades fenicias de la Península Ibérica bajo el poder de Roma*. SPAL Monografías Arqueología 29. Sevilla: Universidad de Sevilla, 2019.

Rad, Gerhard von. *Das fünfte Buch Mose. Deuteronomium*. Das Alte Testament Deutsch 8. Göttingen: Vandenhoeck & Ruprecht, 1964.

Reuter, Eleonore. *Kultzentralisation: Entstehung und Theologie von Dtn 12*. Bonner Biblische Beiträge 87. Frankfurt-am-Main: Anton Hain, 1993.

Richardson, Seth. "Before Things Worked: A 'Low-Power' Model of Early Mesopotamia." In *Ancient States and Infrastructural Power: Europe, Asia, and America*, edited by Clifford Ando and Seth Richardson, 17–62. Philadelphia: University of Pennsylvania, 2017.

Richardson, Seth. "Early Mesopotamia: The Presumptive State." *Past and Present* 215 (2012): 3–49.

Richardson, Seth. "The Mesopotamian Citizen Conceptualized: Affect, Speech and Perception." In *State Formations: Global Histories and Cultures of Statehood*, edited by J. Brooke, J. Strauss, and G. Anderson, 261–75. Cambridge: Cambridge University Press, 2018.

Richardson, Seth. "Mesopotamian Political History: The Perversities." *Journal of Ancient Near Eastern History* 1 (2014): 61–93.

Richter, Sandra. *The Deuteronomistic History and the Name Theology: lĕšakkēn šĕmô šām in the Bible and the Ancient Near East*. Beiträge zur Zeitschrift für die Alttestamentliche Wissenschaft 318. Berlin: de Gruyter, 2002.

Rossi, Benedetta, and Philippe Guillaume. "An Alternative Reading of the Law of the Hebrew Slave (Deuteronomy 15:12–18)." *Res Antiquae* 15 (2018): 3–30.

Sapir-Hen, Lidar, Meirav Meiri and Israel Finkelstein. "Iron Age Pigs: New Evidence on Their Origin and Role in Forming Identity Boundaries." *Radiocarbon* 57, no. 2 (2015): 307–15.

Schiffman, Lawrence H. *Sectarian Law In The Dead Sea Scrolls: Courts, Testimony and the Penal Code*. Brown Judaic Studies 33. Chico, CA: Scholars, 1983.

Schorch, Stefan. “The Samaritan Version of Deuteronomy and the Origin of Deuteronomy.” In *Samaria, Samarians, Samaritans: Studies on Bible, History and Linguistics*. Papers of the sixth international conference of the Société d’Études Samaritaines, Pápa, Hungary, July, 2008, edited by J. Zsengellér, 23–37. Studia Samaritana 6. Berlin: de Gruyter, 2011.

Shai, Itzik, Aaron Tavgar, Matthew Soriano, Deborah Cassuto, Christian Locatell, and Charles Christopher McKinny. “Ten Years of Research at Tel Burna: A Canaanite Cultic Center and Judahite Border Settlement.” *Qadmoniot* 52, no. 158 (2019): 83–91.

Skinner, John. *Prophecy and Religion: Studies in the Life of Jeremiah*. Cambridge: Cambridge University Press, 1922.

Smith, Christopher. “*Leges Regiae* and the Nomothetic World of Early Rome.” *Cahiers des études anciennes* 57 (2020): 91–103.

Sulzberger, Mayer. “The Status of Labor in Ancient Israel.” *Jewish Quarterly Review* 13 (1923): 245–302.

Taylor, Lily Ross. *Roman Voting Assemblies*. Ann Arbor: University of Michigan Press, 1966.

Thareani, Yifat. “Forces of Decline and Regeneration: A Socioeconomic Account of the Iron Age II Negev Desert.” In *The Economy of Ancient Judah in Its Historical Context*, edited by Marvin Lloyd Miller, Ehud Ben-Zvi, and Gary N. Knoppers, 207–35. State College, PA: Pennsylvania State University, 2015.

Thareani-Sussely, Yifat. “The ‘Archaeology of the Days of Manasseh’ Reconsidered in the Light of Evidence From The Beersheba Valley.” *Palestine Exploration Quarterly* 139 (2007): 69–77.

Tigay, Jeffrey. *Deuteronomy*. Philadelphia: Jewish Publication Society, 2003.

Vater, Johann Severin. *Commentar ueber den Pentateuch mit Einleitungen zu den einzelnen Abschnitten, der eingeschalteten Uebersetzung von Dr. Alexander Geddes’s merkwuerdigeren, critischen und exegetischen Anmerkungen, und einer Abhandlung ueber Moses und die Verfasser des Pentateuchs* III. Halle: Waisenhaus, 1805.

Wallenstein, Immanuel M. *The Modern World-System*. 3 vols. New York, London, and San Diego: Academic Press, 1974, 1980, 1989.

Walls, Amanda Nicole. “Israel’s Pagan Passover.” PhD diss., University of Georgia, 2019.

Watanabe, Kazuko. “Adoration of Oath Documents in Assyrian Religion and its Development.” *Orient* 55 (2020): 71–86.

Watanabe, Kazuko. “Innovations in Esarhaddon’s Successor Oath Documents Considered from the Viewpoint of the Documents’ Structure.” *State Archives of Assyria Bulletin* 21 (2015): 173–215.

Wazzana, Nili. “The Law of the King (Deut 17:14–20) in the Light of Empire and Destruction.” In *The Fall of Jerusalem and the Rise of the Torah*, edited by Peter Dubovský, Dominik Markl, and Jean-Pierre Sonnet, 169–94. Forschungen zum Alten Testament 107. Tübingen: Mohr Siebeck, 2016.

Weinberger, Anat. “Provenance of the Clay Artifacts from the Favissa at ’En Ḥaẓeva.” *Atiqot* 68 (2011): 185–89.

Weinfeld, Moshe. *Deuteronomy and Deuteronomic School*. Oxford: Clarendon, 1971.

Welch, Adam. *The Code of Deuteronomy. A New Theory of Its Origin*. London: James Clarke, 1924.

Wellhausen, Julius. *Die Composition des Hexateuchs und der historischen Bücher des Alten Testaments*. 3rd ed. Berlin: G. Reimer, 1899. Repr., as 4th ed., Berlin: de Gruyter, 1963.

Wette, Wilhelm Martin Leberecht de. *Beiträge zur Einleitung in das Alten Testament.* I. *Kritischer Versuch über die Glaubwürdigkeit der Bücher der Chronik mit Hinsicht auf die Geschichte der Mosaischen Bücher und Gesetzgebung: Ein Nachtrag zu den Vaterschen Untersuchungen über den Pentateuch*; II. *Kritik der israelitischen Geschichte.* Halle: Schimmelpfennig, 1806–1807.

Wette, Wilhelm Martin Leberecht de. "Dissertatio Critico-Exegetica qua Deuteronomium a prioribus libris Pentateuchi diversum, alius cuiusdam recentioris auctoris opus esse monstratur." PhD diss., University of Jena. Jena: Etzdorf, 1805.

Winand, Jean. "Words of Thieves." In *Scribal Repertoires in Egypt from the New Kingdom to the Early Islamic Period*, edited by Jennifer Cromwell and Eitan Grossman, 127–52. Oxford Studies in Ancient Documents. Oxford: Oxford University Press, 2018.

Yadin, Yigael. "Beer-Sheba: The High Place Destroyed by King Josiah." *Bulletin of the American Schools of Oriental Research* 222 (1976): 5–17.

Zahn, Molly M. "Genre and Rewriting." In *Genres of Rewriting in Second Temple Judaism: Scribal Composition and Transmission*, edited by Molly Zahn, 56–73. Cambridge: Cambridge University Press, 2020.

Ziffer, Irit. "Altars and Art Objects." In *Beer-Sheba III: The Early Iron IIA Enclosed Settlement and the Late Iron IIA-Iron IIB Cities*, edited by Ze'ev Herzog and Lily Singer-Avitz, 3.1,229–57. Tel Aviv University Nadler Institute of Archaeology Monographs 33. Winona Lake, IN: Eisenbrauns, 2016.

Zwickel, Wolfgang. "The World of Cult Stands." In *Yavneh II: The 'Temple Hill' Repository Pit*, edited by Raz Kletter, Irit Ziffer, and Wolfgang Zwickel, 178–93. Orbis Biblicus et Orientalis, Series Archaeologica 36. Fribourg: Academic, 2015.

Bill T. Arnold

Innovations of the Deuteronomic Law and the History of Its Composition

In the last twenty-five years, scholars have made significant progress on the relationships between the legal corpora of the Pentateuch. In particular, we are now more confident of D's reliance on the Book of the Covenant (hereafter BC), a designation derived from the words ספר הברית in Exodus 24:7; BC being Exodus 20:22–23:33, the oldest portion of which was likely 21:1–22:16.[1] The relationship between the Deuteronomic law and the Holiness Code (hereafter HC), often assumed to be Leviticus 17–26, is more complicated.

But questions remain. In particular, opinions diverge on (1) whether the Deuteronomic innovations were subversive or complementary; (2) the extent of dependence or influence, or in some cases, even the direction of dependence, especially between HC and Deuteronomic law; (3) the closely related methodological question of how to discern which were the anterior texts, or whether anteriority is even important or possible to determine; (4) a further methodological question stemming from redaction criticism regarding the composition history of D and the other legal corpora, especially as these relate to the Tetrateuch, Pentateuch, Hexateuch, or Enneateuch; (5) the role of the Decalogue in this reconstruction, and whether we can have any confidence of its age or the process by which it was incorporated into the corpora, perhaps as an organizing principle for D, or even for the other corpora as well; and finally (6) the very nature of the Deuteronomic law itself. This last question relates, of course, to a much-discussed systemic question about whether the laws of the Pentateuch should be considered actual law or something else altogether, such as theoretical or descriptive treatises.

This investigation makes no attempt to address all these questions, although I believe the results will be related to and have implications for each one. Primarily, I am concerned in this study with the uniqueness of D as compared to the other legal corpora in the Pentateuch and with what this uniqueness may reveal about D's ideological agenda. In particular, I hope to contribute

1 Otto, *Das Deuteronomium*, 236–364; *Deuteronomium*, 1:231–38; Levinson, *Deuteronomy.*

Note: I am indebted to Brent A. Strawn for his suggestions on an early version of this paper, to Paavo Tucker and Aaron Woods for their assistance, and to the editors of this volume for numerous improvements.

https://doi.org/10.1515/9783110713312-006

insight into these research questions by addressing D's *raison d'être*. Why was the Deuteronomic law written? What purposes did it aim to serve in ancient Israel? How tentative must our conclusions be given our differences of opinion on the intractable question of when *Urdeuteronomium* was composed? The study will proceed by investigating unique material in the Deuteronomic laws. This first portion of the paper will interact in large measure with Benjamin Kilchör's 2015 monograph on the topic, highlighting areas especially relevant to the question of D's ideological agenda. Then, based on this fresh analysis of the legal core's unique materials, the investigation will explore the contributions made to our understanding of this agenda. The investigation yields a tentative reconstruction of D's composition, before drawing conclusions about its original purpose and nature as resistance literature in the seventh century BCE.

1 Unique Material in Deuteronomy 12–26

Benjamin Kilchör investigates the chronological relationship (i.e., the possible literary reliance in either direction, as well as the possibility of independence) of BC, the Deuteronomic core (Deut 12–26), and HC.[2] Excluding Deuteronomy 12:1 and 26:16–19, the legal core contains 340 verses, which according to Kilchör's analysis, breaks down as follows: 110 are dependent upon BC and/or HC (32.3 %); 50 are related to texts in BC and/or HC but the direction of dependence is impossible to determine, a category Kilchör calls "reversible" (*Abhängigkeitsrichtung umkehrbar*; 14.7 %); and finally, 180 verses making up unique material having no observable connection with legal texts in the Tetrateuch (*sondergut*; 52.9 %).[3] One does not have to agree with all of Kilchör's decisions to admit that his overall conclusions are sound. First, one needs to consider the methodology used to discern literary dependence, and especially whether the direction of dependence can be determined. Second, one must also consider individual case-by-case texts in which a difference of exegetical detail may result here and

2 Kilchör, *Mosetora*, 317–20.

3 For heuristic purposes, I take as essentially correct Kilchör's proposed *Sondergut* of the Deuteronomic core: **12**:6–12, 17–19, 26, 28; **13**:1, 2, 4–6, 8–13, 15–16, 18–19; **14**:1, 3, 20, 24, 28; **15**:3, 5–11, 13–14, 20–22; **16**:2, 5, 12, 14, 17, 20; **17**:3–4, 7–20; **18**:3, 6–8, 13–14, 17–22; **19**:8–9, 14, 17–20; **20**:1–20; **21**:1–6, 9–17, 19–20, 22; **22**:2, 5–8, 13–21, 23–27; **23**:2–3, 7, 9–10, 13–14, 16–19, 25–26; **24**:1–6, 11; **25**:3–4, 6–10, 17–19; **26**:4, 10–15. In addition to these, there are many places in the Deuteronomic law where he identifies specific lexical or more minor phraseological distinctives. Here, I am only interested in exploring the recurring and more systematic innovations.

there in a difference of opinion about whether a particular verse is reversible, irreversible, or independent altogether. But given these caveats, Kilchör has laid a useful foundation for determining both tightly connected literary dependence between two (or more) texts and also for identifying looser ties between texts that have more indirect allusions and a subtle relationship. Kilchör goes beyond searching out characteristic phraseology of D[4] and "coincidence in language"[5] and moves the inquiry further along by isolating and investigating the innovations of the Deuteronomic law.

In particular, he has adapted the seven criteria of Richard B. Hays, developed originally for New Testament studies, to good effect for his purposes.[6] Further, Kilchör has ventured beyond the attempt to determine the mere presence of literary connections, to determine as much as is possible, the direction of dependence.[7] This portion of his work, of course, cuts against the grain of much contemporary scholarship. Since I agree in a great many details with Kilchör's reasonable approach, I use his conclusions to ask a question about the characteristic purposes of the unique material.

1.1 Deuteronomy 12:1–31 (The "Place" for Yhwh Worship)

Without doubt, Deuteronomy 12 is critical to our understanding of the Deuteronomic law as a whole and serves as the rhetorical cornerstone of the legal core. The chapter is the key to discerning the origins of the legal core, as much as that is possible.[8] After the superscription in 12:1, the chapter has four paragraphs: 12:2–7, the "place" that Yhwh chooses; 12:8–12, the "rest" that Yhwh provides; 12:13–19, local meat consumption; and 12:20–28, provisions for profane slaughter in other locales. This is followed by a concluding "warning against heresies" in 12:29–31, which some have taken as parallel to 12:1–4 in inverse sequence but which may also be an introduction to the laws of sedition in Deuteronomy 13.[9] I take it as axiomatic that the chapter draws upon and interacts with Exodus 20:24b[10] as well as drawing upon Leviticus 17:13–14 and less directly Exodus 23:20–24 (esp. v. 24) and 34:12–14. Thus, the frame of Deu-

4 Weinfeld, *Deuteronomy*.
5 Driver, *Critical Deuteronomy*, 10.
6 Kilchör, *Mosetora*, 31–35; Hays, *Echoes in Paul*; Hays, *Echoes in the Gospels*.
7 Kilchör, "Direction"; Kilchör, *Mosetora*, 35–41.
8 Pakkala, "Date," 388.
9 McConville, *Law*, 64.
10 See Levinson, *Deuteronomy*, 28–52.

teronomy 12 (that is, vv. 2–4 and 29–31) draws on the theme of the Decalogue's prohibition against foreign gods and images.

The chapter introduces a number of innovations in the Deuteronomic law: (1) the focus on eating in the presence of Yhwh together with the whole household in joyful celebration, cf. vv. 7, 12, 17, and 18; (2) the inclusion of the male and female servants and Levites for humanitarian reasons, cf. vv. 12, 18, and 19; and (3) above all of course, the idea of centralization, vv. 8–11 and 26. In addition, it might be observed that the stock Deuteronomic phraseology of "carefully hearing" the words being commanded, and the purpose clause, that "it may go well" may be another innovation of the chapter (v. 28). As the foundation for the rest of the legal core, we shall return to these themes frequently in this survey of the specific innovative texts of the legal materials.

1.2 Deuteronomy 13:1 (Canon Law)

The so-called "canon formula"[11] is connected to 4:2 but in general is also a Deuteronomic innovation, not being found elsewhere in the Pentateuch but perhaps reflected in wisdom texts (Prov 30:5–6; Eccl 3:14, 12:12–13; Rev 22:18–19, and cf. Jer 26:2, 12, 15). While not innovating a law from elsewhere in the Tetrateuch, a strong case can be made that this saying draws upon cuneiform legal tradition in general and even might adapt and transform a particular portion of Esarhaddon's Succession Treaty, § 4.[12] It seems entirely possible the Deuteronomic innovation was intended to summon loyalty to the word of Yhwh, using an Assyrian formula requiring exclusive loyalty to "the word of Esarhaddon," rather than as a narrow understanding of "canon" as a fixation on a closed collection of authoritative texts.[13] The innovation of 13:1 as "canon" law, understood broadly, is established, although caution is advisable when assuming a presumed Assyrian parallel. Recent work on the other proposed connections with EST (i.e., the rest of Deut 13 and Deut 28:15–45, and perhaps Deut 6:5) is suggestive that an Aramaic bridge transmitted a widely used Northwest Semitic curse tradition into the southern Levant, explaining those parallels as other

11 But see Nelson, *Deuteronomy*, 169–70.

12 Levinson, "You Must Not," 12–19; and specific to Esarhaddon's Succession Treaty, see especially Levinson, "Neo-Assyrian Origins," 30–32; Levinson, "Esarhaddon's Succession Treaty"; and Levinson and Stackert, "Between the Covenant Code." The connections with the EST, however, have been contested by some; see Berman, "Historicism," and the rebuttal in Levinson and Stackert, "Limitations." See also Versluis, "'And Moses Wrote,'" 139–41.

13 Versluis, 154–55.

than literary dependency. Several difficulties remain, and some scholars are revising or abandoning altogether the theory of direct oral or written connection with the EST.[14]

1.3 Deuteronomy 13:2–19 (Warnings against Heresy)

The chapter is not dependent upon earlier laws of the Tetrateuch, but most assume it is related in its various paragraphs to the opening of the Decalogue in Deuteronomy 5:6–10[15] or 5:11.[16] Kilchör points out that the chapter has no dependence upon tetrateuchal parallels, and the connection with Exodus 20:3 and 23:13 could just as easily be a dependence upon or shared redactional history with Deuteronomy 5:7.[17] Clearly, however, Deuteronomy 13 paraphrases the first commandment or at least, the three scenarios presented in this chapter could be taken as constituting *kasuistische Ausführungsgesetze* on the prohibition against "foreign gods."[18]

In addition, relative to the focus on "other gods whom you have not known," the recurrence of this phrase (in variations) in vv. 3, 7, and 14 is essentially identified as "direction of dependence is reversible" by Kilchör,[19] and yet this opprobrium of "other gods" whom the Israelites have not previously known characterizes Deuteronomy's preaching against idolatry (18 times). It may be inspired by the First Commandment (5:7) or may just as easily owe its origins to the preaching of Hosea (Hos 13:4).[20] Regardless of the origins or direction of influence, we may accept this focus on "other gods" in the First Commandment and in these warnings against apostasy as an innovation in the Deuteronomic law.

---

14 On the possibility of transmission by means of an Aramaic bridge, see Quick, *Deuteronomy 28*. Alternatively, Diana Edelman argues against a theory of dependence altogether, and explores instead a native monarchic Judahite treaty template as the source for much of this material ("Saying Goodbye").

15 Braulik, *Die deuteronomischen Gesetze*, 32–33.

16 Kaufman, "The Structure," 122–27.

17 Kilchör, *Mosetora*, 96.

18 Braulik, *Die deuteronomischen Gesetze*, 33.

19 It appears he omitted v. 17 in his discussion and list; cf. Kilchör, *Mosetora*, 95–96 and 333.

20 Cf. Weinfeld, *Deuteronomy*, 324.

1.4 Deuteronomy 14:1–21 (Dietary Laws)

Despite the attempt to relate this legal material to the Third Commandment (5:11) by way of phraseological associations with Leviticus 22:32–33,[21] I find the connection too forced to be useful. The obvious connection with Leviticus 11 is complex, and while I assume Deuteronomy 14 is dependent upon Leviticus 11 as its anterior text, the direction of dependence has been debated, and some have taken them as both dependent upon a common source.[22] Though Kilchör notes that abbreviation is not common in Deuteronomy where the discourse develops its central ideas (*Leitgedanken*), whereas reduction and simplification occur in contexts in which differentiation and distinctive regulations are relevant to the book's agenda,[23] I think it highly likely that Deuteronomy 14 was written to simplify and abridge the laws of Leviticus 11 (and perhaps Exod 23:19) in order to provide a new, more easily applicable version of those laws.[24] But regardless of the details of the origins of Deuteronomy 14, the innovation of v. 1 uses an identification clause to emphasize the essential nature of Israel as the "children belonging to Yhwh,"[25] who are therefore not permitted to participate in laceration and ritual tonsure, either shaving a forelock or the beard as mourning rituals, which are rituals well-attested in Canaanite culture.[26] The additional innovative verses in this text were added to round off the literary representation of the dietary laws (vv. 3 and 20).

---

21 Kilchör, *Mosetora*, 96–102.

22 Nihan, "Laws," 401–4. But see Eckart Otto, who argues that "it is simply not necessary to postulate a hypothetical source document. The list of clean and unclean animals in Lev 11:2–23 is taken up in Deut 14:4–20 and supplemented by a list of unclean birds. The key to understanding the re-interpretation of Lev 11 in Deut 14 is the law of Deut 12, which is, indeed, the hermeneutical key not only for Deut 14, but for the entire Deuteronomic Code (Deut 12–26)" ("Deuteronomy," 181).

23 Kilchör, *Mosetora*, 102.

24 Firmage, "Biblical Dietary Laws," 207–8.

25 The nominal clause of identification is modified by the prepositional phrase belonging to Yhwh, showing possession; Arnold and Choi, *Guide*, § 5.1.1 and § 4.1.10f.

26 Pardee, "Ba'lu," 267–68; see Zevit, *Religions*, 664, and Schmidt, *Israel's Beneficent Dead*, 166–78.

1.5 Deuteronomy 14:22–15:23 (Economic Miscellanies: Tithes, Debt Remission, Slave Manumission, and Firstlings)

Based on the use of a monetary tithe in 14:25 and certain redundancies in the text based on the name formula, it is possible to argue that 14:24–26 constitutes a later expansion intended to address changing circumstances, related to "an emerging redistributive economy in which currency was replacing barter-based exchange."[27] With regard to selections devoted to various types of tithes, Kilchör demonstrates that attempts to discern direction of literary influence have mistakenly relied on flawed historical reconstructions.[28] An approach based firstly on literary comparisons, regardless of *a priori* historical assumptions, suggests that Deuteronomy 14:22–29 presupposes the tithe practices of anterior texts in Leviticus 27:30–33 and Numbers 18:21–32,[29] and that vv. 24–26 make certain provisions for Israelites for whom "the place" is too far away for participation. In addition, vv. 28–29 constitute an innovation related to poverty – the triennial tithe must be shared with the landless. This altruistic impulse appears to be a distinctive innovation of the Deuteronomic law.

Similarly, the Deuteronomic innovation related to debt remission (15:1–11) is focused on alleviation of the needs of those who suffer in poverty (v. 4), as well as the desire for Israelites to give generously without attempting to abuse the law of the Shemittah for personal gain (vv. 7–11). The concept of "brotherhood" recurs here as well, serving as a powerful motivation undergirding the ethical demands of Deuteronomic law.[30] The release of slaves (15:12–18) was a concern of Exodus 21:2–11 and Leviticus 25:39–46.[31] The Deuteronomic innovation is focused on a problem identified also in H – that a released slave who fell into poverty through loss of land will not be helped by release in the year

---

27 Richter, "Question," 42. Kilchör identifies vv. 24 and 28 as innovations, which confirms Richter's assessment to some degree (*Mosetora*, 333). The concept (mistaken, in my view) that we should think of these tithes as "taxes" goes back to Wellhausen (*Prolegomena*, 155–59). See Eissfeldt, *Erstlinge*, 48–51. For evidence of tithing as an ancient practice and its distinction from "taxes," see Lundbom, *Deuteronomy*, 482–83.

28 Kilchör, *Mosetora*, 115–16.

29 Kilchör, 116–25.

30 McConville, *God*, 92–93. For an alternative, view, see Guillaume on brotherhood in this volume.

31 Kilchör argues, I think convincingly, that Deut 15:12–18 is a new formulation or application of Exod 21:2–11, while also taking Lev 25:39–46 into consideration ("... unter Berücksichtigung von Lev 25,39–46 handelt" (*Mosetora*, 150). On the Hebrew "slave," see Rossi and Guillaume, "Alternative Reading."

of jubilee unless they also receive the ancestral property back into their possession (Lev 25:41b). Deuteronomic law addresses the problem differently, by insisting the released slave be sent away with provisions of flock and agricultural produce (15:13–14).

The law of the firstborn male animals (15:19–23) draws upon Exodus 22:28–29 [Eng 22:29–30], and has been innovated only (1) by location, either "at the place that Yhwh shall choose" or "within any of your towns" and (2) by manner: with the household and having given attention to the clean or unclean distinction (15:20 and 22). Kilchör concludes that D again presupposes previous laws (Exod 13:2,11–16; 22:28b–29; 34:20; Num 18:15–18) but, at the same time, updates them based on Deuteronomy 12 and that the beneficiaries of these innovations are individuals susceptible to poverty, especially peasant farmers and their families.[32]

1.6 Deuteronomy 16:1–17 (The Pilgrimage Festival Calendar)

The historical and literary connections between Deuteronomy 16 and the numerous Tetrateuch materials have generated an enormous amount of scholarly speculation. Other texts in the Torah related to this chapter are Exodus 12:1–28, 13:1–16, 23:14–17, 34:18–25, Leviticus 23, and Numbers 28–29. After a review of the intricacies between these, Kilchör concludes that Deuteronomy 16 presupposes all the festival laws and that with regard especially to Passover-Maṣṣot (vv. 1–8), the earlier texts have been brought together and interpreted in light of centralization.[33] In fact, here is perhaps the best example of updating based on the centralizing principle.[34] Cutting across all three festivals, among other lesser innovations are modifications that accommodate the new situation after centralization. First, regarding Passover-Maṣṣot (vv. 1–8), the location at "the place" is identified (v. 2) and there follows a specific prohibition against observing the festival "within any of your settlements" (i.e., *bəʾaḥad šəʿārêkā*, "in one of your gates," v. 5). Second, the instruction for observing Shavuot (vv. 9–12) is innovated only in certain details, this time based on parallels to Leviticus 23 instead of Exodus, such as the call for a "freewill offering" (*nədābâ*, v. 10) instead of H's more elaborate proscription of animals and grain (Lev 23:17–20).[35]

32 Kilchör, *Mosetora*, 162.

33 Kilchör, 162–201.

34 Levinson, *Deuteronomy*, 53–97.

35 Kilchör focuses only on the offering for the first barley offering (Lev 23:12–13) but fails to draw the contrast between Deut 16:10 and the even more elaborate offerings for Shavuot in Lev 23:17–20, which would strengthen his argument (*Mosetora*, 194).

In addition, vv. 11–12 continue the Deuteronomic innovation by making Shavuot a joyful festival "before Yhwh" (again, focused on centralization) and mandates that the entire household participate, including children and servants, along with resident Levites, immigrants, orphans, and widows in the care of the Israelite worshipper. The characteristic motive clause recalling that the Israelites were themselves servants in Egypt is present.[36] Third, the law of Sukkot (vv. 13–17) similarly adds the Deuteronomic theme of joy in corporate worship (with the whole household), including the *personae miserae* in one's social orbit (v. 14). In addition, the concluding assertion that all are to give according to the blessings bestowed by Yhwh (v. 17) may be another innovation, again softening the burden of the more elaborate sacrifices required in P and H for those who simply cannot afford them.

1.7 Deuteronomy 16:18–17:20 (Judiciary and Monarchy)

The appointment of judges and *šōṭərîm*-officials (16:18–20) is innovated by the recurring phrase emphasizing conquest and long life on "the ground/land that Yhwh your God is giving you" (cf. 5:16; 16:20; 17:14a; 18:9a).[37] In addition to this, the simple appointment of judges and officials in v. 18a, as distinct from instructions for fair legal pronouncements in the Tetrateuchal parallels, may be considered unique material.[38] There follow brief prohibitions against three unacceptable religious practices (16:21–17:1), which have parallels in Leviticus 19:23a; 26:1; and 22:19–20, respectively. These three essentially restate casuistic laws found in their Tetrateuchal anterior texts and perhaps add the distinctive detail that the last one is "abhorrent" to Yhwh (*tôʿăbat yhwh*).[39]

The prosecution of idolaters (17:2–7) reduplicates the forms and phraseology of the chapter concerned with apostasy (Deut 13:2–19) and continues the distinctive Deuteronomic casuistic form of *kî* introducing the protasis.[40] The possibility that 17:3–4 is unique to Deuteronomic law is raised by a comparison of

36 The celebratory quality of Israel's worship is a persistent theme since Deut 12, where the phrase "you shall eat there before Yhwh your God, and you shall celebrate over all your handiwork" (12:7, and cf. 12:12, 18, 27), announces another hallmark of Deuteronomic law; see Arnold, "Israelite Worship," 168–69.

37 Kilchör, *Mosetora*, 203; Braulik, "Der unterbrochene Dekalog," 181. In this discussion, I am suspending the question of whether these laws on various authorities (judges, kings, priests, and prophets) are extensions of the command to honor father and mother; cf. Kilchör, 201–3.

38 Kilchör, 206–7.

39 Weinfeld, *Deuteronomy*, 267–69 and 323.

40 Levinson, *Deuteronomy*, 103–4.

these verses to the parallels in Numbers 32:13, Leviticus 24:14a, and Numbers 35:30, respectively.[41]

Instructions for the functions of a "high court" (17:8–13) and the law of the king (17:14–20) contain no anterior texts in the Torah and are essentially unique to Deuteronomy.[42] Perhaps the most distinctive feature of the latter of these is the remarkable constriction of the monarchy as an institution. As the only Pentateuchal text devoted to the nature of the monarchy, the duty of the king is to study "a copy of this law" (17:18), whereas the Levitical priest is the source of authority in difficult judicial or legislative cases (17:8–13).[43]

1.8 Deuteronomy 18:1–22 (Priest and Prophet)

The legal pericope devoted to provisions of support for the clergy (vv. 1–8) has a clear parallel in Numbers 18:2–20, to which the phrase "as he [Yhwh] promised them" (v. 2) probably points.[44] In particular, v. 3 appears to be conceptually parallel to Numbers 18:8–11 but without phraseological specifics. This leaves vv. 6–8 as an innovation, dealing as it does with the Levite who leaves the countryside villages for "the place" chosen by Yhwh, where he must have equal status with his priestly brothers.

Deuteronomy's prescription of prophetic authority (vv. 9–22) has two innovative and distinctive portions. First comes a redundant call for wholehearted faithfulness to Yhwh in the face of sorcerers and diviners of all sorts, despite the attraction such practices held for "the nations" in the land prior to Israel's arrival (vv. 13–14). Second is the long, final prediction of a future prophet who will faithfully lead Yhwh's people (vv. 17–22).[45]

---

41 Kilchör, *Mosetora*, 212–13.

42 On the direction of dependence between Deut 17:14 and 1 Sam 8:5, see Müller, "Israel's King," 62–68.

43 Choi, *Traditions*, 68; Strawn, "Reading Josiah," 34–36.

44 See Deut 10:9; Kilchör, *Mosetora*, 216; Milgrom, "Profane Slaughter," 3–4, 11–13. Note the use of the perfect in *ka'ăšer dibber-lô* in 18:2 instead of the participle, which is Deuteronomy's regular way of citing itself, rather than Tetrateuchal intertexts.

45 Kilchör examines parallels between Deut 18:9–14 and, in order, Num 34:2; Lev 18:27a, 21a; Num 23:23a; Lev 19:26b; Exod 22:17; Lev 19:31a; Lev 18:27a, 30; Gen 6:9, and for Deut 18:15–18, he compares Num 12:6; Exod 4:12b, 20:1 *Mosetora*, 220–23, 334.

1.9 Deuteronomy 19:1–21 (Fairness in the Administration of Justice)

Against illegitimate blood revenge, the law provides three asylum cities (vv. 1–13, cf. Exod 21:12–14; Num 35; and also Deut 4:41–43), which is innovated by Deuteronomy only at vv. 8–9 with the notion of land expansion.[46] Deuteronomy's conceptual map of territory promised to the ancestors (Deut 1:7–8; 11:24; 34:1–4) anticipates land expansion in the future, for which three additional asylum cities would need to be named.[47] The fact that Deuteronomy 4:41–43 adds three cities in the Transjordan may also show an awareness of unanticipated land expansion, as reported in Deuteronomy 1–3 (cf. Num 21:21–35). Specifically, the possibility of additional cities needed in the future may be seen in the light of the contrast between uninheritable land (Edom and Moab) and Amorite territories in the Transjordan, which were added through the "accidental conquest" motif, including the allotment of the territories of Sihon and Og to Reuben, Gad, and Half Manasseh (2:1–3:22, esp. 3:8–17).

The paragraph on the displacement of boundary markers and court witnesses (vv. 14–21) contains Deuteronomic innovations at v. 14 and vv. 17–20. The distinctive expression regarding "the land that Yhwh your God is giving you to possess" is not itself characteristic of these innovations but of Deuteronomy more generally, although here it may have been instigated by association with v. 8 and the concept of enlarged territories.[48] The law against false witnesses (vv. 15–21) draws upon several texts, notably Numbers 35:30 and several phrases from the Book of the Covenant and Deuteronomy 13:6, 9, 12; 17:4, 9.[49] The Deuteronomic version assumes the need for two witnesses in capital cases, as in its anterior text (Num 35:30), but innovates the law by taking up the possibility that one of the witnesses is malevolent and therefore provides a process for justice in such cases.

---

46 As before, Kilchör argues that Deut 19:1–13 can be best understood if one presumes that Exod 21:12–14 and Num 35 were known to the Deuteronomic tradent (*Mosetora*, 237).

47 Rainey and Notley, *Sacred Bridge*, 30–31. Jeffrey H. Tigay takes vv. 8–9 as parenthetical, identified here as a Deuteronomic innovation, prompted by the idea of greater distances within the Promised Land (v. 6) so that when the distances increase because of newer territories, additional cities are needed (*Deuteronomy*, 181).

48 Kilchör, *Mosetora*, 237. On the occurrences of the phrase, see Weinfeld, *Deuteronomy*, 341–42, although he omitted (apparently inadvertently) Deut 19:14 from this list. Kilchör also takes the theme of the removal of landmarks as evidence of the influence of wisdom literature (265).

49 Kilchör, 238–41.

1.10 Deuteronomy 20:1–20 (On Warfare)

Rather than a thorough list of rules governing behavior in warfare, these paragraphs establish general priorities by instructing the roles of priests and officers (vv. 2–9) and guarding against cruelty and war crimes against cities and trees (vv. 10–18 and vv. 19–20 respectively). Deuteronomy's laws regarding warfare have no direct parallels to the rest of the Pentateuch.[50] These paragraphs may themselves be taken as innovations by displaying an altruism missing in earlier texts related to warfare.[51]

1.11 Deuteronomy 21:1–23 (Miscellany on Domestic Life)

This chapter is framed by the recurring reference to the ground "that Yhwh your God is giving you" (vv. 1 and 23), although the laws contained in this *inclusio* are quite diverse.[52] The law regarding unsolved murder (vv. 1–9) has no parallel elsewhere in the Tetrateuch, although like the laws on warfare in the previous chapter, this paragraph may be connected to others in Deuteronomy itself, such as those defining the tasks of elders and judges (Deut 16–18) or the administration of justice (19:15–21). This innovation is concerned with absolving the guilt of an innocent village in the case in which a murdered corpse is found close to its gates.

Similarly, the paragraph on female captives of war (vv. 10–14) has no parallel elsewhere in the Tetrateuch, although it is linked thematically and somewhat in its phrasing to Deuteronomy 20 (see Beukenhorst in this volume). Again, the Deuteronomic innovation, if this can be called such, prescribes a specific process by which an Israelite man may marry a female captive that first, provides time for proper mourning of her losses, and second, prohibits divorcing her into slavery. In the same way, the law regarding primogeniture in polygamous families (vv. 15–17) has no anterior texts and appears to be a Deuteronomic innovation to ensure fairness and uniform treatment across all Israelite families.

---

50 Driver, *Critical Deuteronomy*, 236; Kilchör, *Mosetora*, 241; Beukenhorst in this volume.

51 So, e.g., Num 31:17–18 mandates the execution of all but virgins whereas Deut 20:14 allows the capture of all as prisoners; see Kilchör for further differences between Num 31:17–18 and the Deuteronomic law (*Mosetora*, 242).

52 Richard D. Nelson incorrectly says "vv. 1 and 21" (*Deuteronomy*, 255). The laws collected here, like so many others in 21:1–25:19, may in fact be organized and arranged only by a loose associative principle; see Rofé, "Arrangement." Tigay treats all of the disparate laws of 21:10–25:19 as "miscellaneous laws" having mostly to do with private matters as opposed to the preceding collection focused on public officials and "matters concerning the nation as a whole" (*Deuteronomy*, 193).

By contrast, the law of the rebellious son (vv. 18–21) is genetically connected to Exodus 21:15 and 17 and probably intends to supplement those earlier laws by placing responsibility on the parents to execute the punishment.[53] Here we have an example of a Deuteronomic innovation that is directly supplementing BC's regulation (perhaps also aware of H; cf. Lev 20:9), but again, as a protective and altruistic measure.

The final law of the chapter is concerned with the proper disposal of the body of an executed criminal (vv. 22–23). Here we return to the category of a regulation having no parallel text in the Tetrateuch, although Kilchör identifies certain lexical links with Numbers 35:34.[54] The Deuteronomic innovation is once again focused on humanitarian treatment of others, as well as defilement of the land as a result of inhumane conduct.

1.12 Deuteronomy 22:1–29 (Domestic Disputes)

The theory that the Deuteronomic law has a redactional arrangement based on the Decalogue finds expression here in the assumption that the various laws of this chapter are transitional. So, e.g., vv. 1–12 contain diverse materials woven together and standing as transitional between laws focused on the sixth and seventh commandments (of the Jewish ordering).[55] Clearly, these materials contain two specific connections with BC, in which a briefer casuistic law there is given fuller or clearer treatment here: vv. 1–4 supplementing Exodus 23:4–5, and vv. 28–29 supplementing Exodus 22:15–16 [Eng 16–17].[56] Additional innovations in these materials relate to transvestism (v. 5), not capturing a mother bird together with her young (vv. 6–7), care in building a parapet (v. 8), accusations of unchastity (vv. 13–21), and adultery with an engaged woman (vv. 23–27). The point of the laws concerned with mixture taboos is, of course, often discussed and seldom understood, beyond a general assumption that "mixtures seen as violating or blurring natural or social boundaries were thought to generate ritual impurity."[57]

---

53 Kilchör, *Mosetora*, 244. The Deuteronomic innovation perhaps also makes the rebellious son hypothetical only, more as a parenetic instruction than a true legal text, despite its casuistic formulation; see Brichto, "Kin," 32–33.

54 Kilchör, *Mosetora*, 245.

55 Kaufman, "Structure," 135–38. Being the fifth and sixth commandments in the Catholic/Lutheran ordering; see Braulik, "Sequence," 321–22.

56 Other texts may also be in view, as argued by Kilchör, *Mosetora*, 247–48, 253–54.

57 Nelson, *Deuteronomy*, 267, referring to Lev 19:19.

1.13 Deuteronomy 23:1–26 [Eng 22:30–23:25] (Sexual and Social Boundaries)

As we saw with 22:1–12, a paragraph that serves as a transition between the fifth and sixth commandments for the view committed to the decalogic arrangement, so 23:16–24:5 is transitional between the sixth and seventh commandments.[58] In this chapter, the only direct dependence upon BC is the concern with interest (v. 20 [Eng 19]), which builds upon both Exodus 22:24 [Eng 22:25] and Leviticus 25:35–38 in not only guarding against worsening the plight of the poor but in positively establishing a program for poverty prevention.[59]

If Kilchör is correct, then D's innovation in this case is inspired by Leviticus 25:35–38 but is more closely intent on expanding the original prohibition of Exodus 22:24 [Eng 22:25] in order to prohibit interest (*nešek*) charged to any vulnerable Israelite. Therefore, D hopes to avoid poverty altogether. The first prohibition makes specific mention of "the poor" (*heʿānî*) among the people of Israel (Exod 22:24 [Eng 22:25]), while H's rather obscure phraseology implies financial difficulties with the potential for catastrophic ruin.[60] D's innovation, then, in Deuteronomy 23:20–21 [Eng 23:19–20] contributes to a larger agenda of poverty prevention by democratizing BC's prohibition in order to enable the endangered or nearly impoverished Israelite to avoid further loss.

Innovative contributions of the Deuteronomic law in the section of "community laws" (vv. 2–9) involve what appears to be an adaptation of H's prohibition of priests from altar service if they have physical blemishes (Lev 21:16–24) by widening the regulation to laity, excluding men with crushed testicles or a severed penis, both words being distinctive in the Hebrew Bible (23:2; *pəṣûaʿ* and *šopkâ*). These are likely focused on Canaanite customs considered abhorrent to Yhwh and lead, therefore, to the concern in 23:3 against further Canaanite influences.[61] Further, the ban on the inclusion of an Ammonite or Moabite individual in the "assembly of Yhwh" is doubly emphasized (v. 7), whereas provision is made for admitting children of the third generation of Edomites or Egyptians (v. 9). With regard to the sanctity of the war encampment (vv. 10–15), the innovations include a general introduction to the topic (v. 10) as well as explicit instructions for defecation outside the camp (vv. 13–14).

---

58 Braulik, "Sequence," 321–22; Kaufman, "Structure," 138–39.

59 I am therefore in agreement with Kilchor's thorough treatment and conclusions (*Mosetora*, 264–73), and Tigay, *Deuteronomy*, 217.

60 Milgrom, *Leviticus 23–27*, 2,204–9.

61 Kilchör, *Mosetora*, 258.

One remarkable innovation in this chapter is the law about extraditing runaway slaves to other countries (vv. 16–17).[62] The humanitarian thrust of the Deuteronomic law comes to the fore again in this law, which stands in contrast with ancient Near Eastern legal materials, permitting the escaped servant asylum in Israel, including permission to reside "with you, in your midst, ... in any one of your villages," apparently fully incorporated in Israelite society. An important part of the Deuteronomic innovation is the theological foundation for such altruism; namely, that the runaway servant imitates Yhwh in the freedom to select a "place" to reside. Although many interpretive details remain unclear (such as the precise understanding of *qādēš* and *qədēšâ*), the prohibition of prostitution is a Deuteronomic innovation (vv. 18–19).[63] Another innovation of this chapter is the restriction in two brief laws that one may eat from another person's unharvested crops while passing by the field, permitted one does not take advantage by consuming more than they can eat on the spot (vv. 25–26). These prohibitions have in mind both provisions for the needy and fairness to the farmer.

1.14 Deuteronomy 24:1–25:19 (Miscellany on Various Social Concerns)

Among a large group of miscellaneous laws, the Deuteronomic innovations begin with a ban on remarriage (24:1–4), the deferral of a new husband from the military (24:5), and the seizure of essential implements in pledge (24:6). In all these cases, a concern with fundamental fairness is at play.[64]

Exodus 21:20, which is concerned with the beating of servants, may have loosely inspired the Deuteronomic innovation related to flogging (25:1–3), but this is a genuine innovation in the obvious humanitarian concern for excessive punishment.[65] A further innovation occurs in the next law's prohibition against cruel treatment of the threshing ox (25:4).

62 For exegesis on why these are foreign servants escaping to Israel, see Tigay, *Deuteronomy*, 215 and Nelson, *Deuteronomy*, 280.

63 For background on *qādēš* and *qədēšâ*, see Lundbom, *Deuteronomy*, 657–60 and van der Toorn, "Female Prostitution." For a vigorous denial that they connote "sacred prostitution," see several publications by Phyllis A. Bird ("End"; "Prostitution"; "Of Whores"; "Bible," 156–58).

64 The law regulating fairness in exacting a pledge (24:10–13) is a restatement of Exod 22:25–26 [Eng 22:26–27] but broadens the items taken and requires fair treatment of the borrower.

65 For ancient Near Eastern parallels in ancient law, see Lundbom, *Deuteronomy*, 699–700. It goes beyond the evidence to aver "no other ancient Near Eastern source limits the number of strokes" (Tigay, *Deuteronomy*, 230).

The custom of Levirate marriage is the backdrop of Genesis 38 and the book of Ruth[66] and is attested in other ancient legal customs, especially Hittite, and related Assyrian laws as well as laws from Nuzi and Ugarit.[67] The Deuteronomic innovation in 25:5–10 appears to refine the custom as an obligation to ensure the "patrilineal kinship interest tied to land and property" and only secondarily to provide the continuation of the deceased man's posterity, guaranteeing the social wellbeing of the widow.[68] Kilchör has suggested that the innovation is also referring back to Numbers 27:8–11, in which the daughters of Zelophehad are permitted to inherit the property of their deceased father and the sequence is established in the case of a deceased man with no sons: the inheritance passes to a daughter or the man's brothers or his uncles or nearest kinsman within the clan. Whereas Numbers 27:8–11 has the daughters in focus, Kilchör argues that Deuteronomy 25:5 has Numbers 27:8 in view lexically but switches the view to the widow, in order to ensure that she goes to the brother as well as the inheritance to ensure her welfare. [69] I think it likely that Levirate marriage prior to the Deuteronomic innovation of 25:5–10 was a known practice and perhaps a legal assumption, vaguely intended to secure a future for the deceased man who was childless but now required in order also to protect the widow against poverty.

While not a completely new law, the punishment of the woman who improperly intervenes in a fight between her husband and another man (25:11–12) builds upon Exodus 21:18–19, 22–25, and the adaptation of the laws against false weights and measures (25:13–16) are drawn from Leviticus 19:35–37. I agree with Kilchör about the direction of dependence from H to D.[70] The concluding note on Amalekite aggression (25:17–19) is an innovation but also not actually a legal text. It seems likely to be a closure of the miscellaneous laws of Deuteronomy 23–25, serving as an *inclusio* with 23:4–7 [Eng 3–6] or perhaps even a larger structural frame for all of Deuteronomy 12–25, by echoing the words of 12:9–10.[71]

---

66 Brichto, "Kin," 11–21; Braulik, *Die deuteronomischen Gesetze*, 108–9.
67 Lundbom, *Deuteronomy*, 706.
68 Naomi Steinberg has clarified that the birth of a male child as guarantor of the widow's future is a by-product of the levirate law, whereas kinship inheritance interests were primary ("Romancing," 338–40). Her work has also helpfully proposed a spectrum of widowhood in ancient Israel along the lines of three separate categories of widows (342).
69 Kilchör, *Mosetora*, 297.
70 Kilchör, 301–2.
71 Driver, *Critical Deuteronomy*, 287–88; Nelson, *Deuteronomy*, 302.

1.15 Deuteronomy 26:1–15 (Concluding Liturgies)

The liturgy for presenting first fruits (vv. 1–11) quite obviously draws upon Exodus 23:19a (and cf. Lev 19:23–25; 23:9–14) but does so by looking beyond the annual requirement and developing a unique ritual for the unrepeatable event of bringing of first fruits after the conquest of the Promised Land.[72] Innovations, of course, include the centralization formula (v. 2) but also the declaration (v. 3), ritual (v. 4), and confession (vv. 5–10) that constitute the liturgy. As an example of the difficulties in this approach, the call to celebration, together with one's household and the Levite and *gēr* in the country villages, is also distinctive of the Deuteronomic core (12:7, 12:12, 12:18, 14:26–27, 16:11 and 16:14).[73]

The tithe declaration (vv. 12–15), which is unique to Deuteronomy, returns to the specifics of 14:28–29, where the triennial tithe is established. While we cannot be dogmatic about the direction of influence here, we can be confident that the Deuteronomic innovation is the concern for the *tetrad* – the Levite, the *gēr*, the orphan, and the widow – who appear to have landlessness as their common.[74]

2 Ideological Agenda of these Unique Materials

Before turning to an overview of the various themes that recur in the Deuteronomic innovations, one important topic related to structure of the legal core needs addressing. While I have agreed in the main with Kilchör's method and results, I cannot at this time agree with the theory that the Decalogue provided the overall structure for the Deuteronomic law in chs. 12–26, which is central in his presentation. As an example of the difficulties in this approach, the removal of landmarks (19:14) is only placed among commands related to the sixth commandment (murder) by assuming that removal of such landmarks may generate hatred between Israelites. In this way, *ist diese Bestimmung mit dem Tötungsverbot assoziiert*, and the instruction regarding false witnesses must likewise be associated with murder instead of the more logical ninth commandment.[75] This

72 The temporal clause at the beginning of the paragraph (v. 1) distinguishes the ritual envisioned here as unrepeatable, whereas the temporal clause in the next paragraph (v. 12) returns to the cycle of the triennial tithe.

73 Cf. Arnold, "Israelite Worship," 168–69.

74 Awabdy, *Immigrants*, 90–91.

75 So Kilchör, who draws also upon Num 35:26–27 to make the association, which, however, makes no mention of landmarks, only asylum cities (*Mosetora*, 237). On false witnesses (Deut 19:15–21), see p. 238. Many other examples could be given in which I believe the association

goes without raising the complicated question of which sequence of the three possible ways of ordering the Ten Words (now known as Catholic/Lutheran, Protestant/Anglican, or Jewish order) was followed in the organizing structure of Deuteronomy 12–26.[76] Alternatively, Stephen A. Kaufman made the argument many years ago that a decalogic arrangement of the laws in Deuterononomy 12–25 (in his discussion) contains laws "here and there" whose connections with the Ten Words cannot be readily demonstrated by direct dependence but whose location in the current arrangement was due to other structuring principles.[77] But this argument could be turned around; perhaps Deuteronomy 12–26 is primarily arranged by free "association" like other ancient Near Eastern law corpora, and the decalogic arrangement, if indeed it can be accepted as present, is secondary, perhaps as part of this Deuteronomic innovation.

Taking up now the Deuteronomic innovations themselves, we begin with the observation that the concept of cult centralization stands at the heart of the matter, along with its implications for a number of elements of the society. In a sense, this investigation confirms the older interpretation that focuses on Deuteronomy's tenets of one Yhwh, one Israel, one land, one place of worship, and one revelation, which is the Torah.[78] Especially pertinent for our deliberations is the book's overall casting of its individual laws as the "Torah,"[79] reflecting a move from individual "instructions" (plural) to the singular, connoting the disclosure

---

with the Ten Words is in doubt, such as Deut 25:11–12 linked to the ninth commandment by way of associations with 25:5–10, itself already in some doubt (Kilchör, 299–300).

76 Kilchör, 42–52. He has followed the Catholic/Lutheran sequence in ordering Deut 12–26, and is drawing deeply on the work of Braulik (*Die deuteronomischen Gesetze*). Individual exegetical problems abound, such as, e.g., the Deuteronomic law related to warfare, which has been shown recently to be structured by an "associative organizing principle," using the six "laws of war" scattered over four disparate loci, which does not preclude an overarching connection to the Decalogue, although this seems less likely in my view (see below); cf. Bartor, "'When You Go,'" 1–2. Even less likely, it seems to me, is the possibility the laws are structured around the theme of the preservation of life as the center (19:1–21:9) of a chiastic, or palindromic structure; cf. Tsai, *Human Rights*.

77 Kaufman identifies three additional principles known from ancient Near Eastern legal corpora at work in Deut 12–25, besides the overarching decalogic arrangement: (1) general themes, (2) priority, and (3) deliberate concatenation or association of key words, phrases, or motifs ("Structure," 115).

78 Von Rad, *Old Testament Theology*, 1.226–29 and von Rad, *Das Gottesvolk*, 50. Whether or not one can call this a "unified theological conspectus" ("einer einheitlichen theologischen Schau") remains open to debate, as does the assumption that this theological vision begins with 6:4. Even in pre-modern times, the convergence of faith in one Yhwh worshipped in one place by one people, Israel, goes back to Josephus; cf. Amir, "Josephus," 15.

79 Deut 1:5, 4:8, 4:44, 17:18, 27:3, 27:8, 27:26, 28:58, 28:61, 29:20, 29:28, 30:10, 31:9, 31:11, 31:12, 31:24, 31:26, 31:46, 33:4, and 33:10.

of the will of Yhwh *in writing* (4:13 and 10:4). This is likely a move already inspired by the book of Hosea (Hos 4:6, 8:1 and 8:12)[80] and relates further to the agenda of the Deuteronomic laws in general to consolidate worship in one location, among one people, worshiping one Yhwh, by means of one Torah. Indeed, Hosea may have been the original inspiration for cult centralization because of the conviction that the increase of priests and altars in the Northern Kingdom only led to an increase of sin and guilt (Hos 4:7–8 and 8:11). Similarly, Hosea may be responsible for a more comprehensive understanding of "Torah" (Hos 4:6 and 8:12), although broadened considerably in its application in Deuteronomy.[81]

Beyond cult centralization – and beyond specific phraseological distinctives, which in many cases are common to the book as a whole – this survey has identified other ideological features that characterize the Deuteronomic law itself. The distinctive accent of Deuteronomy's opprobrium of idolatry recurs in the legal core as a means of identifying Israel as one people, unified under the banner of exclusive Yahwism. Israel's loyalty to one Yhwh is at times defined over and against the image of idolatry as practised among Israel's neighbors.[82] This becomes a criterion for identifying Israel vis-à-vis Canaanite practices of funerary rites, dietary laws, and other social customs, in order to emphasize the unified nature of Israel as Yhwh's own possession.[83] Furthermore, the worship and service of Yhwh in the Deuteronomic law is expected to be exultant celebration (note the recurrence of the verb *śmḥ* in the legal core, culminating just beyond it at 27:7), especially in the prescription to eat certain meals in the presence of Yhwh at the central sanctuary.[84]

In addition, this investigation has highlighted Deuteronomy's particular interest in tying together its innovations in worship with humanitarian themes, especially the mandate to include one's entire household in the moment of sac-

---

80 Wolff, *Hosea*, 79, 138; Dearman, *Book of Hosea*, 158–59.

81 Von Rad, *Old Testament Theology*, 1.222; Wolff, *Hosea*, 79, 81, 138.

82 If the so-called "canon law" of 13:1 is original in its location, as opposed to being drawn secondarily from 4:2 at a later date, then we may speculate that the Deuteronomic law also innovated Neo-Assyrian ideology to call for exclusive loyalty to the word of Yhwh over and against the Assyrian demand for loyalty to Esarhaddon. In this way, the Deuteronomic law also appears to envision itself with some degree of fixity or finality, although we should not overstate this idea to the exclusion of the possibility of a perceived need for legal adaptation in the future.

83 Various innovations associated with the "community laws" may also be motivated by concerns over too much association with Canaanite practices, or impurity arising from conformity to Ammonites, Moabites, etc.

84 Arnold, "Israelite Worship," 168–69. The presence of a "festive theory" in the legal core may be an overstatement; cf. Braulik, "Joy."

rifice to Yhwh and sharing one's God-given abundance with the *personae miserae* class of individuals.[85] In refining the laws devoted to tithes and debt remission, these Deuteronomic innovations show a particular altruistic impulse for the poor, ensuring that the blessings of the land must be shared with the landless. Lending laws are innovated lightly in order to protect destitute brother-Israelites and to prevent further financial loss. Such altruism extends remarkably to the runaway slave who is granted asylum in Israel. Essential fairness is at play in all these innovations, visible also in regulations related to the freedom to eat from another person's unharvested crops, the deferral of a new husband from military service, and the seizure of essential implements in pledge. We even find among these innovations a concern that fairness be shown to animals (a mother bird or a threshing ox).

The mandate for universal fairness pervades other social institutions. The Deuteronomic laws add little new to the institutions related to judges and officials of the court, but the function of a "high court" itself and the role of the monarch have no correspondence in the Tetrateuch. Innovations related to the court were intended to ensure fairness through new regulations on the displacement of boundary markers, further instructions for the proper role of witnesses, and concerns with the administration of justice in cases of unsolved murder, an executed criminal, or in cases of excessive flogging. In addition, cult centralization contained an inherent danger in creating an appearance of consolidated power in the hands of a monarch, requiring a further innovation severely constricting the notion of kingship. The distinctively Deuteronomic "law of the king" (Deut 17:14–20) expresses a qualified acceptance of the royal institutions but abhors any imitation of the customs of the nations, envisioning instead a human king chosen by Yhwh. This places the law between the older north Israelite traditions that were opposed to kingship and the Deuteronomistic traditions of the exilic period that glorified the Davidic line.[86] Justice was also a concern for the non-Jerusalem Levites. Centralization required the Deuteronomic laws to provide for them since they were formerly associated with the countryside villages, although the details of precisely what is provided and what their future roles would be are unclear (Deut 18:6–8).

With regard to warfare, Deuteronomy's laws are themselves innovations, intended to guard against inhumane treatment and war crimes against cities

85 Arnold, "Israelite Worship," 172. Deuteronomy also innovates in its understanding of how the poor (*'ebyôn* and *'ānî*) relate to other vulnerable individuals in the society. If the system envisioned in Deuteronomy is effective, then immigrants, orphans, and widows would be provided for, and would not be vulnerable to falling into poverty; see Lohfink, "Poverty," 43–45.
86 Rofé, "Ephraimite," 228–29; *contra* Müller, "Israel's King," 73–74.

and trees, defining roles for priests and military officers in preparing and conducting war and ensuring the fair treatment of female captives of war taken by Israelites as wives. Regarding family law, the innovations strive to ensure fair inheritance rights in polygamous families, and perhaps to mitigate the case of the rebellious child. The custom of Levirate marriage is refined not only to ensure one's posterity but to safeguard the well-being of the widow.

An assortment of Deuteronomic laws are related to mixture taboos, which may reflect a priestly concern with ritual purity.[87] Concerns with purity and impurity, perhaps a secondary theme but certainly not unimportant to the Deuteronomic law, may be behind the prohibition of prostitution, remarriage, and instructions for defecation outside the encampment.

Finally, a question raised by this research group is whether Deuteronomy is "utopian."[88] Without going into detail here, I only offer the observation that, as with so much of our work in other details, the answer to this question depends upon definitions. In Paul Ricoeur's theory of "cultural imagination," utopian projection is an instrument of ideological critique.[89] A distinction may be made between ideologies, or in this case, theologies, that define social organization, as opposed to utopias calling established systems of power and structure into question. So, for example, the Deuteronomic "law of the king" is such a utopian vision designed as a check against other ancient ideologies of monarchy. Thus, the use of "utopia" to describe the agenda of the Deuteronomic law is appropriate but needs grounding in historical realia. It will be clear from my conclusions below that I consider the Deuteronomic law "utopian" in the narrower sense of an ideal but nevertheless real reform program for late pre-exilic Judah.

---

87 Clearly these laws are not exclusively devoted to priestly concerns, but I find little to support the idea that they are strictly "lay-related" and certainly are not secularizing; see Arnold, "Israelite Worship" *contra* Weinfeld, *Deuteronomy*, 190–243.

88 In past scholarship, the question arose because of the tension between the vision of a just and righteous Israel as a real program for reform during the time of Hezekiah or Josiah, on the one hand, versus a post-exilic work of imagination, on the other hand, which is unlikely to come to fruition in any real sense; see Perlitt, "Der Staatsgedanke"; Lohfink, "Distribution." Käre Berge applies an understanding of utopia to Deuteronomy's didactic program as falling between "practice" and "dream" ("Literacy," 5–12).

89 Blacketer, "Deuteronomistic Ideology." He carefully defines utopia as "an inventive discourse on social-political structures based upon a rational hope and historically conditioned self-reflection," which thereby represents an ideal, with potential of realization in the present. Understood in this way, the Deuteronomic law is a constitutive ideology of ancient Israel in covenant with Yhwh. Defined as a covenant, such a utopian vision implies also the possibility of a dystopian reality, in which idolatry is pervasive and the essentials of the Torah ethic are ignored.

All of this seems to confirm the notion that the mission of Israel, and indeed, the essential nature of the people of God known as "Israel," which is first defined in Exodus 19–24, is refined theologically in the Deuteronomic law and driven deeper into the elemental identity of the people. This is done first by the convergence of all Israel's tribal "customary law" traditions, which it shared with other ancient Semitic cultures of the time, together with innovated religious observances and regulations into a new formulation of "Torah."[90]

Second, it is also done by the transformation of those tribes themselves, at first a diverse group but now a unity in a new charter, if not a "constitution," which evinces "a concept of political responsibility both of the body politic and of the individual," and through which the divine purpose for a just cosmos is made possible.[91] And this process is begun already in the Deuteronomic innovations, as a theological beginning defining itself as both "statutes and ordinances" envisioning a new social order around a central sanctuary.

3 Conclusions

While most of these data have been identified and widely discussed for many years, this investigation has highlighted the materials unique to the Deuteronomic legal core based on a fresh analysis of their literary relationship to other legal corpora in Exodus, Leviticus, and Numbers, especially highlighting the observations and some of the conclusions of a recent investigation by Benjamin Kilchör. While I have not been persuaded by certain details of Kilchör's treatment, such as the arrangement of the laws according to the Decalogue, I have, however, found myself in agreement in the main with his identification of the

---

90 Greengus, *Laws*, 282–89.

91 McConville, *God*, 74–98. The frequently explored possibility of identifying Deuteronomy as a "constitution" may be technically correct, in my view, but is not altogether satisfying. I agree that Deuteronomy was constitutive in several aspects for ancient Israel, but not it seems, in all aspects. In other words, I think the book was constitutive but not a constitution, because I believe the idea of amendability was foreign to the tradents who gave us Deuteronomy and because the noun "constitution" carries too much baggage in contemporary political theory to capture the essence of Deuteronomy. Instead, the book's own testimony is that it produces something entirely new, the Torah, containing much legal material combined with other sorts of materials in a compelling hortatory tone, and constituting a covenant for Israel. We have no comparable genre to Deuteronomy's Torah, and we shall have to be content with that reality. See, among several other publications on this topic, McBride, "Polity," and for a helpful survey of the scholarship and issues related to Deuteronomy as covenant/treaty, polity/constitution, catechism/Torah, sermon, or a hybrid, see Strawn, "Lincoln."

"special materials" (*Sondergut*) of Deuteronomy when compared to the parallels in the Tetrateuch. Focused attention to these distinctive features of the legal core provides a renewed portrait of the nature and purposes of the Deuteronomic law.

This investigation suggests three conclusions, all of which bear upon the history of scholarship on these research questions and suggest possibilities for future investigation. My comments will fall along the lines of (a) the composition of Deuteronomy's legal core, followed further by brief comments on (b) the purpose for its composition, which is related finally to (c) the nature of Deuteronomy's legal materials.

3.1 Composition

Although far from conclusive, this investigation suggests the following scenario for the composition of the legal core, the materials we now have in Deuteronomy 12–26. First, during the late eighth century BCE, collections of *sepharim* ("texts") were created as new compositions through scribal techniques we may identify as transcription and/or invention.[92] These were genuinely new compositions, although they were likely inspired by older oral traditions (transcription) or by other texts (invention), in which case the older texts inspired a scribe to create by improvising, echoing, or extemporizing from memory. The material realia of text composition in ancient Israel, such as the physical media used (likely papyrus early on, and later leather) and the technical restrictions of text production, lead us to imagine these short, literary texts (*sepharim*) as perhaps circulating separately before being incorporated into a larger discourse.[93] It seems altogether likely that this collection of short *sepharim*, which cannot yet be considered a "document" in any classical sense, was inspired by the Book of the Covenant or some early version of it and perhaps also by social, political, and religious developments in Hezekiah's reign.

Second, this collection of loosely related *sepharim* was developed further by scribes in the early seventh century BCE through processes of compilation,

---

92 On these scribal techniques in antiquity, see van der Toorn, *Scribal Culture*, 109–41, where he also defines other modes of text development that are dependent upon anterior texts: compilation, expansion, adaptation, and integration. For how this relates to the earliest legal materials in Deuteronomy, see Arnold, "Number Switching," 165–66.

93 Arnold, 167, 171–72. For these earliest pieces of Deuteronomic law, we should probably assume the medium was individual sheets of papyrus.

expansion, adaptation, and/or integration.[94] We might not be far from the truth by imagining the original Hezekian *sepharim* collection was expanded by the "special materials" under investigation here into a new composition, one that we may envision for the first time as a genuine "document." It seems also likely that a new beginning was added, which is now Deuteronomy 6:4–5,[95] and that the entire document was partly motivated by anti-Assyrian sentiment in loyal opposition to Manasseh's pro-Assyrian policies (thus, it consisted of 6:4–5[9] and 12:1–26:15*). Like its anterior texts, the Hezekian *sepharim* were inspired by BC and perhaps P materials related to it, so this new document was also influenced by the theology and themes of the Holiness school without directly copying its particulars, and at times, differing from its views.[96] This new document, which I suspect ran through ch. 26, may justifiably be called *Urdeuteronomium*. I suspect it was also characterized by our recurring and familiar labels "statutes and judgments" (*haḥuqqîm wəhammišpāṭîm*, Deut 12:1 and 26:16, and cf. 4:1, 4:5, 4:8, 4:14, 4:45, 5:1, 5:31, 6:1, 6:20, 7:11, and 11:32), which sheds insight into how it was perceived. With regard to physical realia, we may imagine *Urdeuteronomium* as written on a continuous papyrus scroll, assuming for this thought experiment, with Menahem Haran, that literary activity in pre-exilic Israel was mainly done on papyrus and was transitioned to leather at the beginning of the post-exilic period.[97]

Third, in harmony with the consensus of an earlier generation of scholars working on Deuteronomy, we may speculate further that *Urdeuteronomium* was expanded in a Josianic edition (4:44–28:69*). The physical realities of a papyrus scroll required replacing after approximately forty years or so,[98] and it seems likely that the occasion for the transmission from an original Manassite composition to a new leather parchment was also the occasion for an expanded Josianic edition of Deuteronomy.[99] This new edition of Deuteronomy may also have been perceived as "this Torah" (*zōʾt hattôrâ*) in contradistinction to the older edition of statutes and ordinances only (4:44, and cf. 1:5, 4:8, 17:18, 17:19, 27:3, 27:8, 27:26, 28:58, 28:61, 29:20, 29:28, 30:10, 31:9, 31:11, 31:12, 31:24, and 31:26).

---

94 Van der Toorn, *Scribal Culture*, 118–41. Similarly, Stephen Kaufman distinguishes between "original compositions," on the one hand, and scribal techniques dependent upon anterior texts on the other, such as conflation (of several varieties), extended citation, and quotation ("Temple Scroll").

95 *contra* MacDonald, "Date."

96 The influence of the Holiness School was much more extensive than previously thought; see Arnold, "Holiness Redaction"; and Tucker, *Holiness Composition*, 185–89.

97 Haran, "Book Scrolls in Israel"; Haran, "Book Scrolls at the Beginning."

98 Van der Toorn, *Scribal Culture*, 148–49.

99 Arnold, "Number Switching," 179.

It follows then, finally, that this Torah edition from the time of Josiah would have been expanded again in the exilic period with an historical introduction and concluding chapters related to the covenant and the death of Moses in something very like our current book of Deuteronomy.[100]

3.2 Purpose

Based on the ideology and theological themes of the special materials discussed here, a reasonable speculation presents itself regarding the *raison d'être* for a Manassite-era *Urdeuteronomium*, which consisted largely of Deuteronomy's legal core as we have it now. In light of extensive evidence for scribal activity during the late seventh century BCE,[101] it seems entirely likely that enthusiasm for Hezekiah's reforms found continued expression as a conservative movement arising against the religious measures and political alliances of Manasseh during his long reign.[102] Loyal opposition to Manasseh's pro-Assyrian policies would have found fertile soil among the scribes and priestly tradents who preserved, expanded, and integrated older materials handed down from the halcyon days of the late eighth and early seventh centuries BCE. This explains, too, the use of Assyrian parallels in the apostasy laws of Deuteronomy 13, which may have been inserted at this time, and perhaps the similar phraseological coincidences of Deuteronomy 28. With many others, I also assume Hezekiah's reforms that inspired the movement had significant influence from northern refugees, leading to the Shechemite edition in Josiah's day (4:44–28:69*) with its Ebal-Gerizim framing of the legal core in Deuteronomy 11:29–30 and 27:1–13.[103]

3.3 Nature

This Manassite-period *Urdeuteronomium* stood as a monumental outworking of the "single principle, the fundamental duty of 6:5," in the manifold details of

---

100 Assuming as I do that Deut 1–3(4) is neither a new introduction to a supposed Deuteronomistic History nor a supplement integrating the legal core into the narration of the Hexateuch, but instead, an expansion, creating of Deuteronomy an independent book; see Kratz, "Headings," 32–37. For competing views of the dating of Deuteronomic law on the basis of social and economic history, see Naʾaman, "Sojourners" (seventh century BCE) and Knauf, "Observations" (sixth century BCE). See further the debate between Juha Pakkala ("Date"; "Dating") and Nathan MacDonald ("Issues") on the dating of Deuteronomy.
101 Arnold, "Number Switching," 178; Richelle, "Elusive Scrolls."
102 Driver, *Critical Deuteronomy*, li–lii; McConville, *Grace*, 18–20.
103 Knoppers, "Northern Context."

the "statutes and judgments" (framed by 12:1 and 26:16).[104] As an essential call for loyalty to one Yhwh in the face of Assyrian demands for loyalty and service, the Deuteronomic law was resistance literature with both positive and negative aspects. Positively, the innovated Deuteronomic law sought to shape and form a community of Yhwh-loyalists, moulding identities in corporate and individual levels.[105] Negatively, it sought to form the community vis-à-vis Assyrian demands, expressed more generally over and against all religious and societal demands of the surrounding culture, often defined as "the nations" who inhabited the land before Israel. These are two sides of the same coin. The rhetoric of the Deuteronomic law uses binary opposition (i.e., Yhwh not Assyria, centralized cult not local high places) to construct Israel's identity as one people serving one Yhwh.[106] An underlying principle of the whole Deuteronomic law is a genuine-versus-false binary, which unifies Israel as a community under the banner of one Yhwh.[107]

Deuteronomy's legal provisions, either in their canonical form or in any of their earlier iterations, should not be thought of as a legal "code."[108] Indeed, we should think of these laws as academic in nature rather than legislative, for they appear to have been scholarly exercises describing or exploring the law as it was being practised in ancient society, rather than prescribing individual laws themselves.[109] But this raises an interesting question at the foundation of all others addressed by this research group. What precisely was *Urdeuteronomium*?

Various elements in the final form of these laws in Deuteronomy 12–26, and especially in their canonical placement as "the Torah" (1:5; 4:44), have transformed the academic exercise of collecting and studying legal *sepharim* through the concept of divine revelation that distinguishes ancient Israel from all other religious expressions of the ancient Near East.[110] Indeed, Israel's con-

---

104 Samuel R. Driver referred to the singular "commandment" in 5:31 (cf. 7:11 and 19:9) as it relates to 6:5, over and against the plurals of "statutes and judgments" (*Critical Deuteronomy*, 88). Philip Peter Jenson helpfully proposes three "levels" of the laws in Deuteronomy, "the commandment," which is the Shema, the Ten Words at the middle level, and the "statutes and judgments" of Deut 12–26 ("Snakes," 190–92).

105 This understands law as "a form of social and mental conditioning," shaping the vocation of a society; see Burnside, "Spirit." Or to use paradigms known in sociology, the law establishes a pattern-making tendency, or schema, which over time labels certain things as important and others as unimportant, and which is reinforced by human enactment through ritual; see Douglas, *Purity*, 1–90.

106 On the "pragmatics of oppositions," see Burnside, "Strange Flesh," 412–13.

107 Arnold, "Israelite Worship," 173.

108 Markl, "Gottes Gesetz," 49.

109 Westbrook, "Codification"; but see Jackson, "Modelling."

110 Levinson, *Legal Revision*, 22–33.

vergence of religious observances with laws of secular governance "was a novel development, unlike what had long been the situation in the ancient Near East."[111] The nature of Israel's *ius divinum* was authorized theologically by means of embeddedness in a covenant between Yhwh and Israel, making it especially unique when compared to royal legislation in the ancient Near East, despite the Neo-Assyrian background for a covenant-authorized law.[112]

Understanding this distinctiveness does not, in itself, answer the question of precisely what the Deuteronomic law was (or more broadly, the Pentateuchal law in general). Joshua Berman distinguishes between modern statutory law, on the one hand, and common-law traditions on the other.[113] Gerhard von Rad thought the embeddedness of the law in history and event was enough to distinguish it from law in the "normal sense of the term" as an absolute set of demands.[114] Further research is needed to explore the differences between didactic *tôrâ*, in its rich tapestry of legal, hortatory, sapiential, and prophetic elements, on the one hand, and the subsequent *nomos*, with its reductionistic and statutory approach to the law.

Works Cited

Amir, Yehoshua. "Josephus on the Mosaic 'Constitution.'" In: *Politics and Theopolitics in the Bible and Postbiblical Literature*, edited by Henning Reventlow, Yair Hoffman, and Benjamin Uffenheimer, 13–27. Journal for the Study of the Old Testament Supplement Series 171. Sheffield: JSOT Press, 1994.

Arnold, Bill T. "The Holiness Redaction of the Primeval History." *Zeitschrift für die alttestamentliche Wissenschaft* 129 (2017): 483–500.

Arnold, Bill T. "Israelite Worship as Envisioned and Prescribed in Deuteronomy 12." *Zeitschrift für altorientalische und biblische Rechtsgeschichte* 22 (2016): 161–75.

Arnold, Bill T. "Number Switching in Deuteronomy 12–26 and the Quest for *Urdeuteronomium*." *Zeitschrift für altorientalische und biblische Rechtsgeschichte* 23 (2017): 163–80.

Arnold, Bill T., and John H. Choi, *A Guide to Biblical Hebrew Syntax*. Second Edition. Cambridge: Cambridge University Press, 2018.

Awabdy, Mark A. *Immigrants and Innovative Law: Deuteronomy's Theological and Social Vision for the* גר. Forschungen zum Alten Testament 67. Tübingen: Mohr Siebeck, 2014.

Bartor, Assnat. "'When You Go Forth to War against Your Enemies …': Narrative Reading of Deuteronomic Warfare Legislation." In: *The Reception of Biblical War Legislation in*

111 Greengus, *Laws*, 285; see also Otto, "Keilschriftrechtlicher Hintergrund."

112 Markl, "Gottes Gesetz," 49–56, 52, note 9.

113 Berman, "History."

114 Von Rad, *Old Testament Theology*, 1.201.

Narrative Contexts: Proceedings of the EABS Research Group "Law and Narrative," edited by Christoph Berner and Harald Samuel, 1–21. Beihefte zur Zeitschrift für die alttestamentliche Wissenschaft 476. Berlin: De Gruyter, 2015.

Berge, Kåre. "Literacy, Utopia and Memory: Is There a Public Teaching in Deuteronomy?" *Journal of Hebrew Studies* 12 (2012): article 10:1–19.

Berman, Joshua. "Historicism and Its Limits: A Response to Bernard M. Levinson and Jeffrey Stackert." *Journal of Ancient Judaism* 4 (2013): 297–309.

Berman, Joshua. "The History of Legal Theory and the Study of Biblical Law." *Catholic Biblical Quarterly* 76 (2014): 19–39.

Bird, Phyllis A. "The Bible in Christian Ethical Deliberation concerning Homosexuality: Old Testament Contributions." In *Faith, Feminism, and the Forum of Scripture: Essays on Biblical Theology and Hermeneutics,* 127–62. Eugene, OR: Cascade Books, 2015. Reprint of *Homosexuality, Science, and the "Plain Sense" of Scripture*, edited by David L. Balch, 142–76. Grand Rapids, MI: Wm. B. Eerdmans, 2000.

Bird, Phyllis A. "The End of the Male Cult Prostitute: A Literary-Historical and Sociological Analysis of Hebrew *qādēš-qĕdēšîm*." In *Congress Volume: Cambridge 1995*, edited by J. A. Emerton, 37–80. Vetus Testamentum Suplements 66. Leiden: Brill, 1997.

Bird, Phyllis A. "Of Whores and Hounds: A New Interpretation of the Subject of Deuteronomy 23:19." *Vetus Testamentum* 65 (2015): 352–64.

Bird, Phyllis A. "Prostitution in the Social World and Religious Rhetoric of Ancient Israel." In *Prostitutes and Courtesans in the Ancient World*, edited by Christopher A. Faraone and Laura McClure, 40–58. Wisconsin Studies in Classics. Madison, WI: University of Wisconsin Press, 2006.

Blacketer, Tad C. "Deuteronomistic Ideology and Utopia: Paul Ricoeur's Cultural Hermeneutics and Centralization during the Judean State Period." PhD diss., Asbury Theological Seminary, 2019.

Braulik, Georg. *Die deuteronomischen Gesetze und der Dekalog. Studien zum Aufbau von Deuteronomium 12–26*. Stuttgarter Bibelstudien 145. Stuttgart: Katholisches Bibelwerk, 1991.

Braulik, Georg. "The Joy of the Feast: The Conception of the Cult in Deuteronomy, the Oldest Biblical Festival Theory." In *The Theology of Deuteronomy: Collected Essays of Georg Braulik*, 27–65. Translated by Ulrike Lindblad. North Richland Hills, TX: BIBAL, 1994.

Braulik, Georg. "The Sequence of the Laws in Deuteronomy 12–26 and in the Decalogue." In *A Song of Power and the Power of Song: Essays on the Book of Deuteronomy*, edited by Duane L. Christensen, 313–35. Winona Lake, IN: Eisenbrauns, 1993.

Braulik, Georg. "Der unterbrochene Dekalog. Zu Deuteronomium 5,12 und 16 und ihrer Bedeutung für den deuteronomischen Gesetzeskodex." *Zeitschrift für die alttestamentliche Wissenschaft* 120 (2008): 169–83.

Brichto, Herbert C. "Kin, Cult, Land and Afterlife – A Biblical Complex." *Hebrew Union College Annual* 44 (1973): 1–54.

Burnside, Jonathan P. "The Spirit of Biblical Law." *Oxford Journal of Law and Religion* 1 (2012): 1–24.

Burnside, Jonathan P. "Strange Flesh: Sex, Semiotics and the Construction of Deviancy in Biblical Law." *Journal for the Study of the Old Testament* 30 (2006): 387–420.

Choi, John H. *Traditions at Odds: The Reception of the Pentateuch in Biblical and Second Temple Period Literature*. Library of Hebrew Studies/ Old Testament Studies 518. London: T&T Clark International, 2010.

Dearman, J. Andrew. *The Book of Hosea*. New International Commentary on the Old Testament. Grand Rapids, MI: Eerdmans, 2010.
Douglas, Mary. *Purity and Danger: An Analysis of the Concepts of Pollution and Taboo*. London: Routledge, 2002 [1966].
Driver, Samuel R. *A Critical and Exegetical Commentary on Deuteronomy*. International Critical Commentary 5. Edinburgh: T&T Clark, 1895.
Edelman, Diana V. "Saying Goodbye to the Theory of the Influence of Esarhaddon's Sucession *Adê* on Deuteronomy 13 and 28." In *Beside the Ark: Thinking about Deuteronomy outside the Box*. Edited by Diana V. Edelman, Benedetta Rossi, Kåre Berge, and Philippe Guillaume, forthcoming.
Eissfeldt, Otto. *Erstlinge und Zehnten im Alten Testament. Ein Beitrag zur Geschichte des Israelitisch-Jüdischen Kultus*. Beiträge zur Wissenschaft vom Alten Testament 22. Leipzig: Hinrichs, 1917.
Firmage, Edwin. "The Biblical Dietary Laws and the Concept of Holiness." In *Studies in the Pentateuch*, edited by John A. Emerton, 177–208. Vetus Testamentum Supplements 41. Leiden: Brill, 1990.
Greengus, Samuel. "Book Scrolls at the Beginning of the Second Temple Period. The Transition from Papyrus to Skins." *Hebrew Union College Annual* 54 (1983): 111–22.
Greengus, Samuel. *Laws in the Bible and in Early Rabbinic Collections*. Eugene, OR: Cascade Books, 2011.
Haran, Menahem. "Book-Scrolls in Israel in Pre-Exilic Times." *Journal of Jewish Studies* 33 (1982): 161–73.
Hays, Richard B. *Echoes of Scripture in the Gospels*. Waco, TX: Baylor University Press, 2016.
Hays, Richard B. *Echoes of Scripture in the Letters of Paul*. New Haven: Yale University Press, 1989.
Jackson, Bernard S. "Modelling Biblical Law: The Covenant Code." *Chicago-Kent Law Review* 70 (1995): 1,745–827.
Jenson, Philip Perter. "Snakes and Ladders: Levels of Biblical Law." In *Ethical and Unethical in the Old Testament: God and Humans in Dialogue*, edited by Katharine J. Dell, 187–207. Library of Hebrew Bible/Old Testament Studies 528. New York: T&T Clark, 2010.
Kaufman, Stephen A. "The Structure of the Deuteronomic Law." *Maarav* 1 (1978): 105–58.
Kaufman, Stephen A. "The Temple Scroll and Higher Criticism." *Hebrew Union College Annual* 53 (1982): 29–43.
Kilchör, Benjamin. "The Direction of Dependence between the Laws of the Pentateuch: The Priority of a Literary Approach." *Ephemerides Theologicae Lovanienses* 89 (2013): 1–14.
Kilchör, Benjamin. *Mosetora und Jahwetora. Das Verhältnis von Deuteronomium 12–26 zu Exodus, Levitikus und Numeri*. Beihefte zur Zeitschrift für altorientalische und biblische Rechtsgeschichte 21. Wiesbaden: Harrassowitz, 2015.
Knauf, Ernst Axel. "Observations on Judah's Social and Economic History and the Dating of the Laws of Deuteronomy." *Journal of Hebrew Scriptures* 9 (2009): 2–8.
Knoppers, Gary N. "The Northern Context of the Law Code of Deuteronomy." *Hebrew Bible and Ancient Israel* 4 (2015): 162–83.
Kratz, Reinhard G. "The Headings of the Book of Deuteronomy." In *Deuteronomy in the Pentateuch, Hexateuch, and the Deuteronomistic History*, edited by Konrad Schmid and Raymond F. Person, 31–46. Forschungen zum Alten Testament 2 Reihe 56. Tübingen: Mohr Siebeck, 2012.
Levinson, Bernard M. *Deuteronomy and the Hermeneutics of Legal Innovation*. New York: Oxford University, 1997.

Levinson, Bernard M. "Esarhaddon's Succession Treaty as the Source for the Canon Formula in Deuteronomy 13:1." *Journal of the American Oriental Society* 130 (2010): 337–47.

Levinson, Bernard M. *Legal Revision and Religious Renewal in Ancient Israel.* Cambridge: Cambridge University, 2008.

Levinson, Bernard M. "The Neo-Assyrian Origins of the Canon Formula in Deuteronomy 13:1." In *Scriptural Exegesis: The Shapes of Culture and the Religious Imagination: Essays in Honour of Michael Fishbane*, edited by Deborah A. Green and Laura Suzanne Lieber, 25–45. Oxford: Oxford University Press, 2009.

Levinson, Bernard M. "*You Must Not Add Anything to What I Command You*: Paradoxes of Canon and Authorship in Ancient Israel." *Numen* 50 (2003): 1–51.

Levinson, Bernard M. and Jeffrey Stackert. "Between the Covenant Code and Esarhaddon's Succession Treaty: Deuteronomy 13 and the Composition of Deuteronomy." *Journal of Ancient Judaism* 3 (2012): 123–40.

Levinson, Bernard M. and Jeffrey Stackert. "The Limitations of 'Resonance': A Response to Joshua Berman on Historical and Comparative Method." *Journal of Ancient Judaism* 4 (2013): 310–33.

Lohfink, Norbert. "Distribution of the Functions of Power: The Laws Concerning Public Offices in Deuteronomy 16:18–18:22." In *A Song of Power and the Power of Song: Essays on the Book of Deuteronomy*, edited by Duane L. Christiansen, 336–52. Winona Lake, IN: Eisenbrauns, 1993.

Lohfink, Norbert. "Poverty in the Laws of the Ancient Near East and of the Bible." *Texts and Studies* 52 (1991): 34–50.

Lundbom, Jack R. *Deuteronomy: A Commentary.* Grand Rapids, MI: Eerdmans, 2013.

MacDonald, Nathan. "The Date of the Shema (Deuteronomy 6:4–5)." *Journal of Biblical Literature* 136 (2017): 765–82.

Markl, Dominik. "Gottes Gesetz und die Entstehung des Monotheismus." In *Ewige Ordnung in sich verändernder Gesellschaft? Das göttliche Recht im theologischen Diskurs*, edited by Markus Graulich and Ralph Weimann, 49–67. Quaestiones Disputatae 287. Freiburg: Herder, 2018.

McBride, S. Dean, Jr. "Polity of the Covenant People: The Book of Deuteronomy." *Interpretation* 41 (1987): 229–44.

McConville, J. Gordon. *God and Earthly Power: An Old Testament Political Theology, Genesis-Kings.* London: T&T Clark, 2006.

McConville, J. *Gordon. Grace in the End: A Study in Deuteronomic Theology.* Grand Rapids, MI: Zondervan, 1993.

McConville, J. Gordon. *Law and Theology in Deuteronomy.* Journal for the Study of the old Testament Supplement Series 33. Sheffield: JSOT Press, 1984.

Milgrom, Jacob. *Leviticus 23–27: A New Translation with Introduction and Commentary.* Anchor Bible 3B. New York: Doubleday, 2001.

Milgrom, Jacob. "Profane Slaughter and a Formulaic Key to the Composition of Deuteronomy." *Hebrew Union College Annual* 47 (1976): 1–17.

Müller, Reinhard. "Israel's King as *Primus Inter Pares*: The 'Democratic' Re-conceptualization of Monarchy in Deut 17:14–20." In *Leadership, Social Memory, and Judean Discourse in the Fifth-Second Centuries BCE*, edited by Diana V. Edelman and Ehud Ben Zvi, 57–76. Worlds of the Ancient Near East and Mediterranean. Sheffield: Equinox, 2016.

Na'aman, Nadav. "Sojourners and Levites in the Kingdom of Judah in the Seventh Century BCE." *Zeitschrift für altorientalische und biblische Rechtsgeschichte* 14 (2008): 237–79.

Nelson, Richard D. *Deuteronomy: A Commentary*. Old Testament Library. Louisville, KY: Westminster John Knox, 2002.

Nihan, Christophe. "The Laws about Clean and Unclean Animals in Leviticus and Deuteronomy and Their Place in the Formation of the Pentateuch." In *The Pentateuch: International Perspectives on Current Research*, edited by Thomas B. Dozeman, Konrad Schmid, and Baruch J. Schwartz, 401–32. Forschungen zum Alten Testament 78. Tübingen: Mohr Siebeck, 2011.

Otto, Eckart. *Deuteronomium*. 4 vols. Herders Theologischer Kommentar zum AltenTestament. Freiburg im Breisgau: Herder, 2012 and 2016.

Otto, Eckart. *Das Deuteronomium. Politische Theologie und Rechtsreform in Juda und Assyrien*. Beihefte zur Zeitschrift für die alttestamentliche Wissenschaft 284. Berlin: De Gruyter, 1999.

Otto, Eckart. "Deuteronomy as the Legal Completion and Prophetic Finale of the Pentateuch." In *Paradigm Change in Pentateuchal Research*, edited by Benjamin Kilchör, Markus Zehnder, and Matthias Armgardt, 179–88. Beihefte zur Zeitschrift fur Altorientalische und Biblische Rechtsgeschichte 22. Wiesbaden: Harrassowitz, 2019.

Otto, Eckart. "Keilschriftrechtlicher Hintergrund von Rechtssätzen im Buch Deuteronomium." In: Kleber K, Neumann G, Paulus S and Möllenbeck C, editors. *Grenzüberschreitunge. Studien zur Kulturgeschichte des Alten Orients. Festschrift für Hans Neumann zum 65. Geburtstag am 9. Mai 2018*, edited by Kristen Kleber, Georg Neumann, Susanne Paulus, and Christin Möllenbeck, 477–89. DUBSAR: Altorientalistische Publikationen 5. Munster: Zaphon, 2018.

Pakkala, Juha. "The Date of the Oldest Edition of Deuteronomy." *Zeitschrift für die alttestamentliche Wissenschaft* 121 (2009): 388–401.

Pakkala, Juha. "The Dating of Deuteronomy. A Response to Nathan McDonald." *Zeitschrift für die alttestamentliche Wissenschaft* 123 (2011): 431–36.

Pardee, Dennis. "The Ba'lu Myth." In vol. 1 of *The Context of Scripture*, edited by William W. Hallo, 241–74. Leiden: Brill, 1997.

Perlitt, Lothar. "Der Staatsgedanke im Deuteronomium." In *Language, Theology, and the Bible: Essays in Honour of James Barr*, edited by Samuel E. Balentine and John Barton, 182–98. Oxford: Clarendon, 1994.

Quick, Laura. *Deuteronomy 28 and the Aramaic Curse Tradition*. New York: Oxford University Press, 2018.

Rad, Gerhard von. *Das Gottesvolk im Deuteronomium*. Beiträge zur Wissenschaft vom Alten (und Neuen) Testament 47. Stuttgart: W. Kohlhammer, 1929.

Rad, Gerhard von. *Old Testament Theology*. Translated by D. M. G. Stalker. 2 vols. New York: Harper, 1962.

Rainey, Anson F. and R. Steven Notle. *The Sacred Bridge: Carta's Atlas of the Biblical World*. Jerusalem: Carta, 2006.

Richelle, Matthieu. "Elusive Scrolls: Could Any Hebrew Literature Have Been Written Prior to the Eighth Century BCE?" *Vetus Testamentum* 66 (2016): 1–39.

Richter, Sandra L. "The Question of Provenance and the Economics of Deuteronomy." *Journal for the Study of the Old Testament* 42 (2017): 23–50.

Rofé, Alexander. "The Arrangement of the Laws in Deuteronomy." *Ephemerides Theologicae Lovanienses* 64 (1988): 265–87.

Rofé, Alexander. "Ephraimite versus Deuteronomistic History". In *Storia e tradizioni di Israele: scritti in onore di J. Alberto Soggin*, edited by Daniele Garrone and Felice Israel, 221–35. Brescia: Paideia, 1991. Reproduced in *Reconsidering Israel and Judah: Recent*

Studies on the Deuteronomistic History, edited by Gary N. Knoppers and J. Gordon McConville, 462–74. Winona Lake, IN: Eisenbrauns, 2000.

Rossi, Benedetta and Guillaume, Philippe. "An Alternative Reading the Law of the Hebrew 'Slave' (Deuteronomy 15:12–18)." *Res Antiquae* 15 (2018): 1–28.

Schmidt, Brian B. *Israel's Beneficent Dead: Ancestor Cult and Necromancy in Ancient Israelite Religion and Tradition*. Forschungen zum Alten Testament 11. Tübingen: Mohr Siebeck, 1994.

Steinberg, Naomi. "Romancing the Widow." In vol. 1 of *God's Word for our World: Biblical Studies in Honor of Simon John De Vries*, edited by J. Harold Ellens, Deborah L. Ellens, Rolf P. Knierim, and Isaac Kalimi, 327–46. Journal for the Study of the Old Testament Supplement Series 388. London: T& T Clark International, 2004.

Strawn, Brent A. "Lincoln at Gettysburg, Moses at Moab: On the Genre of Deuteronomy as Constitution, Once Again." *Zeitschrift für altorientalische und biblische Rechtsgeschichte* 25 (2019): forthcoming.

Strawn, Brent A. "Reading Josiah Reading Deuteronomy." In *Reading for Faith and Learning: Essays on Scripture, Community, & Libraries in Honor of M. Patrick Graham*, edited by John B. Weaver and Douglas L. Gragg, 31–45. Abilene, TX: Abilene Christian University, 2017.

Tigay, Jeffery H. *Deuteronomy: The Traditional Hebrew Text with the New JPS Translation*. The JPS Torah Commentary. Philadelphia: Jewish Publication Society, 1996.

Toorn, Karel van der. "Female Prostitution in Payment of Vows in Ancient Israel." *Journal of Biblical Literature* 108 (1989): 193–205.

Toorn, Karel van der. *Scribal Culture and the Making of the Hebrew Bible*. Cambridge, MA: Harvard University, 2007.

Tsai, Daisy Yulin. *Human Rights in Deuteronomy: With Special Focus on Slave Laws*. Beihefte zur Zeitschrift für die alttestamentliche Wissenschaft 464. Berlin: De Gruyter, 2014.

Tucker, Paavo N. *The Holiness Composition in the Book of Exodus*. Forschungen zum Alten Testament 2/98. Tübingen: Mohr Siebeck, 2017.

Versluis, Arie. "'And Moses Wrote This Torah': Canon Formulas and the Theology of Writing in Deuteronomy." In *Sola Scriptura: Biblical and Theological Perspectives on Scripture, Authority, and Hermeneutics*, edited by Hans Burger, Arnold Huijgen, and Eric Peels, 137–58. Studies in Reformed Theology 32. Leiden: Brill, 2017.

Weinfeld, Moshe. *Deuteronomy and the Deuteronomic School*. Oxford: Clarendon, 1972.

Wellhausen, Julius. *Prolegomena to the History of Israel*. Atlanta: Scholars, 1994. Reprint of *Prolegomena to the History of Israel*. Translated by J. Sutherland Black and A. Enzies, with a preface by W. Robertson Smith. Edinburgh: Black, 1885.

Westbrook, Raymond. "Codification and Canonization". In *La codification des lois dans l'antiquité. Actes du colloque de Strasbourg, 27–29 novembre 1997*, edited by Edmond Lévy, 33–47. Travaux du Centre de recherche sur le Proche-Orient et la Grèce antiques 16. Paris: De Boccard, 2000.

Wolff, Hans Walter. *Hosea: A Commentary on the Book of the Prophet Hosea*. Hermeneia. Philadelphia: Fortress, 1974.

Zevit, Ziony. *The Religions of Ancient Israel: A Synthesis of Parallactic Approaches*. London and New York: Continuum, 2001.

Philippe Guillaume

Deuteronomy's *Māqôm* before Deuteronomy

1 Introduction

Did Josiah find Deuteronomy? If so, what were the contents of the scroll found in the temple of Jerusalem? Since Wilhelm M. L. de Wette (1805), Josiah's unusual actions seemed "inexplicable except with references to Deuteronomy."[1]

The discovery in 2008–2009 of fragments of Esarhaddon's 672 BCE vassal treaty by the Toronto excavations at Tell Ta'yinat in the North Orontes (in present-day Turkey) supposedly confirms the Neo-Assyrian context of the formation of the earliest layers of Deuteronomy as a reaction to Assyrian or to Egyptian imperialism.[2] Though alternative views are being aired,[3] the Josianic connection remains popular in Deuteronomic scholarship. It provides a rare anchor for the Deuteronomic legal collection in the history of the kingdom of Judah. From this point, a relative chronology can be elaborated for the other biblical collections, depending on their purported relation with the Deuteronomic "code." Hence, the question of Deuteronomy's dating has taken priority over the question of its purpose.[4]

To refocus on purpose, this contribution considers the activities at the "place (*māqôm*) Yhwh has chosen/will choose as a dwelling for his name" as the core of Deuteronomy prescribes them, with no reference to Josiah and Jerusalem. The term "core" is used as a convenient designation for the center of the book – traditionally identified as Deuteronomy 12–26 – with no implication regarding the homogeneity of the contents of that "core." In fact, the short section on tithes in ch. 14 differs significantly from chs. 12 and 26. The latter two chapters portray the *māqôm* as the type of cultic institution that readers of Leviticus and Kings associate with the temple of Jerusalem, although Albrecht Alt had already perceived the weakness of the link with Jerusalem.[5]

Chapter 12 lists eight different kinds of sacrifices and offerings – including tithes – Israelite families are to take to the *māqôm* and eat there with the Levite.

1 Levinson, *Deuteronomy*, 9.
2 For the Neo-Assyrian context, see Steymans, "Die neuassyrische Vertragsrhetorik"; Lauinger, "Esarhaddon's Succession." For Deuteronomy as a reaction to Assyrian imperialism, see Otto, "Born out of Ruins," and as a reaction to Egyptian imperialism, see Crüsemann, *Torah*.
3 Van Seters, *A Law Book*; MacDonald, "Issues"; Pakkala, "Dating."
4 Davies, "Authority," 27, but see Mayes, "On Describing."
5 Alt, "Die Heimat."

https://doi.org/10.1515/9783110713312-007

In ch. 26, a priest receives a basket of first fruits at the *māqôm*, while the Levite is mentioned beside the alien, the widow and the orphan as a beneficiary of the triennial tithes. These "tithes of the third year" presuppose the difference between annual and triennial tithes delineated in Deuteronomy 14:22–29. Chapters 16 and 18 present other differences relative to the number of guests partaking in the *māqôm* banquets. On the one hand, there are *māqôm* celebrations under the watchful eye of the Levites who collect priestly dues (chs. 12, 16, and 18). On the other hand, there are *māqôm* celebrations with no Levite at all (ch. 14). Such celebrations would have no parallel in the Pentateuch or in Kings. This is most likely the reason why a subsequent Levitical writer prefaced the original regulations in ch. 14 with ch. 12 and then placed chs. 16 and 18 after it. A reader or listener would carry over the involvement of the Levites from ch. 12, even though they are not mentioned in ch. 14, and equally would assume their presence from their specific mentions again in chs. 16 and 18. Hence, the *māqôm* celebrations of ch. 14 should be considered on their own account.

2 The Dual Tithing System of Deuteronomy 14:22–29

In eight tight verses, Deuteronomy 14:22–29 delineates an elaborate system of tithes collection and consumption. Two spheres of activities are clearly distinguished: the *māqôm* and the local settlement, "your gates." The *māqôm* is where "you" shall learn to fear Yhwh always. The gates are where "they" – the Levite, the alien (or migrant גר), the widow, and the orphan – are taken care of. The *māqôm* is where one takes the yearly tithes, in kind or in silver equivalent. The gates are where one leaves triennial tithes. At the *māqôm*, "you" eat and drink 10 % of your yearly yield with your household in front of Yhwh in order to learn to fear him always. In your gates, you deliver the tithe of the third year so that you do not abandon the Levite and his needs are satisfied along those of the migrant, the widow, and the orphan.

Gates are the locus of compulsion and taxation,[6] while the *māqôm* is the locus of abundance and joy, precisely because the tithes one takes there are not taxes; instead, the tithe-payers consume their tithes. This is another striking feature of the *māqôm* celebrations, alongside the absence of the Levites and purpose of the festive meal being to learn to fear Yhwh.

6 For a detailed discussion of the synecdochic references cities via their gates as and their functions in Deut, see the contribution by Kåre Berge in this volume.

Neither the *māqôm* nor "your gates" are the locus of charity. Charitable giving is discussed in ch. 15 in relation to neighbors and brothers whose outstanding debts should be remitted. Given the popularity of the expression, *personae miserae,* as a convenient shorthand for the Levite and the *gēr*-orphan-widow triad in Deuteronomic scholarship, it is worth repeating that none of the beneficiaries of triennial tithes are deemed poor or miserable in Deuteronomy.[7] The Levite, the *gēr,* the orphan, and the widow are never identified with the poor and needy (עני ואביון), who constitute a distinct category.[8] Hence, the Levite, the *gēr,* the orphan, and the widow are not *personae miserae*. Nevertheless, they remain a liminal group in "your gates." It is only as the result of a process of supplementation that the strict delimitation of the *māqôm* from the gates is gradually modified, first with the introduction of the Levite at the *māqôm* in ch. 12, then with the addition of *gērîm,* orphans, and widows beside the Levites as guests at the festive meals in ch. 16, and finally with priestly dues allocated specifically to the Levites in ch. 18. This process of supplementation has blurred the specificities of the dual tithing system of ch. 14.

3 A Temple at the *Māqôm*?

Peter Altmann clearly identified the uniqueness of the festive meals of Deuteronomy 14:22–26:[9]

> The DC [Deuteronomic Code] formulation of the tithe overthrows the typical nature of the tithe and tithe feast. Since, as seems to have been the case in Israel and Judah as much as elsewhere in the ancient Near East, the tithe in Israel generally benefited the palace and temple, then the DC meal that benefits those bringing the tribute goes against the fundamental idea of those feasts since tribute functioned as a sign of a submissive bond towards the monarch. Therefore, missing payment amounted to breaking the contract.[10]

Feasting on one's own tithes in front of Yhwh overturns the fundamental notion of tithe feasts. As the portrayal of the king in Deuteronomy 17:14–20 is clearly at odds with the typical nature of kingship in the ancient Near East, it is quite possible that Deuteromomy 14 equally overthrows the typical nature of tithing.

Yet, the notion that Israelites could consume their tithes in front of Yhwh with little or no involvement of any priests has met with much resistance. For

7 See Graber's discussion of the *gēr* in this volume.
8 Lohfink, "Poverty."
9 Altmann, *Festive Meals*, 231.
10 Altmann, *Festival Meals*, 231.

instance, Timo Veijola argued that ch. 14 cannot expect families to squander a tenth of their hard-won yearly production during one trip to Jerusalem. Such a radical and meaningless notion would be utopian, and there is no trace of such a notion in the early history of the institution or later. That the lawgiver, Veijola argued, intended part of the tithes for the sanctuary and the consumption of only a fraction of the tithes by the tithe-payers is so obvious that it needed no telling.[11]

As the aim of the festive meals at the *māqôm* banquets is stated as "rejoicing before Yhwh in order to learn to fear him all your days" (Deut 14:23), the question is whether families would rejoice more when sharing a tenth of their yearly production with the sanctuary than when eating and drinking all of it themselves. The notion of social capital does support the idea that inviting a Levite and some destitute neighbours to share the big meal, as is the case in Deuteronomy 12:12, 16:1, and 16:14, would be felt preferable to gorging on one's tithes alone. The meals would certainly be copious enough for shows of generosity. Generosity generates gains in terms of reputation, especially when it is publicly displayed. Yet, there is a major difference between a few additional guests and having to hand over an amount of one's hard won produce for consumption by others, as is the case in 18:1–8. Gift and tax are not the same. Both represent an immediate loss or revenues – possibly made up later – but one is free, the other compulsory. Compulsion is obvious in ch. 18 and perceivable in ch. 12.

As part of a broader discussion to demonstrate that Deuteronomy 14 depends on Leviticus 27 and Numbers 18, Benjamin Kilchör claims that Deuteronomy's notion of families eating and drinking the whole of their yearly tithes at the *māqôm* is unrealistic, because tithes are *per definitionem* destined to the Levites.[12] Indeed, Leviticus and Numbers earmark tithes for the priesthood, but instead of proving that the Deuteronomic tithes know and depend on Leviticus 27 and Numbers 18, it underlines the uniqueness of Deuteronomy 14:22–29, where the tithes are victuals to be disposed of by the tithe- payers at will. Realistic or not, Deuteronomy's tithing system sticks out in the Pentateuch like a sore thumb, which hardly confirms its dependence upon Leviticus 27 and Numbers 18.

To fit the yearly tithes of Deuteronomy 14:22–29 into the tithes destined for the Levites, Kilchör imagines that the pilgrims are entitled to deduct the expenses incurred during the pilgrimage from the tithes they bring to the *māqôm*. The Levites' actual share is thus what is left of the tithes after the pilgrims ate some as provisions for the journey. If tithes are *per definitionem* destined for the Levites (as per Leviticus and Numbers), the deductions ought to be minimal, but

---

11 Veijola, *Funfte Buch*, 306.

12 Kilchör, *Mosetora*, 120, quoting Eissfeldt, *Erstlinge und Zehnten*, 49–50.

Kilchör is aware that this hardly fits the generosity expressed in Deuteronomy 14:26: eat and drink in the presence of Yhwh as much as you like. Therefore, Kilchör adds that the tithe-payers ought to look after themselves and be allowed to make a second deduction from their tithes, i.e. everything needed for a festive meal.[13]

In fact, Deuteronomy has no place for such parochial calculations. The entire proceeds of the yearly tithes are dedicated to the banquets in front of Yhwh. Of course, there are travel costs as well as major costs inherent in silver exchange, but these costs are shared among all tithe-payers if the feasts are organized at a different place each year (§ 3.2.4). In any case, these costs are part and parcel of the celebrations. This is far more realistic than Kilchör's imagined scheme, which implies that tithe-payers would have good reasons to stay at the *māqôm* as long as the food and drinks they bought there would last. As the aim of the call to eat as much as they wish (כל אשר תאוה נפשך) is to learn to fear God zealously (Deut 14:23), piety would be enhanced and stores at home preserved, at the expense of the Levite's share of the tithes. By comparison, the mere fraction of the yearly tithes of Deuteronomy 14 Kilchör allows to the tithe-payers is miserly.[14] Yet, this scheme is the only crutch to support the notion that the *māqôm* is the central store for the tithes,[15] though the only locations Deuteronomy 14 envisages for storing tithes are in "your gates" so the Levite is not abandoned but can eat and be sated (אכלו שבעו) together with the other beneficiaries of the triennial tithes. This is exactly the notion Deuteronomy 12 and Numbers 18 argue against.

Yet, Altmann still wonders whether the Levites, the resident aliens, the widows, and the orphans may nevertheless be "somehow implicitly" treated as special guests at the *māqôm* celebrations.[16] This is indeed the case in Deuteronomy 16:11–14, and if, for argument's sake, one admits that it is implicitly the case also in ch. 14, the presence of the tithe payers, *gērîm*, widows, and orphans beside the Levites is still far removed from the notion of tithes collected for the benefit of palace and temple. In conclusion, the tithing system of Deuteronomy

---

13 "Einfach gesagt: Die „Spesen" der Reise zum Zentralheiligtum dürfen vom Zehnten abgezogen werden, d. h., die Pilger dürfen sich auf der Pilgerreise vom Zehnten verpflegen. Die Leviten erhalten dann netto den Zehten minus die Wegzehrung. Und hierbei dürfen es sich die Israeliten gut gehen lassen, sie dürfen sich vom Zehnten, den sie abgeben, alles herausnehmen, was zu einem Festessen gehört, alles was das Herz begehrt (Dtn 14:26: כל אשר תאוה נפשך)." Kilchör, *Mosetora*, 120.

14 Kilchör, *Mosetora*, 123: "der Zehnten in Dtn 14,22f selbstverständlich auch an die Priesterschaft geht und lediglich ein Bruchteil davon vom Geber gemäss Dtn 14,23 konsumiert wird …"

15 "die zentrale Sammelstelle des Zehnten": Kilchör, *Mosetora*, 122.

16 Altmann, *Festive Meals*, 236.

14:22–29 is coherent with the kind of life described in Deuteronomy 15, 17, and 19–25 but can only be coherent with the Pentateuch when it is read in light of Deuteronomy 12, 16, 18, and 26.

Since chs. 12 and 16 insist on the presence of Levites at the *māqôm*, are these Levites those living "within your gates," (Deut 14:27) who turn up at the *māqôm* meals as guests, or are they full-time priests collecting foodstuffs from a *māqôm* conceived as a full-fledged temple? In the second case, they would seem to be the only ones entitled to collect the priestly dues specified in Deuteronomy 18:3–4. The next verses, however, insist on equal treatment of the postulated two kinds of Levites (Deut 18:6–8), adding yet another complicating factor with the mention of the sale of what the NRSV renders as "family possessions" (ממכריו על האבות). These "possessions" should not be evoked to reduce their share of priestly dues. Rather than trying to clarify the meaning of these "family possessions," it seems preferable to admit that the text provides no clarification. What it does is to refute any possible argument suggesting that the priestly shares listed in the previous verses may be subject to certain deductions. The writers were evidently under pressure to justify the changes they introduced in a text that was known to present an entirely different view on the revenues of the Levite, i.e., the local Levite whose revenues are delivered at the gate of each settlement and shared with the *gēr*, the orphan, and the widow (Deut 14:27–29). These purported "family possessions" are at loggerheads with the lack of allotment and inheritance adduced in Deuteronomy 14:27 and 29 to justify the Levite's access to a share in the produce of triennial tithes. This contradiction escapes the attention of most readers.

For instance, Juha Pakkala understands the *māqôm* to be a temple, although he is well aware there is only a single mention of the house of Yhwh in the entire book (Deut 23:19) and that the place that Yhwh will choose does not necessarily imply a temple. Nevertheless, he uses the notion of the *māqôm* as a temple in order to date the oldest version of Deuteronomy 12 "in a context where there was no temple," written by an author who "was not sure if there ever would be one. This would perfectly explain the hesitancy in referring to a temple."[17]

If, however, the *māqôm* implies no temple, any argument based on the writer's "hesitancy in referring to a temple" is void. The discussion between Pakkala and Nathan MacDonald focused on the date of Ur-Deuteronomy and for this reason ended up in a stalemate.[18] To overcome the stalemate, one needs to set aside issues of dating and focus instead on the activities at the *māqôm*.

17 Pakkala, "Dating," 294.

18 Pakkala, "Date," prompted the response in MacDonald, "Issues" and then a reply in Pakkala, "Dating."

Tab. 1: Activities and participants at the *māqôm*.

Deut	Activities at the *māqôm*	Participants
12:5–7	Bring your holocausts, sacrifices, tithes and eat in front of Yhwh	you and your households
12:11–12	Bring everything I order: holocausts, sacrifices, tithes ... and rejoice	your sons, daughters, male and female slaves, **and the Levite in your gates**
12:14	offer holocausts and do everything I order	you
12:17–18	Eat tithe of your grain, your wine, and your oil, the firstlings of your herds and your flocks, any of your votive gifts	with your son, daughter, male and female slaves, **and the Levite in your gates**
12:26–27	Present sacred donations, votive gifts, holocausts on the altar and eat the meat of your other sacrifices	you
14:23	Eat yearly tithes	you
14:24–25	Bring silver if too far	you
14:26	Eat and drink whatever you desire	you
15:20	Eat firstlings	you with your household
16:2–7	Sacrifice Passover	you
16:10–11	Present freewill offerings in proportion to blessing, and rejoice	you, your sons, daughters, male and female slaves, **and the Levite in your gates**, and the migrant, orphan and widow among you.
16:14–15	Rejoice, fulfil the days of the pilgrimage	you, your sons, daughters, slaves, and the **Levite**, migrant, orphan and widow **in your gates**
16:16	Not coming empty-handed	all your males
17:8–10	Consult the [Levitical priest/s and/or] judge	you
18:6	A Levite goes from your gates to the *maqom*	to receives portions like his brothers there
26:2	Give a basket of first fruits to the priest in office	you

Compared to Leviticus and Numbers, Deuteronomy displays little interest in sacrificial activities. As would be expected, all mentions of sacrificial practices are found in passages that mention the Levites or a priest at the *māqôm*, i.e. in chs. 12, 16, 18 and 26 (Table 1).

Chapter 12 contains six of the twenty-one occurrences of the term *māqôm*. Another six references appear in the cultic calendar in ch. 16 (Table 1). The tithes and firstlings in the lists of ch. 12 are the only type of offerings mentioned elsewhere in Deuteronomy (14:23; 15:20). Details regarding the other sacrifices are found in Leviticus, not in Deuteronomy. Deuteronomy 12:11 lumps together the tithes of ch. 14 with holocausts and other sacrifices. Hence, it is possible to argue that chs. 12 and 16 were penned to create a link between Deuteronomy and the sacrifices and festivals described in previous books, precisely because no such link existed in a previous version of Deuteronomy.

Nevertheless, Deuteronomy as a whole remains faithful to the dual tithing system of ch. 14. The *māqôm* is never described as a temple. "Your gates" are never deemed illicit places of worship, in sharp contrast to the Deuteronomistic notion of "high places." It is in the context of Kings that the *bāmôt* are problematic,[19] and even more so in the longer account of Josiah's Passover in 2 Chronicles 35, which is "much more 'Deuteronom(ist)ic' than the short note in Kings."[20] Recovering the purpose of Deuteronomy requires focusing on the *māqôm* festivities as ch. 14 imagines them, in isolation from the modifications introduced by chs. 12, 16, and 18.

4 *Māqôm* Banquets according to Deuteronomy 14

The postulated version of Deuteronomy without chs. 12, 16, and 18 focused on Israelite integration. Worship entailed rejoicing in front of Yhwh by eating and drinking one's own yearly tithes. Obviously, the notion of Deuteronomy's *maqom* as "merely" the site of a picnic in front of Yhwh, where every family identifies itself as Israel with no Levites to help (themselves), is simply unthinkable when Deuteronomy is read after or in parallel with the enormous tariffs of Leviticus.

Hence, the change of mood between revelling in front of Yhwh and the sacrifices introduced in ch. 12 is easily missed. The rejoicing (שׂמח) mentioned in Deuteronomy 14:26 is the result of eating and drinking as much as one's desire. The theme of joy is picked up in the two cultic chapters to justify the presence of the Levite (Deut 12:12) and the triad as well (Deut 16:11, 14) at the *māqôm* meals. Whereas Deuteronomy 14:27–29 leaves them behind "in your gates," their presence at the *māqôm* is now compulsory. The compulsion is un-

---

19 Thelle, *Approaches*, 143.
20 Auld, *Life*, 202.

derlined by the expression, "everything I command" (כל אשר אנכי מצוה; Deut 12:11,14).

The originality of the dual tithing system is lost when Deuteronomy is read in the context of Josiah's religious reform:

> In the face of the dismantling of the countryside cultus that Hezekiah began and which Josiah intensified, it was crucial for the Deuteronomic authors to establish for the citizens of Judah that the loss of the local altars did not entail the complete loss of local access to God or, more seriously, that God had abandoned the local sphere. They went out of their way to provide the local sphere with its own integrity. "Yhwh continues to be active and to grant his blessing there."[21]

If Yhwh continues to be active and to grant his blessing at home, why bother travelling to the *māqôm* to get it at the price of transporting 10 % of the yearly produce there? Why shoulder transport costs if, to boot, the farmer and his family are expected to consume as little as possible of the tithes they took to the *māqôm*, leaving the bulk for the priests and Levites? Are the curses and blessings at the end of the book supposed to make reluctant farmers more compliant? This point opens the matter of the difference between theological and economic readings of biblical texts, especially of the Deuteronomic core, which devotes much space to economic matters.

5 The Economy of Deuteronomy's Core

With or without chs. 12; 16, 18, and 26, the main focus of Deuteronomy's core is on food production and distribution, and on credit and trade. The contents of Deuteronomy 12–26 can be broken down as:

23 % about food production and distribution, including carrion and feasts
13.5 % against idolatrous practices
12.5 % about the administration of justice
10 % about marital matters
7.5 % about credit
7 % on the proceeds of war
5.5 % on priestly portions

The other books of the Torah show little interest in the matter of food production and distribution. Leviticus takes for granted an inexhaustible source of

21 Levinson, *Deuteronomy*, 49–50.

foodstuffs and animals ready to be sacrificed to pacify Yhwh and feed his clergy. Apart from chs. 12, 16, and 18, Deuteronomy addresses the needs of the producers of agricultural products. Because religious practices involve expenses in the form of fees, offerings, sacrifices, and time, the condemnation of various religious practices deemed idolatrous (13.5 %) adds up with the 23 % focusing on food production and distribution to reach a good third of Deuteronomy 12–26 (36 %) dedicated to food allocation and wastage reduction.

Another third (30 %) of the material is made up of the administration of justice (12.5 %), marital matters (10 %) and credit (7.5 %), precisely the issues that brought people to litigation in the Judean Desert documents, as in the case of the Babatha widow (93–132 CE).[22]

The last two matters covering more than 5 % of Deuteronomy 12–26 are war (7 %, see Beukenhorst in this volume) and priestly portions (5.5 %). The positive outlook on war and colonization reflects the positive effect of war and colonization in societies with a large pool of unskilled labor, as was the case in Roman Italy:

> The existence of opportunities for unskilled labour, whether in the army, in the cities, or on the farm, coupled with a high level of infant mortality and the lack of any institutions beyond the family to support children or old people, created a clear incentive for having a large family; this implies that the fatality rate on campaign, far from having a fatal effect on the Italian countryside, may have played a vital role in limiting growth and hence maintaining real incomes.[23]

Instead of imagining a world freed from the miseries caused by war, Deuteronomy's core presupposes a vibrant demographic context similar to the Roman context, where war fatalities do not represent a problem for the society as a whole. The brutal environment warfare entails for adult men reduces the age expectancy of adults (compensated for by immigration), raises that of children, and inflates the number of widows and orphans. Despite these "positive" aspects of war, the rules governing war afford every potential fighter the chance to go back home before the battle because of fear, because he acquired a new house, planted a vineyard, became engaged (Deut 20:2–9), had a wet dream (Deut 23:9–11) or was newly married (Deut 24:5). These exemptions reflect economic concerns, making sure that war does not disrupt procreation and agriculture.

Deuteronomy dedicates half of the triennial tithes administered at the local level to the sustenance of widows and orphans so that orphans are raised and given a chance to reach adulthood. The effect on the demographic structure

---

22 Katzoff and Schaps, *Law*.
23 Morley, "Demography," 36.

eliminates generational conflict arising when many men, upon reaching adulthood, still have an active father alive. At Athens, the ratio between men aged 20 and those at 60 might have been 3:1.[24] Elders at the gate occur fourteen times in Deuteronomy 12–26, six of which lie in the framing chapters, yet only twenty-two times in the whole of Genesis–Numbers. There is no hint in Deuteronomy of any animosity toward the elders at the gate, whose authority is respected, suggesting that they are few in each settlement and thus are not seen as an obstacle by younger adult men.

There is no mention of widowers, because men married later than women and died before their wives. Widowhood for women is a major economic issue when shares of communal land are distributed according to the number of adult males. Divorce is a male prerogative. The warrior who married a beautiful captive can divorce her, protecting her from being sold into slavery, though nothing is said about her sustenance thereafter (Deut 21:14). Divorce from an abducted wife is forbidden (Deut 22:29), because abduction is a type of marriage meant to override parental and social veto. The next issue to be considered is why Deuteronomy never names the location of the *māqôm*.

6 A Mobile *Māqôm*?

In 1966 Gerhard von Rad aired the idea that Deuteronomy's silence over the location of the *māqôm* is due to its mobility. He imagined a succession of chosen places operating in turn as the *māqôm*.[25] Stefan Schorch rejects the notion of a mobile *māqôm*, arguing that the "Deuteronomic concept [is] that Israel's entry into the chosen land is the end of wandering and the beginning of a period of general rest."[26] This is not a persuasive objection to the mobility of the *māqôm*. Rather than implying that rest entails sitting under one's own fig tree forever after, rest in Deuteronomy entails leaving the farm behind for a while and travelling to the *māqôm* every year for a big party with family and friends in front of Yhwh. The idea that the *māqôm* cannot possibly represent anything other than the temple of Jerusalem has been pervasive enough to prevent the acceptance of von Rad's suggestion of a mobile *māqôm*.[27]

In fact, the Tabernacle is the epitome of a temporary sacred space circumscribed wherever Israel camped that only lasted for the duration of its stay

24 Akrigg, "Demography," 56.
25 Von Rad, *Deuteronomy*, 94.
26 Schorch, "Samaritan Version," 25.
27 Ska, "Why Does."

there. The mobility of the *māqôm* is coherent with the notion of Yhwh's blessing resulting in the expansion of Israelite territory and the growing distance to be travelled to the *māqôm* (Deut 14:24).

Thanks to Yhwh's blessing, the distance to the place is expected to increase to the point that the cost of the transport of the yearly tithes there would become prohibitive for the Israelites living at the periphery. Were these tithes earmarked to feed the priests of a central sanctuary, which by definition is immobile, producers would be tempted to deduct transport costs from the quantities delivered until they found a closer sanctuary, as is the case in Joshua 22:11. Territorial expansion would consequently be a curse rather than a blessing, and it would split Israel rather than unite it.

On the contrary, if the tithes to be transported to "the place" are destined entirely for the banquets in front of Yhwh, the financial aspects of the blessing reside in changing the location of the yearly gatherings so that it is not always the same farmers who benefit from their proximity to the *māqôm* and the same farmers who bear the greatest transport costs.

The option offered to the distant farmers to change their yearly tithes against silver confirms the writers' concern to ensure fairness and avoid the strife that would inevitably tear the Deuteronomic Israel apart. Fairness, however, can only be obtained if the location of the *māqôm* changes regularly. This is not explicit, but any farmer can figure out the practical implications of Deuteronomy 14:25–26. In short, these verses postulate a self-equalizing system.

7 A Self-Equalizing System

Once a year, every household (rather than males only three times a year according to Deut 16:16) proceeds joyfully to the *māqôm* to revel in front of Yhwh with family and friends. Contrary to the Torah's other books, Deuteronomy's core shows a real concern for logistics, a concern that tends to be ignored by exegetes more at ease with theological matters.

Transport costs are nil for triennial tithes delivered and stored at the local level. Transport costs cannot be ignored for yearly tithes, even though they are dedicated entirely for consumption by the families who take them to the *māqôm*. Increasing in proportion to the distance to the *māqôm*, it is crucial that transport costs are taken into account if the *māqôm* is to function as the nexus holding together the entire Israelite population.

The conversion of yearly tithes into silver is presented as the solution (Deut 14:24–26). No Levite is involved. Each producer is free to decide whether to transport his yearly tithes and yearlings in kind or to sell them and proceed to the *māqôm* with the silver tied to his hand (צרת הכסף בידך Deut 14:25).

Distant farmers could be tempted to divert some of the proceeds of their annual tithes for other purposes, since the quantity of tithed products is greater than the amount of food their households would normally consume at home during that time. In the real world, farmers make sure to produce at the very least 20 % more than their anticipated yearly consumption needs to cover the seeds for the next season and the various taxes, tithes, and duties they have to pay. Farmers also produce excess grain, oil, wine, or livestock for sale or barter to acquire goods they are unable to make themselves. Considering that the annual tithes and firstlings amount to 10 % of the total production of that year, the yearly tithe of Deuteronomy 14 would amount to the food requirements of each family for over a month at home, something that has long been considered problematic.

On the basis of Deuteronomy 16:1–17, Jeffrey H. Tigay calculates a maximum of nine days of presence at the central sanctuary and considers that it would be impossible for the farmers to dispose of over a month's worth of food and drink during these nine days, even if they doubled their normal level of consumption during festivals.[28] Hence, Tigay increases the number of mouths to feed at the *māqôm*, inviting the Levites and the destitute to partake in the banquet. Jack R. Lundbom takes another approach. He equates the *māqôm* with the temple of Jerusalem, where the tithes not consumed during the pilgrimage are stored in the rooms around the temple (see Neh 10:39; 1 Chr 31:11–12).[29] Both approaches miss an essential element of the banqueting spirit: overabundance.[30] The festive spirit transpires in the invitation of Deuteronomy 14:26 for tithe-payers to enjoy all the meats and drinks they might desire. However much the festive meals increased ordinary consumption levels, the system requires an excess of supply in kind to make up for the loss of purchasing power incurred during the exchange of tithes into silver.

The loss of purchasing power varies according to the distance to the *māqôm*, the demand on local markets, and the offer at the *māqôm*. These factors would vary year after year, but they would balance out one another. In a lean year, the amount of silver obtained at home would be higher per quantity than during good years, thus compensating the lesser quantities exchanged. The quantity of victuals obtained at the *māqôm* would fluctuate in the opposite way. During lean years, the rarefaction of produce available at the *māqôm* reduces

28 Tigay, *Deuteronomy*, 143.
29 Lundbom, *Deuteronomy*, 484.
30 Altmann, *Festive Meals*, 221–26.

the purchasing power of the silver, thus offsetting the higher price obtained at home. During good years, the greater quantity of foodstuffs available at the *māqôm* required less silver per unit of quantity, thus compensating for the lower prices obtained for the tithes and firstlings at home. As the number of days spent there is not specified, people would stay together longer when the harvests had been good, returning when left with only what they needed for the return journey.

Despite the flexibility of the duration of the feast, the self-consumption of yearly tithes creates a disparity between the Israelites who brought their tithes and firstlings in kind and those who brought them in the form of silver. The notion of tithes dedicated entirely to the enjoyment of the tithe-payers themselves has been deemed a magnanimous gesture on Moses's part that "makes it as convenient as possible for people who live far from the central sanctuary."[31] In fact, the main beneficiaries of Moses's magnanimity are the farmers who live close to the *māqôm*. The text is silent over the origin of the food available for purchase at the *māqôm*, but the farmers who bore minimal transport costs were in the best position to sell foodstuffs to their distant colleagues, whether the food they sold came from their tithes or from their surplus. *De jure*, it is only surplus that could be sold, but the overabundance mentioned above would make it difficult to distinguish what was earmarked as tithes and what was available for retail. The banquets at the *māqôm* represent an economic system based on the flow of silver from the periphery to the center, though the *māqôm* itself is not an institution meant to hoard that silver, as would be the case with a temple.

Even if other suppliers were present at the *māqôm*, the Israelites living closest to the *māqôm* would find themselves at the receiving end of the flow of silver, while the farmers who live afar and decide to exchange their produce against silver retain none of that silver. Hence, pilgrimage to the *māqôm* would split Israel into two classes of farmers with opposing interests. Those living close to the *māqôm* would enrich themselves directly from the losses incurred by those living far from the *māqôm*.

Resentment would soon arise from the discrepancy of treatment if the same process were repeated year after year. Instead of being a uniting factor, the *māqôm* economy would encourage distant farmers to meet at another *māqôm* closer to home, as the Transjordan tribes are said to have done in Joshua 22. There, it is the threat of war with the other tribes (Josh 22:12) that convinces the Reubenites, Gadites, and Manassites to give up the "altar of great size" they

---

31 Block, *Gospel*, 98.

had built (Josh 22:10). Deuteronomy's solution to maintain the cohesion of Israel through the *māqôm* hinges on the decision taken by the farmers who find themselves in between, neither close nor far from the *māqôm*.

Whatever the yields of any particular year, whatever the size of Israel, the number of farmers bringing their annual tithes in kind would roughly equal the number of farmers bringing their annual tithes in silver. As the demand created by distant farmers at the *māqôm* generates revenues for those who bring their tithes in kind, every farmer carefully weighed out the pros and cons of each option, deciding whether he might offset the cost of transport of his tithes by selling some to more distant colleagues or to save that cost by travelling with silver.

Hence, the *māqôm* economy establishes an invisible line that divides Israel between kind and silver. Every Israelite decides on which side of the line he finds himself, as soon as the next location of the *māqôm* is known. For those living close enough and for those living very far, the decision between kind and silver is obvious. Not so for those in between. They have to base their decision on an estimate of the number of their colleagues living closer to the *māqôm* than themselves and on the number of those living at a further distance than them. As the ability to generate income by selling tithes in kind at the *māqôm* hinges on the correctness of the estimate, the *māqôm* economy is an incentive for every farmer to use his best knowledge of geography and of the current levels of surplus in the land. The incentive ensures that the *māqôm* is supplied with the quantity of foodstuffs required by the families arriving with silver. In this sense, the system is self-equalizing: a rise in prices reduces the quantity demanded at the *māqôm*, while a rise in prices increases the amount brought in kind at the *māqôm*. Suppliers and demanders adjust their behavior to reach equilibrium. At equilibrium, at a given price, the quantity of goods supplied equals the quantity of goods demanded, and there is neither excess supply nor excess demand.

Though supply-demand-equilibrium is a modern concept, markets existed in the ancient world, and those active in them had a certain awareness of it.[32] The portrayal of the token Deuteronomic farmer as engaged in financial transactions with actors well beyond the confines of his village voids any doubts concerning his understanding of basic market forces. The Deuteronomic system presupposes a market in which Israelites could seize opportunities to improve their revenues well beyond basic agricultural activities. The *māqôm* economy relies on every farmer's ability to make the correct decision between tithes in

32 Foldvari and van Leeuwen, "Market Performance."

kind or in silver. This self-equalizing system solves the apparent anomalies that arise from Deuteronomy's prescriptions relative to annual tithes: the over-abundance of foodstuffs consumed at the *māqôm*, the silence of the text over the origin of the food bought at the *māqôm*, the silence over any surplus at the end of the festivities, and the silence over any control of the amounts delivered as tithes.

8 The *Māqôm* as a Distribution Center?

Another issue arises when the second tithing system of ch. 14 is read in light of chs. 16 and 18. According to H. V. Bennett, the centralization of the cult "worked to the disadvantage of the poor by forcing them to travel the great distance to the distribution centre, returning from this site with grain, wine, and meat," which put these persons at the mercy of murderers, rapists, robbers, kidnappers, and other nefarious individuals.[33] In fact, the foodstuffs set aside for the Levites, *gērîm*, orphans, and widows (not for the "poor") are stored "within your gates," which spares transport costs and the dangers on the way to the distant *māqôm* that Bennett imagines. The widow dodging wayfarers with a sack of grain on her back and a couple of orphans hanging at her skirts makes a great story, but it is pure fantasy when triennial tithes are stored locally. For the most efficient mode of operation, it would have been optimal to collect these tithes on a yearly basis at a rate of 3.33 %, delivering them at each settlement's gate, as was the case for Babylonian temple harvests.[34] As for the annual tithes, they are entirely consumed at the *māqôm*, and there is nothing left at the end of the festivities to store.

Instead of a structure with storage facilities, what is needed for the *māqôm* picnics is an open space where every Israelite family can camp for a week or two to enjoy big meals in front of Yhwh, to establish trade contracts, marriages, to exchange news and gossip, to arbitrate disputes, and to prepare raids against neighbors (except Edomites, who are "brothers" [23:8]). The very notion of a general gathering excludes the concept of a city, because no urban center would be able to accommodate the logistics involved. For this reason, the *māqôm* is disassociated from the cities of refuge.[35] The *māqôm* is not conceived as a city. Cities of refuge are carefully set up in the three cantons that are expected to

33 Bennett, "Triennial Tithes," 14–15.
34 Jursa and Schmidl, "Babylonia," 720.
35 Kratz, *Composition*, 123.

form the original Israelite territory (Deut 19:3), while Deuteronomy 12 locates the *māqôm* "in one of your tribes" (Deut 12:5.14) rather than in one of your cities.

9 Arbitration of Difficult Cases

In Deuteronomy 17:8, there is a judge at the *māqôm* who will decide a case that cannot not be arbitrated at the local level. The transfer of the case to the *māqôm* is expressed by the verbs וקמת ועלית, which the NRSV renders as "then you shall immediately go up" but which means more literally, "you will arise and go up." That this formulation implies the existence of a supreme court active throughout the year to which cases could be referred immediately relies heavily on the notion of the *māqôm* as an urban center complete with a temple and an administrative apparatus, which may be precisely what the writer wishes to avoid. The next verse mentions Levitical priests in addition to the judge who will be *in those days* (יהיה בימים ההם Deut 17:9). The term "days" can of course designate an entire year, but it can also refer only to the time spent together at the *māqôm*. The arbitration of difficult cases during the festival would be most effective if it occurred when all Israelite families were gathered to witness the proceedings and hear the verdict. Verdicts pronounced in front of the entire people (כל העם Deut 17:13) are presented as parts of the substance of the learning (למד) taking place at the *māqôm* (Deut 14:23). The law (תורה Deut 17:11–19) is the customary law (משפט), not the written law it became when the core was integrated into the Pentateuch. Instant disclosure of the decisions of the "supreme court" to the whole of Israel gathered at the *māqôm* contributes to establish, maintain, and adapt the customs shared by every member of the Deuteronomic Israel.

10 Festive Meals as Worship

Jacob Milgrom was well aware that Deuteronomy's yearly tithes revert to their producers. Instead of arguing that the producers only ate a fraction of their tithes, he downplayed the originality of the dual tithing system by arguing that the insistence that they be taken to Jerusalem, "endeavoured to maintain their sacred character."[36] Remove Jerusalem or Mt. Gerizim as the site of a perma-

---

36 Milgrom, *Leviticus 23–27*, 2,427.

nent, single *māqôm* and Deuteronomy 14:22–29 is a square peg that fits nowhere in the Torah's round holes.

Puritan predispositions may have played a role in resistance to the notion of eating and drinking to one's desire in front of Yhwh (Deut 14:26) as a way "to learn to fear Yhwh your god all the days" (Deut 14:23). The festive spirit of *māqôm* banquets when Israelite families eat and drink a tenth of what they produced in that year has been identified as dangerously close to orgiastic feasts for Baal or Dionysus. To differentiate the Deuteronomic banquets from these Canaanite celebrations, Paul Humbert could only adduce the fact that the expression *simḥâ gᵉdōlâ* is nowhere used in the book.[37] Unconvinced, Georg Braulik nevertheless reads the *māqôm* as Josiah's temple, hence under the implicit supervision of priests and Levites who would curtail any orgiastic misdeeds.[38]

Timothy M. Willis also notes that the overwhelmingly celebrative tone of worship at the Deuteronomic *māqôm* is "quite striking."[39] But he soon tempers the celebrative tone by stating that the "Deuteronomic laws challenge providers to fulfil their obligations to dependants by bringing the two groups together in worship" and "worship should provide ways of reminding participants that they are obligated to provide for others as God provided for them."[40] As the likely writers of chs. 12, 16, 18, and 26, the Levites would have concurred! But reading the dual tithe system on its own supplies a different reason to rejoice.

Away from the palace, with no Levites collecting 20 % of the animals he slaughters, the Deuteronomic farmer has good reason to rejoice. Like a painting of Peter Brueghel that puts religious processions in the background and foregrounds carousing peasants, the Deuteronomic farmer learns to fear his god (Deut 14:23) by eating and drinking to his heart's desire.[41] The tax burden he has to shoulder is light. Triennial tithes – 10 % every third year – represents a theoretical yearly tax burden of 3⅓ %, similar to the average tax burden in the Roman Empire.[42] No wonder the rewriting put the emphasis on the revenues of the Levites, the most likely candidates for expanding the Deuteronomic core to make it fit their interest, and the most unlikely transmitters of an older form of Deuteronomy with Levites only "within our gates."

---

37 Humbert, "'Laetari,'" 199.
38 Braulik, "Die Freude," 181–82.
39 Willis, "Eat and Rejoice," 283.
40 Willis, 293–94.
41 Altmann, *Festive Meals*, 226–29.
42 Morris and Manning, "Economic Sociology," 137.

11 Conclusion: Forbes Ranking at the Potluck

Were the yearly tithes meant to finance the operation of a temple complete with storerooms and clergy, it would be crucial for that temple to assess the yields of every taxable produce and thus ensure that the due amounts were delivered in full. No such assessment is mentioned, simply because the yearly tithes are not taxes, contrary to the triennial tithes, for which each farmer is to swear that they were delivered in full "in your gates" (Deut 26:12). Annual tithes are entirely consumed by the producers, with all the other Israelite families. Togetherness generates social pressure and worked in the same as when, today, a group is invited to a potluck party. No one wants to look mean publicly. Hence, everyone makes sure to bring aplenty. The same incentive would prevail at the *māqôm* parties, where everyone would throw a big party. Over-abundance is underlined in Deuteronomy 14:26 as eating and drinking "everything you may desire" (בכל אשר תשאלך נפשך). But there is more.

People would comment on the size of every incoming caravan. Each person made sure to parade his best calf and his finest lamb before the slaughter. A breeder made his reputation then and there, which was broadcast immediately Israel-wide, with consequences for the value of one's animals, the best being sought by other breeders for reproductive purposes. Men would roam around each other's tents, comparing animals and products, while women showed off their children. On top of the various other functions discussed above, the yearly gatherings at the *māqôm* functioned as any agricultural fair in rural societies. They were the highlight of the year, eagerly looked forward to. They offered the opportunity to socialize with old friends and make new acquaintances, particularly of the opposite sex. Yearly social interaction and festive meals at the *māqôm* would foster a tight network of families to consolidate Israel's corporate identity.[43] In addition to the arbitration of certain disputes, the festivities would be venues for exchanging news, match-making, marriages, and labor contracts as well as establishing a yearly ranking, a Forbes's list of Israel's millionaires. In kind or in silver, the yearly tithes displayed in front of everyone provided a fairly accurate measure of the net value of one's assets. This rating had direct consequences for economic matters mentioned explicitly in Deuteronomy: credit, trade, self-indenture, hire of labor, election to public offices such as judge and officer, and admission to the *qᵉhal-yhwh* (Deut 23:1–8).

The practical socio-economic model described in the Deuteronomic core turned into a pious fancy when Levites were introduced at the *māqôm* to render

---

43 Davies, "Authority," 35; Altmann, *Festive Meals*, 227–40; Crouch, *Making of Israel*, 132–37.

the core Torah-compatible. At that moment, the festivities at the *māqôm* were regulated according to the cultic calendar of Deuteronomy 16, insisting on the presence of every male three times a year and not empty-handed. As long as the traditional delimitation of the Deuteronomic core is retained, there is little hope for new advances in our understanding of the genesis of Deuteronomy. The recognition that some chapters within Deuteronomy 12–26 function in the same way as the frames and thus belong to the same framing process opens new perspectives. What is left of the earlier version of Deuteronomy now begins at 14:22. Chapters 12–13 and the elaboration of the list of pure and impure animals of Leviticus 11 in Deuteronomy 14:1–21 now introduce the dual tithing system. The aim of this introduction is coherent with the aim of the insertions in the body of the core: the calendar of ch. 16 and the section on the Levites in 18:1–8. The *māqôm* becomes Torah-compatible, though the presence of Levites there hardly matches the Aaronite priesthood in the rest of the Torah. In fact, the last word goes to the priest of Deuteronomy 26:12, who insists that the Levite's proper place is "in your gates," not at the *māqôm*. Hence, Deuteronomy remains an oddity in the Torah. Broadly speaking, the vestiges of the earlier version are found in Deuteronomy 14:22–15:23; 17; 18:9–25:16.

Works Cited

Akrigg, Ben. "Demography and Classical Greece." In *Demography in the Graeco-Roman World: New Insights and Approaches*, edited by Claire Holleran and April Pudsey, 37–59. Cambridge: Cambridge University Press, 2011.

Alt, Albrecht. "Die Heimat des Deuteronomiums." In vol. 2 *Kleine Schriften zur Geschichte des Volkes Israel*, 250–75. Munich: Beck, 1953.

Altmann, Peter. *Festive Meals in Ancient Israel: Deuteronomy's Identity Politics in Their Ancient Near Eastern Context*. Beihefte zur Zeitschrift für die alttestamentliche Wissenschaft 424. Berlin: de Gruyter, 2011.

Auld, A. Graeme. *Life in Kings: Reshaping the Royal Story in the Hebrew Bible*. Ancient Israel and Its Literature 30. Atlanta: Society of Biblical Literature, 2017.

Bennett, Harold V. "Triennial Tithes and the Underdog. A Revisionist Reading of Deuteronomy 14:22–29 and 26:12–15." In *Yet with a Steady Beat: Contemporary U. S. Afrocentric Biblical Interpretation*, edited by Randall C. Bailey, 7–18. SBL Semeia Studies 42. Atlanta: Society of Biblical Literature, 2003.

Block, Daniel. I. *The Gospel according to Moses: Theological and Ethical Reflections on the Book of Deuteronomy*. Eugene, OR: Cascade, 2012.

Braulik, Georg. "Das Buch Deuteronomium." In *Einleitung in das Alte Testament*, edited by Erich Zenger. Kohlhammer Studienbücher Theologie. Stuttgart: Kohlhammer, 2008.

Braulik, Georg. "Die Freude des Festes." In *Studien zur Theologie des Deuteronomiums*, 161–218. Stuttgart: Katholisches Bibelwerk, 1988. ET "The Joy of the Feast." In *The Theology of Deuteronomy: Collected Essays of Georg Braulik O.S.B*, 27–65. Translated by Ulrike Lindblad. BIBAL Collected Essays 2. North Richland Hills, TX: BIBAL, 1994.

Crouch, Carly L. *The Making of Israel: Cultural Diversity in the Southern Levant and the Formation of Ethnic Identity in Deuteronomy.* Vetus Testamentum Supplements 162. Leiden and Boston: Brill, 2014.

Crüsemann, Frank. *The Torah: Theology and Social History of the Old Testament Law.* Translated by A. W. Mahnke. Minneapolis: Fortress, 1996.

Davies, Philip R. "The Authority of Deuteronomy." In *Deuteronomy-Kings as Emerging Authoritative Books: A Conversation*, edited by Diana V. Edelman, 27–47. Ancient Near Eastern Monographs. 6. Atlanta: Society of Biblical Literature, 2014.

Eissfeldt, Otto. *Erstlinge und Zehnten im Alten Testament.* Leipzig: Hinrich, 1917.

Emerton, John. "Priests and Levites in Deuteronomy. An Examination of Dr G. E. Wright's Theory." *Vetus Testamentum* 12 (1962): 129–38.

Foldvari, Peter and Bas van Leeuwen. "Market Performance in Early Economies: Concepts and Empirics with an Application to Babylon." In *A History of Market Performance: From Ancient Babylonia to the Modern World*, edited by Robartus van der Spek, Bas van Leeuwen, and Jan Luiten van Zandern, 19–44. Routledge Explorations in Economic History 68. London and New York: Routledge, 2015.

Hensel, Benedikt. "Deuteronomium 12,13–19: Zur Lokalisierung des einen Maqom." *Biblische Notizen* N. S. 182 (2019): 9–43.

Humbert, Paul. "'Laetari et exultare' dans le vocabulaire religieux de l'Ancien Testament (Essai d'analyse des termes *Sâmaḥ* et *Gîl*)." *Revue d'histoire et de philosophie religieuses* 22 (1942): 185–214.

Jursa, Michael and Martina Schmidl. "Babylonia as a Source of Imperial Revenue from Cyrus to Xerxes." In *Fiscal Regimes and the Political Economy of Premodern States*, edited by Andrew Monson and Walter Scheidel, 715–40. Cambridge: Cambridge University Press, 2015.

Katzoff, Ranon and David Schaps, editors. *Law in the Documents of the Judaean Desert.* Supplements to the Journal for the Study of Judaism 96. Leiden: Brill, 2005.

Kilchör, Benjamin. *Mosetora und Jahwetora: Das Verhältnis von Deuteronomium 12–26 zu Exodus, Levitikus und Numeri.* Beihefte zur Zeitschrift für altorientalische und biblische Rechtsgeschichte 21. Wiesbaden: Harrassowitz, 2015.

Kratz, Reinhard G. *The Composition of the Narrative Books of the Old Testament.* Translated by John Bowden. London: Bloomsbury Academic, 2005.

Lauinger, Jacob. "Esarhaddon's Succession Treaty at Tell Tayinat: Text and Commentary." *Journal of Cuneiform Studies* 64 (2012): 87–123.

Levinson, Bernard M. *Deuteronomy and the Hermeneutics of Legal Innovation.* Oxford: Oxford University Press, 1997.

Lohfink, Norbert. "Poverty in the Laws of the Ancient Near East and of the Bible." *Theological Studies* 52 (1991): 34–50.

Lundbom, Jack R. *Deuteronomy: A Commentary.* Grand Rapids, MI: Eerdmans, 2013.

MacDonald, Nathan. "Issues and Questions in the Dating of Deuteronomy: A Response to Juha Pakkala." *Zeitschrift für die alttestamentliche Wissenschaft* 122 (2010): 431–35.

Mayes, A. D. H. "On Describing the Purpose of Deuteronomy." *Journal for the Study of the Old Testament* 58 (1993): 13–33.

Milgrom, Jacob. *Leviticus 23–27: A New Translation with Introduction and Commentary.* Anchor Bible 3B. New York: Doubleday, 2001.

Morley, Neville. "Demography and Development in Classical Antiquity." In *Demography in the Graeco-Roman World*, edited by Claire Holleran and April Pudsey, 14–36. Cambridge: Cambridge University, 2011.

Morris, Ian and Joe G. Manning. "The Economic Sociology of the Ancient Mediterranean World." In *The Handbook of Economic Sociology*, edited by Neil J. Smelser and Richard Swedberg, 131–59. Princeton: Princeton University Press, 2005.

Otto, Eckart. "Born out of Ruins: The Catastrophe of Jerusalem as Accoucheur to the Pentateuch in the Book of Deuteronomy." In *The Fall of Jerusalem and the Rise of Torah*, edited by Peter Dubovský, Dominik Markl, and Jean-Pierre Sonnet, 155–168. Forschungen zum Alten Testament 107. Tübingen: Mohr Siebeck, 2016.

Otto, Eckart. *Deuteronomium 12,1–23,15*. Herders Theologischer Kommentar zum Alten Testament. Freiburg: Herder, 2016.

Otto, Eckart. *Das Deuteronomium: Politische Theologie und Rechtsreform in Juda und Assyrien*. Beihefte zur Zeitschrift für die alttestamentliche Wissenschaft 284. Berlin: de Gruyter, 1999.

Otto, Eckart. *Das Gesetz des Mose*. Darmstadt: Wissenschaftliche Buchgesellschaft, 2007.

Pakkala, Juha. "The Date of the Oldest Edition of Deuteronomy." *Zeitschrift für die alttestamentliche Wissenschaft* 121 (2009): 394–95. DOI: https://doi.org/10.1515/ZAW.2009.026.

Pakkala, Juha. "The Dating of Deuteronomy: A Response to Nathan MacDonald." *Zeitschrift für die alttestamentliche Wissenschaft* 123 (2011): 431–36. DOI10.1515/ZAW.2011.029.

Rad, Gerhard von. *Deuteronomy: A Commentary*. Old Testament Library. Translated by Dorothea Barton. Philadelphia: Westminster, 1966.

Reuter, Eleonore. *Kultzentralisation. Entstehung und Theologie von Dtn 12*. Bonner biblische Beiträge 87. Frankfurt am Main: Hain, 1993.

Schorch, Stefan. "The Samaritan Version of Deuteronomy and the Origin of Deuteronomy." In *Samaria, Samarians, Samaritans: Studies on Bible, History and linguistics*, edited by József Zsengellér, 23–37. Studia Judaica: Forschungen zur Wissenschaft des Judentums 66; Studia Samaritana 6. Berlin: de Gruyter, 2011.

Seitz, Gottfried. *Redaktionsgeschichtliche Studien zum Buch Deuteronomium*. Beitrage Zur Wissenschaft vom Alten und Neuen Testament 5/13. Stuttgart: Kohlhammer, 1971.

Ska, Jean Louis. "Why Does the Pentateuch Speak So Much of Torah and So Little of Jerusalem?" In *The Fall of Jerusalem and the Rise of Torah*, edited by Peter Dubovský, Dominik Markl, and Jean-Pierre Sonnet, 113–28. Forschungen zum Alten Testament 107. Tübingen: Mohr Siebeck, 2016.

Steymans, Hans Ulrich. "Die neuassyrische Vertragsrhetorik der 'Vassal Treaties of Esarhaddon' und das Deuteronomium." In *Das Deuteronomium*, edited by Georg Braulik, 89–152. Österreichische biblische Studien 23. Frankfurt am Main: Lang, 2003.

Thelle, Rannfrid I. *Approaches to the 'Chosen Place': Accessing a Biblical Concept*. Library of Hebrew Bible/Old Testament 564. London: T&T Clark, 2012.

Tigay, Jeffery H. *Deuteronomy: The Traditional Hebrew Text with the New JPS Translation*. The JPS Torah Commentary. Philadelphia: Jewish Publication Society, 1999.

Van Seters, John. *A Law Book for the Diaspora: Revision in the Study of the Covenant Code*. New York: Oxford University Press, 2003.

Van Seters, John. *The Pentateuch: A Social Scientific Commentary*. Sheffield: Sheffield Academic, 1999.

Veijola, Timo. *Das funfte Buch Moses*. Göttingen: Vandenhoeck & Ruprecht, 2004.

Wette, Wilhelm Martin Lebrecht, de. *Dissertatio critica qua Deuteronomium a prioribus Pentateuchi libris diversum, alius cuiusdam recentioris opus esse monstratur*. Jena: Literis Etzdorfii, 1805.

Willis, Timothy M. "'Eat and Rejoice Before the Lord': The Optimism of Worship in the Deuteronomic Code." In *Worship and the Hebrew Bible: Essays in Honour of John T. Willis*, edited by M. Patrick Graham, Rick R. Marrs, and Steven L. McKenzie, 276–97. Sheffield: Sheffield Academic, 1999.

Graeme Auld

Deuteronomy and the Older Royal Narrative: Some Core Questions

1 Questions about a Deuteronomic Core

Over the ages, readers have recognized the many obvious links between the books of Deuteronomy and Kings. The broad sweep of scholarship holds that the history of Israel from its settlement in Canaan to the fall of Jerusalem to Babylon was told in the books from Joshua to Kings in standards and language drawn from Deuteronomy. More precisely, in the prevailing understanding, the authors of the principal structuring narratives were familiar with the "code" of Deuteronomy (chs. 12–26).

I have challenged this hypothesis in *Life in Kings* (2017), where I advance a three-fold case for recognizing the narrative shared by Samuel-Kings and Chronicles as the core of the royal narrative. My three arguments are as follows. (a) The so-called synoptic material shared between Samuel-Kings and Chronicles is a quite distinctive sub-set of Samuel-Kings. (b) Detached from its present setting(s), this sub-set emerges as an integrated, coherent, and even artistically created text. Finally, (c) the synoptic material was not simply *one* major source alongside others that contributed to Samuel-Kings. It was, instead, its core or alternatively, the seedbed out of which much of Samuel-Kings developed through further exploration of the implications and resources of the older stories. Since the houses of Yahweh and of the king are prominent throughout, I call it the *Book of Two Houses* (henceforth BoTH).

Many nouns, verbs, names, and even whole phrases occur just twice each in the synoptic text – or, where found more than twice, then still are repeated within the accounts of only two kings. Some examples: a shot from a bow only kills Saul and Ahab. The verbs "save" (הושע) and "deliver" (הציל) are used only in narratives about David and Hezekiah; after Saul and David, there is no further mention of Philistines. Many of these pairs occur in clusters. For example: not only "save" and "deliver," but also "scorn" (חרף) and "Yahweh's messenger" (מלאך יהוה) are unique within the synoptic narrative to the accounts of David and Hezekiah. Then, though the verb "prostrate oneself" (השתחוה) occurs four times in BoTH, these clearly form two pairs: one concerns prostration before gods other than Yahweh; the other provides a further link between David and Hezekiah.

https://doi.org/10.1515/9783110713312-008

In my 2017 monograph, I noted some 30 such pairings.[1] However, at the time of completing this contribution, I have identified more than 130.[2] On the one hand, this much larger total strengthens the claim that BoTH was an integrated and artistically purposeful text. On the other, it provides (negative) evidence about the original extent of BoTH. Josiah's successors, the last four kings of Jerusalem, do all feature at the end of Kings and Chronicles; but the shared text relating to them is much sketchier than in the rest of BoTH. Hence, it seems probable that BoTH started with the death of Saul and finished with that of Josiah. In support of this conclusion, not one of the eleven dozen paired links relates to any of these four last kings, while of the kings before Josiah, only Amon is without an explicit link. It is possible that Amon is blamed for serving the same detestable deities that Asa had much earlier removed and that later censors removed their names from 2 Kings 21:21 and 1 Kings 15:13.

Scholarship over many generations has termed chs. 12–26 of Deuteronomy its "code," with the most comprehensive statement about the place chosen by Yahweh at its start and pilgrimage to that place with first fruits at its close. This "code" is also widely reckoned to be its "core." However, several features of Deuteronomy 26:1–15 make me question whether it should be reckoned part of the core of the book.

(1) Its theme of the offerings to be taken to the sanctuary from the produce of the land has already been outlined at 14:22–23; thus, ch. 26 can fairly be described as an expanded statement of the requirement.

(2) That earlier statement of the theme (14:22–23) immediately follows the well-known injunction about the kid and its mother's milk (14:21b). These same themes are paired (though in reverse order) among the *mišpāṭîm* of the so-called Covenant Code (Exod 23:19b, 19a). The link with that code, together with the terseness of the formulation in Deuteronomy 14, are both indications of the priority of Deuteronomy 14 over Deuteronomy 26. The kid, which will not concern us further here, has been usefully discussed by Stefan Schorch and Philippe Guillaume.[3]

(3) Deuteronomy 26:1–15 includes the injunction to prostrate oneself (השתחוה) *before Yahweh* (v. 10). The negative counterpart, *not* to prostrate before *other* gods, is common (see Table A in the Appendix). However, this positive command is not found in any other part of Deuteronomy. In Samuel-Kings, prostration before Yahweh is found only in non-synoptic portions, most of them in 1 Samuel (1 Sam 1:3, 1:19, 1:28, 15:25, 15:30, 15:31, 28:14; 2 Sam 12:20; 2 Kgs 17:36).

1 Auld, *Life in Kings*, 92–93.
2 Auld, "Tracing the Writing of Kings."
3 Schorch, "Young Goat"; Guillaume, "Binding 'Sucks.'"

(4) A fourth criterion, the wording לשכן שמו שם in Deuteronomy 26:2, is discussed below in section 2.

All in all, ch. 26, with its restatement of the first-fruits command that includes the requirement of prostration before Yahweh, should either be reassigned to the outer chapters of Deuteronomy or taken as our first sample of secondary material within Deuteronomy 12–26. Aside from this, I simply accept as a starting point in this paper the opinion about the central chapters of Deuteronomy that is widely shared (though not by Guillaume in this volume).

In my Samuel commentary, I had already argued that most of 1 Samuel (and chs. 1–30 include seven of the nine instances just noted of prostration before Yahweh) was extrapolated from – developed from and projected backwards from – the shared account of Jerusalem's kings.[4] It was a fresh prequel to the older royal story told in BoTH. The development from the major speech of synoptic Solomon (1 Kgs 8//2 Chr 6) to the major speech of non-synoptic Samuel (1 Sam 12) is just one example.[5] In the monograph I claimed that the process of re-appropriating the synoptic royal story continued beyond the prophet Samuel in the same direction – backwards in time – to Moses.[6] Here I will develop my earlier insight further by arguing that the teaching attributed to Moses in Deuteronomy 12 about the place chosen by Yahweh is also indebted to the synoptic account of David and Solomon in BoTH. I note fresh indications of how the whole synoptic narrative of BoTH (and especially the reports about kings Ahaz and Manasseh) may have informed Moses's teaching in Deuteronomy 13 and 18 about prophecy and divination.

The relationship of non-code to code material in Deuteronomy has several similarities to that of non-core to core material in Samuel–Kings. Deuteronomy 1–11 and 1 Samuel 1–30 provide substantial, fresh prequels to the older materials; and there are new tail-pieces in Deuteronomy 27–34 and 2 Kings 24–25. There will also have been many interpolations within the framework of the older materials, some of them quite large. These can be more readily identified in Samuel-Kings, granted that synoptic/non-synoptic corresponds to core/non-core. The core of Samuel-Kings (BoTH) lacked not only the prequel (Samuel and Saul) and the tail-piece (Jerusalem's four last kings) but also most of the story of David and his family in 2 Samuel 9–20, most of the prophetic narratives in 1 Kings 17–2 Kings 10 in which Elijah and Elisha are prominent, and all the connected account of the kings of northern Israel. However, within the Deuteronomic Code (chs. 12–26), we have no similarly objective criterion of verbatim or

4 Auld, *I & II Samuel.*

5 Auld, 103–5, 108–9.

6 Auld, 195–202.

almost verbatim materials found in two separate books for distinguishing between earlier and later or core and non-core; instead, we must operate with clusters of details, as in the above discussion of Deuteronomy 26:1–15.

2 The Place of Divine Choice

Within Deuteronomy, Moses's wording about Yahweh's "choice" (בחר) of a "place" (מקום) appears not only first but also repeatedly in Deuteronomy 12 (vv. 5, 11, 14, 18, 21, and 26). Only in Deuteronomy 16:2, 6, 7, 11, 15, and 16 is the density of usage greater. The other occurrences in Deuteronomy are at 14:23, 24, 25; 15:20; 17:8, 10; 18:6; 26:2; 31:11 (see also Guillaume in this volume). This phrasing re-mints coinage from the divine promise through Nathan to David which, as cited by Solomon, had been extended to include the divine choosing of Jerusalem.

In each of the five synoptic mentions of Yahweh's choice of "the city" (העיר) or Jerusalem, the stated purpose is that his name should "be" there or that he should "set" it there. On four occasions, Kings and Chronicles present the same wording and they differ only on the second.

Tab. 1: Synoptic Mentions of "The City".

1 Kgs 8:16	להיות שמי שם	להיות שמי שם	2 Chr 6:6
1 Kgs 8:29	אמרת יהיה שמי שם	אמרת לשום שמך שם	2 Chr 6:20
1 Kgs 9:3	לשום את־שמו שם	לשום את־שמו שם	2 Chr 7:16
1 Kgs 14:21	לשום את־שמו שם	לשום את־שמו שם	2 Chr 12:13
2 Kgs 21:7	אשים את־שמי לעולם	אשים את־שמי לעולם	2 Chr 33:7

The setting of Yahweh's name in the city of Jerusalem (or indeed anywhere else) is never mentioned in Samuel–Kings outside these five synoptic instances.

The phrase "to set his name there" is also used three times in Deuteronomy in connection with the divine choice of a "place," two of them in ch. 12 (vv. 5 and 21) and the third in 14:24. However, six times (12:11, 14:23, 16:2, 16:6, 16:11, 26:2) we find an alternative formulation never replicated in Samuel-Kings but also found in Jeremiah 7:12 and Nehemiah 1:9: לשכן שמו שם ("to let his name *dwell* there"). Lauren A. S. Monroe has proposed the perfectly cogent argument that שכן in these contexts is a calque of Akkadian *šakanu*, which bears the same sense as Hebrew שים or שום ("set/place").[7]

7 Monroe, *Josiah's Reform*.

However, an alternative and inner-biblical explanation of this variant in Deuteronomy is both perfectly safe and also convergent with a feature of non-synoptic Samuel-Kings often observed in *Life in Kings*. It can be argued that לשכן שמו שם simply draws on and combines two separate elements of BoTH: (a) לשום את־שמו שם (see 1 Kgs 9:3, 14:21; cf. 2 Kgs 21:7) and (b) שכן from 1 Kings 8:12–13//2 Chronicles 6:1–2, a poetic fragment telling that Yahweh had spoken of "dwelling" (שכן *qal*) in darkness, and a house was built for him to live in forever. Combining these two synoptic themes had been eased by עולמים at the end of 1 Kings 8:13 and לעולם at the end of 2 Kings 21:7, both meaning "forever" and functioning as catchwords. Similar talk of Yahweh "dwelling" in the holy "place" had probably been the original intention of Jeremiah 7:3 and 7:7. In unvocalized Hebrew, ואשכנה\ושכנתי אתכם במקום הזה is ambiguous: with the verbs read as *qal*, it means "and I shall dwell with you in this place." However, with the verbs read as *piel* in the standard text, it means "and I shall let you dwell in this place." Assuming a shift from earlier *qal* to current *piel*, a theologically bold promise about Yahweh's presence in the heart of the temple has been tamed to express a promise about Israel continuing in its land. In Deuteronomy, similarly, having the "name" of Yahweh "dwell" in the "place" avoided the bluntness of describing Yahweh (himself) dwelling in the temple, even in darkness.

If לשכן שמו שם is judged secondary to the synoptic formula לשום שמו שם shared with BoTH, two options remain available to us. The primary Deuteronomic legislator could have created this coinage and used it alongside the synoptic formula; or the primary legislator could have adopted the synoptic formula, while the new coinage indicates the work of a subsequent author. The alternative formulations appear in neighboring verses only in Deuteronomy 14:23 and 24. Within Deuteronomy 12 they belong to different paragraphs: לשום is used in vv. 1–7 and vv. 20–28, and לשכן in vv. 8–12. There is consensus over the paragraphing implicit in Deuteronomy 12 (vv. 1–7, 8–12, 13–19, 20–28, 29–31) and wide agreement that the oldest form of the statement about the place of divine choice is within 12:13–18[19], although Simeon Chavel has argued that this paragraph is the latest in the chapter.[8] The final instance of the non-synoptic formula ("to let his name dwell") is found in 26:2, within the restatement of the first fruits topic discussed above. If Deuteronomy 26:1–15 should still be reckoned part of the core of Deuteronomy, it should be seen as part of a secondary (or later) stratum within it and compared with 12:8–12. If לשכן שמו שם was also a secondary addition to 14:23, we should perhaps deduce that Deuterono-

---

8 Chavel, "Literary Development," 316–19.

my 16:1–16, with its three instances of the non-synoptic formula, is also not primary.

Several features of Deuteronomy 12 are clearly related to synoptic 2 Samuel 7 and 1 Kings 8 (and linked passages). However, לשכן שמו שם, though twice as common in Deuteronomy as לשום את־שמו שם, is never found in Kings. Similarly, the chosen *place* (מקום), so common in Deuteronomy and found once in 2 Chronicles 7:12b, is never found in Kings. Instead of reading Kings from the perspective of Deuteronomy, we should read Deuteronomy from the perspective of BoTH. "Place" (מקום) is used in different senses in BoTH, but always "of a location where something of the deity has been invested, whether that be destructive force or more benign choice and commitment."[9] However, in the context of the Jerusalem temple, "place" in BoTH was specifically the "holy of holies" where the ark was deposited. Deuteronomy instead conflated "place" with "house" or "city/Jerusalem."

(a) The divine choice of a "place" from all your sceptres/tribes (מכל־שבטיכם) to set his name there (12:5) recalls BoTH's wording of "a city" (1 Kgs 8:16), "Jerusalem, the city" (1 Kgs 14:21), or "Jerusalem" (2 Kgs 21:7), chosen by Yahweh "from all the sceptres/tribes of Israel" (מכל־שבטי ישראל).

(b) במקום אשר יבחר יהוה באחד שבטיך שם תעלה עלתיך ושם תעשה כל אשר אנכי מצוך in Deuteronomy 12:14 again uses "choose" from BoTH but combines it instead with the unique "one of your tribes/sceptres," which draws on the equally unique באחד שבטי ישראל ("one of the sceptres/tribes of Israel") in synoptic 2 Samuel 7:7.

(c) Deuteronomy 12:21 repeats from 12:5 "the place" and "chosen by Yahweh" and "to set his name there," but without "from all your tribes." The same wording (with "set" and without "from all your tribes") occurs just once more. Only in 12:21 and 14:24 do we find the provision, "if the place is too far from you" (כי־ירחק ממך המקום). If "far" is also an echo of BoTH, it may be recalling the "far land" in Solomon's prayer (1 Kgs 8:41, 46//2 Chr 6:32, 36). In any case, David is the only other user in BoTH of "far," again in connection with "house": "and you have spoken even to the house of your servant from afar" (2 Sam 7:19// 1 Chr 17:17).

Simeon Chavel has argued that Deuteronomy 12:20–28 results from splicing together two originally separate although overlapping formulations: v. 20 originally introduced vv. 22–25, and v. 21 headed vv. 26–28.[10] We have noted that "far" (v. 21) may echo BoTH, and this is also true of "place." However, the corresponding conditional clause that opens v. 20, "if Yahweh your god *widens* your

9 Auld, *Life in Kings*, 77–78.
10 Chavel, "Literary Development," 312–16.

border" (כי ירחיב יהוה אלהיך את גבולך), uses terms not found in BoTH. When "widens your border" is used again in Deuteronomy 19:8, it is much expanded: "… as he swore to your fathers and gives you all the land which he spoke of giving to your fathers." It is now explicit that the phrase refers to the completion of the promised land-taking and that Deuteronomy 12:20 and 12:22–25 mirror 12:8–12.

(d) It is important to note that "you" is plural in the opening paragraphs, Deuteronomy 12:1–7 and 12:8–12, but singular in 12:13–19, 12:20–28, and 12:29–31. The singular "you" also helps to clarify the relationship between the declarations to Israel in Deuteronomy 12:20–28 and the divine promise to David, particularly as represented in 2 Samuel 7:12–16. The correlation is particularly striking at the culmination of vv. 20–28: Israel is addressed in the singular, in terms used of her first king, and charged to do "what is right in the eyes of Yahweh" like every good king that followed him. The synoptic royal story had told of fathers dying and being buried, followed by their sons, and each summarily assessed by whether he had or had not done "what was right in the eyes of Yahweh." In Deuteronomy, Moses speaks in closely related terms: in 12:25, 28 (as also in 4:40), "to you and your sons" is followed by "after you" (אחריך) as in 2 Samuel 7:12 (BoTH), and there with "seed" (זרע) rather than "sons." And in BoTH, the divine promise to David and his *seed* is "forever" (2 Sam 7:13, 16//1 Chr 17:12, 14). "Forever" is used much more densely in synoptic material than in non-synoptic Samuel–Kings (see Table B in the Appendix). The account in 2 Samuel 7//1 Chronicles 17 of the divine commitment to David mediated by Nathan and David's response uses "forever" most densely of all (six times). It is precisely with these several synoptic "forever" passages that Deuteronomy 12 shares so much; and yet it mentions "forever" only in 12:28 (and not even in the related 12:25). This important chapter culminates in 12:28. (As will be noted in Section 4 below, 12:29–31 has a close link with 13:1–6.) In 12:25 and 28, Moses addresses Israel as a singular "you." לך ולבניך is not a common pairing (Exod 12:24; Lev 10:15; Num 18:8, 9, 11, 19; Deut 4:40, 12:25, 12:28; Josh 14:9); but it is almost always linked with עולם, though not in Numbers 18:9 nor Deuteronomy 12:25, and in Deuteronomy 4:40 it is linked with כל־הימים instead. However, there is one crucial difference between the words of Moses and the synoptic narrative – "forever" in Deuteronomy 12:28 is now conditional – "Watch and listen to all these words that I am commanding you in order that it may be well for you and your sons after you forever, *supposing you do what is good and right in the eyes of Yahweh your god* (כי תעשה הטוב והישר בעיני יהוה אלהיך)." The optimism of the older royal ideology represented in BoTH has become blunted.

Just two linked chapters in BoTH have provided several of the key terms in Deuteronomy 12. One narrates the divine promise to David (2 Sam 7) and the other Solomon's actualization of that promise as he dedicates the Jerusalem temple (1 Kgs 8). Viewing this supposed introduction to the core of Deuteronomy from the perspective of BoTH contributes to the analysis of Deuteronomy 12. Positively, Israel (sg) is addressed like one of its (former) kings; and this in turn supports the long-standing critical judgment that the earliest component in Deuteronomy 12 is vv. 13–18. Negatively, vv. 8–12 are stated in language unknown in BoTH: not only the לשכן (let dwell) formula in v. 11, itself part of a secondary combination of elements from BoTH, but also the nouns מנוחה ("rest") and נחלה ("allotment") in v. 9 and the cognate verbs מנחיל ("allot") and הניח ("give rest") in v. 10.

Deriving the wording in Deuteronomy about divine "choice" of a "place" from portions of BoTH also sets a major text-critical issue in a fresh light. Throughout Deuteronomy, and starting from Deuteronomy 12, the MT refers to the place "which Yahweh *will/may choose*" (יבחר יהוה), but the Samaritan text always offers "which Yahweh *chose*" (בחר יהוה) – understood as performative *qatal*, בחר could also be rendered "chooses." Innocent Himbaza has attractively argued for a future perfect interpretation, "which Yahweh will have chosen," of the more original בחר.[11] The linked passages in BoTH also use perfect/*qatal*: דברתי in 2 Samuel 7:7, בחרתי in 1 Kings 8:16, and בחרת in 1 Kings 8:44 and 48. If Deuteronomy borrowed from BoTH, it is natural to suppose that the law-giver simply adopted the perfect/*qatal* from the parent text and produced what we read in the Samaritan text. Only later was the verb adjusted in the MT. Adrian Schenker marshals the evidence from Greek, Coptic, and Latin mss. that the earliest Greek translation of Deuteronomy used the preterite "chose" in agreement with the Samaritan text.[12] Only after the shift in the MT had the LXX been adjusted to agree.

In summary, the following three-stage development is plausible:
(1) Yahweh chooses Jerusalem/the city to set his name there (BoTH).
(2) Yahweh chooses "the place" to set his name there (Deut^1).
(3) Yahweh chooses "the place" to let his name dwell there (Deut^2).

If the older portions of Deuteronomy 12:13–28 were indebted to the completed *Book of Two Houses*, which came to its end with the death of king Josiah, then the purpose of Deuteronomy 12 was not to enjoin *centralization* of "worship" under Josiah or any other king (see also Halpern in this volume). According to BoTH, David and Solomon had already offered holocaust sacrifices in Jerusalem, and BoTH has nothing to report about holocausts offered up elsewhere. A

11 Himbaza, "'Le lieu.'"
12 Schenker, "Textgeschichtliches," 113–16.

Deuteronomic legislator working from BoTH after the fall of Jerusalem had no reason to commend centralization but had every reason to restate principles already normative in BoTH for a new and still emerging situation. The kings had always represented the nation; now without kings, the nation is addressed directly. There had been and must still be a center for key cultic practices. Given the uncertain status of Jerusalem, this center is not (yet) named. The divine promise "forever" is too deeply rooted in the old traditions to surrender; but its restatement now comes with clear conditions.

3 Prophets and Dreamers

It can be argued that both sections of Deuteronomy that deal with prophecy or divination (chs. 13 and 18) were also developed from and respond to (portions of) BoTH.[13] I have described BoTH as "the oldest 'biblical' prophetic narrative."[14] Prophets, along with a seer and men of God, certainly play an important role – from David asking Nathan about building a house for Yahweh to Josiah sending representatives to Huldah after hearing the words from the scroll found in the temple. And Solomon received two divine visions or dreams. However, I prefer now to define the section that dealt with Rehoboam and Jeroboam in BoTH more tightly.[15] If this was more like the "alternative story" preserved in LXX^{BL} than what we read in 1 Kings 12:1–19 (MT and LXX^{A})//2 Chronicles 10:1–19, then neither Ahijah nor Shemaiah was originally styled a "prophet." Furthermore, the religious interpretation now found in 1 Kings 12:15b//2 Chronicles 10:15b had not yet been added, stating that Rehoboam's disregard for the people was "a turn originating from Yahweh in order to establish his word which he spoke through Ahijah the Shilonite." Recognizing as secondary that explicit formulation of word + fulfilment permits a more nuanced view of the earlier role of prophets according to BoTH: they play important parts in the story, but their words do not provide an authoritative interpretation.

The extended story at its heart about Micaiah and the two kings is instructive for two reasons: (a) it pits one "prophet of Yahweh" over against hundreds of prophets who are never said to be in the cause of any other god; and (b) it depicts Yahweh's prophet as involved in Yahweh-inspired deception of the kings. Several significant pairings link the stories in BoTH of Micaiah (1 Kgs

13 Auld, "Divination."
14 Auld, "Isaiah."
15 Auld, "Some Thoughts."

22:5, 22:7, 22:8, 22:17, 22:20, 22:27, 22:28, 22:31) and of Huldah (2 Kgs 22:13, 22:14, 22:18, 22:20, 23:2). Jehoshaphat and Ahab seek (דרש) Yahweh through Micaiah the prophet (הנביא), as only synoptic Josiah will do again through Huldah the prophetess (הנביאה). Small (קט[ו]ן) and great (גדול) are paired only in the Jehoshaphat and Josiah reports. In peace (בשלום) is uttered three times in the exchanges between Micaiah and the king of Israel and reappears only in the response of Huldah to Josiah. Many generations of readers have been surprised at Josiah dying on the battlefield (2 Kgs 23:29–30) after being told by Huldah that he would be gathered to his grave in peace (22:20), but they may have misread the prophetess.

If its author were familiar with BoTH, it is appropriate that Deuteronomy 13:2–6 expresses caution about the advice that might be given by prophets and dreamers of dreams. They might promise things that do not happen; and, even if they do happen, they might go on to encourage following other gods. This would constitute a test from Yahweh. Deuteronomy 18:15–22 returns to the theme of prophets and the danger of following other gods. Moses promises that Yahweh will raise up a prophet like him: he will speak what Yahweh will put in his mouth, and Yahweh will take action against those who do not listen. If the prophet speaks and what is indicated does not happen, then that word was not from Yahweh. It is easier to see these paragraphs in Deuteronomy as responses to the narratives in BoTH about kings and prophets than as statements of the principles that later became operative in these narratives (see also Turton in this volume).

4 King Manasseh's Shadow

Each of these two paragraphs relating to prophets immediately follows a paragraph that deals with "divination" (in the broadest sense) and is also closely related to BoTH – in this case, not to the broad sweep of the narrative, but only its sections on the wicked kings Ahaz and Manasseh.

In BoTH (2 Kgs 21:2//2 Chr 33:2), Manasseh, like Ahaz his grandfather (2 Kgs 16:3//2 Chr 28:3), followed the "abominable actions" (תועבות) of the nations dispossessed before Israel by Yahweh. BoTH uses this abhorrent term only twice. In the case of Ahaz, only one notorious example is cited of his abominations: making his son pass in fire. In the second case, we are also told that Manasseh built altars for Baal, made an Asherah, and built altars for the whole host of heaven (2 Kgs 21:3–5//2 Chr 33:3–5) before, like Ahaz, he "passed his son through fire" (העביר את־בנו באש). This much longer, hostile report goes on to state that Manasseh also practised divination, described in 2 Kings 21:6//

2 Chronicles 33:6 in two pairs of expressions: ועונן ונחש and ועשה אוב וידעונים. Whether there was any relationship between divination and what was done with his son and fire remains an open question.

Tab. 2: Deuteronomy 18 and Parallels.

Deut 18:10–11	Parallels
מעביר בנו־ובתו באש making his son/daughter pass in fire	BoTH on Ahaz and Manasseh
קסם קסמים one divining divinations	(see below)
מעונן ומנחש a soothsayer and an augur	BoTH on Manasseh
ומכשף וחבר חבר and a sorcerer and a charmer of charms	Isa 47:9–12
ושאל אוב וידעני and an *'ôb*-asker and a "familiar"	BoTH on Manasseh
ודרש אל־המתים and one enquiring of the dead	Isa 8:19

These materials are rebuilt in Deuteronomy 18:9–14. The two pairs of terms from BoTH have become eight (18:10–11). However, unlike the case of Manasseh (2 Kgs 21:3–5//2 Chr 33:3–5), there is no mention in Deuteronomy 18 of altar-building for Baal, the making of an Asherah, or the service of the whole host of heaven. Hence, its instruction not to learn to act according to the abominations of these nations (18:9) is now immediately followed by an enhanced list of "divinatory" practices (vv. 10–11) that has not only supplemented the shorter list in BoTH but may also have changed its character.

The two pairs of terms shared with BoTH on Manasseh concern divination in the strict sense: discovering and stating what the future will be. "Enquiring of the dead" (דרש אל־המתים), the new final term, restates the second pair – and is also linked with them only in Isaiah 8:19. But the interpolated pair of terms, shared only with Isaiah 47:9–12, describe sorcery: attempting to change the future. As for קסם, it is quite the commonest of all these terms in the Hebrew Bible (some 30 times, including appearances in Isa 3:2; 44:25). Though normally rendered "divine(r)," it is applied to Balaam, whom the Moabite king recruits to curse Israel and so change Moab's future for the better. If we knew the original import of "making one's son (or daughter) pass in fire," we would know whether sorcery was an original component of the charge-sheet against Ahaz and Manasseh in BoTH. The warning is underscored in vv. 12–14, and only after this comprehensive description of false approach to the deity does Moses present the "prophet like me" that Yahweh will raise up for Israel (18:15–22).

The preceding passage on prophets and dreamers (Deut 13:2–6) also follows a short paragraph related to both Ahaz and Manasseh (Deut 12:29–31). When Yahweh cuts off the nations whose land Israel will settle, Israel should not be ensnared into consulting their gods: the nations had done for their gods every abomination that Yahweh hates – even burning their sons and daughters by fire for their gods. This solitary example given of abominable action is reminiscent of BoTH on Ahaz. However, the threefold mention of "their (unnamed) gods" recalls Manasseh's actions in favor of Baal, Asherah, and the host of heaven. The element of the BoTH critique of Manasseh that we did not find replicated in Deuteronomy 18:9–11 is provided in Deuteronomy 12:30–31 and 13:3. And in case this allusion to Manasseh's actions has not been spotted, his name מנשה (*mnšh*) is immediately played on in 13:4: wherever prophets commend serving other gods, Yahweh is "testing" (*mnsh*/מנסה) Israel. All other instances of נסה in Deuteronomy occur outside chs. 12–26, in 4:34, 6:16, 8:2, 8:16, 28:56, and 33:8.

Each "divinatory-leading-to-prophetic" section of Deuteronomy resumes תועבת הגוים and הוריש from Ahaz and Manasseh in BoTH. This is explicitly so in Deuteronomy 18:9 and 14 and occurs with small modifications in Deuteronomy 12:29–31 (ירש *qal* is used twice in 12:29 and תועבה singular occurs in 12:31). Making another small change, both 12:31 and 18:10 add daughters alongside sons in whatever is done to children "by fire." Deuteronomy 12:31 makes its understanding clear that Canaanites were burning their sons and daughters "to their gods." These are named in 2 Kings 21:3–5 but remain typically anonymous in Deuteronomy. Deuteronomy 13:4 also plays on the name of Manasseh without actually using it. Then Deuteronomy 18:10–11 adopts all the details listed in 2 Kings 21:6 and adds more. The critique of two wicked kings in the older royal narrative has driven the presentation in Deuteronomy of divination and prophecy, both false and true – and not the other way around. Four of the eight terms in the expanded Deuteronomy 18:10–11 (קסם, כשף, חבר, דרש אל־המתים) are neither synoptic nor found elsewhere in Deuteronomy – and this despite the fact that קסם is quite the commonest "divinatory" term in the Hebrew Bible.

There is evidence that the Ahaz and Manasseh narratives from BoTH were influential beyond Deuteronomy. There are striking parallels in a still larger section of Leviticus 18–20. Within Leviticus, "abominations" appear only in these chapters (18:22, 18:26, 18:27, 18:29, 18:30, and 20:13). Not only so – the four divinatory terms used in pairs in 2 Kings 21:6 appear in the same two pairings, לא תנחשו ולא תעוננו (Lev 19:26) and אל־תפנו אל־האבת ואל־הידענים (Lev 19:31), precisely between the mentions in Leviticus 18 and 20 of the abominable "gift" of children. Just as Deuteronomy 12:31 takes the burning (שרף) of children as the prime example of abominable behavior, so, too, the only uses of תועבה in Leviticus follow "giving" children to Molech (18:21, 20:2, 20:3, 20:4, and 20:5). Molech is found elsewhere in the Hebrew Bible only three times: Solomon built a "high place" (במה) for this Ammonite god (1 Kgs 11:7); Josiah's defilement of the Topheth in the Hinnom valley (2 Kgs 23:10) was "lest any man cause his son or daughter to pass in fire to the Molech" (לבלתי להעביר איש את־בנו ואת־בתו באש); and Jeremiah complained against those who had built "high places" for Baal in Hinnom for this purpose (32:35).

From the perspective of BoTH, each positive panel in Deuteronomy 12–13 evokes David and Solomon and is preceded by a warning about continuing in the way of the two most recent evil kings. Deuteronomy 12:5–28 legislate for a central altar, like David and Solomon, "forever"; before this, 12:2–4 warn Israel against behaving like Ahaz and Manasseh and their cultivation of the במות. Deuteronomy 13:2–6 evokes good kings, such as David and Solomon, who were attentive to prophets and dreams, following the warning in 12:29–31 against replicating Ahaz and Manasseh and their abominations.

5 Deuteronomic Core and Non-Core

In each case just discussed, the material is found within the central chapters of Deuteronomy and barely appears beyond their confines. The chosen place is introduced in Deuteronomy 12 (6 times), mentioned 13 times in Deuteronomy 14–18 (14:23, 14:24, 14:25, 15:20, 16:2, 16:6, 16:7, 16:11, 16:15, 16:16, 17:8, 17:10, and 18:6); then, after a substantial gap, there are two final instances in Deuteronomy 26:2 (probably not part of the core: see above) and 31:11 (certainly outside the core). In the royal story, mention of the choice of Jerusalem or "the city" is found in only two non-synoptic contexts: 1 Kings 11:13, 11:32, 11:36, and 2 Kings 23:27. Both of these conclude by re-using synoptic formulae (לשום שמי שם and יהיה שמי שם) – neither adopts the Deuteronomic לשכן שמו שם. That could indicate (but it would be only an argument from silence) that the non-synoptic authors were not yet familiar with the later Deuteronomic usage.

Correlation over prophecy and divination is more complex. Deuteronomy does not mention divination at all outside the central chapters (or indeed prophecy, except for the concluding note about the special prophetic status of Moses in Deut 34:10–12). BoTH features divination only in the case of Manasseh and possibly Ahaz. However, non-synoptic Samuel–Kings includes four mentions and, at least in MT, each uses a form of non-synoptic קסם, apparently now the generic term (נביא experienced a similar development). In 1 Samuel, Philistines consult their priests and "diviners" (6:2); Samuel warns Saul against "divination" (15:23); yet, despite this, Saul asks the medium to "divine" by means of a *'wb*, and she raises up Samuel (28:8). However, in 1 Kingdoms 15:23, the LXX may attest not to קסם but נחש. Finally, in 2 Kings 17:16b–17a, and within a wider critique, fallen (northern) Israel is blamed for behaving in many ways like Manasseh: "they made an Asherah, prostrated themselves to the whole host of heaven, and they served Baal; and they made their sons and daughters pass in fire, divined divinations, and practised augury." Within the first three complaints, serving Baal comes third instead of first with Manasseh. Within the second three, the first and third items are as in the critique of Manasseh, but the second (מעונן) has been replaced by ויקסמו קסמים, presumably under the influence of the enhanced list in Deuteronomy 18:10–11. "Divining divinations" is also in second place there.

6 Conclusion

In each of these topics, chosen place and divination/prophecy, the development appears to have started the same way: moving from BoTH to core-Deuteronomy (no more than Deut 12–25 – but see Table C in the Appendix). Yet, there are differences among them all. The developing critique of "divination" proceeds from synoptic Manasseh, via Deuteronomy 18, to non-synoptic exiled Israel (2 Kgs 17). However, the "choosing" of Jerusalem in non-synoptic portions of Kings is not similarly influenced by Deuteronomy: the chosen "place" plays no part in 1 Kings 11:13, 32, 36 or 2 Kings 23:27. Again, several prophets play a higher, more normative role in non-synoptic Samuel–Kings than any of their counterparts in BoTH. Yet here, the trajectory of development appears to be from BoTH, via non-synoptic Samuel–Kings, to Deuteronomy 18, with its talk of "a prophet like [Moses]."

Non-synoptic materials in Samuel–Kings may find their counterparts either within Deuteronomy 12–25 or within the outer chapters of that book. An example of the first is Samuel's warning about the nature of kingship in 1 Samuel 8 and the law of the king as delivered by Moses in Deuteronomy 17:14–20. One striking instance of a topic found *only* in *non-core* Deuteronomy and *non-synoptic* Kings is the renegade construction of the golden calf and worship before it in Deuteronomy 9:8–21 and 1 Kings 12:25–33.

Mainstream scholarship links the origins of Deuteronomy closely to a reform by Josiah near the end of the monarchy in Jerusalem and reckons that its teachings were drafted in response to the long experience of monarchy. The claims made above are convergent but more specific:

Much of the *wording* at the core of the book called דברים had been influenced by the history of Jerusalem's monarchy as told – as *worded* – in the *Book of Two Houses.*

Appendix: Word Counts

Relationships between Samuel-Kings and BoTH and between the central chapters of Deuteronomy (12–25) and the remainder of that book, and indeed between both, can be sketched in a series of word-counts. Many of the totals tabulated below suggest parallel developments, on the one side from BoTH to Samuel-Kings and on the other from Deuteronomy 12–25 to the whole of Deuteronomy. However, in assessing them, we need to recall that not all materials now in the *central* chapters of Deuteronomy (12–25) had been original components of its *core*.

Life in Kings was so titled because "live," "life," and "alive" or "living" are so sparingly used in BoTH that they provide an excellent indicator of its difference from Samuel–Kings as a whole.[16] As in the synoptic narrative (BoTH), these terms are also used very sparingly in the heart of Deuteronomy. The outer chapters of Deuteronomy comprise roughly twice as much text as the central chapters. Hence, 14 occurrences in chs. 1–11 and 26–34 would reflect a similar density of usage to 7 occurrences in chs. 12–25. Non-synoptic Samuel–Kings is three to four times longer than the synoptic kernel; hence 21 occurrences in non-synoptic Samuel-Kings would reflect a similar density of usage to 6 occurrences in BoTH. The numbers in parentheses in the final two columns of this table and of those that follow indicate the totals across these longer texts, supposing the same level of usage as in their cores. Taking that into account, the "life"-family appears more than twice as densely (32 times) in the outer chapters of Deuteronomy as would be projected from the core (14 times). And in non-synoptic Samuel-Kings, the life-family is used some five times as frequently as a projection from the synoptic core. Development is not simply a matter of increased frequency but also of fresh coinages. For example, "living god" (אלהים חיים or אל חי) is found only in non-core Deuteronomy and in non-synoptic Samuel-Kings.[17]

16 Auld, *Life in Kings*, 29–38.
17 Deut 5:26; 1 Sam 17:26, 17:36; 2 Kgs 19:4, 19:16.

Tab. A: BoTH < Non-BoTH Sam–Kgs *and* Deut 12–25 < Deut 1–11; 26–34.

	BoTH	Deut 12–25	Deut 1–11; 26–34	Non-BoTH Sam–Kgs
חיה etc	6[18]	7[19]	32[20] (14)	c110 (21)
משפט	5[21]	12[22]	25[23] (24)	35[24] (17)
חק[ה]	2[25]	3[26]	26[27] (6)	18[28] (7)
מצוה\ות	2[29]	4[30]	35[31] (8)	19[32] (7)
צוה (subj. Yhwh)	6[33]	4[34]	30[35] (8)	21[36] (21)

18 1 Kgs 8:40, 12:6, 22:14; 2 Kgs 11:12,14:9, 14:17. Here, as in all other BoTH references, mention is made only of the relevant passages in Sam–Kgs and not the synoptic portions in Chr.

19 Deut 12:1,16:3, 16:20, 17:19, 19:4, 19:5, 20:16.

20 Deut 4:1, 4:4, 4:9, 4:10, 4:33, 4:42, 5:3, 5:24, 5:26 (twice), 5:33, 6:2, 6:24, 7:22, 8:1, 8:3 (twice), 28:66 (twice); 30:6, 30:15, 30:16, 30:19 (thrice), 30:20, 31:13, 31:27, 32:39, 32:40, 32:47, 33:6.

21 2 Sam 8:15; 1 Kgs 8:45, 8:49, 9:4, 10:9.

22 Deut 12:1, 16:18, 16:19 17:8, 17:9, 17:11, 18:3, 19:6, 21:17, 21:22, 24:17, 25:1.

23 Deut 1:17 (twice); 4:1, 4:5, 4:8, 4:14, 4:45, 5:1, 5:31, 6:1, 6:20, 7:11, 7:12, 8:11, 10:18, 11:1, 11:32, 26:16, 26:17, 27:19, 30:16, 32:4, 32:41, 33:10, 33:21.

24 1 Sam 2:13, 8:3, 8:9, 8:11, 10:25, 27:11, 30:25; 2 Sam 15:2, 15:4, 15:6, 22:23; 1 Kgs 2:3, 3:[11], 3:28 (twice), 5:8, 6:12, 6:38, 7:7, 8:58, 8:59, 11:33, 18:28, 20:40; 2 Kgs 1:7, 11:14, 17:26 (twice), 17:27, 17:33, 17:34 (twice), 17:37, 17:40, 25:6.

25 1 Kgs 9:4, 9:6.

26 Deut 12:1, 16:12, 17:19.

27 Deut 4:1, 45, 45:6, 45:8, 45:14, 45:40, 45:45, 5:1, 5:31, 6:1, 6:2, 6:17, 6:20, 6:24, 7:11, 8:11, 10:13, 11:1, 11:32, 26:16, 26:17, 27:10, 28:15, 28:45, 30:10, 30:16.

28 1 Sam 30:25; 2 Sam 22:23; 1 Kgs 2:3, 3:3, 13:4, 6:12, 8:58, 8:61, 11:11, 11:33, 11:34, 11:38; 2 Kgs 17:8, 17:13, 17:15, 17:19, 17:34, 17:37.

29 1 Kgs 9:6; 2 Kgs 23:3.

30 Deut 13:5, 13:19, 15:5, 19:9.

31 Deut 4:2, 4:40, 5:10, 5:29, 5:31, 6:1, 6:2, 6:17, 6:25, 7:9, 7:11, 8:1, 8:2, 8:6, 8:11, 10:13, 11:1, 11:8, 11:13, 11:22, 11:27, 11:28, 26:18, 27:1, 27:10, 28:1, 28:9, 28:13, 28:15, 28:45, 30:8, 30:10, 30:11, 30:16, 31:5.

32 1 Sam 13:13; 1 Kgs 2:3, 2:43, 3:14, 6:12, 8:58, 8:61, 11:34, 11:38, 13:21, 14:8, 18:18; 2 Kgs 17:13, 17:16, 17:19, 17:34, 17:37, 18:6, 18:36.

33 2 Sam 5:25, 7:7, 7:11; 1 Kgs 9:4; 2 Kgs 14:6, 21:8.

34 Deut 13:6, 18:18, 18:20, 20:17.

35 Deut 1:3, 1:19, 1:41, 2:37, 4:5, 4:13, 4:14, 4:23, 5:12, 5:15, 5:16, 5:32, 5:33, 6:1, 6:17, 6:20, 6:24, 6:25, 9:12, 9:16, 10:5, 26:13, 26:14, 26:16, 28:8, 28:45, 28:69, 31:14, 31:23, 34:9.

36 1 Sam 2:29; 13:13, 13:14 (twice), 25:30; 2 Sam 17:14; 1 Kgs 8:58, 11:10 (twice), 11:11, 11:38, 13:9, 13:21, 15:5, 17:4, 17:9; 2 Kgs 17:13, 17:15, 17:34, 17:35, 18:6.

Tab. A (continued)

	BoTH	Deut 12–25	Deut 1–11; 26–34	Non-BoTH Sam–Kgs
צוה (subj. Moses)	0[37]	15[38]	39[39] (30)	1[40]
השתחוה (other gods)	2[41]	1[42]	6[43] (2)	10[44] (7)
עבד (other gods)	4[45]	5[46]	13[47] (10)	18[48] (14)
עבד (Yahweh)		1[49]	5[50] (2)	8[51]
ירא את־יהוה	3	10	22 (20)	13 (11)
אהב\אהבה	1	7	16 (14)	25 (4)

Moses is never the subject of "to command" in BoTH and is only once in Samuel-Kings. Prostration before Yahweh is not explicit in BoTH – synoptic 2 Kings 18:22//2 Chronicles 32:12 report the Assyrian envoy telling his Jerusalem hearers that Hezekiah had ordered prostration "before this/one altar" but do not endorse this foreigner's words. Of the 10 non-synoptic instances, 6 belong to just two chapters of 1 Samuel (chs. 1 and 15). Serving (עבד) Yahweh is never mentioned in BoTH; yet its sole mention in the central chapters of Deuteronomy (13:5) comes within a passage partly based on BoTH (section 3 above).

37 In one synoptic *context* (2 Kgs 21:8), Moses is the subject of "commanded" – compare non-synoptic 1 Kgs 8:56 and 2 Kgs 18:12. However, the synoptic parallel in 2 Chr 33:8 is stated differently.

38 Deut 12:11, 12:14, 12:21, 12:28, 13:1, 13:19, 15:5, 15:11, 15:15, 17:3, 19:7, 19:9, 24:8, 24:18, 24:22.

39 Deut 1:16, 1:18, 2:4, 3:18, 3:21, 3:28, 4:2 (twice), 3:40, 6:2, 6:6, 7:11, 8:1, 8:11,10:13, 11:8, 11:13, 11:22, 11:27, 11:28, 27:1 (twice), 27:4, 27:10, 27:11, 28:1, 28:13, 28:14, 28:15, 30:2, 30:5, 30:8, 30:11, 30:16, 31:5, 31:10, 31:25, 31:29, 33:4.

40 2 Kgs 18:12.

41 1 Kgs 9:6; 2 Kgs 21:3.

42 Deut 17:3.

43 Deut 4:19, 5:9, 8:19, 11:16, 29:25, 30:17.

44 1 Kgs 11:33, 16:31, 22:54; 2 Kgs 5:18 (thrice), 17:16, 17:35,19:37,21:21.

45 1 Kgs 9:6, 9:9; 2 Kgs 21:3, 21:21.

46 Deut 12:2, 12:30, 13:7, 13:14, 17:3.

47 Deut 4:19, 4:28, 7:4, 7:16, 8:19, 11:16, 28:14, 28:36, 28:64; 29:17, 25; 30:17; 31:20.

48 1 Sam 8:8, 12:10; 1 Kgs 16:31, 22:54; 2 Kgs 10:18 (twice), 17:12, 17:16, 17:33, 17:35, 17:41, 21:21 (twice).

49 Deut 13:5.

50 Deut 6:13, 10:12, 10:20, 11:13, 28:47.

51 1 Sam 7:3, 7:4, 12:10, 12:14, 12:20, 12:24, 26:19; 2 Sam 15:8.

Tab. B: BoTH > Non-BoTH Sam–Kgs *BUT* Deut 12–25 < Deut 1–11; 26–34.

	BoTH	Deut 12–25	Deut 1–11; 26–34	Non-BoTH Sam–Kgs
תורה	4[52]	3[53]	19[54] (6)	7[55] (14)
עדה\עדות	2[56]		3[57]	2[58] (7)
עמים	3[59]	2[60]	19[61] (4)	4[62] (10)
גוים	6[63]	4[64]	20[65] (8)	14[66] (21)
לעולם	4[67]	1[68]	2[69]	3[70] (14)
כל־הימים	5[71]	4[72]	8[73]	15[74] (17)

תורה plays a much larger part in non-central Deuteronomy than in non-synoptic Samuel–Kings; and עדה\עדות (admittedly rare in Samuel-Kings) is absent from Deuteronomy 12–25.

52 2 Kgs 14:6, 21:8, 22:8, 22:11.
53 Deut 17:11, 17:18, 17:19.
54 Deut 1:5, 4:8, 4:44, 27:3, 27:8, 27:26, 28:58, 28:61, 29:20, 29:28, 30:10, 31:9, 31:11, 31:12, 31:24, 31:26, 32:46, 33:4, 33:10.
55 2 Sam 7:19; 1 Kgs 2:3; 2 Kgs 10:31, 17:13, 17:34, 23:24, 23:25.
56 2 Kgs 11:12, 23:3.
57 Deut 4:45, 6:17, 6:20.
58 1 Kgs 2:3; 2 Kgs 17:15.
59 1 Kgs 8:43, 9:7, 22:28.
60 Deut 13:8 (around you near or far); 20:16 (apparently same as גוים in 15).
61 Deut 2:25, 4:6, 4:19, 4:27, 6:15, 7:6, 7:7, 7:14, 7:16, 7:19, 10:15, 28:10, 28:37, 28:64, 30:3, 32:8, 33:3, 33:17, 33:19.
62 2 Sam 22:48 (=Ps 18:48); 1 Kgs 5:14, 8:53, 8:60.
63 2 Sam 7:23, 8:11; 2 Kgs 16:3, 18:33/19:12, 21:2, 21:9.
64 Deut 15:6, 17:14 (around), 18:9 (of the land), 20:15 (same).
65 Deut 4:27, 4:38, 7:1, 7:17, 17:22, 9:1, 9:4, 9:5, 11:23, 26:19, 28:1, 28:12, 28:65, 29:15, 29:17, 29:23, 30:1, 31:3, 32:8, 32:43.
66 1 Sam 8:5, 8:20; 2 Sam 22:44, 22:50 (=Ps 18:44, 18:50); 1 Kgs 5:11, 11:2, 14:24; 2 Kgs 17:8, 17:11, 17:15, 17:26, 17:33, 17:41, 19:17.
67 2 Sam 7:29, 7:29; 1 Kgs 10:9; 2 Kgs 21:7.
68 Deut 23:7.
69 Deut 5:29, 32:40.
70 1 Kgs 1:31, 2:33; 2 Kgs 5:27.
71 1 Kgs 8:40, 9:3, 12:7, 14:30; 2 Kgs 8:19.
72 Deut 12:1, 14:23, 18:5, 19:9.
73 Deut 4:10, 4:30, 4:40, 5:26, 6:24, 11:1, 28:29, 28:33, 31:13, 31:29.
74 1 Sam 1:28, 2:32, 2:35, 18:29, 20:31, 23:14, 27:11, 28:2; 2 Sam 13:37, 29:14; 1 Kgs 5:15, 11:36, 11:39; 2 Kgs 13:3, 17:37.

Tab. C: BoTH < Non-BoTH Sam–Kgs *BUT* Deut 12–25 > Deut 1–11; 26–34.

	BoTH	Deut 12–25	Deut 1–11; 26–34	Non-BoTH Sam–Kgs
נפש	4[75]	20[76]	13[77] (40)	74[78] (14)
כהן (sg)	8[79]	3[80]	2[81]	51 (27)
כהנים (pl)	5[82]	1[83]	0	40 (18)
הכהנים הלוים		4[84]	1[85]	1[86]
הכהנים בני לוי		1[87]	1[88]	1[89]
הלוי (landless)		7[90]	3[91]	
שבט [ה]לוי		1[92]	1[93]	
הלוים		1[94]	2[95]	2[96]

75 In two pairs of pairs: 1 Kgs 8:48//2 Chr 6:38 with 2 Kgs 23:3//2 Chr 34:31 and 2 Sam 23:17//1 Chr 11:19 with 1 Kgs 3:11//2 Chr 1:11.

76 Deut 12:15, 12:20 (twice), 12:21, 12:23 (twice), 13:4, 13:7, 14:26 (twice), 18:6, 19:6, 19:11, 19:21, 21:14, 22:26, 23:25, 24:6, 24:7, 24:15.

77 Deut 4:9, 4:15, 4:29, 6:5, 10:12, 10:22, 11:13, 11:18, 27:25, 28:65, 30:2, 30:6, 30:10.

78 1 Sam 1:10, 1:15, 1:26, 2:16, 2:33, 2:35, 17:55, 18:1 (twice), 18:3, 19:5, 19:11, 20:1, 20:3, 20:4, 20:17, 22:2, 22:22, 22:23, 23:15, 23:20, 25:26, 25:29, 26:24, 26:24, 28:9, 28:21, 30:6; 2 Sam 1:9, 3:21, 4:8, 4:9, 5:8, 11:11, 14:7, 14:14, 14:19, 16:11, 18:8, 18:13, 19:6; 1 Kgs 1:12, 1:29, 2:4, 2:23, 11:37, 17:21, 17:22, 19:2 (twice), 19:3, 9:4 (twice), 19:10, 19:14, 20:31, 20:32, 20:39 (twice), 20:42 (twice); 2 Kgs 1:13, 1:14, 2:2, 2:4, 2:6, 4:27, 4:30, 7:7, 9:15, 10:24 (twice), 12:5, 23:25. [1 Sam 28 ties; 2 Sam 13 times; 1 Kgs 20 times; 2 Kgs 13 times].

79 2 Kgs 11:9, 11:10, 11:15 (twice), 11:18, 12:3, 22:4, 22:10.

80 Deut 17:12, 18:3, 20:2.

81 Deut 26:3, 26:4.

82 2 Sam 8:18; 1 Kgs 8:6, 8:10, 8:11; 2 Kgs 23:2.

83 Deut 18:3.

84 Deut 17:9, 17:18, 18:1, 24:8.

85 Deut 27:9.

86 In 1 Kgs 8:3, the priests carry the ark into the new temple; but in synoptic 2 Chr 5:3 it is the Levites. When mentioned again in 1 Kgs 8:4, they have become הכהנים הלוים; but in synoptic 2 Chr 5:5, הכהנים והלוים. However, this second mention is not part of the shorter and more original text in 3 Kgdms 8 and so is not here reckoned part of BoTH.

87 Deut 21:5.

88 Deut 31:9.

89 1 Kgs 12:31 – here the negative: priests that were not "sons of Levi."

90 Deut 12:12, 12:18, 12:19, 14:27, 14:29, 16:11, 16:14.

91 Deut 26:11, 26:12, 26:13.

92 Deut 18:1.

93 Deut 10:18.

94 Deut 18:7.

95 Deut 27:14, 31:25.

96 1 Sam 6:15; 2 Sam 15:24.

Except in the outer chapters of Deuteronomy, גוים is at least twice as common as עמים. Both terms are used more densely in non-core Deuteronomy than in the central chapters of that book but less densely in non-synoptic Samuel-Kings than in BoTH. Within BoTH, עמים is found in more central sections and גוים nearer start and end; that may have influenced word-choice in the development of neighboring non-synoptic portions. For example, synoptic 8:43 and 9:7 with עמים bracket non-synoptic 1 Kings 8:53 and 8:60, and 5:14 is also part of the expanded Solomon narrative. Similarly, 2 Kings 17:8, 17:11, and 17:15 mention the "nations" Yahweh dispossessed in favor of Israel and use the same term גוים as we find in the same context just before and after, in synoptic 2 Kings 16:3 and 21:2 and 21:9.

The usage of כל־הימים ("all the days"/"for all time") is remarkably stable across both "core" and "non-core" portions of Deuteronomy and Samuel–Kings. But the usage of "forever" decreases from "core" to "non-core." Later tradition became less optimistic about the older, monarchic claims of "forever."

Like the "life"-family (6.1), נפש is very rare in BoTH and very common in Samuel-Kings; but, unlike חיה\ים, it is relatively commoner in central Deuteronomy than in the outer chapters of the book. However, it is also true that נפש is used in more senses in Deuteronomy than in BoTH, where the four occurrences are in two pairs. Twice in BoTH (2 Sam 23:17; 1 Kgs 3:11) נפש bears the sense of "life'"(as opposed to death), and this is one of the senses found much more often in the central chapters of Deuteronomy (12:23 [twice]; 19:6, 19:11, 19:21, 22:26, 24:6, 24:7, and 24:15) and only once outside (27:25). It is twice paired with "heart" (1 Kgs 8:48 and 2 Kgs 23:3) – and this linking of Solomon and Josiah is replicated in non-synoptic 1 Kings 2:4 and 2 Kings 23:25. We find this usage once in the "code" of Deuteronomy (13:4), but 8 times in the outer chapters (4:29, 6:5, 10:12, 11:13, 11:18, 30:2, 30:6, and 30:10). The "self" with desires appears in Deuteronomy 12:15, 12:20 (twice), 12: 21, 14:26 (twice), 18:6, and 23:25 but outside only in 4:9 and 4:15.

Similarly, the usage of "priest" and "priests" is denser in non-synoptic Samuel-Kings than in BoTH, but this pattern is not at all replicated between the central and outer chapters of Deuteronomy. The table above also illustrates at a glance that BoTH makes no mention of Levites and wider Samuel-Kings only minimal mention of them. By contrast, both Levites and Levitical priests are concentrated in the central chapters of Deuteronomy. Landless Levites are mostly mentioned in the same contexts where the secondary לשכן formula is used. There is no mention at all in the outer chapters of the (landless) "Levite" or of "priest[s]" who are not explicitly "Levitical." From the perspective of the royal narrative, whether synoptic (BoTH) or non-synoptic, priests and Levites may have been central to Deuteronomy, but they were hardly part of its core.

Works Cited

Auld, A. Graeme. *I & II Samuel: A Commentary*. Old Testament Library. Louisville, KY: Westminster John Knox, 2011.

Auld, A. Graeme. "Divination in Hebrew and Greek Bibles: A Text-historical Overview." In *Prophecy and Hellenism*, edited by Hannes Bezzel and Stefan Pfeiffer, 55–67. FAT.2. Tübingen: Mohr Siebeck, 2021.

Auld, A. Graeme. "Isaiah and the Oldest 'Biblical' Prophetic Narrative." In *Prophecy and Prophets in Stories: Papers Read at the Fifth Meeting of the Edinburgh Prophecy Network, Utrecht, October 2013*, edited by Bob Becking and Hans M. Barstad, 45–63. Oudtestamentische Studiën 65. Leiden: Brill, 2015.

Auld, A. Graeme. *Life in Kings: Reshaping the Royal Story in the Hebrew Bible*. Ancient Israel and its Literature 31. Atlanta: Society of Biblical Literature, 2017.

Auld, A. Graeme. "Some Thoughts on the First Jeroboam." *Biblische Notizen* 185 (2020): 45–53.

Auld, A. Graeme. "Tracing the Writing of Kings with Nadav Na'aman and Klaus-Peter Adam." *SJOT* 35 (2021): in press.

Chavel, Simeon. "The Literary Development of Deuteronomy 12: Between Religious Ideal and Social Reality." In *The Pentateuch: International Perspectives on Current Research*, edited by Thomas B. Dozeman, Konrad Schmid, and Baruch J. Schwartz, 303–26. Forschungen zum Alten Testament 78. Tübingen: Mohr Siebeck, 2011.

Guillaume, Philippe. "Binding 'Sucks': A Response to Stephan Schorch." *Vetus Testamentum* 61 (2011): 1–3.

Himbaza, Innocent. "'Le lieu que YHWH aura choisi'. Une perspective narrative, historique et philologique." *Semitica* 58 (2016): 115–34.

Monroe, Lauren A. S. *Josiah's Reform and the Dynamics of Defilement: Israelite Rites of Violence and the Making of a Biblical Text*. Oxford: Oxford University, 2011.

Schenker, Adrian. "Textgeschichtliches zum Samaritanischen Pentateuch und Samareitikon. Zur Textgeschichte des Pentateuchs im 2. Jh. v. Chr." In: *Samaritans: Past and Present: Current Studies*, edited by Menachem Mor and Friedrich V. Reiterer, 105–21. Studia Judaica 53; Studia Samaritana 5. Berlin: de Gruyter, 2010.

Schorch, Stefan. "A Young Goat in its Mother's Milk? Understanding an Ancient Prohibition." *Vetus Testamentum* 60 (2010): 116–30.

Part II: **Case Studies on Textual Units or Themes within *Debarim***

Megan B. Turton

Deuteronomic Law, Deuteronomic Narrative, or Exodus Narrative? The Multivalence and Multiformity of Deuteronomy 18:15–22

1 Introduction

A history of scholarship on Deuteronomy reveals a long-standing tendency to separate the legal provisions in chs. 12–26 from the surrounding framework in chs. 1–11 and 27–34. However, a review of the literature also exposes a debate regarding the precise parameters of the division and the factors that legitimize it. Although genre conceptions of “law” versus “narrative” or “legal” versus “non-legal” contributed to the demarcation of a “core” text and outer frame, a simple separation along those lines has proven problematic. A re-examination of the law-narrative divide and the concept of “core” versus “peripheral” texts is therefore necessary, especially in light of the ongoing redaction of the biblical text whereby older texts are revised and even displaced from their prior settings. The following discussion of the content and function of the law found in Deuteronomy 18:15–22 within its law-code context and its relationship to the narrative of Deuteronomy 5:22–33 and Exodus 20:18–21 illustrates how some legal texts are inextricably connected to the surrounding narrative framework. This phenomenon is further played out in the transmission of the text in the pre-Samaritan manuscripts and the Samaritan Pentateuch.

2 The Issue: Biblical Law and the Deuteronomic “Core”

The legal chapters of Deuteronomy 12–26 are often regarded as an integrated composition known as a “law collection” or even a “law-code” that can be separated from its surrounding literary context. It has been viewed as a distinct

Note: My thanks to Ian Young and Mark O’Brien for commenting on earlier versions of this article. All errors are my own.

https://doi.org/10.1515/9783110713312-009

entity in terms of its genre, being "legal" as opposed to the surrounding framework chapters (1–11; 27–34), which are designated "narrative," "history," "paresis," or some, or all, of the above. The laws have also long been viewed as having differentiated source-redactional origins and history to the surrounding narrative. Thus, in 1805, when Wilhelm M. L. de Wette argued that the book of Deuteronomy was the ספר התורה purportedly discovered in Josiah's reign (2 Kgs 22–23), he postulated that the content of this original book was a law-code (*codicem legum*), particularly those provisions that attempt to effect cult centralization.[1] Julius Wellhausen cemented the isolation of the legal material, theorizing that the newly found scroll contained legislation from chs. 12–26:

> Deuteronomy is the legal expression of the second period of struggle and transition ... the work whose discovery gave occasion to King Josiah to destroy the local sanctuaries was this very book of Deuteronomy, which originally must have had an independent existence, and a shorter form than present.[2]

The introductory discourses in chs. 1–4 and 5–11 and the concluding ones in chs. in 27 and 28–30, respectively, were seen as evidence of two originally separate editions of the law-code, with chs. 31–34 integrating Deuteronomy into a Hexateuch (cf. Josh 24:26). The separation of the laws from the narrative was to have lasting ramifications for subsequent scholarship, as the surrounding framework chapters were assigned in various ways to later Deuteronomistic or post-Deuteronomistic authors and redactors who were deemed to superimpose foreign functions upon the older law text as it was reconfigured to take into account the catastrophic events leading to the exile and the post-exilic period.[3]

However, as early as 1896, Samuel R. Driver challenged the distinction between law and narrative in Deuteronomy when he argued that the language and style of chs. 5–11 do not indicate a different author from chs. 12–26 and concluded that chs. 5–26 and 28 collectively formed the special code of the laws.[4] Gerhard von Rad later contended that Deuteronomy 4:44–30:20 forms a book complete in itself and that Deuteronomic "law" was not truly law but preaching about the commandments.[5] Meanwhile, discoveries in Assyriology within the two genres of law-codes and treaties or loyalty oaths, showed that law, narrative, and other features were often bound in an organic unit.[6]

1 Harvey and Halpern, "W. M. L. de Wette's 'Dissertatio'," 82, n. 59.
2 Wellhausen, *Prolegomena*, 1994, 33.
3 Noth, *Deuteronomistic History*, 12–17; Mayes, *Deuteronomy*, 41–47; Otto, *Das Deuteronomium*.
4 Driver, *Deuteronomy*, lxv–lxvii, 135.
5 Von Rad, *Studies*, 15; *Deuteronomy*, 12, 19–23.
6 Mendenhall, "Covenant Forms," 70.

The ancient Near Eastern Laws of Ur-Nammu, Lipit-Eshtar, and Hammurabi consisted of a collection of legal cases and verdicts also set in a literary framework of prologue and epilogue sections that provided a political context for the compositions, relating the series of laws to the role of the king as the divinely authorized guardian and administrator of justice.[7] Like Deuteronomy, treaty documents from the Hittite Empire contained historical preambles (Deut 1:1–5), historical prologues (Deut 1–4); provisions for depositing the document in the temple and a periodic reading (Deut 31:9–13, 26); blessings and curses (Deut 27–28), *as well* as legal stipulations (Deut 5; 12–26). Thus, they suggested new models to explain the structure, content and rhetoric of Deuteronomy.[8]

Similarly, Neo-Assyrian treaties and loyalty oaths, notably the Vassal Treaty of Esarhaddon (or Esarhaddon's Succession Treaty), contained legal stipulations as well as stipulations of allegiance (see Deut 6:4–7) and lists of curses (see Deut 28), while both the Neo-Assyrian and Sefire treaties also dealt with oath imprecation (see Deut 29: 9–28). These law texts all feature a combination of legal stipulation and non-legal material as primary features.[9]

Developments in the classification of these ancient Near Eastern law texts would also have significant impact upon the understanding of biblical law. It became clear that the ancient Near Eastern "law-codes" did not hold a strictly legislative function but were scribal and, to a certain extent, hypothetical academic treatises on law and royal apologia that had little direct bearing on legal practice.[10]

The nature of biblical law has likewise been reappraised, with a string of publications questioning whether the legal texts were used in any fashion resembling that of legislation or positive law. This began with the Covenant Code, while Deuteronomy was still evaluated as statutory.[11] Other scholars have challenged the legislative nature of all of the biblical laws before the Persian period[12] or the Hellenistic period and later.[13] Increased awareness that both the

---

7 Paul, *Studies*, 11-42; Weinfeld, *Deuteronomy*, 146–57; Roth, *Law Collections*, 2–3; Watts, *Reading Law*, 41–44.

8 Kline, *Treaty*, 27–44; McCarthy, *Treaty and Covenant*, 51–85, 147–205; Watts, *Reading Law*, 40–48; Lundbom, *Deuteronomy*, 20–21.

9 Wiseman, "Vassal-Treaties," i–ii, 1–99; McCarthy, *Treaty and Covenant*, 106–21, 157–205; Weinfeld, *Deuteronomy*, 59–157; Otto, *Das Deuteronomium*, 361–64.

10 Kraus, "Ein zentrales Problem," 283–96; Finkelstein, "Ammiṣaduqa's Edict," 91–104; Bottéro, *Mesopotamia*, 156–84; Westbrook, "Cuneiform," 201–22.

11 Patrick, *Old Testament Law*, 189–90, 200; Westbrook, "Cuneiform," 220; Schmid, "Genesis," 124–25.

12 Fitzpatrick-McKinley, *Transformation*, 166–77; Watts, *Reading Law*, 157–61; Jackson, *Studies*, 70–92.

13 Davies, "'Law'"; Watts, "Ritual Legitimacy," 412–17; LeFebvre, *Collections*, 146–267; Collins, "Transformation," 455–74; Vroom, "Law, Authority," 227–34.

creation and the use of written law was highly literary has meant that its life settings may be removed from those traditionally thought of as "legal." For example, it is evident that within the ancient Near East, Israel included, some written laws were located in and limited to a literary scribal tradition, in which laws continued to be passed on and reworked over long periods of time and space.[14]

With regard to Deuteronomic law, increasingly complex redactional theories have advocated that even Deuteronomy 12 had a lengthy compositional history, including proto-Deuteronomic, Deuteronomic, and several Deuteronomistic elements.[15] Finally, scholarship prioritizing the relationship between law and literature has emphasized that legal and narrative texts within the Pentateuch are inexorably interconnected, especially in the way that they both seek to shape individual and communal identity.[16]

Even so, the legal chapters (12–26) are still referred to as the "core" of Deuteronomy. However, what that term encompasses and whether it may mask conflicting suppositions is not always made clear. Does "core" refer solely to a temporal dimension – a more original Deuteronomy? Ernest W. Nicholson states that there "has been wide agreement among scholars that Deuteronomy owes its present form to several stages of composition ... beginning with an original core (the so-called *Urdeuteronomium*)."[17] Indeed, for many, the program of cult-centralization forms the literary origin of the book of Deuteronomy, so that there is effectively no "Deuteronomy" without it.[18] But, for others like Jack R. Lundbom, the core of the Deuteronomic Code is the casuistic law in chs. 19–25, because the rest is cast largely in homiletic form, even the laws in chs. 13–18.[19]

Might the term "core" refer to a structural position within the center of Deuteronomy as a literary composition? For instance, Duane L. Christensen calls chs. 12–26 the "central core" of a five-part concentric design.[20] Or, does the concept of "core" denote texts that are historically and theologically central to

---

14 Finkelstein, *Ox that Gored*, 1–89, esp. 14–20; Malul, *Comparative Method*; Levinson, *Deuteronomy*; Stackert, *Rewriting the Torah*; Wright, *Inventing God's Law*, 112–22; Teeter, *Scribal Laws*.
15 Reuter, *Kultzentralisation*; Levinson, *Deuteronomy*, 24–28; Person, *Deuteronomic School*, 1–16.
16 Nasuti, "Identity," 9–23; Watts, *Reading Law*, 129, 134–38; Halberstam, "Art," 345–64, esp. 359; Burnside, "Spirit," 129, 137–43; Morrow, *Introduction*, 43.
17 Nicholson, *Deuteronomy*, 5.
18 Reuter, *Kultzentralisation*, 189–91; Levinson, *Deuteronomy*, 9, 13; Schmid, "Deuteronomy,"; Otto, "History," 223; Kratz, "'Peg in the Wall,'" 253.
19 Lundbom, *Deuteronomy*, 26.
20 Christensen, "Deuteronomy," 9.

the message of Deuteronomy?[21] Can "core" texts contain and impart meaning autonomous from the other texts that surround them, or later redactions that transform them? How does the concept of a "core" text fit with the consensus in the field of textual criticism, that biblical texts, even in the latest periods of their transmission, were still fluid and susceptible to both accidental change and purposeful modification?[22] As will now be shown, the legal provision of Deuteronomy 18:15–22 conforms to the conception of a core legal text that is central to the message, purpose, and theology of Deuteronomy – however, this centrality only finds full articulation in the relationship between the legal text and peripheral narrative. Within the pre-Samaritan manuscript group, this multivalence ultimately leads to the text's own instability and multiformity, as it becomes duplicated, spliced into a new sequence, and reinserted outside the Deuteronomic law-code.

3 Deuteronomy 18:15–22 within the Law Code

Deuteronomy 18:15–22 recalls the "prophet like Moses" promise (vv. 15–18) with a test for identifying "false prophets" (vv. 21–22), closing a larger unit of regulations concerning Israel's major office-bearers that runs from Deuteronomy 16:18–18:22.[23] Yet, despite its placement within the seventh of the fifteen legal chapters in 12–26, the literary unit of Deuteronomy 18:15–22 contains elements that do not appear to be particularly legalistic.[24] After the prohibition of the abhorrent practices of the nations and the different forms of divination in Deuteronomy 18:9–14, vv. 15–18 do not simply deal with "typical" features of law such as norms, rules, fundamental principles, or policies.[25] Rather, we are first presented with Moses's narration of past speech between the people, Yhwh, and himself:[26]

21 Braulik, "Sequence," 334.

22 On the textual plurality and pluriformity of the Hebrew Bible in the late Second Temple period, see Tov, *Textual Criticism*, 110–11, 180–90; Ulrich, *Origins*, 34–120; Clines, "What Remains," 76–81; Young, "Biblical Scrolls," 104–7; Segal, "Text," 5–20, esp. 6–7.

23 Driver, *Deuteronomy*, 199–230; Mayes, *Deuteronomy*, 261–62.

24 On Deut 18:15–22 as a literary unit, see Nelson, *Deuteronomy*, 234–36; Lundbom, *Deuteronomy*, 556.

25 For "typical" features of law, see Bartor, *Reading Law*, 7.

26 All of the narrative and law between 4:44–28:68 is presented as Moses's second address to Israel on the plains of Moab.

> The LORD your God will raise up for you a prophet like me from among your own people; you shall heed such a prophet. This is what you requested of the LORD your God at Horeb on the day of the assembly when you said: "If I hear the voice of the LORD my God any more, or ever again see this great fire, I will die." Then the LORD replied to me: "They are right in what they have said. I will raise up for them a prophet like you from among their own people; I will put my words in the mouth of the prophet, who shall speak to them everything that I command.[27]

Through Moses's words, the institution of prophecy is presented as a resolution of the people's fear of direct communication with God. Apart from the initial instruction to heed the prophet, Deuteronomy 18:15–18 is distinctly "un-legal." Instead of regulations about prophets corresponding to those applying to the priests and Levites, the passage relays a pronouncement.[28] We are told how Yhwh will let a prophet whom the people are to listen to emerge from among the people. Consequently, Robert Polzin states that vv. 17–18 are "uncharacteristic of the entire law-code,"[29] and Reinhard Achenbach designates Deuteronomy 18:17–19 not as law but as a prophetic oracle that adds "to the revelation of the Covenant Code and Deuteronomy, a promise of further prophetic, oral revelation."[30]

This segment may be analyzed as a narrative that encloses a story: there is a narrator, the lawgiver Moses, and an addressee, "you," the people. Moses describes a protagonist, the people (also the addressee), who in the past experienced an existential issue – they needed to communicate with God but feared direct communication. The institution of prophecy is presented as a resolution to this conflict. [31]

It is not until after this rationale for the future prophet in vv. 15–18 that vv. 19–22 outline the corresponding regulations:

> Anyone who does not heed the words that the prophet shall speak in my name, I myself will hold accountable. But any prophet who speaks in the name of other gods, or who presumes to speak in my name a word that I have not commanded the prophet to speak – that prophet shall die." You may say to yourself, "How can we recognize a word that the LORD has not spoken?" If a prophet speaks in the name of the LORD but the thing does not take place or prove true, it is a word that the LORD has not spoken. The prophet has spoken it presumptuously; do not be frightened by it.

27 English translations are from the NRSV, unless otherwise specified.
28 So e.g. Barstad, "Understanding," 242, 244.
29 Polzin, *Moses*, 58.
30 Achenbach, "Prophet," 441.
31 Bartor, *Reading Law*, 36, 41.

Verses 19–22 mandate that anyone who does not heed the words that the prophet will speak in Yhwh's name will be "held accountable" by Yhwh himself (אנכי אדרש מעמו). The prophet who speaks in Yhwh's name something he was not commanded to speak or the prophet who speaks in the name of other gods shall die. The test for identifying the difference between true and false prophets and prophecies closes with a command to not be frightened by "it" (לא תגור ממנו) – either the illicit prophecy or the prophet, due to the ambiguity of the pronominal suffix.[32]

Even this more instructional content raises questions concerning its legal efficacy. Relying upon the eventuation of a prophecy to confirm that it is true defeats the aim of prophecy. On a practical level, the true prophet must be recognized before his predictions are realized.[33]

The peculiarity of the "prophet like Moses" unit within its present setting has prompted various attempts to explain its form and presence within the law-code. It is widely thought to be a late exilic or post-exilic addition.[34] This may well be the case – indeed, the present discussion may strengthen this argument – but even as a late addition, its placement *within* the law-code and the meanings that it acquires within that context still require due consideration.[35] The immediate legal context of Deuteronomy 18:15–22 are the previous laws in Deuteronomy 18:9–14, which prohibit the various mantic practices of the nations that are classified as abominations (תועבה). Israel is not permitted to heed (שמע) these practitioners (v. 14); rather, the Israelite people have the prophet who has direct access to Yhwh, who puts his very words in their mouth.[36] Deuteronomy presents "authentic prophecy" as an institution that distinguishes Israel from

---

32 Stackert, *Prophet like Moses*, 136, n. 15.

33 Blenkinsopp, *Prophecy and Canon*, 45–46; Tengström, "Moses," 264; Blenkinsopp, *History of Prophecy*, 157.

34 For an exilic date, see Tengström, "Moses," 263; Blenkinsopp, *History of Prophecy*, 161–63; Otto, "Welcher Bund," 162. A. D. H. Mayes considers v. 14 a transitional link and vv. 15–18 as a late addition to 18:9–13, later than the Deuteronomistic presentation of the Horeb event (5:23–25; 9:9–11). In his view, vv. 19–22 are even later (*Deuteronomy*, 279–80). For postexilic dates, see Nihan, "Moses," 27–36; Achenbach, "Prophet," 440–44. For recent attempts to reassert a pre-exilic date or a setting within D, see Atkins, "Reassessing," 323–41; Stackert, *Prophet like Moses*, 135–40.

35 Despite the myth of "literalism" that seems to pervade the discourse surrounding the interpretation of law, legal texts as a matter of course have multivalent meanings, purposes, and functions. See Barak, *Purposive Interpretation*, 113, 117–18. As such, the functions of the law proposed here do not preclude others.

36 For v. 14 as a connective bridge between Deut 19:9–13 and Deut 18:15–22, see Mayes, *Deuteronomy*, 279–80. Note that the language of ethnic brotherhood is also used twice here; the prophet like Moses must be "from among your/their own people."

the nations, a theme that is also present within the foundational apostasy laws of ch. 13 (vv. 2–6), forming a conclusion to a section of the book comprising Deuteronomy 13–18. The prophet law, therefore, rhetorically confers a unique identity onto Israel vis-à-vis the nations.[37]

As already stated, Deuteronomy 18:15–22 concludes regulations concerning Israel's office-bearers: judges (16:18–20; 17:2–3), kings (17:14–20), priests (18:1–8), and prophets (18:9–22).[38] Within this arrangement, the prophet assumes a special position in the gradation of the various offices of the ideal community. The people appoint (נתן) the judges (16:18). While the people set (שים) the first king chosen (בחר) by Yhwh (17:14–15), subsequent kings are the hereditary descendants of the first (17:20). Similarly, Yhwh has chosen (בחר) the Levitical tribe to serve as priests (18:5), but the office is hereditary and dynastic. In contrast, Yhwh himself legitimates and raises (קום) each individual prophet.[39] This group of laws concerning offices bears the marks of a utopian "constitution," providing the basis for an ideal community that curtails the powers of Israel's authorities and is structured to be governed by Yhwh himself, via the Moses-like prophet.[40] Within this idealistic framework, the prophet assumes the exclusive position of making direct contact with the deity. Yet, at the same time, he is presented as a successor to Moses and, according to Deuteronomy 18:21–22, his prophecy must already be known and verified as accurate in order for him to be deemed a legitimate prophet. The legal provision claims to legitimate the "future" prophets of Israel but, at the same time, severely limits the efficacy of genuinely new prophecy and subordinates past revelations to the Mosaic Torah, which has become the means by which they are authenticated.[41]

---

37 Nihan, "Moses," 29–32; Lundbom, *Deuteronomy*, 555.

38 Driver, *Deuteronomy*, 199–230; Mayes, *Deuteronomy*, 261–62.

39 Braulik, "Zur Abfolge," 77; Nihan, "Moses," 31–32. I follow the majority of modern scholarship and take הנביא here as distributive and not exclusive. Hence, it refers to successive prophets like Moses. So e.g. Driver, *Deuteronomy*, 228–29; Mayes, *Deuteronomy*, 282; Nihan, "Moses," 27.

40 Lohfink, "Distribution," 336–52, esp. 346; Nelson, *Deuteronomy*, 213–37, esp. 213; Levinson, "Deuteronomy's Conception," 68–86, esp. 85–86; contra Halpern, *Constitution*, 226–35; McConville, *Deuteronomy*, 281–85. For a different perspective, see O'Brien, "Deuteronomy 16:18–18:22," 155–72.

41 Lohfink, "Distribution," 349; Levinson, "Deuteronomy's Conception," 80–85; Nihan, Moses," 35; but compare with Lohfink's further comment: "The prophets likewise are bound to Torah – but are perhaps less subordinate to it than parallel to it" ("Distribution," 352). In any case, the impracticality of waiting until a prophet's word comes true in order to know whether the prophet is legitimate points toward a late dating for vv. 21–22 as a principle of basic Deuteronomistic theology that retrospectively assesses known prophets and prophecies

Furthermore, while the verses found in 18:15–18 are certainly unique in their presentation of Moses as self-referential and participating in direct discourse, the use of internal narrative elements within the law of 18:15–22 should not be viewed as something essentially incongruous to a law-code.[42] It is true that only here and for the centralization of the cult in 12:5–8 the "lawgiver" positions himself among the addressees with the first person "I" or "we."[43] However, the ancient Near Eastern model of casuistic law found within all of the law-codes is fundamentally informed by narrative in its presentation of miniature "stories," hypothetical events that involve transformation, conflict, development, and resolution.[44] Indeed, since the 1970s, the "law and literature" movement has fostered increasing recognition that law and narrative and other genres including history are "inseparably related" as reflections of, and participants in, a normative world.[45] Thus, Robert Cover's summary:

> Every prescription is insistent in its demand to be located in discourse – to be supplied with history and destiny, beginning and end, explanation and purpose. And every narrative is insistent in its demand for its prescriptive point, its moral. History and literature cannot escape their location in a normative universe, nor can prescription, even when embodied in a legal text, escape its origin and its end in experience, in the narratives that are the trajectories plotted upon material reality by our imaginations.[46]

Within Deuteronomy 18, vv. 15–18 refer to both "historical" events in the future and the past, the future events being predicated upon the past. Yhwh will raise up a prophet like Moses who should be heeded *because* this is what the people requested at Horeb (ככל אשר שאלת) when they heard the voice of God and requested a mediator because they were afraid that they would die. This is, of course, a reference to the Horeb theophany in Deuteronomy 5:22–33, itself a

(Tengström, "Moses," 264). The king's authority is also undercut and his powers are curtailed in comparison to the usual role of the king in the ancient Near East (Deut 17:14–20). He does not appoint the other officials and, within the description of the judicial system, he does not hear cases (16:18–20; 17:8–13). That the king must have a copy of תורה and must read it suggests his subordination to law (Levinson, "Reconceptualization," 511–34; Lohfink, "Distribution," 346–49).

42 Polzin, *Moses*, 58, 61.

43 Bartor, *Reading Law*, 36.

44 Nasuti, "Identity," 9; Bartor, *Reading Law*, 5–11.

45 See Assnat Bartor, who outlines four main angles from which the interrelationship between biblical law and narrative have been addressed: genre-mixing of law and narrative in the Pentateuch; reflection of familiar narrative or historical tradition in the laws; appearance of legal elements in biblical prose and other literary genres; and narrative reading of the laws (*Reading Law*, 11–13).

46 Cover, "Nomos," 5.

recapitulation of the Sinai theophany in Exodus 20:18–21. After God speaks the Ten Commandments in Deuteronomy 5:6–21 (cf. Exod 20:2–17), the people are reported to be afraid and request that Moses act as an intermediary lest they die. According to the Deuteronomic account of the event, Moses alone received the following laws (the Covenant Code).

By recalling the Horeb revelation and placing the institution of a prophet like Moses back within it, the Deuteronomic regulation becomes imbued with interrelated levels of authority. First, the law emphasizes how it originated in divine speech. Second, the law is presented as God's gracious response to the people's own request and intense fear of death, which not only invokes a sense of collective responsibility for the creation and subsequent upkeep of the law but also alludes to death as the alternative. Third, the law is not presented as a "new law" but as a law that had existed since the antecedent theophany at Horeb. Fourthly and most importantly, it appeals to the general authority of Sinai/Horeb revelation, which Deuteronomy consistently takes for granted.[47]

This means that Deuteronomy 18:15–19, the commandment to heed the prophet like Moses upon fear of punishment, but also 18:20–22, which attempts to ensure that *only* the prophet like Moses should be heeded, is all grounded in the identity-shaping and authoritative past revelation to the community at Sinai/Horeb.[48] To put it another way, vv. 15–18 may be considered a motive clause in which the motivation, reason, justification, or an incentive for a legal provision is given – an answer to the question "Why is the law thus?" or "Why observe this law?"[49]

Motive clauses can come in various forms: they are often grammatically subordinate sentences that follow the legal provision, introduced by various grammatical particles in the forms of conjunctions or prepositions. However, there are also asyndetic motive clauses where causality is not expressed by a particle, but by the simple juxtaposition of clauses. In such cases, it is possible to have a motive clause precede a law as a "prefatory motivation."[50] The content of motive clauses encompasses different types of motivation, ranging from the explanatory, ethical, and religious to the historical.[51] Explanatory clauses

---

47 Stackert, *Prophet like Moses*, 129. On the symbolic significance of Sinai/Horeb as the geographic location of divine revelation and law, see Levenson, *Sinai*, 18; Dozeman, *God on the Mountain*, 69; Markl, "Ten Words," 23–24.

48 Nelson, *Deuteronomy*, 234–36. On the correlative relationship between the prophet like Moses promise segment, and vv. 19–20 and 21–22, see also Nihan, "Moses," 28–29.

49 Doron, "Motive Clauses," 62; Sonsino, *Motive Clauses*, 66; Nasuti, "Identity," 13.

50 Doron, "Motive Clauses," 62–72; Sonsino, *Motive Clauses*, 70–76; contra Gemser, "Importance," 50.

51 Gemser, "Importance," 50–66; Nasuti, "Identity," 13; Watts, *Reading Law*, 66–67; compare Doron, "Motive Clauses," 73–77; Sonsino, *Motive Clauses*, 104–117.

appeal to socially constructed common sense, as within the case of the possible rape of a betrothed virgin, where consent is imputed to the woman because "she did not cry for help in the town" (Deut 22:24). Ethical content is found within the Sabbath commandment "so that your male and female slave may rest as well as you" (Deut 5:14). Religious grounds for obeying a law are found within the תועבה laws, for example, "for whoever does such things is abhorrent to the LORD your God" (Deut 22:5). Finally, motive clauses may have a historical character by urging compliance on the ground of Yhwh's great deeds, such as the second motivation clause of the Sabbath law in Deuteronomy, which urges the performance of the Sabbath day through remembering "that you were a slave in the land of Egypt, and the LORD your God brought you out from there" (Deut 5:15).[52]

Deut 18:15–18 is a prefatory, historical motive clause that lays the groundwork for the following "prophet law" by claiming that is has been provided in gracious response to the people's own communal reaction upon directly encountering God during the terrifying theophany at Sinai/Horeb.[53] Moses reminds the people it is "according to all that you requested" (Deut 18:16). As a rhetorical device, the clause enhances the persuasiveness of the following prophet regulations, hence serving a localized purpose within that legal provision. Within the idealistic laws regulating the various "offices" of Israel, the motivation clause also asserts the superiority of prophecy vis-à-vis all other political and religious institutions whose origins are not traced back to the revelation of the law and the covenant at Mount Sinai/Horeb.[54]

---

52 On historical motive clauses, see further, Gemser, "Importance," 60; Sonsino, *Motive Clauses*, 112–13; Nasuti, "Identity," 12–16.

53 According to Pinchas Doron, there are three other examples of prefatory motive clauses in Deuteronomy (Deut 14:1, 3; 25:17–19), the third of which is also a lengthy historical motivation clause before the command to blot the memory of Amalek: "Remember what Amalek did to you on your journey out of Egypt, how he attacked you on the way, when you were faint and weary and struck down all who lagged behind you; he did not fear God." He does not include Deut 18:15–18 in his discussion of prefatory motivations, but considers 18:15 an additional motive clause to the previous laws prohibiting divinations at 18:9–14 ("Motive Clauses," 71–72). There is nothing to prevent the verse from performing both functions, something that Doron himself seems to be getting at when he states that the previous law against divinations and its motive clause calling the practices תועבה (Deut 18:9–12) is "carried over and elaborated upon in verses 14–15 which are the opening verses of a new law, that of the prophet" (p. 68). The practices of the nations are not only abhorrent but also unnecessary because of Moses the prophet and his successors who were established at Sinai/Horeb. On the connective and contrastive function of vv. 14–15, see also Nelson, *Deuteronomy*, 234; Nihan, "Moses," 28 and n. 16.

54 Nihan, "Moses," 32–33. For Rifat Sonsino, the main purpose of a motive clause is to provide a *raison d'être* for a law, to justify the appropriateness of a *particular* legal prescription, or to

4 Deuteronomy 18:15–22 and Deuteronomy's Narrative Framework

As well as providing force behind an individual law, motive clauses also create links between the laws and the surrounding stories or narrative frameworks of the Pentateuch. As "embedded stories," the mention of historical events that appear in the laws "open a window" onto the frame-story for the law's addressees and for the readers. In Deuteronomy, the most obvious links to the external narrative are the historical motivations that explicitly site incidents from Israel's past experiences in Egypt (Deut 5:15, 15:15, 24:18, 24:22), but also the wilderness wandering (Deut 23:5–6 [ET 23:4–5], 25:17–19). Within all of these instances, the addressee, "you," is prompted to consider their own relationship to the law in light of a series of unfolding events found within the books of Exodus and Numbers, in which they themselves have participated and continue to participate.[55]

In contrast to the aforementioned examples, the recollection of the Horeb theophany in Deuteronomy 18:16–18 does not simply position this particular regulation in relation to the prior event itself but to the narrative framework of Deuteronomy, which contains its own remembrances of Sinai, called Horeb. Here, Sinai/Horeb resonates throughout as the definitive moment of the divine revelation of law to which Deuteronomy, with its new covenant and body of law, must situate itself via various hermeneutical strategies.[56] At the beginning of the book, Deuteronomy presents itself as explication of preceding law in a "superscription" (Deut 1:5–6): "beyond the Jordan in the land of Moab, Moses undertook to *expound* this law (באר את התורה הזאת) as follows: the LORD our God spoke to us at Horeb, saying …"[57] After the laws, blessings and curses

show that the law is just because of a *particular* reason or purpose formulated therein (*Motive Clauses*, 68). The prophetic institution contains is own particular justification in the Sinai/Horeb revelation, but it should not be read in isolation from the other laws of Israel's public offices. Within that greater context, the prophet alone is imbued with Sinaitic authority. "The motivations attached to laws … instruct readers/hearers not only in specific regulations, but also in the law's foundations in Israel's communal experiences and religious ideas" (Watts, *Reading Law* 67).

55 Watts, *Reading Law*, 66. For the notion of the biblical laws and motive clauses containing "embedded stories" within a larger narrative framework, see Bartor, *Reading Law*, 17–22.

56 Levinson, *Deuteronomy*, 151; Markl, "Ten Words," 20–21; Stackert, *Prophet like Moses*, 129; Otto, "Deuteronomy as Legal Completion," 2.

57 Levinson, *Deuteronomy*, 151; Otto, *Deuteronomium 1–11*, 298–328; Otto, "Deuteronomy as the Legal Completion," 2. Admittedly, the meaning of the root באר in the *piel*, and the referent of "this Torah" is not without considerable controversy; see the literature reviewed recently in Edelman, "Metaphor," 317–33. Nevertheless, according to the proposal that Edelman puts for-

(chs. 12–28), a "subscription" positions the previous laws as something like a legislative codicil that is an addition or supplement to the original covenant at Horeb, "These are the words of the covenant that the LORD commanded Moses to make with the Israelites in the land of Moab, besides (מלבד) the covenant that he had made in Horeb" (Deut 28:69 [ET 29:1]).[58]

In the narrative framework of Deuteronomy, the words and commandments of Yhwh delivered by Moses on the plains of Moab were already revealed to him at Horeb, but, apart from the Ten Commandments, are only now conveyed to the people so that they may observe them in the land that they are about to occupy (Deut 4:13–14).[59] Even as Deuteronomy asserts through Moses's discourse in Moab its own covenantal primacy as *the* covenant, it attempts to accomplish this by "re-presenting" Sinai: "The LORD our God made a covenant with us at Horeb. Not with our ancestors did the LORD make this covenant, but with us, who are all of us here alive today (Deut 5:3–4)."[60] In effect, Deuteronomy's laws are presented *as* the Horeb revelation.

Not surprisingly, then, Deuteronomy "re-presents" the Sinai theophany.[61] After the Deuteronomic version of the Ten Commandments, 5:22–33 contains a longer, expanded, and reinterpreted account of the request for Moses to mediate between God and the people found in Exodus 20:18–21.[62] Within the Deuteronomic version, Yhwh speaks the words of the Ten Commandments to the whole assembly, and then it is explicitly stated that he added no more (ולא יסף v. 22).[63] The people are shown God's glory and greatness, and they hear his voice (קול) out of the darkness and fire (vv. 23–24). They express their mortal fear upon

ward that באר is a denominative verb from "well," with the associated meanings "to make clear," "to provide clarity," or even "to make a source of life," the verb still functions to situate Deuteronomic Torah in relation to or against Sinai revelation, as the "direct way to encounter God" (324–30, quote at 329).

58 Levinson, *Deuteronomy*, 151; Nelson, *Deuteronomy*, 238–39.

59 However, the revision of much of the content of the Covenant Code within the Deuteronomic Code points towards the Covenant Code's prior legal authority (cf. Exod 24:3, 7, 12).

60 Najman, *Seconding Sinai*, 32. Similarly, Jeffrey Stackert views Deuteronomy's reuse and reorientation of the Horeb legislation as "relegitimizing" (*Prophet like Moses*, 129–30). Compare with Bernard M. Levinson, who argues that Deuteronomy subverts and abrogates the Exodus laws and thus "circumscribes Sinai" (*Deuteronomy*, 149–53, quote at 153).

61 In addition to Deut 5:22–33, discussed below, see also Deut 5:4–5 and Deut 4.

62 Most scholarship correctly judges Deut 5:22–33 to be dependent upon Exod 20:18–21: Brettler, "'Fire, Cloud,'" 16–17; Blum, "Decalogue," 291; Baden, *Composition*, 133, Stackert, *Prophet like Moses*, 128–35. For a dissenting opinion, see Van Seters, *Life of Moses*, 286–89.

63 In contrast, in Exodus there is ambiguity about whether the people heard the Ten Commandments directly. Exodus 20:1 simply states: "Then God spoke all these words ..." For further discussion of the issues, see Sommer, *Revelation*, 35–41.

hearing the voice of God again (vv. 25–26) and request that Moses alone go near and hear all that Yhwh will say (דבר) and relate to them everything that he says (דבר) so that they may listen and do it (v. 27). Unlike Exodus 20:18–21, Deuteronomy affirms that Yhwh heard the people's request and even approves it with the phrase, "they are right (היטיבו) in all that they have spoken" (v. 28). The following phrasing is difficult, but it expresses Yhwh's hope that the people's frame of mind would continue (והיה לבבם זה להם) and links it to the fear of God (ליראה) and the upkeep of his commandments, all of the days, so that it may go well for the people and their children forever (v. 29). Moses is then instructed to tell the people to return to their tents, but he is to stay in order for God to tell him "all the commandment, the statutes and the ordinances" that he shall teach them, so the people may do them in the land that they will possess (vv. 30–33).

In the reworking of Exodus 20:18–21 in Deuteronomy 5:22–33, and in Deuteronomy in general, the role of Moses as covenant-mediator and lawgiver is pronounced.[64] The Deuteronomic theophany account in ch. 5 elaborates upon and enhances the fear of the people, who believe that they may die upon hearing God again, after they directly encounter his voice and speech. The necessity of a mediator who may hear the words of God is further emphasized by the extended request by the people for Moses *alone* to hear what Yhwh says and relate it back to them. This is now approved by Yhwh himself, who then reiterates that the divine speech to Moses will be nothing less than "all of the commandment, the statutes and the ordinances that you will teach them" (v. 31).

Consequently, it is clear that when Deut 18:16–18 recollects Horeb, it is not just evoking the Sinai event itself, but Deuteronomy's reconfiguring of the theophany and the expanded request for Moses to mediate between God and Israel. The similarity between Deut 18:16–18 and Deut 5:22–33 is not just thematic; the wording is strikingly similar:[65]

Verse 16b is a summary of the people's request for a mediator in 5:23–27, taken almost entirely from 5:25 with some minor changes, including word order and the change from the first-person plural to singular. Verse 17 provides a truncated quote of Yhwh's answer to that question in Deuteronomy 5:28, "they are right in [all] that they have said."

---

64 Polzin, *Moses*, 25–72; Dozeman, *God on the Mountain*, 86; Miller, "'Moses My Servant,'" 301–12; Brettler, "'Fire, Cloud,'" 20, 22–23.

65 The correspondence is so strong that the standard view is that Deut 18:16–18 is textually based upon Deut 5. See Nihan, "Moses," 27; Achenbach, "'Prophet like Moses,'" 442. For a synchronic perspective, see Brettler, "'Fire, Cloud,'" 17, 23.

Tab. 1: Comparison of Deuteronomy 5 and 18.

Deuteronomy 5:25	Deuteronomy 18:16b
ועתה למה נמות כי תאכלנו האש הגדלה הזאת אם יספים אנחנו לשמע את קול יהוה אלהינו עוד ומתנו	לא אסף לשמע את קול יהוה אלהי ואת האש הגדלה הזאת לא אראה עוד ולא אמות
So now why should we die? For this great fire will consume us; if we hear the voice of the LORD our God any longer, we shall die.	If I hear the voice of the LORD my God any more, or ever again see this great fire, I shall die.
Deuteronomy 5:28	**Deuteronomy 18:17**
וישמע יהוה את קול דבריכם בדברכם אלי ויאמר יהוה אלי שמעתי את קול דברי העם הזה אשר דברו אליך היטיבו כל אשר דברו	ויאמר יהוה אלי היטיבו אשר דברו
The LORD heard your words when you spoke to me, and the LORD said to me: "I have heard the words of this people, which they have spoken to you; they are right in all that they have spoken.	Then the LORD replied to me: "They are right in what they have said.

When the law in Deuteronomy 18 repeats the event and the language of the request for a divine mediator in Deuteronomy 5, it creates an intertextual link that invites the reader or addressee to understand the law in light of that narrative. Deuteronomy 5:22–33, as outlined above, already elevates the importance of Moses as the sole recipient and relater of Yhwh's דבר, which will be all of his commandments (צוה vv. 29, 31, 32, 33), the statutes and ordinances (והחקים והמשפטים v. 31). These statutes and ordinances will, of course, include the laws concerning prophets in Deuteronomy 18.[66] Furthermore, within the narrative, Moses is not only the conduit of the divine revelation and divine law but is also promoted as the one responsible for promulgating (דבר) and teaching it (למד) (vv. 27, 31).[67] The very structure of Deuteronomy underscores Moses as the commissioned recipient of God's revelation and the speaker and teacher of Deuteronomic law in the delivery of the four "farewell discourses by Moses."[68] The

66 See the introductory statement at the beginning of the law, אלה החקים והמשפטים (Deut 12:1).
67 For Moses as the teacher of law, see also: 1:5, 4:1, 4:5, 4:14, 6:1.
68 "Abschiedsreden des Mose". See Lohfink, *Höre*, 15–16; Lohfink, "Bund als Vertrag," 218–21; Polzin, *Moses*, 25–72.

narrative framework of Deuteronomy, especially Deuteronomy 5, thus "anticipates" and provides a historical grounding and legitimization for the law of the prophet, which will accord Moses and prophets "like" him the authority to speak words that Yhwh will "put in his mouth": all that Yhwh has "commanded (צוה) him" (18:18).[69] Within the greater complex of Deuteronomy, these commanded words are nothing short of Torah itself (1:5, 4:8, 4:44, 17:11, 17:18–19, 27:3, 27:8, 27:26, 28:58, 28:61, 29:20 [29:21] 29:28 [29:29], 30:10, 31:9, 31:11–12, 31:24, 31:26, 32:46, 33:4, 33:10).[70] According to Eckart Otto, as Moses is established as the paradigmatic mediator of divine revelation, his role as the interpreter of Torah, but also as the scribe who has committed this interpretation into the written book, means that "the role of mediator of divine revelation was assumed by the written *torah* itself."[71] The transcribed Torah assumes Moses's function of mediating the divine will to the generations of addressees in the Promised Land (Deut 31:9, 24; cf. 31:19, 22).

Conversely, within this greater narrative background, the prophet law explicitly draws upon Deuteronomy's theophany tradition and its elevation of Moses as divine mediator and further heightens this authority. Through the context of the law-code, Moses is now attributed with the "institutional" title of prophet הנביא, whom all successive prophets must now be "like" (cf. Deut 34:10: "Never since has there arisen a prophet in Israel like Moses (כמשה), whom the LORD knew face to face.") The attribution of this prophetic supremacy to Moses and prophets like him *within* the law-code means that it is not confined or exhausted by its position in the narrative by a particular time, place or situation. The law, in its second person address "you shall heed him" (אליו תשמעון v. 15), is able

69 Brettler, "'Fire, Cloud,'" 23.

70 It is clear that the law is here participating in a self-legitimizing dialogue. See the following discussion and, on the self-referential nature of Deuteronomy, Olson, *Deuteronomy*, 2, 6, 11, 15, 40, 135, 139, 157. Jean Pierre Sonnet points out that it is not the book of Deuteronomy (or the narrator of) that refers to itself as Torah; rather, it is Moses who qualifies his own speech as Torah (4:8, 17:18, 17:19, 27:3, 27:8, 27:26, 28:58, 28:61, 29:20, 29:28, 30:10, 31:11, 21:12, 21:26, 32:46). These speeches, however, are written down within the book and are therefore witnessed by Deuteronomy (Deut 31: 9, 24). The legitimization of Torah is even furthered by the implication that successive individual prophets that are divinely selected and raised up in the "future" would encompass any of the known prophets found within the Deuteronomistic books and the latter prophets. Their prophecies are now presented as having been verified by Mosaic Torah as "true" prophecy as per Deut 18:21–22, while simultaneously made subordinate to it. The prophets become promulgators and teachers of the Law, and "their books provide an opportunity for further discussion and interpretation of Torah" (Knauf, "King among the Prophets," 133, 144–45). Similarly, Nihan, "Moses," 33–36; Achenbach, "'Prophet like Moses,'" 443; Edelman, "Court Prophets," 55–73; Otto, "Deuteronomy as the Legal Completion," 7.

71 Otto, "Deuteronomy as the Legal Completion," 4–5.

to make a continuing claim beyond the confines of the "historical" situation at hand. It is able to reach beyond the narrated time of the story to future generations.[72] This means that everything that Yhwh commands (כל אשר אצוונו v. 18) the prophet to speak must *continue* to be heeded (ישמע v. 19). The narrative of Deuteronomy 5, which 18:16–17 explicitly invokes, specifies that what Yhwh has commanded the prophet Moses and the prophet like Moses to speak *is the law, the statutes and ordinances*. Therefore, the etiology of the prophetic institution in the legal provision is the etiology of Deuteronomy itself, which is significantly identified as the speech of Yhwh, the Torah expounded by Moses to the people (5:31; also, 1:3–5).[73]

To reiterate, just as Deuteronomy's theophanic narrative shows how Moses is uniquely qualified to impart God's revelation, which is predominantly comprised of divine law, Deuteronomy 18:15–22 makes a legal claim for the prophetic status of Moses and, consequentially, the bulk of Deuteronomy itself (including Deut 5!), which is presented as the *spoken* word of Moses, on behalf of God. This tightly constructed interdependence of law and narrative creates a "hermeneutic circle" in which "each particular can only be understood via the general, of which it is a part, and vice versa."[74] The narrative in Deuteronomy 5 provides the "historical" context of the law and establishes its origins within divine revelation mediated by Moses; the law of Deuteronomy 18:15–22 legally prescribes the mode by which it is revealed (via Moses the paradigmatic prophet) and demands that the words of Deuteronomy make a continual claim upon its addresses as the commandment that "you will heed."

5 Law and Narrative Conflated and Resignified: Deuteronomy 5:22–33 and 18:15–22 in the Pre-Samaritan and Samaritan Pentateuch

The dialectical relationship between the narrative and law texts of Exodus 20:18–21, Deuteronomy 5:22–33, and Deuteronomy 18:15–22 described above exists not just on a theoretical level; the textual history of the Pentateuch physically demonstrates that at least some Second Temple period scribes and exegetes were not

72 Nasuti, "Identity," 10.

73 Nelson, *Deuteronomy*, 235. To be a prophet "like Moses" is, therefore, to subordinate future prophetic messages to Deuteronomic Torah (Stackert, *Prophet like Moses*, 140).

74 Schleiermacher, *Hermeneutics*, 24.

only aware of this intertextual conversation but were willing to further explore, extend, and re-signify the textual associations. The Samaritan Pentateuch and "pre-Samaritan" manuscript from Qumran, 4QpaleoExodus^{m}, show that the Deuteronomic texts were duplicated and conflated together into a new textual sequence and then implanted back into the Sinai pericope at two different locations within the theophany account of Exodus 20.[75] Deuteronomy 5:24b–27, which relates the people describing their mortal fear of the voice of God and the extended request for Moses to mediate, is placed in the middle of the much shorter request at Exodus 20:19 [SP 20:16]. A second addition is made following Exodus 20:21 [SP 20:18], after the people are described as standing at a distance as Moses drew near the darkness to approach God. This is comprised of Deuteronomy 5:28b–29 + 18:18–22 + 5:30–31. Thus, speaking to Moses, Yhwh approves the request of the people and expresses that they should fear him and keep all his commandments (מצותי) so that it may be well for them and their children forever (לעולם). From here, the text of Deuteronomy 18:18–22 relates the promise of a prophet like Moses who must be heeded and the indictment of, and test for, illegitimate prophets. This is followed by the resumption of Deuteronomy 5:30–31 and the instruction from God to Moses that the people should return to their tents but that Moses should stay to hear all the commandment, statutes, and ordinances.

This interpolation of Deuteronomic material into Exodus is not a unique phenomenon in the pre-Samaritan manuscripts. Magnar Kartveit lists thirty-nine major additions; nineteen of these contain material from Deuteronomy inserted into Exodus, Numbers, or another location within Deuteronomy itself.[76] These interpolations have sometimes been labelled harmonizations, that is, additions to the text that are a response to textual discrepancies; here, that would be Deuteronomy's report of speech between the people, God, and Moses that is

---

75 The passages are also extant in Deuteronomy within the Samaritan Pentateuch. For the primary texts, see Skehan, Ulrich, and Sanderson, *Qumran Cave 4*, 53–130; Tal and Florentin, *Pentateuch*. The "pre-Samaritan" Qumran manuscripts are not "Samaritan" but likely a popular textual tradition that circulated in ancient Israel in the late Second Temple period. They contain a "substratum" of the text of the Samaritan Pentateuch to which a layer of further editing was added. The textual variants under discussion here are present in both the "pre-Samaritan" manuscript 4QpaleoExodus^{m} and the Samaritan Pentateuch and are, therefore, not uniquely "Samaritan." See Tov, "Nature," 79–80; Sanderson, *Exodus Scroll*, 266–70. They are also found in 4Q158 (RP^{a}) fragments 6 and 7–8, and (only) the second within 4Q175 (4QTestmonia), lines 1–8. Within both of these latter compositions, the variants have undergone even further change and/or are juxtaposed with different biblical texts that require their own investigation. For transcription of 4Q158 and discussion, see Zahn, *Rethinking Rewritten Scripture*, 29–33, 37–40, 63–67, 245–58; for 4Q175, see White Crawford, *Rewriting Scripture*, 35–36.

76 There is a list provided in Kartveit, "Major Expansions," 123–24; and Kartveit, *Origin*, 310–12.

not actually present in full within the prior account in Exodus.[77] However, the explanation of harmonization, while helpful, is in this case too simplistic and does not adequately represent the impact of the changes.[78]

Magnar Kartveit argues that the pre-Samaritan additions heighten the position of Moses as a reliable mediator of divine messages and, consequentially, the divine law promulgated by him.[79] The two additions in Exodus 20 play a special role in this elevation of Moses's authority. The interpolation of Deuteronomy 5:24–27, as outlined above, contains the people's elaborated request for Moses to act as divine mediator. The second expansion, consisting of the amalgamation of Deuteronomy 5:28–31 and 18:18–22, sanctions the request of the people for a mediator. It not only points to Moses the prophet for this function and a prophet like Moses as the subsequent mediator between God and Israel but also makes it clear that the substance of this prophetic function is now the promulgation of the law.

The placement of the texts suggests that when Deuteronomy 5:29 raises Yhwh's desire that the people fear him and keep his commandments forever, this will be accomplished through the prophet Moses and the prophet like Moses. Indeed, Deuteronomy 5:29 actually expresses this wish through a construction that uses the interrogative מי יתן, "who will give," meaning, "would that" or "oh, that."[80]

> מי יתן והיה לבבם זה להם ליראה אתי ולשמר את כל מצותי כל הימים למען ייטב להם ולבניהם לעלם
>
> Oh, that they had such a mind as this, to fear me and to keep all my commandments always, so that it might go well with them and with their children forever! (Deut 5:29)

In the text-flow of the pre-Samaritan texts, Deuteronomy 18:18 provides the "answer" as to how this will be accomplished: it will be Moses, and only the prophet like Moses, who will speak everything that God commands him (כל אשר אצוונו). Anybody who does not heed these words will be punished (v. 19). Deuteronomy 18:20–22 condemn the prophet who speaks the word that Yhwh has *not* commanded him to speak (לא צויתיו v. 20) and provides that the false prophet is the one whose word does not "take place or prove true" (ולא יהיה הדבר ולא יבוא) and that he has spoken it presumptuously (vv. 21–22). Deuter-

77 Tigay, "Conflation," 68–78; Tov, "Nature," 5–9; White Crawford, *Rewriting Scripture*, 22–23.

78 Segal, "Text of the Bible," 11–17; Kartveit, *Origin*, 275–76; Anderson and Giles, *Samaritan Pentateuch*, 65–67. Later, Emanuel Tov calls them "editorial changes" (*Textual Criticism*, 80–81).

79 Kartveit, "Major Expansions," 118–24 and Kartveit, *Origin*, 276–85; taken up by Anderson and Giles, *Samaritan Pentateuch*, 65–69, 83–90 (with some qualifications).

80 Weinfeld, *Deuteronomy 1–11*, 325.

onomy 5:30–31 then follows, with God instructing Moses to send the people to their tents but for him *alone* to stay to hear *all the commandment* (כל המצוה), the statues and the ordinances that Moses shall teach them so that the people may do them in the land that Yhwh is giving them to possess. The sequence seems to imply that Moses alone has directly heard the direct דבר of Yhwh and is solely qualified to impart his commandment, which are the statutes and ordinances of Mosaic תורה. Subsequent, authentic prophets, as successors of Moses, are necessarily confined to preaching or interpreting the law.[81]

To summarize, these interpolations specify that *from the time of the Sinai event* it was made clear that if the people want to hear and obey the word of Yhwh so that it may go well for them in the land, this should be accomplished through the interpretation and observance of the laws of Moses. By the placement of these texts in Exodus 20:18–21, the authoritative Mosaic תורה now more explicitly includes not just Deuteronomic law but also the Covenant Code, which begins right after this insertion at Exodus 20:22 [SP 20:19]. By inserting the Deuteronomic prophet law and Deuteronomic theophany into Exodus 20, the pre-Samaritan texts drew upon a pre-existing dialectic between Deuteronomic law and Deuteronomic narrative that mutually enhanced the authority of the Mosaic Sinai/Horeb revelation. They additionally planted that dialectic into the Sinai narrative before the Covenant Code, which now, conversely, confers the Deuteronomic authority back into Sinai. This process is, in one sense, the logical outcome of the hermeneutical strategy employed by Deuteronomy in its claim that the words of Yhwh delivered by Moses on the plains of Moab were already revealed at Horeb but were pronounced only when the people were about to enter the Promised Land. The pre-Samaritan manuscript makes what is implicit in the Masoretic Text more explicit.[82]

---

81 Kartveit, *Origin*, 284. Verse 22 and the phrase לא תגור ממנו, "do not be frightened of him/it," appears to conflict with v. 20, which extends the death penalty to the false prophet. Hadi Ghantous contends that v. 22 may be a late concession to "bibliomancy," divination that uses various techniques to select verses or sections out of the prophetic scrolls to dispense oracles ("From Mantle to Scroll," 120–24, 132). If this is the case, 4QpaleoExodus^{m} and the Samaritan Pentateuch ostensibly reject this concession by its insistence on Mosaic Torah as Yhwh's word and commandment.

82 The interpolations in the pre-Samaritan texts do not necessarily indicate that their scribe/s were specifically concerned with affirming or heightening the authority of the Covenant Code, but instead, that this was a logical result of a scribal impulse that consistently seeks to affirm that Moses is a trustworthy relater of history and Yhwh's word. So, if in Deuteronomy Moses claims that during the Sinai/Horeb revelation he was designated a prophet, raised up to speak the words of Yhwh designated as law, then this should be explicitly shown to be true by importing that event into the anterior text.

6 Conclusion: Deuteronomy 18:15–22 and the Deuteronomic "Core"

Some final observations may now be made with regard to the questions posed at the beginning. Firstly, this analysis has not tried to establish whether or not Deuteronomy 18:15–22 was part of an *Urdeuteronomium*. However, we can say that within the law collection in chs. 12–26, it has various functions that are constructed and articulated within that legal-textual landscape. In this sense, the prophet law sits well within the core compositional structure of the Deuteronomic law that, among other things, articulates an ideal government configuration in which the prophet assumes supremacy over other political and religious institutions as the conduit of Yhwh's word. Nonetheless, the prophet is limited by and made accountable to the Mosaic Law. The prophet law is also a central component in the way that Deuteronomy attempts to distinguish the religious and cultic practices of the Israelites from the other nations that do not have a written תורה that may directly and continually communicate the word of God. Moreover, within the legal context, the mandate of a prophet like Moses who speaks God's word that is תורה and must be heeded and the prohibition of inauthentic prophets is able to draw upon the imperative "you will" nature of law to make both an immediate and continual normative claim upon the peoples it addresses.

Deuteronomy 18:15–22 is, additionally, clearly a core text in terms of its centrality to the meaning of Deuteronomy, its message, purpose, and theology. It is also highly literary and idealistic, pointing toward purposes for biblical legal texts that are far richer and more complex than the reductionist function often ascribed to law as a set of practical rules or commands that are laid down and then applied to legal situations. Deuteronomy 18:15–22, in its past mandate for a prophet like Moses who will continue to speak everything to the people that Yhwh commands in the form of the תורה, transports communal Israel from the past to the future: it calls forth a new reality in which the people are in communion with Yhwh and provides the means by which this future may continually be realized through Torah observance and fidelity to Yhwh.[83] Law is itself a mediator between present and future, reality and utopia. The prophet law also seeks to define the community of Israel, which is able through the Mosaic prophets and Mosaic Torah to hear the words and speech of Yhwh forever, over and against the nations that rely on less immediate forms of divine revelation. Law confers identity and constitutes community.

---

83 Burnside, "Spirit," 2–3.

It is also evident that elements of the legal provision itself collapse the distinction between "core" legal texts and "peripheral" narrative, both in terms of their physical positioning within the book as well as their content and purpose. The motive clause – a feature pervasive in Deuteronomic law – that is found in vv. 16–18 uses the embedded narrative of the past historical encounter with God at Sinai/Horeb to legitimize the law's existence and value and to imbue its regulative components with a force it would not otherwise have. The law actually gains its authority and prescriptive character from the narrative. Moreover, the centrality of Deuteronomy 18:15–22 to Deuteronomy is not confined to a legalistic context. In fact, it is only *through* an intertextual dialogue between the prophet law and the extended narrated request for Moses to mediate in Deuteronomy 5:22–33 that *all* the laws of Deuteronomy and the spoken narrative of תורה become sanctioned as mediated prophetic speech from God. Theologically speaking, Deuteronomy 18:15–22 is thus perhaps one of the most core texts of Deuteronomy, but this meaning is only fully articulated via its relationship with narrative.

The two major variants in the pre-Samaritan text both reflect and extend the interrelationship between the Deuteronomic law, Deuteronomic narrative, and Exodus narrative. This, on the one hand, shows that scribes felt free to reconfigure texts to suit their own purposes, disregarding any conception of clear-cut, discrete sources and genres. The seeming disregard for the distinction between law and narrative texts is demonstrated not only by the conflation of narrative and legal prescription from Deuteronomy, but also by its addition into the Exodus account of the theophany. On the other hand, we have seen that this is really an extension of a pre-existing dynamic: law and narrative texts may perform some specific and localized functions within their own contexts, but the hermeneutic of Deuteronomy 18:15–22, for example, is so intertwined with Deuteronomy 5, itself a reinterpretation of Exodus 20, that its full legal significance is only revealed in relation to these narrative texts. And vice versa, the import of the Sinai/Horeb revelation is only truly exposed by the content of the covenantal law. It is therefore likely that the significance and multivalence of Deuteronomy 18:15–22 in relation to the surrounding narrative of Deuteronomy and Exodus contributed to its own textual instability and multiformity.[84] In terms of textual transmission, core texts may in fact prompt their own revision by virtue of their importance. The evidence that scribes continued to (re)interpret legal texts in their transmission in the late Second Temple period, especial-

84 This observation is in line with theories underpinning the rewriting of biblical law. It is their authority that, paradoxically, prompts their revision; so e.g. Levinson, "Human Voice," 35–45; Levinson, *Deuteronomy*, 13–17, 144–57; Stackert, *Rewriting the Torah*, 214–25.

ly in relation to narrative and historical texts, should make us far more cautious about our abilities to unravel complex redactional layers in order to discover a pristine "original" form and function that is divorced from the literary contexts in which we now find them.

Works Cited

Achenbach, Reinhard. "'A Prophet like Moses' (Deuteronomy 18:15) – 'No Prophet like Moses' (Deuteronomy 34:10): Some Observations on the Relation between the Pentateuch and the Latter Prophets." In *The Pentateuch: International Perspectives on Current Research*, edited by Thomas B. Dozeman, Konrad Schmid, and Baruch J. Schwartz, 435–58. Forschungen Zum Alten Testament 78. Tübingen: Mohr Siebeck, 2011.

Anderson, Robert T. and Terry Giles. *The Samaritan Pentateuch: An Introduction to Its Origin, History, and Significance for Biblical Studies*. Society of Biblical Literature Resources for Biblical Study 72. Atlanta: Society of Biblical Literature, 2012.

Atkins, J. D. "Reassessing the Origins of Deuteronomic Prophecy: Early Moses Traditions in Deuteronomy 18:15–22." *Bulletin for Biblical Research* 23 (2013): 323–41.

Baden, Joel S. *The Composition of the Pentateuch: Renewing the Documentary Hypothesis*. New Haven: Yale University, 2012.

Barak, Aharon. *Purposive Interpretation in Law*. Translated by Sari Bashi. Princeton: Princeton University, 2005.

Barstad, Hans M. "The Understanding of the Prophets in Deuteronomy." *Scandinavian Journal of the Old Testament* 8 (1994): 236–51.

Bartor, Assnat. *Reading Law as Narrative: A Study in the Casuistic Laws of the Pentateuch*. Society of Biblical Literature Ancient Israel and Its Literature 5. Atlanta: Society of Biblical Literature, 2010.

Blenkinsopp, Joseph. *A History of Prophecy in Israel*. Louisville: Westminster John Knox, 1996.

Blenkinsopp, Joseph. *Prophecy and Canon: A Contribution to the Study of Jewish Origins*. Notre Dame: University of Notre Dame Press, 1977.

Blum, Erhard. "The Decalogue and the Composition History of the Pentateuch." *The Pentateuch: International Perspectives on Current Research*, edited by Thomas B. Dozeman, Konrad Schmid, and Baruch J. Schwartz, 289–301. Forschungen Zum Alten Testament 78. Tübingen: Mohr Siebeck, 2011.

Bottéro, Jean. *Mesopotamia: Writing, Reasoning, and the Gods*. Translated by Zainab Bahrani and Marc van de Mieroop. Chicago: University of Chicago Press, 1992.

Braulik, Georg. "Zur Abfolge der Gesetze in Deuteronomium 16:18–21:23." *Biblica* 69 (1988): 63–92.

Braulik, Georg. "The Sequence of the Laws in Deuteronomy 12–26 and the Decalogue." In *A Song of Power and the Power of Song: Essays on the Book of Deuteronomy*, edited by Duane L. Christensen, 313–35. Winona Lake: Eisenbrauns, 1993.

Brettler, Marc Z. "'Fire, Cloud, and Deep Darkness' (Deuteronomy 5:22): Deuteronomy's Recasting of Revelation." In *The Significance of Sinai: Traditions about Sinai and Divine Revelation in Judaism and Christianity*, edited by George J. Brooke, Hindy Najman, and Loren T. Stuckenbruck, 15–27. Themes in Biblical Narrative 12. Leiden: Brill, 2008.

Burnside, Jonathan P. "The Spirit of Biblical Law." *Oxford Journal of Law and Religion* 1 (2012): 127–50.
Christensen Duane L. "Deuteronomy in Modern Research: Approaches and Issues." In *A Song of Power and the Power of Song: Essays on the Book of Deuteronomy*, edited by Duane L. Christensen, 3–17. Winona Lake, IN: Eisenbrauns, 1993.
Clines, David J. A. "What Remains of the Hebrew Bible? Its Text and Language in a Postmodern Age." *Studia Theologica* 54 (2001): 76–95.
Collins, John J. "The Transformation of the Torah in Second Temple Judaism." *Journal for the Study of Judaism* 43 (2012): 455–74.
Cover, Robert. "Nomos and Narrative." *Harvard Law Review* 97 (1983): 4–68.
Davies, Philip R. "'Law' in Early Judaism." In *Judaism in Late Antiquity*, Part 3, Vol. 1: *Where we Stand: Issues & Debates in Ancient Judaism*, edited by Jacob Neusner and Alan J. Avery-Peck, 3–33. Handbook of Oriental Studies. Section 1 The Near and Middle East 40. Leiden: Brill, 1999.
Doron, Pinchas. "Motive Clauses in the Laws of Deuteronomy: Their Forms, Functions, and Contents." *Harvard Annual Review* 2 (1978): 61–77.
Dozeman, Thomas B. *God on the Mountain: A Study of Redaction, Theology, and Canon in Exodus 19–24*. Society of Biblical Literature Monograph Series 37. Atlanta: Scholars, 1989.
Driver, Samuel R. *A Critical and Exegetical Commentary on Deuteronomy*. International Critical Commentary 5. Edinburgh: T&T Clark, 1896.
Edelman, Diana V. "Court Prophets During the Monarchy and Literary Prophets in the So-called Deuteronomistic History." In *Israelite Prophecy and the Deuteronomistic History: Portrait, Reality, and the Formation of a History*, edited by Mignon R. Jacobs and Raymond F. Person, Jr., 51–73. Society of Biblical Literature Ancient Israel and Its Literature 14. Atlanta: Society of Biblical Literature, 2013.
Edelman, Diana V. "The Metaphor of Torah as a Life-Giving Well in the Book of Deuteronomy." In *History, Memory, Hebrew Scriptures: A Festschrift for Ehud Ben Zvi*, edited by Ian D. Wilson and Diana V. Edelman, 317–33. Winona Lake, IN: Eisenbrauns, 2015.
Finkelstein, J. J. "Ammiṣaduqa's Edict and the Babylonian 'Law Codes.'" *Journal of Cuneiform Studies* 15 (1961): 91–104.
Finkelstein, J. J. *The Ox that Gored*. Transactions of the. American Philosophical Society 71/2. Philadelphia: American Philosophical Society, 1981.
Fitzpatrick-McKinley, Anne. *The Transformation of Torah from Scribal Advice to Law*. Journal for the Study of the Old Testament Supplement Series 287. Sheffield: Sheffield Academic, 1999.
Gemser, Berend. "The Importance of the Motive Clause in Old Testament Law." In *Congress Volume Copenhagen 1953*, edited by G. W. Anderson, Aage Bentzen, P. A. H. de Boer, Millar Burrows, Henri Cazelles, and Martin Noth, 50–66. Vetus Testamentum Supplements 1. Leiden: Brill, 1953.
Ghantous, Hadi. "From Mantle to Scroll: The Wane of the Flesh and Blood Prophet in the Elisha Cycle." In *Studies in Magic and Divination in the Biblical World*, edited by Helen R. Jacobus, Anne Katrine de Hemmer Gudme, and Philippe Guillaume, 119–33. Biblical Intersections 11. Piscataway, NJ: Gorgias, 2013.
Halberstam, Chaya. "The Art of Biblical Law." *Prooftexts* 27 (2007): 345–64.
Halpern, Baruch. *The Constitution of the Monarchy in Israel*. Harvard Semitic Monographs 25. Chico, CA: Scholars, 1981.

Harvey, Paul B., Jr and Baruch Halpern. "W. M. L. de Wette's 'Dissertatio Critica ... ': Context and Translation." *Zeitschrift für altorientalische und biblische Rechtsgeschichte* 14 (2008): 47–85.

Jackson, Bernard S. *Studies in the Semiotics of Biblical Law.* Journal for the Study of the Old Testament Supplement Series 314. Sheffield: Sheffield Academic, 2000.

Kartveit, Magnar. "The Major Expansions in the Samaritan Pentateuch – The Evidence from the 4QTexts." In *Proceedings of the Fifth International Congress of the Société d'études samaritaines: Helsinki, August 1–4, 2000: Studies in Memory of Ferdinand Dexinger*, edited by Haseeb Shehadeh and Habib Tawa, 117–24. Paris: Geuthner, 2006.

Kartveit, Magnar. *The Origin of the Samaritans.* Vetus Testamentum Supplements 128. Leiden: Brill, 2009.

Kennet, R. H. 1906. "The Date of Deuteronomy." *Journal of Theological Studies* 7 (1906): 481–500.

Kline, Meredith G. *Treaty of the Great King: The Covenant Structure of Deuteronomy.* Grand Rapids, MI: Eerdmans, 1963.

Knauf, E. Axel. "King among the Prophets". In *The Production of Prophecy: Constructing Prophecy and Prophets in Yehud*, edited by Diana V. Edelman and Ehud Ben Zvi, 131–49. London: Equinox, 2009.

Knight, Douglas A. *Law, Power, and Justice in Ancient Israel.* Louisville: John Knox, 2011.

Kratz, Reinhard G. "'The Peg in the Wall': Cultic Centralization Revisited." In *Law and Religion in the Eastern Mediterranean: From Antiquity to Early Islam*, edited by Anselm C. Hagedorn and Reinhard G. Kratz, 251–85. Oxford: Oxford University, 2013.

Kraus, F. R. "Ein zentrales Problem des altmesopotamischen Rechtes. Was ist der Codex Hammurabi?" *Genava* 8 (1960): 283–96.

LeFebvre, Michael. *Collections, Codes, and Torah: The Re-characterization of Israel's Written Law.* Library of Hebrew Bible/Old Testament Studies 451. New York: T&T Clark, 2006.

Levenson, Jon D. *Sinai and Zion: An Entry into the Jewish Bible.* San Francisco: Harper & Row, 1985.

Levinson, Bernard M. *Deuteronomy and the Hermeneutics of Legal Innovation.* New York: Oxford University, 1997.

Levinson, Bernard M. "Deuteronomy's Conception of Law as Ideal Type: A Missing Chapter in the History of Constitutional Law." In *The Right Chorale: Studies in Biblical Law and Interpretation*, 52–86. Forschungen zum Alten Testament 54. Tübingen: Mohr Siebeck, 2008.

Levinson, Bernard M. "The Human Voice in Divine Revelation: The Problem of Authority in Biblical Law." In *Innovation in Religious Traditions: Essays in the Interpretation of Religious Change*, edited by Michael A. Williams, Martin S. Jaffee, and Collett Cox, 35–71. Religion and Society 31. Berlin: de Gruyter, 1992.

Levinson, Bernard M. "The Reconceptualization of Kingship in Deuteronomy and the Deuteronomistic History's Transformation of Torah." *Vetus Testamentum* 51 (2001): 511–34.

Lohfink, Norbert. "Bund als Vertrag im Deuteronomium." *Zeitschrift für die alttestamentliche Wissenschaft* 107 (1995): 215–39.

Lohfink, Norbert. "Distribution of the Functions of Power: The Laws Concerning Public Offices in Deuteronomy 16:18–18:22." In *A Song of Power and the Power of Song: Essays on the Book of Deuteronomy*, edited by Duane L Christensen, 343–49. Winona Lake: Eisenbrauns, 1993.

Lohfink, Norbert. *Höre, Israel! Auslegung von Texten aus dem Buch Deuteronomium*. Die Welt der Bibel 18. Düsseldorf: Patmos, 1965.

Lundbom, Jack R. *Deuteronomy: A Commentary*. Grand Rapids, MI: Eerdmans, 2013.

Malul, Meir. *The Comparative Method in Ancient Near Eastern and Biblical Legal Studies*. Alter Orient und Altes Testament 227. Kevelaer: Butzon & Bercker, 1990.

Markl, Dominik. "The Ten Words Revealed and Revised: The Origins of Law and Legal Hermeneutics in the Pentateuch." In *The Decalogue and its Cultural Influence*, edited by Dominik Markl, 13–27. Hebrew Bible Monographs 58. Sheffield: Sheffield Phoenix, 2013.

Mayes, A. D. H. *Deuteronomy*. Grand Rapids, MI: Eerdmans, 1979.

McCarthy, Dennis J. *Treaty and Covenant: A Study in Form in the Ancient Oriental Documents and in the Old Testament*. Analecta biblica 21a. Rome: Biblical Institute, 1978.

McConville J. Gordon. *Deuteronomy*. Leicester: Apollos and Downers Grove, IL: InterVarsity, 2002.

Mendenhall, George E. "Covenant Forms in Israelite Tradition." *Biblical Archaeologist* 17 (1954): 50–76.

Miller, Patrick D. "'Moses My Servant': The Deuteronomic Portrait of Moses." In *A Song of Power and the Power of Song: Essays on the Book of Deuteronomy*, edited by Duane L. Christensen, 301–12. Winona Lake, IN: Eisenbrauns, 1993.

Morrow, William S. *An Introduction to Biblical Law*. Grand Rapids: Eerdmans, 2017.

Najman, Hindy. *Seconding Sinai: The Development of Mosaic Discourse in Second Temple Judaism*. Journal for the Study of Judaism Supplements 77. Leiden: Brill, 2003.

Nasuti, Harry P. "Identity, Identification and Imitation: The Narrative Hermeneutics of Biblical Law." *Journal of Law and Religion* 4 (1986): 9–23.

Nelson, Richard D. *Deuteronomy: A Commentary*. Louisville: Westminster John Knox, 2002.

Nicholson, Ernest W. *Deuteronomy and the Judaean Diaspora*. Oxford: Oxford University, 2014.

Nihan, Christophe. "Moses and the Prophets: Deuteronomy 18 and the Emergence of the Pentateuch as Torah." *Svensk Exegetisk Årsbok* 75 (2010): 21–55.

Noth, Martin. *The Deuteronomistic History*. Journal for the Study of the Old Testament Supplement Series 15. Sheffield: JSOT Press, 1981.

O'Brien, Mark. "Deuteronomy 16:18–18:22: Meeting the Challenge of Towns and Nations." *Journal for the Study of the Old Testament* 33 (2008): 155–72.

Olson, Dennis T. *Deuteronomy and the Death of Moses: A Theological Reading*. Minneapolis: Fortress, 1994.

Otto, Eckart. *Das Deuteronomium im Pentateuch und Hexateuch. Studien zur Literaturgeschichte von Pentateuch und Hexateuch im Lichte des Deuteronomiumrahmens*. Forschungen zum Alten Testament, 30. Tübingen: Mohr Siebeck, 2000.

Otto, Eckart. *Deuteronomium 1–11*. Herders Theologischer Kommentar zum Alten Testament. Freiburg: Herder, 2012.

Otto, Eckart. "Deuteronomy as the Legal Completion and Prophetic Finale of the Pentateuch." In *Paradigm Change in Pentateuchal* Research, edited by Matthias Armgardt, Benjamin Kilchör and Markus Zehnder, 179–88. Beihefte zur Zeitschrift für altorientalische und biblische Rechtsgeschichte 22. Wiesbaden: Harrassowitz, 2019.

Otto, Eckart. "The History of the Legal-Religious Hermeneutics of the Book of Deuteronomy from the Assyrian to the Hellenistic Period." In *Law and Religion in the Eastern Mediterranean: From Antiquity to Early Islam*, edited by Anselm C. Hagedorn and Reinhard G. Kratz, 211–50. Oxford: Oxford University Press, 2013.

Otto, Eckart. "Welcher Bund ist ewig? Die Bundestheologie priesterlicher Schriftgelehrter im Pentateuch und in der Tradentenprophetie im Jeremiabuch." In *Für immer verbündet. Studien zur Bundestheologie der Bibel*, edited by Christoph Dohmen and Christian Frevel, 161–70. Stuttgarter Bibelstudien 211. Stuttgart: Katholisches Bibelwerk, 2007.

Patrick, Dale. *Old Testament Law*. London: SCM, 1985.

Paul, Shalom M. *Studies in the Book of the Covenant in the Light of Cuneiform and Biblical Law*. Vetus Testamentum Supplements 18. Leiden: Brill, 1970.

Person, Raymond F., Jr. *The Deuteronomic School: History, Social Setting, and Literature*. Studies in Biblical Literature 2. Atlanta: Society of Biblical Literature, 2002.

Polzin, Robert. *Moses and the Deuteronomist: A Literary Study of the Deuteronomic History*, Part One: *Deuteronomy, Joshua, Judges*. New York: Seabury, 1980.

Rad, Gerhard von. *Deuteronomy: A Commentary*. Old Testament Library. London: SCM, 1966.

Rad, Gerhard von. *Studies in Deuteronomy*. Translated by David Stalker. Studies in Biblical Theology 9. London: SCM, 1953.

Reuter Eleanore. *Kultzentralisation. Entstehung und Theologie von Dtn 12*. Bonner biblicshe Beiträge 87. Frankfurt am Main: Hain, 1993.

Roth, Martha. *Law Collections from Mesopotamia and Asia Minor*. 2nd ed. Society of Biblical Literature Writings from the Ancient World 6. Atlanta: Society of Biblical Literature, 1997.

Sanderson, Judith E. *An Exodus Scroll from Qumran: 4QpaleoExod^{m} and the Samaritan Tradition*. Harvard Semitic Studies 30. Atlanta: Scholars, 1986.

Schleiermacher, Friedrich. *Hermeneutics and Criticism and Other Writings*. Translated and edited by Andrew Bowie. Cambridge: Cambridge University, 1998.

Schmid. Konrad. "Deuteronomy within the 'Deuteronomistic Histories' in Genesis–2 Kings." In *Deuteronomy in the Pentateuch, Hexateuch, and the Deuteronomistic History*. edited by Konrad Schmid and Raymond F. Person, Jr., 8–30. Forschungen zum Alten Testament 2. Reihe 56. Tübingen: Mohr Siebeck, 2012.

Schmid, Konrad. "The Genesis of Normativity in Biblical Law." In *Concepts of Law in the Sciences, Legal Studies, and Theology*, edited by Michael Welker and Gregor Etzelmüller, 119–35. Religion in Philosophy and Theology 72. Tübingen: Mohr Siebeck, 2013.

Segal, Michael. "The Text of the Bible in Light of the Dead Sea Scrolls." *Materia giudaica* 12 (2007): 5–20.

Skehan, Patrick W., Eugene Ulrich, and Judith E. Sanderson, eds. *Qumran Cave 4: Palaeo-Hebrew and Greek Biblical Manuscripts*. Discoveries in the Judaean Desert 9. Oxford: Clarendon, 1992.

Sommer, Benjamin D. *Revelation and Authority: Sinai in Jewish Scripture and Tradition*. New Haven: Yale University Press, 2018.

Sonnet, Jean-Pierre. *The Book Within the Book: Writing in Deuteronomy*. Biblical Interpretation Series 14. Leiden: Brill, 1997.

Sonsino, Rifat. *Motive Clauses in Hebrew Law*. Society of Biblical Literature Dissertation Series 45. Chico, CA: Scholars, 1980.

Stackert, Jeffrey. *A Prophet like Moses: Prophecy, Law, and Israelite Religion*. Oxford: Oxford University Press, 2014.

Stackert, Jeffrey. *Rewriting the Torah: Literary Revision in Deuteronomy and the Holiness Legislation*. Forschungen zum Alten Testament 52. Tübingen: Mohr Siebeck, 2007.

Tal, Abraham and Moshe Florentin, eds. *The Pentateuch: The Samaritan Version and the Masoretic Version*. Tel Aviv: Haim Rubin Tel Aviv University Press, 2010.

Teeter, Andrew. *Scribal Laws: Exegetical Variation in the Textual Transmission of Biblical Law in the Late Second Temple Period*. Forschungen zum Alten Testament 92. Tübingen: Mohr Siebeck, 2014.

Tengström, Sven. "Moses and the Prophets in the Deuteronomistic History." *Scandinavian Journal of the Old Testament* 8 (1994): 257–66.

Tigay, Jeffrey H. "Conflation as a Redactional Technique." In *Empirical Models for Biblical Criticism*, edited by Jeffrey H. Tigay, 53–96. Philadelphia: University of Pennsylvania Press, 1985.

Tov, Emanuel. "The Nature and Background of Harmonizations in Biblical Manuscripts." *Journal for the Study of the Old Testament* 31 (1985): 3–29.

Tov, Emanuel. *Textual Criticism of the Hebrew Bible*. 3rd ed. Minneapolis: Fortress, 2012.

Ulrich, Eugene. *The Dead Sea Scrolls and the Origins of the Bible*. Studies in the Dead Sea Scrolls and Related Literature. Grand Rapids, MI: Eerdmans, 1999.

Van Seters, John. *The Life of Moses: The Yahwist as Historian in Exodus-Numbers*. Louisville: Westminster John Knox, 1994.

Vroom, Jonathan. "Law, Authority, and Interpretation in the Ancient World: The Origin of Legal Obligation in Early Judaism." PhD dissertation, University of Toronto, 2017. Now published as *The Authority of Law in the Hebrew Bible and Early Judaism: Tracing the Origins of Legal Obligation from Ezra to Qumran*. Leiden: Brill, 2018.

Watts, James W. *Reading Law: The Rhetorical Shaping of the Pentateuch*. The Biblical Seminar 59. Sheffield: Sheffield Academic, 1999.

Watts, James W. "Ritual Legitimacy and Scriptural Authority." *Journal of Biblical Literature* 124 (2005): 401–17.

Weinfeld, Moshe. *Deuteronomy 1–11: A New Translation with Introduction and Commentary*. Anchor Bible 5. New York: Doubleday, 1991.

Weinfeld, Moshe. *Deuteronomy and the Deuteronomic School*. Winona Lake, IN: Eisenbrauns, 1992.

Wellhausen, Julius. *Prolegomena to the History of Ancient Israel*. Society of Biblical Literature Reprints and Translations. Atlanta: Scholars, 1994. Reprint of *Prolegomena to the History of Israel*. Translated by J. Sutherland Black and A. Enzies, with a preface by W. Robertson Smith. Edinburgh: Black, 1885. Citations are to the 1994 versions.

Westbrook, Raymond. "Cuneiform Law Codes and the Origins of Legislation." *Zeitschrift für Assyriologie* 79 (1989): 201–22.

Wette Wilhelm M. L. de. "Dissertatio critico-exegetica qua Deuteronomium a prioribus Pentateuchi Libris diversum, alius cuiusdam recentioris auctoris opus esse monstratur." PhD thesis, University of Jena, 1805.

White Crawford, Sidnie. *Rewriting Scripture in Second Temple Times*. Grand Rapids, MI: Eerdmans, 2008.

Wiseman, Donald J. "The Vassal-Treaties of Esarhaddon." *Iraq* 20 (1958): 1–99.

Wright, David. *Inventing God's Law: How the Covenant Code of the Bible Used and Revised the Laws of Hammurabi*. Oxford: Oxford University Press, 2009.

Young, Ian. "The Biblical Scrolls from Qumran and the Masoretic Text: A Statistical Approach." In *Feasts and Fasts: A Festschrift in Honour of Alan David Crown*, edited by Marianne Dacy, Jennifer Dowling, and Suzanne Faigan, 81–139. Sydney: University of Sydney, Mandelbaum Publishing, 2005.

Zahn, Molly M. *Rethinking Rewritten Scripture: Composition and Exegesis in the 4QReworked Pentateuch Manuscripts*. Studies on the Texts of the Desert of Judah 95. Leiden: Brill, 2011.

Martijn Beukenhorst

The War Laws in Deuteronomy

> Harsh as some of them are in light of modern ideals (though not modern practices) the [war laws] limit wanton destruction of life and property and are *the oldest known rules of war* regulating the treatment of conquered people and territory.[1]

Warfare does not stand out as a major concern in the main body of decrees and laws in Deuteronomy 12:1–26:16, the so-called Deuteronomic core. These chapters only mention war as a means to attain broader aims. In keeping with the larger concerns of the present volume, this contribution is a case study contributing to the over-arching question about whether or not an earlier independent Deuteronomic core existed that later was framed to obtain the present book.

To answer this question, I begin with a systematic examination of the passages dealing with warfare in the "core" (Deut 20:1–20; 21:10–14; 23:10–15; 24:5), with a stronger focus on the first section (Deut 20:1–20) since it the only one that is fully self-contained. The other passages belong to larger units dealing with other subjects. I then consider relevant parallels in ancient Near Eastern texts, to reveal the specificity of the Deuteronomic approach to war. Finally, I look at the possible influence of the "frame" on the war regulations in the "core," before drawing implications regarding the relation between the core and the frames of Deuteronomy and how likely it is that the core existed independently from the current frames.

1 On Warfare (Deut 20:1–20)

Deuteronomy 20:1–20 consists of three main sections: "preparing the army" (vv. 1–9), "the treatment of defeated populations" (vv. 10–18) and "the treatment of trees near besieged cities" (vv. 19–20). Each section begins with כי + a verb in the imperfect second masculine singular. The three sections are independent but all share the theme of warfare.

1 Tigay, *Deuteronomy*, 185. Italics are mine.

Note: I owe a great debt of gratitude to Prof. Diana Edelman, with whom I studied for a semester at the University of Oslo and who has extensively commented on this article throughout its various stages.

https://doi.org/10.1515/9783110713312-010

The first section addressing the troops has four components: introduction (v. 1), priestly exhortation (vv. 2–4), deferment from battle (vv. 5–8), and military officers taking charge of the troop (v. 9).[2] The *numeruswechsel* between the singular "when you go" (כי תצא) in v. 1 and the plural "when you draw near" (כקרבכם) in v. 2 has prompted Eckart Otto to separate v. 1 from the rest of the passage. Privileging congruence in structure over congruence in content, Otto argues that the discrepancy signals a switch between *erzählten Zeit* and *Erzählzeit.*[3]

Yet, v. 1 fits the rest of the passage and does more than simply situating the passage in the time of Moses. It connects the entire passage to the rest of Deuteronomy, with the mention of an "enemy larger than you" and the reassuring presence of Yhwh as a savior (see also Deut 1:27–31, 7:17–21, 9:1–3, 31:2–6). This theme is common throughout the Hebrew Bible (Josh, Judg and many Pss) and is widespread in ancient Near Eastern literature.[4] It also constitutes the central theme of vv. 2–4, which can be read as a rendering of v. 1 in direct speech.

Verses 5–8 list four reasons for not joining a military campaign. The first three are central points in what the Hebrew Bible considers "the good life." In a letter to the exiles, the character Jeremiah exhorts the Judeans in Babylon to carry out what Deuteronomy 20:5–8 considers valid reasons not to go to war: build a house, plant a vineyard and marry (Jer 29:5–6). These three things appear again in the set of curses in Deuteronomy 28. In v. 30, all three will be taken away. Finally, in 20:9, the officers appoint the leaders of the assembled fighting force.

What is not stated in vv. 1–9 is as interesting as what is stated. The envisaged troops constitute a militia, not a standing army. Ancient Near Eastern kings would lead their army into battle, but here there is no reference to a king. The law of the king in Deuteronomy 17:14–20 is equally silent over the role of the king in war. The appointment of army commanders (שרי צבאות) by the officers (שטרים) in v. 9 further emphasizes the lack of royal involvement. Were this a standing army, one would expect its head to make the speech about legitimate deferments. Thus, the troops envisaged in Deuteronomy 20 are *ad hoc*

2 Tigay, *Deuteronomy*, 186–88. His commentary provides the most extensive division; others tend to give only main divisions. The further analysis of how the Hebrew text creates the divisions is mine.

3 Otto, *Deuteronomium 12–34*, 1,563–65.

4 Otto mentions as an example an inscription by king Zakkur from Ḥamat, where his god Be'elšemajn tells him not to be afraid, because he will save him from the large group of enemies (*Deuteronomium 12–34*, 1,576).

troops that have no connection to any kingdom. Yet, they are to face powerful enemies.

The second section (vv. 10–18) considers the fate of the conquered enemies. Jeffrey Tigay identifies two subsections: the general rules (vv. 10–14) and an exception for cities in the Promised Land (vv. 15–18).[5] Technically, v. 15 marks a transition to the second topic, which begins in v. 16. Some consider vv. 15–18 a later insertion.[6]

Verses 10–14 provide general rules for conquering cities: a choice between war and surrender. Although most biblical translations render *šālôm* here as "terms of peace," immediate surrender is not rewarded by peace but by submission to forced labor (מס). Akkadian and Egyptian cognates of *šālôm* similarly occur in contexts where the meaning "voluntary submission" is clearly indicated.[7]

Verses 15–18 introduce an exception to the principle in the previous verses. Contrary to the cities that are very far from you, no option of surrender is to be offered to the cities of these people that Yhwh is giving you. These must be banned. The *hiphil* of the root *ḥrm* is generally understood in the Hebrew Bible to refer to something that is consecrated to Yhwh by means of destruction.[8] This common understanding is heavily influenced by the Arabic term *ḥarām*, which means "something that is forbidden by religious law."[9] To refer specifically to the destruction of a town, Arabic uses a different root: *ḫrm*.[10] The existence of both roots is attested in other Semitic languages. Since the letter *ḫ* does not exist in Hebrew, both meanings have been subsumed under the single root *ḥrm*. On the one hand, there is destruction, exemplified by

5 Tigay, *Deuteronomy*, 188–89.

6 Otto, *Deuteronomium 12–34*, 1,590.

7 Tigay, *Deuteronomy*, 188–89. Verses 13–14 have a connection to Num 31, the only other passage in the Hebrew Bible that has something resembling regulations for conducting war, although there it is fully embedded within the narrative. In Num 31:9 the Israelites do more or less what Deut 20:13–14 expects them to. Moshe Weinfeld argues for an influence of Num 31 on Deut 20, or at least an influence by the priestly writer he thinks is responsible for this part of Numbers (*Deuteronomy*, 239; *Deuteronomy 1–11*, 28). He argues that the Deuteronomist took a law that was about cultic importance and changed it into a law that focused on morality (*Deuteronomy 1–11*, 25–30). However, Rainer Albertz shows that the influence could also have worked the other way. He argues for a very late redaction of certain passages in Numbers, Num 31 being one of them ("Pentateuchal Redaction," 230–32).

8 Lohfink, "ḥrm," 180–199; see also the discussion in Weinfeld, "Ban," 150, n. 3.

9 In medieval Jewish texts, *ḥrm* has all but shifted to this Arabic meaning.

10 In the Arab world-view as well as ancient Near Eastern ones, all actions concerning war and destruction involve the or a deity, respectively. Nevertheless, this root does not emphasize divine involvement to the same extent as the first.

Sennacherib's destruction in Judah (2 Kgs 19:11). On the other hand, there is consecration to Yhwh through destruction, as in the storming of Jericho (Josh 6:21) or, outside the Hebrew Bible, King Mesha's slaughter of the total population of Nebo for Ashtar-Chemosh.[11]

The meaning of *ḥrm* in Deuteronomy 20:17 fits in the middle of this continuum, reflecting both meanings that are found in Arabic. Verses 16 and 18 show that Yhwh is involved, but there is no explicit reference to any form of dedication or to a ceremony that would imply such an act, as there is in Joshua 6:17. As the Hebrew Bible is constructed within a worldview that credited military victory ultimately to the victor's god, the dedication of a portion of the spoils of war to a sanctuary of that deity would not have required the total destruction of the town's inhabitants, livestock, and goods and the settlement's (re)-dedication to the conquering deity. In Deuteronomy 20:17, the term *ḥrm* also explains the disappearance of the Canaanites, while issuing a warning to remain faithful to Yhwh in the face of other religions, a common theme for Deuteronomy.

The root *ḥrm* in the *hiphil* in combination with a list of Israelite tribes appears in Moses's speech (Deut 7:1–2) and in Joshua 11:12, where the command for destruction comes from Moses and directly from Yhwh in Joshua 11:20. The reference to the command to perform *ḥrm* in the context of the direct speeches by Moses and Yhwh suggests a stronger connection of the Joshua passage with Deuteronomy 7 than with Deuteronomy 20:17, where *ḥrm* has only an indirect connection to Yhwh. The main difference between Deuteronomy 7 and Deuteronomy 20 is the role of the deity. In Deuteronomy 7:2, Yhwh delivers Israel's enemies into Israel's hands so that Israel can *ḥrm* them. While not exactly the same as Joshua 6:17, both texts imply an active act of consecration to Yhwh. In Deuteronomy 20:17, however, Yhwh's command is merely recalled; there is no presentation of its actual pronouncement, possibly because Deuteronomy 20:17 presupposes both Deuteronomy 7 and Joshua 6.

The third section (vv. 19–20) prohibits the cutting down of fruit trees when besieging a city. Tigay argues that felling fruit trees was common practice in ancient Near Eastern warfare.[12] However, as will be demonstrated below, most descriptions of war in the ancient Near East make no mention of this practice, and the ones that do imply that the policy was implemented exceptionally, in order to destroy a given city and prevent reoccupation. The exceptional nature of such destruction of food-producing trees arguably is illustrated by 2 Kings 3:19. Yhwh orders Elisha to destroy every fortified city and every choice city in

---

11 *COS* 2, 137–38. Here, the consecration to the deity is executed through full destruction, with no dedication of spoils to a sanctuary.

12 Tigay, *Deuteronomy*, 190.

Moab, to fell every “good” tree, stop up all water springs, and ruin every inheritable portion of land with stones. Israel complies in 2 Kings 3:25, and the story concludes with the single example of child sacrifice (v. 27) in the Hebrew Bible. One can take the assigning of the series of specific actions to be carried out, in this instance to Yhwh as the ultimate source of authority, to imply that these were extraordinary acts and circumstances rather than routine ones.

2 Marrying a War Captive (Deut 21:10–14)

Because Deuteronomy 20:1 and 21:10 begin with the same words (כי תצא למלחמה על איביך). Jack Lundbom and Eckart Otto see an intended connection between the two texts.[13] In their view, the unit that begins in 20:1 once would have extended to 21:14, before the insertion of 21:1–9 interrupted the original flow. It is just as likely, however, that this shared opening results from the fact that both present conditional regulations on the topic of war. In fact, Deuteronomy 23:10 opens with a similar phrase, the only difference being the replacement of the term “making war” (למלחמה) with “setting up camp” (מחנה) against your enemies, a more specific aspect of waging war. Thus, the opening conditional formula in 21:10 does not imply a direct connection with 20:1, as though it were part of an envelope structure. Instead, it indicates that 21:10–14 is a self-contained regulation.

A second argument for the connection between Deuteronomy 20 and 21 is based on a possible connection between 20:19 and 21:1, both of which use the words שדה, אדם, אדמה, כי.[14] Because the expression באדמה in 21:1 is only used elsewhere in Deuteronomy in 4:18 and Deuteronomy favors the expression בארץ to designate a location “in the land,” Lundbom argues that the use of אדם in 20:19 inspired the use of באדמה instead of בארץ in this section, to make it a nice fit.[15] The argument relies heavily on the uniqueness of the preposition ב in combination with המדא instead of the more commonly found לע; on its own, המדא is common in Deuteronomy. Thus, despite a certain similarity, there are no indications that these words reflect a deliberate change to rearrange the laws in Deuteronomy 21.

The regulation in 21:10–14 is part of a larger set of laws grouped under the common subject of family law that extends to 21:21.[16] The first law focuses on

13 Lundbom, *Deuteronomy*, 579; Otto, *Deuteronomium 12–34*, 1,625–28.

14 Rofé, “Arrangement,” 271. This argument is followed by Lundbom (*Deuteronomy*, 579).

15 Lundbom, *Deuteronomy*, 579.

16 Tigay, *Deuteronomy*, 194.

the marriage of a beautiful captive woman, involving the loss of monetary gain that would have been realized from her sale had the owner not chosen to marry her, and the prohibition to sell her later into slavery. A waiting period of a month before marriage is prescribed to ensure that the foreign woman was not pregnant when she was captured.

The shaving prescribed in v. 12 has generally been understood as part of the mourning of the captive's father and mother in v. 13.[17] A similar shaving is indicated in a text found in Mari about treating captured prisoners.[18] In the Mari text, however, the head of the woman is shaved in order to mark the loss of her previous status, either as a way to humiliate her or to mark her liminal status until new hair indicates her new situation. On analogy, the passage in Deuteronomy also could be referring to a ritual to mark the woman's transition from the status as a foreign captive to that of the wife of an Israelite.

The inability to sell her after a marriage and subsequent divorce has occurred means that the captive has somewhat transcended the status of a slave, although it does not indicate that her marriage to an Israelite makes her an Israelite wife. This law would certainly ensure the long-lasting integration of fertile women and maximize Israelite demographic growth. Since the general attitude toward foreign women in the Hebrew Bible is hostile (e.g. Deut 20:18; Num 31), the uniqueness of Deuteronomy 21 should be underlined, as it betrays a long-term economic motivation in war that differs significantly from the *ḥrm* in Deuteronomy 20:17. In light of ch. 21, the submission of the besieged city in ch. 20 can be viewed as the preferred option for the Israelites, even though the status of the married captive and any future children is left in limbo.[19]

3 Hygiene on Military Campaigns (Deut 23:10–15)

The regulation about the purity of the military camp in Deuteronomy 23:10–15 stresses the importance of keeping away from all bad things (כל דבר רע) because Yhwh is present in the camp. The "bad things" to be avoided are nocturnal emissions – specified as semen in Leviticus 15:16 – and defecation within the camp. It is significant that human excrement is not the subject of any impurity laws in the Torah. Only Ezekiel 4:12–15 reflects the natural revulsion caused

---

17 So, e.g., Tigay, *Deuteronomy*, 194.
18 Du Buit, "Quelques contacts," 576–77.
19 On the different origins of the *gēr*, see Gräber's discussion in this volume.

by excrement and designates it as "impure" (טמא). Since Deuteronomy 23:11 uses the term "pure" (טהור) and since this section is unrelated to what precedes or follows and is a self-contained regulation, the question is whether it constitutes a secondary addition, making up for the absence of excrement in the purity laws in Leviticus and Numbers. This concern for purity certainly marks a clear contrast from the previous passage that condones – if not encourages – marrying a foreigner. At the same time, however, it seems strange that it was not added to the body of purity laws in Leviticus or Numbers instead, where it would have fit more logically.

4 The Man with a "New Wife" (Deut 24:5)

The final war-related passage is 24:5, which specifies a one-year exemption from military duty to any man recently married, regardless of the number of wives. The verse is part of a larger section on matrimonial affairs in 24:1–5. Verse 5 rephrases 20:7, shifting the focus away from the husband who loses his wife when dying in battle towards the wife. Even though the Vulgate and the Peshitta rendered the text as though שמח were a *qal*, the *piel* indicates clearly that it is the husband who is to make his wife happy.

5 War in Ancient Near Eastern Texts

The best-known work in the ancient Near East that resembles a code of laws or regulations is Hammurabi's law "code," composed for the Babylonian king Hammurabi around 1750 BCE. It consists of a prologue, around 300 conditional statements, and an epilogue. The prologue focuses on the appointment of Hammurabi by the gods as a ruler, lawmaker, and protector of the weak and poor, thus granting divine status to the laws, so that breaching them would not only be a crime against Hammurabi but also against the gods. This focus on Hammurabi as the gods' instrument to serve justice is stressed again in the epilogue.

The main body has a very distinctive structure. Each law always begins with a "if" clause, *šumma* in Akkadian, roughly equivalent to the Hebrew כי in legal contexts. The *šumma*-clause sets up a conditional situation followed by a sentence that describes the solution. All examples are in third person. The very first law of Hammurabi provides an excellent example of the way these conditional statements are formulated.

> 1. If (šumma) a man accuses another man and charges him with homicide but cannot bring proof against him (end of šumma-clause), his accuser shall be killed (main clause).[20]

The same conditional structure is found in Deut 20:1.

> When/if (כי) you go to war against your enemies and see horses and chariots and an army greater than yours (end of כי-clause), do not be afraid of them (main clause), because the LORD your God, who brought you up out of Egypt, will be with you.

Deuteronomy contains examples of such conditional statements in second and third person alongside unconditional statements.[21] Thus, it does not mirror the structure used in Hammurabi's law "code" but overlaps with it in the formulation of some of its regulations. Many topics discussed in Deuteronomy 12–26 are also present in the Hammurabi collection, with closeness in wording in some instances.

Hammurabi's "code" (§ 26–41, 102–103) has some laws dealing with war. They consistently focus on how soldiers fit into the public realm and as such, they differ notably from Deuteronomy's war regulations.

> 26. If either a soldier or a fisherman who is ordered to go on a royal campaign does not go, or hires and sends a hireling as his substitute, that soldier or fisherman shall be killed; the one who informs against him shall take full legal possession of his estate.[22]

Other conditional statements mention the possibility of being recruited for the army but do not specify regulations for recruitment. Rather, they describe situations that impact civilians.

> 33. If either a captain or a sergeant should recruit(?) deserters or accepts and leads off a hireling as a substitute on a royal campaign, that captain or sergeant shall be killed.
>
> 34. If either a captain or a sergeant should take a soldier's household furnishings, oppress a soldier, hire out a soldier, deliver a soldier into the power of an influential person in a law case, or take a gift that the king gave to a soldier, that captain or sergeant shall be killed.[23]

---

20 Roth, *Law Collections*, 81.
21 The term "conditional statements" corresponds to the older idea of casuistic law, where a situation is sketched, often introduced by כי, followed by a result. "Unconditional statements" are commands with no explanation or limitations attached. For further consideration of the possible influence of legal collections on "the core," see Edelman in this volume.
22 Roth, *Law Collections*, 86.
23 Roth, 87.

The remaining war regulations acknowledge the existence of an army and regulate its impact on "civilians" but not the workings of the army itself. Laws regulating what would specifically constitute warring activities are rare in ancient Near Eastern law "codes." One example is found in a Hittite manuscript from 1650–1500 BCE, where only a single law out of two hundred relates to war. Like Hammurabi's law "code," these laws differ from Deuteronomy in only using third person conditional statements. Formulations in the second person, however, can be found in other types of Hittite texts:

> 42. If anyone hires a person, and that person goes on a military campaign and is killed, if the hire has been paid, there shall be no compensation. But if the hire has not been paid, the hirer shall give one slave.[24]

A review of other ancient Near Eastern sources that deal with regulations or instructions yields little that can be connected to the Deuteronomic regulations on war. The closest examples are the Hittite instructions to commanders of border garrisons and to the royal guard. As border regions of the Hittite Empire were often recently conquered areas, they had a high potential for rebellion. Commanders are given detailed instructions for what to do and how to do it.

> 16. He (the margrave) must keep an account of the troops of the post and put it in writing. He will know the officers of second, third, and fourth rank in (each) place. And wherever the enemy attacks, the troops are to follow the enemy's track for three days. They are to hold the roads for two days. The margrave must arrest and send before His Majesty anyone who does not kill the enemy, (whether) officer of the second, third, (or) fourth rank.[25]

The instructions to royal guards are equally specific. As they interacted closely with the king, the royal guards were to follow strict rules of behavior. These include very rudimentary things such as what to do when one needed to relieve oneself or how different groups should be dressed. There are also sections on how the groups should be organized and how they should interact in the field.

> 25. After that (there is) again an interval of one IKU. Then two men of a field unit march. They hold spears and (are) either high-ranking or low-ranking officers. They are clothed in good ceremonial garments (and) shoes like *ḫilammi*-officials. A field unit commander and an army bailiff march with them. They hold staffs.
>
> 27. The soldiers who (are) from a field unit keep the peaceful (crowd) lined up on the side. The left (group) keep (it) lined up on the left, the right (group) keep (it) lined up on the

24 Roth, 223.
25 Roth, 222.

> right. They march three IKU apart. If, however, somewhere ahead of one the road (is) narrow, he moves in tighter.[26]

Beyond the "genres" of instructions and collections of conditional regulations, a parallel to the exemption of a newlywed man in Deuteronomy 24:5 appears in the Ugaritic myth of King Keret or Kirta, a son of El. Despite his status as a demigod, he experiences many tragic events. At the start of the epic, Keret's entire family is dead. In a dream, El tells Keret that to obtain an heir, he must attack the kingdom of Udum and marry the king's granddaughter. El gives very detailed instructions on how to do this, and Keret follows them meticulously. In both episodes, the army of Keret is described; everyone is called up to the army, including five categories of those normally exempted. The newly wed bridegroom is explicitly referenced as the last category forced to join the army on this occasion.

El in the dream to Keret
"Muster Ngb and let it come forth,
the host of the troops of Ngb.
And let come forth the assembled multitude,
thy troops, a mighty force:
three hundred myriads;
serfs uncounted,
peasants untold.
They march in thousands *serried,*
and in myriads *massed.*
After two, two march;
after three, all of them.
The solitary man closes his house;
the widow hires herself out;
the sick man is carried in
(his) bed; the one-eyed man *blinks*
with one eye. And even the newly wed bridegroom goes forth: he drives to another
his wife, to a stranger his
well beloved.– (They are) like the locusts

Keret's execution of El's plan
He mu[st]ered Ngb and [it came forth, the host]
of the troops of Ng[b. And there came forth the assembled]
multitude, his [troo]ps, [a mighty force
thr[ee] hundred myriads
They marched in thousands *serried,*
and in myriads *massed.*
After two, two march;
after three, all of them.
The solitary man closes his house;
the widow hires herself
out; the sick man is carried in
(his) bed; the one-eyed man
blinks with one eye.
And *(to them) is added* the newly wed
bridegroom:
he *drives* to another his wife,
and to a stranger <his> well beloved.–"[27]

The conscription of the newlywed reveals how desperate Keret's situation is. It is an action of very last resort, while Deuteronomy signals that his exemption was to be routine. In the same way, the newly wed man drafted by Keret drives

26 Roth, 227–28.
27 Ginsberg, "Legend," 15–16, 18.

his own wife to another man even before the battle, as though all hopes that he would ever return have been given up.

The other Deuteronomic parallel with ancient Near Eastern texts is the prohibition against cutting down fruit trees during a siege in Deuteronomy 20:19–20. Tigay cited four texts to support the view that felling fruit trees was a standard practice during war or a siege. First are the annals of Pharaoh Thutmoses III (fifteenth century BCE). In the account of his campaign in Canaan, Thutmoses III is said to have cut down fruit trees during his siege of Megiddo.

> … [His majesty gave] orders to his army, saying, "Capture w[ell], capture w[ell, Oh my vi]ctorious [army!] Look, [all foreign lands are] placed [in this city according to the decree] of Re today, because very chieftain of all [northe]rn lands is bottled up within it, and because the capture of Megiddo is the capture of 1000 cities, so capture firmly, capture firmly. Lo[ok …] […] troop [comman]ders to equi[p their army in order to inform] every [man] of his position, they have measured [this] city, encircling (it) with a ditch, enclosing (it) with fresh branches of fruit trees."[28]

If the above translation is correct, all the text specifies is the cutting of fresh branches of fruit trees, rather than the use of their trunks to build siege works. The branches could have been used to "decorate" the ditch as a forceful image of the wilting of the hopes of the inhabitants of the besieged city as the siege dragged on.

The Gebal Barkal Stela states that Thutmoses III cut down all the orchards and fruit trees of the cities of an unnamed ruler across the Euphrates.

> He is a king who is valorous like Montu, who captures but no one captures from his hand, who tramples all rebellious foreign lands, there was no one to protect them in that land of Naharin because its lord had fled out of fear. I hacked up his cities and villages and set fire to them, my majesty having reduced them to mounds. They will not be repopulated, my majesty having carried off all their people as prisoners of war and their cattle without limit and their property as well. From it I took grain and plucked barley. I cut down all their orchards and all their fruit trees. Their territory has been cut off, my majesty demolished it, it having turned into […] on which there are no trees.[29]

The tone of this text is more bombastic than is the case with the siege of Megiddo and conveys a notion of total destruction much further north, in an area from which no Pharaoh ever hoped to draw revenues, contrary to Megiddo and Canaan as a whole.

The cutting down of orchards is mentioned as a literary motif on one of the Calah bulls. As a mirror image of Thutmoses's destructive spree in Mesopota-

28 *COS* 2, 12.
29 *COS* 2, 15.

mia, it is now the Assyrian king Shalmaneser III who crosses the Euphrates to lay siege to Damascus ca. 840 BCE.

> In my eighteenth regal year, I crossed the Euphrates for the sixteenth time. Hazael of Damascus trusted in the massed might of his troops; and he mustered his troops in great numbers. He made Mt. Saniru/Senir, a mountain peak, which (lies) opposite Mount Lebanon, his fortress. I fought with him. I decisively defeated him. I felled with the sword 16,000 of his troops, his fighting men. I took away from him 1,121 of his chariots, 470 of his cavalry, together with his camp. In order to save his life he ran away. I pursued after him. I confined him in Damascus, his royal city. I cut down his orchards. I marched to the mountains of Ḫaurāni. I razed, destroyed and burned cities without number. I marched to the mountains of Ba'li-rasi at the side of the sea. I erected a statue of my royalty there.[30]

A similar siege of Damascus by Tiglath-pileser III is reported a century later in the Calah Annals.

> [... of] Rezin [the Damascene ...]. [I captured] heavy [booty] [...] his advisor [...] [(With) the blood of his] war[riors] I dyed a reddish hue the river of [...], raging [torrent]; [...], his courtiers, charioteers and [...], their weapons I smashed; and [...] their horses I [...]. I captured his warriors, archers, shield- and lance-bearers; and I dispersed their battle array. That one (i.e. Rezin), in order to save his life, fled alone; and he entered the gate of his city [like] a mongoose. I impaled alive his chief ministers; and I made his country behold (them). I set up my camp around the city for 45 days; and I confined him like a bird in a cage. His gardens, [...] orchards without number I cut down; I did not leave a single one.[31]

The question is whether the felling of orchards in these last three texts – rather than the leaving of the trunks intact as in the first text – is evidence of a common Near Eastern practice as Tigay has argued, or whether these historical examples are exceptions to a norm that left fruit trees intact during war. Neither Thutmoses, as he camped in front of Megiddo, nor the Israelites, about to enter Canaan in the story-world of Deuteronomy, had an interest in destroying the orchards of cities they were about to conquer. By contrast, Shalmaneser and Tiglath-pileser III may have actually destroyed the orchards around Damascus out of spite, because they failed to conquer the city. Failure led to felling in order to weaken the economic potential of areas that were merely raided but resisted the kind of control necessary to ensure taxation in the form of the collection of regular tribute. It is more likely that felling orchards was the exception to the norm of leaving them intact.

---

30 *COS* 2, 267.
31 *COS* 2, 286.

6 A War between the "Core" and the "Frame" in Deuteronomy

The impending conquest of Canaan by the Israelites is the context of the Deuteronomic "frame"; in particular, Moses's "military speeches" (Deut 1:29–33, 2:24–25, 2:31, 3:21–22, 7:1–5, 7:16–24, 9:1–6, 11:22–5, and 31:1–6), represent one of the four types of "orations" found in Deuteronomy.[32] On the eve of the Israelites' conquest of Canaan, Moses recalls past battles, utters a rallying cry calling for courage, and promises victory in the upcoming battle. The rallying cry is usually the main point of the speech, focusing on the importance of courage and denouncing fear. Yhwh is almost always mentioned as the one who will ensure victory. These "general" military speeches transcend the context of specific battles in the Hexateuch and fit the general Deuteronomistic ideology of total war and the thorough destruction of the Canaanites to avoid religious contamination, as is exactly the case in Deuteronomy 20:15–18. Moshe Weinfeld cited the address to the troops in 20:2 as an example of these speeches in the Deuteronomic "core."[33] In this case, it would be legitimate to view the common distinction between core and frame in Deuteronomy as artificial, at least as regards theology, since a very similar message is found, for instance, in Deuteronomy 7.

That being said, is it possible that some or all of the laws relating to war could have been integral to an independent written legal core, prior to the creation of the narrative frames? On analogy with other ancient Near Eastern legal collections, it could be suggested that the war laws found presently in the "core," none of which deal explicitly with rules for engaging the enemy in battle in warring activities, are there because the larger collection focuses more extensively than other biblical legal collection on the functioning of a civilian society. Matters that affect everyday life, like the exemption of a newly married man from service, the marrying of a female prisoner-of-war, how an enemy population is to be put to use in civilian life if they surrender, or how the fruit trees of a conquered city should not be cut down because they will provide immediate economic benefit under the new regime, could be seen as logical extensions of a civilian-based collection. It is less easy to accommodate the law for cleanliness in a military camp under this rubric, unless one argues that it is anticipating the return home to civilian life of as many conscripts as possible. This is unlikely, however, since the larger concern is the religious purity of the camp, not the physical health of the soldiers.

---

32 Weinfeld, *Deuteronomy*, 45–51.

33 Weinfeld, 54.

Commentators have commonly noted the high level of "humanitarianism" associated with the war regulations.[34] Deuteronomy 20:5–9 and 24:5 in particular could be seen as examples where a humanitarian approach is highlighted over a practical one, but the central role of humanitarian conduct is clear in the other war-related regulations as well. The only exceptions are the regulation for a "pure" camp in 23:10–15 and 20:14–18, which reflects the general ideology in Deuteronomy that the Canaanites should be destroyed. The otherwise strong focus on humanitarianism is common within the book at large.[35] It is apparent, then, that the primary focus of the war regulations in Deuteronomy is on being as "humanitarian" as possible, not on conducting war *per se*. It is noteworthy that many of the war regulations revolve around the central assets of a society at large: children, food, and housing, which, as already noted, also were core Israelite/Samarian/Judahite/Judean cultural norms that defined what was necessary for a "good life": having a wife (and children), building a house, and planting a vineyard. Thus, their inclusion in a collection of other regulations designed for civilian life more generally is not as inconsistent as it might have seemed at first glance.

As it now stands, the war regulations in 20:15–18 and 23:12–14 seem to be incompatible with the "legal core." Any advocate of a pre-existent "legal core" needs to address this issue. The logical resolution would be to argue that these two regulations were added secondarily when the inner or the outer frame was created. Since 4:44–11:32 and 27:1–28:66 already presume a story-world where the Israelites are on the eve of occupying the Promised Land, they could have been added when the "law code" was first framed in the first edition of the book. At the same time, however, they could be associated with the secondary expansion, when a scribe added 1:1–4:43 and 28:67–34:12 as an outer frame. Both frames share the same overall setting. Nevertheless, if either of these stances is taken, then a further consideration would need to be entertained. Might any or all of the other war regulations have been added secondarily or simultaneously as well?

---

34 E.g. Brown, *Message*, 196. He gives Deut 20 the header, "Soldiers with a Difference."

35 Although other books of the Torah have similar "moral" or "humanitarian" laws, Deuteronomy often goes a step further and emphasizes the humanitarian aspect rather than the cultic one. For a fuller discussion, see Weinfeld, *Deuteronomy 1–11*, 19–37. He uses the perceived morality of Deuteronomy to argue for a difference between Deuteronomy and "the priestly school" in the rest of the Torah, which he argues is more focused on the cult than on moral guidelines. Although seeing this as the primary difference between Deuteronomy and the rest of the Torah is probably too one-sided (a discussion too long for this article), Weinfeld shows how the "legal core" of Deuteronomy has a strong focus on doing what is perceived as morally just.

The other way to resolve this inconsistency would be to revise the conception of the three-stage creation of the book by eliminating a pre-existent "legal core." One could then argue that the regulatory section in chs. 12–26 was created by the author of the first set of frames in Deut 4:44–11:32 and 27:1–28:66.[36] In this way, the contextual contingency of the laws would cease to be a problem, and the humanistic tendencies in chs. 12–26 would derive from the person who conceived and penned the first version of the book. However, all of these solutions raise problems of their own, and it is beyond the scope of this article to discuss them in more depth.

7 Conclusion

The regulations in Deuteronomy 20:1–20, 21:5, 23:10–15, and 24:5 are consistent with similar ancient Near Eastern texts belonging to non-regulatory genres: the exemption of newlywed men from conscription, leaving fruit-bearing tress intact during a siege, and consecrating the entire population of a conquered city to one's deity. The story-world of Deuteronomy, which sets Moses's speech on the eve of the occupation of the Promised Land, is a fitting context for all the Deuteronomic war regulations. It is still popular, however, to assume that a "legal core" predates the Mosaic story-world.

The traditional understanding of the formation of Deuteronomy, with a "legal core" to which a frame was added later, can be sustained if the war regulations in Deuteronomy 20–25 make sense without the story-world provided by the "frame." Is that the case? As demonstrated, on analogy with other ancient Near Eastern legal collections that deal with civilian law, most of the regulations in Deut 20:14–18 and 23:10–15 can be viewed as tangentially applicable to a collection of civilian regulations that reflect the assumed cultural prerequisites of the "good life": building a house, planting a vineyard, and having a family. The exceptions are the forced labor imposed on towns that accept the terms of surrender (Deut 20:10–14), the rules to maintain purity in the Israelite military camp (23:10–15), and the utter destruction of the Canaanite cities (Deut 20:15–18). Only this last passage requires the Mosaic fiction and the general ideology that the Canaanites should be utterly destroyed – though little by little (Deut 7:22), since wild beasts seem to be considered even more dangerous than the Canaanites. The first exception is consistent with the humanitarian emphasis found in Deuteronomy and is consistent with "the good life." Nevertheless,

36 For this view, see Edelman in this volume.

20:15–18 and 23:10–15 in particular are enough to show that the so-called "core" has been subject to various additions. Whether all the remaining war laws were once part of the original form of an independent "legal core" or were added as well remains inconclusive. The limits of the ability of biblical exegesis to identify additions are reached at this point.

The war laws cannot provide a definitive answer to whether the traditional hypothesis of a three-stage compositional process for Deuteronomy that involved an independent "legal core" framed twice is more cogent than one that would see a scribe assembling the bulk of chs. 12–26 for the first time when composing one or both sets of narrative frames in a single creative process that yielded the first version of Deuteronomy. The decision between the two positions becomes a matter of opinion based on the emphasis given to different aspects. What is clear, however, is that the extent of any *Urdeuteronomium* is as elusive as its date. If a legal collection ever existed before the framing material of Deuteronomy 1–11 and 27–34, it was not as extensive as what we know today as Deuteronomy 12–26.

Works Cited

Albertz, Rainer. "A Pentateuchal Redaction in the Book of Numbers?" *Zeitschrift für die alttestamentliche Wissenschaft* 125 (2013): 220–33.

Ames, Frank R. "Collateral Duties: Military Objectives and Civilian Protections in Deuteronomy." In *Worship, Women and War: Essays in Honor of Susan Niditch*, edited by John J. Collins, Timothy M. Lemos, and Saul M. Olyan, 173–82. Brown Judaic. Studies 357. Providence, RI: Brown University Press, 2015.

Brown, Raymond. *The Message of Deuteronomy: Not by bread alone*. The Bible Speaks Today series. Leicester, England and Downers Grove, IL: Inter-Varsity 1993.

Collins, John J. "The Agonistic Imagination: The Ethics of War in Deuteronomy." In *Worship, Women and War: Essays in Honor of Susan Niditch*, edited by John J. Collins, Timothy M. Lemos, and Saul M. Olyan, 183–98. Brown Judaic. Studies 357. Providence, RI: Brown University Press, 2015.

Christensen, Duane L. *Deuteronomy 1:1–21:9, Revised*. Word Biblical Commentary 6A. Nashville: Thomas Nelson, 2001.

Du Buit, M. "Quelques contacts bibliques dans les archives royales de Mari." *Revue biblique* 66 (1959): 576–81.

Frevel, Christian, Thomas Pola, and Aaron Schart. *Torah and the Book of Numbers*. Forschungen zum alten Testament 2.62. Tübingen: Mohr Siebeck, 2013.

Ginsberg, H. L. "The Legend of King Keret: A Canaanite Epic of the Bronze Age." *Bulletin of the American Schools of Oriental Research Supplementary Studies* 2/3 (1946): 1–50.

Gordon, Cyrus. "Notes on the Legend of Keret." *Journal of Near Eastern Studies* 11 (1952): 212–13.

Hallo, William W., K. Lawson Younger, Jr., eds. *The Context of Scripture: Canonical Compositions, Monumental Inscriptions, and Archival Documents from the Biblical*

World, Vol. 1: *Canonical Compositions from the Biblical World.* Leiden: Brill, 1997. Cited as *COS* 1.

Hallo, William W., K. Lawson Younger, Jr., eds. *The Context of Scripture: Canonical Compositions, Monumental Inscriptions, and Archival Documents from the Biblical World.* Vol. 2: *Monumental Inscriptions from the Biblical World.* Leiden: Brill, 2000. Cited as *COS* 2.

Hallo, William W., K. Lawson Younger, Jr., eds. *The Context of Scripture: Canonical Compositions, Monumental Inscriptions, and Archival Documents from the Biblical World.* Vol. 3: *Archival Documents from the Biblical World.* Leiden: Brill, 2002. Cited as *COS* 3.

Knoppers, Gary N. "Dissonance and Disaster in the Legend of Kirta." *Journal of the American Oriental Society* 114 (1994): 572–82.

Lundbom, Jack R. *Deuteronomy: A Commentary.* Grand Rapids, MI: Eerdmans, 2013.

Lohfink, Norbert. "*ḥrm*." In *Theological Dictionary of the Old Testament*, vol. 5: *ḥmr–YHWH*, edited by Johannes Botterweck and Helmer Ringgren, 189–99. Grand Rapids, MI: Eerdmans, 1986.

Milgrom, Jacob. *Numbers.* The JPS Torah Commentary. Philadelphia: Jewish Publication Society, 1990.

Niditch, Susan. *War in the Hebrew Bible: A Study in the Ethics of Violence.* New York: Oxford University, 1993.

Noth, Martin. *The Deuteronomistic History.* Journal for the Study of the Old Testament Supplement Series 15. Sheffield: JSOT Press, 1981.

Otto, Eckart. *Deuteronomium 1–11: 1,1–4,43.* Herders Theologischer Kommentar zum Alten Testament. Freiburg im Breisgau: Herder, 2012.

Otto, Eckart. *Deuteronomium 12–34: 12,1–23,15.* Herders Theologischer Kommentar zum Alten Testament. Freiburg im Breisgau: Herder, 2016.

Parker, Simon B. "The Historical Composition of KRT and the Cult of El." *Zeitschrift für die alttestamentliche Wissenschaft* 89 (1977): 161–75.

Plaut, W. Gunther, and David E. S. Stein. *The Torah: A Modern Commentary.* Rev. ed. New York: Central Conference of American Rabbis, 2005.

Rad, Gerhard von. *Deuteronomy: A Commentary.* Translated by Dorothea Barton. Old Testament Library. London: SCM, 1988.

Rofé, Alexander. "The Arrangement of the Laws in Deuteronomy." *Ephemerides Theologicae Lovanienses* 64 (1988): 265–87.

Roth, Martha T. *Law Collections from Mesopotamia and Asia Minor.* 2nd ed. SBL Writings from the Ancient World 6. Atlanta: Scholars, 1995.

Smoak, Jeremy D. "Building Houses and Planting Vineyards: The Early Inner-Biblical Discourse on an Ancient Israelite Wartime Curse." *Journal of Biblical Literature* 127, no. 1 (2008): 19–35.

Tigay, Jeffrey H. *Deuteronomy: The Traditional Hebrew Text with the New JPS Translation.* The JPS Torah Commentary. Philadelphia: Jewish Publication Society, 1996.

Tsai, Daisy Yulin. *Human Rights in Deuteronomy: With Special Focus on Slave Laws.* Beihefte zur Zeitschrift für die alttestamentliche Wissenschaft 464. Berlin: De Gruyter, 2014.

Versluis, Arie. *The Command to Exterminate the Canaanites: Deuteronomy 7.* Oudtestamentische Studiën 71. Leiden: Brill, 2017.

Weinfeld, Moshe. "The Ban on the Canaanites in the Biblical Codes and its Historical Development." In *History and Traditions of Early Israel: Studies Presented to Eduard*

Nielsen, May 8th 1993, edited by André Lemaire and Benedikt Otzen, 142–60. Vetus Testamentum Supplements 50. Leiden: Brill, 1993.
Weinfeld, Moshe. *Deuteronomy 1–11: A New Translation with Introduction and Commentary.* Anchor Bible 5A. New York: Doubleday, 1991.
Weinfeld, Moshe. *Deuteronomy and the Deuteronomic School.* Oxford: Clarendon, 1972.
Wright, Jacob. "Warfare and Wanton Destruction: A Reexamination of Deuteronomy 20: 19–20 in Relation to Ancient Siegecraft." *Journal of Biblical Literature* 127 (2008): 423–58.

Philippe Guillaume

Brothers in Deuteronomy: Zoom in on Lothar Perlitt's *Volk von Brüdern*

1 Introduction

Brotherhood is a fundamental notion in Deuteronomy, where the term אח occurs forty-nine times. In Hebrew, as in English, the term "brother" has a broad range of meanings. Brothers can be siblings sharing one or both parents, intimate friends, members of the same social group, or business partners. Western scholarship, however, has been keen to read Deuteronomy in light of Leviticus and thus to find in Deuteronomy the seeds of concepts that supposedly would eventually flourish in Europe: the separation of state and religion and human rights.[1]

Friedrich Schiller's *Wilhelm Tell* was a powerful source of inspiration for French revolutionaries, for Germans during the Napoleonic wars, and for the Swiss during the Second World War. In the Wilhelm Tell story, the priest Rösselmann exhorts a small assembly of local farmers to resist Habsburg tyranny by taking the solemn oath, "A folk of banded brothers we will be."[2] The oath served as a title for Lothar Perlitt's seminal 1980 article, "'*Volk von Brüdern*': Zur deuteronomischen Herkunft der biblischen Bezeichnung 'Brüder.'"[3] Transposing the narrow Swiss valleys of the Wilhelm Tell story to the valleys below Mount Nebo, where the Israelite mob awaits the signal to enter the Promised Land, the Deuteronomic brother became every "fellow Israelite."

The popularity of the Israelite *Volk von Brüdern* generated inspiring portrayals of Judahites who were to consider one another brothers, including sisters and slaves.[4] A *Bruderethik* supposedly expressed "the special relationship obtaining among members of God's people."[5]

---

1 Otto, "Human Rights"; Otto, *Das Gesetz*, 128; Tsai, *Human Rights*.

2 Translation in Scott (no date). Schiller, *Wilhelm Tell*, Act 2, end of scene 2: "Laβt uns den Eid des neun Bundes schwören. / Wir wollen sein ein einzig Volk von Brüdern ..." Perlitt, "'Ein einzig Volk," 27 notes a similar line in Count Nikolaus Zinzendorf's hymnal: "... nimm Gebet und Lieder /der eingewordenen Brüderschaft ..." (*Gesangbuch*, no. 206, 1) as well as in Plato's *Menexenos*, 239a.

3 Perlitt, "Ein einzig Volk."

4 For brothers: Otto, *Das Gesetz*, 135; for sisters: Reuter, *Kultzentralisation*, 150–53 and Otto, "False Weights," 183; and for slaves: Weinfeld, "Deuteronomy," 34.

5 Levin, "Rereading Deuteronomy," 67.

https://doi.org/10.1515/9783110713312-011

For Christoph Levin, Deuteronomy's brotherhood ethic is the result of a systematic revision of the original features of the Deuteronomic law reflecting the internal morality of the Jewish temple community in the Persian period. Forced to share the country with a population that differed ethnically and religiously, the Jewish temple community developed a morality of its own.[6] If this brotherly ethic is a feature of the Persian period, what original feature did it revise? What were the characteristics of Deuteronomy's brotherhood before the Persian era, or are we to understand that most of the forty-nine occurrences of the word "brother" in Deuteronomy were added during the Persian period in order to set apart the Jewish community from its neighbors?

Levin builds his case upon "the sections of the law book that have as their most immediate subject the ethic of brotherhood and/or the care of the poor",[7] i.e. passages dealing with credit and slaves (15:1–18), false witness (19:16–21), loss of livestock (22:1–4), interest (23:20–21), kidnapping, pledges, and wages (24:7–15), and flogging (25:1–3). Deuteronomy 23:2–9 is not discussed at all, and for good reason. This passage excludes eunuchs, bastards, Ammonites, and Moabites from the *qᵉhal-yhwh*. Though this assembly would have provided a fine hint about the purported Jewish temple community forced to share the country with a population that differed ethnically and religiously, Deuteronomy 23:8–9 grants admission to Edomites and third generation Egyptians into the *qᵉhal-yhwh*, in particular because the Edomite is your brother. Obviously, Edomite brothers as members of the *qᵉhal-yhwh* hardly fit a Jewish temple community trying to distinguish itself from ethnically and religiously different neighbors. Levin would have had to decide whether the Edomite brothers were an original feature of Deuteronomy or if they belonged to a different redactional stage. It was easier to simply ignore 23:2–9.

This chapter provides a systematic analysis of the occurrences of the word אח throughout Deuteronomy to find out how often the brother refers to a fellow Israelite, where in Deuteronomy this sense occurs, which other meanings of the term appear in the book, and what the implications of these other meanings are.

2 *אח* in Deuteronomy

Table 1 lists the 49 occurrences of the term אח, with their renderings in the NRSV.

6 Levin, 70–71.

7 Levin, 51.

Tab. 1: The word אח in Deuteronomy.

Deut	MT	Context	NRSV
1:16.16	שׁמע בין אחיכם ושׁפטתם בין אישׁ ובין אחיו ובין גרו	Arbitration	Give the members of your community a fair hearing, and judge rightly between one person and another, whether citizen or alien.
1:28	אחינו המסו את לבבנו	War	Our kindred made our hearts melt
2:4.8	אחיכם/אחינו בני עשׂו	Edom	your kindred/our kin, the descendants of Esau
3:18.20	תעברו לפני אחיכם בני ישׂראל	War	cross over armed as the vanguard of your Israelite kin
10:9	לא היה ללוי חלק עם אחיו	Land	no allotment for Levi with his kindred
13:7	אחיך בן עמך	Apostasy	your brother, your father's son or your mother's son
15:2.3	לא יגשׂ את אחיו / את אחיך תשׁמט ידך	Debts	a member of the/your community
15:7a	אביון מאחד אחיך באחד שׁעריך בארצך	Loans	a member of your community
15:7b.9	אחיך האביון / לאחיך לעניך	Loans	your needy neighbor
15:11b	אחיך עני ואביון בארצך	Alms?	poor and needy neighbor in your land
15:12	אחיך העברי או העבריה	Antichresis	a member of your community, whether a Hebrew man or a Hebrew woman
17:15.15	אישׁ נכרי אשׁר לא אחיך הוא	King	a foreigner who is not of your community
17:20	רום לבבו מאחיו	King	exalting himself above other members of the community
18:2.7	נחלה לא יהיה לו בקרב אחיו	Prebends	other members of the community/fellow-Levites

Tab. 1 (continued)

Deut	MT	Context	NRSV
18:15.18	נביא מקרבך מאחיך / אחיהם	Prophet	your/their own people
19:18.19	עד שקר ענה באחיו	False witness	another
20:8	לא ימס את לבב אחיו	War	making the hearts of his comrades melt
22:1–4 (6x)	שור אחיך...	Stray animals	neighbor
23:8	כי אחיך הוא	Edom	they are your kin
23:20.21	לא תשיך לאחיך נשך	Loans	to another Israelite you may not charge interest
24:7	נפש מאחיו מבני ישׂראל	Kidnap	other Israelite
24:14	שׂכיר עני ואביון מאחיך או מגרך אשר בארצך בשעריך	Salaries	poor and needy laborers, whether other Israelites or aliens
25:3	ונקל אחיך לעיניך	Punishment	your neighbour will be degraded in your sight
25:5–9 (4x)	כי ישבו אחים יחדו	Undivided estate	When brothers reside together ...
25:11	אנשים יחדו איש ואחיו	Brawl	men in a fight with one another
28:54	תרע עינו באחיו	Famine	begrudge food to his own brother
32:50	אהרון אחך	Sibling	your brother Aaron
33:9	ואת אחיו לא הכיר	Tribe	he ignored his kin
33:16	נזיר אחיו	Tribe	Joseph prince among his brothers
33:24	רצוי אחיו	Tribe	Asher, favorite of his brothers

Faced with the double challenge of inclusive language and brotherly ethics, modern translations tend to render the Deuteronomic brother as a genderless "kin/kindred," a "member of your community," or "an Israelite." In more sensitive matters, however, one has felt a need to broaden the scope of generosity. Hence, the NRSV urges the addressee to give alms and grant loans to a neighbor (Deut 15:7–11), to return the stray animals of one's neighbor (Deut 24:1–4), and to avoid humiliating a guilty neighbor with more than forty lashes (Deut 25:3). Limiting these benevolent measures to brothers appears not to square well with the common understanding of Deuteronomy's brotherly ethics and even less with its purported humanitarianism.

In eleven cases, the Deuteronomic brother is indeed a fellow Israelite, as indicated by direct references to episodes mentioned in the books of Exodus and Numbers (Deut 1:16 twice, 1:28, 3:18, 3:20, 18:15, 18:18)[8] or to the twelve-tribe system: Levi deprived of land among his brothers (Deut 10:9, 18:2), Joseph as prince among his brothers, and Asher the favorite among his brothers (Deut 33:16, 33:24).

The Levites, however, constitute a "brotherhood" of their own. They are granted privileges that set them apart from other Israelites (Deut 18:1–5).[9] Thus, all Israelites are not equal.

In five cases, the word "brother" is used in a narrow sense: for a fellow tribesman (Levi again in 18:7), a true sibling in reference to apostasy (13:7) and to famine (28:54), and to Aaron and Levi (32:50; 33:9).

In two cases, a specification is added to the term "brother." The kidnap of someone belonging to a brother *from the sons of Israel* is liable to the death penalty (24:7). Whether the kidnap of someone who does not belong to an Israelite is liable to a less severe penalty is not clear. What is clear is that the writer felt the need to insist that the owner of the kidnapped person must be an Israelite. Does this mean that a brother need not necessarily be an Israelite? The same question arises in Deuteronomy 17:15, where the king must not be a foreigner who is not your brother (איש נכרי אשר לא אחיך). In this case, the brothers over whom the chosen king should not elevate himself (17:20) may not all be Israelites. Both instances could suggest that some brothers are not fellow Israelites. Who could these non-Israelite brothers be?

According to Eckart Otto, the heavy insistence on the Israeliteness of the king is a reaction against positive descriptions of non-Israelite rulers in Isaiah

---

8 Judges appointed in the wilderness (Exod 18:13–26), Horeb (Exod 20:18), spies sent in Canaan (Numbers 13) and the Transjordan tribes serving as vanguard (Num 32:17–42). On Deut 18:18–22, see Turton in this volume.

9 See Rossi in this volume.

44:28, 45:1 and Jeremiah 25:9, 27:6, and 43:10.[10] An answer from Deuteronomy itself would carry more weight. The Israeliteness of the king is the direct result of the presence of non-Israelite brothers, the sons of Esau and Edomites, encountered three times in the book, in 2:4, 2:8 and 23:8. The Israelite king should be a brother as well as a non-foreigner; otherwise, an Edomite brother would qualify to rule Israel, something Deuteronomy 15:6 warns against: "You will rule over many nations, but they will not rule over you." The presence of Edomite brothers equally explains why the death penalty applies specifically to the kidnap of persons belonging to a brother from the sons of Israel (24:7).

This leaves twenty-five occurrences of the term אח to be discussed point by point to reach a more precise view of the Deuteronomic brotherhood.[11]

3 Other Brothers as Fellow Israelites?

Deuteronomy 15, which deals with money matters, is a pivotal chapter for understanding Deuteronomic ethics. Therefore, I will establish the sense of the remaining 18 passages where אח occur that have not yet been discussed before turning to the seven occurrences of "brother" in ch. 15 and the related one in 23:20–21.

3.1 Brothers in Court (Deut 19:18–19)

In Deuteronomy 19:18–19, the brothers who are to receive a fair hearing (1:16) and the witness who accuses his brother falsely (Deut 19:18–19) can be classified as references to fellow Israelites. The entire passage describes daily life at home among neighbors and brothers. These then bring the count of uses of "brother" to designate an Israelite to thirteen.

3.2 Brothers in Arms (Deut 20:8)

The justification for sending home a timorous fighter in 20:8 uses the same expression found in the disheartening report of the spies concerning the cities

10 Otto, *Deuteronomium 12,1–23,15*, 1,482–84.

11 16 references to Israelites (1:16 twice, 1:28, 3:18, 3:20, 10:9, 17:15 twice, 17:20, 18:2, 18:15, 18:18, 18:20 24:7, 33:16, 33:24) + 5 reference to tribesmen (13:7, 18:7, 28:54, 32:50, 33:9) + 3 references to Edomites (2:4, 2:8, 23:8) + 25 additional occurrences (15:2–12 (7 times), 19:18, 19:19, 20:8, 22:1–4 (6 times), 23:20, 23:21, 24:14, and 25:3–11 (6 times) = 49.

to be conquered in 1:28: "to make our heart melt." Read in light of ch. 1 where the brothers are indeed fellow Israelites, the brothers in arms of ch. 20 are also Israelites. If, however, Deuteronomy 20:5–9 was part of an older core, in that context it could have had in mind *gērîm* liable to military conscription in exchange for land grants within Israel. In this case, the brothers in arms were not necessarily all Israelites. Therefore, these brothers cannot be added to the list of indisputable fellow Israelites.

3.3 A Brother's Stray Animal and Lost Garment (Deut 22:1–4)

The rules regarding the return of lost property use the term "brother" to designate the rightful owner (22:1–4). The NRSV broadens the application of that "law" by rendering אח as "neighbor." Yet, apart from the garment mentioned in v. 3, it is wealthy owners who are more likely to suffer the loss of a bull or cow, a sheep or goat, or a donkey and other property, because they own more assets than ordinary farmers and are unable to supervise them as closely as the owners of smaller flocks would. Delegating the supervision to hired staff was a stopgap solution; remember the parable of the unjust steward (Lk 16:1–13). It is the distance (קרוב) mentioned in v. 2 that makes these rules particularly relevant. Most inhabitants of a given village would have known exactly who owned the few bulls and oxen locally. The presence of a new ox in the village would be immediately known to everyone. An extra sheep or goat may more easily pass unnoticed, though each family literally ear-marked its animals, for instance with a distinguishing slit in one ear.[12] A sheep with a different marking would not escape the attention of neighbors for long and would soon earn its receiver the reputation of a sheep-stealer. Were the mark that of a neighbor, the stray would be immediately returned to its local owner. Only if the mark was unknown locally could the animal be considered a stray.

Distance is again present in v. 4. The over-burdened donkey is transporting goods away from home or to its home settlement. The relevance of the entire passage is proportional to the physical distance that separates the brothers. Though settings within local settlements are not excluded, the brothers in question are more likely to be living in different settlements. They may be siblings or associates, but hardly neighbors who would by definition know the owner of the stray assets. Of course, as siblings, these brothers would be fellow Israelites. As associates, however, one might be one of the omnipresent *gērîm*. Therefore, these six mentions of brothers are not necessarily referring to fellow Israelites.

12 Dalman, *Arbeit*, 185.

3.4 A Brother's Day Laborer (Deut 24:14)

Deuteronomy 24:14–15 stipulates the daily payment of the wages of a poor or needy hired laborer "from your brother" or from "your *gēr*" in your land, in your gates. The particle *mem* in front of "your brother" and in front of "your *gēr*" (מאחיך או מגרך) can be interpreted either partitively or comparatively. The partitive sense is preferred by the majority of scholars, who see it to designate the poor and needy laborer himself, thus constituting "your brother" or your *gēr*. As the *gēr* in Deuteronomy forms, with the orphan and the widow, a group that is most frequently designated as *personae miserae*, the *gēr* as much as the brother in 24:14 is commonly understood as the poor laborer.[13]

In fact, the triad consisting of the *gēr*, the orphan, and the widow is never combined in Deuteronomy with the *'ebyôn* or the *'ānî*.[14] Brothers are encouraged to give alms to a poor brother (Deut 15:11), never to a poor orphan or a poor widow. Therefore, Deuteronomy's *gēr*, orphan, and widow are precisely the categories that should not be designated *personae miserae*, because, with the Levite, they are the exclusive beneficiaries of the triennial tithes.

Whatever the yield of any particular year, they receive their share and thus share the common lot, be it abundance or dearth. Hence, Deuteronomy's *gēr*, orphan, and widow are never destitute, contrary to a brother who may end up in poverty despite the release of his debts (Deut 15:3). Granted, it is somewhat counter-intuitive to understand that brothers are at risk of poverty when orphans and widows are not. It is counter-intuitive to grasp that a brother may need alms but not orphans or widows. Yet, it is exactly what Deuteronomy's brotherly ethics imply. *Gērîm*, orphans, and widows are not brothers. As such, they have no share in communal land. This is why they are beneficiaries of the triennial tithe; they receive a share of the food produced on communal land. Contrary to widows and orphans, however, *gērîm* may cultivate land granted by an imperial overlord (see above point 3.2), but this land would be taken from the vast reserve of previously uncultivated land near Israelite settlements or from the share of communal land previously owned by a local Israelite brother who was executed or exiled for whatever reason.

The failure to understand the implications of the Deuteronomic economy has turned Deuteronomy's brotherly ethics into a mere humanistic stance. For instance, Mark A. Awabdy accepts that "D imagines a society in which one can

---

13 Tigay, *Deuteronomy*, 226–27. McConville, *Deuteronomy*, 362–63.

14 Lohfink 1990, "Das deuteronomische Gesetz," 37; Lohfink, "Poverty," 43; Gräber in this volume.

be a גר, orphan, or widow without being poor and needy,"[15] but he fails to apply this view to the *gēr* in Deuteronomy 24:14. Instead, he reads this verse as a reference to an impoverished native (the brother) and an impoverished *gēr* and argues that although the גר, orphan, and widow do not represent a separate class of the poor, "they have the potential, just as the native does, to become impoverished."[16] In fact, the opposite is true. The *gēr*, the orphan, and the widow are the only ones who are protected from the threat of total destitution. Their revenues will be lower in bad years, just as those of the brothers. The brother, however, has a greater potential of impoverishment because it is proportional to his potential of enrichment obtained from the risky non-agricultural financial activities described in ch. 15.

Reading the *mems* comparatively, v. 14, states that the hireling is poorer and needier (עָנִי וְאֶבְיוֹן) than "your brother" and/or "your *gēr*" who is in your land, inside your gates. In this case, your brother and your *gēr* act as employers, not employees. They may indeed be better off than the hirelings they employ, but not necessarily so. Before or after their own grains, grapes, and olives are harvested, they may well join the harvest gangs working on another's land and orchards. Hence, being a hireling has no implication regarding one's wealth. A hireling may indeed be a true *persona misera* if all he owns is his physical ability to provide labor for others. In Deuteronomy, however, this case may be more relevant to the Hebrew and Hebrewess of 15:12–17 than to the hirelings of ch. 22.

Reading the *mems* partitively is another option. It avoids the pitfalls of the comparative option. "Your brother and your *gēr*" are the employers of the poor and needy day laborers in question. Both must pay the wages of the hirelings daily because they are providing occasional labor beyond their usual economic network, where work days are one currency among others and thus do not require immediate compensation. Like this *gēr*, the "brother" in question here may be any fellow Israelite with a sufficiently large estate to require a hired day laborer or an Edomite brother in the same position. In this case, there is no contradiction between the needy laborer in v. 14 and the eradication of need among brothers in 15:4.

3.5 Only Forty Lashes for a Guilty Brother (Deut 25:3)

The number of lashes to punish a man found guilty is limited to a maximum of forty (25:3) lest "your brother be degraded in your eyes". The case is introduced

15 Awabdy, *Immigrants*, 109, 214.

16 Awabdy, 89.

as a dispute between men (אנשים), but v. 3 applies the limitation of the number of lashes specifically to "your brother," leaving behind the men and the guilty one (הרשע) of the previous verses. Either the maximum of forty lashes applies only to a brother, or the term "brother" designates any guilty man, whether *gēr*, slave, Hebrew, or foreigner. In both cases, the aim is to protect the honor of the guilty one from being degraded beyond repair in the eyes of others. Are these others a narrow circle of equals, or do they include all other men witnessing the flogging? At this stage, both options are possible, but putting the punishment by flogging in relation to capital punishment brings to light some interesting differences.

The death penalty is to take the form of hanging (21:23) or of stoning for any man or woman guilty of idolatry (17:5), for a rebellious son (21:21), an adulteress (22:20), and a betrothed virgin and her rapist (22:24–25). Stonings are public executions at the gate of the local settlement, in the presence of witnesses. Hanging the corpse on a tree makes the public display of the execution last until sunset. Significantly, brothers are never mentioned in reference to capital punishment. This may be incidental. Or, read in light of the limit of forty lashes, it could suggest that the highest punishment to be inflicted on a brother is forty lashes. It is also significant that the flogging of the guilty brother occurs in front of a judge, with no reference to witnesses and no audience beyond other brothers. Gates are not mentioned, as though the flogging is to occur behind closed doors. If more than forty lashes would degrade the brother in the eyes of his brothers, a single lash would degrade him even more in front of his entire village. None of these points is decisive, but they would support the notion of a narrow circle of brothers that deals with its own delinquents in its own way, as it deals with the debts of a defaulter in its ranks (ch. 15). Therefore, Deuteronomy 25:3 cannot be taken as an indisputable case of a brother as a fellow Israelite.

3.6 Partners in Joint Ventures (Deut 25:5–11)

The next cases concern brothers who would often be siblings, though not necessarily so. The first case is the death of a brother who sat or resided together (ישׁבו אחים יחדו Deut 25:4–9) with another brother. "Residing together" implies more than co-residence. It refers to partners working an undivided estate, as would siblings who inherited their father's estate and decided to cultivate it in partnership instead of splitting it between themselves. In the sense of "sitting together," the verb ישׁב has a broader scope that could involve partners who were not necessarily siblings as well. In either case, the death of the heirless partner raises the issue of who inherits his assets. To prevent his assets from passing to a son born after the widow remarried outside the partnership, the surviving partner must "raise the name" of the dead partner by fathering a post-mortem heir through the widow.

The case of the brawling brothers seems unrelated to the previous one, but its placement in v. 11 immediately after the case of the brothers who resided together is not as haphazard as it might otherwise seem. The focus is on the wife of one of the brothers who grabs the genitals, literally the "shameful parts" (מבושים) of her husband's brother. The penalty seems disproportionate, unless the grabbing results in the loss of fertility.[17] What is to be cut off is not the hand but the palm (כף), possibly one or several fingers of the grabbing wife.[18]

The culprit is not any woman and the victim is not any man. The case deals specifically with a woman who grabbed the genitals of her husband's brother. The underlying matter is the same as for the partner who died before fathering an heir: inheritance of the assets. The difference is the timing. The grabbed brother does not die right away, but a successful grabbing would leave him without an heir if he had not already fathered one. The wife of the grabbed brother's opponent is singled out precisely because she is the one whose sons would benefit the most from the infertility of her husband's "brother," be that a sibling or a business partner. Whereas in vv. 4–9 untimely death leaves one brother heirless, in v. 11 the lack of an heir is the result of wilful emasculation. The penalty is harsh precisely because the sterility of the partner is in the interest of the wife of the non-sterile "brother" whose sons would inherit the assets of the entire estate or business rather than only those of their own father if both partners had sons.

The brothers in both cases could be siblings, fellow Israelites, or partners who have pooled assets to set up a *ḫarrānu* business venture.[19] As the matter of genitals arises again in the requirements for admission into the *qᵉhal-yhwh* (Deut 23:2), to which belong Edomite brothers and third generation Egyptians (Deut 23:8–9), in both cases the Israelite partner could happen to be an Edomite brother. Therefore, none of the six occurrences of the word אח in Deuteronomy 25 can be considered an indisputable reference to fellow Israelites.

---

17 As argued by Paul, "Biblical Analogues," 337 against previous suggestions of genital mutilation by Eslinger, "Case of an Immodest Lady," or genital shaving by Walsh, "You Shall Cut Off."

18 Jacobs, "Instrumental Talion," 275.

19 This type of venture involves one or more silent partners who advance capital to one or more acting partners who run the business. The partners usually share profit and losses equally. So e.g. Jursa et al., *Aspects*, 206–14. For examples, see e.g. Pearce and Wunsch, *Documents of Judean Exiles*, nos. 40, 60, and 97.

At this stage, only the two brothers mentioned in Deuteronomy 19:18–19 can be added to the initial twenty-one fellow Israelites identified above, leaving twenty-three potential non-Israelite brothers out of the total of forty-nine: 49 – 23 fellow Israelites + 3 Edomites = 23. So far, fourteen uses of "brother" have been identified as not necessarily referring to Israelites (20:8, 22:1–4 [6 times], 24:14, 25:3–11 [6 times]). The occurrences of the word אח in 15:2–12 and the 23:20–21 remain to be considered.

3.7 Arrears of a Neighbor, Too? (Deut 15:2–3)

The double mention of "his neighbor" in the introductory verse (רעהו 15:2) is the cornerstone of the notion of Deuteronomic humanitarianism and brotherly ethics. Verses 1–2 set out the prescriptions relative to the debt release (*šemiṭṭah*, שׁמטה) at the end of the seventh year. The principle of the release is binding on the writer's brother, addressed as "you": "At the end of the seventh year, you will do a release" (מקץ שׁבע שׁנים תעשׂה שׁמטה, verse 1). Verse 2a continues with third person singular forms:

וזה דבר השמטה שמוט כל בעל משה ידו אשר ישה ברעהו

This is the manner of the release: every creditor is to drop any loan held against *his neighbor*.

The release is designated as outstanding debts held against a *neighbor*. Verse 2b further explains the release procedure by indication of what should *not* be done:

לא יגשׂ את רעהו ואת אחיו כי קרא שׁמטה ליהוה

No one shall press his neighbor and *his brother* when a release for Yhwh has been declared.

Brother and neighbor are mentioned side by side, as though the terms אח and רע were synonymous, although the *waw* between the two direct objects can also be translated "or" instead of "and." The next sixteen verses delineate the practical application of the *šemiṭṭah* and of labor contracts, using over sixty second person singular prefixes and suffixes that all refer to "your brother"; "his neighbor" (רעהו) never occurs again in ch. 15. Yet, exegetes are keen to discover a humanitarian trait in the release of the debts of neighbors, even some consider the words "and his brother" (את אחיו) to be a secondary and thus negligible addition.[20]

20 For the secondary addition, see e.g. Perlitt, "'Ein einzig Volk,'" 33.

Therefore, Deuteronomy's *Volk von Brüdern* is actually a people of neighbors, read more or less consciously in light of the command to love one's neighbor in Leviticus 19:18. On the basis of this argumentation, Christoph Levin reconstructs the growth of Deuteronomy 15 word by word in six steps:

1. the *Vorlage* used by the Deuteronomic editor from Exodus 21:1–11 and 23:10–11;
2. the reworking of these instructions by the Deuteronomic editor;
3. a historical redaction, which inserted Deuteronomy in the Exodus narrative;
4. a covenant-theology revision;
5. a brotherhood ethic revision;
6. a debate over whether or not there shall remain any poor.

Quoting himself, Levin argues that "Deuteronomy's brotherhood ethic did not belong to the original features of the law, as has often been thought, but that it, too, is a later insertion."[21] The thrust of this six-stage development is to ensure that the brotherhood ethics is a development late enough to be attributed to a purported Jewish temple community of the Persian period that developed a morality of its own to differentiate itself from the *goyim* with whom it was forced to share the country.[22] Alternatively, in her article in this volume, Diana Edelman argues that a single creative writer could have produced Deuteronomy by combining various genres.

Whatever the date of ch. 15, Levin rightly notes that the Septuagint ignores the words "his neighbor and" in 15:2 and limits the practical application of the release to "his brother" only:

> ἀφήσεις πᾶν χρέος ἴδιον ὃ ὀφείλει σοι ὁ πλησίον καὶ τὸν ἀδελφόν σου οὐκ ἀπαιτήσεις
> you shall remit every personal debt which your neighbor owes you, and you shall not ask it back of your brother (NETS).

The other textual differences besides the Septuagint reveal a debate over the crucial issue of who exactly should benefit from the *šemiṭṭah*. Two opposite strategies can be seen at work in 15:2, either inflating or deleting.

In light of the Septuagint, it is possible to argue that the Masoretic text reflects the inflationary tendency: the words "his neighbor and" were added to an older form of the Hebrew transmitted by the LXX. In this case, the older Hebrew text of v. 2a set out a general rule (remission of a neighbor's debt) followed by the practical application of that rule to brothers in v. 2b. In light of

21 Levin, "Rereading Deuteronomy," 52, quoting Levin, "Das Deuteronomium."
22 Levin, "Rereading Deuteronomy," 70–71.

Otto's distinction between *lex generalis* and *lex specialis* for slaughter in Deuteronomy 12,[23] it could be argued that the neighbor in v. 2a belongs to the *lex generalis*, while the brother in v. 2b reflects the *lex specialis*. Otto does not do so himself, however; instead, he argues that the Greek translators deleted the second occurrence of the word "neighbor." They supposedly considered it superfluous because it already was mentioned in the first part of the verse.[24]

Otto is correct if, without the second "neighbor," the Greek text is the *lectio facilior*. The juxtaposition of "his neighbor" and "his brother" in v. 2b is awkward. It is clear that the Greek translator separated them by introducing the first clause with ἀφήσεις to make the neighbor the beneficiary of the release of "every personal debt that your neighbor owes you" (ἀφήσεις πᾶν χρέος ἴδιον ὃ ὀφείλει σοι ὁ πλησίον) and then adding, "and you shall not ask it back of your brother" (καὶ τὸν ἀδελφόν σου οὐκ ἀπαιτήσεις).

The argument, however, can be reversed. If the Greek translator improved the version transmitted in the Masoretic text, a clearer reading for the whole of v. 2 would have been obtained by deleting the brother rather than the second neighbor in v. 2b. This is exactly what is attested by a single Hebrew witness mentioned in the critical apparatus of the Biblia Hebraica Stuttgartentia, which suggests one delete ואת אחיו to obtain a smoother reading involving neighbors only. This suggestion contradicts the basic rule of textual criticism, since it is attested by a single manuscript (4QDeut^c^). With no brother at all, Deuteronomy 15:2 would have requested the remission of all debts held against any neighbor, as humanitarian readings do, thus avoiding the issue of the difference between a neighbor and a brother.

The Samaritan Pentateuch provides another take on the issue. In the Samaritan text, the second occurrence of the word רעהו in 15:2b is sometimes attested without the conjunction between "his neighbor" *and* "his brother."[25] The missing copula can be interpreted as a *lapsus calami*, a scribe having simply missed the copula. Or, the missing copula represents an intermediary phase between an older Hebrew version attested in the LXX with no neighbor in v. 2 and the reading attested in the Masoretic text with both "his neighbor and" "his brother" but without the copula:

LXX's Vorlage*	לא יגש את אחיו כי קרא שמטה ליהוה
Intermediary text (one Hebrew ms + SP)	לא יגש את רעהו את אחיו כי קרא שמטה ליהוה
Final text (MT)	לא יגש את רעהו ואת אחיו כי קרא שמטה ליהוה

23 Otto, *Deuteronomium 12,1–23,15*, 1,312.
24 Otto, 1,329.
25 Von Gall, *Der hebräische Pentateuch*, 396.

With no copula, the intermediary text sets the brother in apposition to the neighbor: "no one shall press his neighbor, i.e. his brother" (את רעהו את אחיו), to specify that the beneficiary of the release is actually a brother. With the mere addition of the copula between "his neighbor" and "his brother," the final text extends the release to the debts of neighbors, too.

The Septuagint reflects the apposition of the brother to the neighbor by presenting the *lex generalis* in v. 2a (πλησίον) and then the *lex specialis* (ἀδελφός) in v. 2b. "No one shall press his neighbor, i.e. his brother." The absence of any neighbor in the rest of the chapter shows that the release concerns first and foremost, if not exclusively, the debts held against brothers.

Finally, a single Dead Sea scroll fragment preserves a section of Deuteronomy 15:2. Dated paleographically between 150 and 100 BCE, 4Q30 (4QDeut^{c}) fragment 26, line 4(3) has neither neighbor nor brother in v. 2b: לא] יגש כי קרא שמ[טה. Despite its fragmentary state, this line states "d[o not collect when a release has been called]," clearly omitting את רעהו ואת אחיו.[26]

Is the omission of "his brother and his neighbor" a *lectio facilior* or a *lectio difficilior*? A firm answer would require the full text of v. 2 to know if a neighbor or a brother or both were mentioned in the first part of the verse. Unfortunately, the last two words of v. 2a are not preserved. It begins with וזה ד[בר at line 2. As line 3 begins with v. 2b, it is clear that more than half of the column is preserved and that only a dozen letters are missing. There is space for one or two words where the Masoretic text has eight words (שמוט כל בעל משה ידו אשר ישה ברעהו). There is no way to decide whether there was any brother or neighbor in the void, but it is clear that 4QDeut^{c} transmitted a shorter version of Deuteronomy 15:12, for both parts of the verse:

- With a neighbor in the void, 4QDeut^{c} had the *lex generalis* in v. 2 and the *lex specialis* in the next verses mentioning "your brother."
- With neither neighbor nor brother in the void, 4QDeut^{c} also had the *lex generalis* in v. 2 and the *lex specialis* in the next verses mentioning "your brother."
- With a brother in the void, 4QDeut^{c} had no *lex generalis* in v. 2. The brother was mentioned throughout.

In Deuteronomy 15:2, the identification of textual improvements, either through deletions or additions, is not secure, and the recovery of the earliest form of the verse by comparing the available textual witnesses remains speculative.[27] Nevertheless, with or without neighbor, brother, and copula between them, the

26 Crawford, "4QDeutc," 24; Ulrich, *Biblical Qumran Scrolls*, 211.
27 McCarthy, *Deuteronomy*, 98*.

practical application of the release concerns the debts held against a brother. This brother may be a fellow Israelite, a sibling, a friend, an associate, a fellow tribesman, or even an Edomite.

3.8 No Shortage among Brothers (Deut 15:4)

Recognizing the difference between brothers and Israelites resolves the incoherence between Deuteronomy 15:4, which promises an absence of shortage among brothers, and v. 11a, which recognizes ongoing shortage outside the brotherhood, i.e. "in the land":

> אפס כי לא יהיה בך אביון (Deut 15:4a)
> There will, however, be no one in need among you
>
> כי לא יחדל אביון מקרב הארץ (Deut 15:11a)
> Since there will never cease to be some in need within the land

"Among you" in v. 4 refers to the brothers mentioned in v. 3. The promise of v. 4 is conditioned by the application of the release of a brother's debt, not the debts of neighbors. Brothers are "among you" while neighbors are "in the land" where, according to v. 11, need and shortage prevail.

The difference between the brotherhood and the land justifies two different attitudes regarding the practice of credit:

In the brotherhood	*šemiṭṭah*	no shortage	lend to many *goyim* (Deut 15:2–6)
In the land	no *šemiṭṭah*	shortage	open the hand to brother and needy ones (Deut 15:11)

It may seem counter-intuitive to derive the absence of shortage from the practice of the *šemiṭṭah*. Yet, from an economic point of view, it is crucial to purge the credit market regularly, identify borrowers in dire straits, clean their slates even when no interest is accruing, and protect the actors on the credit market by excluding bad payers.

From a rhetorical point of view, the promises of prosperity conditioned by the application of these measures (Deut 15:4–6) lose all credibility if the *šemiṭṭah* is unable to protect brothers from serious impoverishment. For this reason, it is crucial to identify the beneficiary of alms in v. 11.

3.9 Alms for a Destitute Brother? (Deut 15:11b)

After the recognition that needs and shortages are the rule "in the land" (Deut 15:11a), v. 11b urges the addressee, a brother, to open his hand a second time:[28]

> תפתח את ידך לאחיך לעניך ולאביונך בארצך

The NRSV fuses the three beneficiaries of generosity into a single category: "Open your hand to the poor and needy neighbor in your land," not to "your brother, to your poor, and to your needy in your land," as the text states. This poor and needy neighbor is the result of three presuppositions:
- the brother (אחיך) is any neighbor;
- the words עני and אביון are somewhat synonymous;
- the copula between עניך and אביונך can be ignored.

The distinction between the brother's status before the *šemiṭṭah*, when he is needy (אביון), and after the *šemiṭṭah*, when he has become עני, is missed when the last four words of Deuteronomy 15:11 (לאחיך לעניך ולאביונך בארצך) are compounded into a single category: the poor. The conjunction *waw* between לעניך ולאביונך can be understood either to split the beneficiaries of the open-hand gesture into two distinct categories, לאחיך לעניך and אביונך בארצך, or as setting off the final element in a list of three recipients. In the first case, "your hard-toiling one" would stand in apposition to "your brother," and "your needy one" would be qualified by the adverbial phrase, "in your land." The addressee would be urged to be equally charitable to "your brother, i.e. your hard-toiling one,"[29] and to the "your needy one in your land." In the second case, the brother would be urged to be equally charitable to three categories of persons: "your brother, your hard-toiling one, and your needy in the land." In the first case, charitable gifts rather than loans are to be given to a brother in dire straits who has become a physical laborer to make ends meet; in the second, a brother is to be extended charity long with others who need it, implying through analogy that his circumstances have become precarious but not stating this outright, as in the first instance.

On the one hand, the words עני and אביון are taken as synonyms to designate a poor and needy brother. On the other hand, עני refers to manual labor

---

28 The first time is in v. 7, in order to urge a brother to grant a loan to a needy brother despite the closeness of the release.

29 עני implies hard toil rather than destitution, as does πένης, its Greek equivalent in the LXX. See Coin-Longeray, "Πενία."

rather than destitution, thus setting apart a toiling brother who finds himself excluded from preferential credit conditions following the release of his debts, to a general category of beggars in the land who survive from hand to mouth thanks to charity. Whether in the land himself or equated with others in the land, there is nothing indicating that the brother in question has to be a fellow Israelite.

3.10 A Hebrew Brother? (Deut 15:12–18)

Whereas the issue in Deuteronomy 15:2 is the relationship between "brother" and "neighbor," vv. 12–18 deal with the relationship between brothers and Hebrews:

> כי ימכר לך אחיך העברי או העבריה (Deut 15:12)

Ever since the Septuagint, this Hebrew or Hebrewess have been identified with the brother who precedes them:

> Ἐὰν δὲ πραθῇ σοι ὁ ἀδελφός ὁ Εβραῖος ἢ ἡ Εβραία
> But if your brother is sold to you, whether a Hebrew man or a Hebrew woman (NETS)

The verb πραθῇ is a passive form of πιπράσκω "to be sold,"[30] which renders ימכר as a *niph'al.* העברי and העבריה are then construed as appositives of the subject, אחיך; all three are rendered as nominatives in the Greek.

Though they disagree on the implication of this verse for the relative position of the different biblical legal codes, Bernard M. Levinson and John Van Seters interpret the verb as a reflexive *niph'al*, involving an Israelite who sells her/himself to a fellow Israelite in a case of self-indenture.[31] The brother who sells himself can be a Hebrew *sister* or even an *Israelite* sister, if Hebrew and Israelite are synonymous. Two issues arise from the inclusion of a Hebrewess in the term אח. First, it is not certain that an Israelite or a Hebrew woman could become a contracting partner to a self-indenture agreement without being represented by a male relative. Second, if according to a gender inclusive perspective, "your brother" can be both a male and a female Israelite, the note in 15:17b that "to your female slave, you shall do the same" is redundant.

30 Montanari, *BDAG*, 1,666.
31 Van Seters, *Law Book*, 85; Levinson, "Manumission," 286–87.

Sara Japhet reads ימכר as a passive *niph'al*: "When your brother, a Hebrew man or a Hebrew woman, is sold to you ..."[32] Instead of self-indenture, this case is closer to the sale of a Hebrew slave in Exodus 21:2 (עֶבֶד עברי), except that in Deuteronomy 15, the Hebrew becomes a slave only once the procedure of self-indenture is completed (Deut 15:17). Selling someone into slavery is clear when the verb מכר is combined with expressions such as לעבד (Esther 7:4), לאמה (Exod 21:7), ממכרת עבד (Lev 25:42). In Deuteronomy 28:68, מכר is parsed as a *hitpa'el* followed by לעבדים ולשפחות in order to convey a reflexive meaning, as is also the case in 1 Kings 21:20.25 and 2 Kings 17:17. In 15:12, מכר is not followed by any indicator of slavery. In fact, the verb מכר generally means "to deliver over goods, persons, for the use or possession of others, sometimes for a limited period [...] not necessarily by way of sale."[33]

It is not impossible that Deuteronomy 15:12 would be the sole attestation of מכר in the *niph'al* in Deuteronomy. In an unpointed text, however, ימכר can equally be parsed as *qal*:

> כי ימכר לך אחיך העברי או העבריה
> When a brother delivers to you the Hebrew man or the Hebrew woman

Instead of equating the brother with the Hebrew and the Hebrewess who are selling themselves or being sold to another brother, what is involved is a transaction between a first brother, the subject of מכר (the "seller"), and a second brother, the "purchaser" addressed as לך, with a Hebrew man or woman as the object of the transaction.

The main objection to reading העברי או העבריה as the direct object of the verb מכר "to sell" is the absence of the particle את in front of העברי and העבריה. This argument is not decisive, however, since with a determined noun, as here, את appears very frequently but rarely is necessary to signal the noun's function as the direct object of the sentence or clause.[34] There are at least 13 cases of omission of the particle את in the Deuteronomic core, which shows that its omission in Deut 15:12 would not be exceptional.[35] Consequently, in an unvocalized text, העברי או העבריה can be read as the objects of the sale and אחיך as the subject of the verb מכר, in spite of the absence of the *nota accusativi* in front of העברי. In this case, a different rendering from the NRSV (added in parenthesis) of verse 11 is possible:

32 Japhet, "Relationship," 73.

33 Clines, *DCH* 5, 271.

34 Joüon and Muraoka, *Grammar*, § 125–26; Waltke and O'Connor, *Introduction*, § 10.3; Bekins and Kirk, "Thorny Text," 360.

35 See Deut 14:25, 14:26, 15:12, 15:22, 17:12, 17:16, 19:3, 19:19, 21:9, 22:17, 22:21, 22:22, 22:24, 24:7.

> When your brother (NRSV: a member of your community, whether a Hebrew man or a Hebrew woman) will trade with you a Hebrew or a Hebrewess, and he serves you six years, then in the seventh year you shall send him free from you (NRSV: set that person free).

The addressee ("you") is purchasing the labor of a Hebrew from one of his brothers who owns the labor of the said Hebrew, for instance in order to reimburse an antichretic loan grant to the Hebrew by that brother.[36] The labor contract must not exceed six years, which does not mean that the Hebrew is a slave, nor that he works throughout these years for the purchasing brother. Every workday the Hebrew (and his wife or dependant "the Hebrewess") provides to the purchasing brother repays the loan he received from the first brother as well as the principle or the interest of a debt contracted by the second brother towards the first. Such complex enmeshment of contracts is well attested.[37] Like the release of debts after six years (Deut 15:1–6 discussed below), the aim of the maximum term of six years is to prevent the accumulation of levels of mutual debts to the point that it becomes impossible to decide which party benefits the most, something that inevitably generates resentment, as happens in Genesis 29–31 when Laban makes Jacob serve him for another seven years. In Genesis, the contract is between an uncle and a nephew, an Israelite and an Aramean. In Deuteronomy 15, the brothers are partners, with no indication of any blood and ethnic ties.

The outcome at this point is that none of the seven occurrences of the word אח in Deut 15:1–12 have to refer to Israelites and only to Israelites. One of these brothers may be an Edomite.

3.11 Interest-Free Loans between Brothers (Deut 23:20–21)

Loans of silver, food, or any other staple to "your brother" must not bear interest, in contrast with loans to foreigners (נכרי). Because Edomites or some Edomites are brothers, the corollary is that Edomites are the exception among foreigners. Hence, loans between Israelites and Edomites bear no interest, if and only if they are brothers.

Lending conditions vary according to the relations between lender and borrower and become less and less favorable as the distance increases. Loans be-

36 For the similarity with Jacob's position in regard of Laban see Rossi and Guillaume, "Alternative Reading," 10–11.

37 See for instance Rossi and Guillaume, "Alternative Reading," 10–11 on the (officially unpublished) BaAR 6 contract # 9 between Ahiqam and Enlil-iqiša involving the labor of a female slave.

tween brothers generate no interest (23:19), arrears are remitted during the *šemiṭṭah* (15:3) and loans are not secured by any pledge. Loans to neighbors are secured with a pledge (24:10) and are not subject to the *šemiṭṭah* release. Interest apparently is left to the discretion of the lender since no explicit mention is made of it, while loans granted to foreigners bear interest (23:20), and they are to be recovered by any means (15:23). Therefore, when it comes to loans, brothers may not be equivalent to any fellow Israelite any more than neighbors, who may include *gērîm* and foreign residents besides other Israelites.

3.12 Less than Half the References to Brothers Must Be to Israelites

All in all, the total count of occurrences of the word "brother" in Deuteronomy that refer to Israelites only is twenty-three out of a total of forty-nine, i.e. 46.9 %. Three other occurrences refer specifically to Edomites, while another twenty-three occurrences refer indiscriminately to Israelite or non-Israelites as brothers. Perlitt's notion of a Deuteronomic Israel as a brotherhood excludes the three references to Edomite brothers and the possibility that non-Israelites may be found among the other twenty-three indiscriminate mentions of the word אח. There is, nevertheless, a distinctive *Bruderethik* in Deuteronomy, which one can retrieve by comparing brothers with neighbors in Deuteronomy.

4 Brothers and Neighbors

As shown in Table 1, the New Revised Standard Version uses a dozen different expressions and circumlocutions to render Hebrew אח; seven times, it chooses "neighbor" (Deut 15:11, 22:1–4, 23:4). In the Hebrew text, a neighbor and a brother appear together twice: as potential instigators of idolatry (13:5) and as beneficiaries of a debt release (15:2). Apart from these two cases, Deuteronomy uses the term 'neighbor' (רע) sixteen times in reference to specific contexts:

- a victim of homicide (4:42, chapter 19: verses 4–5 and 11, 27:24)
- a victim of false witness (5:20)
- the husband of a woman who should not be coveted (אשת רעך 5:21)
- an intimate friend (רעך אשר כנפשך 13:7)
- the husband of a raped woman (22:24, 22:26)
- the owner of a vineyard or of a field (23:25–26)
- the owner of a pledge whose house the lender should not enter (24:10)
- the owner of an adjacent cultivated plot (גבול רעהו, 27:17)

While the NRSV's rendering of the term אח as a vague "member of your community" saves defining the nature and the boundaries of that community, rendering the term אח as "neighbor" is outright misleading.[38] Deuteronomy's neighbors occur in ordinary circumstances of daily life: work in neighboring fields and vineyards, securing loans with pledges, and the inevitable consequences of having to rub shoulders with neighbors on a daily basis: accusations of adultery, rape, and encroachment of boundaries and debts.

"Kin," "kindred," and "fellows" are vague enough to designate tribal brothers as well as supra-tribal brothers (Edom). But the sensitivity of modern readers has overruled the actual data when brothers become neighbors, because restricting the *šemiṭṭah* to the debts of brothers (15:9 and 15:11) seems unfair to the neighbor. The same applies to the return of a brother's stray animal (22:1–4) and the limitation of the number of lashes to brothers (25:3). The circumlocutions, "member of your community" (1:16, 15:3, 15:7, 15:12, 17:20, 18:2), "one of your own community" (17:15), and "a neighbor who is a member of your community" (15:2) muddle the difference between brother and neighbor to the point that everyone ends up being the brother of everyone else – except, of course, for the troublesome Edomite, who upsets the portrayal of an Israelite community that differs ethnically and religiously from its neighbors, thanks to a distinctly egalitarian and humanitarian morality of its own.

In fact, Deuteronomy displays a far more nuanced Israel, with neighbors and *gērîm* cohabiting with brothers in every settlement. The difference between brothers and neighbors is especially marked in financial matters. Loans between brothers are subject to debt remission and the prohibition of interest (15:2–3), contrary to loans to neighbors, which are secured with a pledge and probably can bear interest (24:10). For this reason, brothers borrow from brothers but find it advantageous to lend to others, presumably to neighbors and explicitly to foreigners, something that does not easily fit concepts of "humanitarianism." Hence, modern readers and translators feel the need to extend the financial solidarity owed to brothers to "neighbors and members of their community."

Instead of broadening the scope of family solidarity to all Judeans as Otto claims, the Deuteronomic core broadens the circle of Israelite brothers to include Edomites.[39]

---

38 Morrow, *Introduction*, 246–47.

39 Otto, *Das Gesetz*, 126–27.

5 Edomite Brothers (Deut 2:4, 2:8, and 23:8)

The presence of Edomite brothers is the key to designations of the Deuteronomic brother that are otherwise awkward or outright tautological if the brotherhood includes all Israelites or Judeans and only them:

- The tribes to be supported by their Transjordanian brothers are designated the "sons of Israel" in 3:18 because the mention of the sons of Esau in 2:4 and 2:8 (אחיכם בני עשו) renders the meaning of the word "brother" ambiguous.
- The status of brother granted to the Edomite is likely to have exacerbated the debate over the beneficiaries of the *šemiṭṭah*, as indicated by the complicated textual history of Deuteronomy 15:2. Shifting the focus from brothers to neighbors turned the *šemiṭṭah* into an internal Israelite affair, to express "the special relationship obtaining among members of God's people."[40]
- The presence of Edomites within the brotherhood explains the circumlocution regarding the choice of a king among brothers who must not be a foreigner (17:15).
- The use of the expression, "his brother from the sons of Israel," to designate the victim of kidnap in Deuteronomy 24:7 equally presupposes the existence of non-Israelite brothers.

Edomite brothers are a thorn in the flesh of readings that invoke the use of brotherhood to construct a Jewish "religious-ethnic group" or of "a distinctive Israelite identity in avoidance of non-Israelites."[41] Therefore, much effort has been spent on ignoring these troublesome Edomite brothers.

5.1 Diachronic Strategies to Ignore Edomite Brothers

In his oft quoted study of the biblical concept of brotherhood, Perlitt (1980) attributed most of the plural forms of אח to the "brüderliche Organisation der Israelitischen" (1:28, 13:18, 13:20, 10:9, 33:9, 33:16, and 33:24), except those referring to Edom (2:4, 8), which he considered echoes of the pre-state nomadic tribal organization based on blood relationships when Edomites were some kind of related tribe. Therefore, the Edomite brothers are not "Dtn-spezifisch"

40 Levin, "Rereading Deuteronomy," 67.
41 Crouch, *Making of Israel*, 218.

and can thus be safely ignored, though they are a unique feature in Deuteronomy.[42]

Yet, there still are ten plural forms and nineteen singular ones in the Deuteronomic core (chs. 12–26), a ratio that prevents a simple attribution of all plural forms to pre-Deuteronomic traditions and singular ones as typical Deuteronomic traits. Moreover, the expression "your brother" (אחיך) in Deuteronomy 23:8 is a singular form found within what Perlitt considers the historical core of Deuteronomy. The Edomite brother has thus every qualification to become a hallmark of Deuteronomy, except, of course, that he does not fit the portrayal of Israel as a *Volk von einzelnen Brüdern*. Therefore, Perlitt eliminates "your brother the Edomite," explaining in a footnote that "your brother" in Deut 23:8 is a *gentilicium*, a singular form standing *pars pro toto* for a plural form. "Your brother the Edomite" means "your brothers the Edomites." Hence, in his view, the single form אחיך in 23:8 belongs with the plural forms referencing the Edomites in 2:4 and 2:8 in the non-Deuteronomic material, though it is a singular form within the legal core.[43]

Instead of dispatching the Edomite brother into a pre-monarchic limbo, recent exegetes attribute the Edomite brother to a post-exilic elaboration, with the same aim.[44] Pre-Deuteronomic or post-Deuteronomic, they think the Edomite brother has no more place in true Deuteronomic thinking than the Ammonites and Moabites. Therefore, the admission of Edomites into the *qᵉhal-Yhwh* reflects a time when Edomite and Jewish villages may have coexisted in the Negev around Hebron in the first part of the Persian period.[45] If so, the brotherhood of the sons of Esau in ch. 2 and of the Edomite in ch. 23 is highly relevant to the understanding of Deuteronomy, even if Perlitt wrote that they are not. As for the third generation Egyptian, whom 23:8 places on an equal footing with the Edomite brother, he must reflect an undefined time when Egypt was not a threat any more.[46]

For argument's sake, let us accept as factual that, in the Persian or early Hellenistic period, that is, before the Torah became an authoritative document, the Edomite brother was the result of the historical circumstance that part of the territory of monarchic Judah became Edom/Idumea. In this case, the writers wanted to emphasize that Yhwh-worshippers in that territory could be part of

---

42 Perlitt, "'Ein einzig Volk,'" 36.

43 Perlitt, 36 n. 28.

44 Otto, *Deuteronomium 12,1–23,15*, 1,752–61.

45 Römer, *So-Called Deuteronomistic History*, 171.

46 Otto, *Deuteronomium 12,1–23,15*, 1,743.

the pilgrimage celebrations and be eligible for business and marriage arrangements.

The problem is that no Edomites are ever mentioned in relation to pilgrimage celebrations at the *maqom*, the prime venue for business and marriage arrangements and for the assimilation of Israelite norms (see ch. 7 in this volume). Deuteronomy only mentions Edomite brothers and Egyptians in relation to the mysterious *q*ᵉ*hal-Yhwh*. There is nothing in Deuteronomy that allows equating the *q*ᵉ*hal-Yhwh* with Israel as a whole and even less with the *maqom*.[47] The *q*ᵉ*hal-Yhwh* is discussed in ch. 23 only, while the *maqom* festivities are discussed in chs. 12, 14, 16, 18, and 26. The *maqom* festivities involve Israelite families at a place where Yhwh chooses to place his name. No meal, families, tithes, sacrifices, or Levites are mentioned in relation with the *q*ᵉ*hal-Yhwh*. Whereas the *maqom* festivities are inclusive occasions, the bulk of the few verses dedicated to the *q*ᵉ*hal-Yhwh* exclude eunuchs, bastards, Ammonites, and Moabites (23:1–6).

Another problem is that the relevance of the Idumean factor loses much of its force if the bulk of the Deuteronomic core was produced in Israel rather than in Jerusalem. The Idumean argument presupposes de Wette's notion of an *Ur-Deuteronomium* crafted in Jerusalem, even though it dates the insertion of the Edomite brother much later than Josiah's reign. Instead of an argument based on textual evidence, the Idumean argument adds a second presupposition to the premise according to which Israel as a a *Volk von Brüdern* is a hallmark of Deuteronomy.

The exclusion of Ammonites and Moabites in 23:2–7 can be explained as intra-biblical exegesis in light of the story of Lot's daughter in Genesis 19:30–38, and historically as reflections the opposition of Tobiah and Sanballat to Nehemiah's activities. The echoes of Deuteronomy 23:2–7 in Nehemiah 13:1–2 recall the exclusion of Ammon and Moab but avoid any mention of the favorable attitude to Edom and Egypt. Does this mean that Nehemiah was more open to the Edomites and the Egyptians because he ascribed a greater authority to Deuteronomy than modern scholarship does? Instead of ignoring the Edomite brother, Jeremiah 49:7–13 has a list of judgments on Edom following those on Egypt, Ammon, and Moab. Does this mean that the writer or redactors of the book have no qualms in opposing Deuteronomy?[48]

---

47 The *qāhāl* at Horeb (Deut 5:22); and the *yom haqqāhāl* (Deut 9:10, 10:4, 18:16) abstain from reproducing the *q*ᵉ*hal-Yhwh* exactly. The Horeb assembly is designated as the *q*ᵉ*hal*-Israel in Deut 31:30, not as the *q*ᵉ*hal-Yhwh*, because there is no place for any Edomite brother at Horeb. Some translators were aware of the difference between these different assemblies. The *yom-haqqāhāl* in Deut 9:10 is not well attested in the Septuagint tradition, while some versions either ignore the *yom-haqqāhāl* in 10:4 or replace it with "a day in the desert" (ἐν τῇ ἐρήμῳ).
48 For a detailed consideration of this possibility, see ch. 14 by Benedetta Rossi in this volume.

If the presence of Idumeans in southern Jewish villages was the cause of the admission of Edomites into the *q^e^hal-Yhwh*, one needs to explain why Edomite brothers were inserted in Deuteronomy of all places; precisely in the book for whom Israelite brotherhood is supposedly the hallmark, whereas Nehemiah – produced when the presence of Edomites in southern Judah was significant (the case of Jeremiah is less clear) – consciously avoids any mention of Edomites and Idumeans. The aim of the Idumean hypothesis is to explain away the Edomite brother as a late addition to Deuteronomy, an addition to be ignored because it is irreconcilable with the factoid of the hallmark of Deuteronomy. It would have been a wonderful illustration of another factoid, that of Deuteronomic humanitarianism,[49] had "the special relationship obtaining among members of God's people"[50] been extended to the Edomite brother. Admittedly, the Edomite brotherhood as the basis for acceptance in the *q^e^hal-Yhwh* is a crux, due in part to the absence of data on the nature of this assembly.

5.2 Synchronic Strategies to Ignore Edomite Brothers

Synchronic studies use different approaches to downplay Edomite brotherhood. In one of her monographs, Crouch lists Deuteronomy 23:8–9 along the passages in which the "brother language appeals to the idea of Israel as a large extended family and draws on the affective power of such language in efforts to motivate certain kinds of behavior within the community."[51] Edomites and Egyptians would thus be evoked as part of an Israelite family extended to the point that the expected brotherly behavior applies well beyond what usually defines an Israelite community. Crouch is aware of this, and in another volume, she cuts out the Egyptian.[52]

As the plural "sons born to them" in Deuteronomy 23:9a is followed by a singular "he will enter" in 23:9b, the Egyptian is considered secondary, and only the Edomite is to be treated (תעב) as an Israelite.[53] A quote from F. V. Greifenhagen reinforces the exclusion of the Egyptian, since "if the Egyptian can enter the assembly of Yhwh, then the whole process of Israel's separation from Egypt is brought full circle back to its beginnings."[54] Exit the Egyptian;

49 See Arnold in this volume. Weinfeld, "Present State," 34; Otto, "Human Rights"; Tsai, *Human Rights*.
50 Levin, "Rereading Deuteronomy," 67.
51 Crouch, *Israel and the Assyrians*, 117.
52 Crouch, *Making of Israel*, 195–98.
53 Crouch, 197.
54 Greifenhagen, *Egypt*, 195.

the mention of the third generation can now be applied to the Edomite, whose admission into the *q*ᵉ*hal-Yhwh*, though not explicitly stated, implies that he has been resident long enough to assimilate to Israelite norms.[55] The conclusion is quite similar to Perlitt's. The "use of familial language in Deut 23:8 to articulate the Edomite's unusual potential as a future Israelite makes sense in an identity framework in which significant weight can be given to traditions of common descent, provoked by notions of just such a familial relationship with Edom."[56] In other words, after living among Israelites for three generations, these Edomites have become quasi-Israelites, or at least "semiforeigners or half brothers."[57]

In fact, there are no half-brothers or semi-foreigners in Deuteronomy. Were admission into the *q*ᵉ*hal-Yhwh* conditioned by the assimilation of Israelite norms, this principle would apply to Egyptians as much as to Edomites and even more to the *gēr* who resides "within your gates." This is not the case, and Crouch admits that the principle of assimilation is not explicit in the text. What is explicit is that Deuteronomy 23 grants a special status to some Edomites and Egyptians – while Moabites and Ammonites are ranked among the eunuch and the *mamzer*, forever barred from the *q*ᵉ*hal-Yhwh*.

The very negative attitude toward the Ammonite and Moabite may be viewed as an echo of the story of Lot's daughters in Genesis 19:30–38. This genealogical argument would neatly explain the exclusion of Ammonite and Moabite and the admission of Edomites, but it fails to account for the very positive attitude towards the Edomite and the Egyptian. Were genealogical factors the guiding principle for the selection of brothers, Arameans would have an even stronger claim to admission in the *q*ᵉ*hal-Yhwh* than Edomites, but Deuteronomy ignores the Arameans. Moreover, this kind of reasoning attributes much weight to genealogical stories and ethnicity, which usually result from political and economic circumstances, which they justify. Arguing that actual genealogical ties are the cause of the admission of the Edomite and third generation Egyptian is counter-intuitive.

It is hard to avoid the conclusion that the various strategies deployed to ignore the Edomite brother are cases of special pleading. The Edomite brother is a crux, complicated by the absence of indications relative to the nature and activities of the mysterious *q*ᵉ*hal-Yhwh* into which they are admitted. Perlitt's approach to eliminate Edomite brotherhood is too expedient to be convincing. Crouch's arguments are more in line with current exegetical *mores*, but the traditions of common descent it relies upon are too malleable to be used as causes.

---

55 Crouch, *Making of Israel*, 198 n. 240.
56 Crouch, 199.
57 Stulman, "Encroachment," 615 n. 8.

The view that brotherly language draws on the affective power of such language to motivate certain kinds of behavior within the community is certainly correct,[58] but the focus on Israel as a large extended family in which the desired behavior is to take effect is but a first step into the role of the Edomite brother in Deuteronomy. The inclusion of Edomites and Egyptians in the *qᵉhal-Yhwh* remains a crux until Edomite brotherhood is considered outside the confines of familial, genealogical, and ethnic ties. To be sure, the later redefinition of the Edomite brother of Deuteronomy 23:8 along ethnic lines is the burden of the references to "your brother Esau" in 2:2 and 2:8 when the earlier core was "framed". In the process, however, the Egyptian of Deuteronomy 23:8 had to be ignored because he does not fit the context of the Exodus, whose baseline is the escape from the Egyptian house of slavery.

The easy way out is to argue that these references to Esau/Edom as brother are later redactional additions aimed at harmonizing the Pentateuch, the Hexateuch, or the Enneateuch into a single meta-narrative through the additional of internal cross-referencing among the individual books. This may well be the case for brother Esau in Deuteronomy 2:2 and 2:8, but it is far less likely that later redactors insisted that at least some Edomites and even some Egyptians could enter the *qᵉhal-Yhwh*. Given the definition of this assembly outside Deuteronomy, 23:8–9 is a crux that harmonizes nothing. A late redactor who produced a crux that the readers mentioned above felt the need to explain away would be a very poor harmonizer. He added Deuteronomy 2:2–8 because he felt the need to explain away the crux of 23:8–9 that he found in the text he was meant to harmonize. The Edomite and Egyptian members of the *qᵉhal-Yhwh* are the cause rather than the result of a harmonizing redaction. They represent the kind of *lectio difficilior* that critical exegesis must face squarely instead of explaining away.

In fact, scholarship has to ignore the Edomite brotherhood as long as brotherhood is considered from an ethnic point of view. Obviously, there is no place for Edomite brothers within an Israelite ethnicity defined as a people of brothers. Shifting from an ethnic to an economic point of view opens a new horizon.

6 Brothers as Partners

Rather than diluting the *scandalon* of the Edomites brothers as members of the *qᵉhal-Yhwh*, which has been ill-defined as an extended Israelite family, Deuter-

58 Crouch, *Israel and the Assyrians*, 177.

onomy is rather consistent in setting brotherhood in economic contexts. Two-thirds of the uses of brothers in the plural in Deuteronomy occur in relation to prebendaries (18:2, 18:7), loans (15:2–11, 23:20–21), labor contracts (15:12–18, 24:7, 24:14), livestock management (22:1–4), and inheritance (25:5–11). In such contexts, brotherly language takes on a precise meaning of partnership in economic ventures.

The term "brother" was commonly used to refer to business partners in Ugarit (for instance 17.314 in PRU IV, 189) and Mesopotamia.[59] The term "brother" was also used to address business partners at Elephantine, independently from any shared ethnicity. For instance, letter *TAD* 1: A3.10 Berlin 23000 concerns non-Judeans who own a boat, or shares of a boat, in partnership. Spendata, son of Fravatipata, addresses Ḥori son of Kamen and Peṭemachis as brothers, showing that, in Aramaic, the term brother was applied to anyone with whom one had established business dealings or ties, forming a personal economic network.[60] Among individuals unrelated by blood or ethnic ties, the Elephantine papyri seem to distinguish a brother from a companion (אחבר[61] and a colleague (כנת).[62]

The maximum term of seven years for loans between brothers in Deuteronomy 15:1–9 far exceeds the term of loans contracted in ordinary agricultural operations.[63] The Deuteronomic brothers addressed in the core of the book constitute a *Bruderwirtschaft*, which is narrower than the *Volk von Brüdern* of the book's frames. The Deuteronomic core addresses only the wealthiest Israelites.[64] Ordinary fellow Israelites who are not members of the economic elite

59 Oppenheim and Reiner, *CAD*, p. 202. For examples of the potential use of the term ŠEŠ and PAB for Akkadian *aḫu* to mean "colleague, partner," see SAA 8 296, where brothers built a storeroom (Hunger, *Astrological Reports*, 296); SAA 13 27 s.1, where "Thirty-one 'brothers' have released him from the 'locks' of Aššur"; and SAA 13 40 3, where "Good health to my brother (ŠEŠ-ia)" appears in a clear craftsmanship context.

60 Porten and Yardeni, *Textbook*, 48–49.

61 Porten and Yardeni, *Textbook*, 191 text 7.56 line 2.

62 כנת in Porten and Yardeni, *TAD* 2: 2.2:6 (judges), 3.8:38 (right of "one or two"), 6.4:3–4 (right of "one or two"), 7.1.3 (judges), 8.4:2 (judges), 8.5:16 (?), 8.6:7.11 (?); *TAD* 3: 1.1:56.67.99.185, 3.8IIIB:1 (foremen); *TAD* 4: 1.32:14; 3.45:6.

63 Of the 27 usable contracts for barley published in Pearce and Wunsch, *Documents*, a single one has a term of 12 months (No. 61) and one of 10 months (No. 94). Of the eight tablets published in Joannès and Lemaire, "Contrats," and Joannès and Lemaire, "Trois tablettes," two have terms of 11 months (J 1 and J 5). Of the 16 usable contracts involving silver, the longest term is 10 months (again No. 61). The others have terms between less than a month and 7 months. Though not relevant for Palestine, contracts dealing with date follow the same pattern.

64 So Cazelles, "Droit public," 101. Nevertheless, he concludes that the Levitical priests are the keystone of Deuteronomic public law, even though they are ranked among the economically weak (p. 106)!

are referred to as neighbors. Neighbors are not necessarily *gērîm*, neighbors are probably not foreigners, but they are not brothers, either.

There is a possibility that the Deuteronomic *Bruderwirtschaft* includes Edomite partners, as stated in Deuteronomy 23:7. Given the limited data provided about the nature of the *qᵉhal*-Yhwh, how this assembly relates to the *Bruderwirtschaft* must remain an open question.

Only twelve of the 35 occurrences of the word "brother" in the singular in chs. 12–26 do not have an obvious economic context: 13:7 on idolatry, 17:15 (twice) and 17:20 on the king, 18:15 and 18:18 on prophets, 19:18 (twice) on false witnessing, 20:8 on war, 23:8 on Edom, 25:3 on flogging, and 25:11 on the grabbing wife. Yet, apart from the Edomite brotherhood, all the others have more or less direct economic implications. Worship of other gods, kings, and prophets are likely sources of expenses in the form of taxes, sacrifices, or salaries for their services. False witness can have disastrous consequences for an entire household in terms of fines or even capital punishment. War in ch. 20 is viewed as a profitable enterprise. As discussed above (§ 3.6), the infertility resulting from injuries inflicted by the grabbing wife impacts the inheritance of the brother's estate. Deuteronomy 23:2–9 would thus be the single outlier in chs. 12–26 if the Edomite brotherhood has no economic implication and if the *qᵉhal*-Yhwh is a purely religious institution with no financial implications for its members. An Edomite brother as some sort of partner belonging to commercial associations such as those attested at Assur fits the context of chs. 12–26.

Such associations involve rituals of initiation, during which new members take oaths of an ethical nature[65] to bind them and to enforce the highest possible levels of accountability between members. Accountability in commercial ventures and trade consortia is crucial, especially in long-distance trade, where fraud can be potentially more profitable than honesty."[66]

Long distance trade relies upon the price differential in different locations, the potential profit increasing proportionally with the distance between the supplying region and the destination of the transported goods. But long-distance trade combines the costs and risks inherent in transport (attacks of caravans, shipwreck, disease, spoilage) and the risk of price fluctuation inherent in commerce.[67] Splitting the sum invested to finance an overland trade venture among several partners spread the risk borne by each partner, who could invest in several ventures instead of putting all his eggs in the same basket.[68]

---

65 Carroll, "Egyptian Craft Guilds."
66 Greif, "Contract Enforceability."
67 Radner, "Die beiden neuassyrischen Privatarchive."
68 Radner, "Traders," 116.

An association of entrepreneurial merchants to reduce the risk inherent to long-distance trade is attested already in the Old Assyrian period.[69] The Neo-Assyrian *tamkārus* continued to work within royal circles while also acting as private entrepreneurs (EN KASKAL = **bēl ḫarrāni*). Possibly attested already at Ugarit, they definitely were active in Neo-Assyrian times.[70] So far, Neo-Assyrian EN KASKAL trade ventures are only attested from the city of Assur, possibly because it is the sole place where private archives have so far been retrieved.[71] The private traders of Assur equipped caravans to go to the mountainous areas by river and land routes for wine, clothes, and other staples. These traders established *ḫarrānu* partnerships, with contracts recording the total amount of the capital being invested and the number of shares held by each silent partner. The earliest known example found at Assur is dated 717 BCE.[72] The *ḫarrānu* documents from Assur involve a large number of residents.

Two centuries later, contracts recovered from Babylonia name individuals with Yahwistic backgrounds as partners in *ḫarrānu* ventures, sometimes with non-Judeans. I will present four examples that appear to involve investments in more local business opportunities rather than those provided long-distance trade.

CUSAS 61 (508 BCE) records the promise by Zērūtu and his wife to pay a very large amount of barley (13,500 litres) and silver as the principle of a *ḫarrānu* venture named after Yāḫû-šūri, who must have provided the largest share of the capital. The postulated diasporic setting of these tablets explains the association of Judean exiles with non-Judeans. The same applies at Elephantine, where some Judeans take an oath by the name of another deity.[73]

CUSAS 40 (517 BCE) is a partnership contract for a *ḫarrānu* venture involving 2,160 liters of dates belonging to the silent partner, who values it at 30 shekels. When compared with the other known eleven contracts involving dates and the sixteen that involve exchange rates for silver, it is clear this involves a very favorable rate for the owner of the dates in comparison to the value according to the average rate (19 shekels) or the median rate (18.25). The contract becomes effective immediately after the date harvest, and the acting partner is to repay the value in silver seven months later at the time of the barley harvest, exactly

69 Graslin, "Les mécanismes."

70 For Ugarit, see Rainey, "Business Agents," 319; for Neo-Assyrian examples, see Radner, "Traders," 109; for biblical testimony, see Nah 3:16.

71 Radner, "Traders," 118; Postgate, "Some Merchants."

72 Radner, "Traders," 116.

73 For the text, see Pearce and Wunsch, *Documents*, 196–97. For Elephantine, see Porten, *Archives*, 151–86; Greifenhagen, *Egypt*, 236.

when the value of barley is at its lowest yearly rate. The partners share out the profit equally.

The contract CUSA 55 (549 BCE) also is executed after the date harvest. It involves two siblings who will repay 25 shekels of silver to the silent partner four months later at the time of the barley harvest, but they will repay at the value of barley against silver when the contract was established. That value is set during the sowing season, when the demand for barley is highest as farmers buy seeds in order to make their stores last until the next harvest.

CUSAS 97 (518 BCE) involves 32 shekels of silver the acting partner and his wife will repay at an indeterminate date. Another man guarantees that the 32 shekels will be paid back, thus reducing the risk taken by the silent partner, though he also enjoys a half-share of any profit the acting partners may make with that silver.

The amounts of silver involved in these four contracts are beyond what ordinary farmers would have at their disposal. These businessmen are able to benefit from seasonal price variations, usually within the same year, which makes the six full years in Deuteronomy 15 appear as a very long term of credit.

The ban on interest-bearing loans between brothers (Deut 23:20–21) is reflected in extant *ḫarrānu* contracts, where interest is often absent or low.[74] Risk and profit are shared out according to the number of shares held by each partner. Solidarity between the partners is total when the creditor is also one of the shareholders, as is often the case.

The so-called "craftsmen's charter" (YBC 3499) from the Eanna temple at Uruk (unknown year in the reign of Cyrus) mentions an assembly where the craftsmen settled their business.[75] This assembly concerns the affairs of institutional craftsmen, not of private traders. Yet, it is conceivable that Neo-Assyrian private traders who had sufficient capital to invest in *ḫarrānu* ventures as silent partners set up assemblies of their own where they conducted business.

The very limited place Deuteronomy 17 ascribes to the royal office excludes the presence of royal trade agents such as the Neo-Assyrian *tamkārus*. Apart from the house of Yhwh in Deuteronomy 23:19, there are no temples in Deuteronomy. Prebendary personnel would be a good fit for the brotherhood of the Levitical priesthood mentioned in Deuteronomy 17, 18 and 24, but they are never connected to the *q^ehal-Yhwh*. Therefore, the social background of the members of the *q^ehal-Yhwh* is to be sought among entrepreneurs outside any royal and

---

74 Note, however, that the promissory note for barley and silver from a *ḫarrānu* contract in Pearce and Wunsch, *Documents*, 196 (CUSAS # 61, 536 BCE). It includes 20 % interest rate on the barley and 12 shekels interest on a principle of 30 shekels over a long term of 12 months.

75 Payne, "New Evidence," 110–11, line 18.

temple economy, though some private entrepreneurs did undertake managerial tasks for institutions, such as the management of agricultural estates and rent farming.[76] What characterizes non-prebendaries is their concentration as active agents in inter-regional trade ventures, whereas prebendaries often played the role of silent partners, merely providing funds.[77]

Applying the distinction between prebendaries and non-prebendaries to Deuteronomy reveals the blind spot of de Wettian scholarship, which presupposes an exclusively prebendary background – the Jerusalem temple – and ignores private entrepreneurs active beyond institutional boundaries. Yet, private entrepreneurs constitute a major characteristic of the Iron Age economy, in parallel with the development of long-distance trade. Whereas prebendaries had a conservative attitude aimed at preserving their privileges, private entrepreneurs bore the risk of innovation and were more prone to develop partnerships with foreigners in order to raise the required capital.[78] No wonder Deuteronomy 23 urges its audience not to abhor an Edomite brother or third generation Egyptian.

The Edomite brother and the third generation Egyptians of the *q^ehal-Yhwh* may or may not belong to secondary textual expansions interacting with stories of the book of Genesis (Lot, Esau, Joseph) and of the book of Numbers (Balaam). They also or alternatively may reflect a rivalry between different temples (Elephantine, Transjordan, Samarian, or the house of Yhwh in the Idumean ostraca).

To be sure, the Deuteronomic "you" addressing members of a brotherhood narrower than *kol Israel* did not fit the Mosaic fiction. Before it was constructed as a testament of Moses, Deuteronomy had a life of its own, where the speaker was a brother addressing his brothers as equals, contrary to the semi-divine Moses of the Torah who towers above a rebellious populace about which he entertains no illusion over its ability to abide by the laws he is giving it.[79]

7 Conclusion

Of the 49 occurrences of the word "brother" in Deuteronomy, only sixteen (32.6 %) refer necessarily or most likely to ethnic Israelites.[80] The remaining

76 Beaulieu, "Finger in Every Pie"; Jursa, "Business Companies," 253.
77 Jursa, "Business Companies," 63–64.
78 Liverani, "Influence," 134.
79 Blanco Wißmann, *"Er tat das Rechte,"* 204–6; Otto, *Deuteronomium 1–11*, 263.
80 Deut 1:16 (a fair hearing), 1:28 (spies), 3:18, 3:20 (vanguard), 10:9, 13:7, 18:2, 18:7, 33:9, 33:16, 33:24 (Levi, Moses, Aaron, Joseph and Asher), 17:15 (twice), 17:20 (king), 18:15, 18:18 (prophet).

thirty mentions of brothers are not necessarily Israelites but may sometimes include Edomite brothers (2:4, 2:8, 23:8). The efforts to ignore these Edomite brothers are suspect because they presuppose the notion of the Deuteronomic Israel as a *Volk von Brüdern* more than they demonstrate why Edomites cannot be brothers.

The exclusive focus on the ethnic view of brotherhood has caused much misunderstanding. To decide whether a brotherly ethic is an original feature of Deuteronomy or if it is the result of a systematic revision of the original features of the Deuteronomic law,[81] distinguishing two aspects of brotherhood – ethnicity and partnership – is helpful. Applied to the distinction between core and frames within Deuteronomy, partnership and ethnicity fall neatly in each type of material, respectively.

Though Edomite brotherhood is stated explicitly in the core and in the frame, in chs. 12–26 brotherhood pertains predominantly to economic practices. Apart from the idolatrous brother in 13:7, the king who must be a brother and not a foreigner (17:15.15.20), and the tribe of Levi (18:2.7), the other twenty-nine mentions of brothers in chs. 12–26 (29/35, 82.9 %) can include an Edomite business partner involved with elite Israelites operating within the framework of the mysterious *q^{e}hal*-Yhwh (23:8).

In the Deuteronomic frames, brotherhood is defined along ethnic lines. This is evident in the two references to "your brothers the sons of Esau" (2:4.8). The other eight occurrences of the word "brother" in chs 1–11 and 27–34 refer to fellow Israelites. If the frames were meant to insert an earlier core into the Exodus fiction, Levin's claim that Deuteronomy's brotherhood ethic is the result of a systematic revision of the original features of the Deuteronomic law is probably correct.[82] Whether or not this revision is a feature of the Persian period is another matter.[83] All that can be advanced here is that it belongs to the formation of the Torah and the figuration of Deuteronomy as Moses's testament.

Contrary to Levin's view, however, the systematic revision hardly operated in the passages of the core he envisaged. Credit and slaves (15:1–18), false witnessing (19:16–21), loss of livestock (22:1–4), interest (23:20–21), kidnapping, pledges, wages (24:7–15), and even flogging (25:1–3) are indeed fine illustrations of *Bruderethik*, but ethics that can involve Edomites with Israelite investment

81 Levin, "Rereading Deuteronomy," 70–71.

82 Levin, 70–71.

83 While Berge (ch. 4 in this volume) supports a Persian date of composition for the book, Davies (ch. 2 in this volume) proposes an origin of the core, if not the first edition with frames, soon after 722 BCE, in Samerina.

partners. In this case, Deuteronomy's brotherly ethics can hardly set apart the Jewish community from its neighbors and develop a morality of its own.[84]

The morality deployed by Deuteronomy's *Bruderethik* is not distinctive. Gustav Hölscher's oft repeated impracticability of Deuteronomic laws is only correct when they are applied to all levels of society, including neighbors.[85] Within a guild-like circle of investors such as the mysterious *q*ᵉ*hal*-Yhwh, the principles delineated in chs. 15–25 are crucial to preserve the economic viability of partnerships involved in risky financial operations.[86] The release of arrears do not apply to short term loans granted to ordinary Israelites, Hebrews, *gērîm*, or widows, who supply a pledge to reduce the risk of the lender. The regulations (rather than laws) transmitted in the Deuteronomic core are coherent with economic realities, ancient and modern. They foster the prosperity obtained from investment in the sale or trade of wholesale commodities and the processing of raw materials and credit.[87]

Such a reading of Deuteronomy's brotherly ethics is less inspiring for kind-hearted philanthropists than traditional readings, which figure Israel as a people where women and slaves share the same status as any other Israelite. Readers have the choice between seemingly harsh Deuteronomic rules, which closely reflect ancient Mesopotamian practices, and genteel but impractical ones for an Israel in which loans should be granted to the poor because debts need not be paid back since they will all eventually be cancelled. Deuteronomy 15 mentions charitable attitudes, but contrary to Leviticus 19:18 and 19:34, Deuteronomy never urges its audience to love the neighbor and the *gēr* as oneself.

There is, however, one point over which a part of Deuteronomy agrees with Leviticus, precisely the passage that displays a brotherhood that has no room for Edomite brothers: the Levitical brotherhood (18:1–8). The economic context is congruent with the overall context of the core, but instead of delineating brotherly ethics, this passage enumerates priestly portions owed exclusively to a Levitical brotherhood, a brotherhood that appears like a cuckoo's egg in the Deuteronomic nest unless Deuteronomy is read in light of the previous scrolls of the Torah. This very passage may indeed be ascribed to a systematic revision

84 Levin, "Rereading Deuteronomy," 70–71.
85 Hölscher, "Komposition," 195–97; Levin, "Rereading Deuteronomy," 51.
86 As the locus of the brotherhood, the *q*ᵉ*hal-Yhwh* into which the Edomite brother is admitted alongside third generation Egyptians must be distinguished from the yearly gatherings of Israelite families at the *maqom*. For a detailed consideration of these gatherings, see my other article in ch. 7 in this volume.
87 Wunsch, "Debt, Interest."

of the Deuteronomic core. These priestly dues would encapsulate the morality of a Jewish temple community claiming the right to collect meat and wool from the populace.

In this volume, Diana Edelman applies Occam's razor to eliminate speculations involved in the identification of multiple redactors and to view the first edition of Deuteronomy as the work of a single creative writer who assembled a large range of different kinds of materials. She then allows room for subsequent changes made to the book but not for concerted redactions. The fact that Deuteronomy juxtaposes two brotherhoods, a Levitical brotherhood besides a "financial brotherhood," supports Edelman's case, even if she has not endorsed either. This guild appeals to the "financial" brotherhood for its financial support, possibly in the context of rivalry with other priestly dynasties that used other scrolls of the Torah to bolster their own claims. The dual restrictions placed on the Deuteronomic king – that he must be a brother (Deut 17:15) and be subservient to the levitical priests who dictate the Torah (Deut 17:18) – also supports the view of a seamless Deuteronomic narrative.

Edelman's solution, however, runs the risk of downplaying the tensions that exist in the text, which would have certainly been the aim of the redactors if the Levites and Moses were indeed used to frame an earlier Deuteronomic core. Did the Levitical scribes invent the "financial guild" out of whole cloth, or did they recycle a pre-existing "document?" This is a critical question.

Finally, Edelman asks a crucial question: What is gained by postulating an earlier stage over assigning the assembling of the materials in chs. 12–26 to the same person who created the preceding and succeeding narrative material delivered primarily in a set of speeches made by Moses to Israel?

The gain is a return to a reading of Deuteronomy for its own sake as a self-contained document rather than to search for its innovations over against the other biblical "law-codes," as done for instance by Benjamin Kilchör and discussed in Bill Arnold's article in ch. 6 of this volume. Reading Deuteronomy on its own account undermines two additional pillars of Deuteronomic scholarship besides the *Volk von Brüdern*: the notions of centralization and of profane slaughter, as argued by Baruch Halpern in ch. 5 of this volume.

The recognition of the creative ability of the Deuteronomic writer in producing a story-world by assembling a rich palette of apodictic and casuistic statements and motivational clauses certainly entails going beyond the simplistic view of a Deuteronomic core identified as chs. 12–26 that later was enclosed in successive frames. In short, the Deuteronomic story-world is inherently incompatible with the story-world of the rest of the Torah as well as with the story-world of the Deuteronomic history. Is this not a gain in the present state of Hebrew Bible scholarship?

Works Cited

Awabdy, Mark A. *Immigrants and Innovative Law: Deuteronomy's Theological and Social Vision for the* גר. Forschungen zum Alten Testament 2. Reihe 67. Tübingen: Mohr Siebeck, 2014.

Beaulieu, Paul-Alain. "A Finger in Every Pie: The Institutional Connections of a Family of Entrepreneurs in Neo-Babylonian Larsa." In *Interdependency of Institutions and Private Entrepreneurs: Proceedings of the 2nd MOS Symposium, Leiden, December 11–12, 1998*, edited by R. Bogaert, 43–72. MOS Series 2. Istanbul: Nederlands Historisch-Archaeologisch Instituut, 2000.

Bekins, Peter and Alexander T. Kirk. "A Thorny Text: The Use of את and the Subversion of Form in Ezek 2:60." *Vetus Testamentum* 67 (2017): 357–71.

Blanco Wißman, Felipe. *"Er tat das Rechte": Beurteilungskriterien und Deuteronomismus in 1 Kon 12–2 Kon 25*. Abhandlungen zur Theologie des Alten und Neuen Testaments 93. Zürich: Theologischer Verlag, 2008.

Carroll, James L. "Egyptian Craft Guild Initiations." *Studia Antiqua* 5, no. 1 (2007): 17–44.

Cazelles, Henri. "Droit public dans le Deutéronome." In *Das Deuteronomium: Entstehung, Gestalt und Botschaft*, edited by Norbert Lohfink, 99–106. Bibliotheca Ephemeridum Theologicarum Lovaniensium 68. Leuven: Peeters, 1985.

Clines, David J. A., ed. *Dictionary of Classical Hebrew*. 8 vols. Sheffield: Sheffield Academic, 1993–2016. Cited as *DCH*.

Coin-Longeray, Sandrine. "Πενία et πένης: Travailler pour vivre?" *Revue de philologie de littérature et d'histoire anciennes* 75 (2001): 249–56.

Cole, Steven W. and Peter Machinist eds, with contributions by Simo Parpola. *Letters from Assyrian and Babylonian Priests to Kings Asarhaddon and Assurbanipal*. State Archives of Assyria 13. Helsinki: Helsinki University, 1998. Cited as SAA 13.

Crawford, Sidnie White. "4QDeut c." In *Qumran Cave 4 IX Deuteronomy, Joshua, Judges, Kings*, by Eugene Ulrich, Frank Moore Cross, Sidnie White Crawford, Julie Ann Duncan, Patrick W. Skehan, Emanuel Tov, and Julio Trebolle Barrera, 15–34. Discoveries in the Judaean Desert 14. Oxford: Clarendon, 1995.

Crouch, Carly. *Israel and the Assyrians: Deuteronomy, the Succession Treaty of Esarhaddon, and the Nature of Subversion*. Ancient Near Eastern Monographs 8. Atlanta: Society of Biblical Literature, 2014.

Crouch, Carly L. *The Making of Israel: Cultural Diversity in the Southern Levant and the Formation of Ethnic Identity in Deuteronomy*. Vetus Testamentum Supplements 162. Leiden: Brill, 2014.

Dalman, Gustav. *Arbeit und Sitte in Palästina*, Vol. 6: *Zeltleben, Vieh- und Milchwirtschaft, Jagd, Fischfang*. Gütersloh: Bertelsmann, 1939.

Eslinger, Lisle M. "The Case of an Immodest Lady Wrestler in Deuteronomy 25:11–12." *Vetus Testamentum* 31 (1981): 269–81.

Gall, August Freiher von, ed. *Der hebräische Pentateuch der Samaritaner*. Giessen: Alfred Töpelmann, 1914.

Graslin, Laetitia. "Les mécanismes de régulation des marchands mésopotamiens au premier millénaire av. J.-C." In *Les régulations sociales dans l'antiquité*, edited by Michel Molin, 139–56. Rennes: Presses universitaires, 2006.

Greifenhagen F. V. *Egypt on the Pentateuch's Ideological Map: Constructing Biblical Israel's Identity*. Journal for the Study of the Old Testament Supplement Series 361. Sheffield: Sheffield Academic, 2002.

Hölscher, Gustav. “Komposition und Ursprung des Deuteronomiums.” *Zeitschrift für die alttestamentliche Wissenschaft* 40 (1923): 161–255.

Hunger, Hermann. *Astrological Reports to Assyrian Kings*. State Archives of Assyria 8. Helsinki: Helsinki University, 1992. Cited as SAA 8.

Jacobs, Sandra. “Instrumental Talion in Deuteronomic Law.” *Zeitschrift für altorientalische und biblische Rechtsgeschichte* 16 (2010): 263–278.

Japhet, Sara. “Relationship between the Legal Corpora in the Pentateuch in Light of Manumission Laws.” In: Japhet Sara. *Studies in Bible*, 40–74. Jerusalem: Magness, 1986.

Joannès, Francis and André Lemaire. “Contrats babyloniens d’époque achéménide du Bît-abi Râm avec une épitaphe araméenne.” *Revue d’assyriologie et d’archéologie orientale* 90 (1996): 41–60.

Joannès, Francis and André Lemaire. “Trois tablettes cunéiformes à l’onomastique ouest-sémitique.” *Transeuphratène* 17 (1999): 17–34.

Joüon, Paul and Tamitsu Muraoka. *A Grammar of Biblical Hebrew*. Rome: Pontifical Biblical Institute, 2008.

Jursa, Michael. “Business Companies in Babylonia in the First Millennium BC: Structure, Economic Strategies, Social Setting.” In *The Knowledge Economy and Technological Capabilities: Egypt, the Near East and the Mediterranean 2nd Millennium BC–1st Millennium AD*, edited by Myriam Wissa, 53–68. Aula orientalis Supplementa 26. Sabadell, Spain: Editorial Ausa, 2010.

Jursa, Michael, with contributions by Joahnnes Hackl et al. *Aspects of the Economic History of Babylonia in the First Millennium BC: Economic Geography, Economic Mentalities, Agriculture, the Use of Money and the Problem of Economic Growth*. Alter Orient und Altes Testament 377; Veröffentlichungen zur Wirtschaftsgeschichte Babyloniens im 1. Jahrtausend v. Chr. 4. Münster: Ugarit-Verlag, 2010.

Levin, Christoph. “Das Deuteronomium und der Jahwist.” In Fortschreibungen: Gesammelte *Studien zum Alten Testament*, by Christoph Levin, 96–110. Beihefte zur Zeitschrift für die alttestamentliche Wissenschaft 316. Berlin: de Gruyter, 2003.

Levin, Christoph. “Rereading Deuteronomy in the Persian and Hellenistic Periods: The Ethics of Brotherhood and the Care of the Poor.” In *Deuteronomy-Kings as Emerging Authoritative Books: A Conversation*, edited by Diana V. Edelman, 49–72. Ancient Near Eastern Monographs 6. Atlanta: Society of Biblical Literature, 2014.

Levinson, Bernard M. “The Manumission of Hermeneutics: The Slave Laws of the Pentateuch as a Challenge to Contemporary Pentateuchal Theory.” In *Congress Volume Leiden 2004*, edited by André Lemaire, 281–324. Vetus Testamentum Supplements 109. Leiden: Brill, 2006.

Liverani, Mario. “The Influence of Political Institutions on Trade in the Ancient Near East (Late Bronze to Early Iron Age).” In *Mercanti e politico nel mondo antico*, edited by Carlo Zaccagnini, 119–38. Rome: L’Erma di Bretschneider, 2003.

Lohfink, Norbert. “Das deuteronomische Gesetz in der Endgestalt. Entwurf eine Gesellschaft ohne marginale Gruppen.” *Biblische Notizen* 51 (1990): 25–40.

Lohfink, Norbert. “Poverty in the Laws of the Ancient Near East and of the Bible.” *Theological Studies* 52 (1991): 34–50.

McCarthy, Carmel. *Deuteronomy*. Biblia hebraica quinta editione cum apparatu critic novis curis elaborato 5. Stuttgart: Deutsche Bibelgesellschaft, 2007.

McConville, J. Gordon. *Deuteronomy*. Leicester: Apollos, 2002.

Montanari, Franco, ed. *Brill Dictionary of Ancient Greek*. English edition edited by Madeleine Goh and Chad Schroeder. Leiden: Brill, 2015. Cited as *BDAG*.

Morrow, William S. *An Introduction to Biblical Law*. Grand Rapids: Eerdmans, 2017.

Nougayrol, Jean. *Palais Royal d'Ugarit*. Vol. 4. *Textes accadiens des archives sud (archives internationales)*. Mission de Ras Shamra 9. Paris: Imprimerie nationale, 1956. Cited as *PRU* 4.

Oppenheimer, Leo and Erica Reiner, eds. *Chicago Assyrian Dictionary*, vol. 1, *A, Part 2*. Chicago: The Oriental Institute, 1964. Cited as *CAD*.

Otto, Eckart. *Deuteronomium 1–11*. Herders Theologischer Kommentar zum Alten Testament. Freiburg im Breisau: Herder, 2012.

Otto, Eckart. *Deuteronomium 12,1–23,15*. Herders Theologischer Kommentar zum Alten Testament. Freiburg im Breisau: Herder, 2016.

Otto Eckart. "False Weights in the Scale of Biblical Justice? Different Views of Women from Patriarchal Hierarchy to Religious Equality in the Book of Deuteronomy." In *Gender and Law in the Hebrew Bible and the Ancient Near East*, edited by Victor H. Matthews, Bernard M. Levinson, and Tikva Frymer-Kensky, 128–46. Journal for the Study of the Old Testament Supplement Series 262. Sheffield: Sheffield Academic, 1998.

Otto, Eckart. *Das Gesetz des Moses*. Darmstadt: Wissenschaftliche Buchgesellschaft, 2007.

Otto, Eckart. "Human Rights: The Influence of the Hebrew Bible." *Journal of Northwest Semitic Languages* 21 (1999): 1–20.

Paul, Shalom M. "Biblical Analogues to Middle Assyrian Law," in *Religion and Law: Biblical-Judaic and Islamic Perspectives*, edited by Edwin B. Firmage, Bernard G. Weiss, and John W. Welch, 333–50. Winona Lake: Eisenbrauns, 1990.

Payne, Elizabeth E. "New Evidence for the 'Craftsmen's Charter.'" *Revue d'assyriologie et d'archéologie orientale* 102 (2008): 99–114.

Pearce, Laurie E. and Cornelia Wunsch. *Documents of Judean Exiles and West Semites in Babylonia in the Collection of David Sofer*. Cornell University Studies in Assyriology and Sumeriology 28. Bethesda, MD: CDL, 2014. Cirted as CUSAS.

Perlitt, Lothar. "'Ein einzig Volk von Brüdern': Zur deuteronomischen Herkunft der biblischen Bezeichnung 'Brüder.'" In *Kirche: Festschrift für Günther Bornkamm zum 75. Geburtstag*, edited by Dieter Lührmann and Georg Strecker, 27–52. Tübingen: J. C. B. Mohr, 1980. Reprinted in Perlitt, Lothar. *Deuteronomium Studien*, 50–73. Forschungen zum Alten Testament 8. Tübingen: Mohr, 1994.

Porten, Bezalel. *Archives from Elephantine: The Life of an Ancient Jewish Military Colony*. Berkeley: University of California Press, 1968.

Porten, Bezalel and Ada Yardeni. *Textbook of Aramaic Documents from Ancient Egypt*. 4 vols. Winona Lake: Eisenbrauns, 1986–1999. Cited as *TAD*.

Postgate, J. Nicholas. "Some Latter-Day Merchants of Aššur." In *Vom Alten Orient zum Alten Testament: Festschrift W. von Soden*, edited by Manfred Dietrich and Otto Loretz, 403–6. Alter Orient und Altes Testament 240. Neukirchen-Vluyn: Neukirchener Verlag, 1995.

Radner, Karen. "Die beiden neuassyrischen Privatarchive." In *Ausgrabungen in Assur: Wohnquartiere in der Weststadt, Teil 1*, edited by Peter A. Miglus, Karen Radner, and Franciszek M. Stepniowski, 79–133. Wissenschaftliche Veroffentlichungen der Deutschen Orient-Gesellschaft Series 143. Wiesbaden: Harrassowitz, 2016.

Radner, Karen. "Traders in the Neo-Assyrian Period." In *Trade and Finance in Ancient Mesopotamia: Proceedings of the First MOS Symposium (Leiden 1997)*, edited by J. G. Dercksen, 101–26. MOS Studies 1. Leiden: Nederlands historisch-archaeologisch Instituut te Istanbul, 1999.

Rainey, Anson F. “Business Agents at Ugarit.” *Israel Exploration Journal* 13 (1963): 313–21.

Reuter Eleanore. *Kultzentralisation: Entstehung und Theologie von Dtn 12*. Bonner biblicshe Beiträge 87. Frankfurt am Main: Hain, 1993.

Römer, Thomas C. *The So-Called Deuteronomistic History: A Sociological, Historical and Literary Introduction*. London: T&T Clark International, 2007.

Rossi, Benedetta and Philippe Guillaume. “An Alternative Reading the Law of the Hebrew ‘Slave’ (Deuteronomy 15:12–18).” *Res Antiquae* 15 (2018): 1–28.

Scott P. M. *Schiller’s William Tell, translated, with an introduction and notes, by Major-General Patrick Maxwell Scott*. London: Walter Scott, no date.

Stulman, Louis. “Encroachment in Deuteronomy: An Analysis of the Social World of the D Code.” *Journal of Biblical Literature* 109 (1990): 613–32.

Tigay, Jeffrey H. *Deuteronomy*. JPS Torah Commentary. Philadelphia: Jewish Publication Society, 1996.

Tsai, Daisy Yulin. *Human Rights in Deuteronomy: With Special Focus on Slave Laws*. Beihefte zur Zeitschrift für die alttestamentliche Wissenschaft 464. Berlin: de Gruyter, 2014.

Ulrich, Eugene C., ed. *The Biblical Qumran Scrolls: Transcriptions and Textual Variants*. Vetus Testamentum Supplements 134. Leiden: Brill, 2010. And http://dssenglishbible.com/scroll4Q45.htm and http://www.deadseascrolls.org.il/explore-the-archive/image/B-368456.

Van Seters, John. *A Law Book for the Diaspora: Revision in the Study of the Covenant Code*. New York: Oxford University Press, 2003.

Walsh, Jerome. “You Shall Cut Off Her … Palm? A Re-Examination of Deuteronomy 25:11–12.” *Journal of Semitic Studies* 49 (2004): 47–58.

Waltke, Bruce K. and Michael Patrick O’Connor. *An Introduction to Biblical Hebrew Syntax*. Winona Lake, IN: Eisenbrauns, 1990.

Weinfeld, Moshe. “Deuteronomy: The Present State of the Field.” In *A Song of Power and the Power of Song*, edited by Duane L. Christensen, 21–35. Winona Lake: Eisenbrauns, 1993.

Wunsch, Cornelia. “Debt, Interest, Pledge and Forfeiture in the Neo-Babylonian and Early Achaemenid Period.” In *Debt and Economic Renewal in the Ancient Near East*, edited by Michael Hudson and Marc Van De Mieroop, 221–53. International Scholars Conference on Ancient Near Eastern Economies 3. Bethesda, MD: CDL, 2002.

Zinzendorf, Count Nikolaus Ludwig Graf von. *Gesangbuch der Evangelischen Brüdergemeinde*. Hamburg: Friedrich Wittig, 1967.

Benedetta Rossi

"Not by Bread Alone" (Deut 8:3): Elite Struggles over Cultic Prebends and Moses's Torah in Deuteronomy

Introduction

For some time, it has been recognized that one of the peculiar characteristics of Deuteronomy in comparison with the priestly texts (P) is its "lay" character, which Moshe Weinfeld characterizes as "secularization."[1] The almost total absence, even the marginalization of the cult and of cultic regulations in Deuteronomy is striking. Gerhard von Rad describes the book as a divine charge "given to a lay community"; that is why "all that is ritual in the technical sense, so far as it concerns only the cult personnel, is absent."[2] However, one of the thorny issues of Deuteronomy is precisely the priesthood and, in particular, the connection between the Levites and the priesthood.[3]

In the following paper, I shall argue that the Levitical priests represent an emerging scribal elite, bound up with the cult only in a secondary way, in contrast to the religious elite and their cultic privileges. The religious elite in question is represented in particular by the priests who are descended from Aaron. It seems that the Levitical priests responded to the cultic privileges that the Aaronide priests reserved for themselves by contesting them and claiming for themselves an exclusive competence in the Torah of Moses and its authoritative teaching. The background to the dispute apparently was a competition between two groups of personnel serving in the temple (scribal-administrative v. cultic). In the final analysis, the *casus belli* can be ascribed to a reorganization of the prebendary system in favor of the priests, as described particularly in Numbers 18.

In § 1 I shall briefly present the two principal interpretive frameworks for the relationship between the Levites and the priesthood in Deuteronomy. At the same time, I shall highlight five issues that remain unanswered when these two

1 Weinfeld, *Deuteronomy*, 190–243.

2 Von Rad, *Studies*, 13.

3 Some phrases characteristic of Deuteronomy highlight the importance of the issue at stake: "Levitical priests/priests sons of Levi" (7 times in Deuteronomy, which is the book with the most occurrences of the phrase in the Hebrew Bible); "the Levite within your gates" (only present in Deut 12:12,18; 14:27; 16:11, 14).

https://doi.org/10.1515/9783110713312-012

frameworks are applied singly or in tandem. Then, in § 2, I will undertake a fresh evaluation of the relationship between the Aaronide priesthood and the Levitical priests, beginning with the mediatory priestly function of enacting reconciliation with God in 10:6–9 before moving to the system of priestly prebends, with its associated distinctions, in 18:1–8. Next, in § 3 I shall show the strategies through which the Levitical priests presented themselves as a new elite, claiming for themselves an exclusive connection with the Torah and the authority of Moses. Finally, in § 4, based on a comparison with material from the ancient Near East, I shall provide a reconstruction of the background to the rise of the Levitical priesthood and of its possible implications for the composition of Deuteronomy.

1 Levitical Priests: Between Centralization of the Cult and Levitization of the Priesthood. Two Current Frameworks

Typically, scholars adopt two interpretative frameworks to explain the relationship between Levites and the priesthood in Deuteronomy: the centralization of the cult and the idea of the Levitization of the priesthood. Generally, criticism of one of these two interpretative schemes ends up making use of the other.

1.1 Centralization of the Cult

Julius Wellhausen singled out the centralization of the cult.[4] He deduced that the distinction between local Levites (i.e. "within your gates," understood with spatial significance)[5] and Zadokite Levitical priests in the central sanctuary in Jerusalem was a consequence of Josiah's reform.[6] Deuteronomy, which consid-

4 Wellhausen, *Prolegomena*, 121–22, esp. 146–47.

5 "*Levites* in the provincial towns of Judah" (Wellhausen, 143).

6 The abolition of local shrines would have caused the marginalization of the local priesthood (represented by the Levites) in favor of the Levitical Priests (Zadokites) serving in Jerusalem. Ezek 44 "merely drapes the logic of facts with a mantle of morality"; i.e. Ezek 44 ascribes the marginalization of the local priesthood to cultic faults (Wellhausen, 122–24). Deut 18:1–8 compensates for the loss of local places of worship by allowing the provincial Levite to go to Jerusalem to officiate. See also Otto, "Priestertum," 1,647–48. However, the compensation imagined by the Deuteronomist failed. The subordination of Levites to the Zadokite Priests of Jerusalem would be the outcome of this failure (Wellhausen, *Prolegomena*, 146–47). "In this

ers all Levites to be priests, would be the starting point for explaining Ezekiel 44 and P. Ezekiel 44 offers a reason for the downgrading of the local Levites and for the distinction between Levites and Levitical priests. P establishes the subordination of the Levites to the (Aaronide) priests as going back to the time of Moses.[7] As Jaeyoung Jeon observes, Josiah's reform and the centralization of the cult continue to be a widespread framework for interpreting the issue of the Levitical priests in Deuteronomy.[8] However, the position of the Levitical priests performing cultic functions at the *māqôm* needs critical scrutiny.

The Levitical priests are only present at the *māqôm* explicitly in 17:8–9, and their presence does not involve liturgical or cultic service but the administration of justice (// with שפט). The competence of the Levitical priests in 17:8, repeatedly expressed by the root ירה (יורוך, vv. 10.11; התורה, v. 11), is in giving an authoritative word in matters of jurisprudence (דבר המשפט, v. 9).[9] However, in Deuteronomy, the exercise of juridical power by the Levitical priests is not linked exclusively with the *māqôm*. In 21:5, the Levitical priests act locally (v. 1: באדמה אשר יהוה אלהיך נתן לך; v. 2: הערים אשר סביבת החלל) alongside the elders to resolve the case of a homicide without witnesses.[10]

In Deuteronomy 31:11–13, the septennial reading of the Torah of Moses by the Levitical priests takes place at the *māqôm* on the occasion of the feast of Sukkot. On this occasion, the Levitical priests present at the place chosen by Yhwh do not explicitly perform a cultic function but instead, teach and proclaim (קרא, v. 11) the Torah of Moses. Similar to what we have observed for their judicial authority, the legal instructions laid down in Deuteronomy 24:8 (ירה) show that the authoritative instruction by Levitical priests is not linked exclusively to the *māqôm*.

Even the mention of the Levitical priests in 17:18 does not imply their presence in the place chosen by Yhwh. If מלפני הכהנים הלוים (v. 18) is read in a spatial sense ("in the presence of the Levitical priests"), the expression simply indicates supervision by the Levitical priests, without specifying their location.

---

way arose as an illegal consequence of Josiah's reformation, the distinction between priests and Levites" (Wellhausen, 147).

7 Already Wellhausen, 125–26.

8 Jeon, "Levites," 339.

9 I.e. the sentence; so e.g. Driver, *Deuteronomy*, 208. Deut 17:9–11 uses terminology to draw a distinction between the expertise of the judges and that of Levitical priests. Both deal with legal issues (v. 9: דבר המשפט), but the noun משפט never appears as the direct object of the root ירה. It seems reasonable, therefore, to argue that the verb ירה and the noun תורה in vv. 9–11 point to the competencies of Levitical priests.

10 Eckart Otto shows in detail that Deut 21:1–9 is to be considered an example of a legal act (*Rechtsakte*) (*Deuteronomium 12,1–23,15*, 1,642–46).

If the expression מלפני הכהנים הלוים is understood as "in agreement with the copy held by the Levitical priests," it is underlining that custody of the master copy of the Torah is in the hands of the Levitical priests.[11] No details are provided as to the location of the latter.

To sum up, in Deuteronomy, the presence of the Levitical priests at the *māqôm* is bound up with judicial authority and teaching, but it is not forbidden for either task to be exercised in other places than that chosen by Yhwh.

1.2 The Levitization of the Priesthood

Ulrich Dahmen and Reinhard Achenbach take up the terminology of Antonius Gunneweg and emphasize the phenomenon of the Levitization of the priesthood, which they place in the post-Exilic period.[12] From being a disadvantaged class included in the list of *personae miserae* (pre-Exilic Deut), after a post-Exilic rewriting, the Levites were to assume priestly prerogatives. In their view, the subordination of the Levites (*clerus minor*) to the Aaronide priests, descendants of Eleazar (*clerus maior*), as attested in P (Ezek 44; Num 18) and Chronicles, was a reaction to the process of the Levitization of the priesthood.[13]

The idea of a Levitization of the priesthood in Deuteronomy has the advantage of separating the interpretation of the relationship between the Levites and the priesthood from the centralization of the cult.[14] Moreover, it conveniently places the relationship between the Levites and the priesthood against the background of the composition of the Hexateuch and the Pentateuch.[15] Nevertheless, this interpretative model leaves some questions unanswered.

---

11 On the contrary, Samuel R. Driver infers a reference to the central sanctuary from Deut 31: 9, 26 (*Deuteronomy*, 212). See also Wright, "Levites," 327. He admits, however, "though it is not stated, we may infer that they were probably altar clergy."

12 Gunneweg, *Leviten*, 117–38 (esp. 138); Dahmen, *Leviten*, 396–401; Achenbach, "Levitische Priester," 286–95.

13 See the summary in Otto, *Deuteronomium 4,44–11,32*, 990–96 and *Deuteronomium 12,1–23,15*, 1,478–80. Tackling the issue from Deut 18:1–8, Raymond Abba ascribes the distinction between subordinate cultic officials (Levites) and priests to the monarchic period ("Priests," 266–67).

14 See Jeon, "Levites," 339–40.

15 See Otto, "Priestertum," 1,648–49.

1.3 Unresolved Issues

I shall highlight five issues that remain unanswered when the two frameworks of cultic centralization and the Levitization of the priesthood are applied singly or in tandem.

First, Deuteronomy 18:1–2, 5 would have to be considered the first attestation of the Levitical priesthood.[16] If this is the first attestation, ascribed to a dtr hand, how do we explain the presence in 18:1 of the reference to the "fire offerings" (אשי)? This typically priestly lexeme is a hapax in Deuteronomy; it occurs for the most part in Leviticus (41 out of 64 uses) and Numbers (16 out of 64 uses).[17] Moreover, if this is the first attestation of the Levitical priesthood, how are we to interpret the reference to Yhwh's previous pronouncement to them in v. 2: כאשר דבר לו?[18]

Second, the Levitization of the priesthood would provoke the reaction of the Zadokite (Ezek 44) and the Aaronide (Num 18) priesthoods to the claims advanced by the "Levitical priests." However, Reinhard Achenbach claims that the typical area of competence assigned to the Levitical priests in Deuteronomy is the Torah of Moses.[19] In the book, this characteristic competence of the Levitical priests is not connected to the world of the cult but rather, to the sapiential and lay spheres of instruction.[20] On closer inspection, then, the "Levitical priests" of Deuteronomy, with their competence in the Torah of Moses, do not seem to be a threat to the specifically cultic prerogatives of the descendants of Aaron. If this is so, why did the Aaronide priesthood have to react by claiming the priesthood for themselves? Why insist on the subordination of the Levites in the arrangement of the cult by instituting the typically cultic distinction between the temple personnel (Levites as *clerus minor*) and priests (descendants of Aaron as *clerus maior*)? If the intrusion of the "Levitical priests" into cultic questions cannot actually be detected in Deuteronomy, the reason for a reaction on the part of the Zadokite and Aaronide priesthood needs to be seen from a different perspective.

---

16 See Achenbach, "Levi," 439 and "Levitische Priester," 290.

17 Reinhard Achenbach considers the phrase יהוה הוא נחלתו (Deut 18:2), which hints back to Num 18:20, an addition ("Levitische Priester," 292).

18 The etiology of the Levites in Exod 32 ends up being useless for understanding the authoritative divine word hinted at in Deut 18:2.

19 See Achenbach, "Levitische Priester," 287–93.

20 So recognized already by von Rad, *Studies*, 11–24. See also Weinfeld, *Deuteronomy*, 161–66 and "On 'Demythologization'."

Third, the assumption of priestly prerogatives by the Levites is bound up with their competence in the Torah of Moses.[21] However, if this competence is not specifically connected with the world of the cult, why is the appellative כהן used to mark the assumption of this prerogative? Moreover, why would the Levites assume priestly prerogatives for themselves? In other words, the transition from the "Levite within your gates," understood as a *persona misera*, to the Levitical priests remains unexplained.

Fourth, the account of Korah's rebellion (Num 16) and the Levites is to be read as an etiology for the exclusion of the Levites "from the high priest's priestly ministry and cultic and political primacy."[22] In particular, the latter aspect would be reflected in the story of Aaron's rod (Num 17:16–26). If the etiology in Numbers 16–17 combines the exclusion of the Levites from the priesthood with their exclusion from political primacy, clearly the intention is to explain an attempt by the (non-Aaronide) Levites not only to assume the religious leadership (with the priesthood) but also the political leadership of the community. The fact that Korah's challenge is directed against Aaron (the priest) and against Moses, the leader of the community, underlines again the double nature of the rebellion as religious and political.[23]

The degradation of the Levites to the *clerus minor* is considered by those who follow this line of reasoning to be the response to the religious leadership claimed by the Levitical priests. The question of the political leadership claimed by the Levitical priests remains unsolved. Is it possible to find a trace of this double claim to religious and political leadership by the Levites of whom Korah, the descendant of Kohath, is made the spokesman in the etiology of Numbers 17:16–26?

Finally, Harald Samuel recently has made a critical examination of the idea of the Levitization of the priesthood.[24] In Deuteronomy, every Levite is potentially a priest. The expression "Levitical priests," a result of the centralization of the cult, would serve to indicate the actual practice of the priesthood in relation to the central sanctuary.[25] Here, the Levites not only would be priests potentially but also *de facto*. The positions favorable to the Levites, who were understood from the beginning as priests (potential or *de facto*), would then in his view be challenged by a series of additions expressing the priestly reaction

---

21 Achenbach, "Levi"; "Levitische Priester," 285–86.

22 Achenbach, "Levi," 440. According to Christian Frevel, Num 16 already presupposes the priestly hierarchy developed in Num 3 and 8 ("Ending with the High Priest," 149–50).

23 See also Pyschny, "Debated Leadership," 121–28.

24 Samuel, *Von Priestern*, esp. 141–45.

25 Samuel, 142.

to the pro-Levitical position.[26] The inclusion of the Levites among the *personae miserae* would be the clearest result of the priestly opposition to the Levites. The protection envisaged in Deuteronomy 12:19 and 14:27, 28–29 for the "Levite within your gates," together with other disadvantaged categories, makes it difficult to understand the inclusion of the Levite among the *personae miserae* as the result of a position hostile to the Levites. Thus, once again, considering the Levitization of the priesthood on the basis of the centralization of the cult does not seem compelling.

2 A Fresh Evaluation of the Levitical Priests and Their Relationship to Aaronide Priests

To offer a response to these questions and points that lack convincing solutions from an application of the model of Levitization, often due to cultic centralization, I will reconsider the entire relationship between the Aaronide priesthood and the Levitical priests, focusing on Deuteronomy 10:6–9 and 18:1–8.

2.1 The Aaronide Priesthood in Deuteronomy 10:6–9

Deuteronomy 10:6–9 contains references to the Aaronide high priesthood; this is shown by the lexicon and by a series of intertextual references. Even when the similarities of 10:6–9 to the priestly texts of the book of Numbers are generally recognized,[27] there is still a question about the direction of dependence and the type of relationship between the latter and Deuteronomy 10:6–9.[28]

For 10:6–7, it is possible to observe the following three points.[29] 1) Deuteronomy 10:6–7 attests to an exclusive connection with Numbers 33:30–34: the staging posts of B^{e}ne Yaʿaqan; Moser; Gudgod; and Yotbatah are mentioned only in

26 E.g. Deut 10:6–7 added to vv. 8–9. The mention of wilderness posts (vv. 6–7) would aim to detach the institution of Levitical duties from Horeb (Samuel, 21).
27 See already Driver, *Deuteronomy*, 118–21.
28 The crucial relevance of the issue at stake is highlighted by Otto, "Levitisierung," 280.
29 Scholars disagree whether Deut 10:6–9 should be ascribed to a single redactional layer or be seen as two different additions. Otto (*Deuteronomium 4,44–11,32*, 994–95) ascribes the whole of 10:6–9 to a post-exilic rewriting. Among those who are inclined to see two different redactional layers (vv. 6–7 and 8–9), are Driver, *Deuteronomy*, 118–121 (only vv. 6–7 are added); Dahmen, *Leviten*, 23–26, 105–6; Samuel, *Von Priestern*, 21–24.

these two texts.[30] 2) The tradition about the death of Aaron appears in Deuteronomy 10:6, Numbers 20:22–29, and Numbers 33:38–39. 3) The reference to the succession of Eleazar, which is attested in Deuteronomy 10:6, appears in connection with the death of Aaron in Numbers 20:22–29 but is not mentioned in Numbers 33:38–39.

Deuteronomy 10:6–7 combines references to various texts of Numbers; this leads us to the view that Deuteronomy 10:6–7 is later than Numbers 20:22–29 and 33:38–39. Moreover, whereas Numbers 33:30–34 is perfectly integrated into its context, Deuteronomy 10:6–7 is marked by numerous elements of rupture within its context, starting with the voice of the narrator, which replaces the discourse of Moses.[31] Finally, a similar technique of the conflation of texts can be observed in 9:22–23, belonging to the same pericope (Deut 9:7–10:11).[32]

In what follows, I would like to show that Deut 10:6–7 refers to the Aaronide high priesthood in order to question its legitimacy.

In Deuteronomy 10:6, the priesthood of Eleazar (כהן *piel*) is foregrounded. The same root, כהן *piel*, combined with the investiture formula מלא *piel* + obj. יד, is employed in Numbers 3:1–4 with reference to the priesthood of Eleazar. In this case, however, it is stated that Eleazar, with Ithamar, exercised the priesthood in the presence of Aaron (v. 4: ויכהן אלעזר ואיתמר על־פני אהרן אביהם). Numbers 20:22–29 describes Eleazar's succession in conjunction with Aaron's death on Mount Hor. At Yhwh's order (v. 24), Moses clothes Eleazar in Aaron's vestments; Aaron's vestments (described in Lev 8:7–9) are the vestments of the high priest.[33] The transfer of vestments indicates that Eleazar is replacing his father, Aaron, in the office of high priest. Verse 10:6 mentions Eleazar's priesthood (כהן *piel*) in connection with the death of Aaron (v. 6: שם מת אהרן ויקבר שם ויכהן אלעזר בנו תחתיו). The mention of Aaron's death, like the expression תחתיו, signals Eleazar's succession as high priest. Deuteronomy 10:6, therefore, deals with the theme of the Aaronide high priesthood.

By means of some variations from Numbers 33:30–34 and 20:22–29, Deuteronomy 10:6–7 questions the legitimacy of the Aaronide high priesthood. In addition to a variation in the steps of the journey as recounted in Number 33:30–

30 See Budd, *Numbers*, 350. SamPent further stresses the reference to Num 33:30–34 by harmonizing Deut 10:6 with Num 33:31–38 (see McCarthy, *Deuteronomy*, 79*). According to Philip J. Budd, Deut 10:6–7 provides the starting point for the list in Num 33 (*Numbers*, 355). Contrarily, Graham I. Davies considers the itinerary in Num 33 the original ("Itineraries," 6).

31 Already Driver, *Deuteronomy*, 118.

32 Num 11:1–3 and 11:4–35 are linked to Exod 17:2–7, see Otto, *Deuteronomium 4,44–11,32*, 981.

33 Budd, *Numbers*, 228.

34, which is typically stressed by the commentators,[34] Deuteronomy 10:6–7 reworks the notice of Aaron's death.

Aaron's death is recorded in Numbers 20:22–29 and 33:38–39. In 20:22–29, Yhwh announces it in v. 24, and in v. 28, the location of his death is given as Mount Hor (וימת אהרן שם). Yhwh makes it clear that, because Aaron was associated with Moses in the rebellion at Meribah, he will not enter the land promised to the fathers (v. 24). An ascent up the mountain (v. 27) precedes his death; v. 28 records the 30 days of mourning for his death (ויבכו את־אהרן שלשים יום כל בית ישראל). Numbers 33:38–39 (which omits the reference to Eleazar) indicates that Aaron ascends Mount Hor "at the command of Yhwh" (ויעל אהרן הכהן אל־הר ההר על־פי יהוה, v. 38). As a result, the parallel between Moses's death and that of his brother, Aaron (already evoked in Num 20:22–29) is intensified in that book (cf. Deut 34:5: וימת שם משה עבד־יהוה בארץ מואב על־פי יהוה).[35]

Deuteronomy 10:6–7 reduces the parallel between the deaths of Moses and Aaron drawn in Numbers in three ways. First, the site of Aaron's death is shifted from Mount Hor to Moserah (v. 6: ובני ישראל נסעו מבארתבני־יעקן מוסרה שם מת אהרן). In 10:6, Aaron does not ascend a mountain and die thereafter, like Moses. The fact that Deuteronomy 32:50 mentions Aaron's death on Mount Hor, thus establishing a parallel between the latter's death and that of Moses (כאשר מת אהרן אחיך בהרההר), indicates that the variation in Deuteronomy 10:6 is intentional.[36]

Second, the expression על־פי יהוה (Num 33:38 and Deut 32:50) marks the obedience of Aaron and Moses to Yhwh over their deaths. For Aaron, this obedience is bound up with his ascent up Mount Hor (Num 33:38); for Moses, the expression is linked to the verb מות. The reference to Aaron's obedience is absent in Deuteronomy 10:6, however; instead, 9:20 recalls his rebellion.

Third, none of the texts concerning Aaron's death (Num 20:28; 30:38; Deut 32:50) specifies the place of his burial. By contrast, Deuteronomy 10:6 specifies that Aaron was buried in Moserah. According to Eckart Otto, in Deuteronomy 10:6, the name Moserah (מוסרה) is to be understood as a reference to the divine מוסר in 11:2. Yhwh's discipline (מוסר) of his people is explained in 11:3–7 as a punishment for those who, from Egypt onwards, had not acknowledged the deeds of Yhwh (v. 3 mentions Pharaoh and the Egyptians; v. 6 refers to Dathan and Abiram). If this interpretation is correct, Aaron's death at Moserah is linked implicitly to punishment (*mûsar*), and in this "rebellion" he finds his burial. The failure to

34 For an overview, see Otto, *Deuteronomium 4,44–11,32*, 991.

35 According to Budd (*Numbers*, 227), "the account of the death of Moses had probably already been formulated."

36 References to Num 20:22–29 and 30:33–34 rule out the possibility that Deut 10:6 picks up a different tradition about Aaron's death.

mention Aaron's obedience supports this reading. Deuteronomy 10:6 places the succession of Eleazar against this background: ויכהן אלעזר בנו תחתיו (v. 6). In contrast to the account in Numbers 22:20–29, this one lacks any reference to divine or Mosaic legitimacy: the succession is portrayed simply as a hereditary one.

In brief, the uncoupling of Aaron's death from the Mosaic model together with the absence of divinely endorsed legitimation of Eleazar's succession produce the effect of questioning the Aaronide high priesthood.

On closer inspection, Deuteronomy 10:8–9 is pursuing a similar aim.[37] I shall make two points here.

1) In v. 8, the verb בדל *hiphil* is characteristic of priestly language.[38] With reference to the Levites, it occurs in Numbers 8:14 and 16:9 (+ subject Yhwh). In both of these cases, the separation of the Levites occurs in the desert and is linked to the subordination of their service to Aaron and his priesthood. In Deuteronomy 10:9, the separation of the tribe of Levi is performed by Yhwh[39] and is associated with Horeb (בעת ההוא, v. 8 → 10:1). The choice of the whole of the tribe of Levi is thus set in an authoritative place; moreover, it anticipates the succession of Eleazar (v. 6) and is thus freed from subordination to the Aaronide priests. The election of the entire tribe of Levi precedes the institution of the hereditary Aaronide high priesthood.[40]

2) In v. 9, the statement that Levi will have "neither portion nor inheritance with his brothers" (לא־היה ללוי חלק ונחלה עם־אחיו), together with the explanation that "Yhwh is his inheritance" (יהוה הוא נחלתו), refers to a previous pronouncement of Yhwh (כאשר דבר יהוה אלהיך לו). Dahmen shows in detail the possibility of identifying this divine pronouncement with the words addressed by Yhwh to Aaron in Numbers 18:20.[41] In 18:20–21, Yhwh establishes Aaron's pre-eminence over the Levites. The words, "You shall not have any heritage in their land nor hold any portion among them; I will be your portion and your heritage among the Israelites," (v. 20) are a theological legitimation of the prebendary privileges of Aaron and his descendants, which are presented in detail in vv. 8–19. Numbers 18:21 reserves for the Levites the tenth, subsequently

37 For different positions on the relation between vv. 6–7 and 8–9, see n. 30.

38 See Otzen, "בדל," 519–20; Dahmen, *Leviten*, 68.

39 Dahmen (*Leviten*, 29–30) sees in Deut 10:8 a critical stance toward Num 8:14. Here, Levites are separated by Moses; in Deut 10:8, on the contrary, Yhwh himself chooses the Levites.

40 As Christian Frevel highlights, in Deut 10:8 "the assignment of powers does not agree with the Levites' status in Numbers, but is contrastive to it" ("Ending with the High Priest," 144).

41 Dahmen, *Leviten*, 60–66. In his view, the references to Num 18:20 in Deut 10:8 are aimed at criticizing the Aaronidic priesthood (72). Samuel R. Driver contests the identification of the former divine word (Deut 10:9) with Num 18:20. In Num 18:20 Aaron is the recipient of Yhwh's pronouncement; in 10:9 the whole tribe of Levi receives it (*Deuteronomy*, 123–24).

reduced, of an offering for Yhwh that is appointed for Aaron (vv. 28–29). Thus, Numbers 18:20 contains the theological foundation for the prebendal system that privileges Aaron and his descendants, thus legitimizing their privileges over and against the Levites.

The reprise of Numbers 18:20 in Deuteronomy 10:8 is marked by a series of variations that underline the polemical force of the reference. In 10:9, the narrator reports the direct speech of Yhwh to Aaron (Num 18:20). Moreover, the referent of the statement in Deuteronomy 10:8 is no longer Aaron but Levi, i.e. the tribe of Levi ("Levi has no allotment or inheritance with his kindred; the Lord is his inheritance"). In Numbers 18:20, the divine speech was employed to give theological motivation to the tithes due to the sons of Aaron, a feature distinguishing the latter from the Levites. By contrast, Deuteronomy 10:8 provides a theological foundation for "not having portion or inheritance." In 10:9, the condition attributed to the whole of the tribe of Levi arises because (על כן) Yhwh has separated the latter from the rest of the people (בדל *hiphil*) for service. The consequences of "not having portion or inheritance," i.e. the question of the tithes, will be tackled in § 4.

To sum up: Deuteronomy 10:9 examines the causes of the statement addressed to Aaron in Numbers 18:20. The lack of a portion or inheritance alongside the rest of the people, the partial basis for the special status of Aaron's descendants, is destined for the whole of the tribe of Levi and founded on the election of the latter.

A critical attitude toward the Aaronide priesthood and its hereditary privileges is shared by 10:6–7 and 10:8–9. This favors the redactional unity of vv. 6–9. However, we still have to explain the sense of the location of vv. 6–9 in its present narrative context.

Verses 6–9 interrupt Moses's speech and, in particular, the account of the reestablishment of the covenant after the sin at Horeb. Deuteronomy 10:1–5 mentions the rewriting of the tablets and the construction of the Ark in which they are placed. The theme of 9:7–10:11 is the breaking of the covenant, caused by the sin of the calf, and its healing. The sequence in 10:1–5, 10–11 links the possibility of the renewal of the covenant to the intervention of Moses and his intercession at Horeb (9:25–29).

In 10:6–9, the narrator begins to speak, bringing the extra-diegetic addressee into play and extending the temporal perspective to his own time (v. 9: "until this day"). The "today" introduced by the narrator is that of the extradiegetic addressee and can be identified as the time of the Exile.[42] In the today of the

42 See Otto, *Deuteronomium 4,44–11,32*, 995–96.

narrator and of the extradiegetic addressee, it is no longer Moses who mediates reconciliation with Yhwh and the reestablishment of a broken covenant.[43] So, the question becomes, "How is one reconciled with God and how can his covenant be restored?"

Deuteronomy 10:6–9 seems to answer this question by comparing two different ways of re-establishing the relationship with Yhwh and showing the validity of one over the other by contrasting the two. The high priesthood, with the cult and the sacrificial practices, is compared with the Torah of Moses and found inadequate. The link between the high priesthood (Deut 10:6–7) and the reestablishment of the relationship with Yhwh is particularly clear with reference to its role in expiation (Lev 16:32).[44] Numbers 18:1 records a similar function for the Aaronide priesthood in connection with sins of a cultic nature.

The Torah of Moses as an instrument of reconciliation is evoked by the mention of the "Ark of the Covenant" (10:8), the carrying of which was entrusted to the tribe of Levi. In the context of Moses's account of the experience at Horeb, the Ark returns in 10:1, 3, 5. Ordered by Yhwh (10:1) and constructed by Moses (v. 3), the Ark has the role of safekeeping the document of the renewed Horeb covenant, i.e. the tablets written by Yhwh (10:2, 5).

However, the reference to the "today" of the extradiegetic addressee introduced by the narrator (10:8–9) allows us to attribute an added significance to the Ark of the Covenant. The Levitical task of carrying the Ark, which refers to the *fabula* of Deuteronomy in 31:9, is extended in time "until this day." The reference to Deuteronomy 31:9 includes the time in Moab where Moses hands over to the Levites the written Torah, which is to be placed by the side of the Ark (31:9, 25). However, in the (post-)Exilic period of the extradiegetic addressee ("until this day," Deut 10:9), the Ark of the Covenant is no longer present. It is plausible, therefore, that the mention of the Ark of the Covenant, entrusted to the Levites "until this day" (10:9), refers to the Torah of Moses that was entrusted to them (31:9) and, again, available to the extradiegetic addressee.[45] It already contains the Ten Commandments, so that nothing of significance has been lost, just the two artifacts on which the divine words were carved.

In Deuteronomy 30:1–10, the hearing and the custody of the Torah of Moses takes on a specific function with reference to the possible return after the Exile. The memory of the words of the Torah of Moses (30:1) will enable the scattered

---

43 See Otto, 1,001–2.

44 The phrase כהן *piel* + תחת points to an exclusive link between Deut 10:6 and Lev 16:32. The link is highlighted by Weyringer, *Schwelle* (forthcoming).

45 See Otto, *Deuteronomium 4,44–11,32*, 995–96.

people to be reconciled with Yhwh, opening the way for return to the land.[46] Thus, the Torah of Moses and its observance not only represent the document of the covenant in Moab; they offer a valid instrument for restoring the breach of the covenant.[47] After the disaster of the Exile, the memory of the Torah of Moses opens the way for reconciliation with Yhwh.

In summary, Deuteronomy 10:6–9 is inserted in 9:7–10:11 to compare two possible avenues of reconciliation with God: the priesthood and cult, entrusted to the priests descended from Aaron, on the one hand, or listening to and observance of the Torah of Moses, entrusted to the Levitical priests, on other hand. The efficacy of the latter is indicated at the expense of the former. Thus, the polemic against the Aaronide priesthood put forward by Deuteronomy 10:6–9 has as its aim the challenging not only of the institution of the Aaronide priesthood but, even more, its ability to accomplish reconciliation with God cultically and to re-establish the covenant after sin.[48]

So far, the debate between the Aaronide priesthood and the Levitical priests seems to be essentially theological. However, the reference to Numbers 18:20 already points the reader towards the nucleus of the question: the system of prebends and their distribution.

2.2 The Polemic over the System of Prebends (Deut 18:1–8)

Deuteronomy 18:1–8 deals with the maintenance of the Levitical priests, identified in v. 1 as "all the tribe of Levi."[49] Presenting the regulations for the maintenance of the clergy, 18:1–8 is a critical discussion of the interests of the Aaronide priesthood and their claims with respect to the Levites. In particular, the interests of the Aaronide priesthood and the distinction of the latter from the Levites are attested in vv. 3–5 and 6–7. The frames (vv. 1–2 and v. 8) question the prebendary privileges and the division of the clergy found in vv. 3–5, 6–7.[50]

---

46 See Otto, *Deuteronomium 23,16–34,12*, 2,066–68.
47 See Markl, "No Future," 722–24.
48 One question remains open: why not explicitly mention the Aaronidic priesthood when its privileges are discussed? A possible answer may come from the Mosaic authority of the debated priestly texts. The list of the posts of the Exodus itinerary in Num 33 is presented as Moses's writing (33:2), i.e. sharing the same authority as Moses's torah (Deut 31:9). Num 20 and 18 as well are Yhwh's words addressed to Aaron and Moses.
49 The phrase, "all the tribe of Levi," (כל־שבט לוי) occurs rather than the former phrase, "the Levitical priests" (כהנים הלוים); see Driver, *Deuteronomy*, 214.
50 According to Tigay, *Deuteronomy*, 170, Deut 18:1 "counters the view of Leviticus and Numbers that restricts the priesthood to Aaron's family."

Deuteronomy 18:3–5 exemplifies four particular characteristics from the point of view of vocabulary and contents. First, in 18:4, there appears the list of first fruits to be given to the priest (ראשית דגנך תירשך ויצהרך וראשית גז צאנך תתן־לו). The list corresponds to the list of products of the land that is typical of Deuteronomy (7:13; 11:14; 12:17; 14:23; 28:51)[51] but with two variations: the addition of the substantive ראשית and the reference to the "first fruits of the fleece of your flock," a hapax in the Hebrew Bible.[52] In Deuteronomy, the substantive ראשית, used in the sense of "first fruits," occurs elsewhere in 26: 2,10: the first fruits of the products of the soil are destined for Yhwh (cf. also Exod 23:19; 34:26). In 26:4, the priest who sets the basket with the first fruits on the altar has the sole function of witnessing the gift to Yhwh.

Things are different in Numbers 18:12–14: "The best of the oil, the wine, and the grain, their first fruits," which the sons of Israel bring to Yhwh are destined for Aaron by the command of the same deity ("I will give them to you," לך נתתים, v. 12). Whoever is pure in the house of Aaron (v. 13: כל טהור בביתך) can eat it. The distinction between the first fruits appointed by Yhwh for the Aaronides and the tithes appointed for the Levites is established by Numbers 18:21: "to the sons of Levi I am giving all the tithes in Israel as an inheritance (ולבני לוי הנה נתתי כל מעשר בישראל לנחלה)." In Nehemiah 10:38, the Israelites themselves bear witness to this practice: "the first fruit of our coarse meal (ואת־ראשית עריסתינו) and of our offerings, of the fruit of every tree, of wine, and of oil (תירוש ויצהר) we shall bring to the priests (נביא לכהנים) and the tithe of our soil to the Levites (ומעשר אדמתנו ללוים)."[53] Deuteronomy 18:3, which seeks to give the first fruits of the gifts of the land to the priest, reflects a practice and a concern similar to that of Numbers 18.[54]

Second, Deuteronomy 18:3 fixes a portion to be given to the priests in the context of a sacrificial animal (זבח): "you shall give the priest the shoulder,

---

51 So e.g. Dahmen, *Leviten*, 281; Samuel, *Von Priestern*, 120–22.

52 Wool appears as a cultic prebend in contracts from Seleucid Uruk detailing the purchase of multiple/cumulative prebends. In addition to meat, textiles and carded wool are mentioned (see Corò, *Prebende Templari*, 129).

53 In addition to the distinction between priests and Levites indicated by their distinctive income streams (first fruits to the priests; tithes, in general, to Levites), Joseph Blenkinsopp highlights the anti-Levitical position of Neh 10:38–40. An Aaronite priest supervises the Levites collecting the tithe; after completing their work, the Levites are required to give a tenth of their tithe to the priests (*Ezra-Nehemiah*, 317–19).

54 According to Philip J. Budd, Num 18:8–20 aims at defining the prebendary system for the clergy (*Numbers*, 202). However, the different prebendary statuses reinforces and secures the distinction between Aaronide priest and Levites.

the cheeks and the stomach (ונתן לכהן הזרוע והלחים והקבה)."[55] Deuteronomy mentions the slaughter (זבח) of animals and the eating of flesh (אכל) in 12:5, 21 and in connection with the celebration of the Passover (16:2–7). In each of these cases, the eating of the flesh that has been sacrificed is to be done by the one slaughtering the animals. In 12:15, 21, the eating is set within "your gates" and everyone can eat of it until they are full (v. 21: בכל אות נפשך). The fact that both the pure and impure can eat it indicates that there are no restrictions in this connection. In the case of the Passover, too, the eating of the flesh that has been offered is carried out by the one who performs the slaughtering. In no case of the slaughter of flesh does Deuteronomy specify that a portion is appointed for the priest. By contrast, the cuts of flesh destined for the priest from cultic offerings are laid down in Exodus 29:27, Leviticus 10:14–15, and Numbers 18:18 (breast and thigh); in Leviticus 7:32–34, only the thigh is destined for the priest. The substantive זרוע, referring to an animal, occurs only in Deuteronomy 18:3 and Numbers 6:19. In Numbers 6:18–20, the shoulder of the animal is destined for the priest along with the breast and the thigh. In brief: the interests expressed in Deuteronomy 18:3 seem once more to be in dissonance with the rest of the book, whereas they are in line with the interests of P with regard to the portions of the sacrifices to be given to the priest.

Third, the sequence of cuts in 18:3 (הזרוע והלחים והקבה) destined for the priest is a *unicum* in the Hebrew Bible. It has no correspondence in the portions usually assigned to the priest in Leviticus and Numbers. The lists of cuts of meat recorded in Ash 1922.256, however, a temple ordinance for the Eanna temple (Uruk), can provide clues for proposing an interpretation of the biblical text.[56] The lists of Ash 1922.256 are arranged in decreasing order according to the price of the cuts of meat:[57] the most expensive cuts are reserved for the sovereign (l. 2: "A shoulder, the rump and a rib roast"), and then for the priestly

55 For the distribution of sacrificial meat in the Hebrew Bible, see Amadasi Guzzo, "Sacrificie banchetti," 98–108.

56 See McEwan, "Distribution," 187–98 and also Corò, "Meat," 26–63. As Corò highlights, assigning leftovers from the sacrifice marks an evolution of the prebendary system. In order to make the distribution of cultic prebends easier, the allotment of land (prebendary fields) is replaced by the assignment of sacrificial remainders. The development takes place when the prebends, originally assigned from the king, end up being inherited, purchased or sold (*Prebende*, 24).

57 I follow here the transcription and translation of Ash 1922.256 provided by McEwan, "Distribution," 188–94. The text is probably a scribal exercise. This, however, does not downplay its importance "as a historical source for the period of the composition of the original" (McEwan, 194).

hierarchies and the temple officials in decreasing order of importance.[58] From the shoulder (l. 2), the first cut mentioned because it is the most expensive, the list ends with the "rumen, small intestines, the 'colon' and the blood intestines and the lungs" (l. 19), passing through the neck and the head (ll. 12–13).[59] A similar dynamic can be observed in the trio in Deuteronomy 18:3: from the shoulder, one comes to the stomach, passing through the cheeks/jaws of the animal (i.e. part of the head). In light of Ash 1922.256, it is improbable that one and the same category of priest or official received the shoulder (the first cut mentioned) together with part of the head and the stomach, which was one of the cheaper cuts in Ash 1922.256 l. 42. So how are we to understand Deuteronomy 18:3? Presumably, the trio of meat cuts is a summary of the whole division of cuts of meat, beginning with the most expensive (the shoulder) down to the stomach, the least expensive. Thus, this triad is evoking the totality of the animal's flesh assigned to various temple prebendaries, according to different cuts and their different roles (e.g. Ash 1922.256). The fact that the whole animal in Deut 18:3 is destined for the priests only underlines the extension of their privileges.

Fourth, Deuteronomy 18:5 brings to the fore the idea of a continuous priestly ministry (כל הימים) bound up with descent (הוא ובניו). Such a portrayal contrasts with the representation of the priesthood (כהן) elsewhere in Deuteronomy. In the majority of cases, the role of כהן is specified as a temporary office, marked by the expression היה + בימים ההם (cf. 19:17; 26:3–4 and also 17:12 with reference to v. 9). The idea of a hereditary priesthood (כהן *piel*) occurs in Deuteronomy 10:6 with reference to the succession of Eleazar and the Aaronide high priest. Once again, the idea of the priesthood contained in Deuteronomy 18:5 is a close reflection of the Aaronide priesthood (hereditary and continuous) rather than the temporary priestly post attested in the majority of cases in Deuteronomy. The transference of the terminology of the election of the *māqôm* (בחר + subject יהוה) to the person of the priest is a further legitimation of the latter,[60] reinforcing the view that is favorable to priestly interests, and, more precisely, the interests of the Aaronide priesthood as contained in 18:3–5.

To sum up, vv. 3–5 reveal the use of phraseology typical of Deuteronomy (the trio of products of the land and the formula of the election of the *māqôm*). However, the content contrasts with the sacrificial practice (the sacrifice and

---

58 McEwan, 195: "The order in which the terms are listed in the texts is as much influenced by considerations of priestly hierarchy as by anatomical arrangement."

59 The head is mentioned in l. 13 without any detailing of its different parts. Presumably, the whole head was destined to the same person (McEwan, 195).

60 Cf. Otto, *Deuteronomium 12,1–23,15*, 1,490.

eating of the meat and the destination of the first fruits) and the conception of the priesthood attested elsewhere in Deuteronomy. Conversely, the interests represented by vv. 3–5 are close to the interests attested elsewhere in priestly writings (e.g. Num 18), which refer particularly to the interests of the Aaronide priesthood (see Deut 18:5).

Deuteronomy 18:6–7 seems to be responding to a similar logic.[61] The expression הלוי מאחד שעריך (v. 6) is taking up the typical terminology the Deuteronomic code uses to refer to the Levite ("the Levite within your (sing. and pl.) gates"; הלוי אשר בשעריך /- כם, e.g. 12:12, 18; 14:27), assigning it a spatial sense. In particular, vv. 6–7 indicate not only the possibility that the Levite may move to the *māqôm* to carry out cultic functions (v. 7) but also the presence of Levites stationed (v. 7) at the *māqôm* in the presence of Yhwh (הלוים העמדים שם לפני יהוה, v. 7). The function performed by the latter is identified in v. 7 with the same roots, עמד and שרת, that were employed for the priest in v. 5. However, there are some differences: the service of the priest in v. 5 is the result of a particular divine election (כי בו בחר יהוה, v. 5) and is the object of a specific fee (vv. 3–4). By contrast, the Levite enters into service "according to the desire of his heart" (בכל אות נפשו, v. 6) and joins the other Levites who carry out a similar service (v. 7), but there is no mention of specific fees.

The differences between the service of the priest with his rights (vv. 3–5) and that of the Levites at the *māqôm* seem to indicate the Levites are cultic personnel of a lower rank (*clerus minor*), i.e. additional personnel serving before Yhwh with a status and privileges quite different from those of the כהן.[62] Confirmation of this could come from the occurrences of the phrase "all his brother Levites":[63] the phrase occurs elsewhere in the Pentateuch only in Numbers 8:26 and 18:2, 6 in contexts in which the Levites are subordinated to the Aaronide priesthood.

In sum, from what we have seen, Deuteronomy 18:3–5 and 6–7 reflect the interests of the Aaronide priests and implicitly reiterate the difference between them and the Levites who are present at the *māqôm* as additional personnel not

---

61 Driver stresses a contrast between Deut 10:6 and the cities assigned to the Levites in Num 35:1–8 and Josh 21. The institution of Levitical cities cannot have formed an element of Deut 18:6. As a result, he deduces the antecedence of Deut 10:6–8 to P (*Deuteronomy*, 218). However, a comparison with ancient Near Eastern material could capsize this view. As Paola Corò points out, land assignment is an earlier stage in the cultic prebendary system. Land is progressively replaced by movable assets, i.e. mainly remains of sacrifices (*Prebende*, 24).

62 The lack of reference to priestly functions assumed by Levites, who come to the *māqôm*, is also stressed by Abba, "Priest," 266.

63 See Otto, *Deuteronomium 12,1–23,15*, 1,452.

endowed with the same privileges. Such a view of the privileges of the priesthood, with the consequent subordination of the Levites, is called into question in vv. 1–2 and 8 which, by framing the text, change its purpose.

Some elements enable us to consider vv. 1–2 and 8 as redactional frames. Deuteronomy 18:8 can be regarded as an addition to v. 7 for the following three reasons. The vocabulary of vv. 6–7 refers to v. 5 while v. 8 (חלק and אכל) takes up the terminology of vv. 1–2. Verses 6–7 presuppose the "Levite within your gates," but the prerogatives assigned to the subject of v. 8 do not correspond to those of the "Levite within your gates." In fact, the latter is presented as one of the three disadvantaged categories; by contrast, 18:8 refers to a process of sale (מכריו). Finally, the singular Levite in vv. 6–7 becomes pluralized (יאכלו, v. 8).[64]

The vocabulary of 18:1–2 refers clearly to 10:8–9, thus being distanced from the following vv. 3–5: in 18:1, "all the tribe of Levi" (כל־שבט לוי) + "not having portion or inheritance" (לא־יהיה [...] חלק ונחלה עם־ישראל) is attested in 10:9: לא־היה ללוי חלק ונחלה עם־אחיו. The statement, "Yhwh is their inheritance as he said to them" recurs in 18:2 (ונחלה לא־יהיה־לו בקרב אחיו יהוה הוא נחלתו כאשר דבר־לו) and 10:9 (לא־היה ללוי חלק ונחלה עם־אחיו יהוה הוא נחלתו כאשר דבר יהוה אלהיך לו). Syntactic discrepancies in relation to the context (cf., for example, 18:2 with the 3rd masc. sing. suffixes) lead to the conclusion that 10:8–9 is the text to which 18:1–2 refers.[65]

The addition of Deuteronomy 18:1–2 has as its aim the questioning the privileges of the Aaronide priesthood as they are laid down in vv. 3–5. In 18:1, the statement that the Levitical priests have no portion or inheritance with Israel is followed by an explanation concerning what is due to them: "they shall eat the offerings by fire belonging to Yhwh and his inheritance" (אשי יהוה ונחלתו יאכלון). The substantive אשה is typical of priestly vocabulary: almost all its occurrences (57 of 62 uses) are found in Leviticus (41 times) and Numbers (16 times). The lexeme is a *hapax* in Deuteronomy. The substantive אשה generally indicates the portions of a sacrificial offering consumed by fire on the altar, either reserved wholly for Yhwh (e.g. Exod 29:18, 25, 41; 30:20; Lev 1:9; Num 15:10, 13, 14) or else reserved in part for Aaron (e.g. Lev 2:3, 10). Only in Leviticus 7:25 and Deuteronomy 18:1 is the substantive אשה associated with eating (אכל). In Leviticus 7:25, it is prescribed that whoever eats the fat of animals offered to Yhwh as an אשה must be cut off from the community (ונכרתה הנפש האכלת מעמיה). In Deuteronomy 18:1, the possibility of eating the אשי יהוה is granted to the Leviti-

64 The LXX, harmonizes v. 8 with vv. 6–7 by means of a 3rd sing. (LXX: μερίδα μεμερισμένην φάγεται; MT חלק כחלק יאכלו).

65 Cross-references between 18:1–2 and 10:8–9 are stressed by Otto, *Deuteronomium 12,1–23,15*, 1,451.

cal priests, i.e. all the tribe of Levi (לכהנים הלוים כל־שבט לוי) without any internal distinctions. In both cases, it is clear that the animals are not being sacrificed as holocausts because there are meat portions available for consumption after the specified portions have been burnt in fire on the altar. In Joshua 13:14, the אשי יהוה are assigned to the tribe of Levi in return for their lack of an inheritance (לשבט הלוי לא נתן נחלה אשי יהוה אלהי ישראל הוא נחלתו כאשר דבר־לו, v. 14). According to Trent C. Butler, this clarification, inserted in the context of the division of the land as instructions delivered by Moses (13:1), has the purpose of underlining the fulfilment of the prescriptions of Deuteronomy 10:6–9 and 18:1.[66] Joshua 13:14 would, therefore, be following on from Deuteronomy 10:6–9 and 18:1.

Two considerations that press us to review the relationship between the two texts can be examined. First, in Joshua 13:14, the אשי יהוה are destined as an inheritance ("the sacrifices of Yhwh, God of Israel, this is his inheritance," אשי יהוה אלהי ישראל הוא נחלתו); in Deuteronomy 18:1, the syntagma, אשי יהוה, is the direct object of אכל. The same thing happens for the substantive נחלה (i.e. "they will eat the sacrifices of Yhwh and his inheritance"). Compared with Joshua 13:14, the wording of Deuteronomy 18:1 heightens the connection between the tribe of Levi and the sacrifices of Yhwh (אשי יהוה). In brief, the mention of the אשי יהוה in 18:1 and their mandatory consumption by the "levitical priests, i.e. all the tribe of Levi," leads us to understand the extension of a privilege that sometimes is reserved to Aaron and his descendants.[67]

Second, Deuteronomy 18:2 (ונחלה לא־יהיה־לו בקרב אחיו יהוה הוא נחלתו כאשר דבר־לו), like 10:8, refers to the divine words spoken to Aaron in Numbers 18:20.[68] In this case, too, the privilege reserved for Aaron is extended in Deuteronomy 18:2: the recipients are the "Levitical priests, all the tribe of Levi." As observed for 10:8–9, the expression "the tribe of Levi" (attested in Deuteronomy only in 10:8 [שבט הלוי] and 18:2) is underlining the extension of a privilege reserved elsewhere (e.g. Num 18:20–24) for a part of that tribe. The extension of the Aaronide privilege is further underlined in 18:1 by the use of כל (10:8 שבט הלוי; 18:1: כל שבט לוי).

Deuteronomy 18:8 has a function similar to that of 18:1–2. According to a common interpretation, the expression, חלק כחלק, is intended to establish an equivalence between the portion of the Levite who arrives at the *māqôm* "from

66 Butler, *Joshua*, 163. He also calls Num 18:20–24 into question.
67 See also Tigay, *Deuteronomy*, 170; Milgrom, "Profane Slaughter," 11–12.
68 The reference to Num 18:20–24 is highlighted by Otto, *Deuteronomium 12,1–23,15*, 1,451; Tigay, *Deuteronomy*, 170.

your gates" and that of the Levites who are already present there.[69] However, in vv. 6–7, there is no mention of a portion (חלק) appointed for the Levites that could be taken as a point of reference for comparison with v. 8. In addition, in Deuteronomy, the substantive חלק never indicates a portion with reference to the Levite within your gates, who is portrayed rather as "not having a *heleq* or inheritance" (12:12; 14:27, 29). For these reasons, it is improbable that חלק כחלק in 18:8 refers to a portion appointed for the Levite.

In my opinion, the expression, חלק כחלק יאכלו (v. 8), is intended to establish an equivalence between the portion appointed for the "Levitical priests, that is, all the tribe of Levi" (v. 1) and that of the priests (vv. 3–5). The text would be intending to establish an equality in the maintenance of all those belonging to the tribe of Levi. The privileges reserved for the Aaronide priesthood (in vv. 3–5) would thus be extended and so annulled by v. 8. This hypothesis is supported by a consideration of a) the possible referent of the expression חלק כחלק in v. 8 and b) the subject of the verb יאכלו in v. 8.

a) In the majority of its occurrences, the substantive חלק does not indicate a portion of food but a portion of land. In Joshua 14:4, for example, it designates the land possessed by the Levites in the countryside. In 18:8, חלק, the direct object of the verb אכל, indicates, by metonymy, the alimentary products and beasts grown and nurtured on the land that provides sustenance. The summary trio of the products of the land were mentioned as the source of the maintenance of the priest in vv. 3–5. Thus, it is plausible to think that the portions appointed for the priests in vv. 3–5 are the terms of comparison for understanding the חלק כחלק of v. 8.

b) Who is the subject of יאכלו in v. 8? The syntagma, אכל + direct object חלק, occurs elsewhere only in Hosea 5:7 and Amos 7:4 in a metaphorical sense: the portion indicates the land that has been metaphorically devoured by the enemy (Hos 5:7) or by fire (Amos 7:4). By contrast, in Deuteronomy 18:8, the syntagma, אכל + direct object חלק, is to be understood to refer to food and sustenance. The singular expression, חלק כחלק יאכלו (v. 8), with the topicalization of the object, can be explained beginning from 18:1: לא־יהיה לכהנים הלוים כל־שבט לוי חלק ונחלה עם־ישראל אשי יהוה ונחלתו יאכלון. The hendiadys, חלק ונחלה, is clarified subsequently by the explanation, אשי יהוה ונחלתו יאכלון. The direct object, נחלה, precedes the verb, אכל, in emphatic position. Verse 18:1 lacks a repetition of the first substantive of the pair, i.e. חלק. The first member of the hendiadys (חלק) is repeated at the beginning of v. 8, as the direct object in emphatic position in relation to the verb אכל.

69 See for instance Tigay, *Deuteronomy*, 172; Otto, *Deuteronomium 12,1–23,15*, 1,492.

v. 1:	לא־יהיה[...] חלק ונחלה עם־ישראל אשי יהוה ונחלתו יאכלון	They will have no portion or inheritance with Israel; they will eat the sacrifices of Yhwh and his inheritance.
v. 8:	חלק כחלק יאכלו	They will eat an equal portion

Following the connection illustrated above, one can identify the subject of יאכלו (v. 8) as the "Levitical priests, i.e. all the tribe of Levi" (v. 1). Therefore: v. 8 ("they will eat an equal portion") has the objective of assigning to the Levitical priests the same alimentary portion or support assigned to the priests in vv. 3–5. Verse 8 thus sees the abolition of the privileges represented by the priestly prebends in order to re-establish an equality in sustenance, that is, an "equal portion" (חלק כחלק) for all.

The conclusion of v. 8 (לבד ממכריו על־האבות, "besides what he receives from the sale of his goods/paternal patrimony") is difficult to interpret.[70] Nevertheless, certain elements point the way to establishing its meaning. There is mention of additional income (לבד מן), over and above the prebends assigned for the exercise of the cult which, as we saw previously, are foregrounded by the substantive חלק. If this is the case, the expression, מכריו על־האבות would indicate an income alternative to the prebends, obtained, that is, outside the exercise of the cult. In addition, the expression highlights the earnings coming from a sale (מכר) of paternal property (על אבות), presumably obtained as a hereditary possession.

To interpret this expression, Godfrey R. Driver suggested a reference to Akkadian *mkr*, "to lay out, invest." According to Driver, the root, *mkr*, "must once have had the general sense of handling and possessing, acquiring and disposing of property." The substantive *makkūrum* would indicate "that in which a man deals," subsequently identified as a property or goods in a general sense.[71] The context of Deuteronomy 18:1–8, concerning the prebends due for cultic services, can help specify further the nature of the goods mentioned in v. 8.

The documentation originating in Mesopotamia shows that hereditary prebends,[72] with their incomes, were treated as mobile goods, whether for anti-

70 See Otto, *Deuteronomium 12,1–23,15*, 1,434.
71 Driver, "Problems," 77–8.
72 Following Arminius C. V. M. Bongenaar, a prebend or "income right" can be defined as "the right to a fixed income from the temple in return for the performance of services connected to the cult" (see Bongenaar, *Neobabylonian Ebabbar Temple*, 140).

chretic pledges or loans. Moreover, prebends were sold, both as a whole or in part.[73] In light of this, Deuteronomy 18:8 could perhaps be referring to the sale of incomes deriving from prebends that had been received as family property.

To sum up, in Deuteronomy 18:1–8, the system of prebends appointed for the officials of the cult becomes a tool with which to establish, support, and contrast social distinctions among various elites.[74] Verses 3–7 reinforce the distinction between priests and Levites, the latter understood as additional personnel, on the basis of the prebendary privileges received for their service. The interests underlying vv. 3–7 are revealed to be those of the Aaronide priesthood. With 18:1–2, 8, however, these privileges are called into question and extended to "all the tribe of Levi": the right to eat the sacrifices of Yhwh is claimed for each member of the tribe (v. 1), and so an equal portion is prescribed for the (Levitical) priest (v. 8). The advocates of this debate over priestly privilege, already present in 10:6–9, are revealed to be the "Levitical priests" (18:1). Who are they, how are they distinguished, and how are they portrayed in Deuteronomy?

3 The Levitical Priests: A Scribal Elite of *homines novi*

The "Levitical priests" appear in both the legislative section (17:9,18; 18:1; 21:5 [הכהנים בני לוי]) and in the outer frames of Deuteronomy (27:9; 31:9 [הכהנים בני לוי]). In particular, they are portrayed as a scribal elite. By claiming for themselves exclusive competence in the Torah of Moses and systematically constructing a parallel between their authority and that of Moses, the Levitical priests legitimate their supremacy in juridical, political, and religious matters. By illustrating, in order, their claim to juridical, political, and religious authority, I would like to show that the Levitical priests are depicted as *homines novi* on the scene.

The juridical authority of the Levitical priests is the subject of 17:8–13 (which envisages recourse to the *māqôm* court) and of the arrangements about cases of disease of the skin (24:8–9). The parenthesis of 21:5 reiterates the au-

73 See van Driel, *Elusive Silver*, 136–37; Corò, *Prebende*, 39–78; Pirngruber and Waerzeggers, "Prebend Prices," 111–44. Michael Jursa shows that prebends could be sold, leased, or delegated (*Neo-Babylonian Documents*, 33–35). As regards the prebend of the scribes, see Frame and Waerzeggers, "Prebend of the Scribe," 13–20.

74 As Jursa highlights, the prebendary system ends up being "a means of generating (and sustaining) social distinctions" (*Neo-Babylonian Documents*, 32).

thority of the Levitical priests, resolving some ambiguities in connection with their jurisdiction.

In 17:9, the "Levitical priests" are located at the *māqôm* (v. 8) at the court held there (17:9–13). The authority attributed to them is a judicial authority, parallel to that of the judge (v. 9: אל הכהנים הלוים ואל השפט), designated by the lexemes ירה (vv. 10–11) and תורה (v. 11). Verses 10–11 aim at underlining and reinforcing the authority of the Levitical priests, setting it in parallel to that of Moses.

In v. 8, recourse to the *māqôm* court happens when a judgement is "too difficult" (יפלא ממך דבר למשפט). In the desert period, Moses claimed for himself jurisdiction over the most difficult cases: "the case that is too hard for you, you shall bring it before me and I shall hear it (והדבר אשר יקשה מכם תקרבון אלי ושמעתיו)" (Deut 1:17). After entry into the land, Moses's juridical competence for the most difficult cases was to be transferred to the tribunal located at the *māqôm* (17:8).[75] Thus, the exercise of juridical power for the most disputed cases, performed at the *māqôm* court, is portrayed as a continuation of the jurisdiction exercised by Moses in the desert.

In the majority of its occurrences in Deuteronomy (19 of 23 occurrences), the syntagma שמר + ל + עשה underlines the binding authority of Moses's instructions in Moab (esp. חקים ומשפטים, e.g. 4:5; 5:1; התורה הזאת, 31:12) or of the divine prescriptions given at Horeb (5:32). Only in 17:10 and 24:8 is there a reference to the teaching (ירה) of the Levitical priests. The use of the phrase שמר + ל + עשה in 17:10 and 24:8 indicates that the authority of their prescriptions is analogous to that of the Mosaic prescriptions.

The expression סור (לא) + ימין ושמאל occurs in Deuteronomy 5:32 referring to the divine instructions at Horeb. In 17:20 and Josh 1:7 and 23:6, the same expression indicates the attitude required toward the Torah of Moses. In Deuteronomy 17:11, the expression refers to the word pronounced by the Levitical priests.

In Deuteronomy 24:8, the normative nature of the judgement (ירה) of the Levitical priests in cases of cutaneous disease is conveyed by the use of the syntagma שמר + ל + עשה. The Mosaic legitimation of their authority is underlined further: the Levitical priests are the exclusive recipients of instruction from Moses. This instruction is reserved for them (כאשר צויתם) and not shared by Moses with the rest of the community. The community can come to awareness of this supplementary instruction only through the word of the Levitical priests. According to the provision of 24:8, obedience to the instruction of the Levitical priests

75 See Tigay, *Deuteronomy*, 164.

coincides with obedience to Moses's commands (כאשר צויתם תשמרו לעשות). Moses's authority and that of the Levitical priests is, therefore, on the same plane. The LXX and the Samaritan Pentateuch confirm this reading: in fact, the prescription of the Levitical priests is expressed by the substantives תורה (Sam Pent: ככל התורה אשר יורו אתכם) and νόμος (κατὰ πάντα τὸν νόμον ὃν ἐὰν ἀναγγείλωσιν ὑμῖν).

Deuteronomy 21:5 not only reiterates the authority of the Levitical priests but removes all possible ambiguity with regard to the extension of their jurisdiction. The law of 21:1–9 describes the case of a homicide without witnesses. The ritual of the heifer to be conducted by the elders (vv. 3–4, 6–8) is interrupted at v. 5 by the appearance alongside the elders of the "the priests, the sons of Levi"; the fact that the latter do not play any role in the ritual being described testifies to the redactional nature of the parenthesis of 21:5.[76] The vocabulary of 21:5 may indicate the purpose of the addition.

The title, הכהנים בני לוי, occurs elsewhere in Deuteronomy 31:9. In 31:9, "the priests, the sons of Levi," and the elders, who are both recipients of the book of the law of Moses, seem to enjoy the same authority. Before this, 21:5 establishes the superiority of the Levitical priests over the elders; in the final analysis, the authority of the latter is subject to the word of the Levitical priests.

The area of the authority of the Levitical priests is specified as "every dispute and every injury" (כל־ריב וכל־נגע). This pair of substantives refers to 17:8: "when it is too difficult for you to decide between homicide and homicide, plea and plea (דין), injury and injury (נגע), matters of controversy within your gates (דברי ריבת בשעריך)." In 17:8, appeal to the authority of the *māqôm* court, presided over by the Levitical priests and judges, was reserved for particularly difficult cases. Moreover, the Levitical priests exercised their authority at the *māqôm* court alongside the judge. According to 17:8–13, therefore, the juridical authority of the Levitical priests located at the *māqôm* is limited to controversial cases and shared with the judge. Deuteronomy 21:5 introduces a change in perspective: the word of the Levitical priests is final in every case of plea or injury (כל־ריב וכל־נגע), not only in the most complicated cases (as in 17:8). Moreover, the authority of the judge, exercised locally by the elders in 21:3–9, is subordinated in 21:5 to that of the Levitical priests. Finally, their presence is no longer situated exclusively at the *māqôm* (as in 17:8–13): in 21:5, they

---

76 Otto, *Deuteronomium, 12,1–23,5*, 1,633–34. However, as Driver points out, "the presence of the priests appears to be required, not for the purpose of taking part personally in the ceremony (which is performed throughout by the 'elders' of the city concerned), but rather for the purpose of imparting to it a religious character, and of securing that the prescribed rites are properly performed" (*Deuteronomy*, 243).

appear locally as the final authority in a judgement presided over by the elders of the city.

The political authority claimed by the Levitical priests finds clear expression in 17:18 in the context of the law of the king.[77] Deuteronomy 17:18 establishes the connection between the “Levitical priests” and the Torah of Moses in the written form of a *sefer*. In the context of the law of the king in 17:14–20, vv. 18–20 bind the power of the king and the success of his reign (v. 20) to the keeping and observance of the Torah of Moses. On the one hand, the observance of the *sefer hattorah* renders the king similar to “his brothers,” preventing him from raising himself above them (v. 20: לבלתי רום־לבבו מאחיו). On the other hand, the duty imposed by the Torah subjects the king’s power to the authority of the Levitical priests. In a prescription that is unique among the extant evidence from the ancient Near East, the king himself will write a copy of the law that restricts him.[78] Moreover, the master copy of this Torah is not at his disposal: the “Levitical priests” are the guardians of the *sefer hattorah* (v. 18) and supervisors of the writing of the royal copy (v. 18).[79]

What is the aim of this portrayal of the king? Verses 16–20 are not typical of the formulation of the laws;[80] they no longer are addressed to the community (in the 2nd pers. sing. in vv. 14–15), not even the king (who is spoken of in the 3rd pers. sing.). The opening of v. 16 (רק) marks a change in perspective from the previous statements; [81] in particular, vv. 16–20 foreground a series of limitations on the authority of the sovereign.[82] Political authority, which is associated with judicial authority (16:18–17:13) and precedes the arrangements relating to the religious authorities (priests in 18:1–8 and prophets in 18:9–22), is represented after all by a weakened sovereign.

77 Otto ascribes 17:18 to a post-exilic reworking (*Deuteronomium 12,1–23,15*, 1,487–89).

78 Sonnet, *Book*, 77–78. It would be equally possible to translate “one will write for him” (i.e. the king).

79 According to 11Q 19, the priests write the copy of the torah for the king. 11Q 19 56:20–21: “And when he sits upon the throne of his kingdom *they* shall write for him this law according to the book which is before the priests.”

80 Von Rad lists Deut 17:14–20 among the texts for which the “conventional designation of ‘laws’ is utterly unsuitable” (*Studies*, 22–23). Deut 17:14–20 bring traces of “sermon-like” utterances.

81 See Otto, *Deuteronomium 12,1–23,15*, 1,487. More precisely, the adverb רק (v. 18) introduces a contrast with the former statements; when it introduces a clause beginning with a verb, רק forces a countering interpretation of the following clause (so Levinsohn, “רַק and אַךְ,” 90–94). In this case, vv. 18–20 counter the view of the king as a mighty political and military authority.

82 As Nili Wazana stresses, the “law” of the king disempowers the institution of monarchy (“Law of the King,” 176).

An open question remains: if the authority of the sovereign is weakened, what is the political authority to which one can appeal? Clearly not the sovereign, but the Torah of Moses, which the king is bound to copy and observe, and, in the final instance, the Levitical priests, the guardians of the original copy of the Torah and the guarantors of the conformity of the royal copy with this original. In 17:16–20, in the context of the laws on offices, Moses's speech aims at clarifying not just the authority of the Mosaic Torah but also the class to which this authority has been transferred: the Levitical priests.[83]

The claim of the Levitical priests to religious authority is advanced in Deuteronomy 18:1–2 and 8: as we indicated (see § 2.2) in the discussion of the privileges related to the priestly prebends, the Levitical priests aimed at gaining authority in the religious sphere at the expense of the Aaronide priests.

In sum, by means of a series of redactional interventions within the legislative code, the Levitical priests aim to present themselves as the decisive authority in Israel juridically, politically, and religiously. The reference tool that enables them to present themselves as the new elite is their connection with the *Torah* of Moses and its authoritative teaching.

In the frames of Deuteronomy (27:9 and 31:9), it is the narrator who mentions the Levitical priests. The way in which they are portrayed is clear evidence of their authoritative position within the community. In 27:9, the Levitical priests begin to speak along with Moses in order to instruct the people: "Moses and the Levitical priests said to all Israel." The first person singular of v. 10 ("which I [viz. Moses] command you today") not only indicates that the reference to the Levitical priests is plausibly an addition but, above all, renders the latter the spokesmen for Moses and his teaching. Right from the plains of Moab, in the presence of Moses, the Levitical priests are depicted as bearers of his word for the community.[84] The entrusting of the *sefer hattorah*, written by Moses, to the Levitical priests, who bear the Ark of the Covenant, in 31:9, is further confirmation of their position as guardians of the Mosaic tradition. Not only that, the reading of the law of Moses every seven years, intended for the whole community, further underlines the elite position of the Levitical priests. For the generations succeeding that of Moab, access to the Torah of Moses will be possible only through the mediation provided by the Levitical priests.

---

83 A priestly group portrayed the king as a "student" of the Torah in a time where no king was on the throne (see Markl, "Anti-King," 174–75). Levitical priests are deemed responsible for writing this law.

84 The same applies to the elders in 27:1. The relation between the authority of Levitical priests and that ascribed to elders is resolved in 21:5 in favor of the Levitical priest. Deut 21:5 reasserts their preeminence.

To sum up, the Levitical priests break onto the scene as a new elite by means of some targeted strategies. In its written form, the Torah of Moses is employed as an instrument to separate the elite from the community (31:9–13) and to supervise political power (17:14–20). The connection with writing makes clear the scribal *milieu* of the Levitical priests. The systematic construction of a parallel between their authority and that of Moses contributes to reinforcing their leadership in relation to the elders and their authority in the juridical sphere (21:5). This scribal elite is contrasted with the priestly one (the Aaronide priesthood), which is based on the privileges of the cult (10:6–9; 18:1–8). Emphasis on descent from Aaron, with his prerogatives, is replaced by the parallel with Moses and his prerogatives.

The data we have assembled shows that the Levitical priests and their portrayal as an emerging scribal elite is not necessarily being opposed to the centralization of the cult in one place but, more precisely, to the centering of religious power, with its privileges, in the hands of the priests descended from Aaron.

4 A Contest between Two Elites: The Background and the Stakes

The texts of Deuteronomy witness to a contest between two elites. In particular, there is a contrast between two models of constructing and depicting an elite and the interaction between the latter and the community. The first model is represented by the priests descended from Aaron. In this case, the separation of the elite is founded on the cult and its related privileges. In particular, the religious elite is constructed on the concept of separation from the community, determined by a clear boundary between pure and impure. The relationship with the divinity, revelation, and access to its decrees, together with the possibility of reconciliation with the divine, are all mediated by cultic practices performed by the priests. Membership in this elite is established and fixed by inheritance and by sharing in Aaron's genealogy.

The second model of an elite is represented by the Levitical priests, who are depicted as a scribal elite. Separation from the community or from other elite classes is based on specific scribal competences, in particular, a monopoly over the Torah of Moses and a teaching/word that is normative. The relationship with the divinity is no longer regulated by cultic practices but mediated by the Torah of Moses and its practice. Guardianship and observance of the Torah of Moses replace sacrificial practices as the means of reconciliation with God (cf. Deut 10:6–9 and Deut 30).

Described in these terms, the competition between a religious and a scribal elite centers on factors of an ideological and religious nature, especially those that regulate interaction with the community.[85] Closer examination of the texts reveals that other mechanisms are at work that were decisive for provoking the conflict between the two elites.

The study of Deuteronomy 10:6–9 and 18:1–8 has highlighted the centrality of Numbers 18 for the current debate between the Aaronide priesthood and the Levitical priests. The debate with Numbers 18 and the content of Deuteronomy 18:1–8 reveal that the system of prebends is central to the dispute between the Aaronide elite and the Levitical priests. Through words addressed by Yhwh to Aaron, Numbers 18 puts forward a reorganization of the prebendal system; the redistribution of prebends establishes the superiority of the Aaronide priests over the Levites, who are subordinated to them. The subordination of the Levites at cultic sites is reflected more significantly in the reduction of income deriving from their offices. Thus established, the superiority of the Aaronide clergy is sealed in its authority by a divine word fixed as a "perpetual law" and an "inviolable and perpetual covenant" with Aaron and his descendants (v. 19). The redistribution of prebends is followed by the presence of a hereditary high priesthood, obtained by succession (cf. Num 20:22–29 and Deut 10:6–7) that is reserved for Aaron's descendants.

The restructuring of the prebendal system, with the consequent subordination of the Levites (cf. Deut 10:8–9 and 18:1–8), as well as the institution of an Aaronide high priesthood with its privileges seem to be the causes triggering the reaction of the Levitical priests in Deuteronomy and their claims. This is the picture that can plausibly be reconstructed from the texts of Deuteronomy. But what are the causes of the discussion around the privileges? What are the roots of the contest?

A comparison between the biblical information and that provided by sources from the ancient Near East may provide elements for a possible answer. If the competition between the elites attested in Deuteronomy arises from a redistribution of prebends, it is plausible to suppose that the scribal elite, represented by the Levitical priests, could have had a share in this system.

The material coming from the archives of temples in Mesopotamia reveals the portions appointed for the scribes who were employed as administrative personnel in the temple. At Sippar, for example, the scribes received part of the sacrificial meat.[86] As we have observed, the evidence from the ancient Near East reveals that the division of incomes deriving from the cult vary in quality

85 Davies, "Authority," 36–37, n.18.

86 Frame and Waerzeggers, "Prebend of the Scribe," 5.

and quantity and that this establishes a social scale of prestige among the temple personnel.[87] It is possible to suppose, therefore, that the scribes who were employed as temple personnel and who received portions of the sacrificial meat appointed for the priests ended up being equal in importance with the priests themselves, also acquiring their status.[88]

Moreover, we should note the possibility that the administrative personnel (scribes) cooperated with the priests at some cultic sites. In fact, the documentation from the ancient Near East shows the possibility of cumulative prebendary income deriving from various offices.[89] Yet, according to Govet van Driel, scribes were not prebendaries because of their scribal competence but as a result of additional functions they carried out in the temple.[90] Looked at in this light, the scribal elite who were present in the temple alongside the priestly elite and who were on a par with the priests in terms of the distribution of prebends could become an active threat to the prestige of the latter.

Deuteronomy 18:6–7 attests to the presence of the Levites in the temple with general cultic duties but without the mention of a particular income. Despite the fact that the vocabulary makes their duties equal to those of the priests in 18:6–7, the Levites at the *māqôm* do not receive the title, "Levitical priests"[91] or a specific income. On closer inspection, Deuteronomy does not provide any indication to support a "scribal" function of the Levites at the *māqôm*; however, clues for this function are found in Nehemiah.

Nehemiah 13:10 denounces the poor nature of the remuneration appointed for the Levites, a similar situation to that reflected in Numbers 18 and, implicitly, in Deuteronomy 18:6–7. Nehemiah 10:38–39 assigns the Levites the task of collecting locally ("in all the towns") the tithes destined for and to be taken to the temple. This task is a good reflection of a possible scribal and administrative

87 So van Driel, *Elusive Silver*, 148: the prebendary system creates a "tough, resilient, numerically important elite which sometimes managed to maintain its interests until deep into the Hellenistic period, if not to its very end, after the beginning of what we now call the Christian era [...]. The prebendal class probably constituted one of the few recognizable elements of the socio-political structure which could through its own weight up to a degree withstand the monarchy." See also Jursa, *Neo-Babylonian Documents*, 32; Corò, *Prebende*, 23.

88 The analogy with Egyptian lector priests could help stress the plausibility of the proposed reconstruction. See in this regard, Edelman, "Of Priests and Prophets," 107–10. Lector priests (*ḫry- ḥbt*, lit. "the one in charge of the festival rolls," or "scroll-carrier,") operated in the House of Life, located in a separate building within temple complexes. They did not officiate in the cult but rather, served the purpose of education and research in the Houses of Life. I am not assuming the associations she draws with biblical prophets.

89 See Corò, *Prebende*, 86–99.

90 Van Driel, *Elusive Silver*, 38.

91 See Otto, *Deuteronomium 12,1–23,15*, 1,492.

role assigned to the Levites; precisely by virtue of this function, the Levites serve as a link between the countryside ("your gates") and the sanctuary. In the system of collecting and distributing the tithes described in Nehemiah 10:38–39, in each case, a priest, a "son of Aaron" is put in a position of superiority, charged with supervising the activity of the Levites. The system for distributing the tithes represented by Nehemiah 10:38–39 (cf. also vv. 12–47) reflects the superiority of the Aaronide priests over the Levites, which is also revealed in Numbers 18.

Nehemiah 10:38–39 could shed light on the identity and function of the "Levite within your gates" in Deuteronomy. The reconstruction is hypothetical since Deuteronomy does not provide any clue as to the role of the Levite "within your gates," but perhaps it is not without plausibility. Against the background described, the Levite "within your gates" could have had the role of an administrator and local scribe, operating in the city and on behalf of the families.[92] The Levite "within your gates" would not have functioned in a judicial capacity, as hypothesized by Mark Leuchter,[93] but rather, would have placed his administrative and scribal competence at the service of the local communities and, presumably, also, of the temple (or temples?). In brief, it seems plausible that the Levites could have been present at a cultic site as administrative personnel with scribal expertise.

The information we have collected can help reconstruct the circumstances that led to the dispute between the religious elite (Aaronide priests) and the scribal elite (levitical priests) attested in Deuteronomy. In the light of this information, we can hypothesize the following reconstruction. The local Levite (the "Levite within your gates") was a scribe associated with the local structures and dependent on the local families for his maintenance. As a scribe and administrator, he could be a possible link between the higher religious structures and the local towns (cf. the movement of the Levite to the *māqôm* together with the family).

The Levites, scribes, and administrators were linked to the priestly elites by their service in the temple as administrative personnel. Gradually, they progressed within the temple, taking on not only administrative tasks but also cultic duties. The gradual inclusion of an administrative and scribal class within the dynamics of the temple was reflected in a substantial equalization between

92 Johannes Hackl analyzes linguistic features of administrative documents from Judean exiles. He makes the case that scribes who completed a lower level in urban scribal training were employed as scribes in villages in the countryside ("Babylonian Scribal Practices").
93 Leuchter, "Levites in your Gates," 419–25.

scribes and cultic officials in the prebendal system (cf., for example, the temple at Sippar). Perhaps the epithet "Levitical priests" reflects this stage.

The priestly class proper was opposed to the emerging scribal class in the temple, perceiving it as a threat.[94] Their reaction was reflected in a reduction in the Levites' prebends (Neh 13:10) and in the reform of the prebendal system (cf. Num 18), which ended up subordinating the Levites to the Aaronide priests as *clerus minor* (Deut 18:6–7).

The Levitical priests, i.e. Levites acting as scribes but also performing cultic and sacral tasks, contested the opposition of the Aaronides with two strategies of reaction and action. On the one hand, they extended the privileges of the descendants of Aaron (10:8–9; 18:1–2), thus challenging the principle of elite separation based on the redistribution of prebends. On the other hand, they portrayed themselves as a scribal elite, reserving for themselves a monopoly over the Torah of Moses and presenting themselves as the latter's successors with regard to the authoritative nature of their teaching.

One question remains to be answered: why oppose the monopoly of the cult (claimed by the Aaronide priests) with the scribal monopoly of the Torah of Moses? Philip Davies has advanced the theory that the literary enterprise of Deuteronomy originated in the practice of the diffusion of the Torah of Moses as depicted in Nehemiah 8.[95] In particular, he asks, "Should this function of disseminating and regulating *tōrâ* be regarded as postdating the creation of the book of Deuteronomy or as a practice from which the book itself arose?" Davies speculates that Deuteronomy was the outcome of the emergence of the Torah as an authoritative document in the Persian period (cf. Ezra 7:25–26)[96] and, therefore, a reflection of the ceremony in Nehemiah 8. The opposition of the Levitical priests to the pretensions of the Aaronide clergy and their claim to exclusive competence over the Mosaic Torah, as just described, could confirm Davies's theory.

Here is a brief list of elements for comparison. In Ezra-Nehemiah, the Torah of Moses is in the hands of Ezra, a scribe and high priest of Aaronide descent. Even though far from having historical importance, Ezra 7:25–26 reveals the political importance of the Torah of Moses and its authority, which is provided with "official enforcement."[97] In Nehemiah 8:1, the people ask Ezra to bring the

---

94 For a description of the contrast between the emerging scribal elite and the priestly class under Persian rule, see Silverman, *Persian Royal-Judean Elite*, 215–17. Walther Sallaberger and Fabienne Huber Vuillet point out the supervising role of administrators and royal officials in Neo Babylonian and Achaemenid Eanna ("Priester," 638).

95 Davies, "Authority," 35.

96 In particular, Davies, 37–38.

97 Davies, 37.

book of the Torah of Moses that was given to Israel. In Deuteronomy, the Torah of Moses is not in the hands of Israel (Neh 8:1) nor of an Aaronide priest (Ezra) but is consigned to the Levitical priests in the process of its writing by Moses himself (Deut 31:9). Nehemiah 8: 7, 9 depict the Levites of being tasked with explaining and teaching the Torah proclaimed by Ezra; in 8:13, the Levites are assembled under Ezra's supervision to examine the law. In Deuteronomy, competence in the law of Moses, including its reading, interpretation, and application, is reserved for the Levitical priests.

Thus, the opposition of the Levitical priests to the Aaronide priestly elite, based on scribal competence in the Torah of Moses, could be set against the background of the appearance of the Torah of Moses as an instrument of politico-religious legitimation in Ezra-Nehemiah. From this point of view, Deuteronomy would not mark the appearance of the Torah of Moses on the scene but instead, the etiology of its origin and the legitimation of the Levitical priests as its *coryphei*.

Perhaps there remains a final question: how is it possible in practice to live "not by bread alone" (Deut 8:3) but on the Torah of Moses and its teaching? Certainly, the extension of the prebendal privileges to the whole tribe of Levi, described in Deuteronomy 18:8, provides a preliminary answer. However, it is clear that the monopoly of the Torah of Moses and, above all, the hegemony over the community this guaranteed, was reckoned by the newly emerging elite as more advantageous in terms of prestige and authority than the control of the cultic and sacrificial system.

Works Cited

Abba, Raymond. "Priests and Levites in Deuteronomy." *Vetus Testamentum* 27 (1977): 257–67.

Achenbach, Reinhard. "Levitische Priester und Leviten im Deuteronomium. Überlegung zur sog. 'Levitisierung' des Priestentums." *Zeitschrift für altorientalische und biblische Rechtsgeschichte* 5 (1999): 285–309.

Achenbach, Reinhard. "Levi and Levites." *Religion Past and Present* 7 (2010): 439–40.

Amadasi Guzzo, Maria Giulia. "Sacrifici e banchetti. Bibbia ebraica e iscrizioni puniche." In *Sacrificio e Società nel mondo antico*, edited by Cristiano Grottanelli and Nicola F. Parise, 98–108. Roma – Bari: Laterza Editore, 1988.

Blenkinsopp, Joseph. *Ezra–Nehemiah: A Commentary*. The Old Testament Library. London: SCM, 1989.

Bongenaar, Arminius C. V. M. *The Neo-Babylonian Ebabbar Temple at Sippar: Its Administration and Its Prosopography*. Publication de l'Institut historique-archéologique néerlandais de Stamboul 80. Leiden: Nederlands Historisch-Archaeologisch Instituut te Istanbul, 1997.

Budd, Philip J. *Numbers*. Word Biblical Commentary 5. Waco, TX: Word Books, 1984.

Butler, Trent C. *Joshua*. Word Biblical Commentary 7. Waco, TX: Word Books, 1983.

Corò, Paola. "Meat, Prebends and Rank: A Short Note On the Distribution of Sacrificial Meat in Seleucid Uruk." In *Food and Identity in the Ancient World*, edited by Cristiano Grottanelli and Lucio Milano, 257–67. History of the Ancient Near East/Studies 9. Padova: S.A.R.G.O.N. Editrice, 2004.

Corò, Paola. *Prebende Templari in Età Seleucide*. History of the Ancient Near East/ Monographs 8. Padova: S.A.R.G.O.N. Editrice, 2005.

Dahmen, Ulrich. *Leviten und Priester im Deuteronomium. Literarkritische und Redaktionsgeschichtliche Studien*. Bonner Biblische Beiträge 110. Bodenheim: Philo, 1996.

Davies, Graham I. "The Wilderness Itineraries and the Composition of the Pentateuch." *Vetus Testamentum* 33 (1983): 1–13.

Davies, Philip R. "The Authority of Deuteronomy." In *Deuteronomy–Kings as Emerging Authoritative Books: A Conversation*. Edited by Diana Edelman, 27–47. SBL: Ancient Near East Monographs 6. Atlanta, GA: Society of Biblical Literature, 2014.

Driver, Godfrey Rolles. "Two Problems in the Old Testament in the Light of Assyriology." *Syria* 33 (1956): 70–78.

Driver, Samuel R. *A Critical and Exegetical Commentary on Deuteronomy*. The International Critical Commentary. Edinburgh: T&T Clark, 1902.

Edelman, Diana. "Of Priests and Prophets and Interpreting the Past: the Egyptian *ḤM–NṮR* and *ḪRY–ḤBT and the Judahite NĀḆÎʾ*." In *The Historian and the Bible: Essays in Honour of Lester L. Grabbe*, edited by Philip R. Davies and Diana V. Edelman, 103–112. Library of Hebrew Bible/Old Testament Studies 530. New York – London: T&T Clark, 2010.

Frevel, Christian. "Ending with the High Priest: The Hierarchy of Priests and Levites in the Book of Numbers." In *Torah and The Book of Numbers*, edited by Christian Frevel, Thomas Pola, and Aaron Schart, 138–63. Forschungen zum Alten Testament 2. Tübingen: Mohr Siebeck, 2013.

Frame, Grant and Caroline Waerzeggers. "The Prebend of Temple Scribe in First Millennium Babylonia." *Zeitschrift für Assyriologie* 101 (2011): 127–51.

Gunneweg, Antonius H. J. *Leviten und Priestern. Hauptlinien der Traditionsbildung und Geschichte des israelitisch-jüdischen Kultpersonals*. Forschungen zur Religion und Literatur des Alten und Neuen Testaments 89. Göttingen: Vandenhoeck & Ruprecht, 1965.

Hackl, Johannes. "Babylonian Scribal Practices in Rural Contexts: A Linguistic Survey of the Documents of Judean Exiles and West Semites in Babylonia (CUSAS 28 and BaAr6)." In *Wandering Arameans: Arameans Outside Syria: Textual and Archaeological Perspectives*, edited by Angelika Berlejung, Aren M. Maeir, and Andreas Schüle, 125–40. Leipziger altorientalische Studien 5. Wiesbaden: Harrassowitz, 2017.

Jeon, Jaeyoung. "Levites. Hebrew Bible/Old Testament." *Encyclopedia of the Bible and Its Reception, Volume 16*, edited by Christine Helmer, Steven L. McKenzie, Thomas Römer, Jens Schröter, Barry Dov Walfish, and Eric Ziolkowski, 336–46. Berlin – Boston, MA: de Gruyter, 2018.

Jursa, Michael. *Neo-Babylonian Legal and Administrative Documents: Typology, Content, and Archives*. Guides to Mesopotamian Textual Record 1. Münster: Ugarit Verlag, 2005.

Leuchter, Mark. " 'The Levite in Your Gates': the Deuteronomic Redefinition of Levitical Authority." *Journal of Biblical Literature* 126 (2007): 417–36.

Levinsohn, Stephen H. "רַק and אַךְ: Limiting and Countering." *Hebrew Studies* 52 (2011): 83–105.

Markl, Dominik. "No Future without Moses: The Disastrous End of 2 Kings 22–25 and the Chance of the Moab Covenant (Deut 29–30)." *Journal of Biblical Literature* 133 (2014): 711–28.

Markl, Dominik. "Deuteronomy's 'Anti-King': Historicized Etiology or Political Program?" In *Changing Faces of Kingship in Syria Palestine 1500–500 BCE*, edited by Augustinus Gianto and Peter Dubovský, 165–86. Alter Orient und Altes Testament 459. Münster: Ugarit Verlag, 2018.

McCarthy, Carmel. *אלה הדברים: Deuteronomy*. Biblia Hebraica Quinta 5. Stuttgart: Deutsche Bibelgesellschaft, 2007.

McEwan, Gilbert J. P. "Distribution of Meat in Eanna." *Iraq* 45 (1983): 187–98.

Milgrom, Jacob. "Profane Slaughter and a Formulaic Key to the Composition of Deuteronomy." *Hebrew Union College Annual* 47 (1976): 1–17.

Otto, Eckart. "Die post-deuteronomistische Levitisierung des Deuteronomiums. Zu einem Buch von Ulrich Dahmen." *Zeitschrift für altorientalische und biblische Rechtsgeschichte* 5 (1999): 277–284.

Otto, Eckart. "Priestertum. II Religionsgeschichtlich. 1. Alter Orient und Altes Testament." *Religion in die Geschichte und Gegenwart, Volume 6*, edited by Hans D. Betz, Don S. Browning, Bernd Janowski, and Eberhard Jüngel, 1,646–49. Fourth edition. Tübingen: Mohr Siebeck, 2003.

Otto, Eckart. *Deuteronomium 4,44–11,32*. Herders Theologischer Kommentar zum Alten Testament. Freiburg i.B.: Herder, 2012.

Otto, Eckart. *Deuteronomium 12,1–23,15*. Herders Theologischer Kommentar zum Alten Testament. Freiburg i.B.: Herder, 2016.

Otto, Eckart. *Deuteronomium 23,16–34,12*. Herders Theologischer Kommentar zum Alten Testament. Freiburg i.B.: Herder, 2017.

Otzen, Benedikt. "בדל, *bāḏal*." *Theologisches Wörterbuch zum Alten Testament, Volume 1*, edited by Johannes Botterweck, Helmer Ringgren, and Heinz-Josef Fabry, 518–20. Stuttgart: Kohlhammer, 1973.

Pirngruber, Reinhard and Caroline Waerzeggers. "Prebend Prices in First Millennium B. C. Babylonia." *Journal of Cuneiform Studies* 63 (2011): 111–44.

Pyschny, Katharina. "Debated Leadership: Conflicts of Authority and Leadership in Num 16–17." In *Debating Authority: Concepts of Leadership in the Pentateuch and the Former Prophets*, edited by Katharina Pyschny and Sarah Schulz, 115–31. Beihefte zur Zeitschrift für die alttestamentliche Wissenschaft 507. Berlin – Boston, MA: de Gruyter, 2018.

Rad, Gerhard von. *Studies in Deuteronomy*. Studies in Biblical Theology 9. London: SCM, 1953.

Sallaberger, Walther and Fabienne Huber Vuillet. "Priester. A. I. Mesopotamien." In *Reallexikon der Assyriologie und vorderasiatische Archäologie, Band 10*, edited by Erich Ebeling, Ernst F. Weidner, and Michael P. Streck, 617–40. Berlin – Boston, MA: de Gruyter, 2005.

Samuel, Harald. *Von Priestern zum Patriarchen. Levi und die Leviten im Alten Testament*. Beihefte zur Zeitschrift für die alttestamentliche Wissenschaft 448. Berlin – Boston, MA: de Gruyter, 2014.

Silverman, Jason M. *Persian Royal–Judean Elite Engagements in the Early Teispid and Achaemenid Empire: The King's Acolytes*. Library of the Hebrew Bible/Old Testament Studies 690. London – New York: Bloomsbury – T. & T. Clark: 2020.

Sonnet, Jean-Pierre. *The Book Within the Book: Writing in Deuteronomy*. Biblical Interpretation Series 14. Leiden: Brill, 1997.
Tigay, Jeffrey. *Deuteronomy*. Philadelphia: Jewish Publication Society, 1996.
Van Driel, Govert. *Elusive Silver: In Search of a Role for a Market in an Agrarian Environment: Aspects of Mesopotamia's Society*. Publication de l'Institut historique-archéologique néerlandais de Stamboul 95. Leiden: Nederlands Instituut voor het Nabije Oosten, 2002.
Wazana, Nili. "The Law of the King (Deuteronomy 17:14–20) in the Light of Empire and Destruction." In *The Fall of Jerusalem and the Rise of the Torah*, edited by Peter Dubovský, Dominik Markl, and Jean-Pierre Sonnet, 169–94. Forschungen zum Alten Testament 107. Tübingen: Mohr Siebeck, 2016.
Weinfeld, Moshe. *Deuteronomy and the Deuteronomic School*. Oxford: Clarendon, 1972.
Weinfeld, Moshe. "On 'Demythologization and Secularization' in Deuteronomy." *Israel Exploration Journal* 23 (1973): 230–33.
Wellhausen, Julius. *Prolegomena to the History of Israel: With a Reprint of the Article Israel from the Encyclopaedia Britannica*. Atlanta: Scholars Press, 1994.
Weyringer, Simon. *An der Schwelle zum Land der Verheißung. Rhetorik und Pragmatik in Dtn 9,1–10,11*. Beihefte zur Zeitschrift für altorientalische und biblische Rechtsgeschichte. Wiesbaden: Harrassowitz, forthcoming.
Wright, George Ernst. "Levites in Deuteronomy." *Vetus Testamentum* 4 (1954): 325–30.

Daniel Graber

The גר (*Gēr*) in Deuteronomy

1 Introduction

In the Hebrew Bible, the term *gēr* (גר) generally refers to liminal figures within Israel. The *gēr* stands outside the circle of the addressees, though he is not a foreigner (נכרי). To render this particular status, the term *gēr* is commonly translated "alien," "stranger," or "sojourner." This last term is preferable to the previous two, which run the risk of being confused with an outright foreigner.

Ever since Alfred Bertholet's seminal work, a major chasm has been identified regarding the status of the *gēr* in the Pentateuch. In short, the Covenant Code (Exod 20:22–23:22) and the Deuteronomic Code (Deut 12–26) would view the *gēr* as a social category, denoting a low class of displaced Israelites in need of protection and charity, while in the Holiness Code (Lev 17–26) and even more so in later priestly legislation (Num 9–35), the *gēr* would be an outsider seeking integration into the post-exilic Judean community.[1] In line with the objectives of this volume, I will strive to avoid the presuppositions about dates and locations upon which the above views rely and focus on the Deuteronomic treatment of the *gēr*. Etymologically, *gēr* comes from the root גוּר "to migrate." So, to start with, the *gēr* can be viewed as an immigrant.

There are 22 occurrences of *gēr* or *gērîm* in Deuteronomy (Table 1).

Five times, the *gēr* is mentioned together with the Levite, the orphan, and the widow, a tetrad often referred to in Deuteronomic scholarship as *personae miserae* or at least "vulnerable persons."[2] The tetrad is granted the proceeds of tithes delivered every third year "within your gates" (Deut 14:29) as well as, according to 16:11, 16:14, and 26:12–13, an invitation to join the families at the *māqôm* to consume annual tithes there. Johannes U. Ro claims that the *gēr* is considered equal to orphans, widows, hirelings (שכיר), and Levites in Deuteronomy.[3] This can only be correct on a very general level that ignores Deuteronomy's precise exposition of the status of *gērîm*, orphans, widows, Levites, and hirelings.

Six times, the *gēr* is mentioned together with the orphan and the widow but without the Levite (10:18, 24:17–21, 27:19), three times in the legal core (chs. 12–

1 Bertholet, *Die Stellung*, 103–95; Bultmann, *Die Fremde*; Albertz, "From Aliens," 53.
2 For a *persona misera*, see Otto, *Das Deuteronomium*, 291–92. For a vulnerable person, see Glanville, *Adopting the Stranger*, 275.
3 Ro, *Poverty, Law*, 40.

https://doi.org/10.1515/9783110713312-013

Tab. 1: List of the Occurrences of Gēr and Gērîm in Deuteronomy.

גר	προσήλυτος	יתום ואלמנה	לוי	אח	בשעריך
1:16	1:16	–	–	1:16	–
5:14	5:14	–	–	–	5:14
10:18	10:18	10:18	–	–	–
10:19 (2x)	10:19 (2x)	–	–	–	–
–	12:18	–	12:18	–	–
14:21	–	–	–	–	14:21
14:29	14:29	14:29	14:29	–	14:29
16:11	16:11	16:11	16:11	–	–
16:14	16:14	16:14	16:14	–	16:14
23:8	–	–	–	23:8	–
24:14	24:14	–	–	24:14	24:14
24:17	24:17	24:17	–	–	–
24:19	24:19	24:19	–	–	–
24:20	24:20	24:20	–	–	–
24:21	24:21	24:21	–	–	–
26:11	26:11	–	26:11	–	–
26:12	26:12	26:12	26:12	–	26:12
26:13	26:13	26:13	26:13	–	–
27:19	27:19	27:19	–	–	–
28:43	28:43	–	–	–	–
29:10	29:10	–	–	–	–
31:12	31:12	–	–	–	31:12

26), and three times in the frames (chs. 1–1, 27–34). Five times, the *gēr* is mentioned alone. In three cases, his place is given as "within your gates," showing that the core (14:21) and frames (5:15 and 31:12) agree that the *gēr* is no outsider. In fact, he is a "special insider"[4] present "in your midst" (16:11, 26:11 בקרבך) or "in the midst of your camp" beside "your wives and your little ones," a likely reference to the mixed crowd (טף) that went out of Egypt with Israel (Exod 12:37). Finally, the *gēr* is mentioned three times together with a brother (1:16; 23:8; 24:14).

At first sight, the core and frames display a remarkable homogeneity in regard to the place and status of the *gēr*. On closer look, however, differences of emphasis appear within different parts of Deuteronomy.

4 Glanville, *Adopting the Stranger*, 255.

2 *Gēr* and Brother (Deut 1:16, 24:14)

The *gēr* appears in the initial chapter of Deuteronomy, which recalls the episode in Exodus 18 when Moses heeded Jethro's advice and appointed officers over Israel to arbitrate their disputes. Thereafter, Moses was to hear only difficult cases. Whereas there is no mention of any *gērîm* in Exodus 18, Deuteronomy 1:16 innovates with a unique presentation of arbitration procedures:

> שמעו בין אחיכם ושפטתם צדק בין איש ובין אחיו ובין גרו
> Hear between your brothers and judge rightly between a man and his brother and between [a man and] his *gēr!*

The *gēr* here represents a legal category placed in parallel with that of a brother (אח) in relation to a man of nondescript legal status (איש). The parallelism is established by the third person singular pronoun suffixed to the words "brother" (אחיו) and *gēr* (גרו); this is the sole instance when the noun *gēr* bears this pronoun (see Table 2).

The suffix places the *gēr* in the same position as the brother in relation to the man (איש). Since the categories of brother and *gēr* are distinguished, this does not imply that in legal disputes, a *gēr* has the same rights and duties as an Israelite. Fairness (צדק) does not exclude differences in legal standings. It is clear that *gērîm* have close enough interactions with Israelites to be involved in litigation with them and that those called to arbitrate the dispute must hear the *gēr*'s point of view. Yet, it does not imply that the *gēr* can initiate the case as plaintiff.

The legal standing of the *gēr* in Deuteronomy 1:16 can be compared to that of the *gēr* in the legal core, where he also is placed in parallel with a brother in regard to the treatment of hirelings:

> לא תעשק שכיר עני ואביון מאחיך או מגרך אשר בארצך בשעריך (Deut 24:14)
> You shall not oppress a poor and needy hireling from your brother or from your *gēr* in your land in your gates.

Tab. 2: The גר and Its Suffixes in Deuteronomy.

Deut		
1:16	3. sg.	*between a man and his brother or his gēr*
5:14	2. sg.	list of Sabbath rest
24:14	2. sg.	*… whether from your brother or from your*
29:10	2. sg.	list, stands before Yhwh
31:12	2. sg.	list, reading of the Torah

Like the third singular pronoun in 1:16, the particle מן before and the second pronoun singular after the brother (מאחיך) and the *gēr* (מגרך) place them in parallel. The מן particle can express different possibilities. In a partitive sense, the מן particle indicates that the hireling belongs to a work-gang tied to a specific brother or *gēr* as part of the repayment of debt in workdays or assigned to them as beneficiaries of workdays due as *corvée*.[5] In any case, both the brother and the *gēr* are in the position to employ day laborers, and both are called not to oppress them. Or, in a comparative sense of the מן particle, 24:14 insists that the hireling should not be oppressed more than a brother or a *gēr*. Even if the labor is supplied as part of *corvée* work, the employer is nevertheless required to feed the hireling on the particular day (ביומו) when he works for that man. In all cases, it is not the *gēr* who needs protection, it is the hireling. Instead of being depicted as one of the tetrad of *personae miserae*, the *gēr* here is depicted as a person of means who, like a brother, needs additional day laborers because both are farming large enough tracts of land to require external labor to face times of intense activity, such as harvesting. It is possible to infer from the phrase "in your land" (בארצך) added before the common location of the *gēr* "in your gates" (see Table 1) that the *gēr* in question here farms an estate such as those granted by a sovereign to his representatives in the "land for service" system of retribution.[6] This estate, as much as the land lots farmed by "your brother," are located outside the physical boundaries of "your gates," but the sphere of activity and responsibility of the *gēr* in question here is identified with the specific Israelite settlement from which the brother originates.[7] Therefore, this *ger* is indeed a "special insider."[8] He is both attached to a particular Israelite settlement but distinct from its Israelite population. The question is whether this particular category of *ger* is also distinct from the orphan and widow, who share with him and the Levite the proceeds of the triennial tithes.

Whereas 1:16 stresses his legal standing, 24:14 focuses on the economic standing of the *gēr*. His equality with the brother is clearer here. One should resist the temptation to harmonize both passages, because the possibility that ch. 1 corrects ch. 24 cannot be excluded. Notwithstanding, chs. 1 and 24 agree on their depiction of the *gēr* as neither a slave nor a vulnerable laborer but as someone whose position is close to that of a brother. Their closeness is underlined by the

---

5 For concrete examples, see Rossi and Guillaume, "Alternative Reading."

6 Edelman, "Different Sources," 441–45.

7 For an understanding of gates as a synecdoche for urban settlements, see Berge in this volume; for their representing a borough within an urban settlement, see Halpern in this volume.

8 Glanville, *Adopting the Stranger*, 255.

final words of v. 24, "in your land, in your gates" (אשר בארצך בשעריך). The interaction of *gērîm* with brothers occurs on the same turf. They might find themselves hiring the same laborers. In real life, the implication would be that they ought to coordinate their activities so that the available workforce may be hired on different days by brothers and by the local *gēr* so that they do not compete with one another, which would be detrimental to both. If the hiring was done on a voluntary basis, one would need to raise salaries to attract willing laborers. If the hiring was done in the framework of credit, the equivalent value of workdays could be subjected to similar inflationary trends. If it was part of taxation, the hirelings might still prefer to spend the workdays they owe in the fields of the man who treats them best and drag their feet when there is no way to avoid the harder task-master.

3 *Gēr* and Sabbath Rest in the Decalogue (Deut 5:14)

The *gēr* is mentioned after family members and draught and pack animals in the list of those who must abstain from work on the Sabbath for Yhwh (5:14). This command reads like a direct response to the above depiction of the *gēr* as the potential hirer of laborers. Such a *gēr* would find himself in a position to hire non-Israelite workers (such as the Hebrew and Hebrewess of 15:12) on the Sabbath at lower rates than on other week-days, since Israelites would be prevented from doing so, leaving the well-off *gēr* as the sole source of wages every seventh day. This section of the Ten Commandments erects barriers to protect Israelites by barring access to the local non-Israelite labor market at preferential prices to *gērîm*.

The idea that the *gēr* "was a non-threatening presence who *belonged*, to some degree, to Israelite society"[9] needs some reframing. It is precisely because the *gēr* belongs to the socio-economic network of the Deuteronomic world that he represents a threat to the Israelite. He is in a good position to outdo Israelites economically, which is exactly what Deuteronomy 28:43 is painfully aware of (see below). Unless the *gēr* is forced to respect the Sabbath as well, "your male and female slave" may *not* rest as you do (Deut 5:14). They – and possibly "your sons, daughters, donkeys, and oxen" too – are likely to be hired by the local *gēr*, but at a lower rate on the day of the Sabbath for Yhwh. In the absence of

9 Awabdy, *Immigrants*, 48.

Israelite competitors on the labor market, the *gēr* would be the sole provider of day labor for a whole day every week. This factor would be negligible during slack times, but during peak times of ploughing and harvesting, Israelites would be tempted to work at the *gēr*'s farm even for lower wages.

As is often the case in Deuteronomy, economic concerns take priority over "humanitarian" ones. Therefore, Deuteronomy 5:14 includes the *gēr* in the list of those who are forbidden to work, but only "your male and female servants like you" (עבדך ואמאתך כמוך) are singled out as benefitting from a well-deserved rest (Deut 5:14). The writers' concern is not that the *gēr* deserves a day of rest but that his Israelite competitors deserve equal treatment.

4 *Gēr* and Egypt (Deut 10:18–19; 23:8; 26:5)

When Moses addresses the people at the threshold of the Promised Land, he reminds them that Israel had lived as *gērîm* (sole plural reference in Deut) in Egypt (10:19). This becomes the reason why "you" (plural) must love the *gēr* in imitation of Yhwh, who is God of gods and Lord of lords, the great God, mighty and awesome, who is not partial and takes no bribe, who executes justice for the orphan and the widow, and who loves the *gēr* by giving him (לתת לו) food and clothing (לחם ושמלה: 10:18). These verses drive a wedge in the tetrad (see below) and set the *gēr* in a separate category from the orphan and widow. Though he benefits from the proceeds of triennial tithes, as do the Levite, the orphan, and the widow (see below), the *gēr*'s status is unique.[10] He is the object of divine love.

The verb אהב "to love" appears 22 times in Deuteronomy, primarily in commands to love Yhwh (6:5, 10:12, 11:1, 11:13, 11:22, 13:4, 19:9, 30:6, 30:20). The other uses refer to Yhwh's loyalty towards those who love him (5:10, 7:9, 30:16), to Yhwh's love towards the ancestors and the addressees (4:37, 7:13, 10:15, 23:6), and to love between human spouses (21:15–16). Deuteronomy 10:19 is the only instance where Israel is called to love the *gēr*. "Love" is a standard way to express the behavior expected from vassals towards their overlord. Though such commanded love does not exclude the emotional aspect of love, it is an eminently "political" kind of love defined "in terms of loyalty, service and obedience."[11]

10 As recognized by Ramírez Kidd, *Alterity*, 83–84.
11 Arnold, "The Love-Fear Antinomy in Deuteronomy," 553.

Does Yhwh's loving provision of food and clothing specifically for the *gēr* mean that the *gēr* is even more needy than the orphan and the widow? This is what is implied when food and clothing are viewed as "a merism that envisions the totality of Yhwh's provision."[12] In this case, is Yhwh's provision for the orphan and the widow less total and they are left naked while the *gēr* receives clothing? Clothing for the *gēr* is mentioned nowhere else. It is to the Levitical priests that the audience is required to deliver the first fleece (18:4).

Therefore, this divine provision of food and clothing for the *gēr* singles out the special status of the *gēr*, a point obscured by the common bundling of the *gēr* with the triad of *personae miserae*. If, as Norbert Lohfink demonstrated, the Levite, the *gēr*, the orphan and the widow should not be viewed as miserable because they are the exclusive beneficiaries of the triennial tithes and as such they are never associated with the *'ebyôn* and the *'ānî*,[13] food and clothing from Yhwh's love underlines the *gēr*'s superior social standing rather than any inferior economic status. Far from being a wretched individual, he could be an imperial representative who is owed food and clothing from the locals. This special reminder was necessary due to the extra economic burden the *gēr* represents to the audience. The resentment it would likely generate would be at loggerhead with the reverence owed to the social status of the *gēr*. Hence, these highly theological verses are coherent with the presentation of the *gēr* as a person of means in the previous section, and both give the lie to the common notion of the *gēr* as a *persona misera*. Whatever legal overtone love may have, the thrust of 10:17–19 is to set the *gēr* on a different plane than Israelite widows and orphans.

It is possible, therefore, to read this curious interplay of divine and human *gēr*-love as a subtle downplaying of the actual financial burden the *gēr* represents to the audience. The tithes of 14:28 exclude any head-on opposition, but the absence of any explicit mention of anything apart from edibles provides a loophole to leave the provision of clothing to Yhwh, though of course it is the Israelites who supply the wool is for the *gēr*'s clothing. The same Israelites provide the priestly portions for the Levite who travels from his local settlement to the *māqôm* (18:6) With the reference to Egypt in 26:5, these are the only Deuteronomic occurrences of the root גור used as a verb, both of them with Israelites rather than the *gēr* as subjects. In both cases, the matter concerns the extraction of revenues. Whether taxation is presented as divine love or as priestly dues makes little difference to the tax payer.

---

12 Awabdy, 54.
13 Lohfink, "Poverty."

5 The Missing *Gēr* in Deuteronomy 12:18

The Septuagint mentions the προσήλυτος among the partakers of the annual tithes at the *māqôm* where the Masoretic text has the Levite (הלוי). It is remarkable that the critical *apparati* of the *Biblia Hebraica Kittel*, the *Biblia Hebraica Stuttgartensia*, and even more surprisingly, of the recent *Biblia Hebraica Quinta*[14] do not signal this textual variant. Given the tension over the revenues of the Levites within Deuteronomy, this textual variant is highly significant.[15] The difference is reconciled by the comprehensive double list of guests at the *māqôm* feasts in 16:11, 14, which includes the tetrad besides the families. It is therefore difficult to identify whether the Hebrew or the Greek text represents the *lectio difficilior*, since both chs. 12 and 16 eliminate the really difficult notion of the absence of the tetrad at the *māqôm*, which is clearly stated in 14:22–26. Despite the difficulty in identifying the more original reading – levite or *gēr* – the difference reflects the social situation of each group of tradents. The tradents of the Hebrew text sided with the Levite, since they themselves derived some of their income from sacerdotal functions, while the Greek translators sought to present a more proselyte-friendly version of the *māqôm* festivities to their Alexandrian audience.

6 Carrion Given to the *Gēr* (Deut 14:21)

That carrion should be given to the *gēr* or sold to the foreigner (Deut 14:21) is another surprise. It is not listed as a *Sondergut* by Benjamin Kilchör, though it differs greatly from the discussion about carrion elsewhere.[16] Exodus 22:30 simply recommends throwing carrion to the dogs. Only Deuteronomy 14:21 considers the option of giving it to the *gēr* or selling it to a foreigner. In light of the dogs in the Exodus parallel, the gift of carrion to the *gēr* sounds more like an ethnic joke than a display of generosity. In fact, 14:21 only mentions the sale to a foreigner after stating that the *gēr* will eat it (ואכלה). The interest of this verse is not to let the *gēr* somehow recycle Israelite carrion but to insist that he will eat it because he is not holy (קדש) to Yhwh, as Israel is. It remains possible to

---

14 McCarthy, *Biblia hebraica quinta*, 41, 87*.

15 For a detailed discussion of this topic, see Rossi's first contribution in this volume.

16 For its absence from the list of *Sondergut*, see Kilchör, *Mosetora*, 333. For its difference from other discussions of carrion, see Otto, "Die nachpriesterschriftliche Pentateuch," 93; Kilchör, *Mosetora*, 93.

read the gift of carrion to the *gēr*, which entails no direct financial compensation as the sale to the foreigner would, as a way to ingratiate the giver in the eyes of the *gēr*, as any gift would. Presenting a gift of carrion as a charitable act may not be the main effect the writer sought.[17] This passage uses holiness to mark the difference between the *gēr* and the Israelite, casting the *gēr* in the realm of the unholy. It marks a contrast with the obligations of the *gēr* to comply with Israelite *mores* (5:14; 31:12).

7 The *Gēr* in the Tetrad (Deut 14:29; 16:11.14; 26:12–13)

With the Levite, the orphan, and the widow, the *gēr* constitutes a tetrad, each of whose members is entitled to a share of the proceeds of the triennial tithes stored in the gates (14:29; 26:12, 26:13) and is to appear as guests at the *māqôm* (16:11, 14) (Table 3).

The mention that the Levite has neither allotment (חלק) nor inheritance (נחלה) with you does not mean he is destitute. The Levites have some unspecified paternal possessions (18:8). As discussed above, in 1:16 and 24:14, the *gēr* farms enough land to need hirelings. What differentiates the tetrad from brothers is that they have no access to communal land. Such land, usually portioned out according to the number of resident adult males (see Deut 32:9; Jer 37:12; Micah 2:5; Ps 16:6) does not concern gardens, terraces, fallow land and unculti-

Tab. 3: The Deuteronomic Tetrad.

14:29		triennial tithes
16:11		festival of weeks
16:14		festival of booths
24:17		custom, pledge
24:19		gleaning of sheaf
24:20		gleaning of olives
24:21		gleaning in vineyard
26:11		first fruits
26:12		triennial tithes
26:13		triennial tithes
27:19	–	curse

17 Against van Houten, *Alien*, 81.

vated areas that may be put under cultivation at will. There is a real possibility that the *gēr* who employs hirelings has received an estate from an outside ruler in the framework of the land-for-service system.

As such this *gēr*, but not necessarily all *gērim*, is a local representative of an anonymous foreign ruler, a "residing foreign delegate."[18] Representing the interests of an overlord, he enjoyed a high position and would deal with the local elite on an equal footing.

8 The *Gēr* in the Triad (Deut 24:17–21; 27:19)

The *gēr* enjoys gleaning rights with the orphan and widow (24:19–21). These rights probably apply only to the adult *gēr* and to the Israelite orphan and widow, because 24:17 refers to a separate custom involving the גר יתום. The word order prevents reading "the orphan of a *gēr*." "Orphaned *gēr*" is preferable; the same form is repeated in 27:19, so it is not a mistake in either verse.[19] Though this verse comes closer to the Levite-*gēr*-orphan-widow tetrad (see above), it nevertheless retains the odd גר יתום formulation. There is, therefore, no reason to correct it. Instead of referring to a *gēr* and an orphan with a conjunction in between and a widow in the second part of the verse, these verses deal specifically with two separate cases: an orphaned *gēr* and a widow's garment. The prohibition to take the latter's garment as pawn means either that loans granted to a widow are not secured by any pledge or that any pledge apart from clothing is allowed, contrary to loans to neighbors that are secured by a pledge of the borrower's choice (24:10). In any case, loans rather than charitable gifts confirm the status of the Deuteronomic widow as a credit-worthy economic agent and thus not a *persona misera*.

This leaves the case of the *gēr* orphan in this pair, which could represent a family grouping that has lost the male head of household. If this is the case, the orphaned *gēr* is a fatherless *gēr* only, with a mother still alive, contrary to the common use of orphan in English to designate a child who has lost both parents. On the other hand, it is possible that the orphaned *gēr* and the widow have been grouped together for consideration because each has lost their respective head of family, which would then allow orphan to bear its normal Eng-

---

18 Na'aman, "Resident-Alien."

19 For this reason, the Septuagint's προσηλύτου καὶ ὀρφανου, "justice of a guest and an orphan," in both verses is the *lectio facilior*, attempting to make sense of the unusual construct chain.

lish sense. Irrespective of the status of his mother, this child was born a *gēr* because his father was a *gēr*, but his father died while his son was still underaged. As could be expected when non-Israelites such as *gērîm* reside more or less permanently in the midst of Israelites, the birth of children of mixed parentage would represent yet another liminal category from that of the "ordinary" *gēr* usually born elsewhere from non-Israelite parents. The official functions performed within Israelite settlements or the close business association with Israelites granted the *gērîm* a status midway between native Israelites and outright foreigners. The status of a child fathered by a *gēr* but born within an Israelite settlement would be even closer to the native Israelite, all the more so if his mother was an Israelite herself.

Nothing indicates that the widow and orphan who benefit from the proceedings of the triennial tithes (Deut 14:28–29) are non-Israelites. If a widow and an orphan have to be recognized as Israelites to benefit from these tithes, the son of a *gēr* whose father met an untimely death would not be entitled to these tithes, even if his Israelite mother was. As no provision is ever mentioned for him elsewhere, the fatherless *gēr* may indeed be a *persona misera*. The admission that poverty will remain in your land (15:11) refers to him among others, and the "custom of the גר יתום" in 24:17 entails the "opening of your hand" in 15:11. The notion of Deuteronomic humanism is adequate in this case, as it refers to charity rather than the right enjoyed by the Israelite orphan.

9 The *Gēr* as Threat (Deut 28:43–44)

As noted above in the section on the prohibition of the *gēr* from working on the Sabbath, his proximity and his quasi-equality put him in the position of a potential challenger. In the list of curses in Deuteronomy 28, the challenge becomes a punishment for the failure to heed Moses's recommendations and breaking the covenant. The utopian scenario of ch. 15, repeated in 28:12–13,[20] views brothers lending against interest to foreigners and never borrowing from other nations (15:3–6). Instead of simply reversing the scenario, dystopia involves the *gēr*, whose proximity is more threatening than the distant foreigner. It is the *gēr* who becomes the loan shark who turns Israel into the tail (28:44).

20 Awabdy, *Immigrants*, 95.

10 The *Gēr* before Yhwh (Deut 29:10)

Chapter 29 presents a significant downgrading of the *gēr*'s status, as though reassurance was urgent after the devastating potential of the *gēr* in ch. 28. Putting the *gēr* back in his proper place means presenting him as a wood-chopper and water-carrier "in your midst" (29:10) – an obvious reference to the punishment of the Gibeonites in Joshua 9. Mark. A. Awabdy downplays this unfavorable portrayal of the *gēr* by including Israelite women and children with the *gēr*, drawing on images of women at the well in Genesis 24, because Deuteronomic Israelite women are never seen engaged in such tasks. He has to evoke the widow of Sarepta to find women doing wood chores. The question is whether the phrase, "from those who cut your wood to those who draw your water" (מחטב עציך עד שאב מימיך) modifies only the *gēr* in the midst in your camp or if it is "a merism for all service-oriented persons in the Israelite community."[21] If so, why not include "your tribal leaders, your elders, your officials, all the men of Israel" (29:9) in the merism? Apart from the modern verse division, nothing separates "every 'man' (כל איש) of Israel" from "your little ones, your wives and you *gēr*." Nevertheless, the purported Deuteronomic humanism is redeemed by recruiting "your little ones and your women" (טפכם נשיכם plural) to help your *gēr* (גרך singular) chop wood and carry water.

11 The *Gēr* Learning to Fear Yhwh (Deut 31:12)

The last appearance of the *gēr* in Deuteronomy is to require his presence every seventh year at the assembly besides men, women, and the mixed crowd (טף, Exod 12:37 and Deut 29:10). Like the yearly *māqôm*-banquets, the aim of this assembly is to learn to fear Yhwh, though this time, the learning is effected by listening to the recitation of "this torah" (31:11).[22] The difference is underlined by the setting of the assembly during the feast of Sukkoth that occurs concomitantly with the *šmiṭṭah* release (31:10). This is new, as neither the prescriptions relative to the release (15:2–6) nor the festival calendar (16:13–15) connect the *šmiṭṭah* with Sukkoth. This lacing of motifs from chs. 15 and 16 strives to harmonize the different strands within the core to produce a more coherent whole. Nevertheless, if listening to the Torah once every seventh year turns the *gēr* into

---

21 Awabdy, 100.
22 Seitz, *Redaktionsgeschichtliche Studien*, 300–1; Awabdy, *Immigrants*, 105.

a "fully participating member of the religious community,"[23] it is significant that the *gēr* does not become a brother. Awabdy is aware of the discrepancy between Deuteronomy 14:21 (no *gēr* at the *māqôm* except in the Septuaginta) and 31:12. He argues that the discrepancy

> is best explained as a development from the social to the social *and* religious integration of the גר. Deuteronomy 23:2–9 provides the legal mechanism for this religious integration. The קהל יהוה is best understood as the assembly of YHWH's people privileged to hear and observe YHWH's word.[24]

Besides the fact that the קהל יהוה is not mentioned again in Deuteronomy after ch. 23 and the Torah-reading ceremony takes place at the *māqôm* and not at the קהל יהוה, Awabdy is at pains to provide substance to the *gēr*'s religious integration. What Deuteronomy 31 integrates is Deuteronomy in the Pentateuch. The religious integration of the *gēr* was of no concern to the writers, who did not try to erase the discrepancies resulting from the framing of the Deuteronomic core.

12 *The Gēr* and Gates

The phrase "within your gates" (בשׁעריך) appears 16 times in Deuteronomy and only 3 times elsewhere (Exod 20:10; Ezek 26:10; Ps 122:2). In Deuteronomy, the *gēr* within your gates is mentioned four times together with the Levite, the orphan, and the widow: 14:29 (triennial tithes); 16:11 (festival of weeks); 16:14 (Sukkoth) and 26:12 (triennial tithes). Another four times, the expression "within your gates" refers exclusively to the *gēr*: work forbidden on the Sabbath (5:14), a gift of carrion (14:21), wages paid daily (24:14), and listening to the Torah (31:12).

These four references to "your gates" specifically dedicated to the *gēr* underline the particularity of the *gēr*'s status in the Deuteronomic economy. The common designation of *persona misera* is even less appropriate for the *gēr* than for the orphan and the widow. The question is who is this *gēr* whose economic status sometimes seems far above that of a beggar and appears more as a challenge and a threat than an object of pity?

---

23 Corcoran, "Alien," 239.
24 Awabdy, *Immigrants*, 244.

13 Origins of *Gērîm*

The attempts to identify the ethnicity of the Deuteronomic *gēr*, whether he is a displaced Israelite, a displaced Judahite, or an immigrant from elsewhere,[25] are misguided in the sense that they seek "either-or" answers.[26] The above consideration of the Deuteronomic *gēr* indicates that it is applied to a variety of individuals.

Some *gērîm* are immigrants who have been granted land, probably in an imperial "land for service scheme" (24:14; possibly 10:19; 31:12). Their children would have inherited their status. Others are sons of resident Edomites and Egyptians born from Israelite women. As only the third generation is granted membership in the *qᵉhal-yhwh* (Deut 23:9), these second-generation sons would be granted *gēr*-status instead (see above on the fatherless and underage *gēr*). Their own sons would become full-fledged Israelites only or more likely if they were also born from Israelite mothers.[27]

The sons of the attractive war captive who was married rather than sold as booty would also qualify for *gēr* status, being half-breed Israelites from their father's side but still remembered as the sons of a foreign mother. The runaway slaves that are to be welcomed would also be a source of *gērim*.[28] As noted by Davies at the end of his article in this volume, Deuteronomy 23:7 shows that "Being immigrants is no bar to being Israelite ... Ethnicity is the code, except that through intermarriage it necessarily imposes itself anyway."

If the females among the welcomed runaway slaves bore children to their Israelite master – nothing indicates that welcome means manumission – their sons would be *gērim*. The males among those runaway slaves could have found themselves in a position to marry Israelite widows, especially when their economic standing improved their prospects on the "second-hand" marriage market, first towards Israelite widows and divorcees for whom the requirements of endogamy are more relaxed in cases of remarriage than they are for first marriages. There are also daughters for whom, for one reason or another, parents have difficulties finding a suitor. In addition to a poor Israelite man who would pay the bride price in the form of work days, as the patriarch Jacob did, a foreign slave residing among Israelites could represent a viable way out of the predica-

---

25 For the first two options, see Knauf, "Observations," 2; for the third option, see Awabdy, *Immigrant*, 116.

26 For an overview, see Awabdy, 110–16.

27 There is a long tradition going back to Neh, 4QMMT, 4QFlorilegium ... of understanding the admittance restrictions to the *qᵉhal-yhwh* as referring to intermarriage. For a recent discussion and bibliography, see Harrington, "Sexual Relations," 294–98.

28 Dion, Israël, 223.

ment. Sons born from such "second rate" Israelite women – daughters, widows and divorcees – would qualify as *gērîm* rather than slaves despite the bond status of their fathers. The grandsons of these women would probably inherit the *gēr* status of their fathers, unless they were born from full-breed Israelite mothers.

Far from the somewhat unidimensional world of Leviticus and Numbers that focuses on the priesthood and views the other Israelites as suppliers of priestly revenues, Deuteronomy depicts a kind of society that would generate a number of *gērîm* from the second generation onward. While true immigrants might be remembered as foreigners for the rest of their lives, their offspring would gradually acquire an in-between *gēr* status.

The children of Israelite mothers from non-Israelite fathers would typically belong to such an in-between *gēr* status, neither a foreigner nor a full-blooded Israelite. In real life, blood relations are subject to complications through marriage and adoption, which introduce degrees within definitions of family relations and kinship.

Defining the *gēr* as a person "who is from outside of the core family" is as problematic as defining him as someone of "non-Israelite and non-Judahite ethnic origin."[29] These definitions are not inherently erroneous; they simply fail to account for Deuteronomy's portrayal of the *gēr* on several accounts. First, internal Deuteronomic tension prevents drawing a comprehensive and integrated image of the Deuteronomic *gēr*. The tension is more acute over the revenues of the Levite, but this is also related to the status of the *gēr*.

Second, the notion of Deuteronomic humanitarianism tends to blind readers to the variety of situations referred to in the book and their implications. For instance, Yhwh's love for the *gēr* never translates concretely into what modern readers would expect from humanitarianism. The most assured revenue for the *gēr* is his share of the triennial tithes stored within your gates (14:29). Gleaning rights shared with orphans and widows (24:19–21) are not sources of large revenue, although they are not negligible. As for the provision of clothing, it is left to Yhwh himself. The presence of the *gēr* at the *māqôm*-banquets is a matter of debate inside Deuteronomy, as the textual variants in 12:18 show. Who is there besides the revelling families? Is it הלוי or ὁ προσήλυτος? In any case, being invited to the banquets can hardly be viewed as a humanitarian gesture if the *gēr* is indeed poor and destitute. At most, it would provide him with "a good meal sometimes during the year."[30]

29 For the first, see Glanville, *Adopting the Stranger*, 257; for the second, see Awabdy, *Immigrants*, 251.
30 Albertz, "From Aliens," 55.

Finally, the notion of *personae miserae* needs to be challenged by drawing on the implications of Lohfink's demonstration that the tetrad does not represent classes of *personae miserae*.[31] Though Awabdy seems to accept Lohfink's point, he continues to use the *personae miserae* in his study, and he concludes that "Finally, D teaches that Israel's election entails a concomitant responsibility to imitate Yhwh's generosity towards the *personae miserae* גר."[32]

The portrayal of the *gēr* as an employer of hirelings can only be reconciled by (mis-)reading Deuteronomy 24:14 to view the *gēr* as a poor and vulnerable person. In this framework, the passages calling for some equality with brothers can indeed be read as motivated by humanitarianism. The fact that the *gēr* does "not enjoy the status of full citizenship"[33] does not necessarily entail a low economic standing.

To be sure, the *gēr*'s entitlement to the proceeds of triennial tithes and gleanings does seem to support the notion of a poor *gēr*. Viewed in light of the Deuteronomic passage that portrays an affluent *gēr* (24:14), the foodstuffs obtained from triennial tithes and gleanings denote a position of power rather than of weakness. To Israelite orphans and widows, triennial tithes and gleanings represent social relief. To the affluent *gēr*, they represent the proceeds of taxation as much as workdays supplied by the local population on his estate.

14 Conclusion

Can exclusion of the *gēr* contribute to his eventual integration in Israel, in line with Philip Davies's proposal in this volume that the original form of Deuteronomy had a goal of creating a new Israelite identity in the province of Samerina that would integrate the recently settled immigrants post 722 BCE under the new imperial Assyrian regime? Yes, in fact. The confinement "within your gates" (14:27–29) of the *gēr* alongside unlanded Israelites, i.e. the Levite, the widow, and the orphan, is coherent with the claim that Deuteronomy constructs a distinctive Israelite identity by avoiding non-Israelites.[34] The *gēr* looks forward to the time when he will become a brother and will then make it to the *māqôm* as a brother, and when his offspring with be able to join the *qehal-yhwh* (23:9) The welcoming of the tetrad to the feasting held at the *māqôm* (16:11,

31 Lohfink, "Poverty."
32 Awabdy, *Immigrants*, 109, quote from 254.
33 Biddle, Deuteronomy, 182.
34 Crouch, *Making of Israel*, 218.

16:14, and 26:12–13), the "place" where Israelite identity is constructed, logically is a secondary development.[35] The above examination of the *gēr* passages without wearing *personae miserae* glasses uncovers an original vision that hinged on a clear distinction between Israelites and *gērim*. Though they rubbed shoulders on a daily basis, and though some or most of the *gērim* were related to Israelites by marriage and other ties, only the brothers travelled to the *māqôm* with their families, thus elevating Israeliteness as a prize to be coveted.

Works Cited

Albertz, Rainer. "From Aliens to Proselytes." In *The Foreigner and the Law: Perspectives from the Hebrew Bible and the Ancient Near East*, edited by Rainer Achenbach, Rainer Albertz, and Jacob Wöhrle, 53–70. Beihefte zur Zeitschrift für altorientalische und biblische Rechtsgeschichte 16. Wiesbaden: Harrassowitz, 2011.

Arnold, Bill T. "The Love-Fear Antinomy in Deuteronomy 5–11." *Vetus Testamentum* 61 (2011): 551–69.

Awabdy, Mark A. *Immigrants and Innovative Law: Deuteronomy's Theological and Social Vision for the* גר. Forschungen zum Alten Testament 2 Reihe 67. Tübingen: Mohr Siebeck, 2014.

Bertholet, Alfred. *Die Stellung der Israeliten und der Juden zu den Fremden*. Freiburg and Leipzig: J. C. B. Mohr, 1896.

Biddle, Mark E. *Deuteronomy*. Smyth & Helwys Bible Commentary 4. Macon, GA: Smyth and Helwys, 2003.

Braulik, Georg. "Das Buch Deuteronomium." In *Einleitung in das Alte Testament*, edited by Erich Zenger et al., 136–55. 6th ed. Kohlhammer Studienbücher Theologie Stuttgart: Kohlhammer, 2006.

Bultmann, Christoph. *Die Fremde im antiken Juda: Eine Untersuchung zum socialen Typenbegriff 'ger' und seinem Bedeutungswandel in der alttestamentlichen Gesetzgebung*. Forschungen zur Religion und Literatur des Alten und Neuen Testaments 153. Göttingen: Vandenhoeck & Ruprecht, 1992.

Corcoran, Jenny. "The Alien in Deuteronomy 20 and Today." In *Interpreting Deuteronomy: Issues and Approaches*, edited by David G. Firth and Philip S. Johnson, 229–39. Downers Grove, IL: Intervarsity, 2012.

Crouch, Carly L. *The Making of Israel: Cultural Diversity in the Southern Levant and the Formation of Ethnic Identity in Deuteronomy*. Vetus Testamentum Supplements 162. Leiden: Brill, 2014.

Dion, Paul E. "Israël et l'étranger dans le Deutéronome." In *L'altérité: Vivre ensemble différents: Approches interdisciplinaires, approches pluridisciplinaires*, edited by M. Gourges and G.-D. Mailhiot, 211–33. Recherches nouvelle série 7. Paris: Cerf, 1986.

Edelman, Diana V. "Different Sources, Different Views: Snapshots of Persian-Era Yehud Based on Texts and on Archaeological Data." *Estudios Biblicos* 76 (2018): 411–51.

35 For a detailed argument supporting this position, see Guillaume's chapter 7 in this volume.

Glanville, Mark R. *Adopting the Stranger as Kindred in Deuteronomy*. Society of Biblical Literature Ancient Israel and Its Literature 33. Atlanta: Society of Biblical Literature, 2018.

Harrington, Hannah K. "Sexual Relations and the Transition from Holy People to Human Sanctuary in Second Temple Times." In *Sexuality and Law in the Torah*, edited by Hilary Lipka and Bruce Wells, 286–308. Library of Hebrew Bible/Old Testament Studies 675. London: T&T Clark, 2020.

Houten, Christiana van. *The Alien in Israelite Law: A Study of the Changing Legal Status of Strangers in Ancient Israel*. Library of Hebrew Bible/Old Testament Studies 107. Sheffield: Sheffield Academic, 1991.

Kilchör, Benjamin. *Mosetora und Jahwetora: Das Verhältnis von Deuteronomium 12–26 zu Exodus, Levitikus und Numeri*. Beihefte zur Zeitschrift für altorientalische und biblische Rechtsgeschichte 21. Wiesbaden: Harrassowitz, 2015.

Knauf, E. Axel. "Observations on Judah's Social and Economic History and the Dating of the Laws in Deuteronomy." *Journal of Hebrew Scriptures* 9 (2009): 2–8.

Lohfink, Norbert. "Poverty in the Laws of the Ancient Near East and of the Bible." *Theological Studies* 52 (1991): 34–50.

McCarthy, Carmel. *Biblia hebraica quinta*. Vol. 5, *Deuteronomy*. Stuttgart: Deutsche Bibelgesellschaft, 2007.

Na'aman, Nadav. "Resident-Alien or Residing Foreign Delegate?" *Ugarit Forschungen* 37 (2005): 475–78.

Otto, Eckart. *Deuteronomium 1–11*. Herders Theologischer Kommentar zum Alten Testament. Freiburg: Herder, 2012.

Otto, Eckart. *Das Deuteronomium: Politische Theologie und Rechtsreform in Juda und Assyrien*. Beihefte zur Zeitschrift für die alttestamentliche Wissenschaft 284. Berlin: de Gruyter, 1999.

Otto, Eckart. "Die nachpriesterschriftliche Pentateuch Redaktion im Buch Exodus." In *Studies in the Book of Exodus: Redaction–Reception–Interpretation*, edited by Marc Vervenne, 61–111. Bibliotheca Ephemeridum Theologicarum Lovaniensium 126. Leuven: Peeters, 1996.

Ramírez Kidd, José E. *Alterity and Identity in Israel: The גר in the Old Testament*. Beihefte zur Zeitschrift für die alttestamentliche Wissenschaft 283. Berlin: Walter de Gruyter, 1999.

Ro, Johannes Unsok. *Poverty, Law, and Divine Justice in Persian and Hellenistic Judah*. Ancient Israel and its Literature 32. Atlanta: Society of Biblical Literature, 2018.

Rossi, Benedetta and Philippe Guillaume. "An Alternative Reading of the Law of the Hebrew 'Slave' (Deuteronomy 15:12–18)." *Res Antiquae* 15 (2018): 3–30.

Seitz, Gottfried. *Redaktionsgeschichtliche Studien zum Buch Deuteronomium*. Beitrage Zur Wissenschaft vom Alten und Neuen Testament 5/13. Stuttgart: Kohlhammer, 1971.

Benedetta Rossi

Authority, Prestige or Subversion? Jeremiah and the Law Code of Deuteronomy

1 Introduction

The book of Jeremiah is commonly considered to use the "law-code" of Deuteronomy 12–26 as a normative legal referent[1] or an authoritative point of reference for Jeremiah's preaching.[2] Deuteronomy's regulations are evoked to explain the fall of Jerusalem: 13:17 in Jeremiah 21:10,[3] 17:3 in Jeremiah 8:2, and 18:9–10 in Jeremiah 32:35.[4] To condemn institutional figures like kings or prophets, Deuteronomy 17:14 and 17:20 are evoked in Jeremiah 36:24 and 36:30[5] and Deuteronomy 18:18 and 18:20 in Jeremiah 14:14. For the book of Jeremiah, Deuteronomy is foundational, although sometimes the book gainsays Deuteronomy's laws.[6] Dalit Rom-Shiloni describes the book's conflicting stance toward Deuteronomy in terms of transformative exegesis, expansion, actualization, and even reversal.[7] To explain the issue at stake, Nathan Mastnjak distinguishes different layers in the book that contain opposing attitudes to Deuteronomy. Deuteronomy appears as a prestigious classic alluded to in the book of Jeremiah. Later Deuteronomistic layers in it, however, refer back to Deuteronomy as an authority demanding obedience, even though with "occasional transformation and subversion."[8]

The twofold attitude toward Deuteronomic legal material in the book of Jeremiah has been extensively described, but no specific purpose for this contrasting stance has been clearly identified. According to Georg Fischer, the book

1 Mastnjak, *Deuteronomy.*
2 Rom-Shiloni, "Actualisation," 260–61; Rom Shiloni, "Prophets in Jeremiah."
3 Fischer, *Jeremia 1–25*, 639–40.
4 Mastnjak, *Deuteronomy*, 137, 144.
5 Fischer, *Jeremia 26–52*, 299.
6 Fischer, "Aufnahme," 129–39; Fischer,"Einfluss," 266–67.
7 Rom-Shiloni, "Actualization"; Rom-Shiloni,"How Can you Say"; Rom Shiloni,"Compositional Harmonization"; Rom Shiloni,"Forest."
8 Mastnjak, *Deuteronomy*, 228–30; Fioscher, "Prestige."

Note: I express my gratitude to Richard Bautch for reading a draft and for fruitful discussions on this and related topics in Rome. Within the framework of the Oslo Deuteronomy Research Group, it was Philip Davies who suggested I deal with the reception of the Deuteronomic legal core in Jeremiah. I dedicate this contribution to him. Shortcomings are entirely mine.

https://doi.org/10.1515/9783110713312-014

picks up and supersedes Deuteronomy's positions, showing how Yhwh overcomes the dire consequences of Jerusalem's destruction.[9] Eckart Otto goes a step further by setting the dialogue between the two books against the background of a post-exilic debate between priestly and prophetic schools.[10]

In the following, I first debate the authoritative status of the legal "core" of Deuteronomy in Jeremiah, using Jeremiah 34:8–22 as a test case. I shall then argue that the challenge mounted to the Deuteronomic laws in the book is intended to subvert Deuteronomy's claims concerning the role Mosaic Torah is to play after the exile. In particular, the frames of Deuteronomy turn the Mosaic Torah into the only legitimate medium of revelation and the only way to restoration in the post-exilic era. References to Deuteronomy in Jeremiah 3:1; 29:3–14, 17; 30:18; and 31:29–30 oppose and subvert the contention that observance of Mosaic Torah can grant new life after the Exile. Some preliminary remarks on Deuteronomy's authoritative claims and on the dynamic of literary subversion are needed as background to the literary analysis.

2 Establishing and Subverting Authority

Like any other legal text, Deuteronomy's legal core asserts its own authority. The prescriptive style of laws, as well as sanctions imposed on their potential transgressors, make the Deuteronomic legal core binding and, therefore, authoritative for its recipients. "Although the question of Deuteronomy's purpose and potential claim to legal validity is highly disputed, it seems unlikely that it was meant to be a purely academic exercise with no intention whatsoever of influencing the lives of its addressees".[11]

The frames of Deuteronomy (chs. 1–11; 27–34) highlight a twofold purpose for obedience to its legal prescriptions. First, faithfulness to the regulations will allow Israel to prosper and to live a long life in the land they are about to enter (Deut 8:1, 8:6–11). In the story-world, the conditional promise is directed to the intra-diegetic addressees, i.e. Israel gathered in Moab and listening to Moses's speeches on the verge of entering the land to possess it. The consequence of transgressing the first commandment and abandoning Yhwh's instructions will be exile (see Deut 4:25–31; 29:21–27; 28:15; 28:58, and 28:63–64). In addition, however, as Dominik Markl highlights: "While the law is meant for life in the

9 Fischer, "Aufnahme," 137–38.
10 Otto, "Scribal Scholarship."
11 Markl, "'Anti-King,'" 167.

land, its neglect will lead to losing it."[12] Thus, a second purpose for obeying Mosaic prescriptions exists: after losing the land and being scattered among the nations, obedience to Moses's teaching and to the legal core embedded in it will grant return and restoration. Deuteronomy 30:1–10 highlights the pivotal role played by Moses's regulations in offering a change to the exiles.[13] Obedience to Yhwh's voice and to Moses's instructions will lead to the end of exile (30:2–3). Yhwh will gather his people and bring them back to the land of the ancestors (30:2–5). Extra-diegetic addressees (i.e. exiled Israel) form the intended audience here.

In addition to clarifying the twofold aim of observing Moses's teaching and statutes, the frames of Deuteronomy reinforce the authority of the core.[14] Moses's parenetical speeches in Deuteronomy 6–11 and the depiction of Moses as the arch-prophet (34:10–12) emphasize his authority. Depicting Moses as the unique and unsurpassed prophet, his Torah (Deuteronomy as a whole) becomes the only way of securing return and restoration after the Exile (30:1–10). Once the restoration is accomplished, Moses's Toraḥ will provide the only suitable access to divine revelation (31:9–13). Moreover, Deuteronomy 1:5 links Moses's explanation of the Torah in Moab to the Sinai revelation,[15] which further enhances the eminence of Moses's instructions, including Deuteronomy's legal code.[16] The link between Moses's teaching in Deuteronomy and the Sinai pericope can reasonably be ascribed to a post-exilic Pentateuch Redaction.[17] The same Pentateuch Redaction is presumably responsible for the limitation of prophetic ministry to Moses in Deuteronomy 34:10–12.[18] By referencing Deuteronomy's legal prescriptions, the creators of the book of Jeremiah aim at subverting the above-mentioned authoritative claims.

Subversion is an attempt to undermine, criticize, or otherwise "corrode" an ideology, institution, or individual.[19] Literary subversion, in particular, manifests itself as resistance to the dominant power that has been built, conveyed, and reinforced by means of authoritative texts. As Carly Crouch explains,[20] the mechanics of subversion involve a dialogue between two texts (the subversive and the subverted one); a transformative action concerning the subverted text,

---

12 Markl, "Efficacy," 138.
13 So Ehrenreich, *Wähle das Leben*; Markl, "No Future."
14 See Markl, "Deuteronomy's Framework"; Markl, *Gottes Volk*, 36–45.
15 Achenbach, "Grundlinien," 65; Otto, "Mose."
16 See Otto, "Deuteronomy as Legal Completion."
17 Otto, *Deuteronomium im Pentateuch*, 167–75; Otto, *Deuteronomium 1,1–4,43*, 319–21.
18 Otto, *Deuteronomium 23,16–34,12*, 2,284–85.
19 Seibert, *Subversive Scribes*, 16.
20 Crouch, *Israel*, 15–45.

and finally, an audience. Although the relation between the subverting and the subverted text must be highlighted,[21] literary subversion can be "concealed" or "conspicuous."[22] The crucial issue at stake is the identification of the literary techniques employed to challenge the authority of the subverted text. Irony, redactional reworking, omissions, and the twisting of literary conventions are among the strategies Eric Seibert lists.[23]

In addition, prophetic figures and their words were privileged instruments scribes used to criticize "their own régime" without being explicit.[24] "Collections of oracles ascribed to prophets of the past provide an ideal disguise for a contemporary critique that might be either unwise or less authoritative or both to express overtly."[25] To highlight the strategies of subversive discourse used in Jeremiah, the first step is to reconsider whether or not Deuteronomic laws are picked up in the book to explain the judgement against Jerusalem and its elites.

3 Incipient Subversion (Jer 34:8–22 and Deut 15:1–18)

The use of Deuteronomy 15:1 and 15:12 in Jeremiah 34:14 has been extensively investigated. Scholars working in Pentateuchal research have considered Jeremiah 34:8–22 a historical source and pivotal point for the relative chronology of the legal codes in the Pentateuch.[26] Klaas Smelik, on the other hand, rejects any attempt to harmonize Jeremiah 34 with the Torah.[27] Jeremian scholarship used to view Jeremiah 34:8–22 as a Deuteronomistic reworking of Jeremiah's words.[28] Christl M. Maier, however, rejects the presence of a core of the prophet's words within Jeremiah 34:8–22 and highlights the presence of post-exilic reworking.[29] A shared viewpoint among the various interpretive efforts seems to be that book refers back to Deuteronomy as an authoritative source in order to elucidate Zedekiah's manumission of slaves and then provide reasons for

21 Amit, *Polemics*, 93–98; Crouch, *Israel*, 21–22.
22 Seibert, *Subversive Scribes*, 16–19.
23 Seibert, 66–94.
24 Davies, *Search*, 94.
25 Davies, "Judahite Prophecy," 212.
26 Japhet, "Relationship," 63–89; Van Seters, "Law"; Leuchter, "Manumission Laws," 635–53.
27 Smelik, "Cohesion," 250.
28 Duhm, *Jeremia*, 279; Rudolph, *Jeremia*, 222–23; Thiel, *Jeremia 26–45*, 39–43.
29 Maier, *Jeremia als Lehrer*, 260–65.

the judgment against Jerusalem.[30] This interpretation, however, is considered a shortcut by Eckart Otto, who is a dissonant voice on the topic.[31] How is the book of Jeremiah dealing with Deuteronomy?

Bernard M. Levinson views the law hinted at as an authoritative referent in Jeremiah 34:8–22 as an innovative "exegetical blend" from different Pentateuchal laws.[32] However, he fails to take into account possible literary developments within Jeremiah 34:8–11 and, thus, overlooks the differences between the LXX and the MT. The impact of the divergences between Jeremiah 34:8–22MT and 41:8–22LXX on the issue of the relationship with Deuteronomy has been marginal. Yet, taking the MT as the sole source of historical investigation is questionable from a scientific point of view.[33] In fact, a comparison between the LXX and the MT reveals diverging attitudes toward the laws of Deuteronomy.

As regards the relationship of Jeremiah 41:8–22LXX to Deuteronomy 15, three points arise. First, within the narrative account (vv. 8–11), Deuteronomy 15:12 provides an authoritative reference for Zedekiah's release, announced in v. 8 and revoked in v. 10. The lexical reference to Deuteronomy 15:12 is marked by the phrase τὸν Εβραῖον καὶ τὴν Εβραίαν and the cluster ἐξαποστέλλω + adj. ἐλεύθερος:

Jeremiah 41:9: τοῦ ἐξαποστεῖλαι ἕκαστον τὸν παῖδα αὐτοῦ καὶ ἕκαστον τὴν παιδίσκην αὐτοῦ τὸν Εβραῖον καὶ τὴν Εβραίαν ἐλευθέρους πρὸς τὸ μὴ δουλεύειν ἄνδρα ἐξ Ιουδα. "To send off free each his Hebrew male servant and each his Hebrew female servant so as not to have a man from Judah in slavery." Deuteronomy 15:12 reads: ἐὰν δὲ πραθῇ σοι ὁ ἀδελφός σου ὁ Εβραῖος ἢ ἡ Εβραία δουλεύσει σοι ἓξ ἔτη καὶ τῷ ἑβδόμῳ ἐξαποστελεῖς αὐτὸν ἐλεύθερον ἀπὸ σοῦ. "But if your brother is sold to you, whether a Hebrew man or a Hebrew woman, he shall be subject to you six years, and in the seventh year you shall send him out a free person from you." As a result, the cancellation of the slave release (41:10–11) becomes a transgression of the Deuteronomic law hinted at in 41:9.

Second, consistent with v. 9, Jeremiah 41:14 refers back to Deuteronomy 15:12, which Yhwh quotes as an authoritative legal referent: ὅταν πληρωθῇ ἓξ ἔτη ἀποστελεῖς τὸν ἀδελφόν σου τὸν Εβραῖον ὃς πραθήσεταί σοι καὶ ἐργᾶταί σοι ἓξ ἔτη καὶ ἐξαποστελεῖς αὐτὸν ἐλεύθερον. "When six years are complete, you shall dismiss your Hebrew brother, who will be sold to you. And he shall work for you for six years, and you shall send him off free" (Jer 41:14).

---

30 Maier, 278–80; Mastnjak, *Deuteronomy*, 146–52.
31 Otto, "Jeremia und die Tora," 546–49.
32 Levinson, "Zedekiah's Release," 318–25.
33 Müller, *Evidence of Editing*, 4.

Finally, to depict the punishment (vv. 17–20), Jeremiah 41:17 and 41:20 pick up images and terminology from Deuteronomy 28:25–26. Verse 17, καὶ δώσω ὑμᾶς εἰς διασπορὰν πάσαις ταῖς βασιλείαις τῆς γῆς, "I will give you as a dispersion to all the kingdoms of the earth," echoes Deuteronomy 28:25, καὶ ἔσῃ ἐν διασπορᾷ ἐν πάσαις ταῖς βασιλείαις τῆς γῆς, "You shall be in dispersion in all the kingdoms of the earth." Jeremiah 41:20, καὶ ἔσται τὰ θνησιμαῖα αὐτῶν βρῶσις τοῖς πετεινοῖς τοῦ οὐρανοῦ καὶ τοῖς θηρίοις τῆς γῆς, "Their carcasses shall become food for the birds of the air and the wild animals of the earth," draws on Deuteronomy 28:26, καὶ ἔσονται οἱ νεκροὶ ὑμῶν κατάβρωμα τοῖς πετεινοῖς τοῦ οὐρανοῦ καὶ τοῖς θηρίοις τῆς γῆς, "Your corpses will be food for the birds of the sky and for the wild animals of the earth." The punishment is the accomplishment of the curses in Deuteronomy 28. These lexical cross-references stress the authoritative role of the law of Deuteronomy in Jeremiah 41:8–22LXX.

In addition, Jeremiah 41:18 alludes to the golden calf and to the Sinai covenant: καὶ δώσω τοὺς ἄνδρας τοὺς παρεληλυθότας τὴν διαθήκην μου τοὺς μὴ στήσαντας τὴν διαθήκην μου ἣν ἐποίησαν κατὰ πρόσωπόν μου τὸν μόσχον [ὃν] ἐποίησαν ἐργάζεσθαι αὐτῷ. "I will give the men who have transgressed my covenant, those that did not stand by my covenant that they made before me – they made the bull calf to work for it (41:18)."[34] The phrase τὸν μόσχον ἐποίησαν ἐργάζεσθαι αὐτῷ ("They made the bull calf to work for it") points back to Exodus 32:8 (ἐποίησαν ἑαυτοῖς μόσχον "they have made for themselves a calf").[35]

According to Jeremiah 41:18, the transgression committed by the prophet's contemporaries is similar to the golden calf apostasy.[36] The sin committed at Sinai serves as a significant frame of reference for depicting the punishment. The reference to Sinai in Jeremiah 41:18 stresses the authority of the Deuteronomic legal core: those who broke the covenant in the days of Zedekiah by infringing a law of Deuteronomy will receive the same punishment as those who violated the Sinai Covenant.[37]

To recap, Jeremiah 41:8–22 consistently invokes Deuteronomy 15:12–18 as an authoritative reference point by means of lexical cross-references. It depicts the cancellation of the manumission as the transgression of a Deuteronomic

---

34 I follow Adrian Schenker, who considers S* and ms 534 to provide the older form of the shorter Greek version without a relative pronoun ("Was übersetzen wir," 253–57). He sees τὸν μόσχον [ὃν] ἐποίησαν ἐργάζεσθαι αὐτῷ to be an asyndetic explicative clause. The accusatives in Jer 41:19 (τοὺς ἄρχοντας Ιουδα καὶ τοὺς δυνάστας καὶ τοὺς ἱερεῖς καὶ τὸν λαόν) are related to the main verb in v. 18 (καὶ δώσω); the phrase καὶ δώσω αὐτοὺς in v. 20 is a resumptive repetition of the main verb (καὶ δώσω, v. 18).

35 Schenker, 255–56.

36 Schenker, 257; Maier, *Jeremia als Lehrer*, 259.

37 Schenker, "Was übersetzen wir," 253–61.

law, whose authority is rooted in Sinai (v. 18) in order to justify the coming judgment.

Three main features characterize the way in which Jeremiah 34:8–22MT refers back to Deuteronomy 15:12–18. The first is the use of conflated references and an increasing degree of intertextual markedness that can be observed in both the narrative account (vv. 8–11) and the legal reference in vv. 14–16.[38] Similar to the LXX, Jeremiah 34:9a refers back to the slave law in Deuteronomy 15:12–18 with the words העברי והעבריה and the cluster שלח + חפשי. Jeremiah 34:9a reads לשלח איש את עבדו ואיש את שפחתו העברי והעבריה חפשים, "Everyone should set free their Hebrew slaves, male and female."

Deuteronomy 15:12 states כי ימכר לכ אחיך העברי או העבריה ועבדך שש שנים ובשנה השביעה תשלחנו חפשי מעמך, "If your kin, whether a Hebrew man or a Hebrew woman, is sold to you and works for you six years, in the seventh year you shall set that person free."

However, the phrase in Jeremiah 34:9b, לבלתי עבד בם ביהודי אחיהו איש, "so that no one should hold them in servitude, even a Judahite his brother," alludes to the slave legislation of the Holiness Code,[39] with a carefully constructed summary of Leviticus 25:39–46.[40] עבד + ב picks up the initial prohibition of Leviticus 25:39 (וכי ימוך אחיך עמך ונמכר לך לא תעבד בו עבדת עבד, "If your brother with you becomes so impoverished that he sells himself to you, you shall not make him serve as slave"), with a causative nuance to assume the meaning, "to enslave".[41] The cluster אחיהו איש ("each one his brother") alludes to Leviticus 25:46. The awkward position of the noun איש in Jeremiah 34:9 marks the intertextual reference to the closure of the law: ובאחיכם בני ישראל איש באחיו לא תרדה בו בפרך, "But as for your fellow Israelites, no one shall rule over his brother with harshness" (Lev 25:46). [42] References to the beginning and the end of a law point to the entire law.[43]

As is the case in verse 9b, Jeremiah 34:10MT conflates references to Leviticus 25:39–46 with Deuteronomy 15:12–18: וישמעו כל השרים וכל העם אשר באו בברית לשלחאיש את עבדו ואיש את שפחתו חפשים לבלתי עבד בם עוד וישמעו וישלחו. "They obeyed, all the officials and all the people who had entered into the cove-

38 On markedness in intertextuality, see Ben Porat, "Poetics," 107–27; Broich, "Formen"; Holthuis, *Intertextualität*, 108–14.

39 Chavel, "Let my People," 88–93; Fischer, *Jeremia 1–25*, 254.

40 Levinson, "Zedekiah's Release," 321–23.

41 עבד *qal* takes on a causative nuance when followed by the preposition ב; see Levinson, "Zedekiah's Release," 321, n. 22.

42 See Duhm, *Jeremia*, 281; Rudolph, *Jeremia*, 222.

43 So Levinson, "Zedekiah's Release," 321–23.

nant, that all would set free their slaves, male or female, so that they would not be enslaved again; they obeyed and set them free." The phrase לבלתי עבד בם עוד points again to Leviticus 25:39–46;[44] the adverb עוד – absent in Jeremiah 34:9 and Leviticus 25:39 – is, however, consistent with the purpose of the Holiness Code to abolish slavery among fellow Israelites. The cluster שלח + חפשי refers back to Deuteronomy 15:12;[45] the same שלח + חפשי occurs again in Jeremiah 34:11. וישובו אחרי כן וישבו את העברים ואת השפחות אשר שלחו חפשים. "But afterward they turned and took back the male and female slaves they had set free."

Jeremiah 34:14MT shows an analogous tendency, with a combination of references to Deuteronomy 15:1 and 15:12 [46]. Verse 14 reads מקץ שבע שנים תשלחו איש את אחיו העברי אשר ימכר לך ועבדך שש שנים ושלחתו חפשי מעמך, "At the end of seven years each of you must set free every man his brother, who has been sold to you and has served you six years; you must set him free from you." It draws on two statements in Deuteronomy 15: v. 1: מקץ שבע שנים תעשה שמטה. "At the end of seven years you shall make a remission," and v. 12: כי ימכר לך אחיך העברי או העבריה ועבדך שש שנים ובשנה השביעה תשלחנו חפשי מעמך, "If your kin, whether a Hebrew man or a Hebrew woman, is sold to you and works for you six years, in the seventh year you shall let him go free from you."

Hints about slave release (Deut 15:12–18) and debt remission (15:1–11) come together: the opening phrase in Jeremiah 34:14MT (מקץ שבע שנים) points to Deuteronomy 15:1.[47] Then, את אחיו העברי אשר ימכר לך quote almost *verbatim* Deuteronomy 15:12, simply omitting the mention of the "female Hebrew."[48] Further references to Deuteronomy 15:12 in Jeremiah 34:14MT are found in the compound preposition מעמך that follows חפשי. The coordination of *šemiṭṭah* regulations (Deut 15:1–11) with the slave release law (Deut 15:12–18) in Jeremiah 34:14 mirrors the strategy pursued by the Holiness Code, with debt (Deut 15:1–11) and slave release (Deut 15:12–18) occurring in the same year.[49]

44 See already ב + עבד in 34:9.

45 See the phrase חפשי + שלח in 34:9, 14.

46 See Levinson, "Zedekiah's Release," 320.

47 According to Mark Leuchter, the phrase alludes to Deut 31:10, the septennial public proclamation of the law (Deut 31:9–13) ("Manumission," 642–46). Reference to Deut 31:10 in Jer 34:14 would thus aim at depicting the prophet Jeremiah as a preacher of the Levitical Torah. However, in Jer 34:8–22 he is only the recipient of a divine message; any clue about a further communication by the prophet to the people is lacking (See Carroll, *Jeremiah*, 649).

48 Against considering the "female Hebrew" as a later addition in Deut 15:12, see Levinson, "Zedekiah's Release," 320–21, n. 21.

49 So Nihan, "Holiness Code," 88.

Second, from a narrative point of view, Jeremiah 34MT builds a mini-plot in vv. 8–11 that contains references to the Deuteronomic and Holiness Codes to stress the execution (v. 10) and later transgression of the laws (v. 11). Against the background of the people's customary disobedience (see esp. לא + שמע in Jeremiah 11:1–14), the stress on the people's heeding (v. 10: וישמעו) produces a temporary surprise. The sudden negative repentance that follows (v. 11: שוב), however, confirms the customary attitude of the people, while casting a shadow over the former obedience.

The third main feature is the blurring in the MT of the hints to the golden calf incident found in Jeremiah 41:18LXX. Only the noun העגל remains as a trace of the calf. Instead, the noun בתר occurs in Jeremiah 34:18, 19 and in Genesis 15:10, which provides a strong lexical reference to the covenant ritual with Abraham in Genesis 15.[50]

To recap, Jeremiah 34:8–22MT conflates references to the legal core of Deuteronomy and the Holiness legislation. These references are embedded in a mini-plot (vv. 8–11) that describes the people's awkward behavior. A reference to the Abrahamic covenant (Gen 15) appears, while hints to the golden calf and to Sinai are blurred.

A close comparison between Jeremiah 34:8–22MT and 41:8–22LXX shows that lexemes and clusters pointing back to Leviticus 25:39–46 are consistently missing in the Greek text:

v. 9	לבלתי עבד בם ביהודי אחיהו איש	πρὸς τὸ μὴ δουλεύειν ἄνδρα ἐξ Ιουδα
v. 10	לבלתי עבד בם עוד	–
v. 17	לקרא דרור איש לאחיו ואיש לרעהו	τοῦ καλέσαι ἄφεσιν ἕκαστος πρὸς τὸν πλησίον αὐτοῦ

Additional lexical hinges with Deuteronomy 15:12 are lacking in the LXX as well:

v. 10	לשלח איש את עבדו ואיש את שפחתו חפשים	τοῦ ἀποστεῖλαι ἕκαστον τὸν παῖδα αὐτοῦ καὶ ἕκαστον τὴν παιδίσκην αὐτοῦ
v. 14	ושלחתו חפשי מעמך	καὶ ἐξαποστελεῖς αὐτὸν ἐλεύθερον

Moreover, while the MT builds a mini-plot throughout vv. 8–11, the shorter Greek text does not mention the execution of the royal edict (v. 10). As a result, there is no reference to the subsequent "negative" repentance (v. 11):

50 Wijesinghe, *Jeremiah 34,8–22*, 149–56; Maier, *Jeremia als Lehrer*, 274; Fischer, *Jeremia 1–25*, 258.

v. 10	וישמעו כל השרים וכל העם אשר באו בברית [...]	καὶ ἐπεστράφησαν πάντες οἱ μεγιστᾶνες καὶ πᾶς ὁ λαὸς οἱ εἰσελθόντες ἐν τῇ διαθήκῃ [...]
v. 11	וישובו אחרי כן וישבו את העבדים ואת השפחות אשר שלחו חפשים ויכבשום [ק] לעבדים ולשפחות	καὶ ἔωσαν αὐτοὺς εἰς παῖδας καὶ παιδίσκας

Finally, Jeremiah 34:18–19MT contains a reference to Genesis 15 instead of to the golden calf.

The chronological relation between Jeremiah 34:8–22MT and 41:8–22LXX has been widely discussed, with opposite outcomes. According to Hermann-Josef Stipp, in this case, the shorter Greek text represents a later reworking of a previous longer text (MT).[51] According to Adrian Schenker and others, however, Jeremiah 41:8–22LXX is the earlier text;[52] the longer 34:8–22MT has resulted from redactional reworking. Even if the antecedence of one text to the other remains controversial, the textual variants in Jeremiah 41:8–22LXX and 34:8–22MT show coherent redactional purposes.

The textual variants, Jeremiah 41:8–22LXX and 34:8–22MT, display diverging attitudes toward the legal core of Deuteronomy and its authoritative status. The shorter Greek text consistently alludes to the law of Deuteronomy 15 concerning the manumission of slaves as a normative, binding, legal authority. The reference to Sinai in Jeremiah 41:18–19LXX reinforces Deuteronomy's authoritative claim.

On the contrary, three strategies point to the MT's (Jer 34:8–22) subversive attitude toward the law of Deuteronomy. First are the conflated references to Deuteronomy 15:12–18 and Leviticus 25:39–46. Though references to both legal collections are presented simultaneously, the focus on the forbidden enslavement of an Israelite brother in Leviticus 25:39–46 deprives Deuteronomy 15:12–18 of its relevance, since ch. 15 regulates the hiring of Hebrews among Israelite brothers.[53] The comparison Christophe Nihan makes between the slave regulations of the Holiness and Deuteronomic codes further illustrates the issue at hand.[54] The possibility of the slave remaining in his master's household (Deut 15:16–17) becomes unnecessary, because the Israelite returns to his estate. Within this framework, the parting gifts (Deut 15:13–14) also seem to be superfluous.

In Jeremiah 34:8–22MT, references to Leviticus neither replace nor substitute for those in the Deuteronomic legislation. Both are simultaneously present and applied to the same situation. The allusions to the intertwined Leviticus

---

51 Stipp, *Sondergut*, 155–56.

52 See Schenker, "Was übersetzen wir," 253–61.

53 See Rossi and Guillaume, "Alternative Reading."

54 See Nihan, "Holiness Code," 86–88.

25:39–46 and Deuteronomy 15:1–18 deprive the Deuteronomic laws of their authoritative status.[55] The Torah is used to undermine the authority of another statement in the Torah.

Second, the reference to the golden calf (Exod 32:8) and Sinai in the shorter Jeremiah 41:18–19LXX version enhances the prestige of the Deuteronomic Code, in line with the main concern of the Pentateuch Redaction in Deuteronomy. Instead of an allusion to Sinai, Jeremiah 34:18–19MT hints at Genesis 15 to convey a different depiction of what the cancellation of the manumission has transgressed. Instead of a punishment resulting from the transgression of an authoritative law from Deuteronomy rooted in the bilateral covenant at Sinai, it infringes the unilateral covenant of Genesis 15. Therefore, the longer Hebrew text of the book of Jeremiah removes Moses's role as interpreter of the Sinai-Torah – the cornerstone of Deuteronomy's authoritative claim.[56]

The third strategy used in the narrative mini-plot is to have the people's fleeting commitment to the law (Jer 34:9–10MT) strip the Pentateuchal laws of their authority by stressing that they are not enforceable. Because it is immediately obeyed (v. 10), the law seems to be an authoritative reference point. But the law is soon transgressed for no explicit reason, which reveals an ironic posture towards Deuteronomy's legal core. The interplay of the verb שוב in *qal* and *hiphil* (Jer 34:11MT) picks up a typical wordplay in the book, turning it upside down. The usual reference to conversion expressed by the root שוב becomes the turning back from the obedience to a law in Jeremiah 34:11MT.[57]

The three strategies outlined above point to a subversive intent in the book, but it is not limited to the regulations in Deuteronomy alone. A broader issue of Pentateuch Redaction surfaces. The authoritative role of Sinai is downplayed (see Jer 34:18), and references to Leviticus 25:36–49 are used to restrain Deuteronomy's normative authority.

Against this background, I return to the textual relationship between Jeremiah 34:8–22MT and 41:8–22LXX. If the MT has precedence over the shorter Greek translation, the LXX avoided references to Leviticus 25:39–46 and stressed the reference to Sinai, in order to reinforce Deuteronomy's authoritative status. The abridgment would have toned down the irony conveyed by MT. If the MT results from a redactional elaboration of the text translated by the LXX, its subversive intent countered Deuteronomy's authoritative claims, rooted in Sinai revelation, as expressed by the shorter Greek text. In any case, the reference to Deuteronomy 15:1–18 in Jeremiah seems to point to wider issues than simply motivating the destruction of Jerusalem.

---

55 Against Levinson, "Zedekiah's Release," 322–25.

56 See Otto, "Jeremia und die Tora," 546–47.

57 See Fischer, *Jeremia 26–52*, 254–55.

4 Yhwh as Lawbreaker (Jer 3:1 and Deut 24:1–4)

The reference in Jeremiah 3:1 to the law regulating divorce in Deuteronomy 24:1–4 is widely recognized.[58] The prohibition of a former husband to remarry the wife he had previously divorced in 24:1–4 is in tension with Yhwh's offer to Israel to return to her divine husband in Jeremiah 3:12–13 and 4:1–2.[59] The reversal of the Deuteronomic legal tradition supposedly reinforces the prophetic message "on the eve of destruction."[60] The alleged metaphorical reference to Deuteronomy 24:1–4 would underline the spiritual dimension of the law[61] and the value of the offer of repentance.[62] These attempts to downplay the tension between Deuteronomy 24:1–4 and Jeremiah 3–4 run the risk of neglecting the juridical nature of Yhwh's lawsuit against the unfaithful woman[63] and miss the polemical attitude in the book of Jeremiah.

Jer 3:1	Deut 24:1–4
If a man divorces his wife (הן ישלח איש את־אשתו) and she goes from him (והלכה מאתו) and becomes another man's wife (והיתה לאיש־אחר), will he return to her (הישוב אליה עוד)? Would not this land be completely polluted? You have played the whore with many lovers; and would you return to me? Oracle of Yhwh.	[1]When a man takes a wife and marries her, but she does not find favor in his eyes because he finds in her something indecent, and so he writes her a certificate of divorce (וכתב לה ספר כריתת), puts it in her hand, and sends her out of his house (ושלחה מביתו) [2]she then goes out from his house (ויצאה מביתו והלכה) and become another man's wife [3]and the second man hates her and writes her a certificate of divorce (וכתב לה ספר כריתת), puts it in her hand and sends her out from his house (ושלחה מביתו), or if the second man who took her to be his wife dies,[4] her first husband who sent her away cannot take her again to be his wife (לא־יוכל בעלה הראשון אשר־שלחה לשוב לקחתה) after she is rendered unclean; that would be an abomination before Yhwh and you shall not bring guilt on the land Yhwh of your God is giving you as possession.

58 See Holladay, *Jeremiah 1–25*, 112–13; Fischer, *Jeremia 1–25*, 185; Fishbane, *Biblical Interpretation*, 307–12; Rom-Shiloni, "Actualization," 262–67; Mastnjak, *Deuteronomy*, 165–72; Bergland, *Reading*, 109–27. On the basis of the difference between 3:1MT and 3:1LXX, Raymond Hobbs considers the use of Deut 24:1–4 in an "earlier poetic oracle" unlikely. According to him, both Jer 3:1 and Deut 24:1–4 quote a former law ("Jeremiah 3.1–3," 23–24).

59 See Mastnjak *Deuteronomy*, 168–69; Rom-Shiloni, "Actualization," 264–66.

60 Rom-Shiloni, 267.

61 See Rom-Shiloni, 263; Mastnjak, *Deuteronomy*, 165–72.

62 Fishbane, *Biblical Interpretation*, 309–10.

63 Pietro Bovati expounds the juridical nature of the *rîb* lawsuit (*Reestablishing Justice*, 30–166).

The reference to Deuteronomy 24:1–4 in Jeremiah 3:1 opens a section on the possibility of salvation that closes in 4:2. The prophet stops accusing the people and offers salvation.[64]

Since 3:6 breaks the flow of vv. 1–5 while picking up terminology and images from 2:1–37, scholars who deemed the prose of vv. 6–11 later than the poetry of vv. 1–5 considered vv. 6–11 a late development of the divorce motif in vv. 1–5, which they ascribed to Jeremiah himself.[65] The case for dating Jeremiah 3:6–11 later than vv. 1–5 is not cogent, however. The claim that poetry is older than prose is grounded on the old assumption that poetry was a distinguishing feature of prophetic pronouncements.[66] Besides the difficulty in distinguishing prose and poetry in the book of Jeremiah [67] the possibility that the poetry does not come from the prophet himself also tends to be overlooked.[68]

The historicity of the mention of the days of Josiah in Jeremiah 3:6 is also highly debated. It is the only dating of a prophetic pronouncement to Josiah's reign in the whole of the book and the only occurrence of a date within chs. 2–6.[69] The mention of Israel and Judah in vv. 7–8 could have triggered the reference to Josiah in v. 6, which, consequently, could be a secondary addition.[70]

Finally, the references to Jeremiah 2:1–37 in 3:6–11 cannot be counted among the features that distinguish vv. 6–11 from vv. 1–5. Verses 1–5 pick up terminology and images from 2:1–37 as well (e.g. hills as the place of prostitution: שפים in 3:2, גבעה in 2:20; pollution of the land: חנף in 3:1, 2, טמא in 2:7; זנה in 2:20; 3:2–3). Hence, the case for vv. 6–11 being a later addition to vv. 1–5 is weak. Textual differences between the MT and the LXX reveal the critical position towards Deuteronomic law in the book and elucidates the aim of the reference to Deuteronomy in Jeremiah 3:1.

The reference to Deuteronomy 24:1–4 in Jeremiah 3:1MT is consistent with the source text. Deuteronomy focuses on the first husband's obligations and prohibits him from taking the rejected wife again after the termination of her second marriage. Jeremiah 3:1MT accordingly points to the man's responsibility. The marriage metaphor runs throughout the unit 3:1–4:4 (e.g. 3:6, 8, 12). In Jeremiah 3:11–12, Yhwh invites Israel to come back, as he does not want to keep

64 Schmid, *Buchgestalten*, 277.
65 See Duhm, *Jeremia*, 33; Rudolph, *Jeremia*, 25; Holladay, *Jeremiah 1–25*, 77–81.
66 E.g. Duhm, *Jeremia*, vii; xii–xiii; 33.
67 So Beuken and van Grol, "Jeremiah 14,1–15,9," 62.
68 So Lalleman-de Winkel, *Jeremiah*, 46–48, 235; Fischer, *Jeremia: Der Stand*, 86–89. Stulman, Order re-examines the relation between prose and poetry.
69 See Fischer, *Jeremia 1–25*, 188.
70 So Levin, "Noch Einmal," 429–30; *Verheißung*, 184, n. 119.

his anger forever (v. 12). Yhwh takes the initiative and invites the rejected woman (cf. v. 8) to come back to him. The divine attitude toward the woman patently contradicts the prohibition directed to the man in Deuteronomy 24:1–4, hinted at in Jeremiah 3:1MT (הישוב אליה עוד). By mentioning the divorce bill, Jeremiah 3:8 further stresses the divorced status of Israel and deepens the tension between the law of 24:1–4 and Yhwh's willingness to take his people again (Jer 3:11–12). The line of reasoning in the MT highlights that Yhwh's invitation (vv. 11–12) violates the law quoted in 3:1.

Jeremiah 3:1LXX distances itself from the focus on the husband in Deuteronomy 24:1–4 and foregrounds the woman's actions. It prohibits her from going back (μὴ ἀνακάμπτουσα ἀνακάμψει πρὸς αὐτὸν); nonetheless the polluted woman (ἔτι οὐ μιαινομένη μιανθήσεται ἡ γυνὴ ἐκείνη) dares to return to Yhwh, her husband (καὶ ἀνέκαμπτες πρός με, 3:1). The woman's initiative patently breaks the quoted law. Her infringement of a rule from the Torah underlines her accountability.

Whereas in Jer 3:6, 12MT the rebellious female Israel (משובה ישראל) comes to the fore, in 3:6, 12LXX, the female metaphor is blurred. The "house of Israel" (ἡ κατοικία τοῦ Ισραηλ) appears instead of the rebellious woman-Israel.[71] The LXX extensively employs female imagery in vv. 2–5, 8–10, 11, and 13 within the accusation; this, however, suddenly vanishes in 3:6 and 3:12 when Yhwh offers the people a chance to reconcile. The shift is probably purposeful. By turning the MT's female imagery (משובה ישראל, vv. 6, 12) into a reference to the "house of Israel" (ἡ κατοικία τοῦ Ισραηλ, vv. 6, 12LXX), Yhwh does not patently appear as a lawbreaker. According to Jeremiah 3:6, 12LXX, he does not offer an adulterous and rejected woman the chance to come back; instead, he invites the settlement of Israel to turn to him. In short, Jeremiah 3:1LXX presumably revises MT here to improve Yhwh's portrayal in two steps. First, the quote from Deuteronomy 24:1–4 is reworked to stress the woman's exclusive responsibility (she dares to come back against the law), and second, the female image for Israel is erased whenever Yhwh offers a way back to the people (Jer 3:6, 12). In the end, the divine character in the LXX is freed from any charge of breaking the law.

If the LXX indeed reworks an earlier MT *Vorlage*, the aim of the Greek restyling underlines the goal pursued by the quote of Deuteronomy 24:1–4 in Jeremiah 3:1MT. The reference to 24:1–4 in Jeremiah 3:1MT shows that Yhwh himself acts against a law from the Torah in granting a chance for return. As a result, the law is unable to promote any reconciliation between Yhwh and his people;

---

71 The person indexicals in 3:6, 12LXX are consistent with the reference to the "house of Israel" (third or second pl.), while those in 3:6, 12MT continue to refer to a female-Israel by means of third, fem. sing. indexicals.

as a matter of fact, obedience to and observance of the law regulating divorce would never lead Israel back to Yhwh. On the contrary, the infringement of the law raises the prospect of reconciliation and return. In this case, Yhwh is the lawbreaker. The aim of such a subversive reference can be further clarified.

The validity of the people's return is discussed in Jeremiah 3:10; lexemes and clusters provide further clues for explaining the polemical stance toward Deuteronomy 24 in Jeremiah 3:1. The verb שוב, a keyword within Jeremiah 3:1–4:4, is coupled in 3:10 with a double cluster: ב + כל לב and ב + שקר. The phrase בכל לב + שוב has a positive undertone in 24:7, where it indicates the people's advocated return.[72] The same phrase (בכל לב + שוב) expresses the return of the exiles in Deuteronomy 30:2 and 30:10. As regards the direction of dependence, it is plausible to presume that the שוב שבות formula in Deuteronomy 30:1–10 influenced Jeremiah.[73] In both 30:2 and 10, the return to Yhwh is wholehearted (בכל לב + שוב) and parallels Moses's teaching (v. 2) as well as the practice of the commandments and statutes written "in this book of the law" (v. 10).

Two lexical references characterize the debate over the validity of the people's return in Jeremiah 3:6–10. On the one hand, the mention of the bill of divorce (ספר כריתת) in Jeremiah 3:8 points back to Deuteronomy 24:1–4 (וכתב לה ספר כריתת, v. 1); on the other hand, Jeremiah 3:10 alludes to Deuteronomy 30:2 and 30:10. Thus, Jeremiah 3:6–10 picks up references from the core and the frames of Deuteronomy.

Because the case for 3:6–11 constituting an addition to 3:1–5 is not cogent, these observations shed further light on the reference to Deuteronomy 24:1–4 in Jeremiah 3:1. First, Jeremiah 3:1 engages in a critical dialogue with the legal core of Deuteronomy. This dialogue appears to be part of a broader discourse that takes into account both the core and the frames (as shown by Jer 3:6–10). Second, allusions to Deuteronomy 30:2 and 30:10 in Jeremiah 3:10 further define the discourse that lays behind the reference to Deuteronomy 24:1–4 in Jeremiah 3:1. The issue at stake is not the authority of the law *per se* but the role played by Moses's law and its observance in granting and legitimizing the people's return and restoration. By quoting the Deuteronomic Code, Yhwh's behavior in Jeremiah 3:2–13 ends up contradicting the law itself. The strategy displayed by Jeremiah 3:1MT does not simply revise or transform a law. The quote of Deuteronomy 24:1–4 insists that the observance of the law cannot ensure a return. As a result, by means of referring to the legal core, the function of the law is sub-

72 See Fischer, *Jeremia 1–25*, 189–90.

73 So Willi-Plein, "ŠWB," 55–71; Vanoni, "Anspielungen," 390; Ehrenreich, *Wähle das Leben*, 124–27.

verted in the MT text of Jeremiah, as highlighted by the frames of Deuteronomy (see esp. Deut 30:2, 10).

5 Revising Trans-Generational Punishment (Deut 24:16 in Jer 31:29–30)

In picking up Deuteronomy 24:16, Jer 31:30 revises the principle of trans-generational punishment hinted at in 31:29 through a proverb.[74]

> Jeremiah 31:29–30:
> בימים ההם לא־יאמרו עוד אבות אכלו בסר ושני בנים תקהינה
> כי אם־איש בעונו ימות כל־האדם האכל הבסר תקהינה שניו
> In those days, the people will no longer say, "The fathers have eaten sour grapes, and the children's teeth are set on edge." Everyone will die for his own sin; whoever eats sour grapes, his own teeth will be set on edge.
> Deuteronomy 24:16:
> לא־יומתו אבות על־בנים ובנים לא־יומתו על־אבות איש בחטאו יומתו.
> Fathers shall not be put to death for their children, nor children put to death for their fathers; each is to die for his own sin.

Within this framework, Deuteronomy 24:16 serves as a prooftext to reject an "old traditum."[75] A Torah statement (Deut 24:16) contradicts the *māšāl* of 31:29 deemed obsolete.

Something remains unexplained, however. Using a Deuteronomic law as an authoritative text seems at odds with the critical stance against the Mosaic Torah in the following Jeremiah 31:31–34.[76] The stance toward Deuteronomic laws in the book of Jeremiah can be further elucidated by considering the way the trans-generational punishment is revised and the context of the revision in Jeremiah 31:29–30.

The notion of trans-generational punishment alluded in Jeremiah 31:29 by means of a popular saying is delineated in the Decalogue: "I, Yhwh your God, am a jealous God, punishing the children for the sin of the fathers (פקד עון אבות על־בנים) to the third and fourth generation of those who hate me (ועל־שלשים ועל־רבעים לשנאי)" (Deut 5:9). According to Bernard M. Levin-

74 See Fishbane, *Biblical Interpretation*, 335–50; Levinson, *Legal Revision*, 57–88.
75 So Fishbane, *Biblical Interpretation*, 337–38; Mastnjak, *Deuteronomy*, 159–61.
76 See Rossi, "Conflicting Patterns."

son,[77] the Hebrew Bible shows at least two other instances of revision of the trans-generational punishment: Deuteronomy 7:9–10 and Ezekiel 18:1–4.

Deuteronomy 7:9–10 does not present the doctrine of individual retribution (v. 10: [he] repays in their own person those who reject him. He does not delay but repays in their own person those who reject him) as a departure from the traditional doctrine. The "new teaching is presented as consistent with the very doctrine that it rejects."[78] Continuity is the guiding principle, and innovation is disguised as continuity between old and new. Deuteronomy 7:9–10 simply reverses the order of the lexemes of the Decalogue, mentioning the covenant of love to a thousand generations (v. 9) before the immediate repaying of those who hate Yhwh (v. 10). The reverse order of the quote abrogates the principle.[79]

Ezekiel 18:1–4 hints at trans-generational punishment by means of a *māšāl* to facilitate the revision process. There, Yhwh himself takes the floor to abrogate the principle: "As surely as I live, declares says Yhwh the Lord (חי אני נאם אדני יהוה), none of you will repeat this proverb in Israel (אם־יהיה לכם עוד משל המשל הזה בישראל)" (v. 3). Yhwh establishes a contrast between the people's saying (אתם משלים, v. 2) and Yhwh's statement (חי אני נאם אדני יהוה, v. 3). Yhwh's speech and his divine authority invalidate the *māšāl* and, consequently, revoke the trans-generational punishment hinted at by the proverb itself.

Jeremiah 31:29–30 display a third way of revising the principle. The revision is introduced in v. 30 by the cluster כי אם, which is foregrounded also in 16:14–15 and 23:7–8, at the beginning of a community's new saying. Against this background, it is possible to argue that the same cluster in Jeremiah 31:30 also introduces the people's speech.[80] In addition, Jeremiah 31:30 amends the trans-generational principle by hinting back at Deuteronomy 24:16. As a result, the community brings about the revision of the trans-generational punishment in Jeremiah 31:29–30 by means of Deuteronomy 24:16. Jeremiah 31:30 uses the law-code of Deuteronomy to contrast and abrogate a principle from the Decalogue (i.e. a part of the frames of Deuteronomy). Using the Torah against the Torah marks a remarkable change, a theological breakthrough. A short glance at the context of Jeremiah 31:29–30 sheds further light on the book's challenging attitude while further contouring the abovementioned theological breakthrough.

Jeremiah 31:29–30 is part of the framework (30:1–3; 31:27–40) of the Book of Consolation (Jer 30–31); the central issue at stake in 30:1–3 and 31:27–40 is again

77 Levinson, *Legal Revision*, 57–88.

78 Levinson, 75.

79 See Levinson, 75–76; Rom-Shiloni, "Jeremiah and Ezekiel," 217–18.

80 So Schoneveld, "Jeremia XXXI, 29–30," 339–41.

that of return and restoration after the Exile. Deuteronomy 30:1–10 appears again to be relevant for the framework of the Book of Consolation. In particular, the following lexical cross-references show that ch. 30 is a reference point for discussing the return after the Exile: the *Schicksalwendeformel* (Deut 30:3; Jer 30:3), the mention of the land possessed by the fathers (ארץ; ירש; אבות, Jer 30:3; Deut 30:5), and the motif of the multiplication of humans and animals (Jer 31:27//Deut 30:5, 9).[81] The stance in Jeremiah toward Deuteronomy 30, however, is quite critical.

In ch. 30, the return after the Exile depends on observing the Torah and its prescriptions. Yet, an unconditional promise comes into view in Jeremiah 30:1–3; 31:27–34.[82] Jeremiah 31:31–34 exhibit a critical attitude toward the role the Torah plays in restoration. Moses's Torah is surpassed as an instrument of reconciliation and re-establishment of the broken covenant.[83] The reference to trans-generational punishment in Jeremiah 31:29 and its revision in v. 30 should be placed within the broader *discourse* that lays behind the whole framework of the Book of Consolation: i.e. the chance of restoration after the exile and the Torah's role in the process.

To sum up: the law-code of Deuteronomy is picked up in Jeremiah 31:30 against a key text of the Decalogue, hinted at in Jeremiah 31:29 by a proverb. This Torah against Torah game challenges the Torah's function in the process of restoration after the Exile. Against this background, Jeremiah 31:30 challenges the authority of Deuteronomy's legal material: references to legal prescriptions of Deuteronomy highlight their failure to assure renewal in post-exilic times.

6 The Fate of the Apostate City (Jer 30:18 and Deut 13:17)

Jeremiah 30:18 opens a new unit in the Book of Comfort (30:18–31:1) announcing the restoration of the tents of Jacob and describing the rebuilding of the city: ונבנתה עיר על תלה, "the city will be built on her tell." The phrase בנה + עיר, combined with the noun תל, points to Deuteronomy 13:17.[84]

81 Schmid, *Buchgestalten*, 72–73; Otto, "Jeremia und die Tora," 554–56.
82 See Otto, 554.
83 See Otto, 556; Rossi, "Conflicting Patterns," 217–23.
84 See on this regard, Schmid, *Buchgestalten*, 120–21; Fischer, "Aufnahme," 130–37; Fischer, "Einfluss," 261.

Verse 17 states והיתה תל עולם לא תבנה עוד, "[the city] will remain a perpetual ruin never to be rebuilt." Jeremiah 30:18 reads: כה אמר יהוה הנני שב שבות אהלי יעקוב ומשכנתיו ארחם ונבנתה עיר על תלה וארמון על משפטו ישב. "Thus says Yhwh: 'I will restore the fortunes of Jacob's tents and have compassion on his dwellings; the city will be rebuilt on her ruin, and the palace will stand in its proper place.'"

As regards the referent of the noun עיר in Jeremiah 30:18 and Deuteronomy 13:17: the framework of the Book of Consolation and the initial address to Israel and Judah (30:4) support the identification of the city in Jeremiah 30:18 as Jerusalem.[85] The apostate city of Deuteronomy 13:17 that can never be rebuilt also looks backward to Jerusalem's destruction.[86] Against this background, it is possible to infer that Jeremiah 30:18 challenges the fate of Jerusalem announced in Deuteronomy 13:17. According to Jeremiah 30:18, the city (Jerusalem) will not remain a ruin forever. On the contrary, it will be rebuilt precisely upon its ruin (ונבנתה [...] על תלה, Jer 30:18). The contrast abrogates the fate of the apostate city in Deuteronomy 13:13–17.[87]

The critical stance of the book of Jeremiah toward the law-code of Deuteronomy appears again in Jeremiah 30:18, which opens with the *Schicksalwendeformel* (הנני שב שבות אהלי יעקוב) already present in the title of the Book of Comfort (30:3). The formula in v. 18 references Deuteronomy 30:3,[88] where it concerns the return of the exiles. In particular, Deuteronomy 30:1–10 stresses the role that heeding Moses's instructions (v. 1) and divine commands (v. 8) will play in making the return possible.

The reference in Jeremiah 30:18 to the שוב שבות formula in Deuteronomy 30:3 points once more to the *discourse* that lies behind the hint at Deuteronomy 13:17. The abrogation of the law of the apostate city in Jeremiah 30:18 is to be read within the framework of the dialogue about the role of the Torah in legitimizing restoration and return (see esp. Deut 30:1–10). By abrogating Deuteronomy 13:17, Jeremiah 30:18 once more rejects Deuteronomy's claim that obedience to Moses's Torah (i.e. Deuteronomy's core and frames) can secure a future for the people after the exile, as promised in Deuteronomy 30:1–10. Jeremiah 30–31 uses the verb שׁוב to render unconditional the conditional elements of Deuteronomy 30:2 and 30:10.[89] By referring to the Deuteronomic legal core, the book

85 Holladay, *Jeremiah 2*, 177; Fischer, *Jeremiah 26–52*, 135.
86 So also Otto, *Deuteronomium 12,1–23,15*, 1,265–67.
87 See Schmid, *Buchgestalten*, 120, n. 307.
88 See Vanoni, "Anspielungen," 388–90.
89 So Lalleman-de Winkel, *Jeremiah*, 156.

of Jeremiah calls the authority of Mosaic Torah into question and criticizes the claim that its observance can grant restoration after the Exile.

7 New Life in Babylon and the Promised Return (Deut 23:7 and 4:29 in Jer 29:7, 13–14)

In Jeremiah 29, the prophet sends a letter to the exiles with a promise of return (vv. 13–14) while tempering expectations in Judah for a swift return expressed by some prophets (vv. 8–9). The legal core of Deuteronomy, together with the frames, once more provide a foil for depicting restoration as well as for discussing its requirements. In Jeremiah 29:4–8, Yhwh offers the *golah* a prosperous life in Babylon and invites the exiled to establish themselves (v. 5) and to multiply there (v. 6). The exiles are even urged to pray for Babylon (והתפללו בעדה את יהוה) and to seek her prosperity (ודרשו את־שלום העיר אשר הגליתי אתכם שמה).

The uncommon cluster דרש + obj. שלום points to Deuteronomy 23:7 (לא־תדרש שלמם וטבתם כל־ימיך לעולם). The syntagma occurs four times in the Hebrew Bible (Deut 23:7; Jer 29:7, Jer 38:4, and Ezra 9:12). While in Jeremiah 38:4, the שלום refers to the people of Jerusalem, in Deuteronomy 23:7, Jeremiah 29:7, and Ezra 9:12, the שלום to be (or not to be) promoted belongs to enemies (i.e. Ammonites and Moabites in Deut 23:7, people of the lands in Ezra 9:12, and Babylon in Jer 29:7).[90] Lexemes from Deuteronomy 23:7 are taken up in Jeremiah 29:7 and reversed (Deut 23:7 לא דרשו; Jer 29:7 ודרשו) to express the paradoxical exhortation to pursue the prosperity of Babylon, the current enemy of Judah and Jerusalem. Once more, Yhwh contravenes a prescription from Deuteronomy's legal core by offering a renewed life to the exiles. Seeking Babylon's welfare (v. 7) and settling down to multiply there (vv. 5–6) depicts the Exile as a prosperous time, a cradle for Israel's own prosperity.

Jeremiah 29:13–14 also pick up references from the frames of Deuteronomy to depict the chance of return from Babylon: "You shall seek me and find me (ובקשתם אתי ומצאתם) when you shall seek me with all your heart (כי תדרשני בכל־לבבכם). I will let you find me, says Yhwh, and I will change your fortunes (ושבתי את שביתכם) and gather you from all the nations and all the places where I scattered you, says Yhwh, and I will bring you back (והשבתי אתכם) to the place from which I sent you into exile." Deuteronomy 4:29 states: "From

90 See Weippert, "Fern von Jerusalem," 133–39.

there you (pl.) shall seek Yhwh your God (בקשתם אלהיך את־יהוה משם), and you (sg.) will find (him) (ומצאת) if you search after him with all your heart and soul (כי תדרשנו בכל־לבבך ובכל־נפשך)." While the existence of a link between Jeremiah 29:13–14 and Deuteronomy 4:29 is recognized, the direction of dependence remains disputed.[91] Against Gottfried Vanoni and Georg Fischer,[92] Eckart Otto argues for the antecedence of Jeremiah 29:13–14 to Deuteronomy 4:29 on the basis of the *Numeruswechsel* in Deuterohnomy 4:29 and the divergences between Jeremiah 29:13–14MT and LXX.[93] The consistent use of second person plural indexicals in Jeremiah 29:13 can, however, result from the embedding of Deuteronomy 4:29 in the framework of the letter to those exiled, always addressed by a second person plural. The alleged conditional promise of Jeremiah 29:13–14MT depends on the conditional meaning ascribed to כי (LXX ὅτι) and on the assumption that the unconditional promises of Jeremiah 29:10–12 should be ascribed to a different redactional layer. While the distinction of two different layers in Jeremiah 29:10–14 is not indispensable,[94] the כי in Jeremiah 29:13 can also have a causal nuance. In both cases (i.e. conditional meaning or causal one), the logical antecedence of the people's search for Yhwh remains in both Jeremiah 29:13 and Deuteronomy 4:29. The causal or conditional meaning of כי, therefore, does not make a sufficient case for establishing the direction of dependence.

Deuteronomy 4:25–31 could provide further clues for interpreting the relationship between Jeremiah 29:13–14 and Deuteronomy 4:29. Seeking Yhwh (בקש and מצא, Deut 4:29) happens in a situation of grief and anguish (בצר לך, v. 30). According to Deuteronomy 4:27, the people in Exile will decrease until only a few remain (ונשארתם מתי מספר). In Deuteronomy 4:25–31, the Exile is the actualization of the curses of Deuteronomy 28.[95] The customary depiction of the Exile as a time of distress (בצר לך, v. 30) and a time of accomplished words (ומצאוך כל הדברים האלה, v. 30, which refers to the former vv. 26–28)[96] provides a favorable condition for Israel's pursuit of Yhwh (v. 29). The verb שוב (v. 30) stresses the people's return to him. Moreover, Deuteronomy 4:25–31 does not explicitly envision a return to the land. The outcome of seeking Yhwh (בקש and מצא) is that the people will turn to him (ושבת עד יהוה) and obey his voice (ושמעת

91 So, Mastnjak, *Deuteronomy*, 195–200.

92 See Vanoni, "Anspielungen"; Fischer, *Jeremia 26–52*, 99.

93 Otto, "Old and New Covenant," 944–47; Otto "Jeremia und die Tora," 555–56.

94 So Mastnjak, *Deuteronomy*, 198.

95 See Markl, *Gottes Volk*, 41.

96 Otto, relates כל הדברים האלה (v. 30) to the ensuing v. 31, which announces divine mercy (*Deuteronomium 1,1–4,43*, 577–578).

בקלו). In return, Yhwh will offer divine mercy and a willingness not to abandon the people (v. 31); there is no mention of a return to the land. Deuteronomy 30:1–10 bring to completion the dynamic begun in Deuteronomy 4:25–31.[97] In Deuteronomy 30:1–10 the return to the land is the outcome of the people's turning back and heeding Yhwh's voice (Deut 4:29; 30:2).

Quite differently, Jeremiah 29:13–14 sets the quest for Yhwh against the background of a prosperous life in Babylon (29:6–7). Against Deuteronomy 4:27, Jeremiah 29:5–6 look forward to the growth of the people in Babylon. The expected image of exile is twisted in Jeremiah: in Babylon the people can experience the chance of renewal after destruction even before the fall of Jerusalem. According to Deuteronomy 4:26–31 (i.e. grief and sorrow in exile), the starting point of striving for Yhwh is dismantled in Jeremiah 29:14. A comparison between Jeremiah 29:14 and Deuteronomy 4:30 stresses this point further: in Deuteronomy 4:30, the verb שוב indicates that the people return to Yhwh. In Jer 29:14, however, it points twice to Yhwh's action toward the people: he will change their fortunes and lead them back (והשבתי אתכם) to the land. Both Deuteronomy 4:29 and 30:2 (שוב שובת) come into view in Jeremiah 29:14–14,[98] which can be plausibly considered to allude to the two Deuteronomic texts.

According to Nathan Mastnjak,[99] Jeremiah 29:13–14 transforms the conditional promise of Deuteronomy 4:29 to endow the unconditional return with an authoritative point of reference. This interpretation should be reconsidered. Jeremiah's letter to the exiled employs references from both the legal core of Deuteronomy (Deut 23:7 in Jer 29:7) as well as from the framing chapters (Deut 4:29 and 30:2 in Jer 29:13–14). In particular, Jeremiah 29:5–7 twists the customary depiction of the Exile in which Babylon is viewed as the arch-enemy. Inviting the exiles to seek the *šālôm* of Babylon contravenes the prohibition ever to promote the *šālôm* of two other arch-enemies – Ammon and Moab (Deut 23:7). The enemies are not the same, but the notion of seeking the *šālôm* of enemies marks a strong lexical connection between Deuteronomy 23:7 and Jeremiah 29:7.

Divine promise may entail breaking the law. Moreover, the people will seek Yhwh in the land of exile, where they already experience salvation and renewal (Jer 29:5–7). Yhwh will be sought not by experiencing distress and the accomplishment of curses (Deut 4:29–30) but by experiencing salvation (Jer 29:5–7). In short, the conditions for renewal and return (i.e. accomplishment of curses, and consequent grief; turning back to Yhwh; heeding his voice) displayed by

97 See Markl, *Gottes Volk*, 41.
98 See Vanoni, "Anspielungen."
99 Mastnjak, *Deuteronomy*, 199–200.

Deuteronomy 4:29 and 30:1–10 are questioned by a polemical reference to the legal core (Deut 23:7).

8 Conclusion

In light of the examples analyzed above, one can interpret the use of the so called "law-code" of Deuteronomy in the book of Jeremiah through the lens of subversion. References to Deuteronomy's legal prescriptions display literary strategies employed in subversive discourse. Irony is displayed in the narrative-mini plot of Jeremiah 34:8–11 and also in the depiction of Yhwh as a law-breaker (Jer 3:1) or as the one who exhorts Israel to infringe a law (Deut 23:7 in Jer 29:7). Yhwh supercedes Moses, yet ironically, the deity ends up being unfaithful to the laws he gave to Moses. The reuse of the legal material of Deuteronomy in Jeremiah twists literary conventions (e.g. the depiction of exile in Jer 29:5–7) as well as theological *topoi*: if transgressing the law typically deserves judgment (e.g. Deut 28), here, contravening the law opens the way to salvation and renewal.

The dynamic of literary subversion implicitly admits the existence of authoritative texts and ultimately of a dominant power conveyed by those texts. Does the subversive attitude in Jeremiah imply that the "law-code" of Deuteronomy is all-in-all a binding authority for the book? To put it differently, is the target of the subversive stance found in the book the authority of Deuteronomy's laws?

The examples examined above show that in the book Jeremiah, Deuteronomy's legal prescriptions are read through the lens of the frames; Deuteronomy 30:1–10, with 4:29 (in Jer 29:13–14). Hints at the framing chapters of Deuteronomy focus on conditions and requirements for securing return and restoration after exile; observance of Moses's Torah (i.e. teaching and legal instructions given in Moab) play a pivotal role in this regard. In addition, the book hints at the "law-code" of Deuteronomy against the background of a broader range of Pentateuchal texts (e.g. Lev 25, Gen 15 or Exod 32 in Jer 34:8–22). The assertion that obedience to Mosaic Torah is the only way to secure return and restoration after the Exile appears to be the focus of subversion in Jeremiah. Against this backdrop, the power against which subversion is directed in Jeremiah could be that of the scribal circles that establish Moses's Torah as the sole authoritative medium for securing restoration in post-exilic times. In doing so, the book challenges one of the major claims of Pentateuch Redaction.

Since the laws of Deuteronomy are read through the lens of the frames in the book of Jeremiah, the book provides no evidence for the existence of an independent legal "core" older than the framework. This, however, cannot be used as evidence that no such independent legal collection ever had existed. The crucial point here is that no binding authority is ascribed in the book to the legal material of Deuteronomy *qua talis*. Rather, the authority of legal prescriptions comes into view and is subverted only in light of the objectives sketched by the frames.

Works Cited

Achenbach, Reinhard. "Grundlinien redaktioneller Arbeit in der Sinai-Perikope." In *Das Deuteronomium zwischen Pentateuch und Deuteronomistischem Geschichtswerk*, edited by Eckart Otto and Reinhard Achenbach, 56–80. Forschungen zur Religion und Literatur des Alten und Neuen Testaments 206. Göttingen: Vandenhoeck & Ruprecht, 2004.

Amit, Yairah. *Hidden Polemics in Biblical Narrative*. Biblical Interpretation Series 25. Leiden: Brill, 2000.

Ben Porat, Ziva. "The Poetics of Literary Allusion." *PTL: A Journal for Descriptive Poetics and Theory of Literature* 1 (1976): 105–28.

Bergland, Kenneth. *Reading as a Disclosure of the Thoughts of the Heart: Proto-Halakhic Reuse and Appropriation Between Torah and the Prophets*. Beihefte zur Zeitschrift für Altorientalische und biblische Rechtsgeschichte 23. Wiesbaden: Harrassowitz, 2019.

Beuken, Willem A. M. and Harm W. M. van Grol. "Jeremiah 14,1–15,9: A Situation of Distress and its Hermeneutics, Unity and Diversity of Form- Dramatic Development." In *Le livre de Jérémie, le prophète et son milieu, les oracles et leur transmission*, edited by Pierre-Maurice Bogaert, 297–342. Bibliotheca Ephemeridum Theologicarum Lovaniensium 54. Leuven: Peeters, 1997.

Bovati, Pietro. *Re-Establishing Justice: Legal Terms, Concepts and Procedures in the Hebrew Bible*. Journal for the Study of the Old Testament. Supplement Series 105. Sheffield: Sheffield Academic, 1994.

Broich, Ulrich. "Formen der Markierung von Intertextualität." In *Intertextualität: Formen, Funktionen, anglistische Fallstudien*, edited by Ulrich Broich and Manfred Pfister, 31–47. Konzepte der Sprach- und Literturwissenschaft 35. Tübingen: Max Niemeyer, 1985.

Carroll, Robert P. *Jeremiah: A Commentary*. Old Testament Library. London: SCM, 1986.

Chavel, Simeon. "'Let my People go!' Emancipation, Revelation and Scribal Activity in Jeremiah 34.8–14". *Journal for the Study of the Old Testament* 76 (1997): 71–95.

Crouch, Carly L. *Israel and the Assyrians: Deuteronomy, the Succession Treaty of Esarhaddon and the Nature of Subversion*. Society of Biblical Literature. Ancient Near East Monographs 8. Atlanta: Society of Biblical Literature, 2014.

Davies, Philip R. *In Search of 'Ancient Israel'. A Study in Biblical Origins*. Journal for the Study of the Old Testament. Supplement Series 148. Sheffield: Sheffield Academic, 1992.

Davies, Philip R. "Judahite Prophecy and the Achaemenids." In *Assessing Biblical and Classical Sources for the Reconstruction of Persian Influence, History and Culture*, edited by Anne Fitzpatrick-McKinley, 203–216. Classica et Orientalia 10. Wiesbaden: Harrassowitz, 2015.

Duhm, Bernhard. *Das Buch Jeremia*. Kurzer Hand-Commentar zum Alten Testament 11. Tübingen: JCB Mohr (Paul Siebeck), 1901.

Ehrenreich, Ernst. *Wähle das Leben! Deuteronomium 30 als hermeneutische Schlüssel zur Tora*. Beihefte zur Zeitschrift für Altorientalische und biblische Rechtsgeschichte 14. Wiesbaden: Harrassowitz, 2010.

Fischer, Georg. "Aufnahme, Wende und Überwindung dtn/r Gedankengutes in Jer 30 f." In *Jeremia und die "deuteronomistische Bewegung*," edited by Walter Groß, 129–39. Bonner Biblische Beiträge 98. Weinheim: Athenäum, 1995.

Fischer, Georg. *Jeremia 1–25*. Herders Theologischer Kommentar zum Alten Testament. Freiburg im Breisgau: Herder, 2005.

Fischer, Georg. *Jeremia 26–52*. Herders Theologischer Kommentar zum Alten Testament. Freiburg im Breisgau: Herder, 2005.

Fischer, Georg. *Jeremia: Der Stand der theologischen Diskussion*. Darmstadt: WBG, 2007.

Fischer, Georg. "Der Einfluss des Deuteronomiums auf das Jeremiabuch." In *Deuteronomium – Tora für eine neue Generation*, edited by Georg Fischer, Dominik Markl, and Simone Paganini, 247–69. Beihefte zur Zeitschrift für Altorientalische und biblische Rechtsgeschichte 17. Wiesbaden: Harrassowitz, 2011.

Fishbane, Michael. *Biblical Interpretation in Ancient Israel*. Oxford: Clarendon, 1985.

Hobbs, Raymond. "Jeremiah 3.1–3 and Deuteronomy 24.1–4." *Zeitschrift für die alttestamentliche Wissenschaft* 86 (1974): 23–29.

Holladay, William. *Jeremiah 1: A Commentary on the Book of the Prophet Jeremiah Chapters 1–25*. Hermeneia. Philadelphia, PA: Fortress, 1986.

Holladay, William. *Jeremiah 2: A Commentary on the Book of the Prophet Jeremiah Chapters 26–52*. Hermeneia. Minneapolis, MN: Fortress, 1989.

Holthuis, Susan. *Intertextualität: Aspekte einer rezeptionsorientierten Konzeption*. Stauffenburg Colloquium 28. Tübingen: Stauffenburg, 1993.

Japhet, Sarah. "The Relationship between the Legal Corpora in the Pentateuch in Light of Manumission Laws." In *Studies in Bible*, edited by Sarah Japhet, 63–89. Scripta Hierosolymitana 31. Jerusalem: Magnes, 1986.

Lalleman-de Winkel, Hetty. *Jeremiah in Prophetic Tradition: An Examination of the Book of Jeremiah in the Light of Israel's Prophetic Traditions*. Contribution to Biblical Exegesis and Theology 26. Leuven: Peeters, 2000.

Leuchter, Mark. "The Manumission Laws in Leviticus and Deuteronomy. The Jeremiah Connection." *Journal of Biblical Literature* 127 (2008): 635–53.

Levin, Cristoph. "Noch einmal: die Anfänge des Propheten Jeremias." *Vetus Testamentum* 31 (1981): 428–40.

Levin, Cristoph. *Die Verheißung des neuen Bundes in ihrem theologiegeschichtlichen Zusammenhang ausgelegt*. Forschungen zur Religion und Literatur des Alten und Neuen Testaments 137. Göttingen: Vandenhoeck & Ruprecht, 1985.

Levinson, Bernard M. *Legal Revision and Religious Renewal in Ancient Israel*. Cambridge: Cambridge University, 2008.

Levinson, Bernard M. "Zedekiah's Release of Slaves as the Babylonians Besiege Jerusalem. Jeremiah 34 and the Formation of the Pentateuch." In *The Fall of Jerusalem and the Rise of the Torah*, edited by Peter Dubovský, Dominik Markl, and Jean-Pierre Sonnet, 315–27. Forschungen zum Alten Testament 107. Tübingen: Mohr Siebeck, 2016.

Maier, Christl M. *Jeremia als Lehrer der Tora: Soziale Gebote des Deuteronomiums in Forschreibungen des Jeremiabuches*. Forschungen zur Religion und Literatur des Alten und Neuen Testaments 196. Göttingen: Vandenhoeck & Ruprecht, 2002.

Markl, Dominik. "Deuteronomy's Framework in Service of the Law (Deut 1–11; 26–34)." In *Deuteronomium – Tora für eine neue Generation*, edited by Georg Fischer, Dominik

Markl, and Simone Paganini, 271–83. Beihefte zur Zeitschrift für Altorientalische und biblische Rechtsgeschichte 17. Wiesbaden: Harrassowitz, 2011.

Markl, Dominik. *Gottes Volk im Deuteronomium*. Beihefte zur Zeitschrift für Altorientalische und biblische Rechtsgeschichte 18. Wiesbaden: Harrassowitz, 2012.

Markl, Dominik. "No Future without Moses: The Disastrous End of 2 Kings 22–25 and the Chance of the Moab Covenant (Deut 29–30)." *Journal of Biblical Literature* 133 (2014): 711–28.

Markl, Dominik. "Deuteronomy's 'Anti-King'. Historicized Etiology or Political Program?" In *Changing Faces of Kingship in Syria-Palestine 1500–500 BCE*, edited by Augustinus Gianto and Peter Dubovský, 165–86. Alter Orient und Altes Testament 459. Munster: Ugarit-Verlag, 2018.

Markl, Dominik. "The Efficacy of Moses's Prophecies and the Scope of Deuteronomistic Historiography." In *Collective Identity and Collective Memory: Deuteronomy and the Deuteronomistic History in Their Context*, edited by Johannes Ro and Diana Edelman, 121–47. Beihefte zur Zeitschrift für die alttestamentliche Wissenschaft 534. Berlin: de Gruyter, 2021.

Mastnjak, Nathan. *Deuteronomy and the Emergence of Textual Authority in Jeremiah*. Forschungen zum Alten Testament 2.87. Tübingen: Mohr Siebeck, 2016.

Mastnjak, Nathan. "Prestige, Authority and Jeremiah's Bible." *Journal of Religion* 98 (2018): 542–58.

Müller, Reinhard, Juha Pakkala, and Bas ter Haar Romeny. *Evidence of Editing: Growth and Change of Texts in the Hebrew Bible.* Society of Biblical Literature Resources for Biblical Study 75. Atlanta: Society of Biblical Literature, 2014.

Nihan, Cristophe. "The Holiness Code between D and P. Some Comments on the Function and Significance of Leviticus 17–26 in the Composition of the Torah." In *Das Deuteronomium zwischen Pentateuch und deuteronomistichem Geschichtswerk*, edited by Eckart Otto and Reinhard Achenbach, 81–122. Forschungen zur Religion und Literatur des Alten und Neuen Testaments 206. Göttingen: Vandenhoeck und Ruprecht, 2004.

Otto, Eckart. *Das Deuteronomium im Pentateuch und Hexateuch: Studien zur Literaturgeschichte von Pentateuch und Hexateuch im Lichte des Deuteronomiumrahmens*. Forschungen zum Alten Testament 30. Tübingen: Mohr Siebeck, 2000.

Otto, Eckart. "Mose, der erste Schriftgelehrte. Deut 1,5 in der Fabel des Pentateuch." In *L'écrit et l'esprit: Etudes d'histoire du texte et de théologie biblique en hommage à Adrian Schenker*, edited by Dieter Böhler, Innocent Himbaza, and Philippe Hugo, 273–84. Orbis biblicus et Orientalis 214. Fribourg: Academic Press and Göttingen: Vandenhoeck & Ruprecht, 2005.

Otto, Eckart. "Old and New Covenant: A Post-exilic Discourse between the Pentateuch and the Book of Jeremiah: Also a Study of Quotations and Allusions in the Hebrew Bible." *Old Testament Essays* 19 (2006): 939–49.

Otto, Eckart. "Scribal Scholarship in the Formation of Torah and Prophets: A Postexilic Scribal Debate between Priestly Scholarship and Literary Prophecy: The Example of the Book of Jeremiah and Its Relation to the Pentateuch." In *The Pentateuch as Torah: New Models for Understanding Its Promulgation and Acceptance*, edited by Gary N. Knoppers and Bernard M. Levinson, 171–84. Winona Lake, IN: Eisenbrauns, 2007.

Otto, Eckart. "Jeremia und die Tora. Ein nachexilischer Diskurs." In *Die Tora: Studien zum Pentateuch*, edited by Eckart Otto, 515–60. Beihefte zur Zeitschrift für Altorientalische und biblische Rechtsgeschichte 9. Wiesbaden: Harrassowitz, 2009.

Otto, Eckart. *Deuteronomium 1,1–4,43*. Herders Theologischer Kommentar zum Alten Testament. Freiburg im Breisgau: Herder, 2012.

Otto, Eckart. *Deuteronomium 12,1–23,15*. Herders Theologischer Kommentar zum Alten Testament. Freiburg im Breisgau: Herder, 2016.

Otto, Eckart. *Deuteronomium 23,16–34,12*. Herders Theologischer Kommentar zum Alten Testament. Freiburg im Breisgau: Herder, 2017.

Otto, Eckart. "Deuteronomy as the Legal Completion and Prophetic Finale of the Pentateuch." In *Paradigm Change in Pentateuchal Research*, edited by Matthias Armgardt, Benjamin Kilchör, and Markus Zehnder, 179–88. Beihefte zur Zeitschrift für Altorientalische und biblische Rechtsgeschichte 22. Wiesbaden: Harrassowitz, 2019.

Rom-Shiloni, Dalit. "Actualization of Pentateuchal Legal Traditions in Jeremiah: More on the Riddle of Authorship." *Zeitschrift für Altorientalische und Biblische Rechtsgeschichte* 15 (2009): 254–81.

Rom-Shiloni, Dalit. "Compositional Harmonization: Priestly and Deuteronomic References in Jeremiah – an Early Stage of a Recognized Interpretive Technique." In *The Formation of the Pentateuch: Bridging the Academic Cultures of Europe, Israel, and North America*, edited by Jan C. Gertz, Bernard M. Levinson, Dalit Rom Shiloni, and Konrad Schmid, 913–41. Forschungen zum Alten Testament 111. Tübingen: Mohr Siebeck, 2016.

Rom-Shiloni, Dalit. "The Forest and the Trees: The Place of Pentateuchal Material in Prophecy of the Late Seventh / Early Sixth Centuries BCE." In *Congress Volume Stellenbosch 2016*, edited by Louis C. Jonker, Gideon R. Kotzé, and Christl M. Maier, 56–92. Vetus Testamentum Supplements 177. Leiden: Brill, 2017.

Rom-Shiloni, Dalit. "'How Can You Say, 'I am not Defiled …'? (Jeremiah 2:20–25): Allusions to Priestly Legal Traditions in the Poetry of Jeremiah." *Journal of Biblical Literature* 133 (2014): 757–75.

Rom-Shiloni, Dalit. "Jeremiah and Ezekiel: What Might Stand Behind Silence?" *Hebrew Bible and Ancient Israel* 1 (2012): 217–18.

Rom-Shiloni, Dalit. "Prophets in Jeremiah in Struggle over Leadership, or Rather over Prophetic Authority?" *Biblica* 99 (2018): 351–72.

Rossi, Benedetta. "Conflicting Patterns of Revelation: Jer 31,33–34 and Its Challenge to the Post-Mosaic Revelation Program." *Biblica* 99 (2018): 202–25.

Rossi, Benedetta and Philippe Guillaume. "An Alternative Reading the Law of the Hebrew 'Slave' (Deuteronomy 15:12–18)." *Res Antiquae* 15 (2018): 3–30.

Rudolph, Wilhelm. *Jeremia*. 3rd ed. Handbuch zum Alten Testament I/12. Tübingen: J. C. B. Mohr [Paul Siebeck], 1968.

Schenker, Adrian. "Was übersetzen wir? Fragen zur Textbasis, die sich aus der Textkritik ergeben." In *Text und Sinn im Alten Testament: Textgeschichtliche und bibeltheologische Studien*, edited by Adrian Schenker, 247–62. Orbis Biblicus et Orientalis 103. Freiburg: Universitätsverlag and Göttingen: Vandenhoeck & Ruprecht, 1991.

Schmid, Konrad. *Buchgestalten des Jeremiabuches: Untersuchungen zur Redaktionsgeschichte von Jer 30–33 im Kontext des Buches*. Wissenschaftliche Monographien zum Alten und Neuen Testament 72. Neukirchen: Neukirchener, 1996.

Schoneveld, Jacobus. "Jeremia XXXI, 29–30." *Vetus Testamentum* 13 (1963): 339–41.

Seibert, Eric A. *Subversive Scribes and the Solomonic Narrative. A Re-reading of 1 Kings 1–11*. Library of Hebrew Bible/Old Testament Studies 436. New York and London: T&T Clark, 2006.

Smelik, Klaas A. D. "The Inner Cohesion of Jeremiah 34:8–22 on the Liberation of Slaves during the Siege of Jerusalem, and Its Relation to Deuteronomy 15." In *Torah and*

Tradition: Papers Read at the Sixteenth Joint Meeting of the Society for Old Testament Study and the Oudtestamentisch Werkgezelschap, Edinburgh 2015, edited by Klaas Spronk and Hans M. Barstad, 239–50. Oudtestamentische Studiën 70. Leiden: Brill, 2017.

Stipp, Hermann-Josef. *Das masoretische und alexandrinische Sondergut des Jeremiabuches: Textgeschichtlicher Rang, Eigenarten, Triebkräfte*. Orbis Biblicus et Orientalis 136. Freiburg: Universitätsverlag and Göttingen: Vandenhoeck & Ruprecht, 1994.

Stulman, Louis. *Order amid Chaos: Jeremiah as Symbolic Tapestry*. The Biblical Seminar 57. Sheffield: Sheffield Academic, 1998.

Thiel, Winfried. *Die deuteronomistische Redaktion von Jeremia 26–45: Mit einer Gesamtbeurteilung der deuteronomistischen Redaktion des Buches Jeremia*. Wissenschaftliche Monographien zum Alten und Neuen Testament 52. Neukirchen-Vluyn: Neukirchener, 1981.

Vanoni, Gottfried. "Anspielungen und Zitate innerhalb der hebräischen Bibel: Am Beispiel von Dtn 4,29; Dtn 30,3 und Jer 29,13–14." In *Jeremia und die "deuteronomistische Bewegung*, edited by Walter Groß, 383–95. Bonner Biblische Beiträge 98. Weinheim: Athenäum 1995.

Van Seters, John. "The Law of the Hebrew Slave: A Continuing Debate." *Zeitschrift für die alttestamentliche Wissenschaft* 119 (2007): 169–83.

Weippert, Helga. "Fern von Jerusalem. Die Exilsethik von Jer 29,5–7." In *Zion Ort der Begegnung: FS für Laurentius Klein zur Vollendung des 65. Lebensjahres*, edited by Ferdinand Hahn, Angelika Neuwirth, Frank Lothar Hossfeld, and Hans Jorissen, 127–39. Bonner Biblische Beiträge 90. Bodenheim: Athenäum, 1993.

Wijesinghe, Shirley L. *Jeremiah 34,8–22: Structure and Redactional History of the Masoretic Text and of the Septuagint Hebrew Vorlage*. Colombo, Sri Lanka: Centre for Society and Religion, 1999.

Willi-Plein, Ina. "*ŠWB ŠBWT* – eine Wiedererwägung." *Zeitschrift für Althebraistik* 4 (1991): 55–71.

Ancient Citation Index

Biblical Citations

https://doi.org/10.1515/9783110713312-015

Other Ancient Citations

Subject Index

https://doi.org/10.1515/9783110713312-016

Modern Authors Index

https://doi.org/10.1515/9783110713312-017

www.ingramcontent.com/pod-product-compliance
Lightning Source LLC
Chambersburg PA
CBHW031749220426
43662CB00007B/331

* 9 7 8 3 1 1 1 2 6 3 5 4 0 *